Lecture Notes in Computer Science 1331

Edited by G. Goos, J. Hartmanis and J. van Leeuwen

Advisory Board: W. Brauer   D. Gries   J. Stoer

Springer
Berlin
Heidelberg
New York
Barcelona
Budapest
Hong Kong
London
Milan
Paris
Santa Clara
Singapore
Tokyo

David W. Embley   Robert C. Goldstein (Eds.)

Conceptual Modeling – ER '97

16th International Conference
on Conceptual Modeling
Los Angeles, California, USA
November 3-5, 1997
Proceedings

 Springer

Series Editors

Gerhard Goos, Karlsruhe University, Germany

Juris Hartmanis, Cornell University, NY, USA

Jan van Leeuwen, Utrecht University, The Netherlands

Volume Editors

David W. Embley
Brigham Young University, Computer Science Department
3361 TMCB, PO Box 26576, Provo, Utah 84602, USA
E-mail: embley@cs.byu.edu

Robert C. Goldstein
The University of British Columbia, Computing and Communications
6356 Agricultural Road, Vancouver, B.C. Canada V6T 1Z2
E-mail: bob.goldstein@ubc.ca

Cataloging-in-Publication data applied for

Die Deutsche Bibliothek - CIP-Einheitsaufnahme

Conceptual modeling : proceedings / ER '97, 16th International
Conference on Conceptual Modeling, Los Angeles, California, USA,
November 3 - 5, 1997. David Embley ; Robert Goldstein (ed.). -
Berlin ; Heidelberg ; New York ; Barcelona ; Budapest ; Hong Kong
; London ; Milan ; Paris ; Santa Clara ; Singapore ; Tokyo : Springer,
1997
   (Lecture notes in computer science ; Vol. 1331)
   ISBN 3-540-63699-4

CR Subject Classification (1991): H.2, H.4, F.1.3, F.4.1, I.2.4, H.1, J.1

ISSN 0302-9743
ISBN 3-540-63699-4 Springer-Verlag Berlin Heidelberg New York

© Springer-Verlag Berlin Heidelberg 1997
Printed in Germany

Typesetting: Camera-ready by author
SPIN 10645658   06/3142 – 5 4 3 2 1 0   Printed on acid-free paper

Preface

It has been about two decades since the first ER conference was held at UCLA in 1979. Returning ER to UCLA is certainly a special event. Some of us on the original committee, although slightly older, are still here to take part in ER'97. To mark this event, a special symposium, Conceptual Modeling: Historical Perspectives and Future Directions, will be held on the Sunday prior to the conference and is open to all ER'97 registrants. A summary of the symposium will be presented at a pre-conference panel discussion on Monday evening. Both the symposium and the panel will be chaired by Peter P. Chen, originator of the Entity-Relationship model.

The theme of the program has been shifted towards a balance between industry practice and research academics. Therefore, the program for ER'97 has been designed specifically to appeal to consultants and information systems professionals as well as to information technology academics and researchers in computer-company laboratories. As a result, three conference sessions organized by our industry chair, Douglas M. Tolbert, are entirely devoted to presentations by industry-based researchers. A panel session on "Is the Future of Conceptual Modeling Bleak or Bright? " is also included. In response to the call for papers, approximately 93 papers were submitted from 24 countries for review, 30 of which from 18 countries were selected by the program committee for ten paper sessions covering the topics: Activity Modeling, Temporal Modeling, Languages, O-O modeling, Distributed Systems, Automated Design Tools, Integration and Case Studies. Each paper was reviewed by at least three reviewers. I want to take this opportunity to thank the program committee's outstanding job in refereeing the papers, and the program chairs, David W. Embley and Robert C. Goldstein. in composing an excellent program for ER'97.

The keynote speakers for ER'97 are well-known to ER conference participants. Dr. Alan G. Merten, currently the president of George Mason University, will talk about the relevance of information technology at the highest levels of an organization. Dr. Michael L. Brodie is a senior staff scientist at GTE Laboratories. His presentation will describe some industrial-strength information systems problems and possibilities for solving them, coming from the perspective of an organization that maintains 150 terabytes of data and 200 million lines of code.

A tutorial program, coordinated by our dedicated chair, Ashok Malhotra, begins the week's events. Extending and complementing the main program is the post conference workshop, covering the topic of futuristic conceptual modeling.

I want to thank our registration chair, Hua Yang, for handling the registration details and our publicity chair, Stephen W. Liddle, for handling the publicity of ER'97 so well. Our special thanks goes to Alfonso Cardenas for his local arrangements, assuring that the conference will run smoothly, and also for selecting the elegant banquet site to exhibit our beautiful beaches and allow the participants to enjoy their stay in Los Angeles.

Finally, we would like to express our sincere appreciation to all those who contributed to ER'97: the authors, invited speakers, session chairs, tutorial presenters, industrial chairs, and participants.

Westwood, November 1997

Wesley W. Chu,
General Conference Chair

Conference Organization

Conference Chair:
Wesley W. Chu, University of California at Los Angeles

Program Co-chairs:
David W. Embley, Brigham Young University
Robert C. Goldstein, University of British Columbia

Industrial Chair:
Douglas M. Tolbert, Unisys Corporation

Tutorial Chair:
Ashok Malhotra, IBM Thomas. J. Watson Research Center

Local Arrangements Chair:
Alfonso Cardenas, University of California at Los Angeles

Registration Chair:
Hua Yang, University of California at Los Angeles

Publicity Chair:
Stephen W. Liddle, Brigham Young University

Steering Committee Representatives:
Stefano Spaccapietra, Swiss Federal Institute of Technology (Chair)
Bernhard Thalheim, Cottbus Technical University (Vice Chair)
Peter Chen, Louisiana State University (ER'97 Liaison)

Area Liaisons:
Asia: Arbee Chen, National Tsing Hua University
Australia: Igor Hawryszkiewycz, Univ. of Technology, Sydney
Chile/Central Am.: Javier Pinto, Pont. Univ. Catolica de Chile
Europe: Georges Gardarin, University of P. et M. Curie-CNRS
Japan: Yahiko Kambayashi, Kyoto University
Mexico: Alfonso Cardenas, University of California at Los Angeles
Mid East: Peretz Shoval, Ben-Gurion University of Negev
South America: Alberto Laender, Univ. Federal de Minas Gerais

Tutorials:

OML: A Metamodel and Notation for a Pure Object-Oriented Software Development Environment by Brian Henderson-Sellers (Swinburne University of Technology, Australia)

A Roles, Relationships & Responsibilities Model for Developing Workflow Applications by Sidney Decker (KPMG Peat Marwick, USA)

A Rapid, Metamodel-Based Methodology for Information Systems Modeling by David Kerner (USA)

Object-Role Modeling by Gordon C. Everest (University of Minnesota, USA)

Symposium:

Conceptual Modeling: Historical Perspectives and Future Directions
  Ray Liuzzi (US Air Force Rome Laboratory)
  Mike McNeil (BBN Technologies)
  Leah Wong (US Navy NRaD)
  Peter Chen (Lousianna State University)

Workshops:

Conceptual Modeling in Multimedia Information
  James Allan (University of Massachusetts, USA)
  Peter Bruza (Queensland University of Technology, Australia)
  Yves Chiaramella (University of Grenoble, France)
  Norbert Fuhr (University of Dortmund, Germany)
  Ramesh Jain (University of California, San Diego, USA)
  Carlo Meghini (Consiglio Nazionale delle Ricerche, Italy)

Strategies for Collaborative Modeling and Simulation
  Albert M. Selvin (NYNEX Science & Technology, Inc., USA)
  Maarten Sierhuis (NYNEX Science & Technology, Inc., USA)

Cognition and Conceptual Modeling
  Jeffrey Parsons (Memorial Univ. of Newfoundland, Canada)
  Ramesh Venkataraman (University of Maryland, USA)

Behavioral Models and Design Transformations: Issues and Opportunities in Conceptual Modeling
  Stephen W. Clyde (Utah State University)
  Stephen W. Liddle (Brigham Young University)
  Scott N. Woodfield (Brigham Young University)

Program Committee

External Referees

Karl Aberer
Jacky Akoka
Herman Balsters
Marcos Borges
Terje Brasethvik
Robert Chiang
Andreas Christiansen
John M. DuBois
D. Fillippido
Maarten Fokkinga
Steffen Geschke
Teruhisa Hochin
Michael Höding
Jason Kwak
Rynson Lau
Jae Young Lee
Mong Li Lee
Ee-Peng Lim
L.H. Lim
Regina Motz
Vincent Ng

Marc Oste
E. Pitarokilis
Rodolfo Ferreira Resende
Berthier A. Ribeiro-Neto
Sumit Sarkar
Ingo Schmitt
Michael Schrefl
Isamu Shioya
Eriks Sneiders
Daeweon Son
Janis Stirna
P.K. Teo
Can Türker
Henderikus van Rein
Mark W.W. Vermeer
Jonckers Viviane
Jef Wijsen
Jongho Won
Scott N. Woodfield
Irene Woon
Esteban Zimanyi

Table of Contents

Session 1: Keynote Address
From Conceptual Modeler to University President 1
Alan G. Merten (President, George Mason University)

Session 2a: Automated Design
Chair: *Alberto Laender (Universidade Federal de Minas Gerais)*

An Ontology for Database Design Automation 2
V.C. Storey, H. Ullrich, S. Sundaresan

Exploiting Domain Knowledge During the Automated Design of
Object-Oriented Databases 16
M. Lloyd-Williams

Intelligent Support for Retrieval and Synthesis of Patterns for
Object-Oriented Design 30
S. Purao, V.C. Storey

Session 2b: Temporal Modeling
Chair: *Ramez Elmasri (The University of Texas at Arlington)*

A Conceptual Development Framework for Temporal Information
Systems 43
I. Petrounias

Temporal Features of Class Populations and Attributes in Conceptual
Models 57
D. Costal, A. Olivé, M.R. Sancho

Managing Schema Evolution Using a Temporal Object Model 71
I.A. Goralwalla, D. Szafron, M.T. Özsu, R.J. Peters

Session 3: Invited Talk
Chair: *Douglas M. Tolbert (Unisys Corporation)*

Distributed Object Repositories: Concepts and Standards 85
S. Iyengar

Session 4a: Languages
Chair: *Paul Johannesson (Stockholm University)*

Extended SQL Support for Uncertain Data 102
D. Dey, S. Sarkar

Conceptual Queries Using ConQuer-II 113
A.C. Bloesch, T.A. Halpin

Transaction-Based Specification of Database Evolution 127
L. Bækgaard

Session 4b: Activity Modeling
Chair: *Sharma Chakravarthy (University of Florida)*

Well-behaving Rule Systems for Entity-Relationship and Object-Oriented
Models 141
K.D. Schewe

Behavior Consistent Refinement of Object Life Cycles 155
M. Schrefl, M. Stumptner

ActivityFlow: Towards Incremental Specification and Flexible Coordination of Workflow Activities 169
L. Liu, C. Pu

Session 5: Keynote Address
Silver Bullet Shy On Legacy Mountain: When Neat Technology Just
Doesn't Work — or — Miracles To Save The Realm: Faustian Bargains
Or Noble Pursuits 183
Michael L. Brodie (Senior Staff Scientist, GTE Laboratories Inc.)

Session 6a: Applied Modeling
Chair: *Terry Halpin (The University of Queensland)*

A Multi-level Architecture for Representing Enterprise Data
Models 184
D. Moody

Data Model for Customizing DB Schemas Based on Business
Policies 198
J. Sekine, A. Kitai, Y. Ooshima, Y. Oohara

Explaining Conceptual Models – An Architecture and Design
Principles 215
H. Dalianis, P. Johannesson

Session 6b: Object-Oriented Modeling
Chair: *Ling Liu (Oregon Graduate Institute)*

Extending an Object-Oriented Model: Multiple Class Objects 229
T. Hruška, P. Kolenčík

Formal Approach to Metamodeling: A Generic Object-Oriented
Perspective 243
V.B. Mišić, S. Moser

Associations and Roles in Object-Oriented Modeling 257
W.W. Chu, G. Zhang

Session 7a: Theoretical Issues in Modeling
Chair: *Tok Wang Ling (National University of Singapore)*

Property Covering: A Powerful Construct for Schema Derivations .. 271
A. Analyti, N. Spyratos, P. Constantopoulos

Inheritance Graph Hierarchy Construction Using Rectangular
Decomposition of a Binary Relation and Designer Feedback 285
M.M. Gammoudi, J.D. Mendes, W.S. Pinto

Towards an Object Database Approach for Managing Concept
Lattices 299
K. Waiyamai, R. Taouil, L. Lakhal

Session 7b: Experience and Applications
Chair: *Uwe Hohenstein (Siemens AG)*

An Experience of Integration of Conceptual Schemas in the Italian Public
Administration 313
C. Batini, G. Longobardi, S. Fornasiero

Application-Oriented Design of Behavior: A Transformational Approach
Using RADD 323
M. Albrecht, M. Altus, M. Steeg

Session 8a: Distributed Systems
Chair: *Debabrata Dey (University of Washington)*

A Java-Based Framework for Processing Distributed Objects 333
D. Wu, D. Agrawal, A.El Abbadi, A. Singh

Fragmentation   Techniques   for   Distributing   Object-Oriented
Databases 347
E. Malinowski, S. Chakravarthy

An Agent Based Mobile System 361
N. Pissinou, K. Makki, M. Hong, L. Ji, A. Kumar

Session 8b: Panel Discussion

Is the Future of Conceptual Modeling Bleak or Bright? 375
Moderator: Shamkant B. Navathe

Session 9: Invited Talk
Chair: *Douglas M. Tolbert (Unisys Corporation)*

Successful Practices in Developing a Complex Information Model .. 376
P. Thompson, J.W. Sweitzer

Session 10a: Integration
Chair: *Isabelle Comyn-Wattiau (Ecole Supirieure des Sciences Economiques et Commerciales)*

Resolving Constraint Conflicts in the Integration of Entity-Relationship Schemas 394
M.L. Lee, T.W. Ling

A Formal Framework for ER Schema Transformation 408
P. McBrien, A. Poulovassilis

A Generative Approach to Database Federation 422
U. Hohenstein, V. Plesser

Session 10b: Tools
Chair: *Sudha Ram (University of Arizona)*

A Virtual Reality Interface to an Enterprise Metadatabase 436
L. Yee, C. Hsu

A Fully Flexible CAME in a CASE Environment 450
A.N.W. Dahanayake, H.G. Sol, J.L.G. Dietz

A Rapid Development Model for Meta-CASE Tool Design 464
M. Gong, L. Scott, Y. Xiao, R. Offen

Author Index 479

From Conceptual Modeler to University President

Alan G. Merten
President, George Mason University

If business, academic, and governmental organizations ever needed leadership, they need it now. Historically, the leaders of business have come from finance, law, marketing, and other traditional disciplines. The leaders of universities have come from arts and science, law, etc. Rarely have computer scientists or information system professionals rose to the ranks of top management.. There are signs that this is about to change. What are the advantages and disadvantages of leading from a information technology background? Why should we provide leadership? What does a technically educated professional need to do to move to senior, general management positions? What should you expect if and when you get the positions?¡/blockquote¿

An Ontology for Database Design Automation[1]

Veda C. Storey
Department of Computer Information Systems
College of Business Administration
Georgia State University
P.O. Box 4015 Atlanta, Georgia 30302-4015
E-mail: vstorey@gsu.edu
Telephone: (404)-651-3894, Fax: (404)-651-3842

Harald Ullrich
William E. Simon Graduate School of Business Administration
University of Rochester
Rochester, NY 14627

Shankar Sundaresan
316 Beam Building
The Smeal College of Business Administration
Pennsylvania State University
University Park, PA 16802
E-mail: shankar-s@psu.edu

Abstract
Although it is possible to encode a great deal of process knowledge about database design into a system, experience has shown that the contribution of a human designer extends beyond his or her knowledge of database design techniques. The next step in the evolution of automated database design tools is to incorporate knowledge and reasoning capabilities to support this higher level of participation. Doing so, requires some understanding of what different terms mean. This paper presents an ontology that can be used as a surrogate for the meaning of words in a database design system to simulate the contributions that a designer would make to a design session with a user based on the designer's general knowledge. The ontology classifies a term into one or more categories such as *person*, *abstract good*, or *tradable document*. It is comprised of a semantic network, a knowledge base containing information on the meaning of terms that have been classified, an expert system knowledge acquisition component, and a distance measure for assessing the distance between the meanings of terms. The ontology was tested by different types of users on a variety of problems and was shown to be quite effective.

---

[1] This research was supported by the National Science Foundation under Research Initiation Award IRI-9209252 to the first author, a research grant from the College of Business Administration, Georgia State University, and the William E. Simon Graduate School of Business Administration, University of Rochester. The authors with to thank Robert C. Goldstein, Roger Chiang and Deb Dey for useful discussions on this research and Shigetaka Yamakawa for his assistance in analyzing the data.

1 Introduction

Database design tools attempt to capture and represent the data items that are important to the application domain for which the database is being developed. Many of these systems have quite sophisticated rules and heuristics for developing a good design for an application. However, they typically rely on the user for all information about the application [Storey and Goldstein, 1993]. A system guides the user through the process of specifying entities, relationships, and attributes. It then applies its expertise to detect missing or conflicting data, expresses the requirements as a well-formed conceptual model, and translates this into a form suitable for implementation. Database design systems, however, cannot compare, for example, a term that a user provides with one from a system's stock of knowledge about that application domain to ascertain if they are the same. This would require an understanding, or some surrogate, for the meaning of the terms. The objective of this research, therefore, is to: *develop an ontology that can be used as a surrogate for the meaning of words.* The ontology can then be incorporated into other expert systems for database design as an additional module to automatically make comparisons between terms based upon some understanding of their semantics.

2 Database Design Ontology

Any knowledge-based system is based on some abstract, simplified view of the world that is called a conceptualization. An ontology is an explicit specification of such a conceptualization [Gruber, 1993]. If two (or more) parties — humans and/or computer programs — can agree on a common ontology as a specification of their shared domain of interest, the ontology can be used to support communication among them, even though they may use entirely different internal knowledge representation mechanisms. The use of ontologies is found in many different areas: the CYC project [Lenat, 1995]; semantic interoperability [Goh et al., 1994, Sciore, 1994]; conceptual database design [Bergamaschi and Sartori, 1992]; and context interchange [Madnick, 1995]. Research on Naïve Semantics which is "commonsense knowledge associated with words" [Dahlgren, 1988; Dahlgren et al., 1989], is of particular interest.

This section presents our database design ontology. The ontology classifies a term (entity name) into one or more categories such as *person, abstract good* or *tradable document*. The purpose of the ontology is to store and provide information on the meaning of terms, to acquire information regarding the meaning of new terms, and to compare two terms to determine if and how they might be related. The ontology consists of the following components:

- a *semantic network* describing the different categories into which terms can be classified;
- a *knowledge base* containing information on the meaning of terms that have already been classified;
- an *expert system-based knowledge acquisition component* supporting an interactive, dialog-oriented extraction of the meaning of terms from a user; and
- a *distance measure* for assessing the distance between the meanings of terms.

2.1 Semantic Network

The ontology is represented by a semantic network that has 57 leaf nodes corresponding to each of the possible categories into which an entity can be classified. These particular nodes are the result of the classification scheme (discussed below) and some reasonable pruning. Figure 1 shows a small part of the semantic network which consists of the most general categories. Subnodes are connected via "is-specialization-of" links as indicated by the arrows.

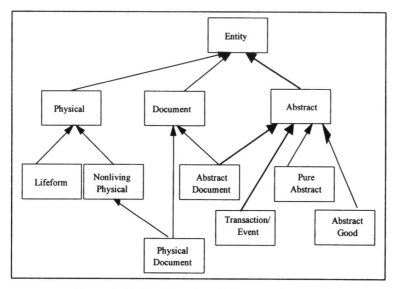

Figure 1: Main categories of the semantic network

Classification Criteria.

Eight criteria were developed to classify a term into one (or more) of the nodes of the semantic network. The objective in developing these eight was to minimize the number of criteria (and hence, the number of questions asked of a user to classify a term) while maximizing the usefulness of the categories of the semantic network. The criteria are: 1) weight (WGT), 2) activity/event (AE), 3) social structure (SS), 4) living (LIV), 5) person (PRS), 6) contains information (INF), 7) permanent location (PL), and 8) bought or sold (BS). For example, it is obvious that the distinction of whether something is a person is important because there are many entities in business applications that are types of people (e.g., *Manager, Employee, Secretary*). "Has weight" helps distinguish concepts that are physical from those that are abstract; "bought/sold" identifies those concepts that are tradable.

Each criterion can take on 3 possible values: "yes" (Y), "no" (N), or "both" possible (B). A value of "both" is most appropriate when there can be more than one classification or the user is uncertain. Every term can be described by these eight attributes and their values. These eight were chosen by first examining other work on ontologies.   Since this research is restricted to database design for business applications, our ontology could be more restrictive than, for example, that required for the CYC project [Lenat, 1995]. Dictionary meanings, as well as thesaurus information were consulted. Informal testing of the system during the development process was also instrumental in finalizing the classification criteria.

The part of the semantic network that classifies transactions or events is shown in Figure 2 and corresponds to:

$$\text{WGT} = \text{N} \qquad \text{(has no measurable weight)}$$
$$\text{AE} = \text{Y} \qquad \text{(is an activity or event)}$$

Then, the transaction/event category is further separated into "service" and "nontradable transaction/event" based on whether 'bought/sold' = Y or N. It is not necessary to consider any of the remaining five criteria (i.e., social structure, living, person, contains information, permanent location).   Note that the actual labels assigned to the categories are not very important because it is intended that the ontology be used internally by a system to compare terms.

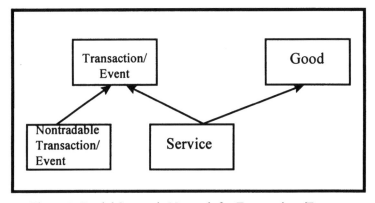

Figure 2: Partial Semantic Network for Transactions/Events

Structure.
There are generalization/specialization hierarchies in the semantic network, such as the part that models *Document* as shown in Figure 3. Based on the user's responses, a term, for example, *Book*, might be classified as a document (the most general document category), even though a more refined classification might be the specialization, "tradable physical document". The user's classification, obviously, is not incorrect. It simply provides less information.

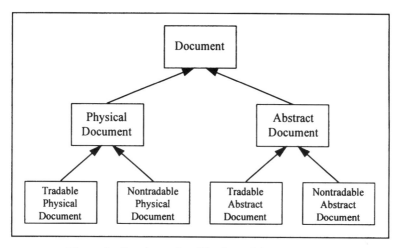

Figure 3: Ontology classification of document

Multiple Classifications.

Multiple meanings are quite frequent; for example, *Chair* might be classified (correctly) as "tradable nonliving physical nondocument" (the chair one sits in) or "person" (the chair of a department) or "pure abstract" (endowed chair). These interpretations can be captured simultaneously. Representative classifications are shown in Table 1.

2.2 Knowledge Base

The knowledge base consists of a set of terms and their classifications. It is possible to start with an empty knowledge base and to build it up. Eventually, this will be expanded to include attributes of terms and other information represented through feature types (common pieces of knowledge about something) as in the Naïve Semantics ontology.

2.3 Knowledge Acquisition Component

The process of classifying a term is a knowledge acquisition process, requiring human input. A user might not be expected to be able to know which classification(s) is most appropriate for a term. We use an expert system to acquire knowledge by asking a series of questions until a term is classified as precisely as possible. The knowledge acquisition expert system consists of:

- an "intelligent" questioning scheme
- rules that help to: i) infer/predict user's answers, ii) optimize the sequence of questions asked, and iii) resolve consistency conflicts in the user's answers.

Table 1: Classification of terms into categories

No.	WGT	LIV	PRS	SS	PL	BS	AE	INF	Result
1		Y		N			N	N	Lifeform
2	Y	Y	Y	N	N		N	N	Person
12		Y	N	N			N	N	Population Group
13			N	Y			N		Social Structure
14			N	Y		Y	N		Tradable Social Structure
16	N		N	N			Y	N	Transaction/Event
17	N		N	N		Y	Y	N	Service
19	N	N	N	N	N				Abstract
20	N	N	N	N	N	Y	N		Abstract Good
22		N	N	N	N		N	Y	Document
23	N	N	N	N	N		N	Y	Abstract Document
24	Y	N	N	N	N		N	Y	Physical Document
25		N	N	N	N	Y	N	Y	Tradable Document
26		N	N	N	N	N	N	Y	Nontradable Document
27	N	N	N	N	N	Y	N	Y	Tradable Abstract Document
28	N	N	N	N	N	N	N	Y	Nontradable Abstract Document
31				N			N		Physical
32			N	N	Y		N		Stationary Physical
33	Y		N	N	N		N		Nonstationary Physical
34				N		Y	N		Tradable Physical
40	Y	N	N	N			N		Nonliving Physical
41		N	N	N	Y		N		Stationary Nonliving Physical
42	Y	N	N	N	N		N		Nonstat. Nonliving Physical
43	Y	N	N	N		Y	N		Tradable Nonliving Physical
44	Y	N	N	N		N	N		Nontradable Nonliving Physical
45		N	N	N	Y	Y	N		Tradable Stat. Nonliving Physical

Questioning Scheme.
The questions the user must answer when classifying a term correspond directly to the 8 criteria on which the categories in the semantic network are based. The questions were formulated to be simple and unambiguous. A maximum of eight questions generates the 57 categories into which an entity could be classified. The questions are illustrated in Figure 4. To each question, a user can respond "yes", "no", or "both". Therefore, there could be 3^8 or over 6400 different answers possible. However, inference rules are used to prune the search tree.

> - Does "purchase order" have a measurable weight?
> - Is "purchase order" an activity or an event?
> - Is "purchase order" a social structure (e.g., a team)?
> - Is "purchase order" living?
> - Does "purchase order" usually have a first name and a last name?
> - Does "purchase order" contain information?
> - Does "purchase order" have a permanent location?
> - Can "purchase order" be bought or sold?

Figure 4: User questioning for "purchase order"

When multiple classifications are possible, or the user is unsure of what the correct response should be, then, the user should respond with "both". For example, a response of "both" to a question asking whether *Customer* is a "person," allows a customer to be either a person or an organization. Then, after further questioning, the classification might be "person" or "tradable social structure". This would be used in a database design to ensure that "person" properties (e.g., SSN, etc.) are not attached to an organization or vice versa.

The questioning scheme is illustrated in Figure 5. The questions are organized so that they are being asked in an intelligent order, which is context-dependent. For example, if the answer to the question "Does it have weight?" is "no", then a user would not be asked whether the term refers to a person.

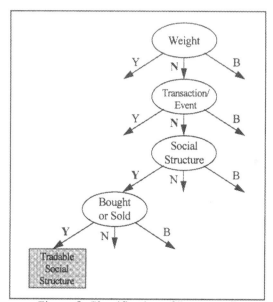

Figure 5: Classification of "company"

Rules.
Four sets of rules help to ensure the correctness of the user's responses, correctness of the classifications, and a dynamic reordering of the sequence of questions asked, based on the user's prior answers, to minimize the number of questions asked.

1. Classification rules identify the minimum number of things needed to establish a category, thus, reducing the number of questions asked. For example:

> *If:* Activity/Event = 'yes'
> Bought/Sold = 'yes'
> ***Then:*** Category = "Service"

> *If:* Living = 'yes',
> Person='no'

> Social Structure = 'yes'
> Bought/Sold = 'B'

Then: Category = "Social Structure"

2. Pruning rules as shown in Figure 6, are based on our knowledge of the real world. For example, if something does not have a weight, then it cannot be a person.

WGT = N	->	PRS = N	SS = Y	->	AE = N
WGT = Y	->	AE = N	SS = Y	->	PRS = N
LIV = Y	->	AE = N	PL = Y	->	PRS = N
LIV = Y	->	INF = N	PL = Y	->	INF = N
LIV = N	->	PRS = N	AE = Y	->	PRS = N
PRS = Y	->	WGT = Y	AE = Y	->	SS = N
PRS = Y	->	LIV = Y	AE = Y	->	WGT = N
PRS = Y	->	INF = N	INF = Y	->	LIV = N
PRS = Y	->	AE = N	INF= Y	->	AE = N
PRS = Y	->	PL = N	INF = Y	->	PRS = N
PRS = Y	->	SS = N	INF = Y	->	PL = N

Figure 6: Rules for pruning of questions asked

3. Conflict resolution rules help to ensure that the user's responses are internally consistent. For example, suppose the user indicates that the concept is living. Then, the response to "contains information" cannot be "yes" so it is changed to the more general answer, "both".

> *If:*   LIV = 'yes'
> INF = 'yes'
>
> *Then*: INF = 'B'

4. Rules for selection of detailed classification select the most detailed classification from a set of established categories. For example, if something is a service, which is a specialization of "transaction/event", then the other main categories, such as social structure, can be ignored.

2.4 Distance Measurement
The ontology is intended to act as a mechanism by which a system can compare two terms (entities) to determine if they are the same, possibly related, or different.

Same: Two entities are candidates to be the same if they have the same ontology classification. For example, both *Plane* and *Airplane* are classified as "tradable, nonstationary, nonliving, physical, nondocument."

Possibly Related: Two entities are possibly related if one is defined as a generalization, specialization, or share common categories. For example, *Document* is a generalization of *Abstract Document*.

Different:. Consider the entities *Flight* and *Flight-attendant*. *Flight* is classified as ``abstract good'' whereas *Flight-attendant* would be classified as "person". Obviously, these entities must be different. This exemplifies that the actual category names are not important.

3 Testing

The ontology was used on a variety of problems by different types of users to test the system for completeness and robustness. Seventeen people participated in the study. Two subjects were considered to be experts in database design, three had medium knowledge, and the remaining subjects were novices. All had the same amount of general knowledge about the tasks. Three diverse types of database design tasks were designed for the testing: 1) Entity names were chosen from sample databases that appear in Microsoft Access™. 2) Database design scenarios were written from which the subjects needed to generate appropriate entity names for a given domain. 3) Nouns from magazine articles were selected. Many of these words would be classified as non-entity names but were included to test the robustness of the ontological classifications. The tasks are summarized in Table 2.

Table 2: Tasks

Access™ applications	Problem descriptions	Magazine articles
Book collection (author, book, quotation, subject, publisher)	Day care center	AT&T introduces USA Direct Service (service, barrier, market, information, business)
Student and classes (student, class, department, instructor, assignment)	Airline	The mining company and the owl that lives underground (owl, ground, capability, community, experience)
Inventory control (employee, inventory transaction, product, supplier, purchase order)	Hotel	COMPAQ advertisement (multimedia, speakers, power, memory, internet)
Time and billing (client, company, payment, time card, project)	Pharmacy	Balance (balance, smoke, youth, brands, samples)
Asset tracking (asset, asset category, maintenance, depreciation, employee)	Consulting company	Interview with Bill Gates (profit, spreadsheet, industry, institution, dream)
Membership (committee, member, member type, organization, payment)	Video rental	Divorce, Chuck-and-Di style (divorce, couple, marriage, knowledge, cocktail)

- Access applications – these are entities taken from the sample databases found in Access™. These were included to provide unbiased examples. They were also intended to verify that the system works for straight-forward cases.

- Problem descriptions – a set of six small database problems were developed. The subjects were required to read a problem description and from this identify five entities. The purpose of this test was to see if the ontology works for cases where there are user-generated entities.

- Magazine articles -- a set of articles from magazines such as *Business Week* and *MacLean's* were selected. Five nouns were underlined for the subjects to consider. The nouns were chosen so that they should be classified into a variety of the categories; for example, they could not all be classified as "pure abstract".

Each subject was asked to use the system for one problem from each of the three different types of design tasks. Each task required 5 terms to be classified for a total of 15 nouns per subject. To overcome any learning that was involved, the subjects were given the tasks so that an equal number did the tasks in the orders: 1-2-3, 2-3-1, and 3-1-2.

The subjects' results were compared to that of experts'. The experts were the researchers who agreed on the most appropriate or most general classification of the test cases. A subject's classification of a term was compared to the experts' as follows:

1. **Same** -- the subject's classification is exactly the same as that of the experts. There may be a single classification of a term or multiple classifications.
2. **Specialization** -- the subject's classification is a specialization of that of the experts'.
3. **Generalization** --the subject's classification is a generalization of that of the experts'.
4. **Overlap** – some, but not all, of the user's categories overlap with those of the experts'. These occur for terms with multiple classifications.
5. **Partial** -- the user's classification is a subset of the experts'.
6. **Partial Specialization** -- at least one of the user's classifications is a specialization of that of the experts'.
7. **Different** – none of the above.
   Examples of each of these are shown in Table 3.

There were a total of 285 classifications. 148 classifications were the same by the subjects as the experts. In 34 cases, the subjects' classifications were specializations of the experts', 20 were generalizations, 18 had overlap, 26 were partially the same, 1 was a partial specialization and 38 were different.

Table 3: User versus expert classifications

Type	Task	Term	User Classification	Expert Classification	Evaluation (User vs Expert)
Access™ application	Time and billing	company	tradable social structure	tradable social structure	same
Problem description	Airline	equipment	tradable stationary nonliving physical nondocument	tradable nonliving physical nondocument	Special-ization
Magazine	Interview with Bill Gates	dream	transaction/ event	nontradable transaction/event	General-ization
Access™ application	Student and classes	Assign-ment	nontradable transaction/ event; pure abstract	nontradable transaction/event; nontradable abstract document	overlap
Problem description	Consulting company	client	person	person, social structure	partial
Access™ application	Access™: member	member	nontradable social structure	person, social structure	partial special-ization
Magazine	Divorce Chuck-and-Di style	divorce	service	nontradable activity/event	different

3.1 Discussion

Approximately 85% of the users' classifications were similar to that of the experts', with over 50% of those being exactly the same. Approximately 35% of the classifications were specializations or generalizations, partial or overlapping. Those classified as partial were perfectly acceptable responses because the user might have had a specific role in mind for a term, whereas the experts had more general meanings in mind. Specializations indicated that the user has a more narrow focus than the experts, whereas gereralizations were the inverse. Approximately 15% of the classifications were different. Some of this (about half) could be explained by the user classifying something incorrectly in a generalization hierarchy. For example, the user might classify something as "nontradable social structure" when it would have been correctly classified as "tradable social structure". The remaining errors were user error. From observing the system in use, these seemed to be attributed to either inexperience on the part of the user or misunderstanding of the application domain. For example, one user considered the term *Book* in both its hardcopy and electronic forms. Another user said that *Book* had a permanent location and seemed to be thinking about books in a library.

As a result of the testing, two of the system's questions, those dealing with whether the concept is a social structure or stores information were re-worded, as shown in Figure 4. For the social structure question the example was added. In general, questions that were the easiest for the users to respond to were those with examples given. Finally, it should be noted that the system was able to classify all terms; there were not any cases where the system was simply unable to make a classification.

4. Application of Ontology

The ontology is being developed for incorporation into a system called the Common Sense Business Reasoner [Storey et al., 1997; 1996]. The objective of the research on the Common Sense Business Reasoner is to develop a capability for acquiring and reasoning with common sense knowledge about the real world to improve database designs. The Common Sense Business Reasoner is intended to interact with a database design system that elicits entities, relationships, and attributes from a user to develop a conceptual model of the user's application. The Common Sense Business Reasoner compares the user's conceptual model to what it knows about the application domain for which the model is being developed and suggests improvements to the design (reasoning). It also acquires additional knowledge from the user's design session (learning). The ontology is used for both the reasoning and the learning functions.

Reasoning is similar to learning, but compares a user's application to the system's knowledge of a domain. There are two types of learning -- within application domain and across application domains. Learning within the same application domain takes place when two or more applications are generalized to form a new node in the system's common sense knowledge base of application domains. Consider, for example, two users' applications for an airline application. User 1's application has the entities *Pilot, Flight-attendant, Airplane, Flight,* and *Passenger,* and the relationships *Pilot flies Flight* and *Passenger takes Flight.* User 2's application consists of the entities, *Pilot, Employee, Plane, Flight, Customer,* and *Ticket,* and the relationships *Pilot assigned-to Flight, Customer buys Ticket,* and *Customer takes Flight.* Based on the ontology alone, the system can conclude:

- *Pilot, Flight-attendant,* and *Passenger* from Airline 1 are candidates to be compared to *Pilot, Employee,* and *Customer* in Airline 2 because their ontology classification is "person".
- *Airplane* and *Plane* can be compared because their ontology classification is: "tradable nonstationary nonliving physical nondocument".

Learning across heterogeneous application domains involves generalizing, for example, *Airline, Railroad,* and *Busline* to a *Transportation* node. The ontology is even more important here because the names of the entities involved can be much different. Figure 7 shows three different application domains that can be generalized to a transportation domain.

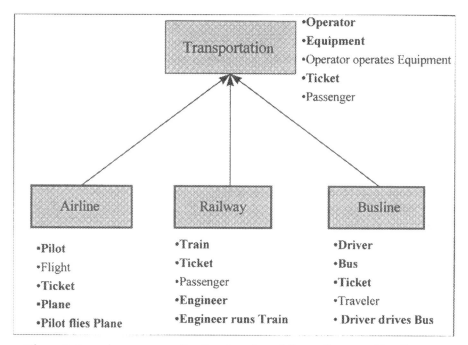

Figure 7: Learning across application domains: airline, railway, and busline are generalized to transportation

- *Pilot, Engineer, Driver, Passenger,* and *Traveler* are all candidates to be the same because their ontology classification is "person". Further work on the part of the system is needed to identify the first three as being comparable.
- *Plane, Train,* and *Bus* are candidates to be the same because their classification is "tradable nonstationary nonliving physical nondocument".

A classification of "not related", for example, for Ticket ("tradable nonstationary nonliving physical document*)* and *Passenger*, ("person") means the system can automatically eliminate some of the options it presents the user.

5. Conclusion

A database design ontology comprising 57 categories into which entities may be classified has been presented. The ontology is represented as a semantic network and is based on eight general classification criteria. Testing of the ontology was carried out on various terms from different application domains. It was found to be effective in over 85% of the test cases. The ontology is language-independent. The knowledge base of classified terms can easily be expanded through use. Observation of the testing showed that the ontology is relatively compact and easy to use. In addition, it allows a term to have multiple classification to capture different meanings. Future research will involve the incorporation of feature types and the integration of the ontology into an expert database design system.

6. Bibliography

1. Bergamaschi, S., and Sartoni, C., ``On Taxonomic Reasoning in Conceptual Design'', *ACM Transactions On Database Systems*, Vol.17, No.3, 1992, pp.385-422.
2. Dahlgren, K., McDowell, J., and Stabler, E. P., ``Knowledge Representation for Commonsense Reasoning with Text'', *Computational Linguistics* , Vol. 15, No. 3, 1989, pp.149-170.
3. Dahlgren, K., *Naive Semantics for Natural Language Understanding* , Kluwer Academic Publishers, The Netherlands, 1988.
4. Goh, C.H., Madnick, S.E., and Sigel, M., ``Context Interchange: Overcoming the Challenges of Large-Scale Interoperable Database Systems in a Dynamic Environment'', *Proceedings of the Third International Conference on Information and Knowledge Management (CIKM-94),* 29~November-2~December 1994, Gaithersburg, Maryland.
5. Gruber, T.R., ``A Translation Approach to Portable Ontology Specifications'', *Knowledge Acquisition*, Vol.5, 1993, pp.199-220.
6. Lenat, D.B., ``CYC: A Large-Scale Investment in Knowledge Infrastructure'', *Communications of the ACM*, Vol.38, No.11, November 1995, pp.33-41.
7. Madnick, S.E., "Integrating Information From Global Systems: Dealing with the 'On and Off-Ramps' of the Information Superhighway", *Journal of Organizational Computing*, Vol.5, No.2, 1995, pp.69-82.
8. Sciore, E., Siegel, M., and Rosenthal, A., ``Using Semantic Values to Facilitate Interoperability Among Heterogeneous Information Systems'', *ACM Transactions on Data Base Systems,* Vol.19, No.2, June 1994, pp.254-290.
9. Storey, V.C. and Goldstein, R.C., ``Knowledge-Based Approaches to DatabaseDesign'', *Management Information Systems Quarterly,* Vol.17, No.1, March 1993, pp.25-46.
10. Storey, V.C., Chaing, R., Dey, D., Goldstein, R.C., Sundaresan, S., and Ullrich, H., "Common Sense Reasoning and Learning for Database Design Systems", *ACM Transactions on Data Base Systems (TODS),* 1997, forthcoming.
11. Storey, V.C., Dey, D., Sundaresan, S., Ullrich, H., and Yamakawa, S., ``Learning Across Application Domains for Database Design Systems''. *Proceedings of the Sixth Workshop on Information Technologies and Systems (WITS'96)*, Cleveland, Ohio, 14-15 December, 1996.

Exploiting Domain Knowledge During the Automated Design of Object-Oriented Databases

Michael Lloyd-Williams

Department of Information Studies
University of Sheffield
Sheffield
S10 2TN
U.K

Recent years have seen the development of a number of expert system type tools who's primary objective is to provide support to a human during the process of database analysis and design. It is generally accepted that these tools, although possessing database design knowledge, are in most cases ignorant of the application domains in which they work, and as such are required to ask what may be regarded as extremely trivial questions in order to elicit the required information. This paper illustrates how domain knowledge representing aspects of these applications may be represented within such tools using a thesaurus approach, and how this knowledge may be exploited by a tool during design processing. It discusses how the technique has been applied to a knowledge based tool designed to support the development of object-oriented databases, resulting in an increase in both the processing efficiency and the overall appearance of intelligence of the tool.

1 Introduction

Recent years have seen the development of a number of expert system tools designed to provide intelligent assistance during the database design process [4, 15, 19]. Such tools are generally intended to act as assistants to human designers [21], being capable of providing guidance, advice, proposing alternate solutions, and helping to investigate the consequences of design decisions.

The effectiveness of existing systems has demonstrated the viability of representing database design expertise in a computer program, but observing such systems in use makes it clear that human designers contribute far more than database design expertise to the design process [20]. Human designers, even when working in an unfamiliar domain, are able make use of their knowledge of the real-world in order to interact with users, make helpful suggestions and inferences, and identify potential errors and inconsistencies [18, 20]. A human designer for instance, would recognize terms such as "*client*", "*customer*" and "*patron*" as being potentially synonymous, regardless of the application domain. Existing intelligent database design tools are unable to identify such situations.

The majority of existing intelligent database design tools do not possess such real-world knowledge, and are therefore required to ask many questions during a design session that may be viewed as being trivial [14, 18]. The representation of real-world knowledge within an intelligent database design tool, coupled with the ability to reason with and make use of this knowledge, can (by reducing the number of trivial questions required) enhance both the appearance of intelligence and the efficiency of such a tool [14]. This paper discusses how such real-world knowledge may be represented and subsequently exploited by an intelligent tool designed to support the development of object-oriented databases; the Object Design Assistant.

2   The Object Design Assistant

2.1 Background Information

Object-oriented databases are a fast developing aspect of the database arena, and have become the focus of much interest and experimental activity in recent years. Indeed, object-oriented technology is viewed by many as being the *"Yellow Brick Road"* to improved productivity, reliability, maintainability, and reusability [16]. Despite this apparent level of popularity of the object-oriented approach, the majority of intelligent database design tools developed to date have concentrated on providing design support for the relational, network, and hierarchical data models [13].

The Object Design Assistant [13, 14] is an example of an intelligent tool designed to provide a coherent support environment for the design of the structural (data) aspects of object-oriented databases. The tool reflects the philosophy of expert system development expressed by Avison & Fitzgerald [1], in that the system represents a computational model of expertise within the domain which *may* reflect aspects of the behaviour of an expert. However, it is not intended to be the functional and behavioural equivalent of an expert. The system is intended to be used primarily by a database analyst/designer who may be non-expert in the process of object-oriented database design, but who is familiar with data modelling concepts. The current version of the system runs in a PC environment, and was developed using Common LISP (Allegro CL\PC).

The Object Design Assistant provides design support for the so called *pure* products of Kotz-Dittrich & Dittrich [12]. That is, products based upon extending object-oriented programming languages to provide functionality for handling persistent objects, rather than those based upon extending existing products to include object-oriented features. The designs produced by the Object Design Assistant exhibit the key object-oriented characteristics [6, 22] of object classes and instances, and the three most popular forms of data abstraction [3, 11]; association, aggregation, and generalization (including multiple inheritance). The designs also satisfy the requirements of the structural aspects of the OMG Object Database Standard *core model* described by Soley & Kent [17].

2.2 Processing Overview

The purpose of the Object Design Assistant is to provide support in the design of object-oriented databases. The main requirement on the part of a user is to provide a description of the application domain in the form of a series of declarative statements, and to subsequently provide information relating to the domain as prompted by the system.

The general procedure followed by the majority of intelligent database design tools supporting specification acquisition is as follows [15].

- Formulate an initial representation of the problem domain
- Use this initial model in order to generate a conceptual model
- Transform the conceptual model into a design model

During a design session, the Object Design Assistant follows this three-step procedure. It is not the purpose of this paper to discuss the Object Design Assistant in depth, however, a brief outline of the method of operation is required in order to illustrate how the domain specific knowledge may be represented and exploited during processing. A overview of the activities performed by the Object Design Assistant therefore follows.

Formulating an initial representation of the problem domain
Problem domain model processing is a three-step process as follows.

- The first step involves the creation of a problem domain model representative of the application domain.
- The second step involves the refinement of this model by detecting and resolving any inconsistencies that may exist (sometimes referred to as *internal* validation).
- The third step involves the confirmation (by the user) of the system's *understanding* of the semantics of the application domain as represented by the problem domain model (sometimes referred to as *external* validation).

The first step requires a set of declarative statements that describe the application domain to be submitted to the Object Design Assistant. This domain description is made up of a series of declarative statements based upon a variation of the method of interactive schema specification described by Baldiserra *et al* [2]. Such statements are based upon the binary model described by Bracchi *et al* [5] in that a statement links together two concepts (ternary relationships are not currently permitted within the domain description). Declarative statements fall into one of three classes of construct, corresponding directly to the structural abstractions of association, generalization, and aggregation. The form of each construct used is as follows, where *A* and *B* represent concepts within the application domain.

- *A verb-construct B* (representing association)
- *A is-a B* (representing generalization)
- *A has B* (representing aggregation)

In addition to these three main construct classes, the system also recognizes statements of the form *A has-property P,* which are used to explicitly define the properties of a concept. Such properties can be thought of as being equivalent to the attributes within a relation (for instance, the concept *BOOK* may have explicit properties *TITLE, AUTHOR* and *PUBLISHER*).

Statements are used to build an initial representation of the application domain which is based upon a variation of a semantic network in consisting of a series of nodes and arcs. An illustration of the declarative statements required from the user in describing an application domain (in this case, a library) follows.

AUTHOR WRITES BOOK
MEMBER BORROWS BOOK
AUTHOR HAS PROPERTY NAME
MEMBER HAS PROPERTY MEMBER-NO
BOOK HAS PROPERTY TITLE

Once constructed, the problem domain model is submitted to a series of refinement algorithms in order to detect and resolve any inconsistencies that may be present. Inconsistencies recognized and resolved at this stage include among others; repeating properties, multi-valued properties, missing arcs, missing nodes, detection of hidden hierarchies, detection of hidden aggregations, synonymous nodes, and synonymous arcs.

The refined problem domain model is then subjected to further processing in order to confirm the system's *understanding* of its structure. Information required during this processing is obtained from the user in the form of responses to a series of system-generated questions. The questions are based upon the system's evolving knowledge of the application domain. Responses are used to update and augment this knowledge. The system's understanding of aspects of the domain may therefore alter at this point, according to user response.

Generating a conceptual model
Conceptual model processing is a also three-step process as follows.

- The first step involves the creation of the conceptual model appropriate to the domain description provided by the problem domain model.
- The second step involves the augmentation of this model by requesting the user to supply additional information.
- The final step involves the specification of any explicit constraints that the user requires to be attached to the conceptual model.

The conceptual model is constructed using the problem domain model as an initial starting point. The concepts of the problem domain model are transformed into a series of object classes and associated properties which represent the application domain from a real-world perspective. The conceptual model is intended to illustrate how the object classes representing the domain are *actually* structured, as opposed to whether it presents the optimum method of structuring.

Once created, the user is requested by the system to supply further information in order to augment the system knowledge of the application domain. The information required during the augmentation processing is obtained from the user in the form of responses to a series of system-generated questions. These questions are based upon the system's evolving knowledge of the application domain as represented by the conceptual model. Responses received from the user are used to update and augment this knowledge. Thus, the system makes use of its existing knowledge of the domain in order to pose questions, the responses to which are used to further augment that knowledge.

Once the conceptual model is complete, the user is presented with the derived object classes, and invited to specify any constraints that apply to the properties of these classes. Constraint specification is performed at the conceptual stage rather than after the final design stage, as the conceptual model is more likely to represent the *user* view of the domain than the more *implementation* (machine) oriented view of the design model. Constraints submitted at this point directly specify some aspect of the application domain, and as such are often referred to as *explicit* constraints [10].

Producing a design model
The final design activity performed is that of design model processing. Design model processing is a three-step process.

- The first step involves the creation of the design model based upon the conceptual model previously created.
- The second step involves the automatic generation of constraints that may be inferred from the evolving design structure.
- The final step is optional, and involves the allocation of data types to properties within the design model.

The design model is constructed using the conceptual model as an initial starting point. The object classes and associated constraints within the conceptual model are transformed into a corresponding series of object classes, constraints, and associated properties which represent the application domain from a perspective more suitable for machine implementation.

Once the design model is complete (in terms of the initial definition of object class structures), a series of explicit constraints are automatically generated in order to support the implicit constraints present within the design structure. Such implicit constraints are often referred to as *inherent* constraints [10] and enforce certain aspects of the domain. Implicit constraints explicitly represented by the system are those relating to relationships between object classes.

The final processing performed upon the design model involves the allocation of data types to properties within the object classes. As certain object-oriented products fall into Fairley's [9] *typeless* category, the allocation of data types to the properties within the evolving design is not a mandatory activity. However, the OMG Object Database Standard core model is *strongly typed* [8], and as the inclusion of data types generally adds to the semantic content of designs, the option of allocating data types is provided (and recommended) by the system.

Once all properties are associated with a data type, the design session concludes. At this point (as is the case if data types have not been allocated), the design model represents the application domain in a form which may be implemented using an object-oriented database product.

3 Exploiting Domain Knowledge During Database Design

Budgen & Marashi [7] argue that any tool that can encapsulate both problem-specific and domain-specific knowledge in order to assist with making decisions during the design process is likely to be helpful. Indeed, the use of domain knowledge by intelligent design tools has been claimed to increase the appearance of intelligence of the tool, increase the efficiency of the tool, and improve the quality and consistency of designs produced [14]. The remainder of this paper illustrates the way in which the Object Design Assistant is able to make use of domain knowledge during the design session in an attempt to realize these benefits, while retaining domain independence.

3.1 Representing Domain Knowledge

Domain knowledge is represented within the Object Design Assistant using a thesaurus type structure [14]. This structure consists of series of concepts and associated synonyms, linked together via abstraction mechanisms corresponding to those recognized by the system (aggregation, association, and generalization). The general format of the domain knowledge as represented by the thesaurus approach is as illustrated in Figure 1.

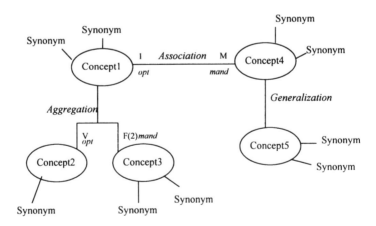

Fig. 1. General method for representing domain knowledge

The fragment of domain knowledge illustrated in Figure 1 consists of five concepts, all of which may be referred to by one or more synonyms. Concepts 1 and 4 are connected by a 1:M association link, with optional and mandatory membership of the link respectively. Concept2 participates in a variable aggregation structure with Concept1, while Concept3 participates in a fixed aggregation structure with Concept1 (two instances of Concept3 per instance of Concept1). Instances of Concept2 may exist without a corresponding instance of Concept1, however instances of Concept3 must be associated with an instance of Concept1. Concept4 has a single subtype Concept5. An illustrative fragment of a domain knowledge structure for use during the development of a university library database is presented in Figure 2.

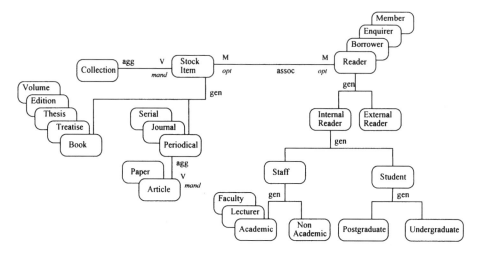

Fig. 2. Fragment of domain knowledge for a university library

It can be seen from Figure 2 that the abstraction mechanisms are categorized rather than being explicitly named. Thus, the use of the thesaurus approach by the Object Design Assistant provides for flexibility, allowing each concept to be referred to by any of a number of associated synonyms, and the abstraction mechanisms linking concepts to take any name provided by the user. For instance, the following declarative statements that may be provided during a design session for a library database would all be recognized by the Object Design Assistant as being semantically equivalent, concerning a single associative relationship between two concepts.

MEMBER BORROWS BOOK
MEMBER LOANS BOOK
READER BORROWS TREATISE
BOOK IS-BORROWED-BY READER

3.2 Exploiting Domain Knowledge During Processing

At various stages of the processing described previously, the Object Design Assistant conducts a dialogue with the user in order to confirm its understanding of the application domain, or to obtain additional information. If domain knowledge is available, the system attempts wherever possible to reason with this knowledge, only resorting to questioning the user if the domain knowledge cannot provide the required information. This use of encapsulated domain knowledge therefore attempts to reduce the amount of dialogue required with the user (in terms of the number of questions asked), thus achieving an increase in efficiency. The appearance of intelligence of the system is also increased, as the system appears to have previous knowledge of the application domain. Certain facts are apparently known by the system without the user having to volunteer such information.

The Object Design Assistant also achieves the implicit objective of making use of domain knowledge whilst retaining domain independence. The tool is not restricted to operating within domains for which encapsulated domain knowledge is available. However, if the encapsulated domain knowledge (or a fragment of this knowledge) does correspond to the application domain in question, then this knowledge is exploited. In this sense, the behaviour of the Object Design Assistant is similar to that of a human designer, asking questions only when it cannot provide the required information from its own knowledge of the domain.

The use of system-encapsulated domain knowledge is transparent to the user as no initial selection of domain is required. Initial investigations [14] indicated that there was a requirement on the part of the user to select an appropriate domain prior to commencing a design session. However, subsequent work has revealed that this need not be the case. The current version of the Object Design Assistant treats its encapsulated domain knowledge as a single concept, which may be reasoned with as a whole, and which exists without the artificial internal barriers to processing created by the partitioning of the knowledge into distinct, mutually exclusive domains.

The processing carried out by the Object Design Assistant when using encapsulated domain knowledge follows the three-step procedure previously described (creating a problem domain model, a conceptual model, and a design model). The processing performed during each of these steps is as follows.

Formulating an initial representation of the problem domain
As is the case when domain knowledge is not available, problem domain model processing is a three-step process.

- The first step involves the creation of a problem domain model.
- The second step involves the refinement of this model, by detecting and resolving any inconsistencies that may exist.
- The third step involves the confirmation of the system's understanding of the semantics of the application domain as represented by the problem domain model.

Domain knowledge is used by the Object Design Assistant during the last of these steps as follows.

When a structure within the problem domain model is categorized as representing a generalization or aggregation structure and no corresponding domain knowledge is available, the user is asked to confirm the semantics of the structure as illustrated by the following dialogue.

ODA > Does the statement FACULTY IS-A READER indicate that;
         FACULTY is a specialized kind of READER ?
         Please Enter Y or N: (or H = help / E = Explanation)
User > y

However, when domain knowledge is available, the system first examines this knowledge in an attempt to confirm the semantics. If the information required is available within the domain knowledge (the structure requiring confirmation is present and therefore the fact in question can be confirmed), then a comment similar to the following is generated to document that this aspect of domain confirmation was performed by the use of system-held domain knowledge.

ODA > ** FACULTY is a specialized kind of READER --> using system held
         domain knowledge
ODA > ** Structure confirmed....

Generating a conceptual model
Conceptual model processing using domain knowledge is a three-step process.

- The first step involves the creation of the conceptual model appropriate to the domain description provided by the problem domain model.
- The second step involves the augmentation of this model by requesting the user to supply additional information.
- The final step involves the specification of any explicit constraints that the user requires to be attached to the conceptual model.

Domain knowledge is used by the Object Design Assistant during the second of these steps as follows.

If no domain knowledge is available, the user is questioned as to the nature of participation (variable or fixed) of each component object class participating in an aggregation structure. If the participation is indicated as being fixed in nature, the system requests the number of component instances involved. The user is also questioned as to whether instances of each aggregate object class may exist without corresponding component object class(es), or whether instances of the component object class(es) may exist independently of the aggregate object class. The following sample is illustrative of the dialogue that takes place.

ODA > Can a READER that usually HAS a NAME exist without a corresponding
         NAME ?

ODA > Please enter Y or N : (or H = help / E = explanation)
User > n
ODA > Can a NAME exist without a corresponding READER ?
ODA > Please enter Y or N : (or H = help / E = explanation)
User > n
ODA > Is the number of NAME's per READER fixed or variable ?
ODA > Please enter F or V :
User > f
ODA > How many NAME's per READER are there ?
User > 1

If domain knowledge is available, the system examines the knowledge in an attempt to obtain the required information. If the information required is available (the aggregation structure under consideration is present), then a comment similar to the following is generated to document that this information was obtained from the domain knowledge.

ODA > ** ARTICLE is a component part of JOURNAL --> using system-held
        domain knowledge
ODA > ** Confirming aggregation details....

For each link object class (representing an association link) within the conceptual model, if no corresponding domain knowledge is available, the user is questioned as to the multiplicity and the membership category of each of the object classes participating in the link. The following dialogue is illustrative of the process.

ODA > Is it possible that a READER CHECKS-OUT more than 1 BOOK ?
ODA > Please enter Y or N : (or H = help / E = explanation)
User > y
ODA > and vice versa ? - Please enter Y or N : (or H = help / E = explanation)
User > y
ODA > Can a READER that usually CHECKS-OUT a BOOK exist without a
        corresponding BOOK ?
ODA > Please enter Y or N : (or H = help / E = explanation)
User > y
ODA > Can a BOOK exist without a corresponding READER ?
ODA > Please enter Y or N : (or H = help / E = explanation)
User > y

If corresponding domain knowledge is available, then a comment similar to the following is generated to document that this information was obtained from that domain knowledge.

ODA > ** READER CHECKS-OUT BOOK --> using system-held domain
        knowledge

ODA > ** Augmenting conceptual model...
ODA > ** Extracting membership participation and cardinality information....

Producing a design model
Processing of the design model when domain knowledge is available is identical to that performed when no such knowledge is in use. This aspect of processing is therefore entirely as described in the previous section.

4 Results to Date

Work to date has concentrated upon developing knowledge structures representing four different application domains (library, health/medical, university, and financial). Although these domains have been developed (and are represented within the system) individually, the system is able to process the knowledge held as a single unit, and if necessary, to make use of fragments of knowledge from different domains within the same design session.

Testing performed on a wide range of example applications has so far produced encouraging results. Where example applications correspond directly to the domain knowledge (ie. the application matches one of the sample domains), reductions in user interaction of between 14% - 36% have been obtained without compromising the designs produced. These figures are based upon measuring only the interactions that contribute directly to the analysis/design process. Interactions that "add-value" to the evolving design but which are not compulsory, or have the potential to vary in number are not included. Such interactions include those used to specify explicit constraints and to allocate data types to properties. The stated figures therefore illustrate the reduction in the minimum number of user interactions required to produce a design. This represents a more consistent and meaningful measurement than would be the case if variable aspects of the process were also counted. In cases where domain knowledge does not directly correspond to the application domain, minor reductions (of up to 2%) in user interaction have occasionally been obtained, illustrating that the system is able to make use of fragments of knowledge where appropriate.

Testing has also demonstrated that the approach is able to recognize and correctly handle certain linguistic subtleties once informed of their existence. For example, the system is able to differentiate between the different meanings attributed to the term *faculty* (used to indicate a member of academic staff in the USA and an element of university organizational structure in the UK), and to handle the use of the different meanings appropriately (if specified appropriately within the domain knowledge).

Despite the encouraging results obtained to date, the use of domain specific knowledge is not claimed to be a panacea. Indeed it is recognized that there are certain aspects of the design process that are best resolved by user interaction. Table 1 summarizes the areas where the domain specific knowledge has been seen to be of benefit during a design session, and the situations that are currently not resolved by the approach.

Table 1. Uses of domain knowledge

Resolved Using Domain Specific Knowledge	Not Resolved Using Domain Specific Knowledge
Confirmation of semantics of relationships between problem domain concepts	Queries relating to concepts and/or relationships between concepts not represented in the domain knowledge
Multiplicity of relationships linking concepts, membership requirements for these relationships (mandatory, optional)	Queries relating to participation in generalization structures not represented in the domain knowledge
Categorization of aggregation structures (fixed, variable, recursive)	Use (by the user) of terms not present in the thesaurus to describe concepts within the application domain

5   Conclusions and Future Work

In general, very little work has taken place in this area to date [13] despite the fact that the use of domain specific knowledge can potentially yield numerous benefits such as increasing the appearance of tool intelligence, increasing efficiency, and improving the quality of resulting designs [14].

This paper has described an approach to representing and exploiting such domain knowledge by an existing intelligent database design tool; the Object Design Assistant. The use of domain knowledge during processing has achieved two of the stated benefits; the enhancement of the appearance of intelligence, and the improvement in performance. The system appears to "know" about certain aspects of the application, and the need for submitting certain trivial questions to the user is removed. This reduction in questioning effects a reduction in processing requirements (certain activities are able to be processed internally by the tool), and hence an increase in efficiency.

The current version of the tool allows for the manual creating updating and augmenting of the domain knowledge as a result of information gained during a design session. An obvious future goal is to automate this process in order that the system can "gain experience" in learning from its design activities, as would a human designer. Current work is concentrating on further developing the Object Design Assistant in order to provide intelligent design support for the functional (behavioural) aspects of object-oriented databases. The logical next step would therefore be to investigate the possibilities of extending the system-held domain knowledge to accommodate both structural and functional aspects.

Acknowledgements

The author wishes to thank the anonymous referees for their helpful and constructive comments on a previous version of this paper.

References

1. Avison, D.E. & Fitzgerald, G. (1995) *Information Systems Development: Methodologies, Techniques and Tools* (second edition), McGraw-Hill.
2. Baldissera, C., Ceri, S., Pelagatti, G. & Bracchi, G. (1979) "Interactive Specification and Formal Verification of User's Views in Database Design", In: *Proceedings of the 5th International Conference on Very Large Data Bases, 1979, Rio de Janeiro, Brazil.* pp. 262-272.
3. Blaha, M., Premerlani, W., & Rumbaugh, J. (1988) "Relational Database Design Using an Object-Oriented Methodology", *Communications of the ACM*, 31(4), 414-427.
4. Bouzeghoub, M. (1992) "Using Expert Systems in Schema Design". In: Loucopoulos, P. & Zicari R. (eds) *Conceptual Modelling, Databases, and CASE,* Wiley, pp. 465-487.
5. Bracchi, G., Paolini, P. & Pelagatti, G. (1976) "Binary Logical Associations in Data Modelling", In: Nijssen, G. M. (ed) *Modelling in Data Base Management Systems*, North-Holland, pp. 125-148.
6. Brown, A. (1991) *Object-Oriented Databases: Applications in Software Engineering.* London: McGraw-Hill.
7. Budgen, D. & Marashi, M. (1990) "Knowledge Use in Software Design". In: Spurr, K. & Layzell, P. (eds) *CASE on Trial,* Wiley, pp. 163-179.
8. Cattell, R.G. (ed) (1994) *The Object Database Standard,* Morgan Kaufmann.
9. Fairley, R.E. (1985) *Software Engineering Concepts*, McGraw-Hill.
10. Formica, A. & Missikoff, M. (1992) "Integrity Constraints Representation in Object-Oriented Databases". In: Pernul, G. & Tjoa, A.M. (eds) *Proceedings of the 11th International Conference on the E-R Approach, Karlsruhe, Germany,* Springer-Verlag, pp. 69-85.
11. Goldstein, R.C. & Storey, V.C. (1994) "Materialization", *IEEE Transactions on Knowledge and Data Engineering,* 6(5), 835-842.
12. Kotz-Dittrich, A. & Dittrich, K.R. (1995) "Where Object-Oriented DBMSs Should do Better: A Critique Based on Early Experience" In: Kim, W. (ed) *Modern Database Systems: The Object Model, Interoperability, and Beyond,* Addison-Wesley, pp. 238-254.
13. Lloyd-Williams, M. (1993) "Expert System Support for Object-Oriented Database Design", *International Journal of Applied Expert Systems*, 1(4), 197-212.
14. Lloyd-Williams, M. (1994) "Knowledge Based CASE Tools: Improving Performance Using Domain Specific Knowledge", *Software Engineering Journal*, 9(4), 167-172.

15. Lloyd-Williams, M. & Beynon-Davies, P. (1992) "Expert Systems for Database Design: A Comparative Review", *Artificial Intelligence Review*, 6(3), 263-283.
16. Sadr, B. & Dousette, P.J. (1996) "An OO Project Management Strategy", *IEEE Computer*, 29(9), 33-38.
17. Soley, R.M. & Kent, W. (1995) "The OMG Object Model" In: Kim, W. (ed) *Modern Database Systems: The Object Model, Interoperability, and Beyond*, Addison-Wesley, pp. 18-41.
18. Storey, V.C. (1992) "Real World Knowledge for Databases", *Journal of Database Administration* 3(1), 1-19.
19. Storey V.C. & Goldstein, R.C. (1993) "Knowledge based approaches to database design". *Management Information Systems Quarterly*, 17(1), 25-46.
20. Storey V.C., Goldstein, R.C., Chiang, R.H.L. & Dey, D. (1993) "A Commonsense Reasoning Facility Based on the Entity-Relationship Model". In: Elmasri, R., Kouramajian, V. & Thalheim, B. (eds) *Entity-Relationship Approach - ER '93*, Springer-Verlag, pp. 218-229.
21. Vessey, I. & Sravanapadi, A.P. (1995) "CASE Tools as Collaborative Support Technologies". *Communications of the ACM*, 37(1), 83-102.
22. Vossen, G. (1990) *Data Models, Database Languages, and Database Management Systems*. Wokingham: Addison-Wesley.

Intelligent Support for Retrieval and Synthesis of Patterns for Object-Oriented Design

Sandeep Purao
Veda C. Storey
Department of CIS, Georgia State University, Atlanta, Georgia 30302-4015
Phone: 404 651 3859, Fax: 404 651 3842, Email: {spurao,vstorey}@gsu.edu

Abstract

Several decades of software engineering research confirm that effective *reuse* is the only realistic approach to meeting the ever-increasing demands on the software industry. Over the last few years, object-oriented paradigm has emerged as the natural foundational technology for reuse approaches, leading to the development of a number of reusable artifacts at different levels of abstraction and granularity. This research focuses on artifacts at one level: 'patterns'. Patterns are groups of objects with stereotypical properties and responsibilities that can be applied by analogy to different domains. In this paper, we present a methodology for automating design of object-oriented systems based on intelligent retrieval and synthesis of reusable patterns. The methodology itself has an object-oriented flavor. It uses a set of techniques and rules aided by heuristics from natural language processing, automated reasoning and learning that are activated, as needed. Effectiveness of the methodology is evaluated using measures such as recall, precision, coverage and spuriousness.

1. Introduction

Although software productivity has steadily increased over the past 30 years, the gains have not been sufficient to close the gap between demands placed on the software industry and what the state of the practice can deliver [Boehm 1987, Cox 1990]. Several decades of software engineering and artificial intelligence (AI) research suggest that *reuse* is the only approach that has a realistic chance of bridging this gap [Lowry and McCartney 1991, Karlsson et al 1995, Krueger 1993, Mili et al 1995]. This involves the automatic design of systems from higher level specifications and reusable components [Setliff 1993]. Realistic applications however, have remained elusive. The introduction and acceptance of object-orientation over the last decade has renewed interest in this area. Reuse is natural with objects, making it especially suited as the foundational technology for a building blocks approach to system development.

Realizing the benefits from reuse, requires: (1) the development of artifacts *for* reuse, and 2) the creation of mechanisms for designing systems *with* reuse [Karlsson et al 1995]. This research focuses on the later, specifically in the context of *Patterns* as the reusable artifacts. Much prior research has focused on the problem of *creating* patterns for reuse. As a result, libraries of patterns are now available for reuse at various stages of software development, such as analysis [Coad et al 1995], design [Gamma et al 1995] and coding [Gamma et al

1995]. However, there does not appear to have been any research directed at the design of systems by automatically retrieving and synthesizing patterns. The objective of this research is:

> *to create a methodology for intelligent retrieval and synthesis of reusable patterns to facilitate automated design of object-oriented systems.*

In doing so, the research directly addresses what is considered to be the most challenging problem in the building blocks approach to system development [Mili et al 1995]. The approach we propose enables system developers to quickly identify relevant patterns, instantiate them for the problem domain and synthesize them into an object-oriented specification. Without such support, the designers are left to their own devices to browse and search through repositories to extract appropriate patterns that they can use in their designs.

2. Reuse

Reuse is natural to human problem-solving behavior. When faced with a problem, we perform a rote recall, followed by a search for analogical similarities. *If* these fail, we turn to analytical heuristics [Lenat et al 1990]. Researchers have recognized that such informal reuse has always been taking place. Formal reuse requires development of tools and techniques *for* and *with* reuse.

2.1 Reusable Artifacts

Reusable artifacts can be identified at different levels of abstraction and granularity. *Templates* are parameterized, domain-independent components. *Classes* correspond to real-life entities, and are more domain-specific. *Patterns* are groups of objects with stereotypical responsibilities and interactions. They represents solutions that can be repeatedly applied in different domains, by analogy [Coad et al 1995]. Application *frameworks* are class collections that capture the common aspects of applications in a certain problem domain [Adler et al 1995]. Mili et al. [1995] identify three factors upon which most classifications of reusable knowledge must rely: (1) the *level of abstraction* – abstract versus concrete, (2) the *stage of development* – design versus coding, and (3) the *nature of knowledge* – artifacts versus skills. This research focuses on patterns, that is, reuse of *abstract artifacts* during *design*. Figure 1 shows the relevance and domain coverage of the four reusable artifacts. *Patterns*, the focus of this research, are highlighted.

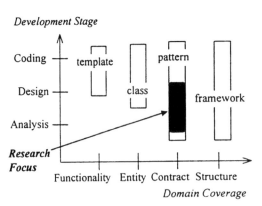

Figure 1. Reusable Artifacts

2.2 Patterns

Patterns, it has been argued, represent the most important form of reuse [Barnes and Bollinger 1991]. A pattern is a group of communicating objects with stereotypical responsibilities [Gamma et al 1995]. Each object contains data definitions (attributes), and behavior descriptions (method signatures). They provide generic design solutions that can be applied by analogy in different domains. For object-oriented system development, patterns are considered to be the key building blocks [Coplien 1996] that can be used early in system development, during design, and later, during construction. Figure 2 shows, in detail, the pattern 'Participant-Transaction', comprised of two objects, and indicates a few others [Coad et al 1995].

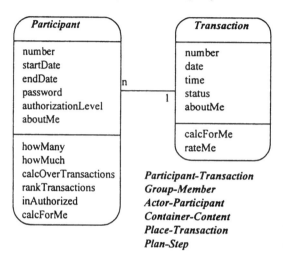

Figure 2. Example Patterns [Coad et al 1995]

2.3 Design *with* Reuse

The problem of designing object-oriented systems with reuse of patterns involves two interlocking tasks: (1) *retrieval* of relevant patterns, and (2) *synthesis* of the retrieved patterns as appropriate in the problem domain being considered. *Retrieval* refers to the search for potentially useful patterns. Automating this process requires encoding the problem space and the solution space, followed by design of a matching algorithm [Mili et al 1995]. *Synthesis* is the composition of retrieved patterns to ensure that, taken together, they satisfy the developer's requirements. The problem of synthesizing the retrieved components to cover the system developer's set of requirements is known as *bottom-up development* [Mili et al 1995]. Bottom-up development requires a specific decomposition of the problem to create slots in which existing patterns can be fitted. It corresponds to a set cover problem [Mili et al 1994a], which is known to be NP-complete [Garey and Johnson 1979]. Both retrieval and synthesis, must be supported as part of an *iterative* development process, that has been shown to be particularly effective for object-oriented systems development [Booch 1995].

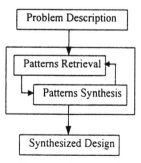

Figure 3. Design *with* Pattern Reuse

3. A Methodology for Retrieval and Synthesis of Patterns

This section presents a methodology for intelligent retrieval and synthesis of patterns for automated design of object-oriented systems. The methodology is dependent upon the availability of libraries of patterns, a number of which have been successfully developed. It automatically retrieves patterns relevant for a given problem, and synthesizes them into a design appropriate for further refinement by the designer. Figure 4 shows the solution architecture of our approach, which uses a set of techniques and rules, aided by some heuristics, to

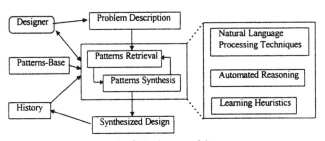

Figure 4. Solution Architecture

facilitate the solution process. The techniques fall into three categories: natural language processing (NLP), automated reasoning (AR) and machine learning (ML).

3.1 Patterns-Base

To store and facilitate the retrieval of patterns, we have developed a hybrid of three widely accepted pattern documentation schemes [Coad et al 1995, Gamma et al 1995, Lea 1994]. This provides the scheme for our patterns-base as shown in table 1. It allows representation of knowledge about patterns at varying levels of abstraction [MIT 1996]. *Known uses* and *Related patterns* provide the most useful information for our purpose. To populate the patterns-base, we have drawn on published and widely available patterns, specifically, those developed by Coad et al [1995]. Their patterns-base consists of 31 different patterns, documentation for which is easily available [Coad et al 1995].

Proposed Scheme	Gamma et al [1995]	Lea [1994]	Coad et al [1995]
Name	Yes	Yes	Yes
Aliases	Yes	Yes	
Purpose	Yes	Yes	
Participants	Yes	Yes	Yes
Attributes			
Responsibilities			
Structure	Yes	Yes	Yes
Collaborations	Yes	Yes	Yes
Applicability	Yes		
Known Uses	Yes	Yes	Yes
Consequences	Yes		
Implementation	Yes		
Sample Code	Yes		
Related Patterns	Yes	Yes	Yes

Table 1: A Pattern-Base for Storing Available Patterns

Three distinct kinds of *Known Uses* are used in the methodology.

Known Uses of Objects. Consider the sample pattern in figure 2. Coad et al [1995] provide as many as 37 known uses for the object Participant, including agent, applicant, and buyer. Similarly, there are 24 known uses for the object Transaction including agreement and assignment

Known Uses of Patterns. There are six different known uses for the pattern, Transaction-SubsequentTransaction, including (1) application-issue and (2) order-shipment.

Known Uses of Patterns in a Context. For the pattern Caller-Dispatcher-CallerBack, examples include: (1) customer-taxi dispatcher-taxi (in a simulation system), (2) inbound call-call back server-call back unit (in a telecommunications system) and (3) requester-job shop-contractor (in a simulation system).

Patterns can be *related* to each other. Four distinct kinds of relationships among patterns are used:

Patterns Sharing a Common Object. These are obvious if the two patterns share a common abstract object. For example, the patterns Place-Transaction and Transaction-Participant are related because they share the object Transaction.

Specific Superimpositions Indicated. Combinations of different objects may also be indicated. For example, the pattern Gatekeeper-Request-Resource indicates that it may be combined with the patterns: (1) Actor-Participant (by equating Participant with Gatekeeper); (2) Participant-Transaction (by equating Participant with Gatekeeper); and (3) Specific Item-Transaction (by equating SpecificItem with Resource).

Objects or Patterns Sharing Known Uses. A third possibility for combining patterns requires searching for the same or similar known uses. For example, the object Container shares the known uses of (1) Airport, (2) Bank, (3) Garage, (4) Hangar, (5) Hospital, (6) Store, and (7) Warehouse with the object Place.

Patterns Sharing Generalized/Specialized Objects from Other Patterns. Combining patterns requires generalization or specialization of objects to identify other objects and patterns related to them. For example, the objects Specific Item and Line Item may be considered as specializations of the object Item, the object Subsequent Transaction may be considered as a specialization of the object Transaction. However, the object Container Line Item may *not* be considered as a specialization of the object Container. These relationships – specializations and generalizations – across objects in different patterns are retained in the patterns-base.

3.2 Sample Problem and Solution

The following sample problem from Coad et al [1995] is used to test the methodology and a comparison made of the result obtained to an expert solution. The concise problem description is stated below along with the synthesized design obtained from our methodology, *with almost no input from the system designer*. Consider the Problem Description for Connie's Convenience Store [Coad et al 1995]:

> "To help each cashier work more effectively during checkout, to keep
> good records of each sale, and to support more efficient store operations"

Based on this meager description, our methodology first identifies the relevant patterns and retrieves them from the patterns-base. They are instantiated for the problem domain by exploiting information available from the 25-word problem description, the information contained in the patterns-base shown above and by applying a number of intelligent heuristics. Based on this instantiation, other information contained in the patterns-base and further application of additional intelligent heuristics, the patterns are concatenated / superimposed to create a graph of patterns. The graph, in figure 5, represents a synthesized object-oriented design for Connie's Convenience Store. Note that no input was required from the system developer, other than the initial 25-word description of the system requirements. The objective is to develop a methodology that, when implemented, will require minimal input from the designer, thus maximizing the automation of the process.

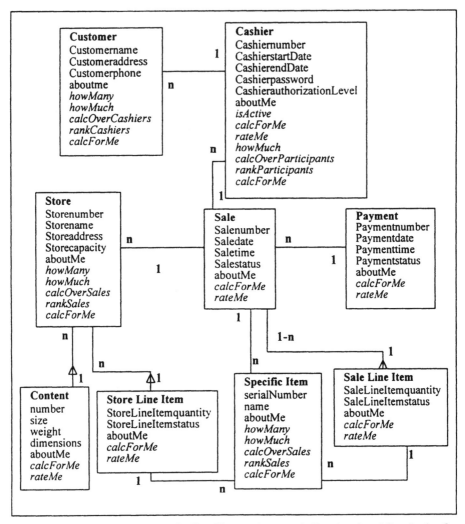

Figure 5. Synthesized Design by Intelligent, Automatic Retrieval and Synthesis of Patterns

The methodology was, therefore, operationalized to *require* minimal designer interaction, with provision for an override capability to the designer.

3.3 Simulated Progression
This section presents a six-step methodology for retrieving and synthesizing patterns to create an object-oriented design. The methodology is illustrated by applying it to the design of a point-of-sale system for a convenience store [Coad et al 1995]. The heuristics used are described in the next section.

Step 1: Parse System Requirements. The description of system requirements for Connie's Convenience Store [Coad et al 1995] is parsed and natural language processing heuristics applied to identify the following as significant words: cashier, checkout, records, sale, store, operations.

Step 2: Match Significant Words to Known Uses. A search is performed for the significant words in the available *known uses* of patterns and objects in these patterns. Known uses of objects are found for three of the seven significant words as shown in figure 6. A search for patterns, based on these objects, is then performed. A total of nine patterns are found, as shown in figure 7. Of these, two (Place-Transaction and Participant-Transaction) are found in patterns by multiple objects. Thus, there are seven unique patterns available for further analysis.

Significant word	Object Identified
cashier	Participant
checkout	– none –
record(s)	– none –
sale	Transaction
store	Place, Container
operations	– none –

Figure 6. Objects Identified

Object Identified	Patterns Identified
Participant	(1) Participant-Transaction
Transaction	(1) Place-Transaction,
	(2) SpecificItem-Transaction,
	(3) Transaction-TransactionLineItem,
	(4) Transaction-SubsequentTransaction,
	(5) Participant-Transaction
Place	(1) Place-Transaction
Container	(1) Container-Content,
	(2) Container-ContainerLineItem

Figure 7. Patterns Identified

Step 3: Instantiate Patterns. The patterns found are instantiated based on information from the problem statement and the *known uses*. For instance, the pattern Participant-Transaction is instantiated as Cashier-Sale. By directly mapping the objects or the instantiations, the patterns are superimposed to create a patterns graph. Note this step requires use of the knowledge available in the patterns base: *patterns sharing common objects* and *patterns sharing known uses*, for example, Place and Container. Figure 8 shows the progression to this point.

Step 4: Apply Instantiation Heuristics. Additional heuristics are applied to investigate and possibly instantiate the objects that remain uninstantiated in the pattern graph. In our example, these include: Actor, Subsequent Transaction, Content and Specific Item. The *Inverse Heuristic* identifies Payment as an instantiation of the object Subsequent Transaction. The *Domain Taxonomies Heuristic* identifies Customer as an instantiation of the object Actor. The remaining objects, Specific Item and Content remain uninstantiated.

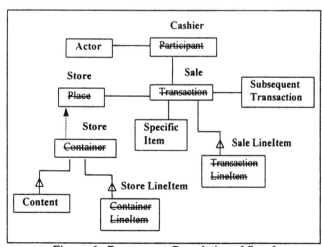

Figure 6. Progress at Completion of *Step 3*

Step 5: Spread the Patterns Graph. Objects available in the pattern graph are used to spread the graph by identifying any additional, related patterns. To identify additional patterns, mutations (specializations / generalizations) of objects in the pattern graph are generated. For our example, the permissible mutations include: LineItem (based on Container Line Item), Item (based on Specific Item). A search is performed in the patterns base using these mutations. This yields two additional patterns that are added to the patterns graph: Item-Line Item and Specific Item - Line Item. Spreading the patterns graph involves checking applicability of patterns that are removed by one / multiple steps from the initial problem statement. This can lead to identifying objects and retrieving patterns that are more likely to be less relevant to the problem at hand. However, this strategy can be profitably used, in iterative fashion, to formulate intelligent *suggestions* that may be confirmed or rejected by the designer. In other words, instead of presenting all the other patterns as possibilities to spread the patterns graph further, the "more relevant" patterns can be identified, instantiated in the context of the problem, and presented to the designer as potentially relevant expansions of the current patterns graph.

Step 6: Rename Instantiated Objects. Based on the instantiated objects, the attributes and behaviors of the objects are renamed. For example, the attributes of Actor (now instantiated as Customer) are renamed as Customername, Customeraddress, Customerphone etc. Where the object represents a superimposition (such as Store, a superimposition of Place and Container), the attributes and behaviors are concatenated before renaming the attributes. This completes the first iteration of the methodology, which produces the synthesized design shown in figure 5.

4. Intelligent Heuristics

We have developed a number of heuristics to intelligently retrieve and synthesize the available patterns. They are classified into the three categories contained in our solution architecture (figure 4).

4.1 Natural Language Processing Heuristics
To identify significant words from the requirements, retrieve patterns based on these, and instantiate them based on the descriptions, we currently employ the techniques given below for parsing the requirements. Additional research is required to adapt results from application of natural language processing techniques to databases, available elsewhere.

Discard Stop Words. This is an accepted technique used by NLP researchers for parsing the description of requirements. A standard list of stop words is available at [MIL 1997], which can be used for this purpose. For the Convenience store example, the following words were discarded (as stop words) using this heuristic: 'to', 'each', 'during', 'to', 'of', 'each', 'and', 'to', 'more.'

Discard Verb Forms. Three specific verb forms are candidates to be discarded. These are: (a) words following the word 'to', (b) words ending in 'ing', and (c) words ending in 'ed'. For the Convenience store example, the following words were discarded using this heuristic: 'help', 'work', 'keep', 'support.'

Discard Adjectives. Two heuristics identify adjectives: (a) words ending in 'ly' and (b) comparatives of size, dimension, and quality as identified by a thesaurus [Merriam-Webster 1978]. For the Convenience store example, the following words were discarded (as adjectives) using these heuristics: 'effectively', 'good', 'more', 'efficient.'

Known Uses of Objects. To identify objects that indicate known uses matching significant words found, we perform a simple parsing of known uses to find a match for the significant word in the known uses of objects. For the Convenience store example, the objects identified are shown in figure 6.

Object-based Pattern Retrieval. To retrieve patterns based on objects identified, we perform a simple parsing of patterns that include the indicated object. This requires a parsing of the pattern name. See the patterns retrieved for the Convenience store example, as shown in figure 7, based on objects identified.

4.2 Automated Reasoning Heuristics

To retrieve additional relevant patterns from the patterns-base, instantiate them for the problem at hand, and synthesize them to produce the required design. We employ the following automated reasoning techniques:

Inverse of Known Uses. This heuristics captures the notion of the inverse for Known Uses. For example, 'sale' and 'purchase' represent inverses of each other. Similarly, 'payment' and 'receipt' are inverses. If a known use for a pattern is available, such as 'purchase-payment', this provides the following possibilities for additional uses: Sale-Payment, Sale-Receipt, and Purchase-Receipt. This provides a pruning of choices presented to the designer.

Domain Taxonomies. A number of domain taxonomies are available from previous research [Glass and Vessey 1996]. Some are based on industry classifications, others are based on application profiles, yet others depend on a layered view of information systems (such as user interfaces, data management) [SIC 1987, DEC 1991]. For the purpose of this research, we adopt DEC's application taxonomy [DEC 1991], which represents a combination of many abstraction levels. Domains in this taxonomy include: distribution of goods, inventory control, order processing, and warehousing. For the Convenience store example, the domain 'Order Processing' is appropriate, which allows instantiation of the object Actor to Customer. Use of domain taxonomies, thus, allows a better approach to exploiting known uses of patterns in context, since the context is provided by the domain taxonomy.

Generalization / Specialization. These heuristics provide rules for intelligent mutation of objects that can be used for 'spreading' the patterns graph. For example, the object 'Container Line Item' may be viewed as a specialization of the object 'Line Item'. Similarly, the object 'Item' may be considered as a generalization of the object 'Specific Item'. However, the object 'Container' should not be considered as a specialization of the object 'Container Line Item.' Meaningful specializations / generalizations of objects are useful for identifying additional potential objects that may be useful for spreading the patterns graph.

Pattern Superimpositions. The patterns for which superimpositions are indicated provide an extension of the known uses of objects as well as patterns. For example, the pattern 'Gatekeeper-Request-Resource' indicates it can be combined with the pattern 'Actor-Participant' by equating 'Participant' with 'Gatekeeper'. This provides a secondary list of known uses for the object 'Gatekeeper,' that is, known uses of the object 'Participant.'

4.3 Machine Learning Heuristics

In an implementation, we will have the added advantage of being able to learn through repeated application of the system. Measures will be accumulated separately, for different domains and at different levels of granularity and used in the identification of relevant patterns. Examples of these are given below. Further research is required to adapt results from machine learning, available elsewhere.

Pattern Affinities. Patterns that do *not* share a common object, but are *often* found to co-exist in a synthesized design will provide a measure of affinity. For example, both 'Group-

'Member' and 'Plan-Step' may be applicable in a number of problem domains. This information will provide additional leads for identification of relevant patterns.

Pattern Indifference. Some patterns may never or rarely co-exist in a synthesized design. For example, the patterns 'Group-Member' and 'Container-Content' may rarely be used together in a synthesized design. This information will provide additional leads for pruning applicable patterns for a given problem.

Instantiation Affinities. Some patterns *often* share a common instantiation. For example, the pattern 'Plan-Plan Execution' may be instantiated as battle plan-battle execution and the pattern 'Step-Step Execution' may be instantiated as tactic-tactic execution. This information will provide additional information about the preferred instantiation of one pattern when instantiation of the other pattern is available.

5. Verification

The synthesized design contained 9 objects (instantiated from 9 patterns) and 10 associations (including aggregation and inheritance) as shown in Figure 5. By contrast, the expert solution contained 10 objects and 11 associations. Since the methodology contained two interlocking tasks, Retrieval and Synthesis, measures to assess both were developed, following the widely accepted notion of type I and type II errors. Retrieval quality was measured by Recall (type I) and Precision (type II), whereas Synthesis quality was measured by Coverage (type I) and Spuriousness (type II). Under each category, we developed finer measures since it is possible to have different levels of acceptability for the generated designs. Also, since the generated designs can vary in degree of accuracy, a finer classification of quality achieved as well as errors committed, was considered more appropriate than a simple binary classification indicated by type I and type II errors. The measures developed and the results obtained from applying them to the convenience store example are shown below.

Retrieval Quality. The errors are indicated by (a) recall – fraction of relevant patterns retrieved, and (b) precision – fraction of retrieved patterns that are relevant.

Appropriate Retrieval	*Statistics*	*Comments*
Patterns Retrieved	9	First pass: 7 plus Spreading: 2.
Patterns Instantiated		
Perfect Matches of Objects	5	Cashier, Store, Sale, Payment, SaleLineItem
Near- Perfect Matches of Objects	3	*Customer* (Person), *StoreLineItem* (Item)
Un-instantiated Objects	1	Content (needed: Register)

Table 2.1: Appropriate Retrieval

Type I Errors (Recall)		
Patterns Missing	0	Some patterns needed recursive application
Objects Missing	2	Session, Register, Cash Drawer
Associations Missing	3	Due to non-recursive application of patterns
Associations *Collapsed*	1	Cashier-*Session*-Sale (Session missing)
Type II Errors (Precision)		
Incorrect Pattern Retrieval	0	
Incorrect Instantiation		
Objects not Required	1	Specific Item
Incorrect Pattern Instantiation	0	

Table 2.2: Type I and Type II Errors in Retrieval

Synthesis Quality. The errors are indicated by (a) coverage – user requirements covered, and (b) spuriousness – incorrect representation of user requirements.

Appropriate Synthesis	Statistics	Comments
Patterns Synthesized	9	
Appropriate Synthesis	8	
Appropriate Superimposition	1	Only one indicated, correctly

Table 3.1: Appropriate Synthesis

Type I Errors (Coverage)		
Patterns not Synthesized	0	
Type II Errors (Spuriousness)		
Associations *Stretched*	1	StoreLineItem-*SpecificItem*-SaleLineItem (SpecificItem added)
Incorrect Associations	0	

Table 3.2: Type I and Type II Errors in Synthesis

As a result of applying the methodology to multiple sample cases, and comparing the results from expert, published solutions, we have discovered that the pattern 'Container-Content' is often applied recursively. This is an apt example of the Pattern Affinities heuristic we expected from repeated applications of the methodology. This implies that in an implementation, it will be necessary to prompt the designer, after the initial application of this pattern, to determine if recursive application is needed.

From the testing, it appears that application of the methodology results in a reasonable preliminary design of an object-oriented system. Further iterations would require designer interaction. Other parameters that would also be important indicators of effectiveness are: length of time needed to produce a design, design quality, ease of use of the methodology and how much design input is required.

6. Conclusion

A methodology has been developed for automatically generating a synthesized object-oriented design for an information system. The approach generates a preliminary design on the basis of a concise, limited natural language statement of the system requirements. The two tasks involved in the process are Patterns Retrieval and Patterns Synthesis. The process is supported by a patterns-base, for which a hybrid scheme has been developed based on previous research. Intelligent heuristics have been developed to maximize the automation of the process. They are grouped in three categories: natural language processing, automated reasoning and machine learning. Performance of the methodology is evaluated using measures of recall, precision, coverage and spuriousness.

We have created a preliminary design for a proposed prototype, which is being developed using Java for use on the world-wide-web. Verification of accuracy of the solutions will be supplemented by experiments with novice developers to assess effectiveness of the methodology on both the process and outcomes. Experience with the prototype so far suggests that the methodology is useful for moderate size problem descriptions. Additional experiments, with larger and more complex system descriptions are needed to further test the methodology and extend it to cover substantially different and larger systems.

References

1. Adler, R. 1995. Emerging Standards for Component Software. In *IEEE Computer*. March. Pp. 68-77.
2. Barnes, B. and T. Bollinger. 1991. Making Reuse Cost-Effective. In *IEEE Software*. January. Pp. 13-24.
3. Boehm, B. 1987. Improving Software Poductivity. In *IEEE Software*. Sept. Pp. 43-57.
4. Booch, G. 1995. *Object-Oriented Analysis and Design*. Benjamin-Cummings.
5. Coad, P. et al. 1995. Strategies and Patterns Handbook: Hypertext Edition   Version 2.0a. Object International, Inc. Available at http://www.oi.com
6. Coplien , J. 1996. *Patterns*. SIGS White Paper Series. ACM Press.
7. Cox, B. 1990. Planning the Software Industrial Revolution. In *IEEE Software*. November. Pp. 25-33.
8. Curtis, B. 1989. Cognitive Issues in Reusing Software Artifacts. In Software Reusability, V II. ed. T. Biggerstaff and A. Perlis, Addison Wesley 1989, pp. 269-287.
9. DEC 1991. *VAX VMS Software Source Book*. Digital Equipment Corp., Maynard, Mass.
10. Frakes, W. B. and B. A. Nejmeh. 1990. An Information System for Software Reuse. In *Software Reuse: Emerging Technology*. IEEE CS Press. Pp. 142-151.
11. Gamma, E. et al. 1995. *Design Patterns: Elements of Reusable Object-Oriented Software*. Addison-Wesley Reading, MA.
12. Garey, M. and D. Johnson. 1979. Computers and Intractabilty. Freeman. SanFrancisco, CA.
13. Glass, R., and I. Vessey. 1996. Contemporary Application-Domain Taxonomies. In *IEEE Software*. July. Pp. 63-76.
14. Karlsson, E. et al 1995. Editor. *Software Reuse. A Holistic Approach*. John Wiley & Sons, Inc.
15. Krueger, C. 1993. Software Reuse. In *ACM Computing Surveys*. Vol. 24. No. 2. June. Pp. 131-184.

16. Lea, D. 1994. Christopher Alexander: An Introduction for OO Designers. In *Software Engineering Notes*. Vol. 19. no. 1. Jan. Pp. 39-46.
17. Lenat, D. et al. 1990. CYC: Toward programs with common sense. In *Communications of the ACM. Special Issue on Natural Language Processing*. Vol. 33. No. 8. Aug. Pp. 30-49.
18. Lowry, M., amd R. McCartney. 1991. eds. *Automating Software Design*. AAAI Press/MIT Press.
19. Merriam-Webster. 1987. *The Merriam-Webster Thesaurus*. Pocket Books. 1978.
20. Mili, H. et al. 1994. Practitioner and Softclass: A Comparative Study of Two Software Reuse Research Projects. In *Journal of Systems and Software*. Vol. 27. May.
21. Mili, H. et al. 1995. Reusing Software: Issues and Research Directions. In *IEEE Transactions on Software Engineering*. June. Pp. 528-562.
22. MIL 1997. List of StopWords. Available at http://arcspk.belvoir.army.mil/moreplus/docs/help/Natural_Language_Search.html
23. MIT 1996. The DaVinci Initiative. Available at http://ganesh.mit.edu/
24. Pree, W. 1995. *Design Patterns for Object-Oriented Software Development*. Addison-Wesley.
25. Prieto-Diaz, R. and P. Freeman. 1987. Classifying Software for Reusability. In *IEEE Software*. Jan. Pp. 6-16.
26. Reifer Consultants 1990. *Productivity and Quality Survey*. El Segundo, CA.
27. Setliff, D. et al. 1993. Practical Software Synthesis. In *IEEE Software*. May. Pp. 6-10.
28. Shicheng, P., R. Hennicker, M. Jarke. 1993. On the Retrieval of Reusable Components. In *Selected Papers from Second International Workshop on Software, Reusability Advances in Software*. Italy, March 24-26.
29. SIC 1987. *Standard Industrial Classification Manual*. Office of Management and Budget.

A Conceptual Development Framework for Temporal Information Systems

I. Petrounias

Department of Computing, Manchester Metropolitan University, John Dalton Building, Chester Street, Manchester M1 5GD, UK, e-mail: I.Petrounias@doc.mmu.ac.uk

Abstract

Conceptual modelling is the activity of describing part of the real world for purposes of communication and understanding. Any conceptual modelling approach aiming to do this accurately must offer support for data changing over time. This paper presents a development framework for Temporal Information Systems. It is based on a Fact Based Model with time support. The mapping of the model onto a relational database is described and an algebra for it is defined, the operations of which operate on facts at the conceptual level. A data definition and manipulation language is defined based on the algebra and operates at the conceptual schema level rather than the database one, thus requiring little or no knowledge from the users about SQL or about how the database itself is organised.

1 Introduction

An area where considerable progress has been made in conceptual modelling is in the extension of existing and the devising of new data models to represent the temporal dimension of data. However, the introduction of time into conceptual models means a more complicated database structure if normalisation rules are still to apply. Users have expressed the desire for temporal functionality, but they have declared that they would be unhappy about moving from existing database platforms and having to invest into new ones [1]. This paper is using an existing conceptual modelling [2] for representing data and presents a framework for temporal application development. It describes an algebra for it, the operations of which apply at the conceptual rather than the database level. Based on the operations defined in that, an interactive temporally extended SQL-based query language is proposed that again applies to the conceptual schema level and requires little or no knowledge of SQL and no knowledge of the database structure. Mapping from a conceptual schema onto a relational database is automatic and queries expressed in that language are translated automatically into extended SQL queries. Section 2 of the paper describes the concepts of the Temporal Fact Based Model (TFBM), section 3 presents a case study that will be utilised to demonstrate the functionality of the proposed approach; section 4 describes the algorithm for mapping a TFBM schema onto a relational database, section 5 presents an architecture for the overall approach, section 6 presents an overview of the algebra for the TFBM, while section 7 concentrates on the interactive language. Finally, section 8 summarises the proposed approach, and presents some ideas about further research in this area.

2 The Conceptual Modelling Language (TFBM)

This section presents the main concepts of the model presented in this paper. The first paragraph deals with the basic notions underpinning the snapshot model, while the second one is dealing with its extension in order to incorporate time.

2.1   Basic Notions Underpinning the Non Temporal TFBM

The proposed approach in this paper is based on the Fact Based Model [3], a general Object Role Model. This model is based on entity types that play various roles in fact types. Fact types can also be objectified and used as entity types participating in other facts. Each entity type is referenced by a reference label. Entity types in the model are non-lexical object types while reference labels are lexical object types. Non-lexical object types are denoting "real life entities" and exist in the information system only through their properties. They have no inherent external representation while lexical object types do have an inherent listable representation. They are used in the information system to "name" the non-lexical object types but not necessary to identify them. The way that a reference label is related to an entity is referred to as reference mode and it is not considered different from a fact. An entity is identified by the various roles that it plays in facts. The only way to distinguish -as it also happens in the real world- between two entity instances of the same entity type that have the same reference label is to follow their participation in facts (identify the entities through their roles in facts). Every entity type appearing in the model is required to participate in at least one fact. The notation used the Fact Based Model and its metamodel are presented in Figure 1 and 2 respectively.

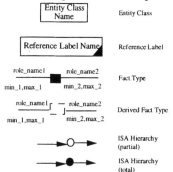

Fig. 1. Notation for the Fact Based Model

2.2   Time in the Temporal Fact Based Model (TFBM)

The most important consideration in the introduction of time in the Fact Based Model is the conceptual model of time employed. The TFBM supports discrete time (a more detailed discussion on the issues can be found in [2]). Temporal elements, based on time periods, were chosen as the most primitive temporal notion. Time periods are still the basic units of representing and reasoning about time for individual instances. However, time intervals are not closed under the set theoretic operations (i.e. union) and, therefore, another level referring to a set of time intervals is required. For example, if we record the employment of a person for various departments and we also like to keep the history of such employments, then if one wishes to know for how long has John been employed by a (any) department, then the result will have to be a set of time intervals which is not an interval itself. This necessitates the introduction of temporal elements. A *temporal element* is a set of time intervals. The set of temporal elements is, therefore, closed under the usual set theoretic operations.

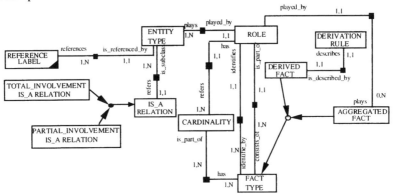

Fig. 2. The Metamodel of the Fact Based Model

To avoid confusion between a point in the continuous model and a nondecomposable unit of time in the discrete model, the term chronon has been proposed [4], [5]. Although the duration of each chronon in a set of times need not be the same, the duration of the chronon is usually fixed by the granularity of the measure of the time being used. The set of chronons is linearly and totally ordered. That is, if we have two chronons t_1 and t_2 then either $t_1 \geq t_2$ or $t_2 \geq t_1$. The formal framework employed as the temporal reasoning mechanism for time periods is based on that of *Interval Calculus* proposed in [6] and later refined in [7]. Time periods can relate to each other with one of thirteen possible relations: before/after, starts_before/starts_after, ends_before/ends_after, costarts/coends,overlaps/overlapped_by, during/contains, same_as. The introduction of temporal elements necessitates the definition of possible relations between temporal elements, that is a description of the possible relationships between all intervals of a temporal element leading to relations between temporal elements. This leads to the following definitions (Figure 3) for the possible relations between temporal elements. A formal definition for these can be found in [2]. In Figure 4, the adopted time period and temporal element semantics are defined. The term Symbol Period is helpful in case the absolute time is not precisely known. The relationship r (and the inverse ri) refers to Allen's relations between time periods, while the relation re (and its inverse rei) refers to the possible relations between temporal elements. Additionally a generic formal calendric system has been defined for the entity Calendar Period that appears in Figure 6 in order to provide for the modelling and reasoning about the usual calendar periods and temporal elements. A detailed discussion and its formalisation can be found in [2].

Time is introduced as a distinguished entity class in the formalism. The other components interact with time in a number of ways. The TFBM supports valid time which is concerned with modelling a time-varying reality; transaction time which is concerned with the storage of information in the database and decision time, that is the time that a particular decision has been taken. Another dimension supported by TFBM is that of Fact Transaction Time. In order to be able to offer the possibility of supporting schema evolution, we need to know when a particular fact type was created, when it was modified and when it was (if it has been) destroyed. What is required is to timestamp with *Fact Transaction time* the fact type in the metamodel, so as to keep the information about its evolution over time. The other types of time described above refer in reality to fact instances and not to the whole fact type. Because the only information bearing mechanism in the model is that of the fact type, it was decided that time should be associated only with facts. The lifespan of an entity, if required, can be found from the union of the time intervals associated with it in the various facts that the entity is participating in. The part of the metamodel of the TFBM that refers to facts is shown in Figure 5.

Relation	Symbol	Symbol for Inverse	Pictorial Example
before	<	>	XXX XX YYY YYY
all_before	a<	a>	XX XX YY YY
starts_before	s	si	XXX XXXX YYY YYYY
all_starts_before	as	asi	XX XXXXX YYY YYYYY
ends_before	e	ei	XXX XXXX YYYY YYYY
all_ends_before	ae	aei	XXX XXXX YYYY YYY
costarts	cs	csi	XXX XXXX YYYY YY
all_costarts	acs	acsi	XXX XXX XX YY YY YYY
overlaps	o	oi	XXXX XXX YYY YYYYY
all_overlaps	ao	aoi	XXX XXX XXX YY YYY YYY
during	d	di	XXXX XXXXXX YYYY YYY
same_as	=		XXX XXX XX YYY YYY YY

Fig. 3. Possible Relationships between Temporal Elements

3   The Case Study

OWN_SHIP is located in an area with certain co-ordinates and is travelling with some speed following a particular course (Figure 6). Its location in the area is given by its longitude and latitude and the area in which it is located has some environmental data. The ship's engines have certain capabilities (i.e. power, propulsion etc.). The ship has a number of weapon systems to defend itself against a possible attack each one with certain capabilities and characteristics (i.e. guns, missiles), information providers (i.e. radars) to detect such an attack, logistic information (i.e. status of available fuel) and data concerning possible damages in OWN_SHIP's systems. At some point in time OWN_SHIP's information providers locate one or more tracks which have certain characteristics (certain type, travelling speed etc.). A system located on the ship will have -based on the information provided- to decide whether or not the detected tracks should be considered as threats to the ship and if they are to formulate a plan in order to prepare a defence against them. In doing so it will have to take into account that the available defence resources might be limited due to possible damages in weapon systems or because the number of threats is too great to defend against or even because some weapons are not usable in the particular situation. Therefore, the system will have to assign priorities to the tracks -depending on their type, distance from OWN_SHIP etc.- in order to deal firstly and be able to use the best available weapons against those that are considered to be the most dangerous ones. Additionally, and because different information providers might give slightly different information about the same tracks, the system after following each track's history must be able to distinguish between 'real' and duplicate tracks.

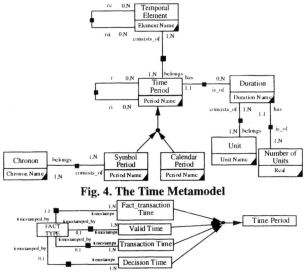

Fig. 4. The Time Metamodel

Fig. 5. Update of Facts with Time in the Metamodel

4   Representation of TFBM on DB Level

This section presents an algorithm for representing a Temporal Fact Based schema onto a relational database platform:

Step 1   For each simple or complex entity class create a relation with its surrogate as primary key and, for every functional dependent and time invarying role of this entity class, append to this relation the corresponding entity class surrogate or reference label name.

Step 2   For each entity class which is subclass of another entity class, replace its surrogate in its corresponding relation with the surrogate of its superclass.

Step 3   For each simple or complex entity class and for every functional dependent and time varying role of this entity (not including the has_component role of complex entities), group in a relation the corresponding entity and time period class surrogates.

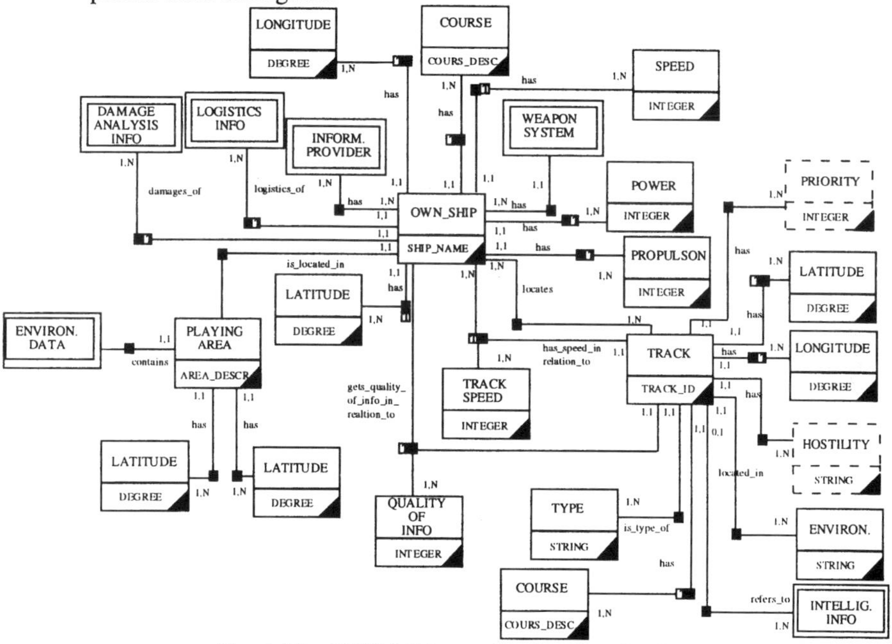

Fig. 6. The TFBM Schema for the Case Study

Step 4   For each fact (except the is_part_of facts of complex entities) with no identifier constraint create a relation with fields all the corresponding surrogates and define as key their combination. Also, if the fact is time-varying then include the time period class surrogates.

Step 5   For each complex entity class do

　Step 5.a Create a relation containing the entity surrogate as the primary key, every functional dependent and time invarying is_part_of component (i.e., if the component is a simple reference label then append itself and otherwise append its surrogate) and finally, composite reference surrogates for the rest of its components.

　Step 5.b For each composite reference surrogate in the previously defined relation, create a separate relation and group in it the surrogates of the complex entity, the component and the time period. If in addition, the composite reference is functionally independent then define as key the combination of all three fields.

The part of the case study that refers to OWN_SHIP can be represented as follows (where the three time surrogates in each timestamped database relation correspond to the valid, transaction and decision time):

Own_Ship (Ship$, Information_Provider$, Weapon_System$, Playing_Area$)
Own_ShiphasLogistics(Ship$, Logistics$, tpv1$, tpt1$, tpd1$)
Own_ShiphasDamage(Ship$,Damage$,tpv2$, tpt2$, tpd2$)

Own-ShiphasLongitude(<u>Ship$</u>,Longitude,<u>tp3v$, tpt3$</u>,tpd3$)
Own_ShiphasLatitude(<u>Ship$</u>,Latitude,<u>tpv4$, tpt4$, tpd4$</u>)
Own_ShiphasCourse(<u>Ship$</u>,Course,<u>tp5v$, tdt5$, tpd5$</u>)
Own_ShiphasSpeed(<u>Ship$</u>,Speed,<u>tp6v$, tpt6$, tpd6$</u>)
Own_ShiphasPower(<u>Ship$</u>,Power,<u>tp7v$, tpt7, tpd7$</u>)
Own_ShiphasPropulsion(<u>Ship$</u>,Propulsion,<u>tpv8$, tpt8$, tpd8$</u>)
Own_ShiplocatesTrack(<u>Ship$,Track$</u>)

The resulting relational schema has flat normalised relations (in third normal form) which can be used directly in the computations. In addition, the algorithm is simple and straightforward, takes into account the cardinality constraints and, complex objects are treated like any other object without providing additional operators. However, due to the flatness of the resulting database schema, join operations will be needed more frequently in order to obtain the combined information.

5   A Framework for Application Development

One of the main problems faced by temporal applications is that conventional query languages do not support temporal operations. Additionally, any use of time will complicate the representation at the database level. Users will need to know not only where exactly the information is stored, but also the information about possible timestamps in the conceptual schema, since the time components will be located in different relations in order to obey the normalisation principles. Furthermore, the majority of current database users would not favour at the moment the introduction of different temporal DBMSs because that would mean abandoning current practices and applications; an expense that most of them would like to avoid. For this purpose, an algebra has been defined for the TFBM followed by a language that allows users to pose queries at the conceptual level without any consideration about how the facts have been stored in a database, have been developed. The language is interactive and based on SQL. It is making use of the mapping algorithm presented above for the transformation of a TFBM schema onto a relational schema. The development of the language has been based on the ORACLE relational DBMS and the pro*C precompiler. The general architecture of the approach is presented in Figure 7.

6   An Algebra for TFBM

An algebra is a collection of high level operators that operate on the concepts of a data model. There are certain requirements that any temporal algebra (irrespective of the model that it refers to) must satisfy (based on [9] for the relational model):

- The temporal algebra must be a consistent extension of a "snapshot" algebra: a temporal algebra should at least be as powerful as a snapshot algebra for the same data model (excluding its temporal modelling aspects) so that queries that were possible when time was not being modelled are not forbidden when it is.
- It should be able for the algebraic operations to be reduced to those of the "snapshot" algebra when there is no mention to time in an expression or query.
- The algebra must possess minimality with respect to the temporal dimension: the temporal information seen by the user should contain only information at

points in time when users record a change, yet the operations should allow the automatic inference of values at other points in time.

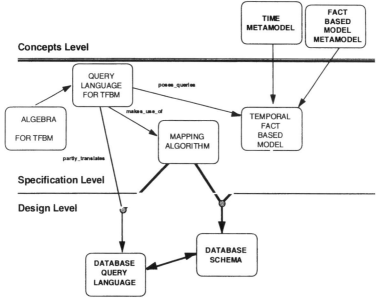

Fig. 7. A Development Framework for Temporal Information Systems

- The algebra must have semantic completeness: operations should be natural with people's intuitive views of time and information over time and powerful as to allow the extraction of temporal information contained in the model.
- The temporal algebra must be specific to the model of time that is employed.

6.1 Definition of an Algebra for the Fact Based Model

The first consideration when defining an algebra for the Fact Based Model is the kinds of objects on which the operations are to be performed, i.e. will the operands be entities, facts, both, etc. Since the only information bearing mechanism in the model are the facts, the algebra's operations will have to be performed on facts or parts of them and also return facts as a result, thus ensuring also that the algebra will remain closed under the defined operations. In the remaining of this section the definition of the various operations will be provided. Most of the examples that appear refer to binary facts because they are the most common ones. However, all the rules, results and explanations apply to unary as well as to facts with arity more than two.

The SELECT operation performs a horizontal selection on a fact type (fact for short) and creates a new fact between the entity types (entities for short) that were involved in the original fact. The newly created fact has the same arity as the old one. The operation might be accompanied by a selection criterion in which case the population of the new fact will refer to only the entities that satisfy the selection criterion. For example, for the fact displayed in Figure 8 the operation $\sigma_{Employee\_Name\ =}$

'John' employment will create a new association between EMPLOYEE and DEPARTMENT (shown in Figure 9 along with the original one and with the new population) the population of which will contain the facts satisfying the condition stated in the conditional part of the operation. The cardinalities of the newly created fact will be for each entity from 0 to the maximum cardinality that it had before in the selected fact. This is because the population of the new fact will be at most the same as the original fact (if there is no selection condition or all fact instances of the original fact satisfy the condition) and the minimum will be 0 (if no instances satisfy the selection condition). The operation is the same and the result as well for facts with more than two entities involved. A selection on a unary fact will return another unary fact (the rule about minimum and maximum cardinalities of the new fact will still be the same) the population of which is defined in the same way as in binary facts.

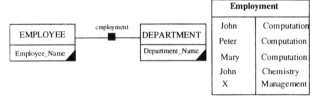

Fig. 8. The Fact Employment

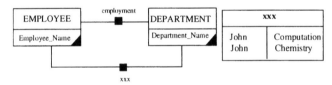

Fig. 9. The Result of the SELECT operation on Fact Employment

The fact that the various types of time are considered as entities participating in the facts means that there is no need for some sort of temporal selection (as in some extended relational algebras) to be defined. The condition, however, might refer to one of the interval relations. Additionally, all rules that were described before still apply, and the result is the same as before when there is no reference to time. This satisfies the first two criteria stated for temporal algebras. All the above considerations apply also when the selection criterion refers to one of the types of time in the fact. In this case there is also a constraint that both the time in the timestamps of the fact and the time given in the selection criterion belong to the same calendar and have the same granularity. Otherwise, the assumption is that there will be two conversion functions (that will "internally" apply) that will convert the timestamps (only for comparison reasons and not changing what appears in the fact) into the calendar and granularity of the selection criterion. When the selection criterion refers to one of the types of time then as part of the condition one can use the possible relationships between time periods. For example, for the fact type EMPLOYMENT an expression could be $\sigma_{Valid\_Time\_Value\ before\ [1989,\ 1990]}$ employment in which case the result would contain the instances for which the time period referring to the valid time is before the period [1989, 1990]. Finally, for nested selection expressions one could also have as part of the selection criterion one of the possible relationships between temporal elements. Their application of those will be similar to that of the previous example.

The PROJECT operation selects vertically part (or whole) of a fact according to the projection criterion given and creates a new fact whose degree is equal with the number of objects that were projected from the original fact. The entities in the new fact will be the ones that were projected. The degree of the new fact is the degree of the original fact decreased by one or more. The project operation does not have any meaning if its applied to unary facts. The cardinalities of the newly created fact will be for each entity from 0 to the maximum cardinality that they had before in the projected fact.

Union compatibility in the TFBM means that two facts must have the same degree and each reference label of each entity in each of the two facts must have a corresponding reference label with the same domain in the other fact. No semantic relationship between the involved fact types is investigated since this is very much application dependent and in practice impossible to achieve.The UNION operation accepts two facts as input and results in a new fact whose degree will be the same one as that of the original facts and its population will be the union of their populations. The cardinalities of the new fact will be (Figure 10):

$$x_1 = min(a_1, a_5) \qquad x_2 = a_2 + a_6 \qquad x_3 = min(a_3, a_7) \qquad x_4 = a_4 + a_8$$

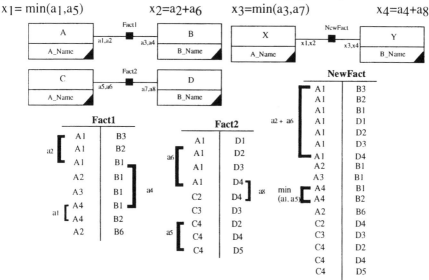

Fig. 10. Cardinalities as a Result of the UNION Operation

The DIFFERENCE operation accepts as input two facts and returns a fact whose population will be the instances of the first fact that were not members of the population of the second fact. The two facts must be union compatible according to the definition provided in the UNION operation. The cardinalities of the newly created fact will be (where the cardinalities refer to those of Figure 10):

$$x_1 = a_1 - a_6 \qquad x_2 = a_2 \qquad x_3 = a_3 - a_8 \qquad x_4 = a_4$$

The inputs to the CARTESIAN PRODUCT operation are two facts and the result a new fact involving all the entities that appeared in the two facts and with degree of the new fact the sum of the degrees of the two individual facts. The population of the new fact consists of all possible combinations of fact instances of the two original facts. If, for example, the Cartesian product was applied to the two original facts of Figure 10 then he cardinalities of the new quadranary fact as a result of the operation would be

$x_1 = a_1 \times a_5 \times a_7$ $x_2 = n$ $x_3 = a_3 \times a_5 \times a_7$ $x_4 = n$
$x_5 = a_1 \times a_5 \times a_3$ $x_6 = n$ $x_7 = a_7 \times a_1 \times a_3$ $x_8 = n.$

The INTERSECTION operation accepts as input two facts and returns a fact whose population will be the instances of the first fact that members of the population of the second fact. The two facts must be union compatible. The cardinalities of the newly created fact will be (cardinalities refer to those of Figure 10):

$x_1 = 0$ $x_2 = min\ (a_2, a_6)$ $x_3 = 0$ $x_4 = min\ (a_4, a_8)$

The algebra presented contained operations that are performed on facts, since facts are the building blocks of the Fact Based Model and they constitute the only information bearing mechanism of the model. The operations that are described possess two fundamental properties: they remain the same when applied to timestamped facts and they do not require the additional introduction of temporally oriented equivalents. Since time has been introduced as a distinguished entity in the Fact based Model, the treatment of timestamped facts is the same as snapshot ones. This keeps the algebra simple and shields the user from unnecessary information regarding the timestamping of facts. The principles of the algebraic operations that have been defined are very close to those defined in the relational algebra which is the most familiar to users. The algebra is also kept closed by defining for every operation one or two facts as input and one fact as output and the populations follow the mathematical properties that apply also to the relational operations. Finally, the algebra does not need to introduce special rules that do not apply to the Fact Based Model in order to cope with special situations, unlike other algebras, i.e. the ERC+ [8] and ERT [10] algebras where, although the algebra operates on entities, there is a special need for an operator between relationships in order to refer to entities that are not linked directly.

7   Data Definition and Manipulation from Conceptual Definitions

This section describes the process for automatically mapping a conceptual schema onto the relational database and the structure of the language based on the previously described algebra that is used for manipulating the created tables and inserted data. Definitions and manipulations remain at the conceptual level and the architecture presented in section 5 is responsible for translating them into data definition and manipulation at the database level.

7.1   Creation of a TFBM Schema

The user is asked to insert the information about a particular application schema, that is the facts, entities that participate in them, cardinalities for the roles that the entities play, information about subtypes and information about whether or not the inserted fact is timestamped. The system then will make use of the mapping algorithm in order to create the necessary database relations. Following the algorithm presented in section 4, when a fact is timestamped an additional relation needs to be created with the surrogates and the time period. In a similar way this is done also when we have facts where the entities are not functionally dependent. The tracing of these different types of relations that need to be created is done via a metadata table that contains information about the fact name, its possible timestamping, entities involved in the fact, cardinalities and subtypes; that relation has the following format

(fact_name,   timestamped,   entity,   min_cardinality,   max_cardinality, level_in_hierarchy, root_of_hierarchy).

The user is also asked to provide information about the name and reference label of each entity involved in a fact. If a fact is timestamped then a relation is created automatically; this relation contains the surrogates of the involved entities and the tp$ surrogate corresponding to the time periods. The time periods for valid, transaction and decision time are stored in another table that contains that surrogate and the start and end of the time intervals for fact instances. For example, assuming that a user wishes to define the fact TRACK is_located_in ENVIRONMENT (non timestamped). Then the relation with the metadata will hold the information

(located_in, N, TRACK, 1, 1, 1, NULL)

(located_in, N, ENVIRONMENT, 1, N, 1, NULL)

The result of those two tuples in the relation that contains the metadata will be the creation of a relation TRACK (track_id, environment_type). When the new fact TRACK has_type will be inserted then the system will locate TRACK as an already defined entity and -because of the 1,1 cardinality between TRACK and TYPE- will modify the existing relation for TRACK by adding another attribute for the TYPE of the track. Therefore, the addition of the tuples

(has_type, N, TRACK, 1,1,1,NULL)   (has_type, N, TYPE, 1,N,1,NULL)

will lead to the modification of the TRACK relation.

7.2   Mappings from Query and Conceptual Level to Database Level

The user is prompted to query the database in a format that follows that of the SQL syntax, but the user queries are based on the Temporal Fact Based schema of the particular application. Then they are transformed automatically onto queries that access the database relations. Additionally, the user is asked to provide the components of a query in an interactive manner and therefore, there is no requirement for him/her to know the database language of the database structure. Special operators have been created in order to cater for relations between intervals and relations between temporal elements. A parser has been created in order to deal with subqueries of any level that involve the temporal operators. The calendar system that is used for time representation and interval comparisons, at the moment, supports the Gregorian calendar system up to the minimum granularity of seconds. Also when intervals of different granularity need to be compared(i.e. month and year), the interval with the highest granularity (year) is converted automatically to the lowest granularity (month). *All* normal SQL queries are allowed and n top the user can specify temporal queries as well. For example, assume that a user wanted to pose the following query to the database: "Find the longitude of a track that was valid at the same time that OWN_SHIP had a latitude of 15^{0}". The whole process of defining the above query is as follows (plain letters denote a system prompts and instructions, while italic letters denote user inputs/choices):

Input all items to be displayed in the following format: Entity.Label
Item 1: *Longitude.degree*
Enter the facts to select from:
Fact 1: *track_has_longitude*
Is there a condition (Y/N): *Y*
Is the condition (N)on temporal or (T)emporal: *t*
Enter time of interest: *1. VALID_TIME*
                            2. TRANSACTION_TIME
                            3. DECISION_TIME
Enter the name of the timestamped fact: *track_has_longitude*
Choose an interval relation: 1. BEFORE
                               2. EQUALS(all interval/time element relations)
Enter 2nd argument of condition: 1. (V)alue
                                 2. (C)olumn
                                 3. *(S)ubquery*
[those arguments correspond to for example salary = 10,000, employee.depno= department.dno and a subquery respectively]
Enter time of interest: *1. VALID_TIME*
                            2. TRANSACTION_TIME
                            3. DECISION_TIME
Enter Fact name: *ship_has_latitude*
Is there a condition (Y/N): *Y*
Is the condition (N)on temporal or (T)emporal: *N*
Enter name of reference label in the format Entity.Label: *Latitude.degree*
Choose an operator: *1. =*
                             2. . ... (all normal comparison operators)
Enter 2nd argument of condition: 1. *(V)alue*
                                 2. (C)olumn
                                 3. (S)ubquery
Enter value: *15*
Is there another condition (Y/N): *N*
Is there another condition (Y/N): *N*
[first question for the condition refers to the subquery, the second to the main query]

The returned query is going to be:

SELECT   Longitude.degree   FROM   track_has_longitude   WHERE track_has_longitude.valid_time   EQUALS   (SELECT   valid_time   FROM ship_has_latitude WHERE Latitude.degree = 15)

8   Conclusions

In this paper a framework for the development of Temporal Information Systems was presented. It starts with a conceptual modelling formalism that is also providing support for the modelling of temporal applications. The modelling formalism is based on facts. There is no distinction between entities and attributes, because such a distinction was considered to be conceptually irrelevant. The only distinction is between lexical and non lexical objects. A time metamodel has been defined for this mode and also an algebra for it and a query language that in contrast to existing temporal languages operates at the conceptual level, thus not requiring from the user's point of view any knowledge of the underlying database. The language is based on SQL but it is also interactive and, therefore, requires no particular knowledge of SQL, but instead prompts the user to insert the relevant information. Current work is concentrating into shortening the time required for inputting a particular query, because although the language has the advantages mentioned before, the time required to define a particular query is admittedly long. Finally, an attempt is made in order to make the query language a graphical one.

References

[1]   Ariav, G., et al, *Special Requirements and Approaches*, Proceedings of the 1st Int. Workshop Towards an Infrastructure for Temporal Databases, March 1994.

[2]   Petrounias, I., Loucopoulos, P., *Time Dimension in a Fact Based Model*, Proceedings of 1st Int. Conference on Object-Role Modelling, Australia, 1994.

[3]   Loucopoulos, P., Petrounias, I., *The Functional Requirements Model and its Metamodel*, UMIST/F_CUBE/8, March 1993.

[4]   Ariav, G., *A Temporally Oriented Data Model*, ACM Transaction on database Systems, 11(4), pp. 499-527, Dec. 1986.

[5]   Clifford, J., Rao, A., *A Simple, General Structure for Temporal Domains*, in Proceedings of the IFIP 8/WG8.1, Working Conference on temporal Aspects in Information Systems, Sophia Antipolis, France, May 1987.

[6]   Allen, J., F., *Maintaining Knowledge about Temporal Intervals*, Communications of ACM, 26(11), Nov. 1983.

[7]   *A Logic Oriented Approach to Knowledge and Databases Supporting Natural Language User Interfaces*, ESPRIT Project 107 (LOKI), Institute of Computer Science, Research Centre of Crete, Greece, March 1986.

[8]   Parent,C.,Spaccapietra,S., *An Entity-Relationship Algebra*, Proceedings of Int. Conference on Data Engineering, Los Angeles, pp.500-507, April 1984.

[9]   McKenzie,E.,Snodgrass,R.,*Evaluation of Relational Algebras Incorporating the Time Dimension in Databases,*ACM Computing Surveys, Vol.23, No.1, March 1991

[10]   Ait-Braham,A., Theodoulidis,B.,Karvelis, G.,*Conceptual Modelling and Manipulation of Temporal Databases*, Proceedings of ER94, Manchester, UK, November 1994

Temporal Features of Class Populations and Attributes in Conceptual Models

Dolors Costal, Antoni Olivé, Maria-Ribera Sancho

Universitat Politècnica de Catalunya, Dept. Llenguatges i Sistemes Informàtics
Jordi Girona Salgado 1-3, Campus Nord, Ed. C-6, E 08034 Barcelona (Catalonia)
e-mail: {dolors|olive|ribera}@lsi.upc.es

Abstract. Constraints play an important role in conceptual modeling. In general, the specification of constraints, both static and transition, must be done in some logic-based language. Unfortunately, the resulting formulas may be complex, error-prone and difficult to read. This explain why almost all conceptual modeling languages have developed a special, easy-to-use syntax (language features) to state the most common constraints. Most features (often with graphical symbols) developed so far are concerned with static constraints (like keys, partitions or cardinalities), and very little work has been done for transition constraints.

In this paper, we identify six temporal features, three related to class populations and three to attributes. The corresponding transition integrity constraints appear in almost any conceptual model and their specification is necessary and important. We believe that our temporal features make their specification simple and practical. We have named each feature, and provide a declarative and procedural formalization for them.

1. Introduction

A conceptual model consists of two (sub)models: The structural and the behavioural model. The first describes the object types characterizing the objects in the domain, their structural relationships, the object attributes and relationships, the derivation rules defining the population of derived object types, or the values of derived attributes and relationships, and the static and transition integrity constraints. The behavioural model describes the event types, the integrity constraints associated with the events, the effect of these events on the Information Base, and the events that must be generated [Bor85].

This paper focuses mainly on the specification of transition integrity constraints. These constraints are conditions that involve facts of two or more states of the Information Base. Usually, they involve facts of only two consecutive states, constraining the transition between them, but in general the constraints may refer to any number of states [ISO82].

In general, the specification of constraints, both static and transition, must be done in some logic-based language allowing, among other things, the use of connectors and quantifiers. Unfortunately, the resulting formulas may be complex, error-prone and difficult to read. This explain why almost all conceptual modeling languages have developed a special, easy-to-use syntax (language features) to state the most common constraints. Most features (often with graphical symbols) developed so far are concerned with static constraints, such as keys, inclusion, exclusion, equality, partition [VeV82] and, above all, cardinality constraints [LEW93].

Transition constraints are considered explicitly in some languages [GKB82, Kun84, SFN+84, WMW89, DHR91], usually expressed in temporal or dynamic logic. However, very little work has been done in selecting some common subset of them, and developing the corresponding syntactic features. Almost the only temporal features that we may find in conceptual modeling languages are the possible definition of mutable vs. immutable (or constant) attributes and relationships, and initial values of attributes [HaM81, JSH+96] and state diagrams [RBP+91, CoD94, Rat97]. In consequence, the designer is forced to specify many transition constraints with complete formulas, or to leave them unspecified.

In this paper, we identify six new temporal features, three related to class populations (section 2) and three to attributes (section 3). We believe that the corresponding transition integrity constraints appear in almost any conceptual model and that their simple specification is necessary and important. We have named each feature, but we have not attempted to propose a graphical symbol for them. We define the temporal features formally, at two levels: declarative and procedural. In the declarative level (sections 2 and 3), the features are related to permissible changes of the Information Base, independent of the transactions that induce the changes. To define features procedurally, we consider that a transaction consists of a number of primitive structural events (section 4), and we determine the conditions such events must satisfy to maintain the Information Base consistent with respect to the temporal features (section 5). Additional detail can be found in [COS97]. Section 6 summarizes our conclusions, and points out future research.

2. Temporal Features of Class Populations

A structural model defines, among other things, a set of classes organized into a class hierarchy through generalization (or specialization). Objects are instances of one or more classes. We assume that, in the general case, an object may change its classes dynamically. The population of a class at a time t is defined as the set of objects that are instance of that class at t.

2.1 Static Features

The most common static features of class populations defined in structural models are class inclusions, partitions and cardinalities. A specialization such as class a ISA class b defines that, at any time, the population of class a is a subset of the population of class b.

Class partitions, such as the partition of class a into classes b and c, define that classes b and c are specializations of class a, and that the population of classes b and c are disjoint. A partial (or incomplete) partition indicates that, at any time, the union of the populations of both classes is a subset of that of class a, while a complete partition defines that, at any time, the union of the populations of both classes is equal to the population of class a [MaO95].

Finally, some languages allow defining constraints on the cardinality of classes [EKW92, LEW93]. These constraints can also be considered static features since they must be satisfied at any time.

2.2 Temporal Features: General Definitions

Temporal features of class populations define some time-dependent constraints that the populations must satisfy. We will define in this Section three of such features. We introduce first the notation we need for their formalization.

We assume that time is discrete, and that time points are expressed uniformly at some level of abstraction (granularity). The lifespan ls of an IS is the temporal interval $ls = (t_i, t_f)$ during which the system exists. Similarly, the lifespan ols of an object o, `ols(o)` = $(t_{o,i}, t_{o,f})$ is the temporal interval during which object o exists. It is obvious that the lifespan of an object must be included in lifespan `ls`. We assume that once an object ceases to exist in the system, it cannot exist again in the future. We usually do not know in advance the exact values of the above time points, but this is unimportant for our purposes: we only need to assume that such values do exist.

We will denote the starting and ending points of a temporal interval `ti` by the functions `startsAt(ti)` and `endsAt(ti)`, respectively. We also use the predicate `belongsTo(t,ti)` to indicate that time point t is included in time interval `ti`.

We use a two-term existence predicate `a(o,t)` to indicate that object o is an instance of class a at time t. Objects can be instances of classes only at times belonging to the lifespan `ls`. In general, an object may be an instance of a class during one or more disjoint and non-consecutive time intervals, called membership intervals. We denote by `mi(o,a)` = $\{ti_1, \ldots, ti_n\}$ the set of membership intervals of object o in class a. It is obvious that the membership intervals of an object o in any class are included in object's lifespan `ols(o)`. On the other hand, there is a correspondence between the existence predicate and the membership intervals, which is captured by the following equivalence:

$\forall O, T(a(O,T) \leftrightarrow \exists TI (TI \in mi(O,a) \wedge belongsTo(T,TI)))$

2.3 Permanent Instances

The permanent instances feature of a class defines whether or not its instances are permanent. A permanent object is an object that, once created, exists until the end of lifespan `ls`. Possible values for this feature are: `[non-]permanent instances`.

Formally, if class a has `permanent instances` then:

$\forall O, T(a(O,T) \rightarrow endsAt(ols(O)) = endsAt(ls))$

The value `non-permanent instances` does not impose constraints on objects' lifespan. It can be seen that if a class has `permanent instances`, then all its subclasses must have also `permanent instances`.

As an example, consider the classes shown in the structural model of Figure 1.

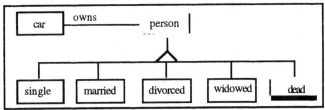

Figure 1. Example of structural model.

Class `car` would have `non-permanent instances`, if we assume that cars may cease to exist at some time. On the other hand, class `person` could be with `permanent instances`, if we assume that persons, once created, are always known to the system. The five subclasses of `person` would also have `permanent instances`.

2.4 Initial Membership

The initial membership feature of a class defines whether or not potential instances of this class must be (must not be) members at object's creation time. Possible values for this feature are `[always|never|sometimes] initially member`.

If class a is `always initially member`, then all objects that are sometime instances of class a must be instances of it at creation time. Formally,

$\forall O, T(a(O,T) \rightarrow a(O, \text{startsAt}(\text{ols}(O))))$

Similarly, if class a is never initially member, then all objects that are sometime instances of class a must not be instances of it at creation time. Formally,

$\forall O, T(a(O,T) \rightarrow \neg a(O, \text{startsAt}(\text{ols}(O))))$

The value sometimes initially member does not impose constraints on membership at object's creation time.

It can be seen that if a subclass of a partition is always initially member, then all other subclasses of the partition must be never initially member.

Note that this feature is orthogonal to the previous one. We can see four of the six possible combinations in the example of Figure 1. Classes car and person are likely to be always initially member, because objects that are cars or persons must be instances of their respective class from the beginning of their existence. Similarly, class single would also be always initially member, since if a person is sometime single then he had to be single when he was created. Classes married, divorced and widowed could be sometimes initially member, if we allow that when a person is known for the first time to the system he may be also instance of one of these classes. Finally, class dead would be never initially member, if we assume that we do not create new persons that are dead at the beginning of their existence in the system.

2.5 Membership Intervals

The membership intervals feature of a class defines some characteristics of the time intervals during which objects may be instances of that class. The three possible values for this feature are: [single[non-]permanent|multiple] membership intervals.

If class a is single (permanent or non-permanent) membership interval then $|\text{mi}(o, \text{classA})| = 1$. In the other case (multiple), the number of time intervals may be greater than 1.

If class a is single permanent membership interval then its objects remain in the class until the end of their lifespan. Formally, we say that the end of their unique membership interval coincides with the end of their lifespan:

$\forall O, TI(TI \in \text{mi}(O,a) \rightarrow \text{endsAt}(TI) = \text{endsAt}(\text{ols}(O)))$

If a class is single non-permanent membership interval then its instances may leave that class before the end of their lifespan.

Note that this feature is orthogonal to the previous ones. We can see several combinations in the example of Figure 1. Classes person and car would be single permanent membership interval, since once an object is classified as person or car, it remains instance of the class until the end of its existence. Similarly, class dead would also be single permanent membership interval (unfortunately). Class single would be single non-permanent membership interval, since persons can only be single during a unique time interval, but may leave this class. Finally, classes married and divorced would be multiple membership intervals, since persons may be married or divorced during several disjoint and non-consecutive time intervals.

2.6 Application

The features can be useful to characterize (part of) the behaviour of roles, which are used in several languages [Per90, GSR96]. In languages using state diagrams (such as those described in [RBP+91, CoD94, Rat97]), some of the temporal features may be inferred from the diagrams. Each state corresponds to a class. If the initial state is unique, then it is always initially member. The other states are never initially member. The final state is single permanent membership interval. The other states are single non-permanent or multiple membership intervals, depending on whether the objects may be in the corresponding state one or more times.

3. Temporal Features of Attributes

3.1 Static Features

Common static features of attributes defined in many conceptual models include single/multivalued attributes, optional/mandatory attributes, functional/total (injective/surjective) attributes [BoC95], participation constraints [LEW93] and other special constraints such as constant, identifier, subset, equality or uniqueness [VeV82].

3.2 Temporal Features: General Definitions

Let attname be an attribute of class a taking values from class b. We use a three-term predicate attname(o1,o2,t) to indicate that the value of attribute attname for object o1 is object o2 at time t. For multivalued attributes, the meaning is that object o2 is one of the attribute values. Objects o1 and o2 must be instances of their corresponding classes at time t. We formalize this as the Temporal Referential Integrity axiom:

$$\forall O1,O2,T(attname(O1,O2,T) \rightarrow a(O1,T) \wedge b(O2,T))$$

Note that we do not consider "null" values to be a special kind of attribute value. Our equivalent concept is that an object does not have a value for a given attribute. On the other hand, it is always assumed that only existing objects can have attribute values or can be attribute values of objects. This is captured by the following implications:

$$\forall O,T(\neg a(O,T) \rightarrow \neg \exists O1\ attname(O,O1,T))$$
$$\forall O,T(\neg a(O,T) \rightarrow \neg \exists O1\ attname(O1,O,T))$$

We will see that, in many cases, it is interesting to define the temporal features of inverse attributes [HaM81]. We do not need special notation for that, but of course the value of such attributes must be syncronised. Thus, if invattname is the inverse of attname in class b, the following equivalence must hold:

$$\forall O1,O2,T(attname(O1,O2,T) \leftrightarrow invattname(O2,O1,T))$$

3.3 Initial Value

The initial value feature of an attribute of a class defines whether or not objects of this class must have (must not have) values for the attribute when the object starts a membership interval in that class. Possible values for this feature are [always|never|sometimes] initially valued.

If attribute attname of class a is always initially valued, then all objects of class a must have a value for attribute attname every time that they start a membership interval in that class. Formally,

$$\forall O,TI(TI \in mi(O,a) \rightarrow \exists O1\ attname(O,O1,startsAt(TI)))$$

Similarly, if attribute attname of class a is never initially valued, then all objects of class a cannot have a value for attribute attname when they start a membership interval in that class. Formally,

$\forall O, TI\ (TI \in mi\,(O,a) \rightarrow \neg\exists O1\ attname\,(O,O1,startsAt\,(TI)))$

The value `sometimes initially valued` does not impose constraints on attribute values at the beginning of membership intervals.

As an example, consider the following class definitions:

```
class person
    name: string;
    phone: integer;
    worksIn: set of project
class married ISA person (multiple membership intervals)
    spouse: person
```

Attributes `name` and `spouse` are likely to be `always initially valued`. Note that `spouse` must be given a value every time a `person` starts a membership interval in `married`. Attribute `phone` might be `sometimes initially valued`, if we assume that we may or may not know a person's phone number when he is created. Attribute `worksIn` could be `never initially valued`, if we assume that when a person is created he is still not working in any project.

3.4 Existence Intervals

The existence intervals feature of an attribute defines some characteristics of the time intervals during which exist values for that attribute. This feature is mainly useful for single valued attributes, and this is the only case we will consider here. The three possible values for this feature are `[single [non-]permanent | multiple] existence intervals`. This feature is orthogonal to the previous one.

If attribute `attname` of class a is `single permanent existence interval`, then it means that once an object o of class a takes a value for attribute `attname` -at some time t belonging to a membership interval `TI ∈ mi (o,a)` - it will keep on having some value for attribute `attname` until the end of the membership interval. Formally:

$\forall O,O1,TI,T(TI \in mi\,(O,a) \land belongsTo\,(T,TI) \land attname\,(O,O1,T) \land$
$\qquad belongsTo\,(T1,TI) \land T1>T \rightarrow \exists O2\ attname\,(O,O2,T1))$

In the example given above, `name` could be an attribute with `single permanent existence interval`. Once an object of class `person` has a `name`, it keeps on having some `name` while the object is classified as `person`. Note that the `name` may change: this feature only requires that some value continue existing for `name`.

A more involved example would be the following attribute:

```
class employee ISA person (multiple membership intervals)
    assignedTo: department (never initially valued,
                    single permanent existence interval)
```

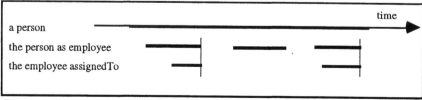

Figure 2. Example of object lifespan, membership intervals and attribute existence intervals

In this case, persons may be employees during several membership intervals, and attribute `assignedTo` is never known when a `person` becomes `employee`, but once known, there is some value for it until he ceases to be employed. The `department` may change during an employee's life. Figure 2 shows graphically the relationship between the three intervals. Note that during the second membership interval, the employee was never assignedTo any department.

If attribute attname of class a is single non-permanent existence interval, then it means that:
- once an object o of class a takes a value for attribute attname, at some time T belonging to a membership interval TI∈mi(o,a),
- and then it ceases to have a value for that attribute during TI,
- it cannot have later (during the same TI) any value for the attribute.

In other words, there is a single existence interval of the attribute, but it may end before the corresponding membership interval. Formally:

$\forall$O,O1,TI,T(TI∈mi(O,a) $\wedge$ belongsTo(T,TI) $\wedge$ attname(O,O1,T) $\wedge$
belongsTo(T1,TI) $\wedge$ T1>T $\wedge$ ¬$\exists$O2 attname(O,O2,T) $\wedge$
belongsTo(T2,TI) $\wedge$ T2>T1 $\rightarrow$ ¬$\exists$O3 attname(O,O3,T2))

A simple example could be the following attribute:

class person (non-permanent instances,
        always initially member, single membership interval)
mother: person (always initially valued,
        single non-permanent existence interval)

In this case, there is a single membership interval. During this interval, the value for attribute mother exists initially, but once a person loses a value for mother he cannot regain it later.

The value multiple existence intervals does not constrain the intervals of attribute value existence.

3.5 Application of Initial Values and Existence Intervals to Optional Attributes

Before continuing with the last feature, it may be interesting to consider the relationship of the previous features with the well-known "optional/mandatory" static feature of single valued attributes.

The two features described above are orthogonal, and each has three possible values, thus originating nine possible combinations. Mandatory attributes correspond to the combination:

always initially valued/single permanent existence interval,

while the other eight combinations correspond to optional attributes. This means that our features may be helpful in providing additional details on why and when a single valued attribute is optional.

3.6 Changeability

Our last temporal feature (which is also orthogonal to the previous ones) deals with changes of attribute values. A feature similar to this one is provided by SDM [HaM81]. We distinguish here between single and multivalued attributes. For single valued attributes possible values are [non-]modifiable. For multivalued attributes we define two sub-features with possible values [insertions [non-] allowed] and [deletions [non-] allowed].

Formally, if a single valued attribute attname of class a is non-modifiable then:

$\forall$O,O1,O2,TI,T(TI∈mi(O,a) $\wedge$ belongsTo(T-1,TI) $\wedge$ attname(O,O1,T-1) $\wedge$
belongsTo(T,TI) $\wedge$ attname(O,O2,T) $\rightarrow$ O1 = O2)

Note that this feature only forbids the changes of values of `attname`. It says nothing with respect to changes from no value for the attribute to some value. The value `modifiable` does not constrain the changes to single valued attributes.

If a multivalued attribute `attname` of class a has `insertions non-allowed`, then the attribute can take values only when an object starts a membership interval in class a. Formally:

$\forall$O,O1,TI,T(TI∈mi(O,a) ∧ belongsTo(T,TI) ∧ attname(O,O1,T)
$\rightarrow$ attname(O,O1,startsAt(TI)))

If a multivalued attribute `attname` of class a has `deletions non-allowed`, then the attribute can take values only when an object starts a membership interval in class a. Formally:

$\forall$O,O1,TI,T,T1(TI∈mi(O,a) ∧ belongsTo(T,TI) ∧ attname(O,O1,T) ∧
belongsTo(T1,TI) ∧ T1 > T $\rightarrow$ attname(O,O1,T1))

The values `insertions allowed` and `deletions allowed` do not constrain insertions and deletions of attribute values.

The following class definition shows a complete example of this feature:

```
class order
    orderNo: integer; (non-modifiable)
    lines: set of orderLine (insertions non-allowed,
                deletions non-allowed)
```

3.7 Composite Temporal Features

In some cases, it may be convenient to give a particular name to a specific combination of values of the three features above, including perhaps values of other features (static or temporal).

For example, a single valued attribute with temporal features:

```
always initially valued
single permanent existence interval
non-modifiable
```

could be called a `constant` attribute. The same name could be given to a multivalued attribute with temporal features:

```
always initially valued
insertions non-allowed
deletions non-allowed.
```

Note that, in general, the features of an attribute are independent of those of its inverse. The following example shows that an attribute may be `constant` while its inverse is not:

```
class person
    parents: set of person inverse of children (constant)
    children: set of person inverse of parents
        (never initially valued, insertions allowed,
        deletions non-allowed)
```

We could give a special name, like `fixed`, to an attribute which is `constant` at both sides:

```
class order
    hasLines: set of orderLine inverse of ofOrder (constant)
class orderLine
    ofOrder: order inverse of hasLines (constant)
```

In this example, the association between an `order` and its `orderLine` is completely `fixed` at creation time, and cannot be changed later.

3.8 Application to Aggregation/Composition

The aggregation (or composition) abstraction, and the part-of relationships are frequently found in conceptual modeling languages. However, their semantics is not always well-clarified and, as a result, their use becomes problematic [dCF92]. In many cases, aggregation is considered a special form of association and its semantics is either language-dependent [KBG89,CoD94,Rat97] or, worst, left (partially) unspecified.

Aggregation has cognitive, static and temporal aspects. Cognitive aspects have been studied in [WCH87,Sto93,MaO95]. Static aspects include the definition of which is the aggregate and which are the parts. The cardinality constraints associated with part-of links have been studied in [Mots93].

Temporal aspects have been less studied. In this respect, we believe that our temporal features may be helpful in clarifying the temporal behaviour of aggregates. In what follows we analyze two recent interpretations of aggregation, and show that they can be fully characterized by our temporal features.

In Syntropy, "aggregation ... mean life-time dependency; in particular, that life-times of the 'parts' are contained within the life-time of the 'whole'. The 'parts' are permanently attached to the whole, and cannot be removed from it without being destroyed. Conversely, destroying the 'whole' destroys the 'parts'" [CoD94, p.39].

A classical example is the "division part of company": "Each division must be associated with a single company, and it must remain associated with that company throughout its life-time. Divisions can be created and destroyed during the life-time of a company, but a division cannot be moved from one company to another. If the company is destroyed, so are the divisions."

Using our temporal features, this semantics is completely captured by:

```
class company (non-permanent instances)
    hasDivisions: set of division inverse of belongsTo
        (insertions allowed, deletions allowed)
class division (non-permanent instances)
    belongsTo: company inverse of hasDivisions (constant)
```

A similar approach is taken by UML: "Composition is a form of aggregation with strong ownership and coincident lifetime of part with the whole. The multiplicity of the aggregate end may not exceed one (it is unshared).The aggregation is unchangeable (once established the links may not be changed). Parts with multiplicity > 1 may be created after the aggregate itself but once created they live and die with it. Such parts can also be explicitly removed before the death of the aggregate" [Rat97, p.53]. In composition, destroying the whole destroys the parts.

Note that, in both cases, deletion of the whole causes the deletion of the parts. This is a necessary consequence in our features, which is formalized in Section 5.

4. Primitive Structural Events

In the two previous Sections, we have defined six new temporal features for conceptual models, and we have given a declarative formalization to them. We now want to provide a procedural formalization. The way we follow is first (in this Section) to define the primitive structural events that change the Information Base (IB), and then (in the next Section) we study the necessary conditions for a transaction (a set of primitive structural events) to satisfy the transition integrity constraints.

We define five kinds of primitive structural events, depending on their effect on the IB: object insertion, object deletion, attribute insertion, attribute update and attribute deletion. For each one of them we formally specify its effect (denoted by E) in the IB and also an applicability axiom (A) that guarantees that the event is productive [VeF85], that is, it ensures that the intended effect does not hold at previous state.

Let c be a class. We use a two term predicate insert_c(X,T) to denote the object insertion primitive structural event corresponding to c. The effect of an insert_c(x,t) is the addition of instance x in object class c at the time instant t (when the event occurs). As can be expected, this event can only be applied if object x was not an instance of c at previous time. Formally,

E: $\forall$X,T(insert_c(X,T) $\rightarrow$ c(X,T))
A: $\forall$X,T(insert_c(X,T) $\rightarrow \neg$c(X,T-1))

Note that an insert_c(x,t) does not distinguish between the case when x is a new object in the system and when x is already a known object and the insertion just adds it to class c. Sometimes we need to make such distinction, and we will assume that there is a most general class object, such that object(x,t) is true if x is an existing object at time t.

In a similar way, we use a two term predicate delete_c(X,T) to denote the object deletion primitive structural event corresponding to c. The effect of a delete_c(x,t) is the removal of the instance x from object class c at the time instant t (when the event occurs). This event can only be applied if object x was an instance of c at previous time. Formally,

E: $\forall$X,T(delete_c(X,T) $\rightarrow \neg$c(X,T))
A: $\forall$X,T(delete_c(X,T) $\rightarrow$ c(X,T-1))

Let attname be an attribute of class c. We use a three-term predicate insert_c_attname(X,Y,T) to denote the corresponding attribute insertion primitive structural event. Its effect consists of the addition of value y for attribute attname of object x at the time instant t (when the event occurs). This event can only be applied if y was not a value for attribute attname of instance x at previous time. Formally:

E: $\forall$X,Y,T(insert_c_attname(X,Y,T) $\rightarrow$ attname(X,Y,T))
A: if attname is single valued, then
$\forall$X,Y,T(insert_c_attname(X,Y,T) $\rightarrow \neg\exists$Z attname(X,Z,T-1))
if attname is multivalued, then
$\forall$X,Y,T(insert_c_attname(X,Y,T) $\rightarrow \neg$attname(X,Y,T-1))

Note that if attname is single valued then the insertion of an attribute value at time t is conditioned to the non existence of any value for that attribute at time t-1.

Attribute update and deletion primitive structural events are defined in a similar way. See [COS97] for details.

Finally, we have to define what happens with objects and attributes existing (or not existing) at previous state of the IB that are not affected by the primitive structural events of a transaction. This is accomplished by the following frame axioms [VeF85, BMR95]:

$\forall$X,T ($\neg$c(X,T-1) $\wedge \neg$ insert_c(X,T) $\rightarrow \neg$c(X,T))
$\forall$X,T (c(X,T-1) $\wedge \neg$ delete_c(X,T) $\rightarrow$ c(X,T))
if attname is single valued
$\forall$X,Y,T ($\neg$attname(X,Y,T-1) $\wedge \neg$insert_c_attname(X,Y,T) $\wedge$
$\neg$update_c_attname(X,Y,T) $\rightarrow \neg$attname(X,Y,T))
$\forall$X,Y,T (attname(X,Y,T-1) $\wedge \neg$delete_c_attname(X,T) $\wedge$
$\neg \exists$Z(update_c_attname(X,Z,T))$\rightarrow$ attname(X,Y,T))
if attname is multivalued:

$\forall X, Y, T \; (\neg\texttt{attname}(X,Y,T-1) \land \neg\texttt{insert\_c\_attname}(X,Y,T) \rightarrow$
$\qquad\qquad \neg\texttt{attname}(X,Y,T))$
$\forall X, Y, T \; (\texttt{attname}(X,Y,T-1) \land \neg\texttt{delete\_c\_attname}(X,Y,T) \rightarrow$
$\qquad\qquad \texttt{attname}(X,Y,T))$

5. Relationship Among Primitive Structural Events

As mentioned before, we consider that a transaction consists of a number of primitive structural events. This section explains how to determine the conditions such events must satisfy to maintain the IB consistent with respect to the transition integrity constraints defined by our temporal features.

More specifically, we present a set of theorems defining the relationships between primitive structural events that maintain the IB consistency. If a transaction respects all the conditions imposed by the theorems then the IB satisfies the transition integrity constraints in the resulting state. The complete set of theorems, together with an intuitive explanation about their meaning, can be found in [COS97]. They can be proved from the features definition given in sections 2 and 3 and the primitive structural event axioms given in section 4. For space reasons we are not able to explain all the theorems in detail. Instead, we will show its application to transaction specification.

5.1 Application to Transaction Specification

Our theorems define constraints on primitive structural events that constitute transactions. These constraints are useful during transaction execution and during transaction definition process. In this last case, they may be applied to assist the process in two manners: *transaction checking* or *transaction repairing*.

Transaction checking consists of: given a transaction specified by the designer, establish whether or not this transaction is consistent with respect to the integrity constraints. Transaction repairing consists of: given an inconsistent transaction (according to transaction checking) obtain one or more sets of primitive structural events such that once added to it constitute consistent transactions. If no such sets of events exist, the transaction is not repairable.

In the next paragraphs, we illustrate the use of the theorems for transaction checking and transaction repairing by means of several examples. All theorems referred in the analysis of the following examples appear in [COS97].

Consider the following class definition:

```
class vendor
    name: string; (always initially valued)
    hasAssigned: set of client; (never initially valued)
```

and a transaction specified with the purpose of inserting a new vendor in the IB:

```
insert_vendor(X,T)
```

Transaction checking establishes that the above transaction is inconsistent. In fact, it violates a single constraint defined by theorem A7 (see [COS97]):

A7. Let `attname` be an attribute defined on c and declared as always initially valued, then:

$\forall X, T(\texttt{insert\_c}(X,T) \rightarrow \exists Y \; \texttt{insert\_c\_attname}(X,Y,T))$

when applied to attribute `name` it comes down to:

$\forall X, T(\texttt{insert\_vendor}(X,T) \rightarrow \exists Y \; \texttt{insert\_vendor\_name}(X,Y,T))$

As a consequence, our transaction is inconsistent because it inserts a vendor without inserting a value for its `name`, being `name` an always initially valued attribute.

The same constraint allows to perform transaction repairing. From it, we deduce that the transaction can be repaired by adding to it the primitive structural event insert_vendor_name(X,Y,T).

As another example, in section 3.8, it has been shown that two recent interpretations of aggregation can be fully characterized by our temporal features. Let's analyze the impact of aggregation on transaction repairing by means of the "division part of company" example. Consider a transaction that deletes a company:

delete_company(X,T)

1- From theorem A17 ([COS97]):

A17. Let c be an object class and attname a multivalued attribute defined on c, then:

$$\forall X,Y,T,TI\,(TI \in mi\,(X,c) \wedge belongsTo\,(T-1,TI) \wedge delete\_c\,(X,T) \wedge$$
$$attname\,(X,Y,T-1) \rightarrow delete\_c\_attname\,(X,Y,T))$$

we have that all existent values of attribute hasDivisions of the company have also to be deleted together with it:

$$\forall X,Y,T,TI\,(TI \in mi\,(X,company) \wedge belongsTo\,(T-1,TI) \wedge delete\_company\,(X,T) \wedge$$
$$hasDivisions\,(X,Y,T-1) \rightarrow delete\_company\_hasDivisions\,(X,Y,T))$$

Applying this to transaction repairing, we obtain the new transaction:

delete_company(X,T)
$\forall Y\,(hasDivisions\,(X,Y,T-1) \rightarrow delete\_company\_hasDivisions\,(X,Y,T))$

2- Now, the new transaction violates a constraint that corresponds to theorem A20, which indicates that when a value of an attribute is deleted, either this value is deleted from its class or the inverse attribute value has to be deleted or the inverse attribute has to be updated:

$$\forall X,Y,T\,(delete\_company\_hasDivisions\,(X,Y,T) \rightarrow$$
$$delete\_division\,(Y,T) \vee delete\_division\_belongsTo\,(Y,T) \vee$$
$$\exists Z\,(update\_division\_belongsTo\,(Y,Z,T) \wedge X \neq Z))$$

Applying this to transaction repairing, three possible transactions appear:

delete_company(X,T)
$\forall Y\,(hasDivisions\,(X,Y,T-1) \rightarrow delete\_company\_hasDivisions\,(X,Y,T))$
$\forall Y\,(hasDivisions\,(X,Y,T-1) \rightarrow delete\_division\,(Y,T))$

or

delete_company(X,T)
$\forall Y\,(hasDivisions\,(X,Y,T-1) \rightarrow delete\_company\_hasDivisions\,(X,Y,T))$
$\forall Y\,(hasDivisions\,(X,Y,T-1) \rightarrow delete\_division\_belongsTo\,(Y,T))$

or

delete_company(X,T)
$\forall Y\,(hasDivisions\,(X,Y,T-1) \rightarrow delete\_company\_hasDivisions\,(X,Y,T))$
$\forall Y\,(hasDivisions\,(X,Y,T-1) \rightarrow update\_division\_belongsTo\,(Y,Z,T) \wedge X \neq Z)$

3- The first possibility has still to be repaired according to theorem A16, which specifies that the deletion of an object from a class implies the simultaneous deletion of all its attributes:

$\forall Y,T\,(delete\_division\,(Y,T) \rightarrow delete\_division\_belongsTo\,(Y,T))$

Then, the transaction must be repaired into:

delete_company(X,T)
$\forall Y\,(hasDivisions\,(X,Y,T-1) \rightarrow delete\_company\_hasDivisions\,(X,Y,T))$
$\forall Y\,(hasDivisions\,(X,Y,T-1) \rightarrow delete\_division\,(Y,T))$
$\forall Y\,(hasDivisions\,(X,Y,T-1) \rightarrow delete\_division\_belongsTo\,(Y,T))$

which is a consistent transaction. This result is coherent with the interpretation taken for aggregation in section 3.8: the deletion of the whole induces the deletion of the parts.

4- The second possibility has also to be repaired according to theorem A3, which specifies that when a `single permanent existence interval` attribute takes a value, it keeps on having value until the end of the object membership interval:
`∀Y,T(delete_division_belongsTo(Y,T) → delete_division(Y,T))`
Then, the transaction is transformed into:

`delete_company(X,T)`
`∀Y(hasDivisions(X,Y,T-1) → delete_company_hasDivisions(X,Y,T))`
`∀Y(hasDivisions(X,Y,T-1) → delete_division_belongsTo(Y,T))`
`∀Y(hasDivisions(X,Y,T-1) → delete_division(Y,T))`

which coincides with the transaction obtained in previous step.
5- The third possibility violates the constraint specified by theorem A6, because `belongsTo is non-modifiable`:

$\forall T\ (\neg\exists Y, Z\ \text{update\_division\_belongsTo}(Y,Z,T))$

As can be seen, this third possibility is not repairable according to the previous constraint.

6. Conclusions

We have described six temporal features that correspond to common transition integrity constraints. Three of them (permanent instances, initial membership, membership intervals) are related to classes, constraining the way how their populations can evolve through time. The other three features (initial value, existence intervals, changeability) are related to attributes, constraining the way how attribute values can change through time. We have shown that these features are orthogonal, and that the features of an attribute are orthogonal to those of its inverse. Our features may be helpful in clarifying the meaning of some concepts. In particular, we have shown that they capture in a simple way the meaning of aggregation/composition, as defined in two recent conceptual modeling languages.

The proposed features are language-independent and, thus, they can be used in any conceptual model. The features correspond to transition integrity constraints that appear in many models, and we have made their specification simple and practical. One possible extension of this work, however, would be the identification and formalization of other important temporal features.

We have formalized the features declaratively and procedurally. The procedural formalization assumes that the Information Base is changed by a set of primitive structural events, and determines the conditions such events must satisfy. The primitive structural events, however, are 'too much' primitive to be practical in behavioural models. In this respect, we would like to determine a set of more complex structural events, consisting of a composition of primitive ones, and meaningful at the behavioural level.

Acknowledgements

We would like to thank the members of the ROSES group and the anonymous referees for their helpful comments. This work has been partially supported by PRONTIC CICYT program project TIC95-0735.

References

[BMR95]   Borgida,A.;Mylopoulos,J.;Reiter,R. "On the Frame Problem in Procedure Specifications",IEEE Trans. on SE,Oct., pp. 785-798.

[Bor85] Borgida,A. "Features of Languages for the Development of Information Systems at the Conceptual Level", IEEE Software, Jan., pp. 63-72.

[CoD94] Cook,S.; Daniels,J. "Designing Object Systems. Object-Oriented Modeling with Syntropy", Prentice Hall.

[COS97] Costal,D.; Olivé,A.;Sancho,M-R. "Temporal Features of Class Populations and Attributes in Conceptual Models-extended version" Report LSI-97-32-R

[dCF92] de Champeaux,D.; Faure,P. "A comparative study of object-oriented analysis methods", JOOP, March/April, pp.21-33.

[DHR91] Dubois,E., Hagelstein,J.; Rifaut,A. "A formal language for the requirements engineering of computer systems", in "From Natural Language Processing to Logic for Expert Systems", Wiley, pp. 269-345.

[EKW92] Embley,D.W.; Kurtz,B.D.; Woodfield,S.N. "Object-Oriented Systems Analysis. A Model-Driven Approach", Prentice-Hall, Inc.

[GKB82] Gustaffson,M.R.; Karlsson,T.; Bubenko jr.J.A. "A Declarative Approach to Conceptual Information Modelling", in Information Systems Design Methodologies: A comparative Review", North-Holland, pp. 93-142.

[GSR96] Gottlob,G.; Schrefl,M.; Röck,B. "Extending Object-Oriented Systems with Roles", ACM TOIS, Vol.14,No.3, pp. 268-296.

[HaM81] Hammer,M.; McLeod,D. "Database Description with SDM: A Semantic Database Model", ACM TODS, Vol.6,No.3, September, pp. 351-386.

[ISO82] ISO/TC97/SC5/WG3. "Concepts and Terminology for the Conceptual Schema and the Information Base", ed. J.J. van Griethuysen.

[JSH+96] Jungclaus,R.; Saake,G.; Hartmann,T.; Sernadas,C. "TROLL-A Language for Object-Oriented Specification of Information Systems", ACM TOIS,Vol.14,No.2, April, pp. 175-211.

[KBG89] Kim,W.; Bertino,E.; Garza,J.F. "Composite Objects Revisited", Proc. OOPSLA 89, pp. 337-347.

[Kun84] Kung,C. "A Temporal Framework for Information Systems Specification and Verification", Ph.D Thesis, The University of Trondheim, Norway.

[LEW93] Liddle,S.W.; Embley,D.E.; Woodfield,S.N. "Cardinality constraints in semantic data models", Data&Knowledge Engineering 11 (1993), pp. 235-270.

[MaO95] Martin,J.; Odell,J. "Object-Oriented Methods. A Foundation", Prentice Hall.

[Mots93] Motschnig-Pitrik,R. "The Semantics of Parts Versus Aggregates in Data/Knowlege Modelling", Proc. of the CAiSE'93, LNCS 685, Springer

[Per90] Pernici,B. "Objects with Roles", Proc. ACM Conf. on Office Information Systems, ACM,New York, 205-215.

[Rat97] Rational Software Corporation, "Unified Modeling Language (UML)", Version 1.0, January.

[RBP+91] Rumbaugh,J.; Blaha,M.; Premerlani,W.; Eddy,F.; Lorensen,W. "Object-Oriented Modeling and Design", Prentice Hall.

[SFN+84] Schiel,U., Furtado,A.L., Neuhold,E.J.; Casanova,M.A. "Towards Multi-level and Modular Conceptual Schema Specifications", Information Systems, Vol.9, No.1, pp. 43-57.

[Sto93] Storey, V.C. "Understanding Semantic Relationships", The VLDB Journal, Vol.2,No.4,Oct., pp. 455-488.

[VeF85] Veloso,P.A.S.; Furtado,A.L. "Towards simpler and yet complete formal specifications", In "Information Systems: Theoretical and Formal Aspects", North-Holland, pp. 175-190.

[VeV82] Verheijen,G.M.A.; Van Bekkum, J. "NIAM: An Information Analysis Method", in "Information Systems design Methodologies: A Comparative Review", North-Holland, pp.537-589.

[WCH87] Winston,M.E.; Chaffin,R.; Herrmann,D. "A taxonomy of part-whole relations", Cognitive Science, 11, pp.417-444.

[WMW89] Wieringa,R.; Meyer,J-J.; Weigand,H. "Specifying dynamic and deontic integrity constraints", Data & Knowledge Engineering, 4, pp.157-189.

Managing Schema Evolution
Using a Temporal Object Model

Iqbal A. Goralwalla[1], Duane Szafron[1], M. Tamer Özsu[1], and Randal J. Peters[2]

[1] Department of Computing Science, University of Alberta
Edmonton, Alberta, Canada T6G 2H1
[2] Department of Computer Science, University of Manitoba
Winnipeg, Manitoba, Canada R3T 2N2

Abstract. The issues of schema evolution and temporal object models are generally considered to be orthogonal and are handled independently. This is unrealistic because to properly model applications that need incremental design and experimentation (such as CAD, software design process), the evolutionary histories of the schema objects should be traceable. In this paper we propose a method for managing schema changes by exploiting the functionality of a temporal object model. The result is a uniform treatment of schema evolution and temporal support for many object database management systems applications that require both.

1 Introduction

In this paper we address the issue of schema evolution and temporal object models. These two issues are generally considered to be orthogonal and are handled independently. However, many object database management systems (ODBMS) applications require both. For example:

- The results reported in [16] illustrate the extent to which schema changes occur in real-world database applications such as health care management systems. Such systems also require a means to represent, store, and retrieve the temporal information in clinical data [3].
- The engineering and design oriented application domains (e.g., CAD, software design process) require incremental design and experimentation [7, 5]. This usually leads to frequent changes to the schema over time which need to be retained as historical records of the design process.

We propose a method for managing schema changes by exploiting the functionality of a temporal object model. The provision of time in an object model establishes a platform from which temporality can be used to investigate advanced database features such as schema evolution. Given that the applications supported by ODBMSs need support for incremental development and experimentation with changing and evolving schema, a temporal domain is a natural means for managing changes in schema and ensuring consistency of the system.

The result is a uniform treatment of schema evolution and temporal support for many ODBMS applications that require both.

Schema evolution using time is the process of allowing changes to schema without loss of information. Typical schema changes include adding and dropping behaviors (properties) defined on a type, adding and dropping subtype relationships between types, to name a few. Using time to maintain and manage schema changes gives substantial flexibility in the software design process. It enables the designers to retrieve the interface of a type that existed at any time in the design phase, reconstruct the super(sub)-lattice of a type as it was at a certain time (and subsequently the type lattice of the object database at that time), and trace the implementations of a certain behavior in a particular type over time.

A typical schema change can affect many aspects of a system. There are two fundamental problems to consider: (1) definition of change semantics, and (2) change propagation. Change semantics is usually defined by specifying of invariants over schema changes. Change propagation deals with reflecting changes to the individual objects by *coercing* them to coincide with the new schema definition. In this paper we primarily consider the consistent handling of the problem of semantics of change using a temporal ODBMS. We describe the necessary modifications that could occur on the schema, and show how the implications of the modifications are managed. Our work is conducted within the context of the TIGUKAT *temporal* ODBMS [10, 6] that is being developed at the University of Alberta. However, the results reported here extend to any ODBMS that uses time to model evolution histories of objects.

The remainder of the paper is organized as follows. In Section 2, we examine some of the previous work on schema evolution. In Section 3, we give a brief overview of the TIGUKAT temporal object model with an emphasis on how histories of objects are maintained. In Section 4, we describe the schema changes that can occur in TIGUKAT, and how they are managed using a temporal object model. In Section 5, we give examples of queries that allow software designers to retrieve schema objects at any time in their evolution histories. Concluding remarks and results of the paper are summarized in Section 6.

2 Related Work

The issue of schema evolution has been an area of active research in the context of ODBMSs [1, 11, 9]. In many of the previous work, the usual approach is to define a set of invariants that must be preserved over schema modifications in order to ensure consistency of the system. The Orion model [1] is the first system to introduce the invariants and rules approach as a more structured way of describing schema evolution in ODBMSs. Orion defines a complete set of invariants and a set of accompanying rules for maintaining the invariants over schema changes. The work of Smith and Smith [18] on aggregation and generalization sets the stage for defining invariants when subtypes and supertypes are involved. Changes to schema in previous works are *corrective* in that once the schema definitions are changed, the old definitions of the schema are no longer traceable. In TIGUKAT, a set of invariants similar to those given in [1] is defined. However, changes to the schema are not corrective. The provision of time in TIGUKAT establishes a natural foundation for keeping track of the changes to the schema. This allows applications, such as CAD, to trace their design over time and make revisions, if necessary.

There have been many temporal object model proposals (for example, [15, 19, 20, 2]). In handling temporal information, these models have focussed on managing the evolution of real-world entities. The implicit assumption in these models is that the schema of the object database is static and remains unchanged during the lifespan of the object database. More specifically, the evolution of schema objects (i.e., types, behaviors, etc) is considered to be orthogonal to the temporal model. However, given the kinds of applications that an ODBMS is expected to support, we have exploited the underlying temporal domain in the TIGUKAT temporal model as a means to support schema evolution.

Skarra and Zdonik [17] define a framework within the Encore object model for versioning types as a support mechanism for changing type definitions. A type is organized as a set of individual versions. This is known as the *version set* of the type. Every change to a type definition results in the generation of a new version of the type. Since a change to a type can also affect its subtypes, new versions of the subtypes may also be generated. This approach provides fine granularity control over schema changes, but may lead to inefficiencies due to the creation of a new version of the versioned part of an object every time a single attribute changes its value. In our approach, any changes in type definitions involve changing the history of certain behaviors to reflect the changes. For example, adding a new behavior to a type changes the history of the type's interface to include the new behavior. The old interface of the type is still accessible at a time before the change was made. This alleviates the need of creating new versions of a type each time any change is made to a type.

3 The TIGUKAT Temporal Object Model

3.1 Fundamentals of TIGUKAT Object Model

The TIGUKAT object model [12, 10] is purely *behavioral* with a *uniform* object semantics. The model is *behavioral* in the sense that all access and manipulation of objects is based on the application of behaviors to objects. The model is *uniform* in that every component of information, including its semantics, is modeled as a *first-class object* with well-defined behavior. Other typical object modeling features supported by TIGUKAT include strong object identity, abstract types, strong typing, complex objects, full encapsulation, multiple inheritance, and parametric types.

The primitive objects of the model include: *atomic entities* (reals, integers, strings, etc.); *types* for defining common features of objects; *behaviors* for specifying the semantics of operations that may be performed on objects; *functions* for specifying implementations of behaviors over types; *classes* for automatic classification of objects based on type; and *collections* for supporting general heterogeneous groupings of objects. Figure 1 shows a simple type lattice that will be used to illustrate the concepts introduced in the rest of the paper.

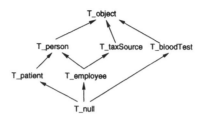

Fig. 1. Simple type lattice.

In this paper, a reference prefixed by "T_" refers to a type, "C_" to a class, "B_" to a behavior, and "T_X< T_Y >" to the type T_X parameterized by the type T_Y. For example, **T_person** refers to a type, **C_person** to its class, *B_age* to one of its behaviors and **T_collection**< T_person > to the type of collections of persons. A reference such as joe, without a prefix, denotes some other application specific reference. The type **T_null** in TIGUKAT binds the type lattice from the bottom (i.e., most defined type), while the **T_object** type binds it from the top (i.e., least defined type). **T_null** is introduced to provide, among other things, error handling and null semantics for the model. In Figures 2-4, the boxes shaded in grey are objects. Objects have an outgoing edge labeled by each applicable behavior that leads to the object resulting from the application of the behavior. A circle labeled with the symbols { } represents a collection object and has outgoing edges labeled with "∈" to each member of the collection.

The access and manipulation of an object's state occurs exclusively through the application of behaviors. We clearly separate the definition of a behavior from its possible implementations (functions). The benefit of this approach is that common behaviors over different types can have a different implementation in each of the types. This provides direct support for behavior *overloading* and *late binding* of functions (implementations) to behaviors.

3.2 The Temporal Extensions

The philosophy behind adding temporality to the TIGUKAT object model is to accommodate multiple applications that have different type semantics requiring various notions of time [8, 6].

Our model represents the temporal histories of real-world objects whose type is **T_X** as objects of the **T_history⟨T_X⟩** type. For example, suppose a behavior *B_salary* is defined in the **T_employee** type. Now, to keep track of the changes in salary of employees, *B_salary* would return an object of type **T_history⟨T_real⟩** which would consist of the different salary objects of a particular employee and their associated time periods.

A temporal history consists of *timestamped objects*. A timestamped object knows its timestamp (time interval or time instant) and its associated value at (during) the timestamp. The following behaviors are defined on the T_history⟨T_X⟩ type:

$$B\_history : \texttt{T\_collection}\langle\texttt{T\_timeStampedObject}\langle\texttt{T\_X}\rangle\rangle$$
$$B\_timeline : \texttt{T\_timeline}$$
$$B\_insert : \texttt{T\_X}, \texttt{T\_timeStamp} \rightarrow$$
$$B\_remove : \texttt{T\_X}, \texttt{T\_timeStamp} \rightarrow$$
$$B\_validObjects : \texttt{T\_timeStamp} \rightarrow \texttt{T\_collection}\langle\texttt{T\_timeStampedObject}\langle\texttt{T\_X}\rangle\rangle$$
$$B\_validObject : \texttt{T\_timeStamp} \rightarrow \texttt{T\_timeStampedObject}\langle\texttt{T\_X}\rangle$$

Behavior *B_history* returns the set (collection) of all timestamped objects that comprise the history. A history object also knows the timeline it is associated with and this timeline is returned by the behavior *B_timeline*. The timeline basically orders the timestamps of timestamped objects [6]. The *B_insert* behavior accepts an object and a timestamp as input and creates a timestamped object that is inserted into the history. Behavior *B_remove* drops a given object from the history at a specified timestamp. The *B_validObjects* behavior allows the user to get the objects in the history that were valid at (during) a given timestamp. Behavior *B_validObject* is derived from *B_validObjects* to return the timestamped object that exists at a given time instant.

Each timestamped object is an instance of the T_timeStampedObject⟨T_X⟩ type. This type represents objects and their corresponding timestamps. Behaviors *B_value* and *B_timeStamp* defined on T_timeStampedObject return the value and the timestamp (time interval or time instant) of a timestamped object, respectively.

4 Management of Schema Evolution by the Temporal Object Model

4.1 Schema Related Changes

There are different kinds of objects modeled by TIGUKAT, some of which are classified as schema objects. These objects fall into one of the following categories: *type, class, behavior, function,* and *collection*. There are three kinds of operations that can be performed on schema objects: *add, drop* and *modify*. Table 1 shows the combinations between the various schema object categories and the different kinds of operations that can be performed in TIGUKAT [12, 14]. The **bold** entries represent combinations that implicate schema changes while the *emphasized* entries denote non-schema changes. In the context of a temporal model, *adding* refers to creating the object and beginning its history, *dropping* refers to terminating the history of an object, and *modifying* refers to updating the history of the schema object. Since type-related changes form the basis of most other schema changes, we describe the modifications that affect the type schema objects. Type modification (depicted at the intersection of the M column and T row in Table 1) includes several kinds of type changes. They are separated into changes in the behaviors of a type (depicted as **MT-AB** and **MT-DB** in Table 1) and changes in the relationships between types (depicted as **MT-ASL** and **MT-DSL** in Table 1). Invariants for maintaining the semantics of schema modifications in TIGUKAT are described in [12, 14]. The invariants are used to gauge the consistency of a schema change in that the invariants must be satisfied both before and after a schema change is performed.

	Operation		
Objects	Add (A)	Drop (D)	Modify (M)
Type (T)	subtyping	type deletion	add behavior(AB) drop behavior(DB) add supertype link(ASL) drop supertype link(DSL)
Class (C)	class creation	class deletion	*extent change*
Behavior (B)	*behavior definition*	**behavior deletion**	change association(CA)
Function (F)	*function definition*	**function deletion**	*implementation change*
Collection (L)	collection creation	collection deletion	*extent change*

Table 1. Classification of schema changes.

The meta-model of TIGUKAT is uniformly represented within the object model itself, providing reflective capabilities [13]. One result of this uniform approach is that types are objects and they have a type (called **T_type**) that defines their behaviors. **T_type** defines behaviors to access a type's interface (*B_interface*), its subtypes (*B_subtypes*), its supertypes (*B_supertypes*), plus many others that are not relevant for the scope of this paper. Since types are objects with well-defined behaviors, the approach of keeping track of the changes to a type is the same as that for keeping track of the changes to objects discussed in Section 3.2. This is one of the major advantages of the uniformity of the object model. The semantics of the changes to a type are discussed in the following sections.

4.2 Changing Behaviors of a Type

Every type has an *interface* which is a collection of behaviors that are applicable to the objects of that type. A type's interface can be dichotomized into two disjoint subsets: the collection of *native* behaviors which are those behaviors defined by the type and are not defined on any of its supertypes; and the collection of *inherited* behaviors which are those behaviors defined natively by some supertype and inherited by the type.

There are three behaviors defined on **T_type** to return the various components of a type's interface: *B_native* returns the collection of native behaviors, *B_inherited* returns the inherited behaviors and *B_interface* returns the entire interface of the type. Types can evolve in different ways. One aspect of a type that can change over time is the behaviors in its interface (i.e., adding or deleting behaviors). To keep track of this aspect of a type's evolution, we define histories of interface changes by extending the interface behaviors with time-varying properties. The definition of the extended *B_native* behavior is

B_native : $\texttt{T\_history}\langle\texttt{T\_collection}\langle\texttt{T\_behavior}\rangle\rangle$. The definitions for behaviors $B\_inherited$ and $B\_interface$ are extended similarly. Each behavior now returns a history of a collection of timestamped behaviors. Adding a new behavior to a type changes the history of the type's interface to include the new behavior. The old interface of the type is still accessible at a time before the change was made. With the time-varying interface extensions, we can determine the various aspects of a type's interface at any time of interest. For example, Figure 2 shows the history of the entire interface for the type $\texttt{T\_person}$.

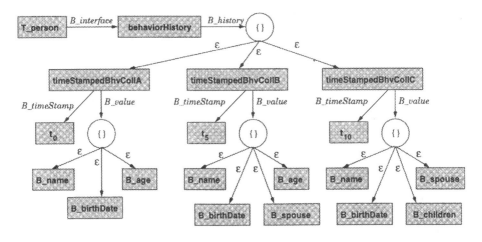

Fig. 2. Interface history of type $\texttt{T\_person}$.

At time t_0, behaviors B_name, $B\_birthDate$, B_age are defined on $\texttt{T\_person}$. The initial history of $\texttt{T\_person}$'s interface is $\{<t_0, \{B\_name, B\_birthDate, B\_age\}>\}$. At time t_5, behavior B_spouse is added to $\texttt{T\_person}$. To reflect this change, the interface history is updated to $\{<t_0, \{B\_name, B\_birthDate, B\_age\}>, <t_5, \{B\_name, B\_birthDate, B\_age, B\_spouse\}>\}$. This shows that between t_0 and t_5 only behaviors B_name, $B\_birthDate$, and B_age are defined and at t_5 behaviors B_name, $B\_birthDate$, B_age, B_spouse exist. Next, at time t_{10}, behavior B_age is dropped from type $\texttt{T\_person}$ and at the same time behavior $B\_children$ is added. The final history of the interface of $\texttt{T\_person}$ after this change is $\{<t_0, \{B\_name, B\_birthDate, B\_age\}>, <t_5, \{B\_name, B\_birthDate, B\_age, B\_spouse\}>, <t_{10}, \{B\_name, B\_birthDate, B\_spouse, B\_children\}>\}$[1]. The native and inherited behaviors would contain similar histories. Using this information, we can reconstruct the interface of a type at any time of interest. For example, at time t_3 the interface of type $\texttt{T\_person}$ was $\{B\_name, B\_birthDate, B\_age\}$,

---

[1] Note that in Figure 2 objects that are repeated in the timestamped collections are actually the same object. For example, the B_name object in all three timestamped collections is the same object. It is shown three times in the figure for clarity.

at time t_5 it was $\{B\_name, B\_birthDate, B\_age, B\_spouse\}$, and at time t_{10} (now) it is $\{B\_name, B\_birthDate, B\_spouse, B\_children\}$.

The behavioral changes to types include the **MT-AB** and **MT-DB** entries of Table 1. These changes affect various aspects of the schema and have to be properly managed to ensure consistency of the schema.

Modify Type - Add Behavior (MT-AB). This change adds a native behavior b to a type T at time t. The **MT-AB** change has the following effects:

  – The histories of the native and interface behaviors of type T need to be updated. The behavior applications $T.B\_native.B\_insert(b, t)$ and $T.B\_interface.B\_insert(b, t)$ perform this update. For example, the behavior application **T_person**.$B\_interface.B\_insert(B\_spouse, t_5)$ updates the interface history of **T_person** when behavior B_spouse is added to **T_person** at time t_5.

  – The implementation history of behavior b needs to be updated to associate it with some function f. This is achieved by the behavior application $b.B\_implementation.B\_insert(f, t)$ (details on implementation histories of behaviors are given in Section 4.3).

  – The history of inherited and interface behaviors of all subtypes of type T needs to be adjusted. That is, $\forall T' \mid T'$ subtype-of $T, T'.B\_inherited.B\_insert(b, t)$ and $T'.B\_interface.B\_insert(b, t)$. For example, the histories of inherited and interface behaviors of the **T_employee** and **T_patient** types (see Figure 1) need to be adjusted to reflect the addition of behavior B_spouse in type **T_person** at time t_5. For the **T_employee** type, this is accomplished using the behavior applications **T_employee**.$B\_interface.B\_insert(B\_spouse, t_5)$ and **T_employee**.$B\_inherited.B\_insert(B\_spouse, t_5)$. Similar behavior applications are carried out for **T_patient**.

Modify Type - Drop Behavior (MT-DB). This change drops a native behavior b from a type T at time t. When a behavior is dropped, its native definition is propagated to the subtypes unless the behavior is inherited by the subtype through some other chain. Many behavior inheritance semantics are possible. One such semantics is that when a native behavior is dropped from a type, all subtypes retain that behavior. This means that if another supertype of the subtype defines this behavior, there is no change. Otherwise, the behavior in the subtype moves from the inherited set to the native set. This is the semantics we are modeling in this paper. If any other behavior inheritance semantics are used, appropriate changes can easily be made to the temporal histories. The **MT-DB** change has the following effects:

  – The native behaviors history of type T changes. The behavior application $T.B\_native.B\_remove(b, t)$ performs this update.

  – The native and inherited behavior histories of the subtypes of T (possibly) change.

4.3 Changing Implementations of Behaviors

Each behavior defined on a type has a particular implementation for that type. The $B\_implementation$ behavior defined on **T_behavior** is applied to a behavior, accepts a type as an argument and returns the implementation (function) of the receiver behavior for the given type. In order to model the aspect of schema evolution that deals with changing the implementations of behaviors on types, we maintain a history of implementation changes by extending the *B_implementation* behavior with time-varying properties − *B_implementation* : T_type → T_history⟨T_function⟩. With this behavior we can determine the implementation of a behavior defined on a type at any time of interest. For example, Figure 3 shows the history of the implementations for behavior *B_age* on type T_person. There are two kinds of implementations for behaviors [12]. A *computed function* consists of runtime calls to executable code and a *stored function* is a reference to an existing object in the object database.

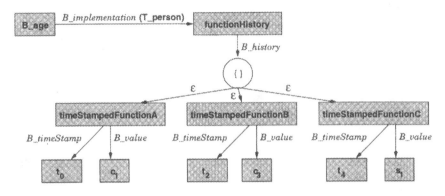

Fig. 3. Implementation history of behavior *B_age* on type T_person.

In Figure 3, we use c_i to denote a computed function, s_i to denote a stored function. At time t_2, the implementation of *B_age* changed from the computed function c_1 to the computed function c_3. At time t_4, the implementation of *B_age* changed from the computed function c_3 to the stored function s_1. All these changes are reflected in the implementation history of behavior *B_age*, which is $\{<t_0, c_1>, <t_2, c_3>, <t_4, s_1>\}$.

Using the results of this section and Section 4.2, we can reconstruct the behaviors, their implementations and the object representations[2] for any type at any time t. For example, the interface of type T_person at time t_3 is given by the behavior application T_person.$[t_3]B\_interface$ which results in $\{B\_name, B\_age,$ $B\_birthDate\}$, as shown in Figure 2. We use the syntax $o.[t]b$ to denote the application of behavior b to object o at time t. The implementation of *B_age* at time t_3 is given by $B\_age.[t_3]B\_implementation(\text{T\_person})$ which is c_3, as shown in Figure 3.

---

[2] Stored functions associated with behaviors allow us to reconstruct object representations (i.e., states of objects) for any type at any time t. This is useful in propagating changes to the underlying object instances. In this paper however, we are concerned primarily with the effects of schema changes on the schema itself.

In this paper we are assuming that there is no implementation inheritance. That is, if the binding of a behavior to a function changes in a type, the bindings of that behavior in the subtypes are unaffected. If implementation inheritance is desired, it can easily be modeled by temporal histories similarly to behavioral inheritance.

4.4 Changing Subtype/Supertypes of a Type

In Section 4.2 we described how the changes in a type's interface was one aspect in which a type evolves. Another aspect of a type that can change over time is the relationships between types. These include adding a direct supertype link and dropping a direct supertype link. The $B\_supertypes$ and $B\_subtypes$ behaviors defined on T_type return the direct supertypes and subtypes of the receiver type, respectively. In order to model the structure of the type lattice through time, we define histories of supertype and subtype changes of a type by extending the $B\_supertypes$ and $B\_subtypes$ behaviors to return a history of a collection of supertypes and subtypes, respectively. Using the $B\_supertypes$ and $B\_subtypes$ behaviors, we can reconstruct the structure of a type's supertype and subtype lattice at any time of interest. To facilitate this, the derived behaviors $B\_superlattice$ and $B\_sublattice$ are defined on T_type. The behavior $B\_superlattice$ is derived by recursively applying $B\_supertypes$ until T_object is reached, while the behavior $B\_sublattice$ is derived by recursively applying $B\_subtypes$ until T_null is reached. In both cases, the intermediate results are partially ordered. Figure 4 shows the supertype lattice history for type T_employee.

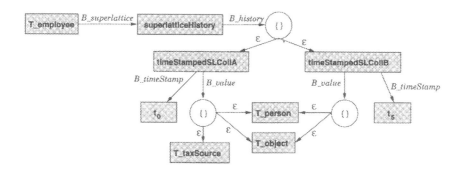

Fig. 4. Supertype lattice history for type T_employee.

At time t_0, the superlattice history of type T_employee included the types T_person, T_taxSource, and T_object. At time t_5, the supertype link between T_employee and T_taxSource is dropped. To reflect this change, the superlattice history of T_employee is updated to $\{<t_0, \{\text{T\_person}, \text{T\_taxSource}, \text{T\_object}\}>$, $<t_5, \{\text{T\_person}, \text{T\_object}\}>\}$.

The relationships between types include the **MT-ASL** and **MT-DSL** entries of Table 1. Similar to the behavioral changes to types discussed in Section 4.2, the relationships between types affect various aspects of the schema and have to be properly managed to ensure consistency of the schema.

Modify Type - Add Supertype Link (MT-ASL). Add a type, say S, as a direct supertype of another type, say T at time t. The **MT-ASL** change has the following effects:

- The history of the collection of supertypes of type T is updated. The behavior application $T.B\_supertypes.B\_insert(S, t)$ performs this update. For example, adding the supertype link between **T_employee** and **T_taxSource** at t_0 necessitates an update to the history of supertypes for **T_employee**.
- The history of the collection of subtypes of type S is updated. In this case, the history of the collection of subtypes of **T_taxSource** has to be updated.
- The behaviors of S are inherited by T and all the subtypes of T. Therefore, the inherited behavior history of T and all subtypes of T is adjusted. The current behaviors of S are inherited by T and all subtypes of T, and timestamped with t. Formally, $\forall b \in S.B\_interface.B\_history.B\_last$, $\forall T' \mid T'$ subtype-of $T, T'.B\_inherited.B\_insert(b, t)$. Behavior B_last returns the collection of behaviors that are currently valid from the interface history of S. Let us assume **T_taxSource** has the behavior $B\_taxBracket$ defined at t_0. $B\_taxBracket$ then has to be added to the history of inherited behaviors of **T_employee**. The history of the inherited behaviors would then be $\{<t_0, \{B\_name, B\_birthDate, B\_age, B\_taxBracket\}>\}$. Behaviors $B\_name, B\_birthDate, B\_age$ are inherited from type **T_person** (see Figure 2), while behavior $B\_taxBracket$ is inherited from type **T_taxSource**.

Modify Type - Drop Supertype Link (MT-DSL). Drop a direct supertype link between two types (a direct supertype link to **T_object** cannot be dropped) at time t. Consider types T and S where S is the direct supertype of T. Then, removing the direct supertype link between T and S at time t has the following effects:

- Adjust the history of supertypes of T and the history of subtypes of S. For example, dropping the supertype link between **T_employee** and **T_taxSource** at t_5 requires updating the history of **T_employee**'s supertypes and the history of subtypes of **T_taxSource**.
- The **MT-ASL** operation is carried out from T to every supertype of S, unless T is linked to the supertype through another chain.
- The **MT-ASL** operation is carried out from each subtype of T to S, unless the subtype is linked to S through another chain.
- The native behaviors of S are dropped from the interface of T. That is, the history of inherited behaviors of T is adjusted.

5 Queries

In this section we show how queries can be constructed using the TIGUKAT query language (TQL) [10] to retrieve schema objects at any time in their evolution histories. This gives software designers a temporal user interface which provides a practical way of accessing temporal information in their experimental and incremental design phases. TQL incorporates reflective temporal access in that it can be used to retrieve both objects, and schema objects in a uniform manner. Hence, TQL does not differentiate between queries (which query objects) and meta-queries (which query schema objects). TQL is based on the SQL paradigm [4] and its semantics is defined in terms of the object calculus. Hence, every statement of the language corresponds to an equivalent object calculus expression. We now give several example queries which illustrate how temporal objects can uniformly be queried using behavior applications without changing any of the basic constructs of TQL.

Example 1. Return the time when the behavior *B_children* was added to the type T_person.
select *b.B_timestamp*
from *b* **in** T_person.*B_interface.B_history*
where *B_children* **in** *b.B_value*
The result of this query would be the time t_{10} as seen in Figure 2.

Example 2. Return the types that define behaviors *B_age* and *B_taxBracket* as part of their interface.
select *T*
from *T* **in** C_type
where (*b1* **in** *T.B_interface.B_history* **and** *B_age* **in** *b1.B_value*) **or**
      (*b2* **in** *T.B_interface.B_history* **and** *B_taxBracket* **in** *b2.B_value*)
This query would return the types T_person, T_taxSource, T_employee, and T_null. The type T_person defines behavior *B_age* natively (see Figure 2), while the type T_taxSource defines behavior *B_taxBracket* natively. The behaviors *B_age* and *B_taxBracket* are inherited by types T_employee and T_null since they are subtypes of T_person and T_taxSource as shown in Figure 1.

Example 3. Return the implementation of behavior *B_age* in type T_person at time t_1.
select *i.B_value*
from *i* **in** *B_age.B_implementation*(T_person).*B_history*
where *i.B_timestamp.B_lessthaneqto*(t_1)
The behavior *B_lessthaneqto* is defined on type T_timeStamp and checks if the receiver timestamp is less than or equal to the argument timestamp. The result of the query is the computed function c_1 as shown in Figure 3.

Example 4. Return the super-lattice of type T_employee at time t_3.
select *r.B_value*
from *r* **in** T_employee.*B_super-lattice.B_history*
where *r.B_timestamp.B_lessthaneqto*(t_3)
The super-lattice of T_employee at t_3 consists of the types T_person, T_taxSource, and T_object. This is shown in Figure 4.

Example 5. Return the types that define behavior B_age with the same implementation as one of their supertypes.

select T

from T **in** $\mathbf{C\_type}$, S **in** $T.B\_supertypes.B\_history$,

$\qquad i$ **in** $B\_age.B\_implementation(T).B\_history$,

$\qquad j$ **in** $B\_age.B\_implementation(S.B\_value).B\_history$

where b **in** $S.B\_value.B\_interface.B\_history$ **and** B_age **in** $b.B\_value$ **and**

$\qquad i.B\_value = j.B\_value$ **and** $i.B\_timestamp = j.B\_timestamp$

This query would return the types $\mathtt{T\_employee}$, $\mathtt{T\_patient}$, and $\mathtt{T\_null}$, assuming the implementation of behavior B_age is not changed when it is inherited by these types.

6 Conclusion

In this paper a uniform treatment of schema evolution and temporal support for object database management systems (ODBMS) is presented. Schema evolution is managed by exploiting the functionality of a temporal object model. The evolution history of the interface of types, which includes the inherited and native behaviors of each type, describes the semantics of types through time. Using the interface histories the interface of a type can be reconstructed at any time of interest. The evolution histories of the supertype and subtype links of types describe the structure of the lattice through time. Using these histories, the structure of the lattice can be reconstructed at any time of interest. The implementation histories of behaviors give us the implementations of behaviors on types at any time of interest. From these, we can reconstruct the representation of objects by examining the stored functions associated with behaviors at a given time. The TIGUKAT query language gives designers a practical way of accessing temporal information in their experimental and incremental design phases.

Our next step is to give a comprehensive treatment to the change propagation problem during schema evolution. That is, devising methods to propagate schema changes to the existing object instances in the TIGUKAT temporal ODBMS. In order for the instances to remain meaningful after the schema has changed, either the relevant instances must be coerced into the new definition of the schema or a new version of the schema must be created leaving the old version intact. Conversion of objects can be optional in our model. Since the evolution history of schema objects is maintained, all the information for older objects is available and we can use this information to continue processing these objects in the old way. Since our model is time based, the old information of the object is available. Thus, even if objects are coerced to a newer schema definition, historical queries can be run by giving an appropriate time point in the history of the object.

References

1. J. Banerjee, W. Kim, H-J. Kim, and H.F. Korth. Semantics and Implementation of Schema Evolution in Object-Oriented Databases. In *Proc. ACM SIGMOD Int'l. Conf. on Management of Data*, pages 311–322, May 1987.

2. E. Bertino, E. Ferrari, and G. Guerrini. A Formal Temporal Object-Oriented Data Model. In *Proc. 5th Int'l Conf. on Extending Database Technology*, March 1996.

3. C. Combi, F. Pinciroli, and G. Pozzi. Managing Different Time Granularities of Clinical Information by an Interval-Based Temporal Data Model. *Methods of Information in Medicine*, 34(5):458–474, 1995.

4. C.J. Date. *A Guide to SQL Standard*. Addison Wesley, 1987.

5. S. Gibbs, D.C. Tsichritzis, E. Casais, O.M. Nierstrasz, and X. Pintado. Class Management for Software Communities. *Communications of the ACM*, 33(9):90–103, September 1990.

6. I.A. Goralwalla, M.T. Özsu, and D. Szafron. Modeling Medical Trials in Pharmacoeconomics using a Temporal Object Model. *Computers in Biology and Medicine - Special Issue on Time-Oriented Systems in Medicine*, 1997. In Press.

7. W. Kim, J. Banerjee, H.T. Chou, and J.F. Garza. Object-oriented database support for CAD. *Computer Aided Design*, 22(8):469–479, 1990.

8. J.Z. Li, I.A. Goralwalla, M.T. Özsu, and Duane Szafron. Modeling Video Temporal Relationships in an Object Database Management System. In *Proceedings of Multimedia Computing and Networking (MMCN97)*, February 1997.

9. G.T. Nguyen and D. Rieu. Schema evolution in object-oriented database systems. *Data & Knowledge Engineering*, 4:43–67, 1989.

10. M.T. Özsu, R.J. Peters, D. Szafron, B. Irani, A. Lipka, and A. Munoz. TIGUKAT: A Uniform Behavioral Objectbase Management System. *The VLDB Journal*, 4:100–147, August 1995.

11. D.J. Penney and J. Stein. Class Modification in the GemStone Object-Oriented DBMS. In *Proc. of the Int'l Conf on Object-Oriented Programming: Systems, Languages, and Applications*, pages 111–117, October 1987.

12. R.J. Peters. *TIGUKAT: A Uniform Behavioral Objectbase Management System*. PhD thesis, University of Alberta, 1994.

13. R.J. Peters and M.T. Özsu. Reflection in a Uniform Behavioral Object Model. In *Proc. 12th Int'l Conf. on the Entity Relationship Approach*, pages 37–49, December 1993.

14. R.J. Peters and M.T. Özsu. An Axiomatic Model of Dynamic Schema Evolution in Objectbase Systems. *ACM Transactions on Database Systems*, 22(1):75–114, March 1997.

15. E. Rose and A. Segev. TOODM - A Temporal Object-Oriented Data Model with Temporal Constraints. In *Proc. 10th Int'l Conf. on the Entity Relationship Approach*, pages 205–229, October 1991.

16. Dag Sjøberg. Quantifying Schema Evolution. *Information and Software Technology*, 35(1):35–44, January 1993.

17. A.H. Skarra and S.B. Zdonik. The Management of Changing Types in an Object-Oriented Database. In *Proc. of the Int'l Conf on Object-Oriented Programming: Systems, Languages, and Applications*, pages 483–495, September 1986.

18. J.M. Smith and D.C.P. Smith. Database Abstractions: Aggregation and Generalization. *ACM Transactions on Database Systems*, 2(2):105–133, 1977.

19. S.Y.W. Su and H.M. Chen. A Temporal Knowledge Representation Model OSAM*/T and its Query Language OQL/T. In *Proc. 17th Int'l Conf. on Very Large Data bases*, 1991.

20. G. Wuu and U. Dayal. A Uniform Model for Temporal Object-Oriented Databases. In *Proc. 8th Int'l. Conf. on Data Engineering*, pages 584–593, February 1992.

Distributed Object Repositories:
Concepts and Standards

Sridhar Iyengar, Repository Architect
Unisys Corporation, Computer Systems Group
Mission Viejo, CA 92691, U.S.A
E-Mail : sridhar.iyengar@mv.unisys.com

1. Abstract

Object technology in general and object frameworks in particular are influencing the evolution of enterprise modeling, software development tool integration, repository architectures and distributed heterogeneous computing. A repository is the basis for data/object sharing and integration for application as well as business objects in an information systems environment.

This paper discusses object oriented repository architectures influenced by OMG CORBA (Common Object Request Broker Architecture) and Microsoft COM (Component Object Model) that supports extensibility and reuse in a distributed application development environment. This paper summarizes key object repository concepts and related work in standardizing core meta data management interfaces and object oriented meta models such as the OMG Meta Object Facility (MOF) and the Unified Modeling Language (UML). This paper has been influenced by R&D efforts at Unisys, IBM, Microsoft as well as on going work at the Object Management Group (Meta Object Facility) and earlier efforts of ECMA PCTE and ANSI X3H4 IRDS repository efforts. Representative architectures for object repositories for CORBA and COM based repositories are briefly described.

All trademarks are owned by respective corporations and organizations.

2. Technology Trends & Standards Influencing Repository Architectures

Repository architectures have been evolving from monolithic to client/server to distributed object paradigms over the last 10 years and tracking similar advances in middleware (system software that is layered between the application and the operating system), databases and applications architectures. The goal of a repository that integrates and manages these design artifacts has remained an elusive one. For an overview of traditional repository concepts please see [13] and [14]. This paper focuses on object orientation and distributed repository concepts and architectures.

One of the more complex problems that have arisen in recent years is that of constructing and managing distributed client/server development environments. This problem is being compounded by the emergence of object and component technology that is increasing the number of casual or business programmers (developers in Visual Basic) at a much faster pace than systems programmers (developers in C++). The rise of Java and the Internet is further accelerating component software technologies such as ActiveX and JavaBeans which also need to cataloged, searched, versioned and managed for effective reuse.

Object & component technology will continue to have a significant impact on application development techniques, Client/Server and Distributed Computing Architectures for the rest of this decade and into the next century. Today, object oriented technology manifests itself primarily in the areas of graphical user interfaces, analysis and design methodologies and programming languages. Object and Object-Relational database technologies are beginning to make an impact in application domains such as CAD, CASE, Geographic Information Systems, Multimedia and Internet, WWW applications that require complex modeling capabilities. The popular relational databases are aggressively moving to add object capabilities to their databases while object database vendors are aggressively moving to support integration with relational databases by adding SQL support which they currently lack. Of course all vendors are integrating with Internet technologies! While the number of object analysis and design methodologies has not shrunk, industry leading methodologists (Booch, Jacobson and Rumbaugh driving the unification) and industry vendors are working with OMG to define the 'Unified Modeling Language - UML' to help accelerate the standardization of object modeling and model interoperability.

The Object Management Group (OMG) has chartered various task forces to standardize interoperable distributed object technologies such as object request brokers, object analysis meta models, repositories and business objects. Of particular relevance to this paper is the work underway in the OMG Object Analysis and Design Task Force and the Common Facilities Task Force in the areas of analysis and design methods and repository/meta object management technologies. Specifically the OMG Object Analysis and Design Task Force (ADTF) is expected to standardize the Unified Modeling Language (UML) as a standard meta model for providing tool interoperability between object analysis and design tools. In addition the ADTF is expected to standardize the Meta Object Facility (MOF) which provides the core meta data APIs for CORBA based design and reuse repositories. Both these standards are expected to be adopted by OMG in 1997. Repository vendors such as IBM, Unisys and Microsoft have also adopted UML as the basis for information modeling in its repository product and this will help interoperability in both COM and CORBA based development environments. Additional standards for exchanging meta data and repository interoperability are being proposed by Electronic Industry Associates Case Data

Interchange Format (CDIF) and the Meta Data Coalition Meta Data Interchange Specification (MDIS).   This   paper   focuses   on   OMG   CORBA   related standardization efforts.

While the industry has been incorporating Client/Server architectures rapidly over the past decade, the advent of distributed object technology as well as the emergence of the Internet as an application development and deployment platform introduces bigger challenges in managing the development and execution environments. The problem of integrating and managing application development environments has historically been a very complex one with some big disappointments (IBM AD/Cycle for example) and some limited successes in very specific domain workbenches (HP SoftBench for example). The problem of integration has become significantly larger due to rapid adoption of component technology on the Microsoft desktop (VBX, OCX - now called ActiveX) and tools such as Visual Basic, PowerBuilder, Delphi etc.) and a requirement to support a variety of client and server platform technologies which support competing object as well as traditional middleware technologies. In the distributed object technology domain, the OMG has standardized on the 'COM/CORBA Interworking' proposal that helps bridge the object interoperability gap in an industry standard manner. CORBA 2.0 standards compliant Object Request Broker (ORB) implementations as well as several products that bridge the COM/CORBA divide are now available from several vendors such as Iona Technologies, Visigenic, Expersoft and BEA.

Many of the technologies and standards efforts mentioned above have so far focused on 'low level' technology and architecture issues. For applications to interoperate and for the dream of application assembly from components to be realized in a heterogeneous environment, the semantics and level of abstraction of these interoperable components and related object models need to be richer. It is this particular problem - meta data driven semantic interoperability - that a new class of object repositories (some available now and some announced for future delivery) from companies such as IBM, Unisys and Microsoft/TI (and more recently Sterling which acquired TI Software) are attempting to address. Lines of business specific object frameworks and the Business Object Framework (BOF) initiative also partially address this problem.

Historically data dictionaries and repositories were used by data administrators, but the recognition and deployment of repository technology in newer domains is now underway. The industry is beginning to see object (and traditional) repositories being used in new domains such as data warehouse management and business object management in addition to the traditional development environment management domain. The recognition that repositories are a key foundation platform technologies are acknowledged by object technology companies, industry consortia such as OMG as well as industry experts [See references 5 through 12].

Object repositories that support extensible meta models and model management environments integrated with distributed object middleware technologies are key to solving the problem of semantic interoperability and component integration across disparate platforms. Distributed object middleware technologies (DCOM/ActiveX and CORBA/Beans) provide basic object and component interoperability, while repositories and standard meta models provide semantic interoperability. Semantic interoperability is a very complex problem and some repositories are beginning to emerge (Unisys Universal Repository, IBM TeamConnection and the Microsoft Repository) for specific domains - typically application development tool integration. A comprehensive multi domain distributed object repository covering the domains of development, run time and systems management technologies is not expected till the end of the decade at the earliest. Successes in individual domains and continued progress in semantic interoperability across domains are expected to gradually ease this complex problem over time. In short just like other technologies (CASE, AI) of the past, object repositories, distributed objects and object frameworks are not panaceas but they are steps forward in solving the problem of managing complex distributed client/server and object environments. The introduction of Microsoft Repository is expected to accelerate the maturation of object repository technology as has been observed in other technology markets that Microsoft has entered. The industry is expected to standardize on UML for object modeling in 1997 and additional standard meta models in the domain of databases, business objects, data warehouse management and software component management are expected in the next couple of years.

The rest of the paper discusses object repository concepts and describes a Distributed Object Repository Architectures that attempts to address the problem of tool, application integration and of necessity object integration in distributed heterogeneous environments. The architecture is neutral to the problem domains and competing object middleware technologies but has been strongly influenced by OMG CORBA. Technologies such as CORBA and OLE/COM, programming languages such as C, C++, COBOL and Java, a variety of database technologies - relational, object and object-relational, a variety of rapid application development tools such as Visual Basic and PowerBuilder will all need to interoperate and have access to technical as well business meta data in a seamless manner. Object repositories & distributed object framework middleware technologies will play a key role in enabling such seamless integration within and across domains.

3. Object Repository Definition & Concepts

The word repository has been overused to mean everything from a file containing information to disk storage to a database that stores specific information. Within the context of this paper, the term repository is not synonymous with a database system. A repository is a specialized, extensible database application that adds value to a database system by being customized to a particular domain such as application development. Thus there are several instantiations of repositories that may in fact have different needs and different architectures. For a brief overview of Object Repository concepts please refer to [7]

This paper proposes an architecture based on distributed object technology that can accommodate integration with existing repositories and tools while meeting the needs of client/server and object component development trends that are well underway. The following working definition of a repository is used in this paper. Note that this is a broader definition of repository than in earlier literature such as [14], but does address the notion of repositories in distributed object environments and builds on earlier definitions. For the purposes of this paper the meta data is defined as descriptive information about data and concepts used in software systems. This meta data can correspond to technology or business concepts.

A distributed object repository (in the world of client/server and object technology) *is a dynamic information system that stores, manages and manipulates technical and business meta data including:*
- *Business Information such as rules, processes, policies, business concepts*
- *Application definitional information such as designs, models, component specifications, meta data definitions for a data warehouse*
- *Operational or run time management information such as database backup schedules, system configurations, software and hardware inventories*

A repository (integrated with distributed object technology) is a framework for developing, integrating, deploying and managing independently developed reusable software components.

This definition is intentionally broad in that it attempts to define repository architectures for multiple domains because it is now recognized that meta data applies to several computing technologies and can in fact be used to correlate and transform information between various domains. While it may seem odd to define a repository in terms of object frameworks (historically repositories have been treated as specialized databases), the nature of object extensibility and the need for installable meta models (developed independently to customize the repository to specific domains) has influenced our design of a framework based repository architecture. The definition of repository used by Microsoft is that of an 'Application Structure Database: a database of descriptive information about the structure of applications...' as in [21]. This definition while it may be pragmatic for a development repository is too restrictive to support enterprise and business use of repositories. However the underlying technology (object model and extensibility) is of necessity domain independent and is more framework like because of the infrastructure of COM and ActiveX.

To classify a product as an object repository implies that object technology is foundational - the architecture, meta model, the API, the persistent store and extensibility must all be object oriented. Of these technologies, the meta model and the Interfaces (API) must be object oriented to ensure interoperability. Ideally the persistent store must be object or object-relational to minimize the impedance mismatch between object oriented meta models and traditional network and relational database technologies. However it is possible to layer object managers on top of relational databases and even simple file systems.

Object-based repositories do not necessarily take such a pure approach and may have an object architecture and may be implemented using OOPLs but may not have an OO meta model. Both implementation approaches are in use today but without an extensible OO meta model and object interfaces, the repository cannot claim to be object oriented. For a detailed discussion of repository evaluation criteria and classification of OO versus Non-OO Repositories and an overview of some representative products please refer to [7].

4. Distributed Object Repository Architectures

The repository architecture is made up of a collection of interacting components and introduces repository terminology and maps these concepts and terms to appropriate OMG CORBA terminology. The repository engine is the implementation of the Repository Services Model the meta model for the repository. The key services in the engine are the Meta Object Facility which the type/model manager and the persistence and version service managers. While this paper describes CORBA based repositories (such as the ones being delivered by OMG member companies), these concepts apply to COM based repositories (such as the once provided by Microsoft) or current repository products that are providing CORBA and COM/ActiveX interfaces. OMG CORBA based repository architecture is the primary focus of this paper because it is the industry standard for distributed object interoperability in heterogeneous environments. More recently Microsoft has implemented a repository based on COM but currently the architecture does not exploit distributed architectures but is upwardly compatible with DCOM (Distributed COM).

This is a necessary step in the transition of traditional technologies (such as data dictionaries and repositories) into OMG CORBA and Microsoft DCOM distributed object infrastructure. For a more detailed explanation of the repository-related terminology the reader is referred to the glossary in [18]. A series of illustrations will be used to show how the OMG Object Management Architecture is used to define a repository reference model that will be used to identify and characterize the services, interfaces, and protocols that comprise the repository architecture. The major components of the Object Management Architecture (OMA see Figure 1) are:

- The **Object Request Broker**, which enables objects to make and receive requests and responses in a distributed environment. The Object Request Broker is specified by the OMG CORBA specifications.

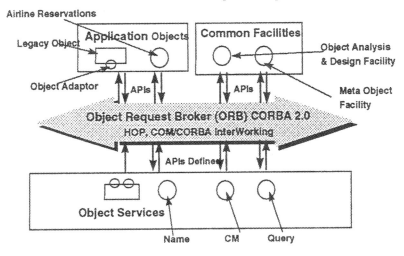

Figure 1: OMG Object Management Architecture

- **OMG Object Services**, are a collection of fundamental OMG standard services (interfaces and objects) that provide basic functions for using and implementing the Repository Facility.
- **OMG Common Facilities**, are collections of compositions of OMG standard services with interfaces that provide general-purpose capabilities useful in many applications. A repository common facility (which includes the Meta Object Facility) is one such facility that is discussed in this paper. Other facilities include print facility, systems management facility etc. More recently OMG is focusing on standardizing domain specific objects (for example, Manufacturing, Telecommunications etc. in the Domain Technical

Committee). Object Services and Common Facilities are standardized in the Platform Technical Committee.

- **Application Objects** are built using collections of common facilities and objects services and are not standardized by OMG. It is assumed that application and tool objects provide user interface and application specific logic.

The repository common facility is an example of a common facility shown in Figure 2

OMG Repository Common Facility

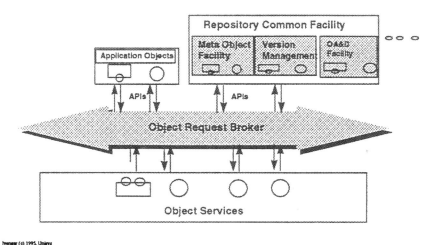

Figure 2: OMG Architecture and the Repository Common Facility

The repository common facility is itself an integrated composition of several object services and other common facilities and will be used in several software domains such as application development, data warehousing and systems management.

An example of a **Repository Common Facility**, which is a collection of objects that implement an object repository, is defined more completely in [12]. The repository object types are stored in the repository meta schema (also referred to as the repository meta model which includes Meta Object Facility) and the instances of these repository object types may either be stored in the repository itself or externally as required by the specific application. The Repository Object types that offer services that extend the behavior of the repository to satisfy the needs defined in the specific schemas (meta-models) for repository-enabled applications are in each of the modules of the repository common facilities (these modules correspond to repository object services or common facilities. The blurry line that exists between object services and common facilities extends into this architecture as well).

The repository facility is defined in terms of interfaces for a set of essential services needed to define, create, manage, activate, and use repository objects. These services constitute the basic enabling technology for repository-compliant facilities, tools, objects, and applications. Interfaces and operations defined for the repository facility are expected to serve as building blocks for specific application and tool domains such as application development, asset management, systems management, data warehouse meta data management etc.

The services of the Repository Facility are intended to align with existing or planned OMG CORBA, Common Object Services, and Common Facilities. In many cases, the existing OMG standards will be used directly as the specification of the corresponding Repository Facility service. New services or facilities (For example Meta Object Facility, Version Management Facility) are expected to be standardized in the future. In other cases, existing object services are either encapsulated to create extended of object services or the interface inheritance mechanism is used to extend the existing interfaces. As an example, the persistence service could be extended to support the capture and persist the date and time that an object was created. As another example, a new 'naming convention verification' interface 'VerifyName' could be added through interface inheritance to support definition and enforcement of naming rules.

The concept of repository schemas and models as extensions to the repository common facility is illustrated in Figure 3 which shows how these content meta models (which is a collective term for technology models, tool models and business models) can be viewed as layers in a repository framework. This architecture is consistent with the traditional four layer meta model architecture used in the definition of the Unisys et al Meta Object Facility submission to OMG [22] as well as the Rational et al Object Analysis and Design Facility submission to OMG [24].

Repository Information Model Architecture

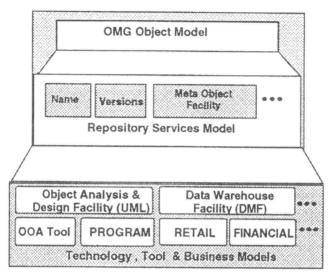

OMG Object Model

Name Versions Meta Object Facility •••

Repository Services Model

Object Analysis & Design Facility (UML) Data Warehouse Facility (DMF) •••

OOA Tool PROGRAM RETAIL FINANCIAL •••

Technology , Tool & Business Models

(C) 1997, Unisys Corporation

Figure 3: Repository Information Model (schema) Architecture

Note that the repository object model which is at the top of Figure 3 is sometimes referred to as **'Repository meta meta model'** and this model describes fundamental repository concepts such as models (synonymous with schema in this document), classes, relationships, events etc. These classes are used to define the repository common facility itself as well as all other repository schemas(meta models such as the UML).

The repository common facility is itself represented as a model (repository schema model) and is the heart of the repository in that it is a composition of key object services and common facilities that constitute the repository. This layer is usually referred to as the **'Repository meta model'** in the repository industry.

The last set of layers corresponds to content models (in that these describe the contents of the repository) that are called **Technology Models, Tool Models and Business Models** which are essentially analogous to CORBA facilities. They are not identical to CORBA facilities because, the definitions include integrity rules, schema related rules, relationships, interfaces which combine together to define a complete schema. The interfaces to a technology model do in fact correspond to the interfaces in a CORBA facility. **Technology models** are sharable by several tools and applications. **Tool Models** on the other hand correspond to the repository schema of a particular tool with value added extensions. Once again an analogy of a tool model to CORBA terms is that the tool model defines the schema that corresponds to a CORBA Application Object. The term **Business Model** in this document refers to a model that describes business (objects) concepts (such as People, meeting, Reservation etc.) as opposed to technical objects (such as file, version, database...).

An example of a repository architecture that shows various types of applications accessing such an architected repository is in Figure 4. The repository object instances themselves can be stored in a variety of data stores (such as object databases, object-relational databases, relational databases, files and so on). The repository federation and distribution services manage federation and access to the actual data. The repository information model layer corresponds to the collection of Repository Common Facility and all the content models that are integrated with and populated in the repository schema. It is crucial for this information to be represented in a language neutral manner so that CORBA IDL can be used as a mechanism for defining the interfaces to all these object types. This enables use of the repository objects by wide variety of development and run time environments.

At the heart of the run time architecture is the object request broker itself. These object interfaces are now available to any application across the network. For supporting repository access to environments where request brokers are not yet prevalent, gateways and bridges can be built to specific proprietary or de facto standard environments. This is also the approach used to map the CORBA concepts to non-object oriented interfaces such as those defined by current repositories on the market. The gateway and bridge approach is also a mechanism that can be used to bridge repository applications that use Microsoft OLE/COM compliant APIs on the desktop to enterprise wide repository services that are implemented using a CORBA infrastructure. OMG has now standardized COM/CORBA interoperability specifications. Note that in a homogeneous environment (say a Microsoft centric environment) such gateways/bridges are not necessary, but most development and execution environments are heterogeneous today.

At the top of figure 4 is the end user view of the repository and here the user accesses a variety of tools in different domains (technical or business) using a choice of interfaces. The tools themselves us the industry standard CORBA based interfaces or other interfaces through various adapters/gateways. Unisys has demonstrated an implementation of a subset of this architecture with its Universal Repository (UREP) product at Object World in August 1995 as a proof of concept. Both IBM and Unisys have products that conform to this architecture and are co-operating to define OMG Meta Object Facility, which is at the core of this architecture. Object repositories that are CORBA compliant are now becoming available.

Distributed Object Repository Architecture

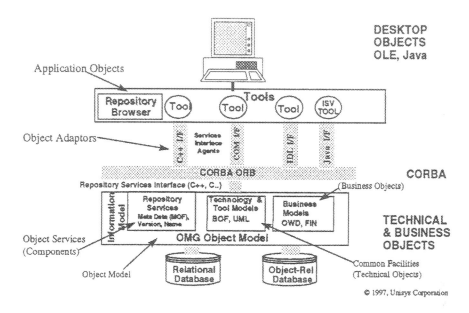

Figure 4 : Distributed Object Repository Architecture

For a comprehensive list of repository related services refer to [10, 11 and 12]. The actual list of repository services and details regarding these services is beyond the scope of this paper. There is general consensus that the most important repository services are:

- Meta Data or Model/Schema management services that support a semantically rich object model (Meta Object Facility addresses this problem)
- Change Management (Version and Configuration management) services
- Tool/Object Integration and Registration services

Of course technology and domain specific meta-models and tools that manipulate these models and instances of models must augment these core repository services. It is these tools - browsers, modeling tools, database tools, compilers, 4GLS etc. and their integration that makes the use of the repository meaningful.

Examples of useful meta-models to standardize include the following:

- Object Analysis and Design (UML is expected to be standardized soon)

- Database and Data Warehouse Technology (SQL92 based)
- Component Discovery and Management (ActiveX and JavaBeans based)
- Transaction Discovery and Management and (CORBA OTS, Tuxedo and CICS based)

Note that except for UML there are no focused efforts in defining standard meta-models for distributed development environments and this is an area of potential future activity in OMG. More recently OMG has started up efforts in standardizing component models. Specific standards for databases and transactions (for example CORBA Object Transaction Service) exist, but standard meta models that build on these core technologies to address broader tool interoperability issues are not available.

A UML representation of the meta-meta model (as part of the Meta Object Facility proposal) submitted to OMG is described in more detail in [22]. This model is being integrated with the models in [23] and the core UML model [24] for the proposed standard that will be submitted to OMG. Note that these models are undergoing revisions prior to final submission to the OMG. Object repository and related development environments from companies such as IBM, Oracle and Unisys are expected to support this standard and conform to the CORBA architecture.

5. Microsoft Repository Architecture

The previous section described in detail the distributed repository architecture influenced by CORBA. This architecture supports COM based tools (including repositories) that use gateways such as the COM/CORBA interworking standard. From the perspective of tool developers this architecture provides the benefits of the enterprise scaleability and heterogeneity of CORBA while supporting the rich development tools that are available in COM based Windows environments. Microsoft has developed a COM based object repository in that all repository interfaces are exposed as COM interfaces. Conceptually the Microsoft repository architecture described in Figure 5 is similar to the CORBA based repository architecture discussed in the previous section. The details of various programmatic interfaces (Microsoft Visual Basic and Visual C++) and the various information models have been simplified in this figure.

A detailed comparison of the two architectures is outside the scope of this paper. The main differences are:
- Object model and object interoperability infrastructure (COM versus CORBA)
- Support of platforms (COM is windows centric, CORBA is available on all industry platforms

- Definition by an industry consortium (OMG) with multiple implementations on various operating system platforms versus definition by a single vendor Microsoft (and some key tool partners) on the Windows platform. The Windows platform restriction for the Microsoft repository is expected to be relaxed in the future.

The basic architecture of the Microsoft Repository includes :

- A persistent store for the objects (a relational database such as Microsoft SQL Server.
- A type interpreter which is used to define and manipulate information models (part of the repository engine)
- Basic repository services such as persistence, transactions (part of the repository engine) exposed as COM interfaces. The repository engine and the information models take advantage of the COM.
- Information Models such the Type definition model - which is the meta-meta model of the Microsoft Repository, Unified Modeling Language (for object modeling tool interoperability), Database Model (for supporting data base and data warehouse management etc.). Microsoft is working with a number of tool and system vendors in defining some of these information models. These information models have been significantly influenced by UML and based on UML.
- Various tools for manipulating information models and instances of information models. All these are repository objects and in fact COM objects
- The repository supports a navigational interface (using programming languages like C++ and Basic) and a query interface (using SQL). The SQL interface by passes the repository engine and is typically used only for querying the database structures. The information model semantics are exposed and enforced only in the navigational interface.

Microsoft Repository Architecture

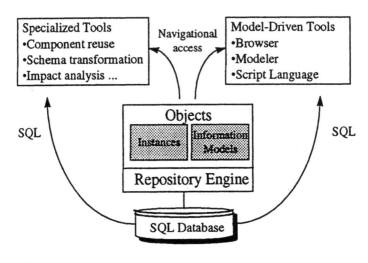

Figure 5 : Microsoft Object Repository Architecture

This paper describes Microsoft repository architecture because it is expected to be a de facto standard in Windows environments for developers of COM based tools. Its technical viability (COM works best on Windows) and success in the broader heterogeneous marketplace remains to be seen. For a good technical overview of the Microsoft Repository see [21] and [25]. For more details on COM see [5]. An additional reason to describe the architecture is to highlight the support of UML in both CORBA and COM based repositories as a significant step in standardizing meta models. Specific architectures of CORBA based repository products from IBM, Unisys and other vendors can be found in references but is generally aligned with the architecture defined in the previous section.

6. Conclusions

The paper highlighted some of the key trends affecting the complexity of development and run time environments and then described the general need for integration of tools and applications in a distributed development environment. A proposal for a distributed object repository architecture based on CORBA and COM technologies was highlighted so as to leverage the strengths of the Microsoft desk top as well as a more heterogeneous UNIX/Enterprise Server environment. The importance of an extensible information model and layered information model architecture as well as support for multiple language interfaces and the importance of Database, O/S and Object Middleware technology independence were highlighted. It is interesting to note that while both Unisys and IBM have released products that are similar in architecture to this paper, OLE and CORBA compliant implementations are expected to be delivered by multiple vendors in the 1997/1998 time frame. All major system and software vendors have either repository development or repository integration efforts underway now. Progress is also being made in standardizing core repository APIs (OMG Meta Object Facility and Microsoft Repository APIs) and industry standard meta models (Unified Modeling Language).

The efforts at OMG by various member companies defining CORBA based open repository standards and the effort at Microsoft who is also working with a number of tool and system vendors to build COM based repository standards will accelerate the pace at which tool and application integration will accelerate. A key challenge is interoperability and convergence between these efforts. While the infrastructure technologies (CORBA and COM) are divergent, consensus on meta models such as the UML which the industry is unanimously supporting (Microsoft included) is a step in the right direction. The same needs to happen with additional meta models and business models.

7. Acknowledgments

The design of the distributed object repository architecture described in this paper has been influenced by efforts in repository architectures at Unisys, Digital, Oracle and IBM Corporations. I thank Unisys Corporation for supporting the research and its developers for implementation of this architecture. I thank the Object Management Group and its member companies for its pioneering work in creating the CORBA architecture and more recently for on going efforts in standardizing the Unified Modeling Language and Meta Object Facility, which are key components of distributed repositories. I also thank the developers of the Microsoft Repository (especially Phil Bernstein) for providing me the information and graphics describing the Microsoft Repository Architecture.

8. References

For an excellent overview of many of the technologies (especially distributed objects) discussed in this paper see [18]. For good overviews of repository technology and implementation issues see [13] and [14]. For papers that are influencing distributed object repository architectures, implementations and technology trends see[9-12, 14] and [16]. For a more detailed overview of the architectures defined in this paper see [12], [16] and [25].

Surf the web pages of Unisys, IBM and Microsoft for detailed information related to specific object repository implementations.

1. OMG Object Management Architecture Guide, September 1992
2. The Common Object Request Broker: Architecture and Specification, CORBA 2.0, March 1995
3. CORBAServices : Common Object Services Specification, March 1995
4. OMG Common Facilities Architecture, November 1995
5. Inside OLE : Kraig Brockschmidt
6. Microsoft Object technology white papers (www.microsoft.com)
7. Object Oriented Strategies, Dec 1995 - OO Repositories : Paul Harmon
8. Patricia Seybold Group's SnapShots, August 1995
9. OMG Common Facilities RFI #3 - Repositories
10. IBM response to OMG RFI#3, OMG document tc/95-11-09
11. Texas Instruments response to OMG RFI #3, OMG document tc/95-11-06
12. Unisys response to OMG RFI#3, OMG TC document tc/95-11-05
13. Bernstein, P.A and U. Dayal, "An overview of repository technology", VLDB 94
14. Implementing a corporate Repository, Adrienne Tannenbaum (Wiley)
15. Object Solutions : Grady Booch
16. Iyengar : Object Repositories, OLE and CORBA - Towards seamless distributed objects, March 1996, Software Development'96 conference proceedings
17. Orfali et al, 1996: The essential distributed object survival guide
18. Unisys Universal Repository Capabilities Guide
19. www.urep.com Unisys Universal Repository
20. www.ibm.com/ad IBM Application Development tools
21. www.microsoft.com/repository Microsoft Repository
22. Unisys et al submission to OMG Meta Object Facility cf/97-01-12, ad/97-08-14, 15
23. Rational et al submission to OMG Object Analysis & Design Facility ad/97-01-14, ad/97-08-10
24. The Microsoft Repository, Philip Bernstein et al , Proceedings of 23rd VLDB Conference, Athens, Greece 1997

Extended SQL Support for Uncertain Data

Debabrata Dey[1] and Sumit Sarkar[2]

[1] University of Washington, School of Business, Box 353200, Seattle, WA 98195
[2] Louisiana State University, College of Business, Baton Rouge, LA 70803
(ddey@u.washington.edu, qmsark@unix1.sncc.lsu.edu)

Abstract. Although the relational model for databases provides a great range of advantages over other data models, it lacks a comprehensive way for handling uncertain data. Uncertainty in data values, however, is pervasive in all real world environments and has received some attention in the literature. Several methods have been proposed for incorporating uncertain data into relational databases; however, these approaches have many shortcomings. In this paper, we discuss a probabilistic extension of the relational model and propose a query language for creation, modification, and retrieval of uncertain data.

1 Introduction

Most modern business information systems rely on database systems for storage and maintenance of volumes of pertinent real world data. However, since uncertainty is pervasive in the real world environments, often the data values (representing the state of the real world) are uncertain. Uncertainty in the data values can arise in many ways. The data item may inherently be uncertain; e.g., only a fraction of all smokers develop cancer. The actual value of a data item may be unknown; e.g., the actual salary of a newly hired employee may be unknown, although one can use other information such as rank, department, job description, and competitive market salary to form an opinion about the salary of the new employee. The data item may not be realized yet; e.g., the instructor for the graduate level database course may yet to be assigned for the next semester. However, if there are only two faculty members who can teach this course, then there is a probability of 0.5 that either will offer that course. Uncertainty may also arise from consolidation or summarization of data or from data heterogeneity. Clearly, information systems require the ability to store, maintain and reason with uncertain data. Unfortunately, such facilities are not available in the popular relational data model and its widely used *structured query language* (SQL). Therefore, it is necessary to extend the semantics of the relational model and SQL so that uncertainty in data items can be represented, and used to make better decisions.

Klir and Folger (1988) identify that there are two types of uncertainties in the real world: uncertainty due to *vagueness* and uncertainty due to *ambiguity*. Uncertainty due to *vagueness* is associated with the difficulty of making sharp or precise distinctions in the real world. For example, subjective terms such as tall, far and heavy are vague. Uncertainty due to *ambiguity*, on the other hand, is associated with situations in which the choices among several precise alternatives are left unspecified. For example, we may know that a person's height is in the range 5–7 feet, but we may not know the exact height of that person. In most business situations, the uncertainty about data arises from *ambiguity*, and not from *vagueness*. If some data item is of interest in an application, it is reasonable to assume that there is a way to measure and collect that data up to the level of precision that is necessary for that application. The uncertainty lies not with the reported value, but with the correctness of the measurement or data collection techniques. These business situations need to be modeled using some kind of uncertainty measure. We feel that the probability measure is the most appropriate measure of uncertainty. Probability theory, due to its wide acceptance, is easier to interpret. Moreover, probability measures have a rich theoretical basis for representing uncertainty; they lend themselves to empirical testability and provide an easy-to-use semantics (Pearl, 1986).

Cavallo and Pittarelli (1987) extend the relational model to represent uncertainty due to *ambiguity* using the probability measure. They restrict the total probability assigned to all tuples in a relation to be exactly one. A resulting limitation is that a separate relation would be required for every object that is known to exist with certainty. On the other hand, if all the information is to appear in a single relation, there is no way of asserting the certainty in the existence of an object. Moreover, they do not provide a query language for this structure. Barbará *et al.* (1992) propose a non-first normal form (non-1NF) extension of the relational model using probability theory. This model poses the usual implementation problem inherent in all non-1NF relations. Second, their method of data organization presumes knowledge of probabilistic independence among attributes which may not be known at design time. Third, their assumption of key attributes always being deterministic is somewhat restrictive. Finally, they also do not provide a non-procedural query language.

Developing relational databases for supporting uncertain data requires three key issues to be addressed. First, a rigorous extension of the relational algebra is required for manipulation of uncertain data items. Second, a non-procedural query language is needed as an easy-to-use interface. Finally, one must address the issues related to implementation, storage, and design. In another paper (Dey and Sarkar, 1996), we have developed a consistent extension of the relational algebra based on probability theory to incorporate uncertain data; this extension overcomes all the shortcomings discussed above. In this paper, we propose an extended relational query language, called probabilistic structured query language, or PSQL in short, for this extended model. Design and implementation issues are ongoing as a part of the bigger project.

The rest of this paper is organized as follows. The structure and meaning of probabilistic relations are discussed in Section 2. Sections 3 and 4 discuss the basic relational operations and the extended query language PSQL. The formulation of probabilistic queries is discussed in Section 5. Section 6 concludes the paper.

2 Structure and Meaning of Probabilistic Relations

Before discussing how uncertain data can be represented using relations, let us first examine how the conventional relational model represents facts about the real world. To illustrate this, consider the relation FACULTY shown in Table 1. In this relation, the first row means that the predicate *FACULTY(3025, James*

Table 1. FACULTY: a Conventional Relation

FAC_ID	name	dept	office	phone
3025	James Lyons	ISDS	2166 Dewey	388-7001
6723	Jack Kivari	Acctg	307A Hylan	388-8002
6879	Julia Apers	Mktg	442C Hylan	388-9921
7691	Tim Prather	Mgmt	242A Hylan	388-7734

Lyons, ISDS, 2166 Dewey, 388-7001) must be assigned a value of "TRUE" (represented by 1). Any predicate not listed in this relation, is assigned a value of "FALSE" (or 0); this is the usual *closed world assumption*. However, when there is uncertainty associated with real world objects, it is not always possible to assign a value of 0 or 1 to these predicates. As a result, the first-order predicate calculus—as well as a conventional relation which may be viewed as a collection of first-order predicates—cannot represent uncertain data.

We address this limitation by using the probability calculus in place of the first-order predicate calculus. Instead of assigning a value of 0 or 1 to a predicate, we assign it a probability. For example, we write

$$\Pr[FACULTY(3025, James\ Lyons,\ ISDS,\ 2166\ Dewey,\ 388\text{-}7001)] = 0.6,$$

to represent the fact that, with a probability of 0.6, there exists a faculty member with the following attribute values: FAC_ID=3025, name=James Lyons, dept=ISDS, office=2166 Dewey, and phone=388-7001. This can be represented in the usual tabular format of a relation by appending a special column called the probability stamp or pS; Table 2 illustrates this representation for a portion of a university database. In this representation, only predicates with non-zero probabilities are explicitly written as tuples or rows; if a predicate is not represented as a tuple, then it has a probability of zero (generalized *closed world assumption*). Thus, a relation captures the joint distribution over all of its non-probability attributes; the probability associated with a particular attribute value can be obtained by appropriate marginalization of this joint distribution. For example, from the first three rows in the FACULTY relation shown in Table 2(a), we can infer that the marginal probability associated with FAC_ID 3025 is one. This implies that this faculty member is known to exist with certainty, although some of the attribute values are not known precisely. The probability that this faculty

Table 2. Extended Relations for a University Database

(a) Relation: FACULTY

FAC_ID	name	dept	office	phone	pS
3025	James Lyons	ISDS	2166 Dewey	388-7001	0.6
3025	James Lyons	Mktg	551A Hylan	388-9901	0.3
3025	James Lyons	Mktg	551A Hylan	388-7001	0.1
6723	Jack Kivari	Acctg	307A Hylan	388-8002	0.5
6723	Jack Kivari	ISDS	307A Hylan	388-7002	0.2
6879	Julia Apers	Mktg	442C Hylan	388-9921	1.0
7691	Tim Prather	Mgmt	242A Hylan	388-7734	0.6

(b) Relation: TENURED

FAC_ID	rank	salary	pS
3025	Assoc	60K	0.2
3025	Assoc	65K	0.4
3025	Full	65K	0.4
6879	Assoc	61K	0.6

(c) Relation: COURSE

COURSE_NO	description	credit
ISD3110	Database Mgmt	3
ACC3501	Internal Audit	4
MKT2100	Intro to Mktg	4
MGT4120	Optimization	3

(d) Relation: OFFERING

FAC_ID	COURSE_NO	room	start	end	enrolled	pS
3025	ISD3110	111A Hylan	10:00A	11:00A	33	0.3
3025	ISD3110	1209 Dewey	09:30A	11:00A	39	0.3
3025	MKT2100	111A Hylan	10:00A	11:30A	33	0.3
6723	ACC3501	107B Hylan	02:00P	03:00P	61	0.6
6723	ISD3110	109A Hylan	01:00P	02:30P	37	0.3
6879	MKT2100	143A Hylan	08:30A	09:30A	53	1.0
7691	MGT4120	1103 Dewey	10:00A	11:00A	23	0.5

member is in the Marketing department is only 0.4 (from the second and the third rows).

It is not mandatory to have pS as one of the columns. For example, the COURSE relation in Table 2(c) does not have the probability stamp. This is a special case of the extended relation, where the probability assigned to each row is exactly one and is not explicitly written. In other words, the first row in this relation is equivalent to the probability calculus statement:

$$\Pr[COURSE(ISD3110, \text{ Database Mgmt, } 3)] = 1.$$

A few restrictions are imposed on these relations so that data integrity can be maintained. We do not allow two distinct tuples with the same values for all non-probability attributes—also called *value-equivalent* tuples—to be present in a relation. Value-equivalent tuples are similar to duplicates in the conventional relational model. Existence of value-equivalent tuples introduces ambiguity about the distribution and are not allowed.

The second restriction is about the primary key of a relation. In the relational model, every tuple in a relation represents a unique object (i.e., an entity or a relationship) from the real world; a *primary key* is a minimal set of attributes that uniquely identifies a tuple, and hence an object. In the probabilistic extension, associated with every object, there may be several tuples representing the complete joint distribution of its attributes. Hence, we retain the *object surrogate* interpretation of the primary key (i.e., unique identifier of real world objects) and discard the notion of the primary key as a unique identifier of tuples. Ideally then, probability stamps associated with a primary key value should add up to one. In that case, the existence of the object (identified by that key value) is certain and the joint probability distribution for all its attributes is completely specified. However, the complete distribution is not necessary in order to store probabilities about attributes. If the existence of the object itself is uncertain, then the probability stamps associated with the key value of that object could be less than one. The modified requirement, then, is that the probability stamps associated with any given key value must add up to no more than one. Furthermore, the primary key and the probability stamp are not allowed to have "null" values.

The third and final restriction is about the foreign keys in a relation (referential integrity constraint). Since the foreign key values in a relation refer to other objects (in the same or a different relation), the probability assignments for a foreign key value cannot be more than the probability of existence of the referred object. For example, in the OFFERING relation, we see that the course with COURSE_NO=ISD3110 is taught by the faculty with FAC_ID=3025 with a probability of 0.6. This is consistent with the axioms of probability theory since the probability of existence of the referred faculty member (FAC_ID=3025) is 1.0 which is greater than 0.6. Similarly, it is also consistent when we consider COURSE_NO as a foreign key in the OFFERING relation since the COURSE relation is deterministic, and the COURSE with COURSE_NO=ISD3110 exists with certainty.

3 Basic Relational Operations

Dey and Sarkar (1996) define the necessary relational operations and the algebra for the above structure. Here, we summarize the three major operations, namely *projection, selection* and *join*.

Projection. The projection operation provides us with the marginal distribution of a subset of attributes. For example, in Table 2, several attributes of faculty members are presented. The user, however, may want to view only the name and department information for all faculty members. This is accomplished by projecting the FACULTY relation onto the attributes FAC_ID, name, dept, and pS. The probability stamps for the resulting tuples are obtained by evaluating the appropriate marginal distribution from the joint distribution stored in the original relation. Thus, the three tuples associated with FAC_ID 3025 in the FACULTY relation in Table 2 result in two tuples for this projection. The probability information in the projected view is consistent with the information stored in the original relation.

Selection. The selection operation is used to identify tuples that satisfy specified conditions on attributes and probability stamps. For instance, we may want to view all tuples with dept='ISDS.' If we perform a selection on the FACULTY relation in Table 2 for this condition, only the first and the fifth tuples would be displayed. We can also include explicit conditions on the probability stamp itself. Further, logical connectives may be used to combine multiple conditions. Such a query, for example, could select tuples with dept='ISDS' and $pS \geq 0.5$. As a result of this query on Table 2, only the first tuple would be displayed. Note that, since the selection operation is defined at the tuple level, just the selection operation cannot provide a list of faculty members in the marketing department with probability of 0.4 or higher. In order to obtain such a list, it is necessary to combine the projection and selection operations.

Join. The join operation between two relations provides the joint distribution of all the attributes in the participating relations. In the join operation, every tuple in one relation is checked for a match (on attributes common to both the relations) with every tuple in the other relation; if a match is found, they are combined to form a new tuple in the resulting relation. The probability stamp of the new tuple is simply the product of the probability stamps of the participating tuples. An important implication of this is that the probability stamp for the resulting relation is a reliable probability measure only when the attributes in the two participating relations are independent. When the attributes are not independent, the distribution represented by the *referenced* relation must be converted to a conditional distribution, with the common attributes used for conditioning. A new relational operation called *conditionalization* allows one to make such transformations (Dey and Sarkar, 1996). The conditionalization operation revises the probability stamps associated with each tuple by changing the marginal probability of the primary key values to unity. In other words, after conditionalization, the relation can be interpreted as the joint conditional distribution of all non-key attributes given the primary key values.

4   The Extended SQL

In this section, we describe the extended syntax of a probabilistic structured query language (PSQL). The create, insert and **update** commands retain their usual syntax. For example, to create the FACULTY relation, we would use:

```
create table FACULTY
      ( FAC_ID smallint primary key,
        name char(20), dept char(5),
        office char(20), phone integer,
        pS ).
```

The only difference is that there is no need to specify the domain for pS which is always $(0, 1]$. Since the basic structure of a relation is like a flat table, we can use the conventional SQL commands for modification of data as well. Therefore, we discuss the extended syntax of select only. The basic form of the conventional select command is:

select attribute_list
  from table_set
    where Query_Condition.

We use this basic form, but introduce a new operator "p" for obtaining the marginal distribution of attributes appearing as its arguments. For instance, "p[FAC_ID,name,dept]" on the FACULTY relation would derive the marginal probabilities for different values of the attributes FAC_ID, name, and dept, based on the joint distribution in FACULTY. Thus, the "p" operator is somewhat similar to *projection*. When explicit conditions are specified for attributes appearing as arguments, the "p" operator calculates the marginal probabilities only for those attribute values that satisfy the given conditions.

Instead of presenting the most general form of the syntax, we illustrate it with the help of example queries. In all these queries, we make use of the relations shown in Table 2.

Query 1: *Name faculty members who are in the ISDS department with a probability more than 0.5.*

select name from FACULTY
  where dept='ISDS' and
    p[FAC_ID,dept] > 0.5.

The result of this query would be *James Lyons*, because he is the only one who satisfies the query condition with a probability greater than 0.5. We make two observations here. First, it is necessary to include the primary key as an argument of the "p" operator so that probability values across different objects are not used in calculating the marginal probabilities. Second, if one is just interested in finding *the names of the faculty members who may be in the ISDS department*, the query condition can be expressed without the probability condition, or with the probability condition "p[FAC_ID,name,dept] > 0." The result of either formulation is: {James Lyons, Jack Kivari}.

Query 2: *What is the probability that James Lyons is in the Marketing department?*

select p[FAC_ID,dept] from FACULTY
  where name='James Lyons' and dept='Mktg'.

Here, the "p" operator is used to display the required marginal probability; it would be calculated in this case by adding the pS-values of the second and the third rows. So the result of this query would be {0.4}.

Query 3: *What is the probability distribution of the department that James Lyons works in?*

select dept, p[FAC_ID,dept] from FACULTY
    where name='James Lyons'.

The result would be: $\{\langle ISDS, 0.6\rangle, \langle Mktg, 0.4\rangle\}$.

Query 4: *Name faculty members who are tenured with a probability of 0.8 or more.*

select name from FACULTY, TENURED
    where (TENURED.FAC_ID=FACULTY.FAC_ID) and
    p[TENURED.FAC_ID] $\geq$ 0.8.

The answer to this query is *James Lyons*.

Query 5: *Name surely tenured faculty members who have a salary less than 62K (with a probability greater than 0.5) or have a rank of "Full Professor" (with a probability greater than 0.2).*

select name from FACULTY, TENURED
    where TENURED.FAC_ID=FACULTY.FAC_ID and
    p[TENURED.FAC_ID] $= 1$ and
    ((salary<62K and p[TENURED.FAC_ID,salary] > 0.5) or
    (rank='Full' and p[TENURED.FAC_ID,rank] > 0.2])).

The result would be *James Lyons* since he is the only one who is surely tenured and he satisfies the condition on rank. If we were interested in *possibly tenured faculty members*, we could drop the probability condition "p[TENURED.FAC_ID] $= 1$" from the above query; the result would be *James Lyons* (satisfying the rank condition) and *Julia Apers* (satisfying the salary condition).

Query 6: *List possible names of faculty members who are teaching 'Intro to Mktg' with a probability greater than 0.5.*

select name from FACULTY, COURSE, OFFERING
    where description='Intro to Mktg' and
    OFFERING.FAC_ID=FACULTY.FAC_ID and
    OFFERING.COURSE_NO=COURSE.COURSE_NO and
    p[OFFERING.FAC_ID,OFFERING.COURSE_NO] > 0.5.

Query 7: *Which courses may be taught by possibly tenured faculty members?*

select COURSE.COURSE_NO, description
    from TENURED, OFFERING
        where COURSE.COURSE_NO=OFFERING.COURSE_NO and
        OFFERING.FAC_ID=TENURED.FAC_ID.

PSQL can support the usual aggregate operations. However, in the presence of probabilistic information, the aggregate operations must be redefined. For example, the AVG operation calculates the expected value of an attribute. In the following query, we group this aggregate information by FAC_ID; this is equivalent to calculating the expected salary of each faculty member.

Query 8: *Find the expected salary of each tenured faculty member.*

```
select FAC_ID, AVG(salary) from TENURED
        group by FAC_ID.
```

Query 9: *What is the probability that a faculty member from the ISDS department is teaching in room 1209 Dewey?*
This query requires the probability distribution from two different relations to be combined into a joint distribution, and is thus similar to *join*. However, the attributes in the relations FACULTY and OFFERING are not independent, since they have the common attribute FAC_ID. Consider the faculty member with FAC_ID=3025; we know that:

$$\Pr[F{=}3025, D{=}\text{'ISDS'}] = 0.6, \text{ and, } \Pr[F{=}3025, R{=}\text{'1209 Dewey'}] = 0.3,$$

where F, D, and R are abbreviations of "FAC_ID," "dept," and "room," respectively. Since these facts are not independent, the desired result cannot be obtained by directly multiplying these numbers. However, assuming conditional independence of the attributes "dept" and "room" (given FAC_ID), the desired joint distribution can be written as:

$$\Pr[F = f, D = d, R = r] = \frac{\Pr[F = f, D = d]\Pr[F = f, R = r]}{\Pr[F = f]}.$$

Thus the above query can be expressed as:

```
select p[OFFERING.FAC_ID,room]*p[FACULTY.FAC_ID,dept]/p[FACULTY.FAC_ID]
        from FACULTY, OFFERING
                where FACULTY.FAC_ID=OFFERING.FAC_ID and
                        dept='ISDS' and room='1209 Dewey'.
```

Another operator called "jointp" directly evaluates the above probability. The above query is then restated as:

```
select jointp[FACULTY.FAC_ID,dept,room]
        from FACULTY, OFFERING
                where FACULTY.FAC_ID=OFFERING.FAC_ID and
                        dept='ISDS' and room='1209 Dewey'.
```

5   Query Formulation with Probabilities

So far we have discussed the extended structure of relations and the extended syntax of PSQL. However, it is not immediately clear how this syntax can be used to retrieve information from the database for use in real world decision making. It is not usual for a user to ask probabilistic queries (i.e., queries with probabilistic conditions) such as: "Name the faculty members who are in the ISDS department with a probability greater than 0.5." It is far more likely that the user would be interested in a simpler query: "Name the faculty members in the ISDS department." Of course, if the stored information were deterministic and complete, we would know with certainty whether a faculty member is in the ISDS department. We could use a simple SQL query to get the desired information:

select name from FACULTY where dept="ISDS".

However, when there is uncertainty with the data, we may not know the departments of different faculty members with certainty. We only have data that represents the probability distribution of department for each faculty member. We would resort to a PSQL query such as:

select name from FACULTY where dept="ISDS" [p > α].

An immediate question that arises is what value of α should the user specify in the above query formulation. In this section, we investigate this from a decision theoretic perspective. We argue that α depends on the value of the query as perceived by the user. Given a query, an object is either relevant to that query, or it is not. In the face of uncertainty, four different outcomes are possible:

1. A relevant object is retrieved: no error.
2. A non-relevant object is excluded: no error.
3. A relevant object is excluded: *Type-I* error.
4. A non-relevant object is retrieved: *Type-II* error.

Let us denote the costs of Type-I and Type-II errors as c_1 and c_2 respectively. If p is the probability that a given object is relevant, then the user should be interested in retrieving it if the expected cost of retrieving it is less than the expected cost of excluding it (Mendelson and Saharia, 1986). In other words: the object should be retrieved if $(1 - p)c_2 < pc_1$. This simplifies to the following retrieval criterion:

$$p > \frac{c_2}{c_1 + c_2} = \alpha.$$

Thus all the user needs to specify is the relative cost of Type-II error which depends on the context in which the query is asked.

6 Conclusions

Although relational databases enjoy a very wide-spread popularity in modern business information systems, they lack the power to model uncertainty in data items. In this paper, we discuss a probabilistic relational model which uses probability theory to express uncertainty about object properties. Our representation of relations abides by first normal form (1NF), and hence is easier to implement. We also present an extension of the structured query language (SQL) so that uncertain data can be manipulated in a fashion consistent with the axioms of probability theory. The extension to SQL requires a few additional operators, and conventional queries retain their usual syntax and meaning.

The explicit representation of uncertainty allows users to incorporate probability thresholds to selectively retrieve information using probabilistic queries. In situations where the user cannot directly provide the probability thresholds, he or she can use a decision theoretic framework for estimating it. Consider, for example, the situation where objects are to be retrieved from the database, but there is uncertainty associated with whether they satisfy the retrieval condition. If a relevant object (i.e., an object that satisfies the query condition in reality) is excluded, a Type-I error is committed. Similarly, a Type-II error is committed by including an irrelevant object. If the relative costs of these errors are known, they may be used to determine the probability threshold. Mendelson and Saharia (1986) show that the total cost of these errors is minimized when the probability threshold is the relative cost of the Type-II error.

Representing probabilistic information in terms of joint probability distributions of several attributes may require a large storage space. Normalizing probabilistic relations based on independence among attributes may reduce the storage requirement to some extent. We will examine how to address this issue by suitably defining a *probabilistic normal form.* Another related issue that will be investigated in the future is the cost-benefit trade-off associated with storing additional data. For, example Mendelson and Saharia (1986) analyze, for deterministic databases, how the cost of data collection and storage can be traded off against the benefits of storing additional amount of data. We will extend their framework for probabilistic databases.

There are several other directions for future research. Issues such as storage structure, access paths and query optimization need to be addressed for successful implementation of the model. We are currently examining these issues so that a prototype probabilistic database management system could be developed.

References

1. Barbará, D., Garcia-Molina, H. and Porter, D., "The Management of Probabilistic Data." *IEEE Transactions on Knowledge and Data Engineering*, 4(5), pp. 487-502, October 1992.
2. Cavallo, R. and Pittarelli, M., "The Theory of Probabilistic Databases." *Proceedings of the 13th VLDB Conference*, pp. 71-81, Brighton, 1987.
3. Dey, D. and Sarkar, S., "A Probabilistic Relational Model and Algebra." *ACM Transactions on Database Systems*, 21(3), pp. 339–369, 1996.
4. Klir, G.J. and Folger, T.A., *Fuzzy Sets, Uncertainty, and Information*, Prentice-Hall, 1988.
5. Mendelson, H. and Saharia, A.N., "Incomplete Information Costs and Database Design." *ACM Transactions on Database Systems*, 11(2), pp. 159–185, 1986.
6. Pearl, J., "Fusion, Propagation, and Structuring in Belief Networks." *Artificial Intelligence*, 29, pp. 241-288, 1986.

Conceptual Queries Using ConQuer–II

A. C. Bloesch[1] and T. A. Halpin[2]

[1]InfoModelers Inc.
110 110th Ave NE
Bellevue WA 98004, USA
email: anthonyb@infomodelers.com

[2]School of Information Technology
The University of Queensland
Australia 4072
email: halpin@it.uq.edu.au

Abstract: Formulating non-trivial queries in relational languages such as SQL and QBE can prove daunting to end users. ConQuer is a conceptual query language that allows users to formulate queries naturally in terms of elementary relationships, operators such as "and", "or", "not" and "maybe", contextual for-clauses and object-correlation, thus avoiding the need to deal explicitly with implementation details such as relational tables, null values, outer joins, group-by clauses and correlated subqueries. While most conceptual query languages are based on the Entity-Relationship approach, ConQuer is based on Object-Role Modeling (ORM), which exposes semantic domains as conceptual object types, allowing queries to be formulated via paths through the information space. As a result of experience with the first implementation of ConQuer, the language has been substantially revised and extended to become ConQuer–II, and a new tool, ActiveQuery, has been developed with an improved interface. ConQuer–II's new features such as arbitrary correlation and subtyping enable it to be used for a wide range of advanced conceptual queries.

1.   Introduction and Related Work

A conceptual schema expresses the structure of an application model using concepts familiar to end users, thus facilitating communication between modeler and subject matter experts during the modeling process. Once declared, a conceptual schema can be mapped in an automatic way to a variety of DBMS structures. Although CASE tools are often used for conceptual modeling and mapping, they are rarely used for querying the conceptual model directly. Instead, queries are typically formulated either at the external level using forms, or at the logical level using a language such as SQL, QBE or OQL based on the generic data model (e.g. relational or object-oriented) supported by the DBMS.

Form-based interfaces are limited to simple queries, which can rapidly become obsolete as the external interface evolves. For relational databases, SQL and QBE are more expressive; but non-trivial queries and even queries that are trivial to express in natural language (e.g. who does not speak more than one language?) can be difficult for non-technical users to express in these languages. Moreover, an SQL or QBE query often needs to be changed if the relevant part of the conceptual schema or internal schema is changed, even if the meaning of the query is unaltered. Finally, relational query optimizers ignore many semantic optimization opportunities arising from knowledge of conceptual constraints.

Logical query languages for post-relational DBMS's (e.g. object-oriented and object-relational) suffer the same problems but to a greater extent. For example, their additional structures (e.g. bags and lists) lead to greater complexity in both user formulation and system optimization. Although some proponents of object-oriented query languages such as OQL [4] describe them as conceptual, this is a mistaken viewpoint (e.g. consider their complex fact structures and dereferencing mechanisms). Languages for pre-relational systems are even lower-level, and hence are totally unsuitable for end users.

For such reasons, many *conceptual query languages* have been proposed to allow users to formulate queries directly on the conceptual schema itself. Several of these were surveyed in our earlier paper [2] and others are mentioned in [21], for example Super [1;22], Hybris[24], ERQL[17] and CBQL[16;20;25]. By and large, current conceptual query language tools based on ER or deductive models are challenging for naïve users, and their use of attributes exposes their queries to instability, since attributes may evolve into entities or relationships as the application model evolves.

This instability is avoided by using a query language based on Object-Role Modeling (ORM), a conceptual modeling approach that pictures the application world in terms of objects that play roles (individually or in relationships), thus avoiding the notion of attribute. ORM has a number of closely related versions (e.g. NIAM [26], FORM [9], NORM [7] and PSM [14]) and is similar to the Object-Relationship Modeling (also given the acronym "ORM") approach used in OSM (Object-oriented Systems Modeling) [8]. ORM facilitates detailed information modeling since it is linguistically based, is semantically rich and its notations are easily populated. An overview of ORM may be found in [10; 13], a detailed treatment in [9] and formal discussions in [11; 12].

The use of ORM for conceptual and relational database design is becoming more popular, partly because of the spread of ORM-based modeling tools, such as InfoModeler from InfoModelers Inc. However, as with ER, the use of ORM for conceptual queries is still in its infancy. The first significant ORM-based query language was RIDL [19], a hybrid language with both declarative and procedural aspects. Although RIDL is very powerful, its advanced features are not easy to master, and while the modeling component was implemented in the RIDL* tool, the query component was not supported. Another ORM query language is LISA-D [14], which is based on PSM and has recently been extended to Elisa-D [23] to include temporal and evolutionary support. LISA-D is very expressive but it is technically challenging for end users. Recently an approach based on query by navigation with a stratified hypermedia architecture was proposed to formulate ORM queries as LISA-D path expressions[15], but to date no LISA-D tool has actually been implemented. The basic concept of query by navigation is also exploited in our ActiveQuery tool, but its design is substantially different in other respects.

Like ORM, the OSM approach avoids the use of attributes as a base construct. A prototype has been developed for graphical query language OSM-QL [8] based on this approach. For any given query, the user selects the relevant part of the conceptual schema, and then annotates the resulting subschema diagram with the relevant restrictions to formulate the query. Negation is handled by adding a frequency constraint of "0", and disjunction is introduced by means of a subtype-union operator. Projection is accomplished by clicking on the relevant object nodes and then on a mark-for-output button. One of the strengths of OSM-QL is its support for quantified conditions. For example, to restrict employees to those that speak at least 3 and at most 5 languages, one simply adds the frequency constraint "3:5" to the Employee end of the relationship Employee speaks Language.

While our version of ORM includes similar frequency constraints in the modeling notation (e.g. "3-5"), ConQuer–II instead uses a count function which can be used to construct a frequency constraint. Once such a constraint has been defined in ConQuer–II, it can be called as a macro in later queries.

From our research of conceptual query tools, we believe OSM-QL to be closest in power and ease of use to our own. Based on the published details [8] of OSM-QL, it appears that ConQuer–II is more expressive and also easier for novice users. For example, it is unclear whether OSM-QL can support arbitrary projections (e.g. of functions such as count) or arbitrary correlations, and there does not appear to be the equivalent of our "maybe" operator (corresponding to conceptual left outer joins). We use "not" and "or" instead of 0 frequencies and subtype unions, and do not require the user to have any familiarity with the conceptual schema or our diagram notation. Another fundamental difference between the OSM-QL tool and our tool is that we map any ConQuer–II query into a sequence of one or more SQL queries for execution on the user's commercial DBMS (Informix, Oracle, MS Access, etc.). In contrast, the OSM-QL prototype implements the query only in terms of its own database language.

The name "ConQuer" derives from "CONceptual QUERy". The first version of ConQuer was commercially released in InfoAssistant, a Windows-based tool that has received positive industry reviews. Based on our own experience and user feedback, we redesigned the language and user interface for greater expressibility and usability. The new tool is called ActiveQuery, and should be available by late-1997 from InfoModelers as an OLE control for Windows applications. As well as complying with Microsoft's user interface standards, the tool provides an intuitive interface for constructing almost any query that might arise in an industrial database setting. Typical queries can be constructed by just clicking on objects with the mouse, and adding conditions.

The rest of this paper provides an overview of ConQuer–II as supported by ActiveQuery. Section 2 explains how the language is based on ORM, and illustrates how queries are formulated and mapped to SQL. Section 3 describes ConQuer–II's improvements to ConQuer. Section 4 discusses the query engine. Section 5 outlines the formal semantics. Finally section 6 summarizes the main contributions and outlines future research.

2. Formulating and Mapping Conceptual Queries

A discussion of the first version of ConQuer (ConQuer–I) and its associated tool may be found in [2]. At that stage, queries were allowed only on schemas that had been reverse engineered (see Fig 1). While the reverse engineering was automatic, the default names generated for schema components were based on the relational schema and were thus often unintuitive. Further, the domain information was based on foreign keys and thus was often incomplete. A separate tool (FactBuilder) allowed domain and predicate text to be improved, and domains to be merged.

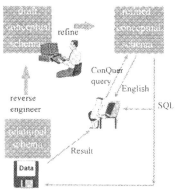

Fig 1. Existing databases may be reverse-engineered then queried.

The ConQuer–II query tool is completely new. Queries are now based on InfoModeler's meta-data, allowing InfoModeler based conceptual models to be directly queried. ConQuer–II queries are automatically translated into English (allowing users to validate the query) and automatically translated into back-end specific, SQL chain queries (for curious users, and to retrieve query results from the designated database).

2.1. The Underlying ORM Framework

We now briefly illustrate and motivate the ORM modeling framework on which ConQuer–II queries are based. Fig 2 is a simple ORM schema fragment. Object types are shown as named ellipses. Entity types have solid ellipses with their simple reference schemes abbreviated in parenthesis (these references are often unabbreviated in queries). For example, "Academic (empnr)" abbreviates "Academic is identified by EmpNr".

If an entity type has a compound reference scheme, this is shown explicitly using an external uniqueness constraint (a circled "P" denotes primary reference). For example, a degree is identified by combining its degreecode (e.g. "PhD") with the university that awarded it (e.g. UCLA). Value types have dotted ellipses (e.g. "Degreecode"), and a "+" indicates numeric reference.

Predicates are shown as named role sequences, where each role is depicted as a box. A role is just a part in a relationship. In the example, all the relationships are binary (two roles) except for the ternary (three role): Academic was awarded Degree in Year. Predicates may have any arity (number of roles) and may be written in mixfix form. A relationship type not used for primary reference is a fact type. An *n*-ary relationship type has *n*! readings, but only *n* are needed to guarantee access from any object type. Fig 2 shows forward and inverse readings (separated by "/") for some of the relationships.

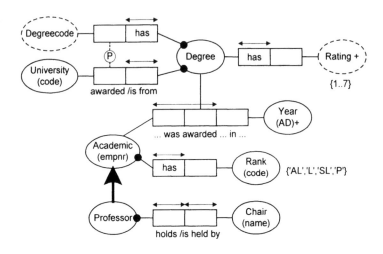

Fig 2. An ORM conceptual schema.

An arrow-tipped bar across a role sequence depicts an internal uniqueness constraint. For example, each academic has at most one rank, but the same rank may apply to more than one academic, and an academic may be awarded a given degree in at most one year. A black dot connecting a role to an object type indicates that the role is mandatory (i.e. each object in the database population of that object type must play that role). The possible values for a value type may be listed in braces beside the relevant type (e.g. Rank and Rating). Subtypes are connected to their supertype(s) by arrows, and given formal definitions (e.g. Professor). Subtype definitions themselves form one class of named ConQuer–II queries. ORM has many other kinds of constraint [9], but these are ignored in this paper since they are not germane to our discussion.

No use is made of attributes. This helps with natural verbalization, simplifies the framework, avoids arbitrary or temporary decisions about whether some feature should be modeled as an attribute, and lengthens the lifetime of conceptual queries since they are not impacted when a feature is remodeled as a relationship or attribute. This *semantic stability* of ORM models, and hence ORM queries, gives it a major advantage over ER, OO and lower level approaches. For examples illustrating this claim, see [2].

Since ORM conceptual object types are semantic domains, they act as semantic "glue" to connect the schema. This facilitates not only strong typing but also query navigation through the information space, enabling joins to be visualized in the most natural way. When desired, attributes (e.g. degree_awarded) can be introduced as derived concepts, based on roles in the underlying ORM schema. Various abstraction mechanisms can also be applied to support queries at a higher level [3].

2.2. Sample Queries and SQL Mapping

Although ConQuer–II queries are based on ORM, it is not necessary for the user to be familiar with ORM or its notation. The query is shown in textual (outline) form (basically as a tree of predicates connecting objects) with the underlying constraints hidden, since they have no impact on the meaning of the query. Moreover, the user can construct a query without any prior knowledge of the schema.

On opening a model for browsing, the user is presented with an object pick list. When an object type is dragged to the query pane, another pane displays the roles played by that object in the model. The user drags over those relationships of interest. Clicking an object type within one of these relationships causes its roles to be displayed, and the user may drag over those of interest, and so on. In this way, users may quickly declare a query path through the information space, without any prior knowledge of the underlying data structures. Users may also initially drag across several object types. The structure of the underlying model is then used to automatically infer a reasonable path through the information space.

Items to be displayed are indicated with a tick "✓": these ticks may be toggled on/off as desired. The query path may be restricted in various ways by use of operators and conditions. As a simple example, consider the query: *For those academics who were awarded a degree that has a rating above 5, list the academics and those degrees.* This may be set out as the following ConQuer outline:

Q1 ✓Academic
　　　└ was awarded ✓Degree in Year
　　　　　└ has Rating > 5

In terms of the ORM schema in Fig 2, this query is a path from Academic through Degree to Rating, extended by a path through the system predicate ">" to the object 5, and then a projection is made on Academic and Degree, which are dereferenced to their identifiers for display of the result. Moving through an object type (e.g. Degree) corresponds to a conceptual join. Since Degree has a composite identification scheme this maps to a composite join in SQL.

Degree (degreecode, university, rating)

Awarded (empnr, degreecode, university, awardyear)
　　　　　↓
Academic (empnr, rank, [chair][1])
　　1 **exists iff** rank = 'P'

Fig 3. The relational schema mapped from the ORM conceptual schema in Fig 2.

Using the Rmap algorithm [9; 18], our conceptual schema maps to the relational schema shown in Fig 3 (for simplicity, domains and value constraints are omitted). Keys and uniqueness constraints are indicated by underlining. Optional columns are shown in square brackets. A subset constraint (e.g. foreign key constraint) is shown as a dotted arrow. By default, Rmap absorbs functional relationships of subtypes into their supertype table. Here the numbered qualification on chair enforces the subtype definition and the relevant mandatory role constraint.

The SQL generated for query Q1 is shown below. Notice how the conceptual query shields the user from details about Degree's composite reference scheme. Here the relational join is a result of the same degree playing two roles which map to separate tables, with no foreign key connection. In contrast to our semantic domain approach, some query tools require foreign keys to perform a join, and even force the user to specify what kind of join (e.g. inner or outer) is associated with a foreign key connection: the limitations of such an approach are obvious.

```
S1      select X1.empnr, X1.degreecode, X1.university
        from Awarded X1, Degree X2
        where X1.degreecode = X2.degreecode and
            X1.university = X2.university and
            X2.rating > 5
```

Basic queries, mappings and semantic optimization for ConQuer were discussed in [2]. We now illustrate some of the new features introduced in ConQuer–II. Connections from a subtype to a supertype appear as an "is" predicate, which may be navigated like any other predicate. For example, the following query asks for those academics who were not awarded any degree from the University of Queensland (UQ) but are professors who hold the informatics chair. The verbalization generated for the query provides a more natural reading. For example, "and" is inserted for conjunctions, the "not" operator is moved after "was", and pronouns and articles are added.

```
Q2      ✓Academic
            ⊢ is Professor
            |           ⊔ holds Chair = Informatics
            ⊔ not was awarded Degree in Year
                        ⊔ is from University = UQ
```

Based on the default relational schema in Fig 1, the following SQL code is generated:

```
S2      select X1.empnr
        from Academic X1
        where X1.chair = 'Informatics' and
            X1.empnr not in (select X2.empnr from Awarded X2
                        where X2.university = 'UQ')
```

If the mapping of the actual model is modified to store the chair fact type in a separate table for professor, the conceptual query remains unaltered although the SQL generated is now different (in the first from-clause of S2, Academic is replaced by Professor)—another example of semantic stability.

ConQuer used a "maybe" operator to perform conceptual left outer joins but ignored any conditions after the operator. ConQuer–II extends the semantics of "maybe" to evaluate such conditions. For example, the following query lists each academic as well as their degrees (if any) that are worth more than a 5 rating.

Q3   ✓Academic
            └─ **maybe** was awarded ✓Degree in Year
                        └─ has Rating > 5

In SQL-92 this can be translated as a single SQL query as follows:

S3   select X1.empnr, X2.degreecode, X2.university
        from Academic X1 left outer join (
                select * from Awarded X2, Degree X3
                where X2.degreecode = X3.degreecode and
                X2.university = X3.university and
                X3.rating > 5)
            on X1.empnr = X2.empnr

Unfortunately, target DBMS's are rarely orthogonal in their support for joins, so in practice this query is translated as a sequence of SQL queries, where the inner join is first computed and the intermediate result is used as the right-hand argument of the outer join in the final query.

The next two examples are based on a different schema concerning employees. ConQuer included basic support for functions and grouped queries, but had complex rules for disambiguation, and required conditions to be added in separate windows. ConQuer–II now has much greater support for such queries, provides for-clauses to disambiguate the grouping criteria, and enables full queries, including all conditions, to be entered on the one query pane. For example, query Q4 lists each department and those of its employees whose maximum individual rating exceeds the average of his/her department (each employee may have many ratings). Notice how the different grouping criteria are captured in the for-clauses. We leave it as an exercise for the interested reader to provide the SQL.

Q4   ✓Department
            └─ employs ✓Employee
                        └─ achieves Rating
                                    └─ **max**(Rating) **for** Employee >
                                    avg(Rating) **for** Department

The most significant enhancement to ConQuer–II is its ability to deal with *correlations* of arbitrary complexity. For example, consider the query: *Who owns a car, and does not drive more than one of those cars (that he/she owns)?*. In English, correlation is often achieved through pronouns. Here there is a correlation on cars ("those") as well as employees ("he/she"). This query may be formulated as Q5. When an object type is referenced more than once in the query body, the system automatically provides subscripts that the user can modify. Object variables with identical subscripts are correlated. This is used here to correlate cars (Car_1). The for-clause has only one instance of Employee in the query body to reference, so no subscripts are needed to perform the correlation for employees.

Q5   ✓Employee
            ├─ owns Car_1
            └─ **not** drives Car_1
                        └─ **count**(Car_1) **for** Employee > 1

Equivalent SQL is shown below. Because the correlation stems from a function argument inside a negated function subquery, the correlation concerns membership in a set, not just equality with an outer instance (see italicized code).

```
S5          select X1.empnr
            from Owns X1
            where X1.empnr not in (
                select X2.empnr
                from Drives X2
                where X2.car in (select X3.car from Owns X3
                                 where X3.empnr = X1.empnr)
            group by X2.empnr
            having count(X2.car) > 1)
```

ConQuer–II is capable of far more complex queries than cited here. In this paper we are more concerned with a clear exposition of our basic approach and its rationale rather than with providing a complete coverage of the language. The next two sections provide an overview of the query engine and formal semantics.

3.   Improvements in Conquer–II

The design of ConQuer–II focused not only on the weaknesses of ConQuer but also the weakness in the design process that caused them. The most important design decision was to keep ConQuer–II semantics as simple and as standard as possible. To reduce the chance of error and speed development of the SQL generator, it was decided to use compiler techniques as much as possible since they embody a wealth of experience in a similar domain.

The new design sought a semantically clear and well founded core language. Sorted finitary first-order logic with schema comprehension proved ideal. Basing the SQL generation on an unambiguous orthogonal core language greatly simplified the generator's design. ConQuer–II's query representations like outline queries are supported by translating them into the core language before further processing. Once again, the clear semantics of ConQuer–II greatly simplified the task.

Because the query language is based around a well understood logic, there is a well developed literature to draw upon. For example, languages like ConQuer–II have a well developed theory of the power of various constructs, making it clear which constructs are needed to improve expressive power. Further, semantic optimization algorithms are readily available for ConQuer–II like languages.

ConQuer–II's outline queries reflect the constructs available in the core language. For users of outline queries, the major ConQuer–II extensions are support for arbitrary variable correlations, quantifiers, arbitrary grouping criteria, reuse of queries (macros) and the removal of many artificial restrictions on queries.

In ORM terms, ConQuer–II queries define derived predicates. Thus existing queries may be reused as if they were predicates in the conceptual model. The user interface of ActiveQuery does not distinguish between these derived predicates and the conceptual model's predicates. This presents users with a uniform interface where they may reuse queries to form more powerful queries.

Our experience with constructing queries using InfoAssistant highlighted several weaknesses with the old user interface. Consequently, ActiveQuery's user interface was redesigned. All query information is now displayed with the query rather than hidden in property sheets, arbitrary expressions may now be used in queries, and support has been added for handling large schemas (e.g. conceptual paths may be inferred from their endpoints).

4. The ConQuer–II Query Engine

ConQuer–II is based on the domain relational calculus or, equivalently, sorted finitary first-order logic with schema comprehension. ConQuer–II extends the logic with various constructs to make queries easier to express. For example, ConQuer–II has a modal-like operator *maybe* that corresponds to a conceptual left outer join, and also has summary functions like maximum.

These extensions undermine the first-order basis of ConQuer–II and make it referentially opaque (i.e. the value of an expression cannot be derived solely from the value of its immediate parts). However, there is a straightforward translation of ConQuer–II queries into a first-order language. Thus, ultimately, these extensions are just a matter of convenience rather than a fundamental change in the power or basis of the language. Internally ConQuer–II queries are expanded to the base logic before any processing is done.

ConQuer–II queries consist of a sequence of named set comprehensions and operations (*subqueries*). Each subquery may refer to earlier subqueries with the final subquery returning the result set of the overall query.

Tools that use the ConQuer–II query engine translate between their external representation and ConQuer–II. For example, ActiveQuery translates between an English-like linearized version of ConQuer–II and ConQuer–II. QBE-like, English text, form based, and direct interfaces are all planned as future interfaces to the ConQuer–II query engine.

There is little research experience in implementing query engines like ConQuer–II's. However, the implementation of translators for programming languages is well understood. Since the task of translating ConQuer–II queries into SQL is similar to programming language translation, it was felt prudent to base the ConQuer–II query engine on programming language translators.

Internally, ConQuer–II queries are represented as abstract syntax trees. Attributes may be associated with nodes, and mechanisms exist for computing synthesized and inherited attributes as well as transforming nodes. Most of the SQL translation is done through visitor classes which calculate attributes and perform tree transformations. In order to simplify SQL translation, ConQuer–II queries are first translated into an abstract SQL dialect and then transformed into the backend-specific SQL. Currently, Informix (Online, SE and Universal), Oracle, DB2, MS SQL Server, Sybase SQL Server, MS Access, FoxPro, Paradox, d-Base, SQL Anywhere and generic ODBC databases are supported. This approach mimics the intermediate languages often used in multi-platform compilers.

The ConQuer–II query engine is written in C++ and consists of about 25 000 lines of code, 15 000 lines of comments, 12 000 blank lines and 210 classes. Further, the ConQuer–II query engine shares some 83 000 lines of code with InfoModeler. ActiveQuery adds some 35 000 lines of, essentially GUI, code based on Microsoft's MFC library.

5.   A Semantics for ConQuer–II

ConQuer–II is a sugared version of sorted finitary first-order logic with set comprehension (Q). In this section, a semantics, based on bag comprehension, is given for ConQuer–II's extensions to Q. The treatment is necessarily brief, but it should be clear how the semantics could be completely formalized. Note that conceptual nulls can never occur, so there is no need to use Lukasiewicz's (or any other) three valued logic.

A ConQuer–II query may be interpreted as specifying the contents of a set, via set comprehension. For example, the query: *Which cars are red?* would correspond to the expression:

$$\{x : \text{Car} \mid \exists\, y : \text{Color}; z : \text{ColorName} \,(\, x \text{ has } y \wedge y \text{ has colorname } z \wedge z = \text{'red'} \,)\}$$

In general, a ConQuer–II query corresponds to the straightforward translation of the query into Q with the ticked object types quantified over by the set comprehension operator and the non-ticked object types by an existential quantifier (unless already bound by a quantifier).

Care must be taken in interpreting the "maybe" operator. Expressions of the form "maybe α", where α is some path expression, should be translated as:

$$\alpha' \vee (\neg\, \alpha \wedge x_1 = \square \wedge x_2 = \square \wedge \dots \wedge x_n = \square)$$

where α' is the translation of α; $x_1, x_2, \dots, x_n$ are the selected object types in α; and $\square$ is a blank in the result set (relationally a null).

A semantics for the summary (bag or aggregate) functions of ConQuer–II can be given as follows. For a given aggregate expression $\mathcal{F}(\alpha_1, \dots, \alpha_n; \gamma_1, \dots, \gamma_m)$ (where $\alpha_1, \dots, \alpha_n$ are arguments and $\gamma_1, \dots, \gamma_m$ are grouping criteria) construct a labeled bag $\mathcal{S}$ corresponding to the ConQuer–II query where all expressions involving summary functions have been elided and the bag's tuples consist of the object types in the function's grouping criteria $(\gamma_1, \dots, \gamma_m)$ and the arguments to the function $(\alpha_1, \dots, \alpha_n)$.

For example, consider the query: *What are the branches and total salary costs of branches with a total salary cost of more than $1 000 000?*, which may be expressed in outline form as:

✓ Branch
   └ employs Employee
        └ earns ✓ **total**(Salary) for Branch > 1 000 000

The corresponding labeled bag is:

$$\textbf{let } S = [\![x : \text{Branch}, y : \$value \bullet z : \text{Employee}, w : \text{Salary} \mid$$

$$x \text{ employs } z \wedge z \text{ earns } w \wedge w \text{ has } \$value \, y]\!].$$

Where the notation $[\![x_1{:}\tau_1, \ldots, x_n{:}\tau_n \bullet x_{n+1}{:}\tau_{n+1}, \ldots, x_m{:}\tau_m \mid \rho]\!]$ means the bag formed by discarding $x_{n+1}, \ldots, x_m$ from the tuples in the set $\{x_1{:}\tau_1, \ldots, x_m{:}\tau_m \mid \rho\}$ (i.e. projecting on $x_1, \ldots, x_n$). The query is thus equivalent to:

$$\{x : \text{Branch}, u : \Re \mid \langle x \rangle \in S_1 \wedge u = (\Sigma_{\langle x', y \rangle \in S} \, y \mid x = x') \wedge u > 1\,000\,000\}$$

where $\Re$ is the set of reals; $S_{i, j, \ldots, k}$ is a set of tuples made up of the i'th, j'th, ..., k'th entries in each tuple of the bag S; and $(\Sigma_{\langle x, y, \ldots, z \rangle \in S} \, \alpha \mid \rho)$ is, for each $\langle x, y, \ldots, z \rangle$ in of the bag S, the sum of every α such that ρ holds.

In general, for a given grouping criterion each object type in the criterion and the arguments of the corresponding aggregate functions are quantified over by the bag comprehension, a conjunct links selected object types to the corresponding elements of S, a series of conjuncts specifies the value of each aggregate function and a series of conjuncts corresponds to any conditions involving aggregate functions.

6.   Future Plans

This paper has discussed ConQuer–II, an ORM-based conceptual query language that enables end users to formulate queries in a natural way, without knowledge of how the information is stored in the underlying database. The benefits of this approach were highlighted and a semi-formal semantics provided.

The main extension planned for the ConQuer–II query engine is recursive completeness. First-order languages like ConQuer–II lack the expressive power of recursive languages. The most probable extension is some kind of fixed-point operator. Clearly, the ConQuer–II query engine could no longer target just SQL dialects and would need to target stored procedure languages.

The ConQuer–II query engine is designed to support object-relational extensions to RDBMS's. In the future, support for these extensions will become part of ConQuer–II. However, support for collection types represents a significant challenge since some queries, involving columns containing collection types, expressible in ConQuer–II require very complex procedural code to be generated. By contrast, row types, and user defined objects and functions can be easily supported.

ORM has a rich constraint language. The ConQuer–II query engine makes use of these constraints to produce more efficient SQL than would otherwise be possible. Much more powerful semantic optimizations are planned for the future. Because of ConQuer–II's first-order basis and clean semantics it will be possible to make use of the very efficient and powerful techniques that have been developed by the automated theorem proving community.

ConQuer–II seems ideal for expressing *ad hoc* constraints in an ORM model. Extensions to InfoModeler (InfoModelers Inc.'s conceptual modeling tool) are planned that would allow *ad hoc* constraints and derivation rules to be constructed with ActiveQuery. ConQuer–II's backend independence and semantic stability mean that such constraints and derivation rules can be expected to retain their meaning under schema transformations and across a variety of backends.

InfoModeler allows users to mix IDEF1X (an ER dialect) models with ORM models. IDEF1X models are internally represented as ORM models but displayed as IDEF1X models. A future release of InfoModeler will allow users to annotate IDEF1X models with the missing predicate text. Thus ActiveQuery will support both ER, ORM and mixed ER/ORM based conceptual queries. Such queries are already possible, but IDEF1X users must be content with the default predicate text.

References

1. Auddino, A., Amiel, E. & Bhargava, B. 1991 'Experiences with SUPER, a Database Visual Environment', *DEXA'91 Database and Expert System Applications*, pp.172-178.

2. Bloesch. A.C. & Halpin, T.A. 1996, 'ConQuer: a conceptual query language', *Conceptual Modeling – ER'96*, Springer LNCS, no. 1157, pp. 121–33.

3. Campbell, L.J, Halpin, T.A. & Proper, H.A. 1996, 'Conceptual schemas with abstractions: making flat conceptual schemas more comprehensible', *Data and Knowledge Engineering*, vol. 20, Elsevier Science, pp. 39-85.

4. Cattell, R.G.G. (ed.) 1994, *The Object Database Standard: ODMG–93*, Morgan Kaufmann Publishers, San Francisco.

5. Date, C.J. 1996, 'Aggregate functions', *Database Prog. & Design*, vol. 9, no. 4, Miller Freeman, San Mateo CA, pp. 17-19.

6. Date, C.J. & Darwen, H. 1992, *Relational Database: writings 1989-1991*, Addison-Wesley, Reading MA, esp. Chs 17-20.

7. De Troyer, O. & Meersman, R. 1995, 'A logic framework for a semantics of object oriented data modeling', *OOER'95: Object-Oriented and Entity-Relationship Modeling*, Springer LNCS, no. 1021, pp. 238-49.

8. Embley, D.W., Wu, H.A., Pinkston, J.S. & Czejdo, B. 1996, 'OSM-QL: a calculus-based graphical query language', Tech. Report, Dept of Comp. Science, Brigham Young Univ., Utah.

9. Halpin, T.A. 1995, *Conceptual Schema and Relational Database Design, 2nd edn*, Prentice-Hall Australia, Sydney.

10. Halpin, T.A. & Orlowska, M.E. 1992, 'Fact-oriented modelling for data analysis', *Journal of Inform. Systems*, vol. 2, no. 2, pp. 1-23, Blackwell Scientific, Oxford

11. Halpin, T.A. & Proper, H.A. 1995, 'Subtyping and polymorphism in Object-Role Modeling', *Data and Knowledge Engineering*, vol. 15, Elsevier Science, pp. 251-81.

12. Halpin, T.A. & Proper, H. A. 1995, 'Database schema transformation and optimization', *OOER'95: Object-Oriented and Entity-Relationship Modeling*, Springer LNCS, no. 1021, pp. 191-203.

13. Halpin, T.A. 1996, 'Business Rules and Object-Role Modeling', *Database Prog. & Design*, vol. 9, no. 10, Miller Freeman, San Mateo CA, pp. 66-72.
14. Hofstede, A.H.M. ter, Proper, H.A. & Weide, th.P. van der 1993, 'Formal definition of a conceptual language for the description and manipulation of information models', *Information Systems*, vol. 18, no. 7, pp. 489-523.
15. Hofstede, A.H.M. ter, Proper, H.A. & Weide, th.P. van der 1996, 'Query formulation as an information retrieval problem', *The Computer Journal*, vol. 39, no. 4, pp. 255-74.
16. Jarke, M., Gallersdörfer, R., Jeusfeld, M.A., Staudt, M., Eherer, S., 1995, *ConceptBase—a Deductive Object Base for Meta Data Management*, Journal of Intelligent Information Systems, Special Issue on Advances in Deductive Object-Oriented Databases, vol. 4, no. 2, 167-192.
17. Lawley, M. & Topor R. 1994, 'A Query Language for EER Schemas', *ADC'94 Proceedings of the 5th Australian Database Conference*, Global Publications Service, pp. 292-304.
18. McCormack, J.I., Halpin, T.A. & Ritson, P.R. 1993, 'Automated mapping of conceptual schemas to relational schemas', *Advanced Inf. Sys. Eng: CAiSE'93*, Springer LNCS, no. 685, pp. 432-48.
19. Meersman, R. 1982, 'The RIDL conceptual language', Research report, Int. Centre for Information Analysis Services, Control Data Belgium, Brussels.
20. Mylopoulos, J., Borgida, A., Jarke, M. & Koubarakis, M., 1990, *Telos: a language for representing knowledge about information systems*, ACM Transactions Information Systems vol. 8, no 4.
21. Ozsoyoglu, G. & Wang, H. 1993, 'Example-based graphical database query languages', *Computer*, vol. 26, no. 5, pp. 25-38.
22. Parent, C. & Spaccapietra, S. 1989, 'About Complex Entities, Complex Objects and Object-Oriented Data Models', *Information System Concepts—An In-depth Analysis*, Falkenberg, E.D. & Lindgreen, P., Eds., North Holland, pp. 347-360
23. Proper, H.A. & Weide, Th. P. van der 1995, 'Information disclosure in evolving information systems: taking a shot at a moving target', *Data and Knowledge Engineering*, vol. 15, no. 2, pp. 135-68, Elsevier Science.
24. Rosengren, P. 1994, 'Using Visual ER Query Systems in Real World Applications', *CAiSE'94: Advanced Information Systems Engineering*, Springer LNCS, no. 811, pp. 394-405.
25. Staudt, M., Nissen, H.W., Jeusfeld, M.A. 1994, *Query by Class, Rule and Concept*. Applied Intelligence, Special Issue on Knowledge Base Management, vol. 4, no. 2, pp. 133-157
26. Wintraecken, J.J.V.R. 1990, *The NIAM Information Analysis Method: Theory and Practice*, Kluwer, Deventer, The Netherlands.

Transaction-Based Specification of Database Evolution

Lars Bækgaard

Department of Information Science, the Aarhus School of Business
Fuglesangs Allè 4, DK-8210 Aarhus V, Denmark
Email: lb@hha.dk

Abstract: We present a two-layer language for the specification of database evolution in terms of transaction-based, dynamic integrity constraints. The first language layer is based on first-order logic and it is used to express dynamic constraints in terms of queries on the transaction history of a database. The second layer uses a customizable combination of text and graphics and its semantics are defined in terms of the first-order language. Our language is orthogonal to state-based constraint languages and it can be used as a supplement to these. Also, our language can be used in combination with all object-based or entity-based data models. We use examples to illustrate the use of the specification language.

Key Terms: Database evolution, database integrity, dynamic constraint specifications, transaction-based constraint specifications.

1. Introduction

In this paper we present a language for the specification of the evolution of operational databases. Typically, operational databases are characterized by a high volume of update transactions each modifying a few database objects. Potentially, each update transaction is capable of violating database integrity. In order to maintain database integrity it is necessary to specify and enforce a set of integrity constraints (Formica and Missikoff 1992), (Hall and Gupta 1991), (Martin, Abida et al. 1992), (Motro 1989), (Mück and Vinek 1989), (Ngu 1990), (Simon and Valduriez 1984), (Stonebraker 1975).

Traditionally, integrity constraints have been specified in terms of database states. Some approaches support the specification of integrity constraints in terms of one database state (Brodie 1980) whereas other approaches support the specification of constraints in terms of relationships between two or more database states (Castilho, Casanova et al. 1982), (Cervasato and Eick 1992), (Chomicki 1992), (Kung 1985), (Lipeck 1986), (Lipeck and Saake 1987) (Vianu 1988)], (Wieringa, Meyer et al. 1989).

The transaction-based specification of object life cycles in terms of transaction histories is supported by systems development methods like JSD (Jackson 1983). In such approaches regular expressions are used to define legal transaction sequences (Bækgaard 1993), (Kappel and Schrefl 1991), (Rosenquist 1982). Transaction-based approaches are characterized by a much more loose coupling between constraint specifications and database schemes than are state-based specification languages.

However, we argue that regular languages are inappropriate as general specification languages.

Our specification approach is transaction-based and it supports the specification of regular expressions over transaction names as a special case. We use a two-layer, customizable language. The first layer is textual and based on first-order logic that is used to formulate constraints in terms of queries on transaction histories. The second layer uses customizable graphical symbols and its semantics are defined in terms of first-order queries on transaction histories.

Our specification approach is flexible in a number of ways. *First*, our specification language is independent of the structure of database objects. It can be used to supplement object-based models (Kim and Lochocsky 1989), (Kim 1995) and entity-based data models (Hammer and McLeod 1981), (Shipman 1981). It can even be used to supplement record-based models like the relational model (Codd 1970) if certain attributes are used as immutable surrogates (Khoshafian and Copeland 1986). *Second*, our language is independent of the specification of transaction bodies (Brodie and Ridjanovic 1984), (Gray 1981), (Leonard and Luong 1981), (Ngu 1984), (Qian 1988). *Third*, our specification approach supports the definition of customized graphical specification symbols. Consequently, the specification language can be tailored to specific specification needs.

The paper is organized as follows. In Section 2 we illustrate the limitations of regular expressions and we motivate the need for a more powerful specification approach. In Section 3 we present a data model that supports the specification of transaction preconditions in terms of queries on transaction histories. In Section 4 we define the syntax and semantics of a customizable graphical specification language. In Section 5 we illustrate the use of our specification language by means of examples. In Section 6 we conclude the paper and suggest directions for future research.

2. Motivation

Systems development methods like JSD (Jackson 1983) supports the specification of transaction-based, dynamic constraints in terms of regular expressions over transaction names.

In Figure 1 we have specified the dynamics of library borrowers as a graph that is equivalent to a regular expression over the transaction names Join, Borrow, Return, and Quit. Figure 1 is interpreted in the following way. The sequence of transactions in which a particular Borrower object participates must define a path in the specified graph. The first transaction must be Join and the last transaction must be Quit. In-between Join and Quit a particular Borrower object can participate in any sequence of Borrow and Return transactions. The fact that Join and Quit are underlined means that a specific Borrower object can participate in at most Join transaction and at most one Quit transaction.

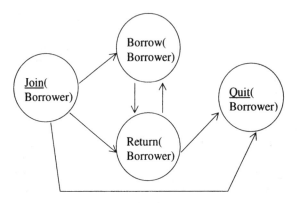

Figure 1 Library borrower as regular expression.

In Figure 2 we have used our specification approach to define the dynamics of library borrowers. In addition to the four transaction types in Figure 1 we have added a Reserve transaction.

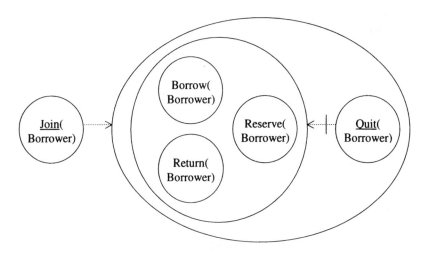

Figure 2 Library borrower.

Figure 2 is interpreted as follows. The transaction Quit is admissible for a particular Borrower object, o, if o has participated in a Join transaction in the past. The transactions Borrow, Return, and Reserve are admissible for a particular Borrower object, o, if o has participated in a Join transaction in the past and if o has not participated in a Quit transaction in the past.

A comparison of Figure 1 and Figure 2 indicates the fact that regular expressions are inappropriate in situations where the transactions are relatively independent. In such situations the regular expression approach forces the designer to specify transaction independence in terms of a possible huge set of explicit paths. This will become evident if the Reserve transaction as added to the specification in Figure 1.

In Section 3-4 we present a specification language that facilitates specifications like the one in Figure 2. Our language facilitates the specification of regular expressions over sets of transaction names as a special case.

3. Queries on Transaction Histories

In this section we present a first-order logic language that can be used to formulate transaction preconditions in terms of queries on transaction histories. We use such preconditions to constrain the sequencing of the transactions that create, modify, and destroy objects. In Section 4 we use the first-order logic language to specify the semantics of graphical symbols like the ones used in Section 2.

3.1 States and Transactions

We model database evolution as a state/transaction sequence where transitions between successive database states are caused by atomic update transactions. This is illustrated in Figure 3 where each s_i represents an explicit database state and each t_j represents an update transaction causing a transition from state s_{j-1} to state s_j. The state s_0 is an empty, initial state.

Figure 3 Database evolution.

A database state is a collection of object classes. An object class is a named set of objects. An object is composed of an immutable, globally unique object identifier and a body. The expression o.OID denotes the object identifier of the object o. The symbol $Borrower_{id}$ denotes the set of object identifiers for objects in the object class named Borrower.

Our specification language is independent of the specification of object bodies. If the underlying data model is a semantic data model like SDM (Hammer and McLeod 1981) or a structural object-oriented model like Telos (Mylopoulos 1992) the object body contains a set of state attributes. If the underlying data model is a behavioral object-oriented data model (Kim 1995) the object body contains the possible object behavior specified as a set of services in addition to the state attributes. Each object is a member of one or more classes. Objects can join and quit object classes dynamically.

We use our specification language to formulate dynamic constraints in terms of queries on the transaction histories of database objects. A database transaction is an execution of a transaction definition. Each transaction definition is composed of a type and a body. Our specification language is independent of the specification of transaction bodies (Brodie and Ridjanovic 1984), (Gray 1981), (Leonard and Luong 1981), (Ngu 1984), (Qian 1988). The type of a transaction is composed of a name and a set of formal parameters. The parameters define the possible transaction participants. For example, the expression Borrow (x: $Borrower_{id}$, y: $Book_{id}$) defines the type of a borrow transaction in a library database.

3.2 Transaction Histories

We use queries on transaction histories to facilitate the specification of transaction preconditions. Each object has a transaction history that can be described in terms of the sequence of transactions that has affected the object. We describe the transaction history as a set with the following structure.

HIST: {TRANS}
TRANS: (TNAME, TIME, OBJECTS)
OBJECTS: {(OID, ONAME)}

Each element in HIST represents a historical transaction occurrence. For such an element, *trans*, the expressions *trans*.TNAME, *trans*.TIME, and *trans*.OBJECTS denote the name of the transaction type, the commit time, and the set of identifiers (*trans*.OBJECTS.OID) and class names (*trans*.OBJECTS.ONAME) for the participating objects, respectively. We assume that time stamps are unique.

HIST is updated whenever a transaction commits. For example, when the transaction Borrow (oid_{13}, oid_{22}) commits at time 070797.1154 the following element is added to HIST.

("Borrow", 070797.1154, {(oid_{13}, "Borrower"), (oid_{22}, "Book")})

3.3 Preconditions

We define preconditions as functions with the following type.

Oid $\rightarrow$ Boolean

Precondition functions have this type because we use them to control the evolution of individual objects. All free variables in the definition of such a function must refer to Oid or to an element in HIST.

We use the following notation to specify a precondition for a specific transaction type/object class pair. The symbols *tname*, *oname*, and *p* denotes a transaction type name, an object class name, and a precondition function, respectively.

PRE *(tname, oname)* = *p*

Such a specification is interpreted in the following way. $p(o.\text{OID})$ must evaluate to true in order for an object, *o*, from the object class named *oname* to participate in a transaction of the type named *tname*.

When a transaction is submitted for execution the specified preconditions for all participating objects are evaluated. The transaction is admitted if and only if all these preconditions evaluate to true.

In order to facilitate the definition of precondition functions we define function generators with the following type. The domain Value denotes one of the domains Boolean, Integer, Real, or String.

Parameters → (Oid → Value)

All free variables in the definition of a function generator must refer to Parameters, to Oid, or to an element in HIST.

3.4 Sample Function Generators

The following examples illustrate the definition of function generators. The symbols *oname*, *tname*, *oid*, and *trans* denote an object class name, a transaction type name, an object identifier, and a transaction history element, respectively.

The function generator COUNT has the following type and definition.

COUNT: (String, String) → (Oid → Integer)

COUNT[*tname, oname*](*oid*) =
    CARDINALITY{*trans*∈ HIST | (*oid, oname*)∈ *trans*.OBJECTS ∧
    trans.TNAME=*tname*)}

For example, COUNT["Borrow", "Borrower"] is a function that returns the number of times a specific object has participated in a Borrow transaction as a Borrower object. COUNT["Borrow", "Borrower"] has the following type and definition.

COUNT["Borrow", "Borrower"]: Oid → Integer

COUNT["Borrow", "Borrower"](*oid*) =
    CARDINALITY{*trans*∈ HIST | (*oid*, "Borrower")∈ *trans*.OBJECTS ∧
    trans.TNAME="Borrow")}

The function generator LAST has the following type and definition.

LAST: (String, String) → (Oid → Boolean)

LAST[*tname₁, oname₁*] (*oid*) =
    {*trans₁*∈ HIST | (*oid, oname₁*)∈ *trans₁*.OBJECTS ∧
    trans₁.TNAME= *tname₁* ∧ *trans*.TIME =
    MAXIMUM{*time* | ∃ *trans₂*∈ HIST, *oname₂*: *time=trans*.TIME ∧
    (*oid, oname₂*)∈ *trans₂*.OBJECTS}}≠∅

For example, LAST["Return", "Book"] is a function that returns true if and only if the most recent transaction in which a specific object, *o*, has participated is a Return transaction and if *o* has participated as a Book object. LAST["Return", "Book"] has the following type and definition.

LAST["Return", "Book"]: Oid → Boolean

LAST["Return", "Book"](*oid*) =
    {*trans₁*∈ HIST | (*oid*, "Book")∈ *trans₁*.OBJECTS ∧
    trans₁.TNAME="Return" ∧ *trans*.TIME =
    MAXIMUM{*time* | ∃ *trans₂*∈ HIST, *oname₂*: *time=trans*.TIME ∧
    (*oid, oname₂*)∈ *trans₂*.OBJECTS}}≠∅

The function generator EXISTS has the following type and definition.

EXISTS: ((String, String) → (Oid → Boolean))

EXISTS[*tname, oname*](*oid*) =
    {*trans*∈ HIST | (*oid, oname*)∈ *trans*.OBJECTS ∧
    trans.TNAME=*tname* }≠∅

For example, EXISTS["Borrow", "Book"] is a function that returns true if and only if a specific object has participated in a Borrow transaction as a Book object in the past. EXISTS["Borrow", "Book"] has the following type and definition.

EXISTS["Borrow", "Book"]: Oid → Boolean

EXISTS["Borrow", "Book"](*oid*) =
    {*trans*∈ HIST | (*oid*, "Book")∈ *trans*.OBJECTS ∧
    trans.TNAME="Borrow"}≠∅

3.5 Aggregation of Function Generators

We use the rules in Table 1 to aggregate precondition functions.

Input expression	Aggregated expression
$(Oid \rightarrow Boolean_1) \wedge (Oid \rightarrow Boolean_2)$	$Oid \rightarrow (Boolean_1 \wedge Boolean_2)$
$(Oid \rightarrow Boolean_1) \vee (Oid \rightarrow Boolean_2)$	$Oid \rightarrow (Boolean_1 \vee Boolean_2)$
$\neg(Oid \rightarrow Boolean)$	$Oid \rightarrow \neg(Boolean)$
$(Oid \rightarrow Nummber_1) + (Oid \rightarrow Number_2)$	$Oid \rightarrow (Number_1 + Number_2)$
$(Oid \rightarrow Number_1) - (Oid \rightarrow Number_2)$	$Oid \rightarrow (Number_1 - Number_2)$
$(Oid \rightarrow Number_1) * (Oid \rightarrow Number_2)$	$Oid \rightarrow (Number_1 * Number_2)$
$(Oid \rightarrow Number_1) / (Oid \rightarrow Number_2)$	$Oid \rightarrow (Number_1 / Number_2)$
$-(Oid \rightarrow Number)$	$Oid \rightarrow -(Number)$
$(Oid \rightarrow Value_1) > (Oid \rightarrow Value_2)$	$Oid \rightarrow (Value_1 > Value_2)$
$(Oid \rightarrow Value_1) < (Oid \rightarrow Value_2)$	$Oid \rightarrow (Value_1 < Value_2)$
$(Oid \rightarrow Value_1) = (Oid \rightarrow Value_2)$	$Oid \rightarrow (Value_1 = Value_2)$

Table 1 Aggregation of precondition functions.

The following example illustrates the use of Table 1.

EXISTS["Buy", "Book"] $\wedge$ LAST["Return", "Book"]$(oid) =$
    $(\{trans \in HIST \mid (oid, "Book") \in trans.OBJECTS \wedge$
    $trans.TNAME="Buy"\} \neq \emptyset) \wedge$
    $(\{trans_1 \in HIST \mid (oid, "Book") \in trans_1.OBJECTS \wedge$
    $trans_1.TNAME="Return" \wedge trans_1.TIME =$
    $MAXIMUM\{time \mid \exists trans_2 \in HIST, oname_2: time=trans.TIME \wedge$
    $(oid, oname_2) \in trans_2.OBJECTS\}\} \neq \emptyset)$

This aggregated precondition function returns true if and only if a specific object, o, has participated in a Buy transaction as a Book object in the past and if the most recent transaction in which o participated was a Return transaction in which o participated as a Book object.

4. A Graphical Specification Language

In this section we show how to specify the semantics of a graphical constraint language in terms of preconditions specified as queries on transaction histories.

Figure 4 defines the syntax and semantics of a graphical symbol for the specification of preconditions. For each graphical symbol the syntax is defined above the line and the semantics are defined below the line. Each p denotes a precondition function as defined in Section 3, each *oname* denotes an object class name, and each *tname* denotes a transaction type name.

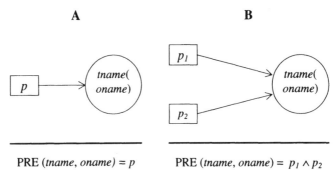

$$\text{PRE } (tname, oname) = p \qquad \text{PRE } (tname, oname) = p_1 \wedge p_2$$

Figure 4 Precondition.

Figure 4 (A) is interpreted in the following way. An *oname* object, *o*, can participate in a *tname* transaction if and only if $p(o.\text{OID})$ evaluates to true. Two or more preconditions are implicitly combined using logical and ($\wedge$) as defined by the aggregation rules in Table 1.

Figure 5 defines the syntax and semantics of a graphical symbol for the specification of immediate predecessors. Figure 5 (A) is interpreted in the following way. An *oname* object, *o*, can participate in a *tname* transaction if and only if the most recent transaction in which *o* participated was a $tname_1$ transaction in which *o* participated as an $oname_1$ object. Figure 5 (B) is interpreted in the following way. An *oname* object, *o*, can participate in a *tname* transaction if and only if the most recent transaction in which *o* participated was a $tname_1$ transaction in which *o* participated as an $oname_1$ object or if the most recent transaction in which *o* participated was a $tname_2$ transaction in which *o* participated as an $oname_2$ object.

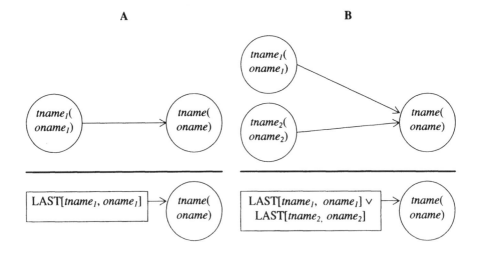

Figure 5 Immediate predecessors.

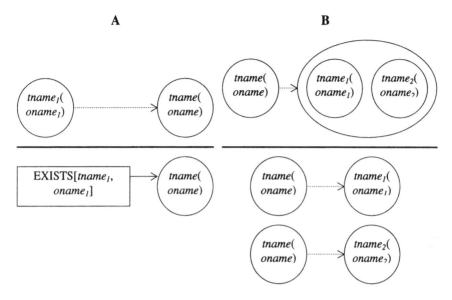

Figure 6 Enabling, non-immediate predecessors.

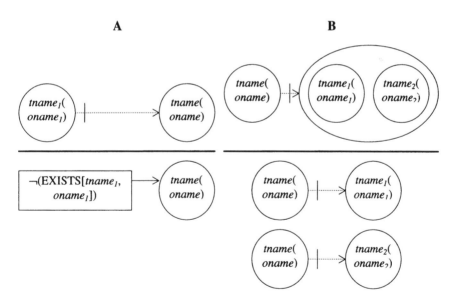

Figure 7 Disabling, non-immediate predecessors.

Figure 6 defines the syntax and semantics of graphical symbols for the specification of enabling, non-immediate predecessors. The dotted arrows indicate non-immediate predecessors. Figure 6 (A) states that an *oname* object, *o*, can participate in a *tname*

transaction if and only if o has participated in a *tname$_1$* transaction as an *oname$_1$*
object in the past.

Figure 7 defines the syntax and semantics of graphical symbols for the specification
of disabling, non-immediate predecessors. Figure 7 (A) states that an *oname* object, o,
can participate in a *tname* transaction if and only if o has not participated in a *tname$_1$*
transaction as an oname$_1$ object in the past. Figure 8 defines a graphical symbol that
can be used to ensure that objects can participate in a transaction of a certain type at
most one time.

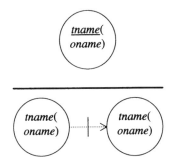

Figure 8 Single-occurrence events.

5. Specification Examples

In this section we use specification examples from a library to illustrate the use of our
specification language. Reserve is an independent transaction that is not returned by
the function LAST.

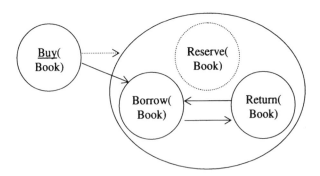

Figure 9 Library book.

The specification in Figure 9 implies that the first transaction in which a Book object
participates must be a Buy transaction. A particular Book object can participate in at

most one Buy transaction. Then, the Book object must participate in an alternating sequence of Borrow and Return transactions starting with a Borrow transaction. In-between the Borrow and Return Transactions the Book object can participate in Reserve transactions.

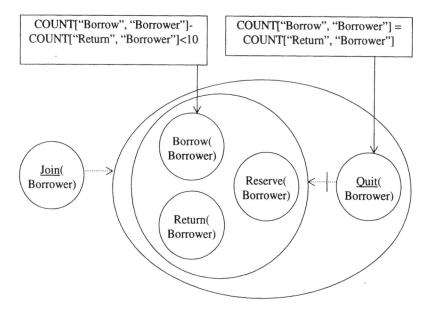

Figure 10 Library borrower.

The specification in Figure 10 implies that the first transaction in which a Borrower object participates must be a Join transaction. Then, the Borrower object can participate in any sequence of Borrow, Return, and Reserve transactions. The number of currently borrowed books is not allowed to exceed 10. Finally, the Borrower object can participate in a Quit transaction if all borrowed books have been returned.

Figure 11 Role modeling in library.

Figure 11 is interpreted as follows. A Librarian object can participate in a Hire transaction if and only if the object has not participated in a penalty transaction in the past. This illustrates that our specification language can be used to define constraints that relate the various roles objects may play during their time of existence.

6. Conclusion

We have presented a two-layer language that supports the specification of database evolution in terms of transaction-based, dynamic integrity constraints. The basic layer of our language is based on first-order logic. The underlying idea is to specify dynamic database constraints in terms of the transaction history. We have used the basic layer to define the semantics of a graphical language for transaction-based specification of database evolution.

Our two-layer language is orthogonal to existing state-based specification languages. Consequently, it can be used as a supplement to these languages. Our language can be used as a supplement to any data model that supports immutable object identifiers or immutable surrogates. Our language is characterized by a very loose coupling between constraint specifications and other schema elements like transaction specifications and object type definitions. Potential application areas include value chain specification, product flow specification, quality control systems, work flow specification, and process-based role modeling.

Future work includes further experiments with application areas, development of analysis tools that can support formal analysis of the consistency and correctness of specifications, and development of efficient implementation methods. Currently, we are extending our language with an event triggering mechanism.

References

Brodie, M. L. (1980). "The Application of Data Types to Database Semantic Integrity." Information Systems 5: 287-296.

Brodie, M. L. and D. Ridjanovic (1984). "On the Design and Specification of Database Transactions". Topics in Information Systems. On Conceptual Modeling. M. L. Brodie, J. Mylopoulos and J. W. Schmidt, Springer-Verlag: 277-312.

Bækgaard, L. (1993). "Specification and Efficient Monitoring of Transaction Dependencies. Ph.D. Thesis". Department of Mathematics and Computer Science, Aalborg University.

Castilho, J. M. V. D., M. A. Casanova, et al. (1982). "A Temporal Framework for Database Specifications". 8th International Conference on Very Large Databases, Mexico City, Mexico.

Cervasato, I. and C. F. Eick (1992). "Specification and Enforcement of Dynamic Consistency Constraints". CIKM'92. ISSM International Conference on Information and Knowledge Management, Baltimore, Maryland, USA.

Chomicki, J. (1992). "History-Less Checking of Dynamic Integrity Constraints". 8th International Conference on Data Engineering, Tempe, Arizona, USA, Computer Society Press.

Codd, E. F. (1970). "A Relational Model of Data for Large Shared Data Banks." Communications of the ACM 13(6): 377-387.

Formica, A. and M. Missikoff (1992). "Adding Integrity Constraints to Object-Oriented Models". CIKM'92. ISSM International Conference on Information and Knowledge Management, Baltimore, Maryland, USA.

Gray, J. (1981). "The Transaction Concept. Virtues and Limitations". VLDB'81. 7th International Conference on Very Large Databases, Cannes, France.

Hall, G. and R. Gupta (1991). "Modeling Transition". 7th International Conference on Data Engineering, Kobe, Japan, Computer Society Press.

Hammer, H. and D. McLeod (1981). "Database Description with SDM. A Semantic Database Model." ACM Transactions of Database Systems 6(3): 351-386.

Jackson, M. (1983). *System Development*, Prentice-Hall.

Kappel, G. and M. Schrefl (1991). "Object/Behavior Diagrams". 7th International Conference on Data Engineering, Kobe, Japan, Computer Society Press.

Khoshafian, S. and G. P. Copeland (1986). "Object Identity". Object-Oriented Programming Systems, Languages, and Applications-86, ACM.

Kim, W., Ed. (1995). *Modern Database Systems. The Object Model, Interoperability, and Beyond*, Addison-Wesley.

Kim, W. and F. H. Lochocsky, Eds. (1989). *Object-Oriented Concept, Databases, and Applications*, ACM Press, Addison-Wesley Publishing Company.

Kung, C. H. (1985). "On Verification of Temporal Database Constraints". SIGMOD'85. International Conference on Management of Data, Austin, Texas, USA.

Leonard, M. and B. Y. Luong (1981). "Information Systems Design Approach Integrating Data and Transactions". VLDB'81. 7th International Conference on Very Large Databases, Cannes, France.

Lipeck, U. W. (1986). "Stepwise Specification of Dynamic Database Behaviour". SIGMOD'86. International Conference on Management of Data, Washington, D.C.

Lipeck, U. W. and G. Saake (1987). "Monitoring Dynamic Integrity Constraints Based on Temporal Logic." Information Systems 12(3): 255-269.

Martin, H., M. Abida, et al. (1992). "Consistency Checking in Object-Oriented Databases. A Behavioral Approach". CIKM'92. ISSM International Conference on Information and Knowledge Management, Baltimore, Maryland, USA.

Motro, A. (1989). "Integrity = Validity + Completeness." ACM Transaction on Database Systems 14(4): 480-502.

Mück, T. and G. Vinek (1989). "Modeling Dynamic Constraints Using Augmented Place Transition Nets." Information Systems 14(4): 327-340.

Mylopoulos, J. (1992). "Conceptual Modeling and Telos". Conceptual Modeling, Databases, and CASE. An Integrated View of Information Systems. P. Loucopoulos and R. Zicari, John Wiley & Sons.

Ngu, A. H. H. (1984). "Transaction Modeling". 5th International Conference on Data Engineering, Los Angeles, USA, Computer Society Press.

Ngu, A. H. H. (1990). "Specification and Verification of Temporal Relationships in Transaction Modeling." Information Systems 15(2): 257-267.

Qian, X. (1988). "A Transaction Logic for Database Specification". SIGMOD'88. International Conference on Management of Data, Chicago, Illinois, USA.

Rosenquist, C. J. (1982). "Entity Life Cycle Models and their Applicability to Information Systems Development Life Cycles." Computer Journal 25(3).

Shipman, D. W. (1981). "The Functional Data Model and the Data Language DAPLEX." ACM Transactions on Database Systems 6(1): 140-173.

Simon, E. and P. Valduriez (1984). "Design and Implementation of an Extendible Integrity Subsystem". SIGMOD'84. International Conference on Management of Data, Boston, USA.

Stonebraker, M. (1975). "Implementation of Integrity Constraints and Views by Query Modification". SIGMOD'75. Workshop on Management of Data, San Jose, California, USA.

Vianu, V. (1988). "Database Survivability Under Dynamic Constraints." Acta Informatica 25: 55-84.

Wieringa, R., J.-J. Meyer, et al. (1989). "Specifying Dynamic and Deontic Integrity Constraints." Data & Knowledge Engineering 4: 157-189.

Well-behaving Rule Systems for Entity-Relationship and Object Oriented Models

Klaus-Dieter Schewe

Technical University of Clausthal, Computer Science Institute,
Erzstr. 1, 38678 Clausthal-Zellerfeld, Germany
schewe@informatik.tu-clausthal.de

Abstract. Integrity Maintenance is considered one of the major application fields of rule triggering systems (RTSs). In the case of a given integrity constraint being violated by a database transaction these systems trigger repairing actions. However, it has been shown that for any set of constraints there exist unrepairable transactions, which depend on the closure of the constraint set. Even if unrepairable transactions are excluded, this does not restrain the RTS from producing undesired behaviour.

Analyzing the behaviour of RTSs leads to the definition of *critical paths* in associated rule hypergraphs and the requirement of such paths being absent. It is shown that this requirement can be satisfied if the underlying set of constraints is *stratified* and that this is always the case for the structural constraints in Entity-Relationship and object oriented models. Moreover, in both cases there is no ambiguity for the selection of rules.

1 Introduction

Active databases (ADBs) aim at extending relational (or object oriented) DBMS by *rule triggering systems* (RTSs), i.e. by sets of rules which on a given *event* and in the case of a *condition* being satisfied trigger *actions* on the database (ECA-rules). Events can be external events, time conditions or internal events resulting from operations on the database. Conditions are usually given by boolean queries that have to be evaluated against the database. The action part consists of a sequence of basic operations to insert, delete or update tuples (or objects respectively) in the database.

The work in [2, 3, 7, 14, 15] and partly in [4] considers the problem to enforce database integrity by the use of RTSs. The results concern the generation of repairing ECA-rules and partly the analysis of the resulting RTS. This analysis concentrates on the *termination* of the rule system, the independence of the final database state from the chosen selection order of the rules (*confluence*) and on *consistency*.

These requirements are not sufficient for a reasonable rule behaviour, because it is easy to define an RTS that empties the database in case of any constraint violation. Therefore, we claim an additional requirement, which informally means that the intended effect of a transaction may not be turned into its opposite by the RTS.

In this paper we first investigate general problems with RTSs and show that these cannot occur in simple Entity-relationship- and object oriented schemata. The first problem concerns the existence of unrepairable transactions that are determined by the closure of the constraint set. Next we analyze how to obtain RTSs that definitely repair constraint violations by a (repairable) transaction without invalidating its intended effect. Given an RTS we first associate with it a *rule hypergraph* which corresponds to the possible sequences of triggered rules. Next we define *critical trigger paths* in these hypergraphs that correspond to the propagation of conditions. Indeed it can be shown that the existence of a single critical trigger path makes the RTS work incorrectly for at least one transaction.

Next, we analyze constraint sets in order to detect whether it is possible to define an RTS of repairing actions such that the critical trigger paths in its associated hypergraph can only invalidate unrepairable transactions. For this we first introduce *stratified* constraint sets that satisfy this condition. There also exists a necessary and sufficient condition for the RTS to work correctly, but due to its NP-hardness we do not consider it in this paper.

Instead of this we apply our results to the case of specific Entity-Relationship and object oriented models and demonstrate that structurally determined constraint sets in these cases are always stratified. Furthermore, it will be shown that in these cases ambiguities arising from different execution orders can also be detected.

The work presented in this paper extends previous research in [12] in that theoretical investigations about the strength and weaknesses of the rule triggering approach for integrity maintenance have been directly tied in with consistency in Entity-Relationship and object oriented models.

2 Rule Systems for Consistency Maintenance

Let us first consider the relational datamodel with *integrity constraints* given by formulae in *implicative normal form*

$$\mathcal{I} \equiv p_1(\mathbf{x}_1) \wedge \ldots \wedge p_n(\mathbf{x}_n) \Rightarrow q_1(\mathbf{y}_1) \vee \ldots \vee q_m(\mathbf{y}_m) \ , \tag{1}$$

with predicate symbols p_i, q_j, which correspond either to a relation of the schema or are comparison predicates $(=, \neq, \leq, <)$. Variables on the left hand side are assumed to be universally quantified, those occurring only on the right hand side are assumed to be existentially quantified (with all $\forall$-quantifiers preceding all $\exists$-predicates).

Moreover, we assume that there is at least one relation symbol on the left hand side of each such $\mathcal{I}$. Moreover, $\mathcal{I}$ should contain at least two relation symbols. The first restriction guarantees the empty database to be consistent, i.e. it satisfies all constraints $\mathcal{I}$, and the second one just states that there is no explicit constraint which requires a relation p to be always empty. We may always write $\mathcal{I}$ in clausal form.

We use the following abbreviations for the most common kinds of constraints:

functional dependency $R_i : A_j \rightarrow A_k$: Whenever the values of attribute A_j in relation R_i coincide for two tuples, the values of attribute A_k must also be equal:

$$R_i(\ldots, A_j : x_j, \ldots, A_k : x_k^1, \ldots) \wedge R_i(\ldots, A_j : x_j, \ldots, A_k : x_k^2, \ldots) \Rightarrow x_k^1 = x_k^2 \ .$$

inclusion dependency $R_i[A] \subseteq R_j[B]$: The values of attribute A in relation R_i always form a subset of the values of attribute B in R_j:

$$R_i(\dots, A : x, \dots) \Rightarrow R_j(\dots, B : x, \dots) \ .$$

exclusion dependency $R_i[A] \parallel R_j[B]$: The sets of values of attribute A in relation R_i and of attribute B in R_j are always disjoint:

$$R_i(\dots, A : x, \dots) \wedge R_j(\dots, B : y, \dots) \Rightarrow x \neq y \ .$$

2.1 ECA-Rules

For the ECA-*rules* we use the notation ON ⟨event⟩ IF ⟨condition⟩ DO ⟨action⟩ with ⟨event⟩ corresponding to an internal event, i.e. an insert- or delete-operation. ⟨condition⟩ is a formula to be evaluated against the actual database state, written as a negation $\neg\mathcal{I}$ for a constraint $\mathcal{I}$ in implicative normal form (1). ⟨action⟩ is a sequence of basic insert- or delete-operations to be triggered, i.e. to be executed if the event occurred and the condition is satisfied.

In this paper, the assumed execution model for ECA-rules relies on a deferred modus, i.e. the system RTS of rules is started after finishing a transaction. Furthermore, we do not assume any order of the rules. Instead of this the execution model relies on demonic non-determinism, i.e. if the events of several rules $r_1, \dots, r_n$ occur and their conditions evaluate to *true*, any of these r_i may be executed unless it is undefined.

Given a single constraint $\mathcal{I}$ in implicative normal form (1) we already get minimum requirements for repairing rules. If a relation symbol p occurs on the left hand side (right hand side) of (1), then each insert- (delete-)operation on p may violate (1), hence give rise to event-parts. The corresponding condition-part is simply $\neg\mathcal{I}$. However, for the action-part there are still several alternatives.

We call a system of ECA-rules *complete* iff for all these cases of events and conditions there exists at least one repairing rule, i.e. whenever the rule is selectable in some database state, the execution of the action part will establish $\mathcal{I}$ as a postcondition. However, we exclude those rules which simply invalidate the event. For transactions we simply consider sequences of insert- and delete-operations.

2.2 A Motivating Example

Let us first illustrate consistency enforcement using a small fragment of the example used in [3, 10].

Example 1. Let us now define a schema with some simple functional and inclusion constraints. For simplicity we omit all types. The relation schemata are

WIRE = { wire_id, connection, wire_type, voltage, power } ,
TUBE = { tube_id, connection, tube_type } and
CONNECTION = { connection, from, to }

These are used to express that there are tubes between two locations and wires in these tubes. In addition consider the following constraints:

$FD_1 \equiv$ WIRE : wire_id $\rightarrow$ connection, wire_type, voltage, power
$FD_2 \equiv$ TUBE : tube_id $\rightarrow$ connection, tube_type
$FD_3 \equiv$ CONNECTION : connection $\rightarrow$ from, to

$ID_1 \equiv$ WIRE[connection] $\subseteq$ TUBE[connection]
$ID_2 \equiv$ TUBE[connection] $\subseteq$ CONNECTION[connection]

The first three functional dependencies express that the values of wire_id, tube_id and connection are unique in relations over WIRE, TUBE and CONNECTION respectively. The latter inclusion constraints express that there is no wire nor tube without a corresponding tuple in a relation over CONNECTION.

Then the following relations define an instance of the schema:

WIRE

wire_id	connection	wire_type	voltage	power
4711	HH-HB	Koax	12	600
4814	HH-H	Tel	12	600

TUBE

tube_id	connection	tube_type
8314	HH-H	GX44
8511	HH-HB	GX44
023	HB-H	T33

CONNECTION

connection	from	to
HH-H	Hamburg	Hannover
HH-HB	Hamburg	Bremen
HB-H	Bremen	Hannover

It is easy to see that this instance satisfies the constraints above.

Now consider the operation $insert_{\text{WIRE}}(t)$. This may lead to a violation of constraint ID_1, in which case we must add a tuple to TUBE. Hence it can be replaced by

$insert_{\text{WIRE}}(t)$;
        IF connection$(t) \notin$ TUBE[connection]
        THEN $insert_{\text{TUBE}}(?, \text{connection}(t), ?)$
        ENDIF

Here the question marks stand for arbitrarily chosen values of the corresponding data type.

Similarly, the operation $delete_{\text{TUBE}}(t)$ may also violate ID_1. Therefore, we may replace $delete_{\text{TUBE}}(t)$ by

$delete_{\text{TUBE}}(t)$;
        IF connection$(t) \in$ WIRE[connection] $-$ TUBE[connection]
        THEN FOR ALL t' WITH connection$(t') = $ connection(t) DO
                    $delete_{\text{WIRE}}(t')$
        ENDFOR
        ENDIF

In order to enforce FD_2 we may then replace $insert_{\text{TUBE}}(t)$ by

IF $\forall t' \in$ TUBE . tube_id$(t) \neq$ tube_id(t')
THEN $insert_{\text{WIRE}}(t)$
ENDIF

Let us now add the exclusion constraint $ED \equiv WIRE[wire\_id] \parallel TUBE[tube\_id]$. In order to enforce this constraint insertions into one of WIRE or TUBE should be followed by deletions in the other. The resulting transactions are

$insert_{WIRE}(t)$;
FOR ALL $t' \in$ TUBE WITH $tube\_id(t') = wire\_id(t)$ DO
$\qquad delete_{TUBE}(t')$
ENDFOR

and

$delete_{TUBE}(t)$;
FOR ALL $t' \in$ WIRE WITH $wire\_id(t') = tube\_id(t)$ DO
$\qquad delete_{WIRE}(t')$
ENDFOR

If we now take together FD_2, ID_1 and ED we must be very careful. E.g., if we execute $insert_{WIRE}(8511,HH\text{-}HB,Koax,12,600)$ on the instance above, we may first delete the tuple $(8511,HH\text{-}HB,GX44)$ in TUBE in order to enforce ED and then the two tuples $(4711,HH\text{-}HB,Koax,12,600)$ and $(8511,HH\text{-}HB,Koax,12,600)$ in WIRE in order to enforce ID_2. The resulting instance would be (omitting CONNECTION):

WIRE

wire_id	connection	wire_type	voltage	power
4814	HH-H	Tel	12	600

TUBE

tube_id	connection	tube_type
8314	HH-H	GX44
023	HB-H	T33

Thus, the "effect" of the original operation, i.e. insertion of a tuple into WIRE, is completely destroyed. The new effect is a deletion in WIRE and TUBE. □

2.3 The Problem of Unrepairable Transactions

Let us first demonstrate the insufficiency of a naive RTS approach using a second trivial example. In "real" applications as in the previous subsection the situation of Example 2 will not occur in such an obvious way, but there are always implied and in general not detectable constraints leading to analogous problems.

Example 2. Take two unary relations p and q and the constraints $\mathcal{I}_1 \equiv p(x) \Rightarrow q(x)$ and $\mathcal{I}_2 \equiv p(x) \wedge q(x) \Rightarrow false$. This implies p to be always empty, hence insertions into p should be abolished. Then we obtain the following repairing rules:

$$R_1 : ON\ insert_p(x)\ IF\ \neg\mathcal{I}_1\ DO\ insert_q(x)$$
$$R_2 : ON\ delete_q(x)\ IF\ \neg\mathcal{I}_1\ DO\ delete_p(x)$$
$$R_3 : ON\ insert_p(x)\ IF\ \neg\mathcal{I}_2\ DO\ delete_q(x)$$
$$R_4 : ON\ insert_q(x)\ IF\ \neg\mathcal{I}_2\ DO\ delete_p(x)$$

If we try to execute a transaction $insert_p(a)$ on a database state satisfying $q(a)$, then we successively trigger the rules R_3 and R_2 with the effect of only deleting a in q. This contradicts the original intention of the transaction. □

In order to analyze the unintended behaviour in Example 2 consider a set Σ of constraints in implicational normal form. Let Σ^* denote the (semantic) *closure*, i.e. $\Sigma^* = \{\mathcal{I} \mid \Sigma \models \mathcal{I}\}$. Now let $\mathcal{I} \in \Sigma^*$ be non-trivial, i.e. it does not hold in all database states. Write $\mathcal{I}$ in implicational normal form

$$\mathcal{I} \equiv p_1(\mathbf{x}_1) \wedge \ldots \wedge p_n(\mathbf{x}_n) \Rightarrow q_1(\mathbf{y}_1) \vee \ldots \vee q_m(\mathbf{y}_m)$$

and let $p_{i_1}, \ldots, p_{i_k}$ and $q_{j_1}, \ldots, p_{j_\ell}$ denote the relation symbols on the left and right hand sides of $\mathcal{I}$ respectively. We may define a transaction T by

$$\mathrm{delete}_{q_{j_1}}(\mathbf{y}_{j_1}); \ldots; \mathrm{delete}_{q_{j_\ell}}(\mathbf{y}_{j_\ell}); \mathrm{insert}_{p_{i_1}}(\mathbf{x}_{i_1}); \ldots; \mathrm{insert}_{p_{i_k}}(\mathbf{x}_{i_k}) \ .$$

If we start T with values for the $\mathbf{x}_i$ and $\mathbf{y}_j$ such that the additional conditions on the left hand side of $\mathcal{I}$ are satisfied, whilst the additional conditions on the right hand side are not, T will always reach a database state satisfying $\neg\mathcal{I}$. This effect of T is intentional and hence the only reasonable approach to integrity maintenance in this case is to disallow such transactions.

More formally, the *effect* of a transaction T in a state σ is given by the strongest (with respect to $\Rightarrow$) formula $\mathbf{Eff}_\sigma(T) = \psi$ such that $\models_\sigma wp(T)(\psi)$ holds. Here $wp(T)(\psi)$ denotes the weakest precondition of ψ under the transaction ψ, i.e. starting T in initial state σ will reach a final state τ satisfying ψ.

Since we only consider sequences of insertions and deletions, $\mathbf{Eff}_\sigma(T)$ can always be written as a conjunction of literals, i.e. in negated implicational normal form, with the positive literals corresponding to insertions and the negative ones to deletions. In addition, we may consider the effect of a sequence $T; RTS$, where T is a transaction and RTS a system of rules. We say that RTS *invalidates the effect* of T iff $\not\models \mathbf{Eff}_\sigma(T) \wedge \mathbf{Eff}_\sigma(T; RTS)$ holds for some state σ.

Then it is justified to call a transaction T *repairable* with respect to the constraint set Σ iff $\neg\mathbf{Eff}_\sigma(T) \notin \Sigma^*$ holds for at least one state σ. Then a complete terminating system RTS of ECA-rules always invalidates the effect of a non-repairable transaction T. Hence the first problem is to detect (and exclude) non-repairable transactions. In order to decide whether a given transaction T is repairable or not, we must be able to decide, whether $\neg\mathbf{Eff}_\sigma(T)$ is in the closure Σ^*. Hence the implication problem for constraints must be decidable.

Note that our treatment ignores the termination problem. Non-terminating transactions have to be excluded as well, but this problem is independent from the repairability problem, since non-termination of RTSs occurs as an orthogonal problem.

2.4 The Problem of Critical Paths

Let us ask, whether we can always find a complete set of repair rules for all repairable transactions. For this we introduce the notions of *associated hypergraphs* and *critical trigger paths*.

Let $S = \{p_1, \ldots, p_n\}$ be a relational database schema and $RTS = \{R_1, \ldots, R_m\}$ a system of ECA-rules on S. Then the *associated rule hypergraph* (V, E) is constructed as follows:

- V is the disjoint union of S and RTS. We then talk of S-vertices and RTS-vertices respectively.

- If $R \in RTS$ has event-part Ev on $p \in S$ and actions on $p_1, \ldots, p_k$, then we have a hyperedge from p to $\{R\}$ labelled by $+$ or $-$ depending on Ev being an insert or delete, and a hyperedge from $\{R\}$ to $\{p_1, \ldots, p_k\}$ analogously labelled by k values $+$ or $-$.

Figure 1 shows the associated rule hypergraph of Example 2 in which case we have a simple graph.

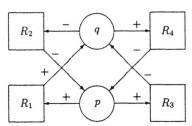

Fig. 1. Associated Rule Hypergraph

So far we ignore the condition part of the rules. These come into play if we consider critical trigger paths in associated hypergraphs. These are defined in several steps starting from paths in the associated hypergraph which correspond to possible sequences of ECA-rules with respect only to their event- and action-parts. Secondly we attach formulae to the S-vertices in the path in such a way that pre- and postconditions of the involved rules are expressed. Then we talk of *trigger paths*.

A maximal trigger path with contradicting initial and final condition will then be called *critical*. Then imagine a transaction with an effect implied by the initial formula, i.e. that there is an initial state such that running the transaction in this state results in a state which satisfies the initial condition of the trigger path. Executing this transaction followed by the rule triggering system along the critical trigger path will then turn the effect of the transaction into its opposite. This means that the RTS invalidates the effect of at least one transaction.

Let $G = (V, E)$ be the rule hypergraph associated with a system RTS of rules. A *trigger path* in G is a sequence $v_0, e_1, v_1', e_1', \ldots, e_\ell', v_\ell$ of vertices and hyperedges with the following conditions:

- $v_i \in S$ holds for all $i = 0, \ldots, \ell$,
- $v_i' \in RTS$ holds for all $i = 1, \ldots, \ell$,
- e_i is a hyperedge from v_{i-1} to v_i' and
- e_i' is a hyperedge from v_i' to V_i with $v_i \in V_i$ and the same label as e_{i+1}.

We call ℓ the *length* of the trigger path.

In addition we associate with each vertex $v_i \in S$ $(i = 0, \ldots, \ell)$ a formula φ_i in negated implication normal form such that $\models \varphi_i \Rightarrow cond(v_{i+1}')$ holds for the condition part $cond(v_{i+1}')$ of rule $v_{i+1}' \in RTS$ and $\models \varphi_i \Rightarrow wp(A_{i+1})(\varphi_{i+1})$ holds for the action-part A_{i+1} of rule v_{i+1}' $(i = 0, \ldots, \ell - 1)$. Furthermore, there is no

$e_{\ell+1} \in E$ from v_ℓ to $v'_{\ell+1}$ with the same label as e'_ℓ such that $\models \varphi_\ell \Rightarrow cond(v'_{\ell+1})$ holds.

Then a trigger path is *critical* iff $\models \neg(\varphi_0 \wedge \varphi_\ell)$ holds. Such a critical trigger path is called *non-admissible* iff there is a consistent state σ and a repairable transaction T such that $\mathbf{Eff}_\sigma(T) \Leftrightarrow \varphi_0$ holds.

Critical trigger paths for the associated rule hypergraph in Figure 1 are sketched in Figure 2. Note that in this case both critical trigger paths are not non-admissible.

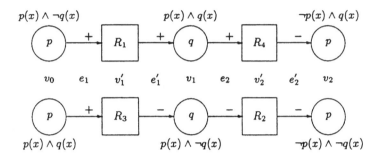

Fig. 2. Critical Trigger Paths

If a critical trigger path is not non-admissible, then only a non-repairable transaction can be invalidated by running the rules in the trigger path. Since we exclude non-repairable transactions, we only have to consider non-admissible trigger paths. After these remarks we are able to state our next result (for a proof see [12]).

If RTS is a complete set of rules associated with a set Σ of constraints and let $G = (V, E)$ be the associated rule hypergraph, then G contains an non-admissible critical trigger path iff there exists a consistent database state σ and a repairable transaction T such that executing T in σ and consecutively running RTS invalidates the effect of T without leaving the database unchanged.

3 Well-behaving Rule Systems

Let us now ask for constraint sets that allow to define complete RTSs which exclude non-admissible critical trigger paths in their associated hypergraphs. Let us start with a simple example.

Example 3. Take again two unary relations p and q and the constraints $\mathcal{I}_1 \equiv p(x) \Rightarrow q(x)$ and $\mathcal{I}_2 \equiv q(x) \Rightarrow p(x)$ which implies p to be always equal to q. Then we obtain the following repairing rules:

$$R_1 : \text{ON insert}_p(x) \text{ IF } \neg\mathcal{I}_1 \text{ DO insert}_q(x)$$
$$R_2 : \text{ON delete}_q(x) \text{ IF } \neg\mathcal{I}_1 \text{ DO delete}_p(x)$$
$$R_3 : \text{ON insert}_q(x) \text{ IF } \neg\mathcal{I}_2 \text{ DO insert}_p(x)$$
$$R_4 : \text{ON delete}_p(x) \text{ IF } \neg\mathcal{I}_2 \text{ DO delete}_q(x)$$

In this case there are no non-admissible critical paths in the associated rule hypergraph. We omit further details. □

3.1 The Stratification Condition

Let us now investigate the reason for the absence of non-admissible critical trigger paths in Example 3. This leads us to the notion of a *stratified* set of constraints.

The motivation behind this is as follows: In Example 3 insertions (deletions) on a relation p only trigger insertions (deletions) on q and vice versa. This should be sufficient for not invalidating an effect once it has been established. The corresponding constraints can therefore be grouped together.

A set Σ of constraints in implicative normal form (1) on a schema S is called *stratified* iff we have a partition $\Sigma = \Sigma_1 \cup \ldots \cup \Sigma_n$ with pairwise disjoint constraint sets Σ_i called *strata* such that the following conditions are satisfied:

(i) If L is a literal on the left hand side (right hand side) of some constraint $\mathcal{I} \in \Sigma_i$, then all constraints $\mathcal{J} \in \Sigma$ containing a literal L' on the right hand side (left hand side) such that L and L' are unifiable also lie in stratum Σ_i.

(ii) All constraints $\mathcal{I}$, $\mathcal{J}$ containing unifiable literals L and L' either on the left or the right hand side must lie in different strata Σ_i and Σ_j.

Our next result (for a proof see [12]) states that stratified constraint sets always give rise to RTSs without non-admissible critical trigger paths in the associated rule hypergraph.

If Σ is a stratified constraint set on a schema S, then there exists a complete RTS such that for any repairable transaction T on S the RTS does not invalidate the effect of T.

It can be shown that there also exists a necessary and sufficient condition for the absence of non-admissible critical paths, called *locally stratified*, but checking that condition is NP-hard, whereas checking stratification can be done in polynomial time.

3.2 Entity-Relationship Normal Form

Finally, we may ask for cases where stratified constraint sets occur. Recall from [8] that a relational database schema S with constraint set Σ is in *Entity-Relationship normal form* (ERNF) – and hence is equivalent to an ER-schema – iff

- all inclusion constraints in Σ are key-based and non-redundant,
- there is no cycle of inclusion constraints in Σ,
- each relation schema $R \in S$ is in BCNF with respect to the functional dependencies in Σ^* and
- there are only inclusion and functional dependencies in Σ^*.

If a relational database schema S with constraint set Σ is in ERNF, then it is easy to see that Σ is stratified. Furthermore, we only obtain an acyclic set of functional and inclusion constraints, for which the implication problem is decidable [1]. Hence we are able to detect also unrepairable transactions.

Hence, following the design approach of Mannila and Räihä in [8] leads to schemata without any problems concerning consistency enforcement by RTSs.

Example 4. Let us look at the following constraints

$$\mathcal{I}_1 : \quad p(x,y) \Rightarrow q(x,z) \quad \text{and}$$
$$\mathcal{I}_2 : \quad q(x,z) \wedge q(y,z) \Rightarrow x = y \quad .$$

Then this set of constraints corresponds to the Entity-Relationship diagram [13] in Figure 3. Obviously, the constraint set is stratified. However, if we add a third constraint

$$\mathcal{I}_3 \quad \equiv \quad p(x,z) \wedge q(y,z) \Rightarrow \textit{false} \quad .$$

it is easy to see that the new set $\{\mathcal{I}_1, \mathcal{I}_2, \mathcal{I}_3\}$ of constraints is not stratified. In terms of the Entity-Relationship diagram in Figure 3 $\mathcal{I}_3$ corresponds to an exclusion constraint B‖D.   □

Note that Example 4 captures the essentials of the motivating practical example.

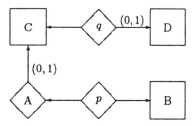

Fig. 3. Entity-Relationship constraints

3.3 The Object Oriented Case

A similar situation arises for the object oriented datamodels. The OODM investigated in [11] distinguishes between objects and values. Types are used to describe immutable sets of values with (type-)operations predefined on them. Type systems are prescriptions for the syntax and semantics of permitted type definitions.

We may always consider type systems that consists of some *base types*, *type constructors* and a *subtyping* relation. Moreover, *recursive types*, i.e. types defined by equations, and *predicative types*, i.e. types defined by restricting formulae, are included.

E.g., base types could $BOOL$, INT, ID or OK, where ID is an abstract identifier type without any non-trivial supertype and OK is the trivial type, and type constructors could be record types $(a_1 : \alpha_1, \ldots, a_n : \alpha_n)$ and finite set types $\{\alpha\}$.

We may use base types and constructors to define new types by nesting. In addition, we may build parameterized types letting type variables in constructors be uninstantiated. Then a type T is called *proper* iff the number of its parameters is 0. T is called a *value type* iff there is no occurrence of ID in T. If T' is a proper type occurring in a type T, then there exists a corresponding *occurrence relation* $o : T \times T' \rightarrow BOOL$ with $o(v_1, v_2) = true$ iff v_2 occurs in v_1 at the position indicated by the position of T' in T. Each subtype relation $T_1 \leq T_2$ as above defines a *subtype function* $T_1 \rightarrow T_2$ on the corresponding sets of values.

The *class* concept provides the grouping of objects having the same structure and behaviour. Structurally this uniformly combines aspects of object values and references. Behaviourally, this abstracts from operations on single objects including their creation and deletion.

Since identifiers can be represented using ID, values and references can be combined into a representation type, where each occurrence of ID denotes references to some other class. Therefore, we may define the structure of a class using parameterized types.

If T is a value type with parameters $\alpha_1, \ldots, \alpha_n$ and if the parameters are replaced by pairs $r_i : C_i$ with a reference name r_i and a class name C_i, the resulting expression is called a *structure expression*. A *class* consists of a class name C, a structure expression S, a set of class names $D_1, \ldots, D_m$ (called *superclasses*) and a set of *operations*. We call r_i the *reference* named r_i from class C to class C_i. The type derived from S by replacing each reference $r_i : C_i$ by the type ID is called the *representation type* T_C of the class C.

A database *schema* S is given by a finite collection of type and class definitions such that all types, classes and operations occurring within type definitions, structure definitions and operations are defined in S.

Then an *instance* D assigns to each class C a value $D(C)$ of type $\{(ident : ID, value : T_C)\}$ such that the following conditions are satisfied:

- For each class C identifiers must be unique.
- The set of identifiers in a subclass C is a subset of the one in the superclass C'. Moreover, if $T_C \preceq T'_C$ with subtype function $f : T_C \rightarrow T'_C$, then $(i, v) \in D(C) \Rightarrow (i, f(v)) \in D(C')$ holds.
- For each reference r from C to D identifiers j occurring in a value v of an object in C with respect to the occurrence relation o_r, i.e. $(i, v) \in D(C)$ and $o_r(v, j)$ hold, must occur in $D(D)$.

From these definitions it is easy to see that constraints arising from the OODM are basically unary inclusion constraints. Therefore, if a relational database schema S with constraint set Σ arises from flattening an OODM schema, then it is easy to see that Σ is stratified. Furthermore, we obtain that the implication problem is decidable [6] and in turn we are able to detect also unrepairable transactions.

4 Conflict Resolution

Referential actions are special rules to cope with violations of a foreign key constraint $R_1[X] \subseteq R_2[Y]$. Note that all inclusion constraints in Entity-Relationship and object oriented models considered so far have this form. As in SQL we only consider the case of delete- and update-operations on R_2, i.e. we consider the deletion (or update) of a tuple $t_2 \in \mathcal{I}(R_2)$. If this leads to constraint violation, there must be at least one tuple $t_1 \in \mathcal{I}(R_1)$ with $t_1[X] = t_2[Y]$. The following actions have been suggested:

cascade: Also delete t_1 (or update the values for the attributes in X such that the constraint violation dissappears). If there is more than one such tuple, the action is applied to all of them.

set null: Set the values for the attributes in X to a null value.

restrict: Reject the deletion or update on R_2 and roll back.

In the first two cases we have a reaction by propagation, since referencing tuples also disappear from the instance.

4.1 The Problem of Ambiguity

Assume that we have associated a referential action with all constraints in I. Then the problem occurs that the final result of an operation depends on the order of applying referential actions.

A *propagation path* (for short: *p-path*) is a sequence $R_n[X_n], \ldots, R_1[X_1]$ such that there are constraints $R_{i-1}[Y'_{i-1}] \subseteq R_i[Y_i]$ in I with $X_i \subseteq Y'_i \subseteq Y_i$ for $i = 2, \ldots, n$, all these constraints are associated with a referential action of kind cascade or set null and $R_{i-1}[X_{i-1}] \subseteq R_i[X_i]$ is in I^*.

A *restriction path* (for short: *r-path*) is a sequence $R_n[X_n], \ldots, R_1[X_1]$ such that there are constraints $R_{i-1}[Y'_{i-1}] \subseteq R_i[Y_i]$ in I with $X_i \subseteq Y'_i \subseteq Y_i$ for $i = 2, \ldots, n$, where $R_1[Y'_1] \subseteq R_2[Y_2]$ is associated with a referential action of kind restrict and all other constraints are associated with a referential action of kind cascade or set null, and $R_{i-1}[X_{i-1}] \subseteq R_i[X_i]$ is in I^*.

A p-path $R_n[X_n], \ldots, R_1[X_1]$ is called a *phantom* iff there is an r-path $R'_m[X'_m], \ldots, R'_1[X'_1]$ with $R'_m = R_n$, $X'_m = X_n$ and an inclusion constraint $R_1[X_1] \subseteq R'_1[X'_1]$ in Dep^*.

A schema S has a *conflict* iff there is a p-path $R_n[X_n], \ldots, R_1[X_1]$ corresponding to constraints $R_{i-1}[Y'_{i-1}] \subseteq R_i[Y_i]$, a r-path $R'_m[X'_m], \ldots, R'_1[X'_1]$ corresponding to constraints $R'_{i-1}[Z'_{i-1}] \subseteq R'_i[Z_i]$ with $R_n[X_n] = R'_m[X'_m]$ and $R_1[X_1] = R'_1[X'_1]$, an instance $\mathcal{I}$ and tuples $t_n, \ldots, t_1$ in $\mathcal{I}(R_n), \ldots, \mathcal{I}(R_1)$ with $t_i[Y_i] = t_{i-1}[Y'_{i-1}]$ and tuples $t'_m, \ldots, t'_1$ in $\mathcal{I}(R'_m), \ldots, \mathcal{I}(R'_1)$ with $t'_i[Z_i] = t'_{i-1}[Z'_{i-1}]$ such that $t_n = t'_m$ and $t_1 = t'_1$ hold. A conflict is called a *phantom* iff the involved p-path is a phantom.

It is easy to see that the condition $t_1 = t'_1$ can be omitted, since the existence of tuple sequences satisfying all other conditions implies the existence of tuples as claimed in the definition.

If there is a conflict, then a deletion or update for the tuple $t_n = t'_m$ violates the constraints $R_{n-1}[Y'_{n-1}] \subseteq R_n[Y_n]$ and $R'_{m-1}[Z'_{m-1}] \subseteq R'_m[Z_m]$. Executing the corresponding referential actions violates the "next" foreign key constraints along the p-path or r-path respectively. Depending on the order of the referential actions the tuple $t_1 = t'_1$ is either deleted according to the actions along the p-path and consequently no constraint violation for $R'_1[Z'_1] \subseteq R'_2[Z_2]$ may occur or it leads to a rollback according to the actions along the r-path. This is the core of the ambiguity problem.

However, if it is a phantom conflict, we also have a r-path $R_k''[X_k''], \ldots, R_1''[X_1'']$ with $R_k'' = R_n$ with foreign key constraints $R_{i-1}''[U_i'] \subseteq R_i''[U_i]$ and $X_k'' = X_n$ and an inclusion constraint $R_1[X_1] \subseteq R_1''[X_1'']$. Hence there are also tuples $t_k'', \ldots, t_1''$ with $t_i''[U_i] = t_{i-1}[U_i']$. Hence the tuple t_1'' enforces a rollback and there is no ambiguity. The work presented in [9] contains simple examples for real and phantom conflicts.

Thus, the *ambiguity problem* is to decide for a given schema S together with a set $Dep = K \cup I$ of minimal key and referential key constraints has a non-phantom conflict or not.

4.2 The Decidability Result

In order to show that ambiguity as defined above is decidable, we first recall that implication for inclusion dependencies alone is decidable [1]. Thus, we can compute all p-paths and r-paths. Since a conflict corresponds to a "diamond" with a p-path and a r-path, the existence of conflicts is obviously decidable and we only have to discard phantom p-paths. For this we have to decide, whether an arbitrary inclusion constraint $(R_1[X_1] \subseteq R_1'[X_1']$ in the definition of phantom p-paths) is in Dep^*.

Thus, the existence of non-phantom conflicts is decidable iff for any inclusion constraint ψ it is decidable whether $Dep \models \psi$ holds. Note that the proof of a general undecidability result in [9] is wrong.

We know that for arbitrary sets of functional and inclusion constraints the implication problem $Dep \models \psi$ is undecidable [5], but the special implication problem, where Dep only contains functional and unary inclusion constraints, is decidable [6]. The same holds for acyclic sets of inclusion constraints. Thus, these two well-known results from dependency theory just capture the situation of Entity-Relationship and object oriented models.

5 Conclusion

In this paper we investigated rule triggering systems (RTSs) for maintaining consistency arising from implicit constraints in Entity-Relationship and object oriented models. The first result assures the existence of non-repairable transactions. In order to disallow such transactions the constraint implication problem must be decidable, which is the case for both models. In the first case we are in the situation of acyclic inclusion constraints, whereas in the second case we only obtain unary inclusion constraints.

Secondly, we analyzed critical trigger paths in rule hypergraphs associated with RTSs. We could show that the existence of critical trigger paths leads to RTSs which may invalidate the effect of some transactions, even if these are repairable. Such a behaviour can be excluded for stratified constraint sets, which holds for the constraint sets arising from Entity-Relationship and object oriented models.

Thirdly, we investigated the ambiguity problem for rules for the case that rollback is allowed is the action part. This again can be reduced to the decidability problem for constraint implication, hence holds for the chosen models.

To summarize, the general applicability of RTSs for integrity maintenance is limited, if we assume that the intended effects of user-defined transactions should be preserved. Fortunately, conflicts do no occur or can be detected efficiently if we only consider constraints arising from conceptual design with Entity-Relationship and certain object oriented models.

References

1. M. A. Casanova, R. Fagin, C. H. Papadimitriou. Inclusion dependencies and their interaction with functional dependencies. *Journal of Computer and System Sciences* 28 (1), 29-59, 1984.
2. S. Ceri, J. Widom: *Deriving Production Rules for Constraint Maintenance*, Proc. 16th Conf. on VLDB, Brisbane (Australia), August 1990, 566-577
3. S. Ceri, P. Fraternali, S. Paraboschi, L. Tanca: *Automatic Generation of Production Rules for Integrity Maintenance*. ACM ToDS, vol. 19(3), 1994, 367-422.
4. S. Chakravarty, J. Widom (Eds.): *Research Issues in Data Engineering — Active Databases*, Proc., Houston, Februar 1994
5. A. K. Chandra, M. Y. Vardi. The implication problem for functional and inclusion dependencies is undecidable. *SIAM Journal of Computing* 14, 671-677, 1985.
6. S. S. Cosmadakis, P. Kanellakis, M. Y. Vardi. Polynomial-time implication problems for unary inclusion dependencies. *Journal of the ACM* 37, 15-46, 1990.
7. M. Gertz, U. W. Lipeck: *Deriving Integrity Maintaining Triggers from transaction Graphs*, in Proc. 9th ICDE, IEEE Computer Society Press, 1993, 22-29
8. H. Mannila, K.-J. Räihä: *The Design of Relational Databases*, Addison-Wesley 1992
9. J. Reinert. Ambiguity for referential integrity is undecidable. In G. Kuper, M. Wallace (Eds.). *Constraint databases and applications*, 132-147, Springer LNCS 1034, 1996.
10. K.-D. Schewe, B. Thalheim: *Consistency Enforcement in Active Databases*, in S. Chakravarty, J. Widom (Eds.): *Research Issues in Data Engineering — Active Databases*, Proc., Houston, Februar 1994
11. K.-D. Schewe and B. Thalheim. Fundamental concepts of object oriented databases. *Acta Cybernetica*, vol. 11(1/2), Szeged 1993, 49 - 84.
12. K.-D. Schewe, B. Thalheim: *Active Consistency Enforcement for Repairable Database Transitions*, in S.Conrad, H.-J. Klein, K.-D. Schewe (Eds.): Integrity in Databases, Proc. 6th Int. Workskop on Foundations of Models and Languages for Data and Objects, Schloß Dagstuhl, 1996, 87-102, available via http://wwwiti.cs.uni-magdeburg.de/~conrad/IDB96/Proceedings.html
13. B. Thalheim: *Foundations of entity-relationship modeling*, Annals of Mathematics and Artificial Intelligence, vol. 7, 1993, 197-256
14. S. D. Urban, L. Delcambre: *Constraint Analysis: a Design Process for Specifying Operations on Objects*, IEEE Trans. on Knowledge and Data Engineering, vol. 2 (4), December 1990
15. J. Widom, S. J. Finkelstein: *Set-oriented Production Rules in Relational Database Systems*, in Proc. SIGMOD 1990, 259-270

Behavior Consistent Refinement
of Object Life Cycles

Michael Schrefl[1] and Markus Stumptner[2]

[1] Institut für Wirtschaftsinformatik, Universität Linz, Altenbergerstr.69 A-4040 Linz,
Austria. email: schrefl@dke.uni-linz.ac.at
[2] Institut für Informationssysteme, Technische Universität Wien, Paniglg. 16, A-1040
Wien, Austria. email: mst@dbai.tuwien.ac.at

Abstract. This paper examines the inheritance of object life cycles that
are specified by behavior diagrams. A behavior diagram of an object type
models possible life cycles of its instances by states, activities and arcs
corresponding to places, transitions and arcs of Petri Nets. In an inheritance hierarchy, subtypes specialize the life cycle of supertypes by
extension, i.e., adding states and activities, and (the focus of this paper)
refinement, i.e., decomposing states and activites into substates and subactivities.
The main contribution of this paper is the identification of necessary
and sufficient rules for checking behavior consistency between a behavior
diagram of a type and a refined subtype, as well as for the combination
of extension and refinement.

Keywords: object-oriented design, object life cycle, inheritance

1 Introduction

One of the central aspects of object-oriented systems is inheritance. Inheritance
defines a relationship between two object types, where one object type called the
subtype inherits structure and behavior from the other one called the supertype.
The inherited structure and behavior may be further specialized in the subtype.
Subtypes may extend supertypes by new features or redefine inherited ones. Applying inheritance to features requires a clear understanding of what it is that
is actually inherited. In particular, it is common to distinguish between individual operations and more comprehensive properties. Several object-oriented
design methods, such as OMT [10], OOSA [5], and OBD [7] model the behavior
of object types at two interrelated levels of detail: at the activity level and at
the object type level. For example, behavior diagrams [7] specify at the activity
level the signature of an activity by identifying types and preconditions of input
parameters as well as the type and the postcondition of the return value. At the
object type level, object behavior is specified in terms of object life cycles that
identify legal sequences of states and activities.

Inheritance of activities corresponds to inheritance of operations in programming languages, which is fairly well understood [3, 15]. Recently, more attention has been directed towards examining inheritance of object-life cycles, i.e., how the life cycle of a subtype should relate to the life cyle of its supertype. We have been studying inheritance of object life cycles in the realm of behavior diagrams [6, 7, 12, 1] which are based on Petri nets. A behavior diagram of an object type represents the possible life cycles of its instances by activities, states, and arcs corresponding to transitions, places, and arcs of Petri nets. Subtypes may specialize the behavior diagram of supertypes in two ways: by extension and refinement. Extension means adding activities, states, and arcs. Refinement means expanding inherited activities and states into subdiagrams. Activities of behavior diagrams can be further described by activity specification diagrams, activity realization diagrams, and activity scripts. The additional diagram types are not needed in this paper; see [1, 7] for details.

In [13], we have already presented a set of complete rules for checking the consistency of lifecycles for objects whose behavior diagrams are created by *extension* of the behavior diagrams of a supertype. This work was driven by the principle that a subtype should either preserve the "observable behavior" or the "invocable behavior" of its supertype, as classified by Ebert and Engels [4]. The notion of observable behavior is given by the assumption that if one ignores the parts of the lifecycle specific to the subtype, the lifecycle of an instance of the subtype should appear just as a lifecycle of an instance of the supertype. The notion of invocable behavior corresponds to the assumption that any sequence of operations that is invocable on a supertype instance should also be invocable on a subtype instance.

This paper deals with the definition of consistency requirements for the *refinement* of behavior diagrams. Our initial work on refinement [12] introduced a set of structured refinement primitives. In this paper we take a more general approach based on labeling states and activities in the diagram. The idea of labeling states and activities is inspired by the way in which in business processes guided by paper are executed: different copies of a business form are given different colors. Each business activity handles one or several copies of a form, it may collect several copies of a form from different input boxes, and it may distribute several copies of a form to different output boxes. In this analogy, labels in behavior diagrams correspond to the colors given to different copies of the form. Note that, if an activity has been refined, its original description in the supertype is "abstract" (which is why it had to be refined) and it cannot be invoked on an object (cf. [12]). Therefore the notion of invocation consistency is not applicable to refined subtypes. This paper deals exclusively with guaranteeing observation consistency.

Many papers have been published on behavior and equivalence preserving refinements of Petri nets (cf. [2] for a survey), but as it turned out, behavior consistency for refinement is much easier to check for labeled behavior diagrams than for Petri nets in general.

The paper is organized as follows: Section 2 provides a short introduction to relevant concepts of Object/Behavior Diagrams. Section 3 describes behavior consistent refinement. Section 4 considers extension and refinement together. Section 5 summarizes the main points of the paper. Proofs have been omitted for space reasons and can be found in [14].

2 Behavior Diagrams

Object/Behavior diagrams are an object-oriented graphical design notation for the design of object-oriented databases [1, 6, 7]. Object/Behavior Diagrams represent the structure of objects in object diagrams and their behavior in behavior diagrams. In this paper, we restrict our attention to behavior diagrams, which depict the behavior of instances of an object type by a set of states, a set of activities, and a set of arcs connecting states with activities and vice versa. Each of the states represents a particular period, each of the activities an event in the life cycle of the instances of the object type. All possible life cycles of instances of an object type have a single start state called the *initial state* and a common set of completion states called *final states*. The principal idea behind behavior diagrams stems from Petri Nets [9]. States correspond to places of Petri nets, activities to transitions.

Definition 1 (Behavior Diagram)
A behavior diagram $B_O = (S_O, T_O, F_O, \alpha_O, \Omega_O)$ *of an object type* O *(the subscripts are omitted if* O *is understood) consists of a set of states* $S \neq \emptyset$, *a set of activities* $T \neq \emptyset$, $T \cap S = \emptyset$, *and a set of arcs* $F \subseteq (S \times T) \cup (T \times S)$, *such that* $\forall t \in T: (\exists s \in S: (s, t) \in F) \land (\exists s \in S: (t, s) \in F)$ *and* $\forall s \in S: (\exists t \in T: (s, t) \in F) \lor (\exists t \in T: (t, s) \in F)$. *There is a distinguished state in* S, *the* initial state $\alpha \in S_O$, *where for no* $t \in T : (t, \alpha) \in F$ *(and which is the only state with that property); and there is a set of distinguished states of* S, *the* final states Ω, *where for no* $s \in \Omega$ *and no* $t \in T : (s, t) \in F$.

Instances of an object type which reside in states correspond to individual tokens of a Petri net. We say an activity $t \in T$ *consumes* a token (or object) from a state $s \in S$ iff $(s, t) \in F$, and $t \in T$ *produces* a token into $s \in S$ iff $(t, s) \in F$. In addition, we say a state $s \in S$ is a *prestate* of an activity $t \in T$ iff $(s, t) \in F$, and $s \in S$ is a *post state* of $t \in T$ iff $(t, s) \in F$. Due to the underlying Petri net semantics a behavior diagram determines the legal sequences of states and activities, and thus the legal sequences in which activities may be applied: an activity may be applied on an object if the object is contained in every prestate of the activity. If an activity on some object has been executed successfully, the object is contained in every post state of the activity but in no prestate unless that prestate is also a post state. Unlike Petri nets, where a transition is automatically fired if every prestate contains a token, an activity in a behavior diagram must be explicitly invoked for an object which is in every prestate of the activity. In addition, and unlike Petri nets, activities take time. Therefore, during the execution of an activity on an object, the object resides in an implicit state named after the activity. This state is referred to as *activity state*. Thus, we can say that every instance of an object type is at any point in time in one or several (activity) states of its object type, which are jointly referred to as *life cycle state*.

Definition 2 (Life cycle state) *A life cycle state (LCS) σ of an object type O is a subset of $S \cup T$. We denote the initial LCS $\{\alpha\}$ by A. An activity $t \in T$ can be started on a life cycle state σ if the set of prestates of t is contained in σ. The start of activity t on LCS σ yields the life cycle state $\sigma' = \sigma \setminus \{s \in S \mid (s,t) \in F\} \cup \{t\}$. An activity $t \in T$ can be completed on a life cycle state σ if t is in σ. The completion of activity t on σ yields the life cycle state $\sigma' = \sigma \setminus \{t\} \cup \{s \in S \mid (t,s) \in F\}$.*

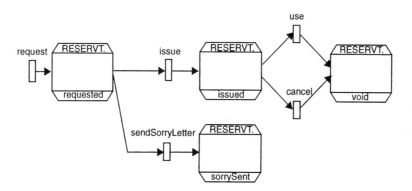

Fig. 1. Behavior diagram of object type RESERVATION

Example 1. Figure 1 shows the behavior diagram of object type RESERVATION. Activities are depicted by vertical bars. States are depicted by rectangles which are labeled by the name of the object type they describe at the top and the name of the state at the bottom. For simplicity, the initial state α is not shown, and is also not indicated in subsequent examples. Also, final states are not marked visually. It is assumed that every activity for which no prestate is shown has the initial state as prestate and that every state which is not the prestate of any activity is a final state. □

A behavior diagram of an object type specifies all legal sequences of life cycle states. A particular sequence of life cycle states of an object type is referred to as *life cycle occurrence* of that object type.

Definition 3 (Life cycle occurrence) *A life cycle occurrence (LCO) γ of object type O is a sequence of life cycle states $\sigma_1, \ldots, \sigma_n$, such that $\sigma_1 = A$, and for $i = 1 \ldots n - 1$ either $\sigma_i = \sigma_{i+1}$, or there exists an activity $t \in T$ such that either t can be started on σ_i and the start of t yields σ_{i+1}, or σ_i contains t and the completion of t yields σ_{i+1}. Any subsequence of γ is called* partial LCO.

Example 2. A possible life cycle occurrence of object type RESERVATION is [{request}, {requested}, {issue}, {issued}, {cancel}, {void}] (cf. Figure 1). □

It is often more convenient to denote the sequence of starts and completions of activities that cause a life cycle occurrence than to list the resulting sequence of life cycle states.

Definition 4 (Reachable life cycle states) *The set of life cycle states reachable from LCS σ, written $R(\sigma)$, contains every LCS σ' of O that can be reached from σ by starting or completing any sequence of activities in T.*

Example 3. Given the behavior diagram of object type RESERVATION, $R(\{issued\}) = \{\{cancel\}, \{use\}, \{void\}\}$ (cf. Figure 1). □

As in [13], we only consider behavior diagrams which are safe, activity-reduced, and deadlock-free. *Safe* means that the completion of an activity never leads to a contradictory state, i.e., a state that the object is already in, *activity-reduced* means that for every $t \in T$ there exists some potential lifecycle occurrence where t is used, and *deadlock-free* means that for every life cycle state σ in $R(\alpha)$, either some $t \in T$ can be started or σ contains only final states. See [13] for a formal definition of these concepts.

3 Consistent Refinement

In this section, we first introduce labeled behavior diagrams and define behavior consistency for refinements of labeled behavior diagrams. Then, we identify necessary and sufficient rules for checking behavior consistency. Before we define labels formally, we will give some introductory remarks.

When activities or states of a behavior diagram are refined into subdiagrams, a major problem is to ensure that if an object leaves one state (or activity state) of a subdiagram and enters a state (or activity state) outside the subdiagram, the object leaves the subdiagram entirely, i.e., it leaves all states and activitity states in the subdiagram. This is a requirement imposed by the notion of refinement: Leaving the abstract state must be equivalent to leaving *all* refined substates since by definition. if an object is still in one of the refined substates, it has not left the abstract state.

For refinements of Petri nets, a common way to ensure that an object leaves a subnet entirely is to (1) refine a transition into a subnet with an initial transition and a final transition, where the subnet is well-formed in that the final transition consumes all tokens in the subnet, and (2) to refine a place by splitting first the state into an input place, a transition, and an output place, and by refining the transition as under (1) above (cf. [19]). Because this approach (as well as its extensions to multiple, alternative initial transitions and multiple, alternative final transitions, cf. [2]) considers transitions and places in isolation, it is not practicable for behavior modeling, where activities and states have to be refined jointly (such that arcs may connect states and activities of different subnets, cf. [12]). In [12] a set of structured refinement primitives for activities and states was introduced which ensure that an object leaves the refinement of an activity or state always entirely. Here, we follow a more general approach based on the labeling of activities, states, and objects. The labeling is used to explicitly mark parts of an object's lifecycle that deal with a particular refined aspect of the original object. An object may simultaneously be in different states but with different labels. If an object is inserted into some state carrying some set of labels the object must be inserted into the state with that set of labels. As we will see, the labeling is used to check whether an object leaves a state again with the set of labels with which it entered the state.

3.1 Labeled Behavior Diagrams

The idea of labeling states and activities is inspired by the way in which in business processes guided by paper work, various carbon copies of a form are given different colors. Each business activity handles one or several copies of a form, it may collect several copies of a form from different input boxes, and it may distribute several copies of a form to different output boxes. A *label* in a labeled behavior diagram corresponds in this analogy to the color given to some copy of a form, an object corresponds to one filled-in form representing a particular business case, and the labels given to an arc identify those copies of a form that are delivered by a business activity to an output box or are taken by a business activity from an input box. We now give a formal definition of this concept. Later, we will use labels to ensure that if an object leaves a subnet that represents the refinement of an activity or state, it leaves the subnet entirely.

Definition 5 (Labeled Behavior Diagram)
A labeled behavior diagram (LBD) $B = (S, T, F, \alpha, \Omega, L, l)$ of an object type O is defined as a behavior diagram $\hat{B} = (S, T, F, \alpha, \Omega)$ with the addition of a set of labels L and a labeling function l which assigns a non-empty set of labels to every arc in F, i.e., $l : F \to 2^L \setminus \{\emptyset\}$. Each outgoing arc of the initial state α carries all labels, i.e., $l(\alpha, s) = L$ for $(\alpha, s) \in F$.

Definition 6 (Labeled life cycle state) *A labeled life cycle state (LLCS) $\bar{\sigma}$ of an object type O is a subset of $(S \cup T) \times L$. We denote the initial labeled life cycle state by $\bar{A} = \{(\alpha, x) \mid x \in L\}$.*

Example 4. A possible (very simple) labeled life cycle occurrence of object type LRESERVATION_WITH_PAYMENT is [{(request,r),(request,p),(request,f)}, {(requested,p),(requested,r),(requested,f)},({{(sendSorryLetter,p),   (sendSorryLetter,r), (sendSorryLetter,f), {(sorrySent,r),(sorrySent,p),(sorrySent,f)}] (cf. Figure 2).   □

In the following, we use the notation $^\bullet t$ and $t^\bullet$ to refer to the incident states of an activity: $^\bullet t = \{s|(s,t) \in F\}$, $t^\bullet = \{s|(t,s) \in F\}$; and we extend l to activities and states. For $e \in ((S \cup T) \setminus \{\alpha\})$, we define that $l(e) = \cup_{\exists (f,e) \in F} l(f,e)$, and for α, we define $l(\alpha) = L$.

Definition 7 (Start and completion of a labeled activity) *A labeled activity $t \in T$ can be started on a labeled life cycle state $\bar{\sigma}$, if $\{(s,x) \mid s \in {}^\bullet t \wedge x \in l(s,t)\} \subseteq \bar{\sigma}$. Starting t then yields $\bar{\sigma}' = (\bar{\sigma} \setminus \{(s,x) \mid s \in {}^\bullet t \wedge x \in l(s,t)\}) \cup \{(t,x) \mid s \in {}^\bullet t \wedge x \in l(s,t)\}$. An activity t can be completed on a LCS $\bar{\sigma}$, if $\{(t,x) \mid s \in t^\bullet \wedge x \in l(t,s)\} \subseteq \bar{\sigma}$. Completion of t then yields $\bar{\sigma}' = (\bar{\sigma} \setminus \{(t,x) \mid s \in t^\bullet \wedge x \in l(t,s)\}) \cup \{(s,x) \mid s \in t^\bullet \wedge x \in l(t,s)\}$.*

The definitions of a labeled life cycle occurrence (LLCO) $\hat{\gamma}$ and partial LCO are analogous to Definition 3. The definition of the set of reachable labeled life cycle states $R(\bar{\sigma})$ for a given $\bar{\sigma}$ is analogous to Definition 4.

We restrict our discussion to a meaningful subclass of labeled behavior diagrams, namely those behavior diagrams which observe the label preservation, the unique label distribution, and the common label distribution properties.

Definition 8 (Label preservation) *A labeled behavior diagram B observes the* label preservation *property if for every $t \in T$ the incoming and the outgoing arcs carry the same set of labels, i.e., $\bigcup_{s \in {}^\bullet t} l(s,t) = \bigcup_{s \in t^\bullet} l(t,s)$.*

Definition 9 (Unique label distribution) *A labeled behavior diagram B observes the* unique label distribution *property if for every activity the label sets of all incoming arcs are disjoint and the label set of all outgoing arcs are disjoint, i.e.,*
(a) $s \in S, s' \in S, t \in T : s \neq s' \wedge (s,t) \in F \wedge (s',t) \in F \Rightarrow l(s,t) \cap l(s',t) = \emptyset$, and
(b) $s \in S, s' \in S, t \in T : s \neq s' \wedge (t,s) \in F \wedge (t,s') \in F \Rightarrow l(t,s) \cap l(t,s') = \emptyset$.

Definition 10 (Common label distribution) *A labeled behavior diagram B observes the* common label distribution *property if all incident arcs of a state carry the same label set, i.e.,*
(a) $s \in S, t \in T, t' \in T : (s,t) \in F \wedge (s,t') \in F \Rightarrow l(s,t) = l(s,t')$,
(b) $s \in S, t \in T, t' \in T : (s,t) \in F \wedge (t',s) \in F \Rightarrow l(s,t) = l(t',s)$, and
(c) $s \in S, t \in T, t' \in T : (t,s) \in F \wedge (t',s) \in F \Rightarrow l(t,s) = l(t',s)$.

To restrict our discussion to behavior diagrams satisfying these properties is meaningful in practice. The label preservation property reflects, in the analogy with business forms, that once an individual form for a business case has been created, each activity in the business process does not consume or produce new copies of the form, the unique label distribution property ensures that some copy of a form is requested by an activity from at most one input box and is delivered by the activity to at most one output box, and the common label distribution property ensures that a box holds always the same copies of a form (e.g., the yellow and pink carbon copy). From here on, we will assume that these properties will always be satisfied by the diagrams under study, and therefore these properties will be reflected in the states contained in $R(\bar{A})$.

Example 5. Figure 2 shows a labeled behavior diagram of object type LRESER-VATION_WITH_PAYMENT with the labels r ("registration"), p ("payment"), and f ("refund"). Note that the diagram satisfies the label preservation, unique label distribution, and common label distribution properties.

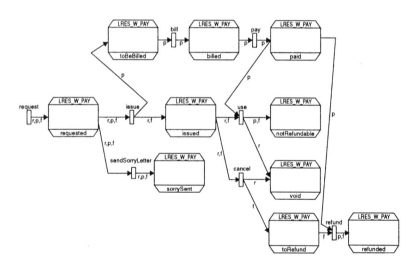

Fig. 2. Behavior diagram of object type LRESERVATION_WITH_PAYMENT

3.2 Consistent Refinement

A labeled behavior diagram is refined by expanding activities and states into subdiagrams. We capture this refinement at the design level by a refinement function h that maps each state or activity of a subdiagram to the activity or state that is replaced by the subdiagram. Similarly, a label may be refined by mapping it to several sublabels, which corresponds in our form analogy to splitting a form into several copies.

The refinement function is explicitly declared by the designer, just as in many object-oriented systems the position of an object type in a type hierarchy is explicitly declared by a "isSubtypeOf" relationship. The refinement function becomes the identity function for those activities, states, and labels which are not refined. We require by definition that the refinement function is surjective for labels, which means in our forms analogy that no copy of the form may get lost in the refinement.

Definition 11 (Refined LBD's)
A labeled behavior diagram $B' = (S', T', F', \alpha', \Omega', L', l', h_B)$ *that is a* refinement *of another LBD* $B = (S, T, F, \alpha, \Omega, L, l)$ *is a labeled behavior diagram with an associated* refinement *function* h_B *which has the following properties:*[3]

$h : S' \cup T' \cup L' \mapsto S \cup T \cup L$ *(h is total)*
(1) $x \in L \Rightarrow \exists x' \in L' : h(x') = x$
(2) $x \in L' \Rightarrow h(x) \in L$
(3) $e \in S' \cup T' \Rightarrow h(e) \in S \cup T$
(4) $h(e) \in S' \cup T' \cup L' \Leftrightarrow h(e) = e$
(5) $h(\alpha') = \alpha$

Example 6. Figure 3 shows a labeled behavior diagram of object type LRESERVA-TION_WITH_ALTERNATIVE_PAYMENT that refines the labeled behavior diagram of object type LRESERVATION_WITH_PAYMENT of Figure 2.

Considering a life cycle state of a subtype at the level of the supertype means abstracting from the refinement. For refinements, the abstraction of a life cycle state plays the role which the restriction of a life cycle state plays for the extension of a type.

Definition 12 (Abstraction of a labeled life cycle state)
The abstraction of a labeled life cycle state $\bar{\sigma}'$ *of an object type* O' *to object type* O, *written* $\bar{\sigma}'/_O$, *is defined as* $\bar{\sigma}'/_O = \{(h(e'), h(x')) | (e', x') \in \bar{\sigma}'\}$. *The restriction of a life cycle occurrence* $\bar{\gamma}' = \bar{\sigma}'_1, \ldots, \bar{\sigma}'_n$ *of object type* O' *to object type* O, *written* $\bar{\gamma}'/_O$, *is defined as* $\bar{\sigma}_1, \ldots, \bar{\sigma}_n$, *where for* $i = 1 \ldots n : \bar{\sigma}_i = \bar{\sigma}'_i/_O$.

In [13] we have identified several kinds of behavior consistency. As noted in the introduction, this distinction cannot be applied to refinement the same way as to extension, because if an activity has been refined its original description in the supertype is "abstract" (that is why it had to be refined) and it cannot be invoked on an object (cf. [12]). We define behavior consistency for refinement in the sense of observation consistency.

---

[3] We write h instead of h_B if B is understood

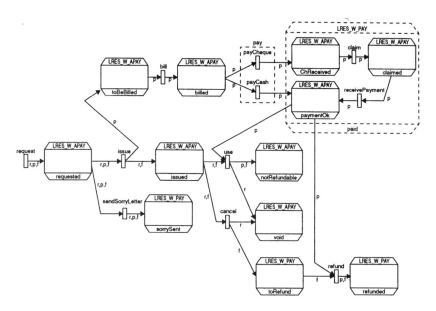

Fig. 3. LBD LRESERVATION_WITH_ALTERNATIVE_PAYMENT

Definition 13 (Behavior consistent refinement)

A LBD $B_{O'} = B' = (S', T', F', \alpha', \Omega', L', l', h_B)$ is a behavior consistent refinement *of a LBD $B_O = B = (S, T, F, \alpha, \Omega, L, l)$, if for every labeled life cycle occurrence $\bar{\gamma}'$ of object type O', $\bar{\gamma}'/_O$ is a labeled life cycle occurrence of B.*

3.3 Checking Behavior Consistency

Rules to check whether a labeled behavior diagram $B_{O'}$ consistently refines a labeled behavior diagram B_O are the rules of *Pre- and post state satisfaction* and the rule of *Pre- and post state refinement.* (cf. Figure 4). Assume an activity t has been refined into a subdiagram N. Then, the rule of *Pre- and post state satisfaction* requires (a1) that if an activity in subdiagram N consumes from a state in subdiagram $N' \neq N$, then it consumes all sublabels of the label associated with N', and (a2) that if an activity of subdiagram N consumes from a state outside N, the activity consumes from all states (or their subdiagrams) from which the activity t has been consuming. Rules (b1) and (b2) are the counterparts to (a1) and (a2) for post states. The rule of *Pre- and post state refinement* requires that any arc in $B_{O'}$ crossing two subdiagrams is reflected by an arc in B_O such that the arc labels in the behavior diagram of the subtype are refinements of the corresponding arc in the behavior diagram of the supertype. In the formal definition, $h^{-1}(e) = \{e' \in S' \cup T' \cup L' | h(e') = e\}$.

Example 7. The labeled behavior diagram of object type LRESERVA-TION_WITH_ALTERNATIVE_PAYMENT (cf. Figure 3) is a consistent refinement of the LBD of object type LRESERVATION_WITH_PAYMENT (cf. Figure 2).

R1. Pre- and post-state satisfaction

(a1) $t \in T, s \in S, t' \in T', s' \in S'$:
$$h(t') = t \wedge h(s') = s \wedge (s,t) \in F \wedge (s',t') \in F' \wedge x \in l(s,t) \wedge x'' \in h^{-1}(x)$$
$$\Rightarrow \exists s'' \in S' : h(s'') = s \wedge (s'',t') \in F' \wedge x'' \in l'(s'',t')$$

(a2) $t \in T, s \in S, \hat{s} \in S, t' \in T', s' \in S'$:
$$h(t') = t \wedge h(s') = s \wedge (s,t) \in F \wedge (s',t') \in F' \wedge (\hat{s},t) \in F$$
$$\Rightarrow \exists \hat{s}' \in S' : h(\hat{s}') = \hat{s} \wedge (\hat{s}',t') \in F'$$

(b1) $t \in T, s \in S, t' \in T', s' \in S'$:
$$h(t') = t \wedge h(s') = s \wedge (t,s) \in F \wedge (t',s') \in F' \wedge x \in l(t,s) \wedge x'' \in h^{-1}(x)$$
$$\Rightarrow \exists s'' \in S' : h(s'') = s \wedge (t',s'') \in F' \wedge x'' \in l'(t',s'')$$

(b2) $t \in T, s \in S, \hat{s} \in S, t' \in T', s' \in S'$:
$$h(t') = t \wedge h(s') = s \wedge (t,s) \in F \wedge (t',s') \in F' \wedge (t,\hat{s}) \in F$$
$$\Rightarrow \exists \hat{s}' \in S' : h(\hat{s}') = \hat{s} \wedge (t',\hat{s}') \in F'$$

R2. Pre- and post-state refinement

(a) $s' \in S' \wedge t' \in T' \wedge (s',t') \in F' \wedge h(s') \neq h(t') \wedge x' \in l'(s',t')$
$$\Rightarrow (h(s'),h(t')) \in F \wedge h(x') \in l(h(s'),h(t'))$$

(b) $s' \in S' \wedge t' \in T' \wedge (t',s') \in F' \wedge h(s') \neq h(t') \wedge x' \in l(t',s')$
$$\Rightarrow (h(t'),h(s')) \in F \wedge h(x') \in l(h(t'),h(s'))$$

Fig. 4. Rules for checking behavior consistency of refinements

Theorem 1 *A labeled behavior diagram* $B' = (S',T',F',\alpha',\Omega',L',l',h_B)$ *is a behavior consistent refinement of a labeled behavior diagram* $B = (S,T,F,\alpha,\Omega,L,l)$ *if and only if rules R1 and R2 of Figure 4 are obeyed.*

4 Consistent Specialization

We consider specialization of the behavior of an object type as a concatenated application of refinement and extension. For labeled behavior diagrams, refinement means replacing activities and states by subdiagrams and replacing labels by a set of sublabels. Extension means adding new activities and new states. And for LBD's, extension means also the possibility of adding new labels, which corresponds in our form analogy to adding another carbon copy to a form.

Behavior consistent refinement has been treated in the previous section. To support specialization by concatenating refinement and extension, we revisit behavior consistent extension as presented in [13] and present a set of rules to check whether a labeled behavior diagram B' is a behavior consistent extension of another labeled behavior diagram B.

Definition 14 (Restriction of a labeled life cycle state) *The* restriction *of a LLCS $\bar{\sigma}'$ of an object type O' to object type O, written $\bar{\sigma}'/_O$, is defined as $\bar{\sigma}'/_O = \{(e,x)|(e,x) \in \bar{\sigma}' \wedge e \in (S \cup T) \wedge x \in L\}$. The restriction of a LLCO is defined as the sequence of restrictions of the states in the original LCO (cf. [13]).*

Definition 15 (Observation consistent extension of LBD's) *We refer to a labeled behavior diagram $B' = (S',T',F',\alpha',\Omega',L',l')$ as an* observation consistent extension *of a labeled behavior diagram $B = (S,T,F,\alpha,\Omega,L,l)$, if for every LLCO $\bar{\gamma}'$ of object type O', $\bar{\gamma}'/_O$ is a LLCO of B.*

Rules to check whether a labeled behavior diagram $B_{O'}$ is an observation consistent extension of another behavior diagram B_O are given in Figure 5. The rule of *partial inheritance* corresponds to the same rule for unlabeled behavior diagrams [13] and requires additionally that (1) all labels are inherited by the subtype and (2) that inherited arcs inherit all labels. The rule of *immediate definition of labels* corresponds to the rule of *immediate definition of pre- and post states* in [13] and requires that an arc inherited by the subtype may not receive a label already defined for the supertype, i.e., a label in L. The rule of *no label deviation* replaces the rules of *parallel extension* in [13]. Part (a) and (b) require that arcs incident to activities added at a subtype carry only new labels, i.e., labels in $L' \setminus L$. Part (c) and (d) require that arcs incident to states added at a subtype carry only new labels. Part (c) and (d) are actually redundant. They follow from the other rules, and the unique label distribution property.

Example 8. The labeled behavior diagram of object type LRESERVA-TION_WITH_PAYMENT (cf. Figure 2) extends the LBD of object type LRESER-VATION (the latter is obtained from Figure 1 by adding a label r to each arc).

Theorem 2 *A labeled behavior diagram $B' = (S',T',F',\alpha',\Omega',L',l',h_B)$ is an observation consistent extension of a labeled behavior diagram $B = (S,T,F,\alpha,\Omega,L,l)$ if and only if rules E1', E2' and E3' of Figure 5 are obeyed.*

5 Conclusion

Whereas inheritance of operations is fairly well understood in the literature, no common understanding of inheritance of object life cycles exists. This paper has treated specialization of object life cycles through extension and refinement in the realm of Object/Behavior diagrams [6, 7]. Complete rules for checking the consistency of extending behavior diagrams were given in [13]. In a similar vein,

E1'. Partial inheritance
    (a) $\alpha' = \alpha$, $L \subseteq L'$
    (b) $t \in T' \wedge t \in T \wedge (s,t) \in F \Rightarrow (s,t) \in F' \wedge l(s,t) \subseteq l'(s,t)$
    (c) $t \in T' \wedge t \in T \wedge (t,s) \in F \Rightarrow (t,s) \in F' \wedge l(t,s) \subseteq l'(t,s)$
E2'. Immediate definition of labels
    (a) $(s,t) \in F' \wedge s \in S \wedge t \in T \wedge x \in L \wedge x \in l'(s,t) \Rightarrow (s,t) \in F \wedge x \in l(s,t)$
    (b) $(t,s) \in F' \wedge s \in S \wedge t \in T \wedge x \in L \wedge x \in l'(t,s) \Rightarrow (t,s) \in F \wedge x \in l(t,s)$
E3'. No label deviation
    (a) $(s,t) \in F' \wedge t \in T' \wedge t \notin T \Rightarrow l'(s,t) \cap L = \emptyset$
    (b) $(t,s) \in F' \wedge t \in T' \wedge t \notin T \Rightarrow l'(t,s) \cap L = \emptyset$
    (c) $(s,t) \in F' \wedge s \in S' \wedge s \notin S \Rightarrow l'(s,t) \cap L = \emptyset$
    (d) $(t,s) \in F' \wedge s \in S' \wedge s \notin S \Rightarrow l'(t,s) \cap L = \emptyset$

Fig. 5. Rules for checking behavior consistency for extensions of LBD's

different authors have been involved with searching inheritance rules for object descriptions in terms of state diagrams [4, 11], automata [8], or concurrent object-oriented languages (e.g, [17, 18]). Liskov and Wing [16] have developed an approach that expresses subtype relations in terms of implications between pre- and postconditions of individual operations plus additional constraints. It provides explicit criteria for individual operations, but is not used for the description of complete lifecycles. Previously, inheritance of object life cycles had been discussed in the area of object-oriented specification methods (e.g., OMT [10] and OOSA [5]), but in a somewhat more informal manner.

This paper builds on the approach of [13] by examining under which conditions a behavior diagram B' of an object type O' consistently refines the behavior diagram B of its supertype O. To facilitate this test, we have used a special variant of behavior diagrams, labeled behavior diagrams (LBD's). Labels can be envisioned as copies of a form which undergo different sublifecycles and, thus, labeling of arcs must be done in a way to preserve the number of labels in the behavior diagram. When an activity (or state) is refined into a subdiagram all labels handled by this activity (or which are stored in this state, resp.) must jointly enter and may only jointly exit the subdiagram.

The behavior diagram of a supertype O is *specialized* by concatenating refinement and extension. For labeled behavior diagrams, refinement provides also the possibility to replace a label by a set of sublabels — which corresponds to splitting a form into sections — and extension provides also the possibility to add new labels. The strict separation of extension and refinement can help to clarify what actually happens when object types are "specialized".

Acknowledgments: The authors wish to express their gratitude to Markku Sakkinen and Peter Bichler for their insightful comments, and to Günter Preuner for his rigorous examination of the paper and proofs.

References

1. P. Bichler, M. Schrefl "Active Object-Oriented Database Design Using Active Object/Behavior Diagrams", in *IEEE RIDE-ADS'94*, 1994.
2. W. Brauer, R. Gold, and W. Vogler, "A Survey of Behaviour and Equivalence Preserving Refinements of Petri Nets," Springer LNCS 483, pp. 1–46, 1991.
3. P.S. Canningen, W.R. Cook, W.L. Hill, and W.G. Olthoff, "Interfaces for Strongly-Typed Object-Oriented Programming," in *Proc. OOPSLA'89,*, ed. N. Meyrowitz, pp. 457–467, 1989.
4. J. Ebert and G. Engels, "Observable or Invocable Behaviour - You Have to Choose!" *Technical Report*, Koblenz University, 1994.
5. D.W. Embley, B.D. Kurtz, and S.N. Woodfield, *Object-Oriented Systems Analysis - A Model-Driven Approach*, Yourdon Press, 1992.
6. G. Kappel and M. Schrefl, "Using an Object-Oriented Diagram Technique for the Design of Information Systems," in *Proceedings of the International Working Conference on Dynamic Modelling of Information Systems*, ed. H.G. Sol, K.M. Van Hee, pp. 121–164, North-Holland, 1991.
7. G. Kappel and M. Schrefl, "Object/Behavior Diagrams," in *Proc. 7th Int. Conf. IEEE Data Engineering*, pp. 530–539, 1991.
8. B. Paech and P. Rumpe, "A new Concept of Refinement used for Behaviour Modelling with Automata," *Proc. FME'94*, Springer LNCS 873, 1994.
9. J.L. Peterson, "Petri nets," in *ACM Computing Surveys*, pp. 223–252, 1977.
10. J. Rumbaugh, M. Blaha, W. Premerlani, F. Eddy and W. Lorensen, *Object-Oriented Modelling and Design*, Prentice-Hall, 1991.
11. G. Saake, P. Hartel, R. Jungclaus, R. Wieringa, and R. Feenstra, "Inheritance Conditions for Object Life Cycle Diagrams," in *EMISA Workshop*, 1994.
12. M. Schrefl, "Behavior Modeling by Stepwise Refining Behavior Diagrams," in *Proc. 9th Int. Conf. Entity-Relationship Approach*, pp. 113–128, 1990.
13. M. Schrefl and M. Stumptner, " Behavior Consistent Extension of Object Life Cycles," in *Proceedings OO-ER 95*, pp. 133–145, Springer LCNS 1021, Dec. 1995.
14. M. Schrefl and M. Stumptner, "Behavior Consistent Refinement of Object Life Cycles," *Institutsbericht, Inst. für Wirtschaftsinformatik, Universität Linz*, Austria, 1997.
15. P. Wegner and S.B. Zdonik, "Inheritance as an Incremental Modification Mechanism or What Like Is and Isn't Like," in *Proc. ECOOP'88*, ed. Gjessing S. and Nygaard K., pp. 55–77, Springer LNCS 322, 1988.
16. B. Liskov and J.M. Wing, "A Behavioral Notion of Subtyping," *ACM Transactions on Programming Languages and Systems*, 16 (6) pp. 1811–1841, 1994.
17. S. Matsuoka and A. Yonezawa, "Analysis of Inheritance Anomaly in Object-Oriented Concurrent Programming Languages," in *Research Directions in Concurrent Object-Oriented Programming*, ed. G. Aga, P. Wegner, and A. Yonezawa, pp. 107–150, ACM Press, 1993.
18. O. Nierstrasz, "Regular Types for Active Objects," in *Object-Oriented Programming Systems Languages and Applications (OOPSLA), Special Issue of SIGPLAN Notices*, vol. 28, Dec. 1993.
19. I. Nierstrasz and T. Murata, "A method for stepwise refinement and abstraction of Petri nets," in *J. Computer and System Sciences*, vol. 27, pp. 51–76, 1983.

ActivityFlow: Towards Incremental Specification and Flexible Coordination of Workflow Activities

Ling Liu and Calton Pu

Department of Computer Science & Engineering
Oregon Graduate Institute
P.O.Box 91000 Portland, Oregon 97291-1000 USA
{lingliu,calton}@cse.ogi.edu

Abstract. We introduce the ActivityFlow specification language for incremental specification and flexible coordination of workflow activities. The most interesting features of the ActivityFlow specification language include (1) a collection of specification mechanisms, which provides a workflow designer with a uniform workflow specification interface to describe different types (i.e., ad-hoc, administrative, or production) of workflows involved in their organizational processes, and helps to increase the flexibility of workflow processes in accommodating changes; (2) a set of activity modeling facilities, which enables the workflow designer to describe the flow of work declaratively and incrementally, allowing reasoning about correctness and security of complex workflow activities independently from their underlying implementation mechanisms; (3) an open architecture that supports user interaction as well as collaboration of workflow systems of different organizations.

1   Introduction

The focus of office computing today has shifted from automating individual work activities to supporting the automation of organizational business processes. Such requirement shift, pushed by the technology trends, has promoted the emergence of a new computing infrastructure, workflow management systems (WFMSs), which provides a model of business processes, and a foundation on which to build solutions supporting the coordination, execution, and management of business processes. One of the main challenges in today's WFMSs is to provide tools to support organizations to coordinate and automate the flow of work activities between people and groups within an organization, and to streamline and manage business processes that depend on both information systems and human resources.

Over the past few years, many workflow management systems have become available on the market, or developed in research labs world wide [8, 10, 3]. Although there are more and more successes in the workflow research and development, it is widely recognized [8, 10] that there are still technical problems, ranging from inflexible and rigid process specification and execution mechanisms, and insufficient possibilities to handle exceptions, to the need for uniform interface support for various types of workflows (i.e., ad-hoc, administrative, or production workflows)[1], for dynamic restructuring of business processes, process status monitoring, automatic enforcement of consistency and concurrency control, and recovery from failure, and for improved interoperability between different workflow servers.

In this paper we concentrate our discussion on the problem of flexibility and extensibility of process specification and execution mechanisms. We introduce the ActivityFlow specification language for structured specification and flexible coordination of workflow activities. The most interesting features of the ActivityFlow specification language include:

- a collection of specification mechanisms, which allows the workflow designer to use a uniform workflow specification interface to describe different types (i.e., ad-hoc, administrative, or production) of workflows involved in their organizational processes, and helps to increase the flexibility of workflow processes in accommodating changes;
- a set of activity modeling facilities, which enables the workflow designer to describe the flow of work declaratively and incrementally, allowing reasoning about correctness and security of complex workflow activities independently from their underlying implementation mechanisms; and
- an open architecture, which supports user interaction as well as collaboration of workflow systems of different organizations.

2 Basic Concepts of ActivityFlow

2.1 Business Process vs Workflow Process

Business processes are collection of activities that support critical organizational and business functions. The activities within a business process have a common business or organizational objective, and are often tied together by a set of precedence dependency relationships. One of the important problems in managing business processes (by organization or human) is how to effectively capture the dependencies among activities and utilize the dependencies for scheduling, distributing, and coordinating work activities among human and information system resources efficiently.

A workflow process is an abstraction of a business process, and it consists of *activities*, which correspond to individual process steps, and *agents*, which execute these activities. An agent may be a human (e.g., a customer representative), an information system, or any of the combinations. A notable difference between business process and workflow process is that a workflow process is an

---

[1] Ad-hoc workflows are controlled by users at run time. Users can react to situations not considered at workflow design stage. Administrative workflows are those workflows where activities are mainly performed by humans. Production workflows are predefined and use a great deal of complex information structures, and involve application programs and automatic activities [3, 7].

automated business process, namely the coordination, control and communication of activities is automated, although the activities themselves can be either automated or performed by people [10].

A workflow management system (WFMS) is a software system which offers a set of workflow enactment services to carry out a workflow process through automated coordination, control and communication of work activities performed by both human and computers.

2.2 Reference Architecture

Figure 1 shows the WFMS reference architecture provided by the Workflow Management Coalition (WfMC) (see http://www.aiai.ed.ac.uk/WfMc/). A

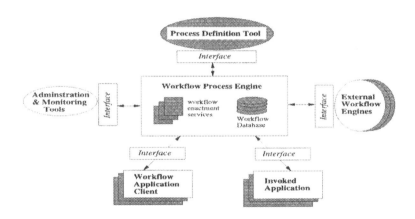

Fig. 1. Reference Architecture of Workflow Management Coalition

WFMS consists of an engine, a process definition tool, workflow application clients, invoked applications, and administration and monitoring tools. The process definition tool is a visual editor used to define the specification of a workflow process, and we call it workflow process schema in ActivityFlow. The same schema can be used later for creating multiple instances of the same business process (i.e., each execution of the schema produces an instance of the same business process). The workflow engine and the surrounding tools communicate with the workflow database to store, access, and update workflow process control data (used by the WFMS only), and workflow process-specific data (used by both application and WFMS). Examples of such data are workflow activity schemas, statistical information, and control information required to execute and monitor the active process instances. Existing WFMSs maintain audit logs that keep track of information about the status of the various system components, changes to the status of workflow processes, and various statistics about past process executions. This information can be used to provide real-time status reports about the state of the system and the state of the active workflow process instances, as well as various statistical measurements, such as the average execution time of an activity belonging to a particular process schema, and the timing characteristics of the active workflow process instances.

ActivityFlow discussed in this paper can be seen as a concrete instance of the WfMC reference architecture in the sense that in ActivityFlow concrete solutions are introduced for process definitions, workflow activity enactment services, and interoperability with external workflow management systems. In this paper our main focus is on the ActivityFlow process definition facilities, including the ActivityFlow meta model (see Section 2.3), the ActivityFlow workflow specification language (see Section 3) and graphical notation for ActivityFlow process definition (see Section 3.4).

2.3   ActivityFlow Meta Model

The ActivityFlow meta model describes the basic elements that are used to define a workflow process schema which describes the pattern of a workflow process and its coordination agreements. In ActivityFlow, a workflow process schema specifies activities that constitute the workflow process and dependencies between these constituent activities. Activities represent steps required to complete a business process. A step is a unit of processing and can be simple (primitive) or complex (nested). Activity dependencies determine the execution order of activities and the data flow between these activities. Activities can be executed sequentially or in parallel. Parallel executions may be unconditional, i.e., all activities are executed, or conditional, i.e., only activities that satisfy the given condition are executed. In addition, activities may be executed repeatedly, and the number of iterations may be determined at run-time.

A workflow process schema can be executed many times. Each execution is called a workflow process instance (or a workflow process for short), which is a partial order of activities and connectors. The set of activity precedence dependency relationships defines a partial order over the given set of activities. The connectors represent the points where the control flow changes. For instance, the point where control splits into multiple parallel activities is referred to as *split point* and is specified using a split connector. The point where control merges into one activity is referred to as *join point*, and is specified using a split connector. A join point is called AND-join if the activity immediately following this point starts execution only when all the activities preceding the join point finish execution. A join point is called OR-join when the activity immediately following this point starts execution as soon as one of the activities preceding the join point finishes execution. A split such that it can be statically (before execution) determined that all branches are taken is called AND-split. A split which can be statically determined that exactly one of the branches will be taken is called OR-split. Figure 2 lists the graphical representation of AND-split, OR-split, AND-join, and OR-join.

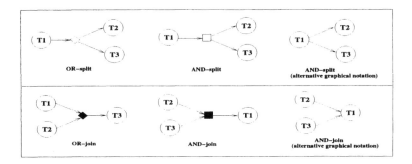

Fig. 2. Graphical representation of AND-split, OR-split, AND-join, and OR-join

The workflow process schema also specifies which agents can execute each workflow activity. Such specification is normally done by associating *roles* with activities. A role serves as a "description" or a "place holder" for a person, a group, an information system, or any of the combinations required for the enactment of an activity. Formally, a role is a set of agents. Each activity has an associated role that determines which agents can execute this activity. Each agent has an activity queue associated with it. Activities submitted for execution are inserted into the activity queue when the agent is busy. The agent follows its own local policy for selecting from its queue for next activity to execute. The most common scheduling policies are priority-based and FIFO. The notion of a role facilitates load balancing among agents and can flexibly accommodate changes in the workforce and in the computing infrastructure of an organization, by changing the set of agents associated with roles.

Figure 3 shows a sketch of the ActivityFlow meta model using extended ER diagram. The following concepts are basics of our activity-based process model:

- *a workflow process*: consists of a set of activities, a role and a collection of information objects to be accessed from different information resources.
- *an activity*: is either an *elementary* activity or a composite activity. The execution of an activity consists of a sequence of interactions (called events) between the performer and the workflow management system, and a sequence of actions that change the state of the system.
- *an elementary activity*: represents a unit of work that an individual, a machine, or a group can perform in an uninterrupted span of time. In other words, it is not decomposed any further in the given domain context.
- *a composite activity*: consists of several other activities, either elementary or composite. The nesting of activities provides higher levels of abstraction that help to capture the various structures of organizational units involved in a workflow process.
- *a role*: is a place holder or description for a set of agents, who are the authorized performers that can execute the activity. The concept of associating roles with activities not only allow us to establish the rules for association of

activities or processes with organizational responsibilities, but also provide a flexible and elegant way to grant the privilege of execution of an activity to individuals or systems that are authorized to assume the associated role.

- *an agent*: can be a person, a group of people, or an information system, that are granted memberships into roles and that interacts with other agents while performing activities in a particular workflow process instance.
- *information objects*: are the data resources accessed by a workflow process. These objects can be structured (e.g., relational databases), semi-structured (e.g., HTML forms), or unstructured (e.g., text documents). Structured or semi-structured data can be accessed and interpreted automatically by the system, while unstructured data cannot and thus often requires human involvement through manual activities.

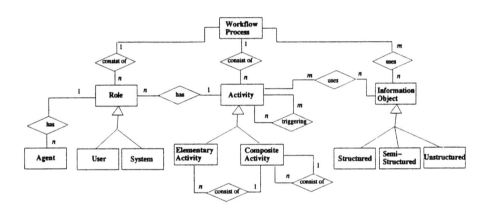

Fig. 3. ActivityFlow meta model

Important to note is that activities in ActivityFlow can be manual activities, performed by users without further support from the system; automatic activities, carried out by the system without human intervention, or semi-automatic activities, using specific interactive programs for performing an activity.

2.4 The Running Example

To illustrate the ActivityFlow meta model, we use a telephone service provisioning process in a telecommunication company. A synopsis of the example is described below.

Assume a telephone service provisioning workflow consists of the following eight activities, each corresponds to a step in the telephone service provisioning process. An instance of this telephone service provisioning workflow is created when an operator collects from a client the information needed to carry out the connection installation service. The client information required includes client name, address, kind of service and requested options. Figure 4 illustrates this example which we will use in the rest of the paper. The activity T_1:ENTER REQUEST

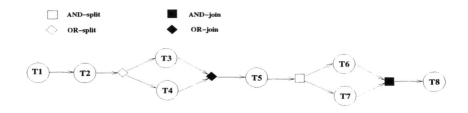

Fig. 4. Telephone Service Provisioning Workflow Process

verifies the service request and creat service order in the client database and service order database. The next activity T_2:CHECK RESOURCE uses the service order created by T_1 and consults the facilities database to determine whether existing facilities can be used for establishing the service. If existing facilities can be used, the activity T_3:ALLOCATE CIRCUIT is executed. Otherwise, a human field engineer is selected to execute the activity T_4:INSTALL NEW CIRCUIT, which may involve manual changes to some switch and the installation of a new telephone line. Once T_3 or T_4 is completed, the activity T_5:VERIFY INSTALLATION is executed to verify if the installation was successful. Then the T_6:activity UP-DATE DIRECTORY and the activity T_7:PREPARE BILL are executed in parallel to update the telephone directory database and generate billing information, respectively. Finally, the activity T_8:GENERATE SUMMARY is executed to generate some summary data about the provisioning of the new telephone service.

2.5 Advanced Concepts

ActivityFlow provides a number of facilities to support advanced concepts such as a variety of possibilities for handling errors and exceptions. For example, at the activity specification stage, we allow the workflow designers to specify valid processes and the compensation activities. At run-time additional possibilities are offered to support recovery from errors or crashes by triggering alternative executions defined in terms of user-defined compensation activities or system-supplied recovery routines.

Time dimension is very important for the deadline control of workflow processes. In ActivityFlow we provide a construct to allow the workflow designer to specify the maximum allowable execution durations for both the activities (i.e., subactivities or component activities) and the process (i.e., top activity). This time information can be used to compute deadlines for all activities in order to meet an overall deadline of the whole workflow process. When an activity misses its deadline, special actions may be triggered. Furthermore, this time information plays an essential role in decisions about priorities and in monitoring deadlines and generating time errors in the case that deadlines are missed. It also provides the possibility to delay some activities for a certain amount of time or to a specific date.

The third additional feature is the concept of workflow administrator (WFA). Modern business organizations build the whole enterprise around their key business processes. It is very important for the success of process-centered organizations that each process has a WFA who is responsible for monitoring the workflow process according to deadlines, handling exceptions and failures which cannot be resolved automatically. More specifically, he/she is able to analyze the current status of a workflow process, make decisions about priorities, stop and resume a workflow process, abort a workflow process, dynamically restructure a workflow process, or change a workflow specification, etc.. A special workflow client interface is needed which offers functionality to enable such workflow process administrator to achieve all these goals.

3 Activity Flow Process Definition Language

3.1 Main Components of a Workflow Specification

In ActivityFlow, a workflow process is described in terms of a set of activities and the dependencies between them. Activities are specified by activity templates or so called parameterized *activity patterns*. An activity pattern describes concrete activities occurring in a particular organization, which have similar communication behavior. An execution of the activity pattern is called an instantiation (or an activity instance) of the activity pattern.

Activities can be composed of other activities. The tree organization of an activity pattern α is called the *activity hierarchy* of α. The set of activity dependencies specified in the pattern α can be seen as the cooperation agreements among activities that collaborate in accomplishing a complex task. The activity at the root of the tree is called *root activity* or *workflow process*, the others are subactivities. We use activities to refer to both the process and its component activities when no distinction needs to be made.

A typical workflow specification consists of the following five units:

- *Header*: The header of an activity specification describes the signature of the activity, which consists of a name, a set of input and output parameters, and the access type (i.e., **Read** or **Write**). Parameters can be objects of any kind, including forms. We use keyword *In* to describe parameters that are inputs to the activity and *Out* to describe parameters that are outputs of the activity. Parameters that are used for both input and output are specified using keyword *InOut*.
- *Activity Declaration*: The *activity declaration* unit captures the general information about the activity such as the synopsis (description) of the task, the maximum allowable execution time, the administrator of the activity (i.e.,

the user identifier (UID) of the responsible person), and the set of compensation activities that are used for handling errors and exceptions and their
triggering conditions.

- *Role Association*: This unit specifies the set of roles associated with the
  activity. Each role is defined by a role name, a role type, and a set of agents
  that are granted membership into the role based on their responsibility in
  the business process or in the organization. Each agent is described by agent
  ID and role name. We distinguish two types of roles in the first prototype
  implementation of ActivityFlow: user and system, denoted as USER and SYS
  respectively.
- *Data Declaration*: The *data declaration* unit consists of the declaration of the
  classes to which the parameters of the activity belong and the set of messages (or methods) needed to manipulate the actual arguments. Constraints
  between these messages are also specified in this unit [5].
- *Procedure*: The procedure unit is defined within a **begin** and **end** bracket.
  It describes the composition of the activity, the control flow and data flow
  of the activity, and the pre- and post-condition of the activity. The main
  component of the control flow includes activity execution dependency specification, describing the execution precedence dependencies between children
  activities of the specified activity and the interleaving dependencies between
  a child activity and children of its siblings or between children activities of
  two different sibling activities. The main component of the data flow specification is defined through the activity state transition dependencies.

3.2 Dynamic Assignments of Agents

The assignment of agents (humans or information systems) to activities according to the role specification is a fundamental concept in WFMSs. At run time,
flexible and dynamic assignment resolution techniques are necessary to react
adequately to the resource allocation needs and organizational changes. ActivityFlow uses the following techniques to fulfill this requirement: (1) When the
set of agents is empty, the assignment of agents can be any users or systems
that belong to the roles associated with the specified activity. When the set of
agents is not empty, only those agents listed in the associated agent set can have
the privilege to execute the activity. (2) The assignment of agents can also be
done dynamically at run time. The activity enactment service engine will grant
the assignment if the run time assignment meets the role specification. (3) The
assignment of agents can be the administrator of the workflow process to which
the activity belongs, as the workflow administrator is a default role for all its
constituent activities.

The role-based assignment of agents provides great flexibility and breath of
application. By statically and dynamically establishing and defining roles and
assigning agents to activities in terms of roles, workflow administrators can control access at a level of abstraction that is natural to the way that enterprises
typically conduct business.

```
ACTIVITY TELESERVPROV
PARAMETER
      In: ClientId:CLIENT,
      In: Start:POINT,
      In: End:POINT,
      Out: CircuitId:CIRCUIT
ACCESS_TYPE Write
SYNOPSIS
      Telephone service provisioning
MAX_ALLOWABLE_TIME 3 weeks
ADMINISTRATOR
      UID: 0.0.0.337123545
EXCEPTION_HANDLER
      none
ROLE_ASSOCIATION
      Role_name: Tele_Service Officer
      Role_type: User
      Agent_Set:
            (UID: 0.0.0.135678221),
            (UID: 0.0.0.355983145);
DATA_DECLARATION
      import class CLIENT,
      import class POINT,
      import class CIRCUIT;
      import class SUMMARYTABLE;
BEGIN
      COMPOSITION
            T₁: ENTERREQUEST(InOut: ClientId:CLIENT, In: Start:POINT, End:POINT)
            D: INSTALLCIRCUIT(In: Start:POINT, End:POINT, Out: Status:Boolean)
            T₆: UPDATEDIRECTORY(InOut: ClientId:CLIENT)
            T₇: PREPAREBILL(InOut: ClientId:CLIENT, In: CircuitId:CIRCUIT)
            T₈: GENERATESUMMARY(In: ClientId:CLIENT, CircuitId:CIRCUIT, Out: Sum:SummaryTable)
      EXECUTION_DEPENDENCY
            ExeR₁: T₁ precede D
            ExeR₁: D precede T₆, T₇
            ExeR₂: T₆, T₇ precede T₈
      INTERLEAVING_DEPENDENCY
            ILR₁: T₁ precede T₂
            ILR₂: T₅ precede T₆, T₇
      STATE_TRANSITION_DEPENDENCY
            STR₁: abort(D) enable abort(TeleServProv)
END
```

Fig. 5. An Example specification of the top activity TELESERVPROV

3.3   Control Flow Specification: Activity Dependencies

In ActivityFlow, we provide four constructs to model various dependencies between activities. They are **precede, enable, disable,** and **compatible**. The construct **precede** is designed to capture the temporary precedence dependencies and the existence dependencies between two activities. For example, "A **precede** B" specifies a *begin-on-commit* execution dependency between the two activities: "B cannot begin before A commits". The constructs **enable** and **disable** are utilized to specify the enabling and disabling dependencies between activities. One of the critical differences between the construct **enable** or **disable** and the construct **precede** is that **enable** or **disable** specifies a triggering condition and an action being triggered, whereas **precede** only specifies an execution precedence dependency as a precondition that needs to be verified before an action can be activated, and it is not an enabling condition that, once satisfied, triggers the action. The construct **compatible** declares the compatibility of activities A_1 and A_2.

Consider the telephone service provisioning workflow example, a sample specification of the top activity TELESERVPROV is presented in Figure 5.

3.4 A Formal Model for Flow Procedure Definition

In this section we provide a graph-based model to formally describe the procedure unit of a workflow specification in ActivityFlow. This graph-based flow procedure model provides a formal foundation for ActivityFlow graphical user interface, which allows the end-users to model office procedures in a workflow process using iconic representation.

In ActivityFlow, we describe an activity procedure in terms of (1) a set of *nodes*, representing individual activities or connectors between these activities (e.g., split connector, join connector described in Section 2.3), and (2) a set of *edges*, representing signals among the nodes. Each node in the activity flow procedure is annotated with a trigger. A trigger defines the condition required to fire the node upon receiving signals from other nodes. The trigger condition is defined using the four constructs described in Section 3.3. Each flow procedure has exactly one begin node and one end node. When the begin node is fired, an activity flow instance is created. When the end node is triggered, the activity flow instance terminates.

Definition 1. *(activity flow graph)*
An activity flow graph is described by a binary tuple $< N, E >$, where

- N is a finite set of activity nodes and connector nodes.
  - $N = AN \cup CN \cup \{bn, en\}$, where $AN = \{nd_1, nd_2, ..., nd_n\}$ is a set of activity nodes, $CN = \{$AND-split, OR-Split, AND-join, OR-join, Iterator$\}$, bn denotes the begin node and en denotes the end node.
  - Each node nd_i $(i = 1, .., n)$ is described by a quadruple (NT, NN, TC, NS), where
    NT is the node type. An activity node has two types: *simple* and *compound*. A connector node has three types: split, join and spawn.
    NN denotes the node name.
    TC is the trigger condition of the node.
    NS is one of the two states of the node: *fired* or *not fired*.
- $E = \{e_1, e_2, ..., e_m\}$ is a set of edges.
  - Each edge is of the form $nd_i \longrightarrow nd_j$.
  - An edge $e_{ij} : nd_i \longrightarrow nd_j$ is described by a triple $(EN, DPnd, AVnd, ES)$, where EN is the edge name, $DPnd$ is the departure node, $AVnd$ is the arrival node, and ES is one of the two states of the node: *signaled* and *not signaled*.

We call e_{ij} an outgoing edge of node nd_i and incoming edge of node nd_j. □

For each node nd_i, there is a path from the begin node bn to nd_i. We say that a node nd_i is reachable from another node nd_j if there is a path from nd_i to nd_j.

Definition 2. *(reachability)*
Let $G = < N, E >$ be an activity flow graph. For any two nodes $nd_i, nd_j \in N$, nd_j is reachable from nd_i, denoted by $nd_i \overset{*}{\longrightarrow} nd_j$, if and only if one of the following conditions is verified:

(1) $nd_i = nd_j$.

(2) $nd_i \longrightarrow nd_j \in E$.

(3) $\exists nd_k \in N, nd_k \neq nd_i \wedge nd_k \neq nd_j$ s. t. $nd_i \overset{*}{\longrightarrow} nd_k \wedge nd_k \overset{*}{\longrightarrow} nd_j$. $\qquad \square$

A node nd_j is said to be *directly reachable* from a node nd_i if the condition (2) in Definition 2 is satisfied. To guarantees that the graph $G = < N, E >$ is acyclic, the following restrictions are placed:

(1) $\forall nd_i, nd_j \in N$, if $nd_i \longrightarrow nd_j \in E$ then $nd_j \longrightarrow nd_i \notin E$.

(2) $\forall nd_i, nd_j \in N$, if $nd_i \overset{*}{\longrightarrow} nd_j$ then $nd_j \overset{*}{\longrightarrow} nd_i$ does not hold.

To illustrate the definition, let us recast the telephone service provisioning workflow procedure described in Figure 5 in terms of the above definition:

- $N = \{Begin(T), T_1, D, T_6, T_7, T_8, End(T)\}$
- $E = \{Begin(T) \longrightarrow T_1, T_1 \longrightarrow D, D \longrightarrow T_6, D \longrightarrow T_7, T_6 \longrightarrow$ AND-join, $T_7 \longrightarrow$ AND-join, AND-join $\longrightarrow T_8, T_8 \longrightarrow End(T)\}$
- $TC(Begin)$: NeedService
  $TC(T_1)$: NeedService
  $TC(D)$: $commit(T_1)$
  $TC(T_6)$: $Status(D) =$ true
  $TC(T_7)$: $Status(D) =$ true
  $TC($AND-join$)$: $terminate(T_6) \wedge terminate(T_7)$
  $TC(T_8)$: $commit(T_6) \wedge commit(T_7)$
  $TC(End)$: $commit(T_6)$

Note that NeedService is a boolean variable. When a new telephone service request arrives, NeedService is true. Figure 6 shows the use of the ActivityFlow graphical notations to specify this activity flow procedure. When a node

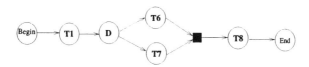

Fig. 6. Graphical representation of the flow procedure of top activity TELESERVPROV

is clicked, the node information will be displayed in a quadruplet, including node type, name, its trigger and its current state. When an edge is clicked, the edge information, such as the edge name, its departure and arrival nodes, and its current state, will be displayed. From Figure 6, it is obvious that activity node T_8 is reachable from nodes T_1, D, T_6 and T_7, and activity nodes T_6 and T_7 are reachable from nodes T_1 and D respectively.

An activity flow procedure G is instantiated by an instantiation request issued by an agent. The instantiation request provides the initial values of the data items (actual arguments) required by the parameter list of the flow. An activity flow instantiation is valid if the agent who issued the firing satisfies the defined role specification.

Definition 3. *(valid flow instantiation request)*
Let $G = < N, E >$ be the activity flow and $u = (agent\_oid, role\_name)$ be an agent requesting the activity flow instantiation T of α. The flow instantiation T is valid if and only if $\exists \rho \in Role(G)$ such that $role\_name(u) = \rho$. □

When the agent who initiates a flow instantiation request is not authorized, the instantiation request is rejected, and the flow instantiation is not created.

When a flow instantiation request is valid, a flow instantiation, say T, is created by firing the begin node of T. A node can be instantiated or triggered when all the incoming edges of the node are signaled, its trigger condition is evaluated to be **true**. When a node is triggered, a unique activity instance identifier is assigned, and the node state is set to **fired**. In ActivityFlow, all the nodes are initialized to **not_fired** and all the edges are initialized to **not_signaled**.

In ActivityFlow, we use the term conditional rollback to refer to the situations which require to revisit the nodes previously terminated or not fired. Conditional rollbacks are a desirable functionality and encountered frequently in some business processes. We provide an iterator connector for realization of conditional rollbacks. We also define the termination property and precedence preserving property to guarantee the correctness of workflow execution. Due to the space limitation, the details are omitted here. Readers may refer to [6] for further discussion.

4 Conclusion

We have described the ActivityFlow approach to workflow process definition. Interesting features of ActivityFlow are the following. First, we use a small set of constructs and a collection of mechanisms to allow workflow designers to specify the nested process structure and the variety of activity dependencies declaratively and incrementally. The ActivityFlow framework is intuitive and flexible. Additional business rules can be added into the system simply through plug-in agents. The associated graphical notations bring workflow design and automation closer to users. Second, ActivityFlow supports a uniform workflow specification interface to describe different types (i.e., ad-hoc, administrative, or production) of workflows involved in their organizational processes, and to increase the flexibility of workflow processes in accommodating changes.

Research and development for ActivityFlow continue along several dimensions. On the theoretical side we are investigating workflow correctness properties and the correctness assurance in the concurrent execution of activities. On the practical side, we are building value-added *adapters* on top of existing transaction processing systems [1] to support extended transaction models and ActivityFlow specifications. In addition, we are exploring the enhancement of process design tools to interoperate with various application development environments.

The implementation architecture for the first prototype of ActivityFlow is based on the World Wide Web (WWW) technologies. We use the HTML (Hyper-Text Markup Language) to represent information objects required for workflow processes and to integrate different media types into a document. The HTTP server translates the requests from the users in the HTML forms to calls of the corresponding procedures of the prototype system of ActivityFlow using a CGI interface or a Java interface. The prototype implementation consists of three main components: *the workflow agent interface toolkit, the workflow activity engine*, and *the distributed object manager*. Readers who are interested in detailed implementation issues may refer to [6, 1, 11].

Acknowledgement This work was partially carried out when the first author was with the University of Alberta. Our thanks are also due to Roger Barga, David Buttler, Yooshin Lee, Kirill Richine, Wei Tang, and Tong Zhou for their implementation endeavour on various components that form the basis for the ActivityFlow project.

References

1. R. Barga and C. Pu. A practical and modular implementation technique of extended transaction models. In *Proceedings of the 21st International Conference on Very Large Data Bases*, Zurich, September 1995.
2. A. K. Elmagarmid. *Database Transaction Models for Advanced Applications*. Morgan Kaufmann, 1992.
3. D. Georgakopoulos, M. Hornick, and A. Sheth. An overview of workflow management: From processing modeling to workflow automation infrastructure. *Distributed and Parallel Database*, 3(2):119–152, 1995.
4. M. Hsu and C. Kleissner. Objectflow: Towards a process management infrastructure. *Distributed and Parallel Databases*, (4):169–194, 1996.
5. L. Liu and R. Meersman. The basic building blocks for modeling communication behavior of complex objects: an activity-driven approach. *ACM Transactions on Database Systems*, 21(3):157–207, June 1996.
6. L. Liu and C. Pu. ActivityFlow: A formalism for incremental specification of workflow activities. Technical Report TR97, University of Alberta.
7. J. McCarthy. There is more than one kind of workflow software. *Computerworld*, November 2 1992.
8. C. Mohan. *Advanced Transaction Models - Survey and Critique*. Tutorial presented at the ACM SIGMOD international conference, 1994.
9. A. Sheth. *Workflow Automation: Applications, Technology and Research*. Tutorial presented at the ACM SIGMOD international conference, 1995.
10. A. Sheth,G. Georgakopoulos, S.Joosten, M. Rusinkiewicz, W. Scacchi, J. Wildedn, and A. Wolf. Report from the nsf workshop on workflow and process automation in information systems. *ACM SIGMOD Record*, 25(4):55–67, December 1996.
11. T. Zhou, C. Pu, and L. Liu. Adaptable, efficient, and modular coordination of distributed extended transactions. In *Proceeding of the International Conference on Parallel and Distributed Databases*, 1996.

Silver Bullet Shy on Legacy Mountain: When Neat Technology Just Doesn't Work

– or –

Miracles to Save the Realm: Faustian Bargains or Noble Pursuits

Michael L. Brodie
Senior Staff Scientist
GTE Laboratories, Incorporated, USA

The software crisis is very much alive almost 30 years after it was first defined. Only now, it is beyond crisis proportions and is eating into our GNP. With a problem so large and wide-spread, most organizations have not really addressed it. Large organizations have built massive legacy mountains of data and code; 150 terabytes of data and 200 million lines of code is not unusual for a North American telephone company. Over the past decade the information systems community has produced some brilliant ideas, including the following:

client/server	legacy systems
business processes re-engineering	wrappers
workflows	repositories
distributed object computing	cooperative ISs
World Wide Web	COTS
inheritance	class libraries
polymorphism	agents
re-use	business objects and rules
interoperability	object-oriented type systems and languages
ontologies	electronic commerce

These revolutionary ideas have been the basis for promises of orders of magnitude improvements in productivity so as to address the software crisis. There have been rare cases in which success has been achieved. In general, however, they have made almost no impact on industrial-strength problems. More widespread success may well be achieved in some years (e.g., 20 for relational DBMSs). They cannot be applied now in vanilla programming shops with vanilla staff. In the next five years, large organizations will attempt to level legacy mountain. What are the real problems, and how can you help? Will research play a role? This talk will outline some industrial-strength information systems problems in legacy mountain, attempt to address them with some of the above ideas, and discuss why the attempts might have failed and why these brilliant ideas are so hard to put into practice.

A Multi-Level Architecture for Representing Enterprise Data Models

Daniel Moody

Simsion Bowles & Associates
1 Collins St., Melbourne, Australia 3000.
Email: dmoody@sba.com.au

Abstract. One of the most serious limitations of the Entity Relationship Model in practice is its inability to cope with complexity. With large numbers of entities, data models become difficult to understand and maintain. The problem becomes unmanageable at the enterprise level, where models typically consist of hundreds of entities. A number of approaches have been proposed in the literature to address this problem, but none have achieved widespread acceptance in practice. This paper proposes a simple and natural extension to the Entity Relationship Model which allows enterprise data models to be represented at multiple levels of abstraction, from a one page overview down to primitive entities and relationships. The model may be organised into any number of levels, depending on its complexity. The technique is based on the organisation of a city street directory, which is a practical solution to the problem of representing a large and complex model in everyday life.

1. INTRODUCTION

The Problem Addressed

One of the most serious practical limitations of the Entity Relationship Model is its inability to cope with the size and complexity of data models encountered in real world situations (Simsion, 1989). Feldman and Miller (1987) argue that this is the primary reason why data modelling techniques have not realised their full potential in practice. With large numbers of entities, data models become difficult to understand and maintain. The problem becomes unmanageable at the enterprise level, where models typically consist of hundreds of entities. The complexity of enterprise data models is a major barrier to their acceptance and use in practice (Shanks, 1996).

Psychological evidence shows that due to limits on short term memory, humans have a strictly limited capacity for processing information—this is estimated to be "seven, plus or minus two" concepts (Miller, 1956; Newell and Simon, 1972). If the amount of information exceeds these limits, information overload ensues and comprehension degrades rapidly (Lipowski, 1975). Empirical studies show that application data models consist of an average of 120 entities, while enterprise data models consist of an average of 1200 entities (Maier, 1996). Clearly, models of this size are well beyond the limits of human information processing.

The understandability of data models is of critical importance in the requirements analysis process, so that users can participate in the development of the model and verify its correctness (Moody and Shanks, 1994; Feldman and Miller, 1986). For this reason, decisions regarding the presentation of data models are far from trivial and should be approached with as much care as decisions on the content of the models.

Outline of this Paper

This paper proposes an extension to the Entity Relationship model to cope with the size and complexity of Enterprise Data Models. The method described is based on the approach proposed by Moody (1991) but has evolved as a result of use in practice. The method is also applicable in any situation where data models become too large to fit easily on a single page. However the primary emphasis is on enterprise data models because this is where complexity becomes unmanageable.

The outline of the paper is as follows. Section 2 looks at methods which have previously been proposed in the literature. Section 3 examines a city street directory as an example of a successful solution to the problem of representing large and complex models in another domain. Section 4 describes a method for representing enterprise data models based on the street directory organisation. The application of the method is illustrated using a simple example. Finally, Section 5 concludes the paper.

2. PREVIOUS RESEARCH

This section reviews methods for representing large data models which have been previously proposed in the literature.

Structured Entity Charts

Martin (1983) proposes a representational scheme in which entities are arranged into hierarchical clusters vertically down the page, with relationships within a cluster shown by indentation rather than by explicit links. The major weakness of this method is that the model is shown as a single interconnected diagram, making it difficult to follow the links between clusters, which may extend over many pages. It also represents a significant departure from the widely used and understood Entity Relationship representation.

Subject Oriented Schemata

This is a technique developed by Lockheed Missiles and Space Company for organising large Entity Relationship models (Gilberg, 1986). It represents large data models as a number of subject-oriented data models (called subschemata), each of which is shown on a separate page. A major weakness of the method is that it involves a high degree of overlap between models, leading to problems of validation and maintenance. It is also difficult to gain an overview of the model as a whole.

Clustered Entity Models

Feldman and Miller (1987) aggregate entities into higher level clusters called information areas to produce a hierarchy of models at different levels of abstraction. A major weakness of this method is that it leads to uncontrolled levels of redundancy between separate entities clusters. It also violates one of the basic principles of hierarchical organisation by allowing objects at different levels of abstraction to appear on the same diagram (Klir, 1983; Flood and Carson, 1988). Experience with this method in practice shows that it leads to models which are more difficult to understand than the original (unclustered) model.

Structured Data Models

Simsion (1989) describes a technique which allows data models to be presented at a number of different levels of abstraction using the mechanism of generalisation (Smith and Smith, 1978). The lowest level model is a fully detailed Entity Relationship model, with the higher levels representing progressively more generic models. At each level of abstraction, the standard Entity Relationship representation is used. A problem with this approach is that at the highest level it leads to extremely abstract concepts that users find difficult to relate to (Moriarty, 1992; Moody, 1996b). Also, the rules for carrying out the levelling are not well-defined, and rely heavily on the modeller's ability to make appropriate generalisations.

Clustered Entity Relationship Models

Teory et al (1989) extends Feldman and Miller's (1987) representational method to include several new conventions such as level numbering, and also define a formal clustering algorithm. However this method suffers from the same problems as Feldman and Miller's original formalism.

Levelled Entity Relationship Models

Gandhi, Robertson and Gucht (1994) define a method for representing large data models using information hiding concepts. This method is based on the Nested Entity Relationship Model of Carlson et al (1990). The major weakness of this method is that it introduces a diagrammatical representation which differs significantly from the standard Entity Relationship model, and fundamentally changes its interpretation.

Financial Services Data Model

Allworth (1996) describes a technique used to represent an enterprise architecture for banking and finance. Like structured data models (Simsion, 1989) it uses generalisation rather than aggregation as an abstraction mechanism. It consists of three levels: the top level model (A level) is a set of high level classifications of data; the second level models (B level) are represented as generalisation hierarchies; while at the third level (C level), standard Entity Relationship diagrams are used.

Requirements of a Representational Approach

All of the methods reviewed have their problems, and none have achieved widespread acceptance in practice. Our criteria for a successful solution to the problem are:

- ◆ Understandability to users: The major consideration in developing representations for models is to enhance human comprehension (De Marco, 1978; Sowa, 1984; Simon, 1982). To do this effectively, the representational method must take into account the nature and limitations of human information processing (Davis and Olsen, 1984).

- Ease of use: In many of the methods proposed, the rules for applying them are either unclear or overly complex. Practitioners choose methods based on whether they are useful rather than if they are theoretically "sound" (Flood and Carson, 1988). In general, the simpler and easier the method is to use, the more likely that it will be adopted in practice.

- Transparency: A major problem with many of the methods proposed is that they significantly change the widely accepted and used Entity Relationship representation. Radical change will be resisted by the profession because of their familiarity with the existing representation. This can be seen by the fact that despite the hundreds of proposals in the literature to extend the Entity Relationship Model, the notations used in practice have changed very little since its original formulation. Another problem with introducing new representations is that they cannot be supported by commercially available CASE tools.

3. STREET DIRECTORY ORGANISATION

Analogical Reasoning

In considering how to represent enterprise data models, a natural starting point is to look at how large models are handled in other disciplines. This is an example of analogical reasoning, a problem solving approach in which a solution is found by looking at how a similar problem has been solved in another domain. The solution to this second problem, the exemplar, can then be used as a basis for developing a solution to the original problem.

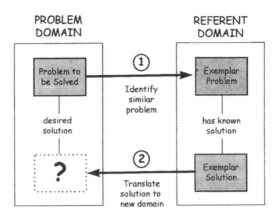

Figure 1. Analogical Reasoning as a Problem Solving Approach

A number of authors have discussed the use of analogical reasoning as a research approach. Polya (1957) discusses the use of analogy in heuristic reasoning and in mathematical discovery. Poincare (1913) describes the use of analogy in mathematics and physics and his own use of analogy in his work on Fuchsian functions. Ladd

(1987) discusses the use of analogy in economics and as a general strategy for scientific research. Analogical reasoning is also one of the primary strategies used in systems research (Klir, 1985; von Bertalannfy, 1964).

An Exemplar Problem

A street directory is a simple, yet very effective solution to the problem of packaging a large and complex model in a way that people can easily understand and use. It serves as an ideal exemplar for representing enterprise data models for the following reasons:

a) Both types of models have a diagrammatical representation which takes the form of a large, interconnected network. They also have similar problems of size: a street directory typically has thousands of different streets, localities, landmarks and other objects to represent, and limited space on each page to show them.

b) A major consideration in the representation of both types of model is understandability to non-experts. Just as an enterprise data model should be understandable by non-technical users, a street directory needs to be easily understood by anyone, not just other map-makers.

c) Proven in practice: The street directory organisation is a practical solution which has evolved over a long period of time, and has worked successfully for many years. Evidence of the maturity of the solution can be seen in the consistency of its structure from year to year, from one map maker to another, and even across different countries.

As shown in Figure 2, a street directory consists of three major components:

- A key map, which provides an overview of the region covered by the directory
- A set of numbered detail maps, showing parts of the region in full detail.
- References between the maps to show how they fit together

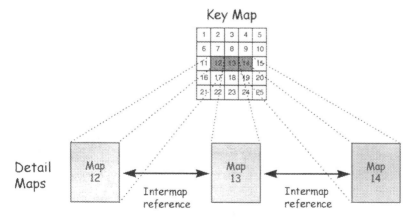

Figure 2. Street Directory Components

Key Map

The key map provides an overview of the total region covered by the directory, and shows how it is divided into detail maps. Figure 3 shows the key map for the London A-Z, one of the most widely used and successful street directories in the world.

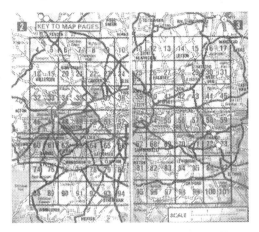

Figure 3. Key Map for the London A-Z

Detail Maps

Each detail map is numbered and shows a subset of the region on a single page. The region is partitioned into maps in such a way that each map shows the maximum amount of detail without sacrificing readability. Figure 4 shows a detail map from the London A-Z.

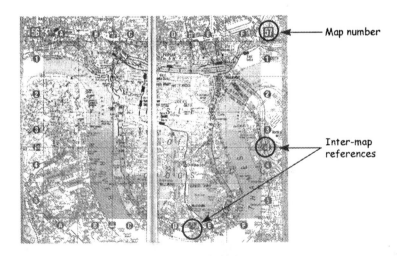

Figure 4. Detail Map, showing cross references to other maps

To assist navigation between maps, inter-map references are shown at the borders of each detail map, which indicate the numbers of adjacent maps to the north, south, east and west. Inter-map references are bi-directional—if map 5 refers to map 2, map 2 will refer back to map 5. In addition, there is a small amount of overlap between adjoining maps (a 1cm border around each map). This provides useful context for showing how maps fit together and also helps in navigating between maps.

4. LEVELLED ENTITY RELATIONSHIP MODELS

Overview of the Method

The problem of representing a city street directory is solved by decomposing it into parts of manageable size. The key map provides an overview of the whole region, while each detail map shows a part of the region in full detail. We use a similar approach in packaging enterprise data models, as shown in Figure 5. The enterprise data model is decomposed into subsets of manageable size called *subject areas*. A high level diagram, called the Context Data Model, shows how the model is divided into subject areas, while each Subject Area Data Model shows part of the model in full detail. Foreign entities are used to show cross-references between subject areas.

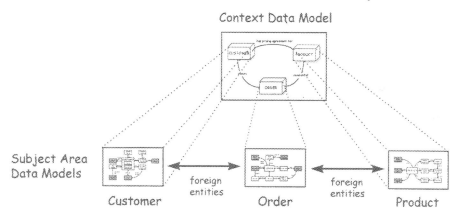

Figure 5. Enterprise Data Model Architecture

A simple three step procedure is described for producing a levelled enterprise data model from a standard Entity Relationship model. An example is used to illustrate the use of the technique.

Step 1: Partition the Data Model into Subject Areas

The first step in producing a levelled enterprise data model is to divide it into subject areas. The guidelines which should be used in partitioning the model are:

1. Each entity should be assigned to one and only one subject area. This minimises redundancy between subject areas.

2. Each subject area should be of manageable size (7+/-2 entities). Because the human mind is limited in the amount of information it can comprehend at one time, the size of subject areas should be limited to a maximum of nine entities

should *not* be included in the count of entities, since they are subcategories within a single entity type.

3. Each subject area should be named after one of the entities on the subject area, called the *central entity*. This ensures that entities are grouped on the basis of logical relationships rather than functional (processing) relationships. Functional areas, although the most obvious way of clustering entities, do not provide a stable basis for partitioning the data model (Martin, 1983). Central entities should also be the entities of greatest significance to the business.

4. The total number of subject areas should be minimised. The complexity of a system is defined by the number of parts and the number of relationships between them (Klir, 1983). Breaking the model down into too many parts will generally make it more rather than less complex.

5. Relationships which cross subject area boundaries, called *boundary relationships,* measure the interconnectedness or *coupling* between subject areas. This is an important measure of the quality of the decomposition of any system (Simon, 1982). Coupling should be minimised to increase the independence of subject areas. A simple measure of the coupling of a decomposition is the number of relationships within each subject area (*internal relationships*) divided by the number of boundary relationships. As a general rule, the total number of internal relationships should be at least twice the number of boundary relationships.

Figure 6 shows an example data model partitioned into subject areas. Central entities are shaded and boundary relationships highlighted on the diagram. Subject areas are called *adjoining* areas when there is a boundary relationship between them.

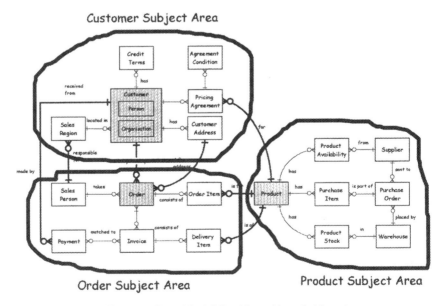

Figure 6. Example Data Model Partitioned into Subject Areas

The partitioning shown in Figure 6 satisfies the partitioning rules defined previously:

1. The subject areas form non-overlapping subsets of the entities in the original model.

2. Each subject area is named after the central entity (shaded on the diagram)

3. Each subject area consists of a maximum of nine entities (6,6,7)

4. The entities could not be partitioned into fewer subject areas without breaking rule 3

5. There are more than twice as many internal relationships (17) as there are boundary relationships (7).

Step 2: Produce Context Data Model

The Context Data Model provides an overview of the model, showing all the subject areas and how they fit together. Each subject area is shown as a three dimensional box, with relationships shown using arrows. The Context Data Model for the partitioned data model of Figure 6 is shown below.

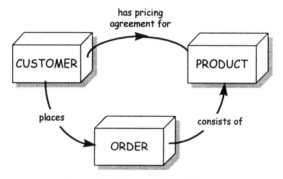

Figure 7. Context Data Model

Any shape could be used instead to represent subject areas. For example in Moody (1996a), graphical images are used. The most important thing is to differentiate between the symbols used for subject areas and those used for entities to avoid confusion. A relationship is generally shown between subject areas on the Context Data Model when there is a boundary relationship between them at the next level (adjoining subject areas). However there is no need to show all boundary relationships between subject areas—only the most important ones should be shown. This is similar to the way the key map on the street directory only shows the major connecting routes between maps. Like the key map, the context data model is a summary diagram only.

The context data model is in fact wholly redundant—all information shown on the context diagram is duplicated at the next level down (on subject area data models). However it provides important context for understanding the data model as a whole. The context diagram uses the mechanism of *aggregation* (Smith and Smith, 1977) to create higher level objects (subject areas) from the primitive entities and relationships of the enterprise. This is precisely the same abstraction mechanism used to group attributes into entities, and so is a natural extension to the Entity Relationship approach.

It is also natural from the point of view of human information processing, since it is the same mechanism used by humans to deal with large amounts of information. The ability to recursively develop information saturated "chunks" is the key to man's ability to deal with complexity on a day to day basis (Flood and Carson, 1988; Uhr et al, 1962). Other authors (eg. Simsion, 1989; Allworth, 1996) have used generalisation as a mechanism for dealing with complexity in large data models, but this is less natural from a human cognition viewpoint (Moody and Osianlis, 1996).

Step 3: Produce Subject Area Data Models

Each Subject Area Data Model shows a part of the enterprise data model which is small enough to be shown on a single page. Subject area data models are represented as standard Entity Relationship models, with the following differences:

* The central entity is shown in the centre of the diagram, and is larger than all other entities
* Foreign entities are used to show relationships to entities on other subject areas

Whenever an entity on a Subject Area Data Model has a relationship to an entity on another subject area (as part of a *boundary relationship*), the second entity is shown as a *foreign entity*. Foreign entities are represented using shaded boxes, with their primary subject area in brackets. In the example data model, there is a boundary relationship between the Customer entity (Customer Subject Area) and the Payment entity (Order Subject Area). Figure 8 shows how this relationship would be shown on the Customer Subject Area Data Model:

Figure 8. Foreign Entity Reference (Customer Subject Area)

The same relationship would be shown on the Order Subject Area Data Model as:

Figure 9. Foreign Entity Reference (Order Subject Area)

Foreign entities thus act as bi-directional links between subject areas. While an entity must be assigned to one and only one subject area (its *primary subject area*), it may appear on any number of subject areas as a foreign entity. Foreign entities should be shown on the outside of subject area diagrams since they are used as entry and exit points into the subject area. (Note: Foreign entities are not included in the count of entities on a subject area because they are included for linking purposes only).

Figures 10, 11 and 12 on the next page show the Subject Area Data Models which result from the example data model.

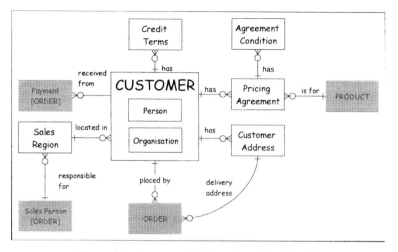

Figure 10. Customer Subject Area Data Model

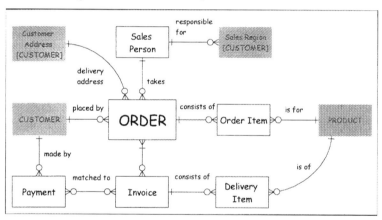

Figure 11. Order Subject Area Data Model

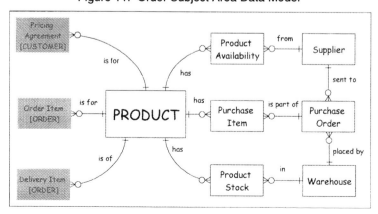

Figure 12. Product Subject Area Data Model

The street directory uses overlap at the boundary of maps and intermap references to show relationships between detail maps. This method uses redundancy in a similar way, by duplicating boundary relationships between adjoining subject areas. All other relationships (internal relationships) appear only on a single subject area.

Foreign entities provide a simple and intuitive mechanism for navigating between different parts of the model, which mirrors the use of foreign keys in the relational model (Codd, 1971). The simplicity of the relational model results from the fact that relationships between tables are shown by common attributes (foreign keys) rather than explicit links (Date, 1986). The simplicity of the approach described in this paper lies in the fact that relationships between subject areas are shown by common entities (foreign entities) rather than explicit connectors. There is no need to introduce any new constructs, which would increase the complexity of the diagrams (Simsion, 1989).

Foreign entities provide useful context to show how subject areas fit together, and assist in navigating between them. An important practical advantage of using foreign entities is that all an entity's relationships are shown on its primary subject area. This is especially important from the purposes of mapping the data model into a database schema, to ensure that all logical access paths are included in the database design (Dumpala and Arora, 1983; Nijssen and Leung, 1987; Dawson and Parker; 1988; Teory et al, 1986).

Extending the Model to Multiple Levels

Given a maximum of nine entities on each subject area data model and the same on the context data model, two levels of abstraction only allows for data models up to 80 entities. At the enterprise level, where data models may consist of hundreds of entities, more than two levels of abstraction will therefore be required. Three levels will cater for data models up to about 700 entities, and four levels up to 5,000. At each level, diagrams are limited to nine objects, to keep complexity manageable.

Comparison With Street Directory Representation

The representational method described in this section corresponds very closely to the street directory organisation:

- The context data model corresponds to the key map in the street directory. The key map shows how the region is divided into detail maps, while the context diagram shows how the model is partitioned into subject areas.
- Subject areas correspond to the detail maps in the street directory. Both show a manageable subset of the underlying model on a single page. However subject areas are named while detail maps are numbered.
- Foreign entities, which are entities duplicated between adjoining subject areas, correspond to the overlap between adjoining detail maps.
- Subject area references shown inside foreign entities correspond to inter-map references in the street directory. These references provide links between subject areas to aid navigation.

5. CONCLUSION

This paper has presented a simple and natural extension to the Entity Relationship model to cope with the complexity of enterprise data models. This method is also applicable in any situation where data models get too large to be easily understood. In terms of the criteria defined in Section 2, the method compares favourably with methods previously proposed in the literature:

- Understandability to users: The method is closely based on the organisation of something almost everyone has used at some time in their lives—a city street directory. Because this is such a familiar concept, non-technical users can understand data models represented in this way with very little explanation.

- Ease of use: A major strength of the method is that it is much simpler to use than any of the methods previously proposed. A simple three step procedure is described for producing a multi-level enterprise model from a standard ("flat") Entity Relationship model. Experience shows that it can be learnt and applied successfully by both experienced and novice data modellers in a one hour workshop session.

- Transparency: The method requires only minimal changes to the widely accepted representation of the Entity Relationship model. At the level of subject area data models, only the constructs of the standard Entity Relationship model are used (entities and relationships). The method can also be supported by most commercially available CASE tools with little or no modification.

REFERENCES

1. Allworth, S., "Using Classification Structures to Develop and Structure Generic Industry Models", *Proceedings of the First Australian Data Management Conference*, Data Management Association (DAMA), Melbourne, Australia, December 2-3, 1996.

2. Bubenko, J.A. Information Systems Methodologies - A Research View, in Olle, T.W., Sol, H.G., Verrijn-Stuart, A.A. *Information Systems Design Methodologies: Improving The Practice.* North-Holland, 1986.

3. Carlson, C.R., Ji, W. and Arora, A.K., The Nested Entity Relationship Model, *Entity Relationship Approach to Database Design and Querying*, North Holland, 1990.

4. Codd, E.F., A Relational Database Model for Large Shared Data Banks, *Communications of the ACM*, 13, 6, 1971.

5. Date, C.J., *Relational Database: Selected Writings*, Addison-Wesley, 1986.

6. Davis, G.B. and Olsen, M.H., *Management Information Systems: Conceptual Foundations, Structure and Development*, McGraw-Hill, 1985.

7. Dawson, K.S. and Parker, L.M.P., From Entity-relationship Diagrams to Fourth Normal Form: A Pictorial Aid to Analysis, *The Computer Journal*, Vol. 31, No.3, 1988.

8. De Marco, T., *Structured Analysis and System Specification*, Yourdon Press, 1978.

9. Dumpala, S.R. and Arora, S.V., Schema translation using the Entity-Relationship Approach, In Chen, P.P. (ed.) *The Entity-Relationship Approach to Information Modelling and Analysis*, North-Holland, 1983.

10. Feldman, P. and Miller, D., Entity Model Clustering: Structuring a Data Model by Abstraction, *The Computer Journal*, Vol. 29, No. 4,1986.

11. Flood, R.L. and Carson, E.R., Dealing With Complexity: An Introduction to the Theory and Application of Systems Science, Plenum Press, 1988.

12. Gandhi, M., Robertson, E.L. and Van Gucht, D., Levelled Entity Relationship Model, *Proceedings of the Thirteenth International Conference on the Entity Relationship Approach*, Manchester, December 14-17, 1994.

13. Gilberg, R.F., A Schema Methodology for Large Entity-Relationship Diagrams, in Chen, P.P. (ed.) *Proceedings of Fourth International Conference on the Entity Relationship Approach, 1986.*

14. Klir, G.J., *Architecture of Systems Problem Solving*, Plenum Press, 1985.

15. Leung, C.M.R. and Nijssen, G.M. From a NIAM Conceptual Schema into the Optimal SQL Relational Database Schema, *Australian Computer Journal,* May, 1987.

16. Lipowski, Z.J., Sensory and Information Inputs Overload, *Comprehensive Psychiatry*, Vol. 16, 3, May/June, 1975.

17. Martin, J., *Strategic Data Planning Methodologies*, Prentice-Hall, 1983.

18. Miller, G., The magical number seven, plus or minus two: Some limits on our capacity for processing information, The *Psychological Review*, March, 1956.

19. Moody, D.L. and Shanks, G.G., "What Makes A Good Data Model? Evaluating the Quality of Entity Relationship Models", *Proceedings of the Thirteenth International Conference on the Entity Relationship Approach*, Manchester, December 14-17, 1994.

20. Moody, D.L., "A Practical Methodology for the Representation of Large Data Models", *Proceedings of the Australian Database and Information Systems Conference*, University of N.S.W., Sydney, Australia, February, 1991.

21. Moody, D.L., "Graphical Entity Relationship Models: Towards A More User Understandable Representation of Data", *Proceedings of the Fifteenth International Conference on the Entity Relationship Approach*, Cottbus, Germany, October 7-9, 1996a.

22. Moody, D.L., and Osianlis, A., "Bringing Data Models to Life: An Interactive Tool for Representing Entity Relationship Models", *Proceedings of the Seventh Australasian Conference on Information Systems*, Hobart, Australia, December 11-13, 1996.

23. Moriarty, T., "Where's The Business?", *Database Programming and Design*, July, 1993a.

24. Newell A., and Simon, H.A., *Human Problem Solving*, Prentice-Hall, 1972.

25. Rescher, N., *The Primacy of Practice*, Blackwell, 1973.

26. Shanks, G.G., "Enterprise Data Architectures: A Study of Practice", *First Australian Data Management Conference,* Melbourne, Australia, December 2-3, 1996.

27. Simon, H.A. *Sciences of the Artificial*, MIT Press, 1982.

28. Simsion, G.C, A Structured Approach to Data Modelling, *The Australian Computer Journal*, August, 1989.

29. Smith, J.M. and Smith, D.C.P., Database Abstractions: Aggregation and Generalization, *ACM Transactions on Database Systems*, Vol. 2 No. 2, 1977.

30. Sowa, J.F. *Conceptual Structures: Information Processing in Mind and Machine,* Prentice-Hall, 1984.

31. Teory, T.J., Wei, G., Bolton, D.L., and Koenig, J.A., ER Model Clustering as an Aid for User Communication and Documentation in Database Design, *Communications of the ACM*, August, 1989.

32. Teory, T.J., Yang, D. and Fry, J.P., A Logical Design Methodology For Relational Databases Using The Extended Entity Relationship Model, *ACM Computing Surveys*, 18, 2, 1986.

Data Model for Customizing DB Schemas Based on Business Policies

Jun Sekine, Atsushi Kitai, Yoshihito Ooshima and Yasuhiro Oohara

NTT Information and Communication Systems Laboratories
1-1 Hikarino-oka, Yokosuka, Kanagawa, Japan.
E-mail: {sekine, kitai, oshima, oohara}@nttjog.isl.ntt.co.jp

Abstract. One of the goals of data modeling has been to uniquely identify the data semantics of target applications and describe them in database schemas. In contrast to this approach, this paper proposes a data model that allows description of variable parts in data semantics and how each variable part is dependent on business policies. This is useful when describing database schemas for common software components that are used in applications with different business policies. A set of alternatives chosen from a specified set of business policies is converted to a set of primitives that describes how variable parts should be customized, thus enabling users to generate a database schema meeting some specific application requirements. The primitives uniformly describe a variety of customizations, such as inclusion and exclusion of database elements, changes in the characteristics of a database elements, and the composition of database elements. The model also serves as a basis of collecting and organizing a variety of business policies. Users can have a global view of how a database schema is affected by different business policy alternatives. A case study has shown that this model is applicable to real database schemas.

1 Introduction

Database design research has long been focusing on describing the data semantics of target applications, and a number of semantic data models [9, 21, 16, 1, 26] have been proposed. According to these proposals, one of the most important tasks in database design is to uniquely identify the data semantics of the target applications and describe them in database (or conceptual) schemas using a data model. This approach works well when the target applications are fixed and their requirements are clear enough. However, this is not necessarily ensured when describing a reusable database schema that can be used for a variety of target applications. We found two problems with this approach when trying to design a database schema for a common reusable software component used in different applications in the same business domain. The first was a divergence of the data semantics due to the divergence of the business policies behind each application. For example, we had difficulty in determining which relationship to define or what multiplicity a relationship should have because different applications have different business policies affecting some parts of the database schema or others.

The other problem is the satisfiability of business policies, meaning that it is difficult to know if a database schema meets the business requirements of an application. Specifications for database schemas may be useful for this purpose, but because they are often written in technical terms, translating them into business terms is often time-consuming. These problems become more important as reusable software components are becoming more popular with the emergence of plug-and-play components in the market.

Three approaches can be taken to resolve the first problem: designing a general database schema that covers all possible variations of business policies, preparing a different database schema for each different set of business policies, or customizing a single database schema based on business policies. The first approach is taken in conventional database design methodologies, especially in the area of schema integration [2, 29, 12]. However, the result of this approach could be redundant database schemas that are difficult to use and not necessarily optimal in terms of performance and storage size. The second approach is taken in proposals for storing specifications in a repository for reuse [7, 22, 11], but the cost of storing and organizing the repository is sometimes high. It is also difficult for users to have a global view of what is stored in the repository and how business policies affect database schemas. This paper takes the third approach, i.e. customization of a database schema, and proposes a data model called Business-Policy-driven Customization (BPC) model for it. The BPC model resolves the first problem by allowing description of variable parts in database schemas and also resolves the second problem by describing the relationships between the variable parts and business policies affecting them.

In the BPC model, each variable part in a database schema is uniformly described as a database policy, such as the existence of a database element, the existence of certain characteristics in a database element and the composition of two database elements, and each database policy has more than one alternative. The BPC model also allows description of business policies, such as whether corporate organizations are allowed as contractors or not, and each business policy has more than one alternative. Since each business policy alternative is related to one or more database policy alternatives, all the variable parts in a database schema are determined by choosing one or more business policy alternatives.

Using this construct, the BPC model allows the description of database schemas applicable to a wide range of applications. Users who are not necessarily experts in database design can give business policy alternatives necessary to customize the database schemas. In addition, the BPC model can be used as a basis of collecting and organizing a variety of business policies. Users can have a global view of business policies. The BPC model tries to describe database schemas that are as flexible and reusable as software components often called frameworks [30, 5, 28] or design patterns [14].

This paper is organized as follows. Section 2 discusses related works and their issues. In Section 3, the target data model generated through customization is briefly defined. In Section 4, details of the BPC model and the customization process using it are presented. Section 5 proposes a graphical notation of the model, and Section 6 presents some results of a case study. Section 7 concludes the paper by discussing the model's status and open issues.

2 Related Works

Related works can be summarized according to how they describe variable parts in database schemas or software specifications and how they describe business policies and their relationships to the variable parts. Regarding the description of variable parts in database schemas, no proposal has been made in data modeling. In requirements engineering, on the other hand, Fugini [13, 27] has introduced the concept of role in an enhanced ER model for including or excluding a group of attributes from object classes. Using a guidance mechanism, users can determine which roles to include, and thus customize software specifications. Fugini's proposal also allows several operations, including specialization, decomposition and composition of specifications, but these operations must be used by users at their own risk. This is in contrast to our approach, where database designers determine which parts are to be customized. We take this approach to ensure the quality and consistency of the customized database schemas. Castano [7, 8] and Bellinzona [3] proposed information structures for guiding customization of specifications. These structures, however, use natural language for guidance, and therefore, they cannot be used for automatic customization of specifications. In network management, a model for specifying managed objects called GDMO [17] has been standardized. The GDMO allows inclusion, exclusion and modification of attributes and behaviors by using the conditional package concept. It also allows separation of object definitions from data type definitions, enabling customization of data type definitions without affecting object definitions. However, this must be done by users at their own risk. Furthermore, an extension of GDMO [18] introduces the concept of relationship, but it does not allow customization of relationships.

Regarding the description of business policies, there have been many proposals [20, 6, 27, 25] in requirements engineering that define models for describing requirements, but none of them clearly separate business policies that can be understood by users from technical policies that can only be understood by engineers. Neither can they describe variations on business policies. Ramesh [24] and other researchers [15, 10, 23, 19] have proposed mechanisms to record design issues and the decisions made on them during design phases for later use in maintaining specifications. Although this information is useful to programmers, it is a mixture of business and technical decisions, and unorganized, thus it is difficult to use it for reusing specifications.

The BPC model tries to uniformly describe variable parts in database schemas and business policies, with a clear separation of these two, and to enable customization of database schemas by enhancing Fugini's role concept [13] and GDMO's conditional package concept [17].

3 Target Data Model

In this paper, an object-oriented data model is chosen for describing target database schemas. This section describes the database elements common to object-oriented models [27, 20, 25, 4] and the enhancements we introduce to reflect business needs and simplify the customization of the BPC model. First, we introduce the following concepts used in one or other object-oriented models (see Fig. 1 for graphical notation):

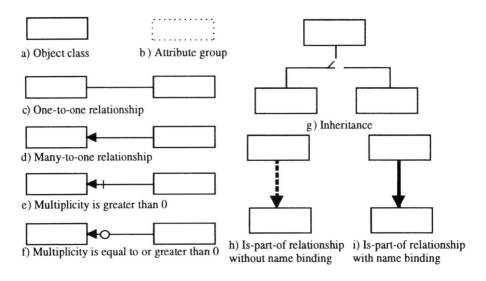

Fig. 1. Object-oriented data model notation

1) *Object class and instance*: An object class has instances. A virtual object class is an object class that does not have any instances and is used as a template for its subclasses.

2) *Attribute and domain*: An object class has attributes. Each attribute has its name and domain. A domain is mapped to either one or a set of object classes or data types. An attribute can be either a class attribute or an instance attribute. An attribute may have a null value, indicating that its value is not known. An object identifier is a special instance attribute that identifies an object instance across all objects in a database. An object identifier is not printable, which means that its value has no meaning to users.

3) *Relationship*: A relationship can be defined for a pair of object classes. Multiplicity of an object class is defined for each object class participating in the relationship. Maximum multiplicity can be either 1 or many, and minimum multiplicity can be either 0 or 1. It is also possible to define any value for the maximum and minimum multiplicities. An is-part-of relationship is a special

relationship that represents a relationship between an assembly class and its part classes.

4) *Inheritance*: Multiple inheritance is allowed for object classes.

5) *Integrity constraints*: Integrity constraints on object classes or attributes can be defined.

In addition to these concepts, the following concepts are introduced here as enhancements:

6) *Key*: Although the concept of key is not common in object-oriented models, we introduce it as an important concept, especially for users without a technical background. This is in contrast to the object identifier concept used by database designers. These two concepts coexist, serving different purposes. A set of values for attributes contained in a key uniquely identifies an instance within an object class and its subclasses. A key is defined for each non-virtual object class, and possibly for a virtual object class. To make the most of polymorphism and to view instances of an object class and its subclasses uniformly, the following constraints are imposed on keys:

a) If an object class has a key, all its subclasses have the same key. This is different from GDMO, which allows subclasses to have different keys.

b) Multiple inheritance is allowed for an object class only if all of its superclasses have the same key or at most one of its superclasses has a key.

A relationship between two object classes is represented by including either (or both) a key or an object identifier of one object class to the other object class. (See Section 4.4 for details.)

7) *Attribute group*: An attribute group is a group of attributes. It is introduced to make description of the inclusion and exclusion of attributes from an object class easier. Fugini's concept of role [13] is similar. Attribute groups do not have instances of their own and do not have keys.

8) *Name binding*: In GDMO [17], the hierarchy of is-part-of relationships and the name binding structure are the same. This means that if object class B is part of object class A, the key of B is the combination of the key of A and the relatively distinguished name (RDN) of B, where the RDN consists of one or more attributes of object class B. However, our investigation into real applications has shown that this is too restrictive, since there are cases where the key of B is determined independently of the is-part-of relationship. To better describe this situation, we classify is-part-of relationships into two categories, i.e., is-part-of relationships with and without name binding. The former represents the situation that GDMO assumes, and the latter represents the situation where keys are determined independent of is-part-of relationships.

The behavioral part of the object-oriented data model has been omitted since it is out of scope of this paper.

4 BPC Model

This section describes the BPC model and the customization process using it.

4.1 BPC Model Architecture

The BPC model consists of three parts: business policy description, database policy description, and database elements.

Business policy description consists of business policies and their alternatives. A business policy (BP) is a decision point required to build an application. It must be a decision point on which a user with no technical background can decide and that can be described in the form of a question to users. For example, "Should corporate contractors be dealt with?" is a BP, but "Does the relationship between Contractor and Contract object classes exist?" is not a BP. More than one BP usually exists for a database schema and each BP has more than one alternative, which we call a business policy alternative (BPA). There are two types of BPs, enumerated BPs and variable BPs. An enumerated BP has a fixed number of BPAs. Users can choose zero, one, or more BPAs from a BP. Constraints on the minimum and maximum numbers of BPAs that users may choose can be described. A variable BP, on the other hand, may have an unlimited number of alternatives. However, this is represented as having one BPA with a variable part in it. Take a service ordering application for example. The following BPs and BPAs may be specified:

Enumerated BP examples:

BP1: Are corporate organizations allowed as contractors for the service?
BPA11: Yes

BPA12: No

BP2: What is the unit of service suspension?
BPA21: Contract

BPA22: Service user

BP3: Do you have to register users for each contract?
BPA31: Yes, each contract must have its users.

BPA32: No, once registered by a contract, all other contracts from the same contractor can refer to the users information.

Variable BP example:

BP4: How many users are allowed in one contract?
BPA41: <n> users

The BPs and BPAs can be interdependent. There are BPs and BPAs that are valid only when other BPAs are chosen. This is described by the valid conditions for the BPs and BPAs. It is also possible to group BPs to form another BP. In this case, choosing a set of BPAs in the latter is interpreted as choosing a set of corresponding BPAs in the former. This hierarchy of BPs and BPAs is introduced to reduce the cost of addressing all the BPs at customization. For example, the BP "Is billing functionality required or not?" may affect many other BPs. By just choosing the BPA "No" for this BP, the cost to users for customization can be reduced.

Database policy description consists of database policies and their alternatives. A database policy (DBP) is a technical policy that addresses how a database element may be customized and can be described by a technical question for database designers. Each DBP has more than one alternative, called a database policy alternative (DBPA). There are also two types of DBPs, enumerated DBPs and variable DBPs. An enumerated BP corresponds to one or more enumerated DBPs, and a variable BP corresponds to a variable DBP. The DBPs related to the example BPs are shown below:

BP1:
  DBP11: Does "Corporate Contractor" object class exists?
  DBP12: Do you need to merge "Private Contractor" and "Contractor" object classes?

BP2:
  DBP21: Should attribute group "Service Suspension" be included in "Contract" object class?
  DBP22: Should attribute group "Service Suspension" be included in "User" object class?

BP3:
  DBP31: Does a relationship exist between "Contractor" and "User" object classes?
  DBP32: Does a relationship exist between "Contract" and "User" object classes?

BP4:
  DBP41: What is the maximum multiplicity of the relationship between "Contract" and "User" object classes?

The database elements are described using the data model shown in Section 3. Each BP has an impact on one or more DBPs. Once a valid set of BPAs is chosen for each BP in a database schema, one and only one DBPA is chosen for each DBP related to the BP, enabling the customization of the database schema. For example, each BPA in BP3 are related to DBPAs of DBP31 and DBP32 as follows:

BPA31: DBP31 ⇒DBPA "No",   DBP32 ⇒DBPA "Yes"
BPA32: DBP31 ⇒DBPA "Yes", DBP32 ⇒DBPA "No"

A database schema described using the BPC model is called a BPC schema. When a BPC schema does not support a BPA, there is no corresponding DBPA for the BPA. This is valuable information for clarifying the limitation of a BPC schema. It is also useful to record even a BP with only one BPA to clarify the situation where the BPC schema is applicable.

The BPC model architecture is illustrated in Fig. 2 as a metadata structure using the graphical notation shown in Fig. 1.

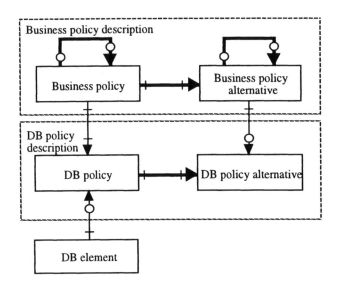

Fig. 2. BPC model architecture

4.2 Database Policy Constraints

Although, it is sufficient for database designers to choose all the DBPAs for each of the corresponding BPAs, this is not cost effective if the number of DBPAs is large. A more sophisticated method for specifying the correspondence is shown in this section.

If all and only all the valid sets of BPAs for a BP satisfy some constraint on their corresponding DBPAs, it is possible to reduce the cost of specifying all the relationships between BPAs and DBPAs by specifying just some of the DBPAs for each BPA and then determine other DBPAs using the constraint. We call this constraint a BP constraint.

BP constraints are Boolean expressions that have a truth value. Boolean expressions may be logical operations, such as the conjunction (and), disjunction (or), and negation (not), of other Boolean expressions or Boolean terms. Boolean terms consist of relational expressions with relational operators, such as "equal to" or "greater than," and arithmetic expressions. Arithmetic expressions are arithmetic operations of other arithmetic expressions or values. Values are either constants or variables. A variable has a value that is dependent on the set of alternatives chosen for a DBP or BP. The following variables can be used:

1) DBP_Val(k): the value of a DBPA chosen for the k-th DBP. Each DBPA is assigned a unique integer number within the DBP.

2) BP_Val(k): the value of a BPA chosen for the k-th BP. Each BPA is assigned a unique integer number within the BP. This is valid only when the number of BPAs chosen for the DBP is one.

3) BP_Min(k), BP_Max(k): the minimum and maximum values of BPAs chosen for the k-th BP.

4) BP_Count(k): the number of BPAs chosen for the k-th BP.

Using this construct, the BP3 constraint, for example, can be written as (DBP_Val(31)=1 and DBP_Val(32)=0) or (DBP_Val(31)=0 and DBP_Val(32)=1). With this constraint, database designers only need to specify the value of DBP_Val(31). Then, the value of DBP_Val(32) is deduced using the BP constraint.

Although BP constraints do not include any information on individual BPAs and DBPAs, they are useful in understanding the overall impact of BPs on DBPs and the relationships between DBPs.

4.3 Database Policy Types

In this section, three types of DBPs are presented: DBPs on existence, characteristics, and the composition of database elements.

1) DBPs on existence of database elements: This type of DBP represents whether a database element exists or not. Either an object class, a relationship, an inheritance, and an attribute group can be specified for this type of DBP.

2) DBPs on characteristics of database elements: This type of DBP represents whether a database element has some characteristics or other as follows:

Subtype A: Is the database element an object class or an attribute group?

Subtype B: Can the attribute have a null value or not?

Subtype C: Is the minimum multiplicity of the relationship 0 or 1?

Subtype D: Is the maximum multiplicity of the relationship 1 or many?

Subtype E: Is the relationship an is-part-of relationship or not?

Subtype F: Does the is-part-of relationship have name binding with it or not?

Subtype G: What is the key of the object class?

Subtype H: What is the domain (data type and length) of the attribute?

Subtype I: What is the minimum and maximum multiplicities of the relationship?

Subtype J: What is the integrity constraint on the object class (or the attribute)?

Note that subtypes A through F are enumerated DBPs, while subtypes G through J can be either enumerated DBPs or variable DBPs, depending on whether a fixed number of alternatives are specified or not.

3) DBPs on composition of database elements: Our case study has shown that more than one object classes or attribute groups are often merged depending on BPs. To describe this, we introduce a DBP describing whether two object classes or attribute groups related by a relationship or inheritance are merged into one or not. This type of DBP has additional parameters for specifying the source and destination of composition operation. There are two types of compositions:

a) Composition of object classes or attribute groups related by relationships
If the source database element is an attribute group, all the attributes in the attribute group are independently merged into the destination database element. On the other hand, if the source database element is an object class, that object class is merged into the destination database element as an attribute with the object class as its domain. The name of the attribute is given by an additional parameter of the DBP. If the multiplicity of the relationship at the source database element is many, the source database element is merged as a set.

b) Composition of object classes related by inheritance
All the attributes of the source object class are independently merged into the destination object class.

In both cases, duplicated attributes are removed and the name and key of the new database element are equal to those of the destination database element.

4.4 Customization Process

Target database schemas are generated by choosing BPAs and then customizing the BPC schemas based on them. However, we need to have an additional step because there are implementation-specific issues to be resolved in the actual generation of target database schemas (Fig. 3).

Step 1: Business policy-based customization

Users refer to BPs and BPAs to choose a set of BPAs for each BP. This is done in two phases. In the first phase, only enumerated BPs are presented to users, and their BPAs are chosen by them as described in Section 4.1. Then, BPAs are determined for variable BPs. Separation into two phases is done because enumerated BPs have more impact on determining the overall structure of BPC schemas. Through these phases, all unnecessary database elements including all attribute groups not merged into object classes are dropped. Composition is done as described in Section 4.3. If two object classes have an is-part-of relationship with name binding between them, the key of the part class is determined by the key of its assembly class.

Step 2: Implementation policy-based customization

As shown below, it is possible to represent relationships in different ways. We, therefore, have to decide which alternative to take. This is independent of business policies but dependent on implementation of target application systems, including which DBMS to use. For example, if a one-to-many relationship R exists between object classes A and B, this relationship can be represented in one or more of the following ways:

a) B has the object identifier of A

b) B has the key of A

c) A has a repeating set of the object identifier of B

d) A has a repeating set of the key of B. If R is an is-part-of relationship with name binding, Object class A has only a repeating set of the RDNs of B.

Once the implementation policy is determined for each relationship, it can be represented using attributes as shown above.

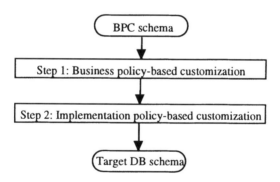

Fig. 3. Customization process

5   Graphical Notation of BPC Model

Graphical notation of BPC schemas helps users understand BPs and their impact on a database schema. This section describes the graphical notation of BPC schemas, called the BPC diagram. Because the amount of information contained in a BPC schema is large, it is not practical to represent all the information in it. We, therefore, present only important information affecting the overall structure of BPC schemas. The BPC diagram includes BPs, relationships between BPs and DBPs, and DBPs, in addition to database elements usually presented in object-oriented diagrams [25], such as object classes, attribute groups, relationships, and inheritance. For the DBPs on characteristics of database elements, only subtypes A through F are presented. Attributes, BPAs, and DBPAs are also omitted.

The actual notation is as follows: First, DBPs described above are represented as open circles or triangles attached to the database elements to which they are related, as shown in Fig. 4. Then, the relationships between BPs and DBPs are represented in two ways. If a BP constraint satisfies the conditions described below, it can be converted to a simpler logical formula, and the structure of this logical formula is presented in the BPC diagram:

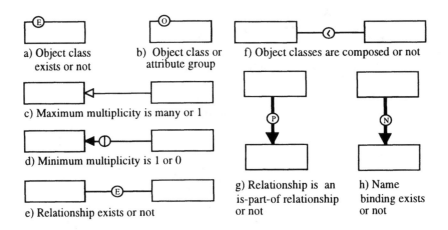

Fig. 4. Database policy notation

Conditions:

a) The BP constraint includes only DBP_Val as variables.

b) All the DBPs used in the BP constraint are enumerated DBPs and have only two DBPAs each.

If these conditions are met, we can assign truth or false values, instead of integers, to all DBPAs, and all Boolean terms in the BP constraint can be replaced by variables of the form DBP(k), where DBP(k) is the truth value of k-th DBP. Logical operators in the BP constraint are represented by open boxes and logical operations are represented by broken lines connecting related DBPs (see Fig. 5). Finally, the name of the BP is placed near the top level logical operator of the BP constraint or the DBP. If the above conditions are not met, the DB constraint is not presented and only the name of the BP is shown near each database element related to it, as shown in Fig.5 (h).

Take BP3 for example, the BP constraint is described as DBP(31) exclusive-or DBP(32), where DBP(31) denotes a Boolean term representing the existence of a relationship between "Contract" and "User" object classes, and DBP(32) denotes a Boolean term representing the existence of a relationship between "Contractor" and "User" object classes. This is graphically represented as shown in Fig. 6.

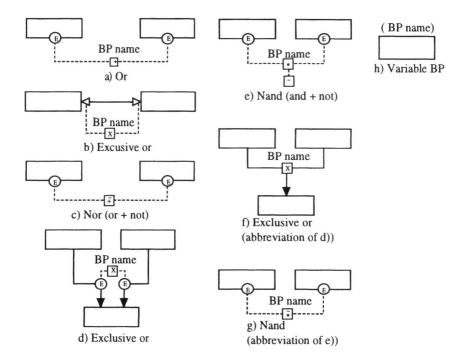

Fig. 5. Business policy constraint notation

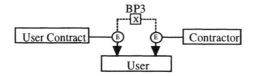

Fig. 6. Graphical notation of BP3

6 Case Study

We have applied the BPC model to a common database schema that is a part of a reusable component for telecommunications service operations, including service ordering and billing. It took us 8 months with 10 people to analyze two different database schemas serving different application systems and design the common database schema. One database schema for service ordering has 7 relational tables with 128 attributes, while the other database schema has 15 relational tables with 159 attributes. Through our analysis, we found that 72 % of the attributes of the first database schema also exist in the second database schema. Then, we enhanced the common part of the two database schemas to cover billing functionality and serve the third application system. The enhanced database schema has 75 object classes and 636 attributes.

During the development of the enhanced database schema, we investigated how many database elements are dependent on BPs and DBPs. The results are as follows: There are 82 BPs, 204 BPAs and 129 DBPs. We observed that all BPs and DBPs related to the static aspect of the database schema could be written using this model. There are 16 DBPs on existence of object classes and 14 on relationships, and there are 3 DBPs on characteristics of object classes and 37 on relationships (30 for multiplicity and 7 for the type of relationship). The number of DBPs on composition of object classes is 58. The number of variable DBPs is only one. These results show that DBPs on compositions and characteristics of relationships are dominant in the database schemas.

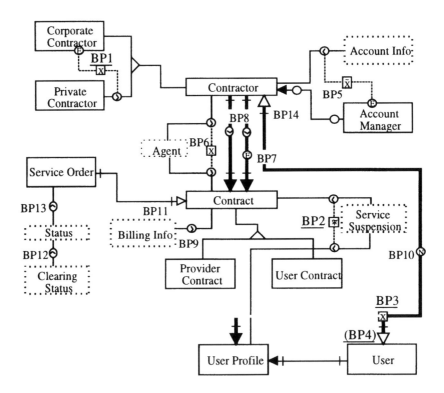

Fig. 7. Example BPC schema

Fig. 7 shows a part of the database schema, including the example BPs shown in Section 4. For example, BP1 is represented as exclusive-or of a DBP on existence of "Corporate Contractor" object class and a DBP on composition of "Private Contractor" and "Contractor" object classes. BP2 is represented as negation of conjunction operation of a DBP on composition of "Service Suspension" attribute group and "Contractor" object class, and a DBP on composition of the same attribute group and "User Profile" object class. By investigating the BPC diagram, we can easily know that the "User" object class may be affected by BPs, 3, 4, 10, and 14, and the "Contractor" object class may be affected by many more BPs.

7   Concluding Remarks

In this paper, we have tried to solve the problem of the divergence of data semantics by allowing the description of variable parts in database schemas, and the problem of satisfiability of business policies by describing how the variable parts are related to business policies. Regarding the description of variable parts of database policies, the BPC model tries to offer a uniform way of describing decision points on database schemas as DBPs. The types of DBPs proposed in this paper cover a variety of customization including those presented in Fugini's proposal and GDMO and are enhanced to describe a wider range of database elements and their characteristics. The applicability of the model has been demonstrated by a real example. This flexibility allows description of database schemas applicable to a wide range of applications. Future study items include:

1) More flexible customization: In contrast to Fugini's approach [13], we did not allow users to freely customize BPC schemas because it is difficult to ensure the consistency and quality of the result of the customization. However, the mixture of both approaches could result in a more flexible model.

2) Higher level semantics for customization: During our case study, we noticed that special combinations of DBPs sometimes arise, such as "compose two object classes if the multiplicity of the relationship connecting them is 1" or "compose two object classes if there is only one subclass for an object class." The benefit of defining these combinations as higher level DBPs for complex object classes should be investigated.

3) Description of behavioral part of object classes

4) Formal description of BP constraints: Reseach in integrity constraints could be used to enhance and formally describe BP constraints.

Regarding the description of business policies, the BPC model provides a framework for describing BPs and their alternatives. Using this framework, we can collect and organize variations of BPs and gain a better understanding of target applications. During our case study, we could actually find inconsistent and missing BPs as a result of describing the BPC schema. It is also useful for the impact analysis of database schemas. Further study items include automatic checking of inconsistencies in a BPC schema and a methodology and technology for identifying relevant BPs and BPAs, including extraction of BPs and DBPs from design information presented in [24, 15].

With regard to the BPC diagram, we believe that it is sufficient to understand the overall structure of a BPC schema, despite the fact that the semantics presented by the BPC diagram is limited to part of the BPC model and the number of applications we tried so far is small. In our case study, it actually helped us find missing and inconsistent BPs. We plan to refine its notation through further case studies.

We are now developing a customization tool based on this model. We believe that this modeling technology, including ours, will become more important as reusable software components become more popular.

References

1. Abiteboul, S. and Hull, R.: IFO; A Formal Semantic Database Model, in *Proc. ACM SIGACT-SIGMOD Symposium on Principles of Database Systems*, pp. 119-132, 1984.

2. Batini, C. and Lenzerini, M., A Comparative Analysis of Methodologies for Database Schema Integration, *ACM Computing Survey*, Vol. 18, No. 4, pp. 323-364, 1986.

3. Bellinzona, R., Fugini, M. G., and Pernici, B., Reusing Specifications in OO Applications, *IEEE Software*, No. 3, pp. 65-75, March 1994.

4. Booch, G., *Object-Oriented Design with Applications*, Benjamin/Cummings, 1991.

5. Birrer, A. and Eggenschwiler T., Frameworks in the Financial Engineering Domain: An Experience Report, in *Lecture Notes in Computer Science*, Vol. 707, pp. 21-35, Springer-Verlag, 1993.

6. Brien, P. M., Niezette, M. et al., A Rule Language to Capture and Model Business Policy Specifications, in *Proc. 3rd International Conference on Advanced Information Systems Engineering (CAiSE'91)*, pp. 307-318, 1991.

7. Castano, S, De Antonellis, V. and Zonta, B., Classifying and Reusing Conceptual Schemas, in *Proc. 11th International Conference on Entity-Relationship Approach (ER'92)*, pp. 121-138, 1992.

8. Castano, S, De Antonellis, V. and San Pietro, P., Reuse of Object-Oriented Requirement Specifications, in *Proc. 12th International Conference on Entity-Relationship Approach (ER'93)*, pp. 339-351, 1993.

9. Chen, P. P.: The Entity-Relationship Model-Toward a Unified View of Data, *ACM Transactions on Database Systems*, Vol. 1, No. 1, pp. 9-36, 1976.

10. Conklin, J. and Begeman M. L., gIBIS: A Hypertext Tool for Explanatory Policy Discussion, *ACM Transactions on Office Information Systems*, Vol. 6, No. 4, pp. 303-331, 1988.

11. Constatopoulos, P. and Pataki, E., A Browser for Software Reuse, in *Proc. 4th International Conference on Advanced Information Systems Engineering (CAiSE'92)*, pp. 304-326, 1992.

12. Duwairi, R. M., Fiddian, N. J. and Gray, W. A., Schema Integration Meta-Knowledge Classification and Reuse, in *Proc. 14th British National Conference on Databases (BNCOD 14)*, pp. 1-17, 1996.

13. Fugini, M. G., Guggino, M. and Pernici, B., Reusing Requirements through a Modeling and Composition Support Tool, in *Proc. 3rd International Conference on Advanced Information Systems Engineering (CAiSE'91)*, pp. 50-78, 1991.

14. Gamma, E., Helm, R, et. al., *Design Patterns: Elements of Reusable Object-Oriented Software*, Addison-Wesley, 1995.

15. Hamada, M. and Adachi, H., Recording Software Design Process for Maintaining the Software, in *Proc. 17th Annual International Computer Software and Applications Conference (COMPSAC)*, pp. 27-33, 1993.

16. Hammer, M. and McLeod, D.: Database Description with SDM; A Semantic Database Model, *ACM Transactions on Database Systems*, Vol. 6, No. 3, pp. 351-386, 1981.

17. ISO/IEC, *Information Technology - Open Systems Interconnection - Structure of management information - Part 4: Guidelines for the definition of managed objects*, 10165-4, 1992.

18. ISO/IEC JTC1/SC21 N-9225, *Open Systems Interconnection - Structure of Management Information - Part 7: General Relationship Model*, 1995.

19. Jarke, M. and Rose, T., Managing Knowledge about Information System Evolution, in *Proc. ACM International Conference on Management of Data (SIGMOD)*, pp. 303-311, 1988.

20. Jungclaus, R., Saake, G., Hartmann, T. and Sernadas, C., TROLL-A Language for Object-Oriented Specification of Information Systems, *ACM Transactions on Information Systems*, Vol. 14, No. 2, pp. 175-211, 1996.

21. Nijssen, G. M.: A Gross Architecture for the Next Generation Database Management Systems, in *Modelling in Data Base Management Systems*, Nijssen, G. M. (ed.), North Holland, pp. 1-24, 1976.

22. Park, S. and Palmer, J. D., A Feature Based Reuse Library, in *Lecture Notes in Computer Science*, Vol. 945, pp. 495-499, Springer-Verlag, 1994.

23. Pinheiro, F. A. C. and Goguen, J. A., An Object-Oriented Tool for Tracing Requirements, *IEEE Software*, No. 3, pp. 52-64, 1996.

24. Ramesh, B. and Dhar, V., Supporting Systems Development by Capturing Deliberation During Requirements Engineering, *IEEE Transactions on Software Engineering*, Vol. 18, No. 6, pp. 498-510, 1992.

25. Rumbaugh, J., Blaha, M., et al., *Object-Oriented Modeling and Design*, Prentice Hall, 1991.

26. Shipman, D. W.: The Functional Data Model and the Data Language DAPLEX, *ACM Transactions on Database Systems*, Vol. 6, No. 1, pp. 140-173, 1981.

27. Theodoulidis, C., Wangler, B. and Loucopoulos, P., Requirements Specification in TEMPORA, in *Lecture Notes in Computer Science*, Vol. 436, pp. 264-282, Springer-Verlag, 1990.

28. Sonnenberger, G. and Frei, H. P., Design of a Reusable IR Framework, in *Proc. ACM SIGIR*, pp. 49-57, 1995.

29. Thieme, C. and Siebes, A., An Approach to Schema Integration Based on Transformations and Behaviour, in *Proc. 6th International Conference on Advanced Information Systems Engineering (CAiSE'94)*, pp. 297-310, 1994.

30. Vlissides, J. M. and Linton, M. A., Unidraw: A Framework for Building Domain-Specific Graphical Editors, *ACM Transactions on Information Systems*, Vol. 8, No. 3, pp. 237-268, 1990.

Explaining Conceptual Models —
An Architecture and Design Principles

Hercules Dalianis
Paul Johannesson
Department of Computer and Systems Sciences
Stockholm University and the Royal Institute of Technology
Electrum 230, S-164 40 Kista, Sweden
email: {hercules, pajo}@dsv.su.se

Abstract

An important activity in requirements engineering is validation, which is the process of checking whether a model correctly represents a piece of reality and the users' requirements. One technique for supporting validation is explanation generation which combines paraphrasing of a specification with question–answer facilities that interactively support a user in exploring a model. In this paper, we propose an architecture and design principles for constructing explanation generation systems for conceptual models. The architecture is partly based on Toulmin's argumentation model, which provides a framework for structuring arguments. We argue that this architecture assists in building explanation generation systems that are highly interactive, provide an adequate amount of information for different user categories, and support a wide range of validation techniques.

1 Introduction

Requirements engineering is the branch of systems engineering concerned with eliciting and specifying the functionality of large and complex software-intensive systems. Put simply, requirements engineering focuses on the early phases of the systems development life-cycle. The result of requirements engineering is a requirements specification, which plays several roles in the process of systems engineering. First, it is the basis for and part of a contract between requirements holders and systems developers. Secondly, it is an architectural, implementation independent drawing of the future system to be built. Thirdly, it provides an explicit basis for reasoning with and among the clients about various qualities of the system.

Requirements engineering consists of several related activities. First, the acquisition of requirements through observation, interviews, analysis of texts, reverse engineering, group work, co-development, etc. Secondly, the modelling and specification of requirements. Thirdly, the analysis of requirements, which includes validation and verification. Finally, communication and documentation of the results of requirements engineering, where traceability and information management are needed.

By validation is meant the process of checking whether a model correctly represents a piece of reality and the users' requirements. Verification, on the other hand, concerns formal properties of a model, such as syntactical correctness, consistency, and completeness. While verification often can be automated, validation is inherently an informal process requiring subjective, human judgement. In this informal process, it is essential that different types of stakeholders participate, including people with limited knowledge of modelling and systems design. However, people who are unfamiliar with modelling languages may have severe difficulties in understanding and validating a model. Furthermore, the sheer size and complexity of a model may make it difficult even for experienced designers to validate a model.

In order to ease the validation process, several different techniques have been proposed. One approach is to introduce *graphical symbols*, [Kung93], or *user defined concepts*, [Mylopoulos90]. Another approach is to *paraphrase* parts of a conceptual model in natural language, [Rolland92], [Dalianis92], [Dalianis96]. In order to validate large models, a technique called *complexity reduction* has been proposed, which presents views of a conceptual model and hides irrelevant details, [Seltveit93]. *Model simulation* is still another technique, which can be used for observing and experimenting with the dynamic properties of a model, [Harel92], [Zave84]. A validation technique similar to model simulation is *model planning* that allows users to explore a model by constructing plans, i.e. operation sequences that result in states where certain conditions hold, [Costal96]. *Explanation generation* techniques have been used to integrate the techniques mentioned above and provide a uniform interface to the users. Explanation generation extends paraphrasing by including question–answer facilities that interactively support a user in exploring a model. Model simulation can be complemented by explanation generation that guides a user through the execution and explains the system's behaviour in more detail. Explanation generation has previously been used mainly for expert systems, e.g. the Explainable Expert System (EES), [Moore91], which provides natural language explanations of rule-based systems based on Rhethorical Structure Theory, [Mann87]. Recently, there has also been an interest in using explanation generation for validating conceptual models. The most comprehensive work on explanation generation for validating conceptual models seems to be [Gulla96], which discusses an explanation component for CASE environments. This component provides a natural language interface to complex model information and integrates model simulation by explaining a model's behaviour by relating trace information to properties of the model.

The purpose of this paper is to outline an architecture and design principles for an explanation component for object-oriented conceptual models. The work reported upon in this paper extends previous work by providing explanation generation not only for static parts of a model, history traces, and simulation, but also for planning. Another difference is that our work focuses on the interaction between users and systems in the explanation process and provides guidelines for the design of interactive dialogue structures. The structure of the paper is as follows. Section 2 introduces the modelling language and notation used throughout the paper as well as a number of examples. Section 3 outlines the architecture of an explanation component. Sections 4, 5, and 6 elaborate on this architecture by discussing explanations of history traces, simulations, and plans, respectively. Section 7 summarizes the paper and gives suggestions for future work.

2 The Delphi Language

The modelling concepts and notation used in this paper are based on the language Delphi, [Höök93]. Delphi is a conceptual modelling language developed by Ericsson Utvecklings AB, where the language has been used for defining specifications of telephone services. The language is supported by a development environment including tools for verification and validation. The formal semantics of Delphi is given by means of first order logic and state machines, which makes it possible to carry out advanced analyses on Delphi specifications. We give here only an informal overview of Delphi as this is sufficient for the purposes of the paper.

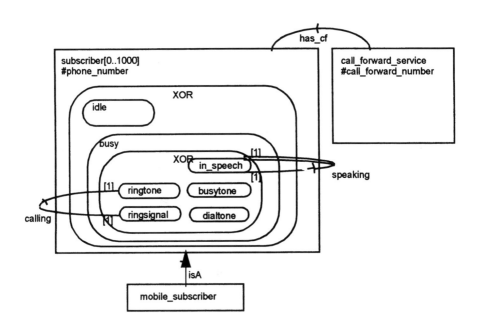

Fig. 1. A Delphi static model

A Delphi specification consists of two parts: a *static model* describing static, structural aspects and a *dynamic model* describing behavioral aspects. The static model describes the *entity types* that exist in a system, their properties, and their relationships. The static model can also include static constraints, called *invariants*, that put restrictions on allowable states. The dynamic model consists of a set of *dynamic rules* that define the state transitions of the system. A dynamic rule consists of a stimulus, conditions, and conclusions. The informal semantics of a dynamic rule is that if a stimulus occurs in a state and the conditions are true in this state, then the conclusions will be true in the next state.

An example of a Delphi specification is shown in Figure 1 (the static model) and Figure 2 (the dynamic model). This specification defines POTS (Plain Old Telephone Service) extended with the service Call Forward. The static model includes three entity types: subscriber with the property phone_number, mobile_subscriber that is a subtype of subscriber, and call_forward_service with the property call_forward_number. The model specifies the set of states of a subscriber, e.g. a subscriber may be idle, have ringtone, or have dialtone.

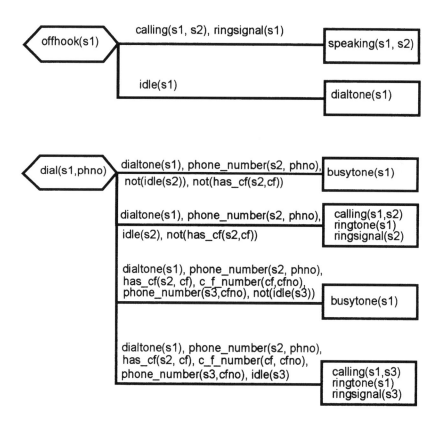

Fig. 2. A Delphi dynamic model

The static model also graphically defines several invariants. For example, if a box is included in another box, the state corresponding to the first box is a substate of the state corresponding to the second box. This means that the static model defines that any subscriber who has `ringtone`, `ringsignal`, `dialtone`, `busytone`, or is in speech is also `busy`. The XOR notation indicates that the substates are exclusive, e.g. a subscriber cannot simultaneously have `ringtone` and `busytone`, nor can she be both `busy` and `idle`. Furthermore, the static model defines a number of relations between subscribers, e.g. that one subscriber can be `calling` another. The model also expresses the invariant that if one subscriber calls another, then the first subscriber must have `ringtone` and the second `ringsignal`. Furthermore, the model specifies cardinality constraints for the relations.

The dynamic model consists of two dynamic rules. For each rule, the stimulus is shown within a hexagon, the conditions are placed along a line, and the conclusions are shown within a rectangle. The second rule contains four branches; the first branch states that dialling to a busy subscriber without call forward results in busytone; the second branch states that if one subscriber dials a phone number and the subscriber with this phone number is idle and does not have call forward, then the dialling subscriber will get ringtone and the other one ringsignal; the third and fourth branches state that dialling to a subscriber with call forward results in busytone if the subscriber forwarded to is busy, and otherwise in ringtone at the dialling subscriber and ringsignal at the other one.

A Delphi specification can have instantiations, or *fact bases*, describing a number of entities and their properties and relations at a particular point in time. Some examples of fact bases, which will be used in later sections, are given below.

Fact base A

subscriber(john)
phone_number(john, 625118)
idle(john)
subscriber(mary)
phone_number(mary, 500198)
idle(mary)

Fact base B

subscriber(john)
phone_number(john, 625118)
subscriber(mary)
phone_number(mary, 500198)
calling(mary, john)
ringtone(mary)
ringsignal(john)

Fact base C

subscriber(john)
phone_number(john, 625118)
subscriber(mary)
phone_number(mary, 500198)
speaking(mary, john)
in_speech(mary)
in_speech(john)

Fact base D

subscriber(john)
phone_number(john, 625118)
has_cf(cf1)
call_forward_service(cf1)
idle(john)
subscriber(mary)
phone_number(mary, 500198)
idle(mary)

3 Architecture for an Explanation Generation System

A basic problem in explaining conceptual models is that of identifying forms of explanations and dialogue structures that effectively support users in understanding the models. Experience has shown that it is not particularly effective to simply paraphrase large fragments of a conceptual model, as people easily get lost in a long text and may even find it unfocused or irrelevant, [Gulla96]. Much more effective are short texts, or visualizations, that answer focussed questions about the structure or behaviour about a model in the context of a particular use case. Especially effective are answers that combine information from different parts of the conceptual model, e.g. from the fact base as well as from the dynamic rules, [Dalianis92]. In order to design an adequate explanation component, two fundamental issues have to be addressed. First, what types of questions and explanations should be supported? Secondly, how should the dialogue between user and system be structured?

When exploring a conceptual model, a user should be able to ask several different types of questions about constructs in the model. There seem to be, at least, four different types of questions in this context. The first type of question is the structural question that asks about the structure of a construct, its properties and relationships to other constructs as well as the constraints pertaining to the construct. The second type of question is the causal question that asks about the cause of a construct, i.e. the events that have made it to come into existence. The third type is the reason question that asks about the reason for a construct, i.e. why the construct has been introduced and what purpose it serves. Finally, there is the procedural question that asks how something is carried out.

A user should not only be allowed to ask isolated questions about a model and get answers, but also to engage in a more structured dialogue with the system involving follow-up questions and more detailed explanations. In order to design such dialogues, some kind of argumentation model is needed as foundation. An attractive candidate for this purpose is Toulmin's argumentation model, [Toulmin59], which describes the structure of arguments. The starting point of an argument is a *claim*, which is a sentence asserting some proposition. This claim is related to *grounds* supporting the claim; the grounds should provide the required basis for accepting the claim. If a presumed listener to the argument is not convinced by the grounds given for the claim, further grounds can be given in support. If the listener is still not convinced, the argument may continue with a *warrant*, i.e. a relation between a ground and a claim showing that the grounds are indeed relevant for the claim. A warrant has usually the form of a general rule that is applicable to the case at hand. If grounds and warrant should not be sufficient to convince the listener, further supportive arguments can be given in the form of *backing*. Backing is used to show that the warrant is reliable and relevant in the context. Normally, backing takes the form of rules at a higher level than the warrant. However, grounds, warrant, and backing may not invariably lead to the required claim – *qualifications* such as "usually" and "possibly" may then be used to clarify the relationships between grounds and claim. If the claim does not follow with certainty from the grounds, an argument may describe the circumstances where the claim does not hold – these are called *rebuttals*. An argument can thus schematically be described as shown in Figure 3 below.

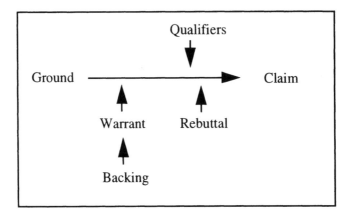

Fig. 3. Toulmin's argumentation model

A major benefit of Toulmin's argumentation model for the purpose of explaining conceptual models is that it can guide the gathering of information from different components of the conceptual model. For example, in an interactive approach, if the user questions the grounds for a specific claim, the warrant can include additional information from the conceptual model and form the basis for a more detailed explanation. In this way, Toulmin's model provides a simple and informative explanation structure that gives an adequate amount of information at the right time and level. Explanations designed according to Toulmin's model are probably most useful for claims on the instance level, i.e. claims about particular objects and their relationships. If a claim is on the instance level, it is natural to structure the argument about the claim in such a way that the grounds are also on the instance level, the warrant on the schema level, and the backing on the meta schema level. This structure gives a correspondence between the central parts of Toulmin's model and the components of a conceptual model. This correspondence can be used to organize the explanation of model constructs as shown in the following sections.

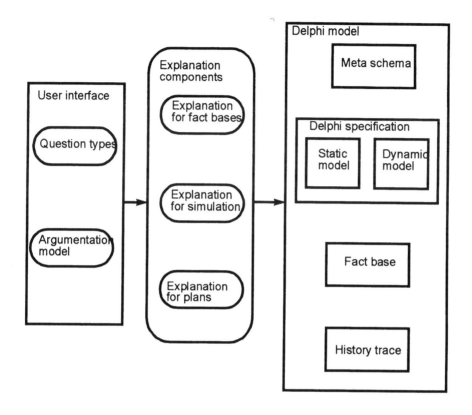

Fig. 4. Architecture of an explanation system

The architecture of an explanation system is outlined in Figure 4. In the rightmost box, the components to be explained are displayed; in addition to explaining a Delphi specification, it is possible to explain the Delphi meta schema, fact bases, and history traces. The explanation component provides three different validation techniques: explanation of instance level information in the fact base, explanation of the results of simulation, and explanation of plans, i.e. sequences of operations for achieving certain goals. All these validation techniques utilize and combine information from several model components, in particular from the fact base and the history trace. The dialogue between user and system is managed by the user interface, which offers the user a set of different questions for initiating explanations. The user interface also uses Toulmin's argumentation model for structuring the system's explanations.

The architecture above suggests the following two design principles for constructing an explanation generation system:

- For each construct in a model, determine which types of questions can be asked about it: structural, causal, procedural, and reason. For each type of question, determine which sources of information that must be used to provide an answer.
- For each model construct and question type, determine how the answer can be divided into smaller units based on the components of Toulmin's argumentation model. Furthermore, determine which follow-up questions are applicable.

In the following sections, we will show a number of examples illustrating how these design principles can be applied.

4 Explanation for Fact Bases

Structural question – combining static model and fact base

Explaining fact bases involves answering questions about why specific facts hold true in the current state of the system. A basic question to ask about a fact base is:
– Why does this fact hold?
This question can be interpreted in two ways. First, it can be seen as a structural question asking whether the fact holds as a consequence of other facts and invariants. Secondly, it can be interpreted as a causal question asking for the event, or sequence of events, that caused the fact to hold. For the structural question, there will be an answer only if there is an invariant that provides a sufficient condition for the fact to hold. In such a case, the simplest answer to the fact will be just to display that part of the information base that causes the fact to hold – this corresponds to giving the grounds in Toulmin's argumentation model as explained in Section 3. A more elaborate answer would include the relevant invariant(s) as well as a part of the information base – giving the invariant(s) would correspond to providing a warrant for the fact to be explained. These ways of explaining a fact are illustrated in the example below:

Example 1. Based on fact base B.

    USER: *Why is John busy?*
    SYSTEM: Because John has ringsignal. (Grounds)
    USER: *I do not understand.*
    SYSTEM: Whenever a subscriber has ringsignal, he is busy. And John has ringsignal and is therefore busy. (Warrant)

Causal question – combining dynamic model, history trace, and fact base

The causal question about a fact requires for answer an event or a sequence of events, which means that the history trace of the system must be consulted. Also in this case, an answer can be more or less elaborate. The simplest answer is to provide the event(s) that caused the fact to hold – corresponding to the grounds. The more elaborate alternative is to include also the conditions and conclusions of the relevant dynamic rules in the answer – corresponding to a warrant. These alternatives are exemplified in the following:

Example 2. Based on fact base C.

> USER: *Why is John speaking with Mary?*
>
> SYSTEM: Because John made offhook. (Grounds)
>
> USER: *I do not understand.*
>
> SYSTEM: Whenever a subscriber is calling another subscriber and the second subscriber makes offhook, then the subscribers start speaking with each other. And in this case, Mary was calling John, and John made offhook. (Warrant)

Causal question – larger parts of a history trace

A special problem in answering causal questions about a fact is to determine how many events to include in the answer. In some cases, it is sufficient to include just one single event, namely the event that introduced the fact due to the conclusion part of the corresponding event rule. In other cases, however, several events are needed to account for a fact, for example when the fact is derived from other facts introduced by distinct events. It may also be appropriate to provide a complete event sequence for explaining a fact when the event that introduced the fact is part of a larger use case; in such a situation, all events in the relevant use case should be provided in the explanation. An example of this is given below:

Example 3. Based on fact base C.

> USER: *Why is John speaking with Mary?*
>
> SYSTEM: Because Mary made offhook and dialled John, and John made offhook. (Grounds)
>
> USER: *I do not understand.*
>
> SYSTEM: If a subscriber is idle and makes offhook and then dials another subscriber, who is idle and does not have call-forward, and this subscriber makes offhook, then the subscribers start speaking. And Mary was idle, made offhook and dialled John, who was idle and did not have call-forward. (Warrant)

5 Explanation for Simulation

Procedural question – combining dynamic model and fact base

Simulation means to execute dynamic rules in the conceptual model and explore the consequences of these executions. The simplest simulation consists of executing one single dynamic rule, and the basic question is a procedural question asking how the dynamic rule was executed. The answer will tell which branch in the rule was chosen and which conclusions the execution gave rise to. The answer can be more or less detailed, including only facts about the conclusion (grounds) or specifying the dynamic rule (warrant). This is illustrated in the following example:

Example 4. Based on fact base B.

USER: *What happens if John makes offhook?*

SYSTEM: John and Mary will be speaking with each other. (Grounds)

USER: *I do not understand.*

SYSTEM: Whenever a subscriber is calling another subscriber and the second subscriber makes offhook, then the subscribers start speaking with each other. And in this case, Mary was calling John, and John made offhook. (Warrant)

Procedural question – with rebuttal follow-up question

A slightly more complex simulation consists of the execution of a dynamic rule and a particular fact. The natural question to ask is a causal question asking whether the fact will hold after the execution or not. If the answer is yes, this case reduces to the same one as a causal question about a fact in the fact base. But if the answer is no, it is natural to continue with a follow-up question that amounts to a rebuttal, i.e. asks for circumstances under which the specified execution would indeed make the fact true. Thus, the answer to this question would describe the circumstances under which the execution of the dynamic rule would follow another branch that resulted in the fact to hold – if such a branch exists. An example of this case is the following:

Example 5. Based on fact base D.

USER: *If Mary dials John, will he get ringsignal?*

SYSTEM: No, he will not. (Grounds)

USER: *Under which circumstances would he get ringsignal?*

SYSTEM: If John did not have call forward, he would get ringsignal. (Grounds)

USER: *I do not understand.*

SYSTEM: If a subscriber calls another subscriber who is idle and does not have call-forward, then that subscriber will get ringsignal. Mary dialled John, who was idle but he had call-forward, and therefore he did not get ringsignal. (Warrant)

6 Explanations for Planning

A classical planning problem has the following form: given a description of the problem domain, an initial state and a goal, find a plan that leads from the initial state to a final state where the required goal holds. The plan will consist of zero, one or more operations. Previous work on planning for conceptual model verification and validation has focussed on how planning can be used to check that a model satisfies certain desirable properties, such as satisfiability, liveliness of predicates, and non-redundancy of constraints, [Costal96]. We will here outline how planning can be used also for interactive exploration and explanation of a model.

Causal question – combining dynamic model and fact base

A basic question about the future states of an information base is the following:
- How can this fact be made to hold?

An answer to this causal question would consist of an event sequence such that starting from the current information base and carrying out the events results in an information base where the requested fact holds.

Example 6. Based on fact base A.

> USER: *How can Mary become speaking with John?*
>
> SYSTEM: Mary makes offhook, dials John, and John makes offhook. (Grounds)
>
> USER: *I do not understand.*
>
> SYSTEM: If a subscriber is idle and makes offhook and then dials another subscriber, who is idle and does not have call-forward, and this subscriber makes offhook, then the subscribers start speaking. And Mary is idle, so if she makes offhook and dials John, who is idle and does not have call-forward, then they will become speaking. (Warrant)

Reason question – combining dynamic model and fact base

The planning question above is similar to the causal question in Section 4, as both require an event sequence as answer. However, the planning question is different in the way that it becomes meaningful to ask reason questions about the answer. For example, one could ask: "Why is this event included in the sequence?" An answer to this type of question would take the form: "This event is included because it ensures that these facts are true, and this is needed for the following event, occurring later in the sequence, to happen." In order to produce this answer, one has to consult the conclusion part of the dynamic rule that is the subject of the question, and the condition parts of all dynamic rules of the events coming later in the sequence.

Example 7. Based on fact base A.

> USER: *How can Mary become speaking with John?*
>
> SYSTEM: Mary makes offhook, dials John, and John makes offhook. (Grounds)
>
> USER: *Why is the event "dials John" included?*
>
> SYSTEM: Because this event results in the fact that Mary is calling John, and this is required if the event of John making offhook is to result in Mary and John becoming speaking. (Grounds)

This kind of validation through explanation for planning can be continued with explanation for simulation, e.g. by asking whether substituting one event in a plan with another event will result in the same goal holding true. In this way, the explanation component should provide a uniform interface to different kinds of validation techniques and allow for their combination.

7 Concluding Remarks

In this paper, we have discussed explanation generation systems for conceptual models and proposed an architecture as well as design principles for constructing such systems. These principles will assist a designer in building explanation generation systems that are highly interactive, provide an adequate amount of information for different user categories, and support a wide range of validation techniques. In the examples in the previous sections, we have shown only explanations expressed in natural language. However, an adequate explanation component should combine natural language with graphical representations. These representations should provide a user with a graphical view of a system and allow her to obtain explanations of its various components by means of point and click interaction. When a user clicks at a component to have it explained, the system should display a menu of the types of explanations applicable for this particular component – these types are given by the four types of questions introduced in Section 3. The system will then display an explanation combining a graphical view with text.

Another line of research is to investigate the usefulness of a more complex argumentation model than Toulmin's. One candidate for this purpose is Rhetorical Structure Theory (RST), [Mann87], which is a model for describing the structure of coherent text. The basic idea of RST is that a segment of text has a central item, called a nucleus. This nucleus is supported by other segments of text, called satellites, that are related to the nucleus in different ways. For example, a satellite may be a causal link or express evidence for the nucleus, or state a condition that must hold if the nucleus is to be accepted. A main advantage of using RST for explaining conceptual models is that it provides a basis for constructing more coherent natural language output, [Gulla96]. However, using RST has the drawback that it requires a customization for each domain or application, since the typical RST relations do not have any immediate correspondences to conventional conceptual modelling constructs. This is in contrast to Toulmin's model where there are natural correspondences between the model's components and conceptual modelling constructs. These correspondences make it easy to apply Toulmin's model for any specification expressed in an object oriented conceptual model. RST may, therefore, be less attractive for these types of models, but can be useful for semantically richer models that provide, for example, constructs for time and intentionality.

References

[Costal96] D. Costal, E. Teniente, T. Urpi, and C. Farre, "Handling Conceptual Model Validation by Planning", *7th International Conference on Advanced Information Systems Engineering, Springer*, 1996.

[Dalianis92] H. Dalianis, "A Method for Validating a Conceptual Model by Natural Language Discourse Generation", *CAISE-92 International Conference on Advanced Information Systems Engineering*, Loucopoulos P. (Ed.), Springer LNCS 593, pp. 425 - 444, 1992.

[Dalianis92] H. Dalianis, *Concise Natural Language Generation from Formal Specifications*, Ph.D. thesis, Department of Computer and Systems Sciences, Royal Institute of Technology, Stockholm, 1996.

[Gulla96] J. A. Gulla, "A General Explanation Component for Conceptual Modelling in CASE Environments", *ACM Transactions on Information Systems*, vol. 14, no. 2, pp. 297 - 329, 1996.

[Harel87] D. Harel, "Statecharts: a Visual Formalism for Complex Systems", *Science of Computer Programming*, vol. 8, no. 3, pp. 231 - 274, 1987.

[Höök93] H. Höök, *A General Description of the Delphi Language*, Ellemtel internal report, 1993.

[Kung93] D. Kung, "The Behavior Network Model for Conceptual Information Modelling", *Information Systems*, vol. 18, no. 1, pp. 1 - 21, 1993.

[Mann87] W. Mann and S. Thompson, "Rhetorical Structure Theory: Description and Construction of Text Structures", in *Natural Language Generation: New Results in Artificial Intelligence, Psychology and Linguistics*, Ed. M. Nijhoff, pp. 85 - 95, Dordrecht, 1987.

[Moore91] J. Moore and W. Swartout, "A Reactive Approach to Explanation: Taking the User's Feedback into Account", in *Natural Language Generation in Artificial Intelligence and Computational Linguistics*, pp. 1 - 48, Dordrecht, 1991.

[Mylopoulos90] J. Mylopoulos, A. Borgida, M. Jarke and M. Koubarakis, "Telos: Representing Knowledge about Information Systems", *ACM Transactions on Information Systems*, vol. 8, no. 4, pp. 325-362, 1990.

[Rolland92] C. Rolland and C. Proix, "Natural Language Approach to Conceptual Modeling", in *Conceptual Modeling, Databases and CASE: An Integrated View of Information Systems Development*, Ed. P. Loucopoulos and R. Zicari, pp. John Wiley, New York, 1992.

[Seltveit93] A. Seltveit, "An Abstraction-based Rule Approach to Large-scale Information Systems Development", in *5th International Conference on Advanced Information systems Engineering*, Ed. pp. 328 - 351, Springer Verlag, 1993.

[Toulmin59] S. Toulmin, *The Uses of Arguments*, Cambridge University Press, 1959.

[Zave84] P. Zave, "The Operational versus the Conventional approach to Software Development", *Communications of ACM*, vol. 27, no. 2, pp. 104 - 117, 1984.

Extending an Object-Oriented Model: Multiple Class Objects

Tomáš Hruška and Petr Kolenčík*

Department of Computer Science and Engineering
Faculty of Electrical Engineering and Computer Science
Technical University of Brno
Božetěchova 2, 612 66 Brno, Czech Republic
{hruska,kolencik}@dcse.fee.vutbr.cz

Abstract. Experiences of both researchers and practitioners with the development of object-oriented database systems help us to evaluate the real contributions of object-oriented modeling principles and show the limits and possibilities of improvements of the object-oriented model. One of the research areas where such a need was recognized concerns the class membership. In most object-oriented data model objects must belong to a single most specific class. However, the real world situations often break this presumption. The aim of this paper is to discuss the issues relating to an extension of modeling concepts to capture the objects that can belong to the multiple most specific classes. Our final objective is to present a framework for the formal object-oriented models that will provide the rigorous theoretical tool to solve issues concerning conflicts that can arise in structural components of objects. Most importantly, we show that the structural conflicts can be solved from the context determined by the static typing.

1 Introduction

The real world situations often break the common presumption of the object-oriented design where objects have a structure determined for all lifetime. In the conceptual design, we often use the multiple inheritance for the model situations in which entities can play several roles. However, this approach does not see an object as a single entity acquiring and discarding roles. According to [14], this approach to the object typing leads to the loss of the possibility to build highly abstract data models because it does not correspond to the actual way the real world entities behave. These problems influence the design, implementation and application level of the object-oriented database systems. For an appropriate study of these questions, some theoretical tools were used (see [2]) to avoid any unexpected conflicts.

To illustrate, consider a database of persons at a university. Suppose that a public library represents a part of this university. A person can play a lot of different roles, such as employee, a student, a teacher or a reader. The roles played by the objects can change during their lifetime.

---

* Supported by the grant of the Czech Grant Agency No. 102/96/0986 Object-Oriented Database Model and by the grant of the Czech Ministry of Education No. 0630 Modeling of Inheritance in the Object-Oriented Database Model.

Assume that there are stored personal codes of students and distinct codes of readers in the database. Furthermore, suppose that a former reader enters this university. The system should automatically resolve conflicts in the attribute *code*. Of course, many cases of this situation may occur, and the database designer should not be forced to rewrite each time the database scheme to get a new class defined by the multiple inheritance. For example, the new class would be forced for the role of *student–reader*. The preferred solution lies in the existence of objects being of the two (generally more) types.

They are two basic reasons for this solution. First, we avoid the combinatorial explosion of the classes defined by using the multiple inheritance (in the cases when many classes can be combined). Second, we do not want to define some new functionality for the combined class. We just expect that it possesses attributes of both students and readers. However, we must decide how to manage the name conflicts due to the presence of attributes and methods of the same name. For this purpose, we deal with the *multiple inheritance* modeling. The multiple inheritance will be then used to represent the *multiple class objects*.

We present another approach to solve the problem of the multiple class objects by using the *category theory* (CT). In their manifestos [3,6], Diskin and Goguen pointed out that the category theory is the formalism especially suited for this purpose. According to these manifestos, we try to show that the approach based on CT brings more simplicity and clarity, in addition, makes the reasoning easier. Specifically, we show, that the structural conflicts can be solved from the context determined by the static typing. Advantages of CT will be illustrated in terms of the formal database model called LDM (Limit Data Model, see Sect. 2), designed to support the development of the object-oriented database system at the author's department.

The main reason for using CT as a formal tool for the object-oriented modeling is that it offers a formal, graphical and powerful abstract language for the modeling of objects (this idea is developed especially in [4]). This property gives a new view and helps to see nontrivial properties which would be difficult to discover otherwise (examples can be found in [5, 10, 11, 13]).

Moreover, all categorical constructions specify objects in terms of their relationship to other objects, and this specification results in a clearer declarative approach with an immediate operational equivalent. In this paper, we use only the basic notions of the category theory (see [1]). The original ideas were introduced in [8, 9, 7]. Here, we focus on the problem of an attribute access for the classes defined by the multiple inheritance and the semantics of the operations creating objects and acquiring and discarding their types.

The paper is organized as follows. Section 2 gives the definition of the inheritance in LDM with an emphasis on the multiple inheritance, attribute access, and disambiguity resolution. Section 3 explains, how to create objects with a single most specific class. Section 4 deals with the semantics of the type changing operations *acquire* and *discard*. Finally, Section 5 presents the semantics of the attribute access for the objects with multiple most specific classes together with the proof that conflicts can be resolved using the static typing in LDM.

2 Inheritance in the Limit Data Model

In general, the database intention is modeled as category $\mathcal{D}_I$ in LDM. In $\mathcal{D}_I$, the categorical objects represent *classes* while arrows with additional conditions are used to model an *aggregation, inheritance, relationships* and *methods*.

The database objects are modeled as tuples defined as a product. Within this framework, we can refer to the class attributes only through the projections (this expresses the principle of an encapsulation). To bring attributes from the superclass to the name space of its subclass, as required by the inheritance, we need a device of an arrow composition that is essential in CT. According to [1] we use the notation $g \circ f(x)$ for a morphism $g(f(x))$. Moreover, in a category the objects and the arrows are not named; therefore, we will introduce a labeling function assigning meaningful names to projections that will enable us to model inheritance.

Hereafter, we use the labeling π_{name}^{Class} for the projection accessing the attribute *name* of the class *Class*. Disambiguities caused by the multiple inheritance will be solved by using $\pi_{Super::name}^{Class}$ denoting the attribute *name* of the class *Class* inherited from the superclass *Super*. Finally, the projection that defines a type coercion to the superclass will be written as $\pi_{Class:Super}$. For each subclass, we need to define composite arrows that enable to access the attributes inherited from the superclass and assign appropriate names to the composite projections following the labeling schema.

To give a deeper insight to the problems caused by the multiple inheritance, consider an example of the class *person* $P^p : \{name\}$, *student* $S^p = P^p \times \text{int} : \{(name, code)\}$ and *lecturer* $L^p = P^p \times \text{int} : \{(name, code)\}$, both *student* and *lecturer* inheriting from *P*. The class *teaching assistant* $TA^p = L^p \times S^p : \{(name, L::code, S::code)\}$ inherits from *lecturer* and *student*.

According to the strong typing of CT, p in *Class*^{p} indicates that this categorical object represents purely the database objects belonging to *Class*, not to its subclasses (as required by the principle of the class polymorphism in the object-oriented languages). We call the classes denoted as *Class*^{p} *pure classes*.

The attribute *name* is placed once in the class TA^p even if it is inherited twice through the classes S^p and L^p. On the contrary, the attribute *code* must be in two copies in TA^p because it can potentially carry two distinct values. Otherwise, if the attribute *code* had always the same value for *students* and *lecturers*, it should be defined in the class *person* only once because it is meaningful and unique for each person. In fact, this principle expresses the semantics of the *virtual base classes* as defined in [12].

Formally, we describe the virtual base classes in a way of category theory which express equations by using of commutative diagrams. Consider Fig. 1. In this figure the diamond of the multiple inheritance for TA^p commutes with the meaning that the composite arrows on two paths leading to P^p give the same results: $\pi_{S:P} \circ \pi_{TA:S} = \pi_{L:P} \circ \pi_{TA:L}$. This means that we can assign a single name to these two equivalent projections referring to the shared attribute *name* $\pi_{name}^{TA^p} = \pi_{name}^{S^p} \circ \pi_{TA:S} = \pi_{name}^{L^p} \circ \pi_{TA:L}$. As a result, we ensure that P^p is the virtual base class and, in essence, the attribute *name* in S^p and L^p denotes the same thing. This construction, which is well known in the category theory, is called *pullback*. Therefore, the *pullback* enables to model the notion of virtual base classes.

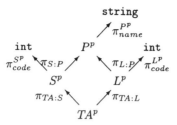

Fig. 1. The diamond of multiple inheritance for teaching assistants.

2.1 Naming Problem

The strength of the object-oriented model lies in the inheritance construction. On the contrary to the aggregation, the inheritance enables to derive a new class, based on some existing one, bringing inherited attributes to its name space. However, for the classes defined by the multiple inheritance it is not sometimes possible to place all inherited names into one naming space. The inheritance is in LDM modeled by using the product construction, arrow composition and projection labeling. The arrow composition will be always unique but the problem of the assigning of unique names to the composite projections should be carefully examined.

Considering the previous example, this problem concerns TA^p, where we need to distinguish two distinct attributes *code*. The corresponding projections $\pi_{code}^{S^p} \circ \pi_{TA:S}$ and $\pi_{code}^{L^p} \circ \pi_{TA:L}$ are always disambiguous but we can not add just the name *code* to the name space of TA because this name denotes two different things. The problem of projections labeling will be called the *naming problem*. The conflicting attributes *code* can be distinguished by using the double colon notation $S::code$ and $L::code$.

In general, the naming problem can be resolved as follows. For each class, we define composite projections that access all attributes inherited from the superclasses through the following *naming algorithm*:

Algorithm 1 (Naming Algorithm)

For all classes Sup that are superclasses of $Class$ so that have their projections for the attributes already defined and labeled **do**:

1. **if** for any class $X \in \mathcal{D}_I$ $\exists Y \in \mathcal{D}_I$, $X \neq Y$, both distinct from Sup, such that the class Sup contains projections labeled $\pi_{X::name}^{Sup^p}$ and $\pi_{Y::name}^{Sup^p}$

   then $$\pi_{S::name}^{Class^p} = \pi_{X::name}^{Sup^p} \circ \pi_{Class:Sup},$$
   where S is the *source class* of *name* in which the conflict causing attribute *name* was defined for the first time (it can be induced from the composition of the projections);

   otherwise, we know that Sup contains the attribute *name* in the forms $S::name$ or *name* only (where S could be the unique superclass of Sup if the attribute *name* comes from it). Therefore, we define a labeling of this projection as

$$\pi^{Class^p}_{Sup::name} = \pi^{Sup^p}_{name} \circ \pi_{Class:Sup};$$

2. **then**, we define the projections for the attributes that $Class$ adds itself with $\pi^{Class^p}_{name}$;

3. **finally**, we can identify some common attributes in the form $Sup_1::name$ and $Sup_2::name$ and define a new label $name$ for projections satisfying the commutativity requirement $\pi^{Class^p}_{Sup_1::name} = \pi^{Class^p}_{Sup_2::name}$. We assign the new label $name$ also for projections with unique label $\pi^{Class^p}_{Sup::name}$ (if there arises the name conflict, we report an error message). □

This is precisely what C++ does. To avoid disambiguities, we can always say which inheritance path is meant using the double colon notation with the direct superclass and the attribute name $Sup::name$. However, if a conflict has already occurred in the superclass, we distinguish the attributes by specifying the source class that they come from (without the possibility to write the whole path). In our example, the projections can be computed and labeled as follows:

$$\mathbf{P} : \pi^{P^p}_{name} : P^p \to \texttt{string}$$

$$\mathbf{S} : \pi^{S^p}_{code} : S^p \to \texttt{int} \qquad\qquad \mathbf{L} : \pi^{L^p}_{code} : L^p \to \texttt{int}$$
$$\pi^{S^p}_{name} \equiv \pi^{S^p}_{P::name} = \pi^{P^p}_{name} \circ \pi_{S:P} \qquad \pi^{L^p}_{name} \equiv \pi^{L^p}_{P::name} = \pi^{P^p}_{name} \circ \pi_{L:P}$$

The first projection $\pi^{P^p}_{name}$ for the class $person$ is named according to the second step of the naming algorithm. When we finish the labeling process for the projection of the class $person$ we can proceed it for its subclasses. With respect to their structure, classes $student$ and $lecturer$ are very similar. The attribute $name$ can be accessed through the projection with two equivalent names $\pi^{S^p}_{name}$ and $\pi^{S^p}_{S::name}$ assigned in the first (the branch **otherwise**), and the third step of the naming algorithm.

More interesting naming process runs for the class $teaching\ assistant$ defined by the multiple inheritance:

$$\mathbf{TA^p} : \pi^{TA^p}_{name} \equiv \pi^{TA^p}_{S::name} \equiv \pi^{TA^p}_{L::name} = \pi^{S^p}_{name} \circ \pi_{TA:S} = \pi^{L^p}_{name} \circ \pi_{TA:L}$$
$$(\text{according to the commutative condition})$$
$$\pi^{TA^p}_{S::code} = \pi^{S^p}_{code} \circ \pi_{TA:S}$$
$$\pi^{TA^p}_{L::code} = \pi^{L^p}_{code} \circ \pi_{TA:L}$$

The attribute $name$ coming from the class $person$ can be accessed by using the composition of the projections (following again the branch **otherwise** in the first step of the naming algorithm and then the third step). In this case, we have three possibilities of labeling this composed projection according to the commutativity condition required for the diamond of the multiple inheritance in Fig. 1. However, the attribute $code$ has not these properties since it has two different sources S and L in the inheritance hierarchy, so we will leave the two projections, referring to two different things, with distinct labels.

2.2 Class Polymorphism

The inheritance significantly differs from the aggregation also in the following way. An object of a subclass of a class can be used in all places where the class can stand. This is an important property of the object-oriented model that enables to reuse a code and data structures. In our model, this kind of class polymorphism is expressed by using categorical objects called the *generalized classes*, which will be in the text denoted by using the superscript g. They are defined through the cocone construction with the inclusion arrows i.

Simply expressed, for each class we define an categorical object whose type represents the union of the types of its subclasses. For example, in the case of the university database, the category $\mathcal{D}_I$, representing the schema of the database, will have the structure shown in Fig. 2, where the upper square is required to commute. The inclusion arrows leading to the upper square can be easily induced from the inheritance hierarchy in the bottom.

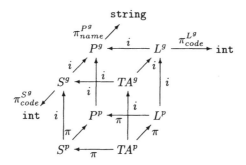

Fig. 2. Inheritance hierarchy of the university database.

The categorical object S^g can be viewed as an union of the sets S^p (*student* tuples) and TA^g (*assistant* tuples). Similarly, the object P^g represents union of the sets S^g, L^g and P^p. The commutativity condition for the upper square ensures that P^g is the union (not the disjoint union) of S^g and L^g (they have TA^g as intersection). This construction is in the category theory known as the *pushout*. This means that disjoint extents of S^g and L^g can be expressed using the pushout.

Within this framework, the classes are represented as the generalized classes, which are themselves defined as an union of the pure classes (i.e. the categorical objects with the superscript p that represents the tuples of one type that are stored in the database). Therefore, the naming scheme should be extended for generalized classes as well. For each generalized class, we define the projections as *sums of projections* of the union components giving it the same label in the subscript. For example, we get $\pi_{name}^{S^g} \equiv \pi_{P::name}^{S^g} = \pi_{name}^{S^p} + \pi_{name}^{TA^p}$ and $\pi_{code}^{S^g} = \pi_{code}^{S^p} + \pi_{S::code}^{TA^p}$. First, this categorical construction of the sum of morphisms in **Set** (the category of sets and mappings between them) determines the set to which an element $o \in S^g$ belongs (with respect to the disjoint union $S^g = S^p \cup TA^p$); then it uses the projection defined for the determined set ($\pi_{name}^{S^p}$ for the objects from S^p and $\pi_{name}^{TA^p}$ for the objects from TA^p).

Now, having defined the generalized classes, the semantics of the object identification can be described in a category as an injective mapping from objects to the set of OIDs that are currently in use (in a length explanation can be found in [7]). OIDs are essential in the object-oriented model for representation of references to the database objects, collections of objects and extents of classes. They also play an important role when introducing persistence into the object-oriented database model.

3 Creating the Database

So far, we have dealt only with the *metadata* of the database and expressed the database schema as a category $\mathcal{D}_I$. Next, we explain how to describe the actual data stored in the database and formalize the semantics of the operations that enable us to create the objects and change their types.

Specific objects (tuples with complex structure) derived from the class definition $\mathcal{D}_I$ are formalized as a *model* of the database intention in the **Set**. **Set** is the category of sets and mappings between them [1]. In the category theory, it is formally represented by using a *functor* D, to another category $\mathcal{D}_E$ representing the content of the database or the database extension.

The functor is defined as a pair of functions. One of them assigns the objects of the first category to the objects of the second category, and the second function does the same job for arrows. Informally, in our case the functor D defines the appropriate mappings from classes of $\mathcal{D}_I$ to their extents in $\mathcal{D}_E$, OIDs to the natural numbers (e.g.), the morphisms to the methods. The commutative conditions of $\mathcal{D}_I$ are required to be preserved also in $\mathcal{D}_E$.

Any transaction consisting of a method invocation or an operation *update, new* or *delete* is expressed as a change of D according to the results given by the function in $\mathcal{D}_E$ used to implement the operation defined in $\mathcal{D}_I$. In this way, we can introduce the notion of persistence into the inherently functional language of the category theory.

The semantics of *new* can be specified in the following way: we define a new functor, $D' : \mathcal{D}_I \rightarrow \mathcal{D}_E$, that satisfies $D'(c) = D(c)$, for all classes $c \in \mathcal{D}_I -$ $\{Class\}$, and redefine its value for $Class$ by adding a new tuple, obj, to the set $D'(Class) = D(Class) \cup \{obj\}$. However, obj needs to be added also to the extents of all the superclasses of the class $Class$: $\forall Sup \in \mathcal{D}_I$, such that $\exists \pi_{Class:Sup} D'(Sup) = D(Sup) \cup obj$.

For example, we show how to create a new object obj of the type S^p initialized to $obj = (James, 007)$ (the first attribute denotes the name of the student and other denotes his code in the database). The state of the database before the execution of *new* is shown in Fig. 3. For simplicity, we have omitted object identifiers in this figure.

Recall that the diamond in Fig. 3 is the upper square in Fig. 2, which represents the database intention $\mathcal{D}_I$. D maps the classes to their actual extents in the database represented by $\mathcal{D}_E$. Let us show how these extents are composed by using the sum construction; for instance, the tuple $(Paul, 002, 002)$, representing a teaching assistant, is included to the extents of all classes in the hierarchy. Similarly, *Mark* and *Tom* are included also to the extent of *persons*. Finally, P^g contains all the tuples in our small database.

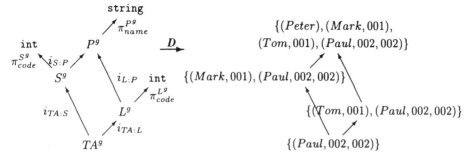

Fig. 3. The database schema $\mathcal{D}_I$ and the content $\mathcal{D}_E$ before the operation *new*.

The invocation of *new* for James with the personal code 007 will have the following effect on the database expressed as a change of D to D' (see Fig. 4):

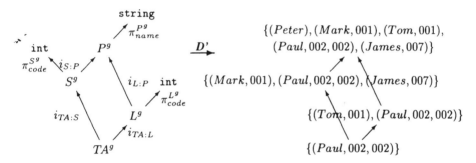

Fig. 4. The database schema $\mathcal{D}_I$ and the content $\mathcal{D}_E$ after the operation *new*.

4 Semantics of Flexible Objects

We have given the formal specification of *new* that creates the objects based on some type existing in the inheritance hierarchy of $\mathcal{D}_I$. In this section we explain how to change the role played by an object; then, we study how it affects the types of objects.

The role-attribute model proposed in [14] defines the conditions on which an object can acquire and discard roles. This definition implies an existence of two corresponding operations. Operation *acquire* extends the type of an object with a new type and *discard* removes the type from an multiple class object. The effect of the first operation, acquiring new type B for an object of type A, is equivalent to the construction of a new object, $A \times B$, with added attributes B. Notice that its type corresponds to the type resulting from the multiple inheritance with the superclasses A and B. However, this class is neither named nor directly accessible. Therefore, we call it *product class*.

On the other hand, the second operation can remove some attributes that are defined as a part of the type that this object discards. Because the structure of objects in such model can change, we call them *flexible objects* or *multiple class objects*. In this section, we define the semantics of these two type of changing operations.

We will define the effect of *acquire* as a change of the database schema $\mathcal{D}_I$ adding the corresponding class defined by the multiple inheritance. However, this is expressed theoretically because the strong typing of the category theory requires an existence of the type corresponding to the structure of the multiple class objects for the sake of consistency. The implementation does not require any change in the database metadata catalogue, and the designer can choose whether the existence of multiple class objects is hidden to the users.

In [2], the authors expressed the type of multiple class objects in terms of its most specific classes. This expression is useful because the system can more easily analyze the effect of *acquire* and *discard* on the structure of objects. In general, *acquire* for an object $obj \in C_1 \times C_2 \times \ldots \times C_n$ and a new role of A takes this object of type $C_1 \times C_2 \times \ldots \times C_n$ and transforms it to an object, obj', of type $C_1 \times C_2 \times \ldots \times C_n \times A$. If we omit the inheritance hierarchy and corresponding commutative conditions (corresponding to the notion of the virtual base class), this operation adds all the attributes of A to the object obj. The additional commutative conditions imposed on the inheritance hierarchy restrict the actual attributes added to the product to those defined as the product of most specific classes of the object.

There are three possibilities to influence the structure of obj by A. First, A can be the supertype of some C_i. Then, the structure and the type of this object remains the same. Second, A can be the subtype of some classes $C_1, \ldots, C_n$. This case means that these classes can be removed from the product while the class A can be added. Finally, if A is not the subclass or superclass of any C_i, the product can be extended by A.

The semantics of *acquire* can be defined by using the product construction with additional commutative conditions as required by the inheritance hierarchy. An example of the multiple class object *reader-student* is shown in Fig. 5 ($R \times S^p$ has the meaning of $(R \times S)^p$). In this example, R^p represents *readers* and PS^p *postgraduate students*.

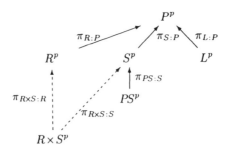

Fig. 5. Multiple class object $R \times S^p$ before invocation of the operation *acquire*.

The three distinct possibilities of classes that can be acquired for $R \times S^p$ in the bottom are P^p, PS^p or L^p. Operation *acquire* P does not change the structure of $R \times S$-object because it already contains all the features of P. The other two possibilities of acquiring of PS and L affect the structure of $R \times S$-object (see Fig. 6).

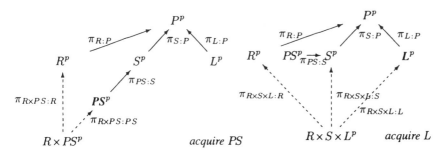

Fig. 6. Illustration of the operation *acquire*.

The operation *discard* works in the reverse order. We can study all distinct cases depending on the relationship between the object type $obj \in C_1 \times C_2 \times \ldots \times C_n$ and discarded type A. If A is not in the supertype or the subtype relationship with any C_i, the structure and the type of the object remain the same. If A occurs in the product $C_1 \times C_2 \times \ldots \times C_n$ as class C_i then obj' has the structure $C_1 \times C_2 \times \ldots \times C_{i-1} \times C_{i+1} \times \ldots \times C_n$.

However, this is not the only possible functionality. For example, we can consider $obj \in R \times S$ and *acquire* type PS getting $obj \in R \times PS$. Now an invocation of *discard* PS would cause the object obj to have the type of R: $obj \in R$ although we expected to get the type it had before applying of *acquire*.

Neither it is also clear what happens if A occurs in the subclass or superclass relationship with some C_i. In this case, the type of obj can remain the same or be restricted. At this time, we prefer removing all the classes C_i that coincide with A or that are in the superclass or subclass relationship with it. We are aware of the fact that the possibility of reversing *acquire* is disabled (we can not return to the preceding state of database).

5 Conflicts and Their Solution

In the previous sections, we have not dealt with the problem of the attribute access for the objects having multiple most specific classes. The present section continues with the use of the category theoretical means as explained in the Sect. 2.

As demonstrated in the previous sections, there is no problem with conflicts concerning the structure of the class state in the category theoretical framework. By using the commutativity conditions, we specify which attributes are essentially the same and which are not.

However, the core of the conflict lies in the naming problem caused by the flat naming space for the classes defined by the multiple inheritance. However, in the case of product classes (used to the model multiple class objects), we choose another policy for the naming because we suppose that the user has not direct knowledge about attributes of such classes. If he wants to access objects with the multiple most specific classes he should use a reference defined only for some existing base class. This context for attribute access gives as natural means for conflict solution.

Before dealing with the conflict resolution, we briefly explain how objects can be accessed by using references in LDM. Conceptually, objects are referenced through their identifiers which are themselves not accessible by a user. Therefore, the objects can be directly denoted by variables or indirectly by expressions containing the attribute access or the method invocations starting from an object-denoting variable. Since the category theory is a strongly typed language we have an unique type associated with each object reference (see [2]). In this section, we show how to use this type to determine the context in which attributes are accessed and, thus, solve possible conflicts.

Recall that the attributes of the product classes $A \times B$ composed from A and B are accessible only through the generalized classes A^g and B^g. For A, it is defined as a disjoint union $A^g = A^p \cup A \times B^p$ and, similarly, for B. Therefore, it remains to define the labeling for the product classes of $A \times B$. Then, we can prove that there is no conflict concerning the attribute access.

The problem arises from $A::attr$ and $B::attr$, which were brought to the product class through the multiple inheritance. The type of the generalized class used to access the multiple class object (in our case, A^g or B^g) determines the *context*, and we must choose the right projections to compose $\pi_{attr}^{A^g}$. There are two possibilities – $\pi_{attr}^{A^g} = \pi_{attr}^{A^p} + \pi_{A::attr}^{A \times B^p}$ or $\pi_{attr}^{A^g} = \pi_{attr}^{A^p} + \pi_{B::attr}^{A \times B^p}$. The first, and the second term defines, how $\pi_{attr}^{A^g}$ is translated for A and $A \times B$-objects, respectively. For example, naming scheme for generalized classes of the university database discussed in the previous sections and the product class $S \times L$ can be computed as follows:

$$\pi_{name}^{S^g} = \pi_{name}^{S^p} + \pi_{name}^{S \times L^p}$$
$$\pi_{name}^{P^g} = \pi_{name}^{S^p} + \pi_{name}^{L^p} + \pi_{name}^{P^p} + \pi_{name}^{S \times L^p} = \pi_{name}^{S^g} + \pi_{name}^{L^g} + \pi_{name}^{P^p}$$

It means that $\pi_{name}^{P^g}$ is for the objects of type S translated as $\pi_{name}^{S^g}$, for the L-objects as $\pi_{name}^{L^g}$ and for the object of type P as $\pi_{name}^{P^p}$. The projections $\pi_{name}^{S \times L^g}$, $\pi_{S::code}^{S \times L^g}$ and $\pi_{L::code}^{S \times L^g}$ are not defined in the database because the system is not aware of the class $S \times L$. This class serves only for the sake of typing consistency in the model category $\mathcal{D}_E$. Nevertheless, we define these projections and labels as shown later on to give the semantics for the context dependent solution of the name conflicts.

The attribute *code* that causes potential conflict is more interesting. It is not defined for the class P. For the other classes, the projections are

$$\pi_{code}^{S^g} = \pi_{code}^{S^p} + \pi_{S::code}^{S \times L^p} \qquad\qquad \pi_{code}^{L^g} = \pi_{code}^{L^p} + \pi_{L::code}^{S \times L^p}$$

It means that $\pi_{code}^{S^g}$ is for the objects belonging to S equal to $\pi_{code}^{S^p}$ (see Fig. 7) while for the objects belonging to $S \times L^p$ as $\pi_{S::code}^{S \times L^p}$. Similarly, we define sums of morphisms for L. Notice the definition of the sum of morphisms $\pi_{code}^{S^g}$, which determines that in the context of S we always access the attribute $S{::}code$ for both kinds of objects belonging to the class S or $S \times L$. Similarly, the attribute $code$ in the context L means $L{::}code$ for L and $S \times L$-objects.

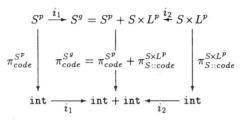

Fig. 7. Composing the sum of morphisms for the product classes.

Therefore, the property of the sum of morphisms offer us how to distinguish attributes $S{::}code$ and $L{::}code$ by using the context in which the object is accessed through the reference. The different attributes $code$ of $S \times L$-objects will be accessed depending on the context in which the object is referred. By using a variable of the type S^g, access to the attribute $code$ will be translated through the sum of morphisms $\pi_{code}^{S^g}$ as $\pi_{S{::}code}^{S \times L^p}$ while through the morphism $\pi_{code}^{L^g}$ as $\pi_{L{::}code}^{S \times L^p}$. Generally, we extend the naming scheme for the generalized classes to cover the product classes by the following step:

Algorithm 2 (Context Dependent Access)

We generate labels for product class $P \times B^p$ by using the *naming algorithm* (see Algorithm 1). **For each** attribute $name$ in B satisfying one of the following conditions **do**:

1. **if** $name$ was inherited to B and does not cause any conflict, and

    if the attribute $name$ does not exist in P, we extend both sums of morphisms $\pi_{name}^{B^g}$ and $\pi_{X{::}name}^{B^g}$ by adding the morphism $\pi_{B{::}name}^{P \times B^p}$,

    otherwise, we extend both sums of morphisms $\pi_{name}^{B^g}$ and $\pi_{X{::}name}^{B^g}$ by the morphism $\pi_{S{::}name}^{P \times B^p}$ (S is the source class of the attribute $name$ in B);

2. **if** $name$ causes a conflict in B and was distinguished by using the prefix $S{::}name$, we extend the sum of morphisms $\pi_{S{::}name}^{B^g}$ by adding the morphism $\pi_{S{::}name}^{P \times B^p}$ (S is the source class for that attribute $name$);

3. **otherwise**, $name$ was defined in B for the first time (i.e. it was not inherited and therefore has no prefix in B), we extend the sum of morphisms $\pi_{name}^{B^g}$ by $\pi_{B{::}name}^{P \times B^p}$.
   □

Proposition 1 Let the product class $P{\times}B$ be a subclass of B (there exists the projection $\pi_{P \times B{:}B} : P{\times}B^p \to B^p$). Then, each access to the attribute $name$ of the $P{\times}B^p$-object, defined in the context of the base class B^g as the sum morphism $\pi_{name}^{B^g}$ or $\pi_{X{::}name}^{B^g}$ (with respect to the Algorithm 2), is unique. □

This proposition follows from the Algorithm 1 and 2. We show that for each attribute access in the context of B there exists an unique projection in $P \times B$ denoting the same attribute. The core of the problem is to find the corresponding prefixes of the attributes in the subclasses. We have four possibilities how the prefixes can change. If the attribute $name$ was inherited from X to B and does not cause any conflict in B, we must find out what prefix this attribute will have in $P \times B^p$. If $name$ does not cause any conflict in $P \times B^p$, we know that the prefix B can be used to distinguish this attribute. Therefore, $name$ can be accessed by using $\pi_{B::name}^{P \times B^p}$. Otherwise, we should use $\pi_{S::name}^{P \times B^p}$, where S is the source class for this attribute, because every conflicting attribute is distinguished by the first step of the naming algorithm using its unique source class..

If there was any conflict caused by $name$ in B, $name$ is distinguished using the prefix denoting the source class of this attribute. This prefix will never change in the subclasses. Therefore, $name$ can be accessed in the context of B by using the sum of morphisms $\pi_{S::name}^{B^g}$ only and we add the projection $\pi_{S::name}^{P \times B^p}$. Finally, if the attribute $name$ was defined in B, B is the unique source for this attribute. This means that we can always find the projection $\pi_{B::name}^{P \times B^p}$ in $P \times B$.

Recall that any attribute name conflict is caused only by the need of the consistent flat naming scheme for the classes in the inheritance hierarchy. It can be resolved in the compile time through the static typing. In the case of product classes the naming algorithm is applied to determine which attribute is meant in different contexts, but the names themselves cannot be used to access attributes directly through product classes.

6 Conclusion and Further Investigation

This paper has discussed an introduction of flexible objects into OODB model as required by the real world situations. It has presented an approach to the formal object-oriented models based on the *category theory* that provides theoretical tools to model the semantics of operations *new*, *acquire* and *discard*.

In terms of LDM, we have investigated issues concerning the name conflicts arising from the multiple class membership of objects. Two algorithms, which are essential to the definition of an object with the multiple most specific classes, were presented.

The *naming algorithm* was used to distinguish attributes of the same name in the classes defined by the multiple inheritance. We have defined the semantics of the operation *new*. The operations *acquire* and *discard* were proposed as the basic means for changing the roles of multiple class objects. Most importantly, we showed that structural conflicts concerning these objects can be resolved from the context determined by the static typing.

However, only the structural components of the objects were studied; a reformulation of the naming algorithm and product classes for methods represents an open investigation area. This can be easily done because methods are in LDM treated in a similar way as attributes; however, the problem of method dispatching makes this case more complicated. It seems that neither preferred class approach nor the argument specificity approach [2] satisfy the real needs of the database systems because the semantics of the dispatching itself still remains to be an open problem.

Acknowledgements

The ideas presented in this paper have been influenced by the discussions with Michal Máčel. The authors would also like to thank Alexander Meduna for his useful comments.

References

1. BARR, M., WELLS, C.: Category Theory for Computing Science. Prentice Hall, 1995.
2. BERTINO, E., GUERRINI, G.: Objects with Multiple Most Specific Classes. In Proceedings of 9th European Conference ECOOP'95 on Object-Oriented Programming, W. G. Olthoff, Ed., vol. 952 of LNCS, Springer, 1995, pp. 102–126.
3. CADIS, B., DISKIN, Z.: Algebraic Graph-Oriented = Category Theory Based. Manifesto of categorizing database theory. Tech. Rep. 9406, Frame Inform Systems, Riga, Latvia, 1994.
4. CADIS, B., DISKIN, Z.: Databases as graphical algebras: Algebraic graph-based approach to data modeling and database design. Tech. rep., Frame Inform Systems, Riga, Latvia, 1996.
5. CADIS, B., DISKIN, Z.: Variable Sets and Functions Framework for Conceptual Modeling: Integrating ER and OO via Sketches with Dynamic Markers. In Proceedings of 14th International Conference OOER'95 on Object-Oriented and Entity-Relationship Modelling, M. P. Papazoglou, Ed., vol. 1021 of LNCS, Springer, 1995, pp. 226–237.
6. GOGUEN, J.: A Categorical Manifesto. Mathematical Structures in Computer Science, 1(1):49–67, 1991.
7. HRUŠKA, T., KOLENČÍK, P.: Semantics of Object Identification in Object-oriented Database Model. In Proceedings of Scientific Conference Electronic Computers and Informatics, Faculty of Electrical engineering and Informatics of Technical University Košice, 1996, pp. 243–249.
8. KOLENČÍK, P.: Classes in Object-Oriented Model as Categorical Objects. In Sborník prací studentů a doktorandů, FEECS TU of Brno, 1996, pp. 75–77.
9. KOLENČÍK, P.: Methods in The Object-Oriented Model as Sums of Morphisms. In Proceeding of International Conference MOSIS'97, vol. 2, ISBN 80–85988–17–8, 1997, pp. 83–88.
10. NÉLSON, D., ROSSITER, B.: Prototyping a categorical database in P/FDM. In Second International Workshop on Advances in Databases and Information Systems ADBIS'95, 1995.
11. PIESSENS, F., STEEGMANS, E.: Categorical data-specifications. Theory and Applications of Categories, 1:156–173, 1995. Available at http://www.tac.mta.ca/tac/.
12. STROUSTRUP, E.: The annotated C++ reference manual. Addison Wesley, 1992.
13. TUIJN, C.: Data Modeling from a Categorical Perspective. PhD thesis, Antwerpen University, 1994.
14. VELHO, A. V., CARAPUCA, R.: From Entity-Relationship Models to Role-Attribute Models. In Proceedings of 12th International Conference ER'93 on the Entity-Relationship Approach, R. A. Elmasri, V. Kouramajian, and B. Thalheim, Eds., vol. 823 of LNCS, Springer, 1994, pp. 257–270.

Formal Approach to Metamodeling: A Generic Object-Oriented Perspective

Vojislav B. Mišić[1] and Simon Moser[2]

[1] The Hong Kong University of Science and Technology,
Clear Water Bay, Kowloon, Hong Kong, email: vmisic@cs.ust.hk,
on leave from University of Belgrade, Yugoslavia.
[2] CSSE/COTAR, Swinburne University of Technology, 1 John St.,
Hawthorn Vic 3122, Australia, email: moser@acm.org.

Abstract. Formal methods and metamodeling are promising ways to cope with the ever increasing size and complexity of modern software systems: the former should provide the means to write precise, unambiguous, and provably consistent descriptions of system properties, while the latter should lead to a better understanding of the software development process through metamodeling the descriptions produced in the course of the software development process. In this paper, we propose to use both formal methods and metamodeling, in order to combine their advantages. A generic metamodel of object-oriented systems is presented and specified, using the Z formal notation. Other known models may easily be mapped to our model, as demonstrated on the OMG core object model. The formal notation facilitates the specification of various constraints and consistency checks, a number of which are shown in detail.

1 Introduction

One of the promising ways to improve both quality and productivity in software development is through the use of formal methods. The ability to specify system properties in a precise and rigorous way, and to actually prove that an implemented system satisfies its requirements, has been invaluable in the design and implementation of many software and hardware systems, regardless of their size [3, 4]. A number of formal specification techniques have been proposed thus far, most of them based on some well-developed mathematical notation. One of the most popular among them is Z [13], which has been used with success throughout academia and industry [4].

Metamodels, the other promising avenue we focus our attention on, have been known and used in database area for quite some time (e.g., in [2]). While the so-called domain (or business) models provide the foundation for the design and development of database oriented applications, metamodels (i.e., the domain models of the domain models) provide the foundation for the design and development process itself. Metamodeling has only recently started to receive more attention in the broader area of software engineering, where it has been used as a vehicle towards a better understanding, and even standardization of the software production process [8, 14]. It effectively imposes a layered structure on the set of system modeling tools and techniques, with the metamodel as the foundation upon which a number of models may be developed.

None of these approaches were, however, fully formal. This paper undertakes a fully formal approach to metamodeling, based on a well-established formal notation. Formal metamodeling should provide improved clarity and precision of specifications and better validation capabilities, which in turn should lead to better control of time, effort, and product quality within the software process. At a more mundane level, this approach could prove useful in the development of data dictionaries and CASE tools.

The paper is organized as follows. Section 2 introduces, via the usual mix of formal Z text and informal English explanations, the generic metamodel of object-oriented systems. Sections 3 and 4 discuss further refinements in the model, namely, classes and their features, together with notions of inheritance, feature sharing, and subtyping, scoping of description objects with emphasis on different types of feature scoping, and method parameters. As other object models are subsumed by the metamodel described here, we show (in Section 5) the derivation of the OMG core object model as a special-ization of our metamodel. Some issues of syntactic and semantic checks of the model are discussed in the Section 6. The last Section concludes the work and presents some directions for future development of the metamodel [3].

2 The Basic Metamodel of Object-Oriented Systems

In a true object-oriented system, everything is an object; consequently, the process of object-oriented system development consists of a sequence of steps in which the objects are created, modified, refined, and (sometimes) deleted. These objects are actually descriptions (and, later, the implementation as well) of various parts of the system, at different levels of abstraction. These concepts will now be briefly explained and described in a rigorous way using the Z formal notation; we assume that the reader is familiar with both the principles of the object-oriented approach and the basics of Z (at the level of [6] and [13], respectively).

Each description object has an external and an internal part, both of which contribute to the description of the system as a whole. The external part of a description object 'represents' it in communication with other objects – other objects may reference it through its external part. The internal part 'implements' the object, its structure and behavior, the details of which are (possibly) hidden from other objects.

Hence, we start with the basic sets of objects, their interfaces, and implementations:

$[Object, ExtPart, IntPart]$

which need not be defined any further in Z (as is the case with basic ontological concepts, such as a 'thing' [14]). The relationship between these sets may be described with the following schema.

---

[3] The metamodel presented in this paper is subject to ongoing development and will probably have evolved by the time this paper appears in printed form. Please contact one of the authors for information on the most recent version of metamodel definitions.

$\boxed{\begin{array}{l} \text{\textit{BasicDefinitions}} \\ \textit{represents} : \textit{Object} \rightarrow \textit{ExtPart} \\ \textit{implements} : \textit{Object} \rightarrow \textit{IntPart} \\ \hline \forall\, O : \textit{Object} \bullet O \in \text{dom } \textit{represents} \vee O \in \text{dom } \textit{implements} \end{array}}$

Although both the external and internal part are optional, at least one must be present: language constructs and some library objects may exist, and may be used (and reused) without knowing anything about their internal part, and some objects (for example, elements of an array) may be used without being assigned a specific name. The predicate requires at least one of the parts to be present.

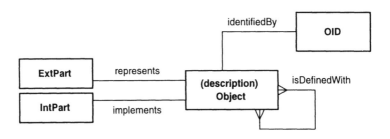

Fig. 1. The fundamental metamodel of an object-oriented system.

Since the external part, or some component thereof, is used to reference the object it represents, we could require it to be unique within the system.

$\boxed{\begin{array}{l} \text{\textit{Uniqueness}1} \\ \text{\textit{BasicDefinitions}} \\ \hline \forall\, E : \textit{ExtPart} \bullet (\exists_1\, O : \textit{Object} \bullet E = \textit{represents}(O)) \end{array}}$

Alternatively, we may allow different description objects to have the same interface (e.g., several equally named methods may exist in a class hierarchy – which is a special case of polymorphism). In this case, if the reference through an external part (which is usually the preferred manner of access) does not point to a single object, some other means of unique identification must be provided. A simple (albeit not very practical) solution in accordance with the principle of object identity [1], is to assign a unique, possibly machine-generated, identifier to each object.

$\boxed{\begin{array}{l} \text{\textit{Uniqueness}2} \\ \text{\textit{BasicDefinitions}} \\ \textit{identifiedBy} : \textit{OID} \rightarrowtail \textit{Object} \\ \hline \forall\, oid_1, oid_2 : \textit{OID} \bullet \\ \quad \textit{identifiedBy}(oid_1) = \textit{identifiedBy}(oid_2) \Rightarrow oid_1 = oid_2 \end{array}}$

As all objects have identifiers, *identifiedBy* is a partial surjection; moreover, it is an injection as well, since different identifiers are mapped to different objects (i.e., no two objects can have the same identifier). Yet another uniqueness constraint (and its implications) will be discussed later, in the context of scoping rules.

Objects are defined in terms of other objects; however, the association is many-to-many, which means that the *isDefinedWith* relationship must be a plain relation.

isDefinedWith : *Object* × *Object*

The set of objects and their descriptions, captured by their external and internal parts, forms, then, the description of the system. This generic metamodel is presented in Fig. 1, using a simplified form of ER graphical notation, where objects are represented as rectangles, and connections as lines between them. Connection names should be read in left-to-right order, e.g., 'an External Part represents a Description Object'. The cardinality of connections is depicted with 'crow feet' at appropriate ends of the line.

3 Refining the Model: Classes and Features

In order to enable the metamodel to be used for modeling actual system implementations (e.g., object-oriented designs and programs), some additional concepts need to be introduced.

Notable among the objects are classes and their features, each of which belongs to a single class. Features may be dynamic or static, i.e., methods or variables. The methods may take parameters, and may produce side effects by sending messages to other objects (some more details will be presented later).

The implementation of a class includes both interface and implementation of its features; we will refer to the features that belong to a class as its 'local' features. (A *LocalSet* of a class is the set of all of its local features.)

```
_ ClassesAndFeatures _____
  Class, Feature ⊂ Object
  hasFeature : Feature → Class
  LocalSet : Class × 𝔽 Feature
 _____
  disjoint⟨Class, Feature⟩
  ∀ F : Feature • ∃₁ C : Class • C = hasFeature(F)
  ∀ C : Class • LocalSet(C) = {F : Feature | C = hasFeature(F)}
```

Classes have unique external parts, even without OIDs:

∀ C_1, C_2 : *Class* • *represents*(C_1) = *represents*(C_2) ⇒ $C_1 = C_2$

Features may be either (instance) variables, or methods, but not both at the same time:

⟨*Variable, Method*⟩ partitions *Feature*

Besides its local features, a class may be allowed access to the features of other classes (variables as well as methods) via inheritance, which is a kind of description.

Multiple inheritance is allowed, therefore *inheritsFrom* is only a relation; if only single inheritance was allowed, it would be a partial function. Finally, we may define children of a class as the set of all classes inheriting from it, and its offspring (children, children's children, . . .) as the transitive closure of the *Children* relation:

Inheritance ———————————————————————————
ClassesAndFeatures
$inheritsFrom : Class \times Class$
$Children, Parents : Class \times \mathbb{F}\, Class$

———————————————————————————————————————
$\forall\, C_1, C_2 : Class \bullet (C_1, C_2) \in inheritsFrom \Rightarrow (C_1, C_2) \in isDefinedWith$
$\forall\, C : Class \bullet Children(C) = \{CC : Class \mid (C, CC) \in inheritsFrom\}$
$\forall\, C : Class \bullet Offspring(C) = Children^+(C)$

(Parents and ancestors of a class may be defined in an analogous manner.)

Inheritance provides feature sharing, since all features of a class may be accessed by all classes which inherit from it, either directly, or indirectly; hence, the full set of features of a class could be obtained by combining the features inherited from its ancestors with those that belong to that class proper. (This point will be elaborated in more detail in the next Section.)

As features are objects in their own right, they can be uniquely identified by their *OIDs*: the *FullSet* of a class will contain a single instance of any feature available to that class, even in the presence of multiple inheritance. On the other hand, it may be convenient to access a feature by its interface part rather than OID – provided we are able to uniquely determine the feature we are referring to. (This opens the possibility to allow feature override[4], i.e., to allow multiple features to have the same interface).

A class also acts as a type for its instances: it provides a template for them, and (at the same time) acts as a factory capable of generating new instances upon request. Not all classes have instances, but each instance must belong to a single class.

ClassesAsTypes ———————————————————————
ClassesAndFeatures
$CInstance \subset Object$
$isTypeFor : Object \rightarrowtail Class$

———————————————————————————————————————
$\forall\, O : Object \bullet O \in CInstance \Rightarrow O \in \mathrm{dom}\, isTypeFor$

Classes may also participate in a subtyping relationship: a class is considered a direct subtype of some other class when it offers at least the same features to its clients. Subtyping may be (and usually is) actually implemented through inheritance, yet the two relationships are conceptually different, and must be considered separately. Note that a class may have a number of supertypes (e.g., he class of *BMW 850ci* cars is a subtype of [the classes of] BMW cars, of 12-cylinder-engine cars, of sports cars, and of

---

[4] The term does seem more precise and more general – and it is already used in Z – than the term 'overload' used by the C++ community.

a number of other classes as well). On the other hand, the number of classes that a given class inherits from is usually low: most classes inherit from a single parent class only.

Subtyping

$ClassesAndFeatures$
$isSubtypeOf : Class \times Class$
$SubTypes, SuperTypes : Class \times \mathbb{F}\ Class$

$\forall\ C : Class \bullet SubTypes(C) = \{C_1 : Class \mid (C, C_1) \in isSubtypeOf\}$
$\forall\ C : Class \bullet SuperTypes(C) = \{C_2 : Class \mid (C_2, C) \in isSubtypeOf\}$

Structures equivalent to ancestors and offspring sets may be defined easily – but that is left as an exercise to the reader.

4 Further Refinement: Scoping

The metamodel should support the principle of information hiding – one of the corner-stones of the object paradigm – by limiting the visibility of objects to as narrow a scope as possible. An object 'covers' another object means that the latter is known only within the local name space of the former. As any object may be covered by a single other object only, $covers$ is a partial function which effectively defines a hierarchy.

$covers : Object \nrightarrow Object$

Scoping introduces additional possibilities for object referencing, as we may require all description objects to have unique interfaces (i.e., $ExtParts$) but only among the set of objects covered by the same 'covering' object.

Uniqueness3

$BasicDefinitions$

$\forall\ O_1, O_2 : Object \bullet$
$\quad covers(O_1) = covers(O_2) \Rightarrow represents(O_1) \neq represents(O_2)$
$\forall\ O_1, O_2 : Object \bullet$
$\quad O_1, O_2 \notin dom\ covers \Rightarrow represents(O_1) \neq represents(O_2)$

Of course, a feature may only be covered by the class it belongs to – other possibilities do not make much sense.

$\forall\ F : Feature \bullet F \in dom\ covers \Rightarrow covers(F) = hasFeature(F)$

In case an even finer granulation of scoping rules, such as the distinction between `private` and `protected` features in C++, has to be provided, we could distinguish features which are inheritable from those which are not. In order to do that, we define private features as those which are covered by the classes they belong to. Features which are not private, are considered public. Some of the private features are inheritable (i.e., `protected` in C++ terms), while others are not (`private` in C++ terms).

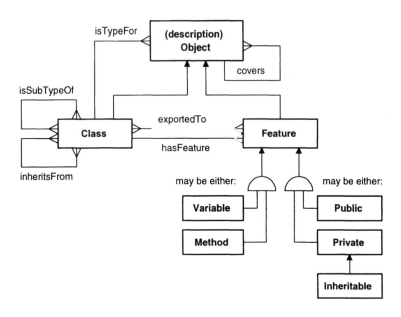

Fig. 2. An enhanced metamodel: objects, classes, and features.

MoreFeatures _____

$Private, Inheritable \subset Feature$

_____

$Private = \{F : Feature \mid F \in \text{dom } covers\}$
$Public = Feature \setminus Private$
$Inheritable \subseteq Private$

The introduction of scoping rules necessitates a slight change in our definition of inheritance-based feature sharing: among the features of a class, all public features, as well as all private but inheritable features, are available to all of its offspring classes.

InheritedFeatures _____

Inheritance
MoreFeatures
$inheritedTo : Class \times Feature$

_____

$\forall F : Feature;\ C : Class \bullet$
$\quad (C, F) \in inheritedTo \Rightarrow \exists SC : Class \bullet$
$\qquad (SC, F) \in belongsTo \wedge (SC, C) \in inheritsFrom^{+} \wedge F \in Inheritable$

Moreover, we could model the mechanism of selective feature export defined in Eiffel [6] or its close relative, the `friend` mechanism of C++, by introducing another relationship between classes and features.

$exportedTo : Class \leftrightarrow Feature$

Of course, any feature could be exported to any other class: the whole purpose of the export mechanism is to defeat the normal scoping rules. (This is why all authors recommend caution when the selective export feature is used, while some even consider it to be contrary to the principles of the object paradigm.)

The enhanced metamodel which includes classes and features of classes, as well as the other concepts defined above, is shown in Fig. 2. Lines with arrows connect subtype entities to their supertypes.

We are now able to define what features are accessible for a class: a class may access all local features, all features inherited from its ancestor classes, and all features (of other classes) which are designated as public, and features (of other classes) made explicitly available to it.

$AccessibleFeatures$ _____

$Inheritance$

$mayAccess : Feature \times Class$

$\forall F : Feature;\ C : Class \bullet$

$\quad (F, C) \in mayAccess \Rightarrow$

$\quad F \in Public \vee (C, F) \in (belongsTo \cup inheritedTo \cup exportedTo)$

Note that the predicate part of the $Uniqueness3$ schema gives rise to certain difficulties in referencing nonlocal features: namely, it does not prohibit several of them to have the same external parts, and any reference (within the implementation part of other objects) which uses the external part only, might be a source of ambiguity. However, the uniqueness of references may be regained by simply qualifying the feature reference with the reference to the class it belongs to (provided that classes are not covered at all); the proof of this is, however, beyond the scope of this paper.

Every method has a number of formal parameters attached. Two among these must always be present, either explicitly, or implicitly: the formal receiver and the formal return value (in accordance with the accustomed practice, a single return value is assumed).

$FParameter \subset Object$

$returnedBy : Method \rightarrow FParameter$

$isReceiverFor : Method \twoheadrightarrow FParameter$

Other formal parameters are optional, and they stand for arguments which are supplied at invocation.

$isSuppliedTo : Method \leftrightarrow FParameter$

Our metamodel could easily be extended to include actual and formal parameters, as well as their relationship; this discussion, however, is beyond the scope of the present paper.

5 Mapping Other Models: The OMG Core Object Model

The generality of our approach enables other (both object-oriented and classical) system models to be easily represented as specializations of our metamodel, by simply renaming of concepts and adding appropriate constraints (where necessary) to cater for the specifics of that particular model. As an example, we will use the so-called core object model from the Common Object Request Broker Architecture (CORBA) standard [10], as defined by the Object Management Group (OMG) [11]. The concepts of the OMG model will be presented through their informal definitions (all quoted text in this Section has been taken literally from [12]), which are then mapped to the concepts of our metamodel in a formal manner. It may be interesting to note that Z has already been used to model some concepts of the OMG core object model [5], though in a somewhat different context.

The OMG core model is a multi-level model, since different concepts belong to different meta-levels (although the term is never actually used). Types and operations defined on them are considered as highest-level concepts. A type 'characterizes the behavior of its instances by describing the operations that can be applied to those objects' (each operation belongs to a single type). Hence, we may establish a correspondence between OMG types and our classes, and between OMG operations and our methods.

$$omgType \subset Class$$
$$omgOp \subset Method$$
$$characterizedBy : omgOp \rightarrow omgType$$

Then, the $characterizedBy$ function is actually a subset of the previously defined $hasFeature$ function:

$$\forall T : omgType;\ O : omgOp \bullet (O, T) \in characterizedBy \Rightarrow (O, T) \in hasFeature$$

Note that these are not new concepts; rather, they are just different names for the concepts which have already been introduced in previous Sections.

Concepts on the highest level have interfaces, but not implementations (which belong to the lower level): each operation in the core model 'has a signature, which consists of a name, set of parameters, and a set of results'. Such behaviour is not forbidden in our metamodel:

$$\nexists T : omgType \bullet T \in \text{dom}\ represents$$
$$\nexists O : omgOP \bullet T \in \text{dom}\ represents$$

Methods in our metamodel have a name (or, more precisely, an external part which includes the name), the formal receiver parameter (which corresponds to the mandatory first parameter of the operation signature in the OMG model), and a single return parameter. Therefore, after we establish the correspondence

$$omgPar \subset FParameter$$

the only real difference (apart from those that require renaming) is that, instead of a total function $returnedBy : Method \rightarrow FParameter$, as defined in our model, we should use a relation:

$omgReturnedBy : omgOp \leftrightarrow omgPar$

'The set of operations signatures defined on a type is called the type's interface', which corresponds to our concept of external part. This may be modeled as:

$\forall\, T : omgType \bullet$
$\quad omgTypeSignature(T) = \{O : omgOp \mid (O, T) \in hasFeature \bullet Signature(O)\}$

The use of a set for $omgTypeSignature$ provides an elegant vehicle of imposing certain constraints on the model: namely, the OMG model requires distinct methods to have different signatures.

Each type and operation in the OMG core model can have many different implementations (which stems from the fact that the model was devised with distributed system architectures and applications in mind). In the same manner as above, we might map type implementations and methods to the implementations ($IntParts$) of our metamodel; alternatively, we might map OMG type implementations to our classes, and OMG methods to our methods.

$omgClass \subset Class$
$omgMethod \subset Method$
$characterizedByMethod : omgMethod \leftrightarrow omgClass$

In this latter case, the $characterizedByMethod$ function would again be a subset of the $hasFeature$ function. Note that the two possible mappings are not in contradiction, since description objects and implementations are not required to be distinct subsets of the $Object$ basic set.

The concepts at different levels (types and operations) must be connected to their implementations: these functions (which have the 'omg' prefix) are subsets of the $implements$ function.

$omgTypeFor : omgClass \rightarrow omgType$
$omgOpImpBy : omgMethod \rightarrow omgOp$

Furthermore, a class must have the same interface as its corresponding type:

$\forall\, TC : omgClass \bullet$
$\quad represents(TC) = represents(omgTypeFor(TC))$

in which case the use of object identifiers becomes a necessity. This part of the OMG core model is presented in Fig. 3; for clarity, the concepts pertaining to the OMG model are shown in gray, and the concepts they have been mapped to are shown 'behind'.

However, there is a restriction on the methods that characterize a given type implementation: these methods must implement the operation of the corresponding type.

$\forall\, M : omgMethod \bullet$
$\quad characterizedBy(omgOpImpBy(M)) = omgTypeFor(characterizedByMethod(M))$

Types and operations, as well as their implementations, are not objects in the OMG sense. Objects in the OMG model are instances of their types; they have distinct identifiers 'independent of an object's properties or behavior ... that provide a means to refer

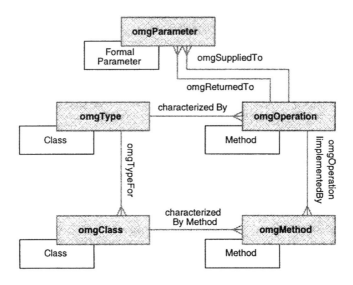

Fig. 3. Types, operations, and their implementations in the OMG core object model.

to the object'. A type can have several implementations, hence the 'combination of a type and one of [its] implementations . . . is termed a class'; an individual 'object, at any given point of time, is an instance of one class'. It is, therefore, convenient to define the *omgInstance* as the subset of the *CInstance* set (which is, in turn, a subset of the *Object* set), with the appropriate connections to the type and operation implementations.

$$omgInstance \subset CInstance$$
$$mayBeInvokedBy : omgInstance \nleftrightarrow omgMethod$$
$$isTypeOf : omgInstance \rightarrow omgClass$$

The core model defines subtyping as the mechanism 'by which objects of one type are determined to be acceptable in contexts expecting another type', and inheritance as the vehicle which 'allows a type to be defined in terms of another type'. Moreover, it relates subtyping and inheritance: whenever two classes participate in a specialization relationship, they also participate in an inheritance relationship (although the reverse is not true). The standard definitions of subtyping and inheritance apply, with the additional constraint expressed as:

$$\forall C_1, C_2 : omgClass \bullet (C_2, C_1) \in isSubtypeOf \Rightarrow (C_2, C_1) \in inheritsFrom$$

This part of the OMG model is presented in Fig. 4.

Other concepts from the OMG core model may be described with equal ease; however, the full details are beyond the scope of this paper.

In summary, the OMG model can be faithfully mapped without introducing additional concepts in our metamodel; the only significant changes were to relax one constraint, and

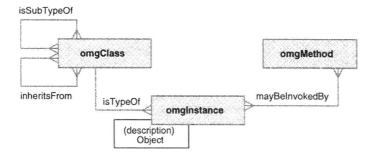

Fig. 4. Objects as instances in the OMG core object model.

introduce two additional ones. Even such a short example offers enough evidence that the genericity of our approach enables other system models to be accommodated with precision and clarity. This holds not only for models based on the object paradigm, but for models based on other paradigms as well. It should be noted that all applications and consistency checks available to our metamodel would, then, be available to the mapped-in metamodels as well (unfortunately, even a small demonstration would exceed the space limitations of this paper). Some examples of metamodel mapping are presented in [8]; yet others have been used to furnish the formal basis for different software meeasures [7, 9].

6   Checking for consistency

One of the major advantages of using formal methods is that it enables checking of consistency and syntactic, as well as semantic, correctness of specifications. Certain design errors and inconsistencies can be found which are hard (and costly) to find in later phases, and some classes of errors may be totally eliminated. This check could even be performed mechanically with a suitable mechanical tools (e.g., a theorem prover), in much the same way the syntactic correctness of a program is checked by the compiler. Of course, semantic constraints may also be checked, but they must be explicitly defined by the designer. We will now show a number of the constraints which must be satisfied in our metamodel (but note that the list is representative, rather than exhaustive).

Some constraints are built-in through the particular specification construct used. For example, the schema *ClassesAndFeatures* contains the line

$hasFeature : Feature \rightarrow Class$

in its declaration part, meaning that *hasFeature* is a total function mapping features to classes; 'total function' means that each member of the *Feature* set is related to some member of the *Class* set through the *hasFeature* relationship:

$\forall F : Feature \bullet \exists_1 C : Class \bullet C = hasFeature(F)$

which may also be expressed as 'the domain of the *hasFeature* function are all members of the *Feature* set':

$$\mathrm{dom}\ hasFeature = Feature$$

Many other statements, both in declaration and predicate parts of the schemas, contain similar constraints which are implicit in the particular definitions used.

Other constraints, stemming from the actual semantics of the metamodel, must be specified explicitly. For example, a class may define scope for its own features only, not for features that belong to other classes:

$$\forall\, C : Class, F : Feature \bullet C = covers(F) \Rightarrow C = hasFeature(F)$$

A particularly interesting class of constraints concerns cyclical definitions, which are undesirable in some cases. Consider, for example, the inheritance mechanism. Since a class inherits features from its parent class(es), the inheritance structure must not contain any cycles, otherwise an infinite loop would result. The constraint that no class may inherit from itself, either directly, or via one or more intermediate objects, may be expressed with the following schema:

$$\forall\, C : Class \bullet C \notin Parent^+(C)$$

A similar check may be written for the subtyping relationship. One may be tempted to generalize similar constraints to objects themselves, for example, by prohibiting cyclical structures in object definition via the *isDefinedWith* relation. This, however, would be counter-productive, since it would automatically ban recursive methods (functions), among other things.

Other constraints could be defined as required: for example, we might prohibit a class from inheriting from another class, and being its supertype at the same time. It may be written in several equivalent ways, one of which is:

$$\nexists\, C_1, C_2 : Class \bullet (C_1, C_2) \in isSubtypeOf \wedge (C_2, C_1) \in inheritsFrom$$

As a final example, we will define the constraint that a feature may be used to define a class only if it is accessible to that class:

$$\forall\, C : Class;\ F : Feature \bullet (F, C) \in isDefinedWith \Rightarrow (F, C) \in mayAccess$$

Note that the implication operator is unidirectional, hence not all features accessible to a particular class are actually used to define it.

A number of other constraints may be defined in order to ensure the internal consistency, as well as syntactic and semantic correctness of the metamodel. it is generally held that the availability of a succinct specification should make life easier for the implementors and testers alike, and eventually lead to the production of systems with better quality.

7 Conclusion

A formal description of a generic object–oriented system metamodel is presented. The use of the well-known Z notation provides concise, complete, and unambiguous description of the structure and properties of the metamodel. The generality of this approach enables the same metamodel to be used at various abstraction levels, from preliminary study to implementation. Moreover, the metamodel is general enough to subsume other system models based on the object paradigm: they may easily be derived by appropriate refinement of the metamodel's basic components, as shown on the example of the OMG core object model. The formal approach should also prove beneficial for the purposes of testing—at all levels—since various constraints may be expressed in a concise and rigorous manner. Further development is under way in the metrics area, where the metamodel is being used as the basis for deriving measures of system size and complexity.

References

1. R. G. G. Cattell. *Object Data Management*, revised edition. Addison-Wesley, Reading, MA, 1994.
2. R. ElMasri and S. B. Navathe. *Fundamentals of Database Systems*, 2nd edition. Benjamin/Cummings, Redwood City, CA, 1995.
3. A. Hall. Seven myths of formal methods. *IEEE Software*, 7(5):11–19, Sept. 1990.
4. I. Hayes, editor. *Specification Case Studies*, 2nd edition. Prentice Hall, Hemel Hempstead, UK, 1993.
5. I. S. C. Houston and M. B. Josephs. A formal description of the OMG's Core Object Model and the meaning of compatible extension. *Computer Standards & Interfaces*, 17(5–6):553–558, 1995.
6. B. Meyer. *Object-Oriented Software Construction*. Prentice Hall, Hemel Hempstead, UK, 1988.
7. V. Mišić and S. Moser. From metamodels to metrics: a formal object-oriented approach. Submitted to *TOOLS Asia Conference*, Beijing, China, Sept. 1997.
8. S. Moser. *Measurement and Estimation of Software and Software Processes*. PhD Thesis, University of Berne, Switzerland, Nov. 1996.
9. S. Moser and V. Mišić. Measuring class coupling and cohesion: a formal metamodel approach. Submitted to *Asia Pacific Software Engineering Conference APSEC'97*, Hong Kong, Dec. 1997.
10. The common object request broker: Architecture and specification, revision 2.0. OMG Document 91.12.1, Object Management Group, July 1995.
11. R. M. Soley, editor. *Object Management Architecture Guide, Revision 3.0*, 3rd edition. John Wiley and Sons, New York, June 1995.
12. R. M. Soley and W. Kent. The OMG object model. In W. Kim, editor, *Modern Database System: The Object Model, Interoperability, and Beyond*, chapter 2, pages 18–41. ACM Press and Addison-Wesley, 1995.
13. J. M. Spivey. *The Z Notation: A Reference Manual*. Prentice Hall, Hemel Hempstead, UK, 1989.
14. Y. Wand and R. Weber. An ontological model of an information system. *IEEE Transactions on Software Engineering*, 16(11):1282–1292, Nov. 1990.

Associations and Roles in Object-Oriented Modeling*

Wesley W. Chu and Guogen Zhang
{wwc, gzhang}@cs.ucla.edu

Computer Science Department
University of California, Los Angeles, CA 90095

Abstract. We present an extended ER model with entity, role, and association as the basic constructs for object-oriented modeling. The purpose of the constructs is to support object evolution and extension for long lived objects. A class hierarchy consists of a static part and a dynamic part. The static part is a classification of entity classes, while the dynamic part is the role classes played by entities. The interaction among objects are captured with association classes. Based on the observation that entities play roles in association with other entities, we provide a unified view on roles in associations and roles as an extension to objects. The proposed modeling constructs help developers better understand the interrelationship among entities, thus result in flexible implementations for dynamic systems.

1 Introduction

Object-oriented systems provide more constructs than relational systems to model and support application semantics. However, in the current object-oriented models there is a lack of direct association support and a lack of systematic support for dynamic object evolution. In this paper, we introduce an entity-role-association modeling framework. *Entity* classes will be used to capture the static ISA hierarchy of the fundamental objects being modeled in the system. *Role* classes will be used to capture the ISA hierarchy of roles that entities can dynamically assume throughout their lifetime in the system. Further, the *association* class construct is introduced to explicitly model the relationships entities can participate in as they evolve through various roles during their lifetime. Altogether, our entity-role-association model provides a useful extension to OO modeling that supports dynamic object evolution. In our model, all the instances of entity classes, roles classes, and association classes are objects.

Relationships among entities is one of the fundamental constructs in semantic modeling as indicated in the original Entity-Relationship (ER) model [Chen76] and later extensions [TYF86, HK87, PM88]. The relationships in the original ER can be viewed as refined into different relationships in later extensions, such

---

* This research is supported in part by DARPA contracts No. 30602-94-C-0207, No. N66001-97-C-8601, and US Air Force contract No. F30602-96-1-0255.

as ISA relationship and others. *Association* is the term commonly used to refer to the interaction among objects [Rat97]. The associated objects are the *roles* of the association. In object-oriented systems, objects interact with each other by sending and reacting to messages. Real world entities are usually modeled by objects, and the state and other properties of associations often have to be encapsulated into the role objects involved. However, the properties of interactions, or associations, can be captured and represented in separate "association objects".

Tanzer [Tan95] presented a critique on the current practice of using regular instance variables for associations. The main problems of using regular classes and pointer/reference instance variables for associations are: (1) For classes with existing objects, it is not easy to insert an instance variable for a new association. (2) Constructing association instances using regular classes for polymorphic associations needs typecase testing on the roles. (3) Using direct multiple dispatching [Ing86] or the visitor pattern [GHJV95] to achieve multiple polymorphism for associations is a complex scheme. Further, it requires the methods to be added into role classes, thus increases code dependencies among modules, and is only partially extensible. In this paper, we propose *association class* construct for complex association modeling and support, and provide implementation schemes to resolve these issues.

We have used the role concept within the context of associations above. Let us now introduce another role concept in *object with roles* for dynamic aspects of objects [GSR96, RS91, Pern90, Alba93, WCL97]. In traditional class-based object-oriented systems, an object is uniquely represented by an instance of the most specific class in the class hierarchy that the object qualifies. Sometimes the static ISA relationship results in complex class hierarchies, and causes problems for object evolution. *Object with roles* is a way to remedy these problems. Under this extension, an object has an instance corresponding to the base (role) class, and a set of role objects that the object is currently playing. An object can acquire roles or drop roles dynamically. A role implicitly inherits the properties of its player. Object with roles extension provides object-oriented systems with more flexibility and expressive power.

For example, a person in a university can be a student. He can also be an employee if he is a TA or RA. The traditional class hierarchy is shown in Fig. 1a. If John was only a student at the beginning, he was represented by an instance of "Student" class. But later he became a TA, and had to be represented with an instance of "Student-Employee" class, while keeping the same object identity, which is a problem. An instance of "Student" cannot become an instance of "Student-Employee" without change of its object identifier. If we create a new instance, all the references to the old object will have to be changed to the new instance, which is very costly if not impossible[2]. If both instances are kept, there will be some redundancy, causing potential inconsistency. We call this *object reclassification anomaly*. Using objects with roles, "Person" can be an entity class, and "Student" and "Employee" are two role classes of "Person"

---

[2] Some systems use becomes to support this. But a new object needs to be created.

(Fig. 1b). Thus John can be represented by a `Person` object with a `Student` role at first. He acquired the employee (TA) role when he became a TA later. Multiple inheritance is also avoided in this case.

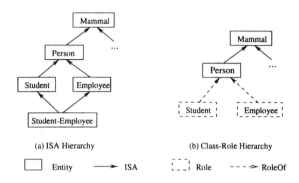

Fig. 1. ISA hierarchy and Class-Role hierarchy

Current research on *object with roles* and associations does not connect these concepts together. Based on the observation that an entity can play a role in association with other entities, we propose to unify the role concepts in *object with roles* and in *associations*. Thus roles can be unified both conceptually and in implementation under the entity-role-association scheme.

The paper is organized as follows. In section 2, we give an overview on modeling using entity-role-association. In section 3, we discuss association classes and their features. In section 4, we discuss the relationships of associations related to roles. Then in section 5, we discuss the relationships between players and roles. An application example is presented in section 6. And finally, a comparison of other related work is presented in section 7.

2 Modeling with Entities, Roles, and Associations

In our approach, the ISA relationship is subdivided into subclassing and role-playing, the entity classes constitute a static classification hierarchy while the role classes are dynamic aspects the entities can assume. The roles are played by objects, which can be entities or other roles.

The entity classes are those that reflect the static aspects of the real-world objects. The relevant entity classes are classified into a class hierarchy, in which classes have the partial order ISA relationship.

Role classes capture the temporal and evolutionary aspects of the real-world objects. The role classes themselves may also have class hierarchies to factorize the common properties with the ISA relationship. The semantics of ISA relationship for role classes are the same as the regular class inheritance (subclassing). For example, `Undergraduate` ISA `Student`, and `Graduate` student ISA `Student`. The player classes and role classes are related through RoleOf relationships, e.g.

`Student` is RoleOf `Person`, `ProjectManager` is RoleOf `Employee` as shown in Fig. 2.

Objects assume roles in their associations with other objects. Associations may have attributes for states and a set of methods, collectively called *properties*, in addition to the roles involved. Association classes are used to capture the properties of associations among objects with specific roles. The number of roles participating in an association is called the *arity* of the association. Association classes among the same set of classes may form a hierarchy.

Fig. 2a shows the student-employee example with associations for `Taking` and `Offering` courses. Note that `Student` and `Employee` are both roles of `Person` and roles in associations `Taking` and `Offering`. It also shows that a `ProjectManager` is a role of an `Employee`. Fig. 2b shows an example of medical image feature relationships for the tumor in a patient's brain, where a microlesion evolves to macrolesion and its spatial relationship with the lateral ventricle changes from disjoint to invading.

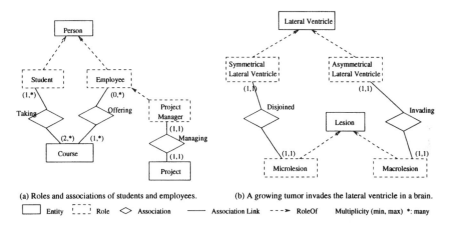

Fig. 2. Examples modeled by entity-role-association constructs.

The basic integrity constraints related to associations are:

1. Referential integrity: the role objects referenced in an association must exist and have the right types. This is a constraint on individual instances.
2. Multiplicity: the number of association instances of the same class in which each role can participate. The multiplicity of each role is specified with a (*min*, *max*) pair (as shown in Fig. 2), meaning that a role has to participate in the associations at least *min* times and at most *max* times. The multiplicity is a constraint on collections of instances.

Based on the properties, associations can be divided into different kinds: (1) Simple associations: A simple association is a simple link that does not have any particular properties of its own. An example of a simple association is *PartOf* relationship. (2) Complex associations: A complex association is one that has its own properties. Instances of associations are used to capture the interrelations among objects. (3) Polymorphic associations: Polymorphic associations are the same kind associations, but for different role classes they have different properties. These associations classes constitute a class hierarchy. For an association instance and a given message to it, the behavior depends on the types of roles involved in the association. For instance, a borrower borrowing a loan item from a library is modeled by `Borrowing` association class, and `loan_period()` is a method of the association. `Loan_period()` depends on the borrower classes and the loan item classes.

The entity-role-association scheme provides flexible basic model constructs. Other high-level objects can be built on top of these basic constructs, e.g. by grouping related objects. As a result, it can be used to specify dynamic and evolving OO systems.

3 Association Classes and Their Features

We first propose a scheme for the association class definition, then discuss the object-oriented characteristics for the association classes. To focus on the association construct and its properties, we ignore the RoleOf relationship on the role class side in this section. We use a simple library model as shown in Fig. 3 to illustrate association features.

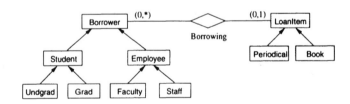

Fig. 3. A simple library model with association features.

An association class can be defined with its role classes, instance variables, and methods. For example, Fig. 4 shows for the `Borrowing` association class between `Borrower` and `LoanItem` for the library example in Fig. 3. The role classes in the order they appear in the association class definition constitute the *tuple of role classes* for the association.

All the association classes in a hierarchy for the "same" type of associations have the same name. For instance, if we want to capture the specialties of the association in different cases. For example, the "same" methods `loan_period` for `Borrowing[Borrower, Periodical]` and `Borrowing[Faculty, Book]` are different, and they would be defined as association classes as follows:

```
association Borrowing[Borrower, LoanItem]{...};
```

```
// association class name and the tuple of role classes:
association Borrowing[Borrower, LoanItem]
{   // normal attributes
    Date    loanDate;
    Date    dueDate;
    Date    returnDate;
    // methods
    virtual int loan_period() { ... }
};
```

Fig. 4. An association class definition for the simple library model example.

```
association Borrowing[Borrower, Periodical]:
            Borrowing[Borrower, LoanItem]{...};
association Borrowing[Faculty, Book]:
            Borrowing[Borrower, LoanItem]{...};
```

We now discuss the characteristics of object-orientation for the association classes. The major differences between association classes and regular classes are on the classification and polymorphism.

The constructors for association instances require a tuple of role instances that corresponds to the tuple of role classes declared in the association class. It is feasible that the constructors of the association classes are polymorphic, based on the role classes. With polymorphic constructors, it is unnecessary to do typecase testing on roles when constructing association objects. It puts more restrictive classification limit on the association instances.

We shall present two other major features – inheritance and polymorphism in the following sections.

3.1 Inheritance of Association Classes

One usage of inheritance is to specialize a class while allowing the subclass to inherit common properties from its superclass. Association class inheritance has its own features.

Implicit Inheritance. An association class defined for some role classes in class hierarchies is applicable to tuples of their corresponding subclasses.

For the library example (Fig. 3), because [Undgrad, Book] ≺ [Borrower, LoanItem], the association class Borrowing[Borrower, LoanItem] defined in Fig. 4 is applicable to tuple [Undgrad, Book]. Similarly, the same holds for tuple [Grad, Periodical].

Explicit Inheritance. The explicit inheritance of association classes is mainly used to override the implicitly inherited association class properties, therefore the following special rules apply to the explicit association class inheritance: (1) The subclass must have the same name as the superclass. (2) The subclass has the same arity as the superclass. (3) The tuple of role classes in the subclass are more specific than that of the superclass.

The following example shows how a subclass can be defined.

```
association Borrowing[Undgrad, Book] :    // subclass
            Borrowing[Student, LoanItem] // superclass
{   ...
    virtual int loan_period() { ... }    // overriding
};
```

3.2 Multiple Polymorphism of Messages on Associations

Given a message on an association instance, there are the following two message dispatching cases:

1. If the method is explicitly defined on the association class of the instance, then the defined method is invoked.
2. If the method is not explicitly defined on the corresponding class of the instance, then the implicitly inherited method will be invoked.

The method invoked depends on the role class tuple of the association instance, thus is *multiply polymorphic*. To determine a unique method to invoke for a message, the explicitly defined association methods must satisfy the unambiguity requirement. For the library example, if we have loan_period() explicitly defined on Borrowing[Borrower, Book] and on Borrowing[Undgrad, LoanItem], to avoid ambiguity, loan_period() must be explicitly defined on Borrowing[Undgrad, Book]. An algorithm can help check if this requirement is met.

For any polymorphic methods that satisfy the unambiguity requirement, we can determine a unique and most specific method to invoke for a message.

4   The Relationship Between Associations and Roles

When implementing associations, depending on the requirements and constraints, there are two alternatives: intrinsic associations and extrinsic associations. Intrinsic associations provide a direct navigation path from role instances to the association instances, while extrinsic associations allow new associations defined on existing objects. Both alternatives can be realized as extensions atop "traditional" OO systems.

4.1   Intrinsic and Extrinsic Associations

In the intrinsic associations (Fig. 5a), roles are tightly coupled with the associations they participate in. An instance variable within each of the role classes is used for each association class, either single-valued or set-valued, depending on the multiplicity of the role in the association. It is similar to the traditional instance variable approach except that the instance variable now refers to the association objects.

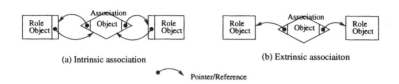

(a) Intrinsic association   (b) Extrinsic associaiton

● ➤ Pointer/Reference

Fig. 5. Intrinsic and extrinsic binary association instances with roles.

If the role classes have already been defined and we want to add more associations but do not want to make changes to the role classes, or do not want to add additional variables and methods to role classes for sparse associations, we can use the extrinsic association (Fig. 5b). In such associations, no variables are used within role classes for associations, instead, a collection of all association instances is maintained, and the relationships from role objects to association objects is recovered by explicit join between role objects and the association instance collection. We call a collection of all the instances of the same association class an *association extent*.

For example, we can maintain the collection for the Borrowing associations, which can be defined or generated like this:

```
Multiplicity multi[] = {MANY, MANY};
extent<Borrowing>  borrowing(multi);
          // for a many-to-many association Borrowing
```

An association extent is a special collection class with integrity enforcement. The association extent also needs to support associative search, join with roles, and probably aggregate functions.

The advantages for the extrinsic association are flexibility in adding new associations to existing classes, and centralized integrity maintenance for each association class. Extrinsic associations also reduce code dependencies among modules using the same roles. Polymorphism can be utilized without adding methods into existing classes.

4.2 Interdependencies Between Roles and Associations

The referential integrity requires that the roles referenced in associations exist. Therefore when an association instance is to be created, the roles either exist or should be created at the same time. When a role is deleted, the deletion is cascaded to all the associations that the role is involved. An application may require that the deletion of a role be prohibited if there are still existing associations involving the role.

On the other hand, a role may exist without participating in any associations, that is, in the multiplicity of the role $min = 0$. For example, the borrower role for a student belongs to this case, because a student is a borrower even he is not currently borrowing any books. A role may be required to be involved in associations for the role to exist, i.e. $min > 0$ for the role. A project manager role in Fig. 2 belongs to this case, since a project manager is an employee who manages a project.

Since there are references to roles in associations, the navigation from an association to roles is always direct. However, navigation from a role to the association may not always be possible. Depending on the implementation scheme, the navigation from a role to associations can be direct (intrinsic associations) or indirect (extrinsic associations with extents).

5 The Relationship Between Players and Roles

A player of a role can be an entity or another role, which is ultimately played by an entity. Depending on the situation and functionality requirements, a role may be incorporated into an entity as a base role, and an entity may or may not be aware of some or all of the roles it is currently playing. An entity may be only shared by the extrinsic roles for redundancy elimination.

A base role is a role played by an entity for its entire lifetime in the system. Thus, if the entity is not playing the base roles, it would not be included into the system. Therefore there is no need to separate the base roles from the entity. For example, Employee is usually considered as a base role and is not separated from Person in a company personnel system.

Often it is unnecessary for the player to keep track of all the roles it is playing. Thus, there are links only from the roles to the player. The roles cannot be accessed directly from their player. We call these *extrinsic roles* to the player (Fig. 6a). The typical supporting scheme for extrinsic roles is the inheritance by delegation [Taiv96]. That is, messages that are not part of direct interface of the role are forwarded (delegated) to the player. The user of the role object treats the role instance the same way as the role class inherits the player class in subclassing. For instance, a student is a member of the student body, but he is also a member of a club. The club member role can be modeled by an extrinsic role.

When a player needs to know the specific roles that it is playing, the roles are *intrinsic*, and the behavior of the player depends on these roles. The roles may be only referenced by the player, i.e. unidirectional from the player to the roles. In this case, roles are just part of states of the player (Fig. 6b). When the relationship between the player and roles are bidirectional (Fig. 6c), in addition to being accessed from inside the player object, the intrinsic roles can also be referenced by other objects. For example, the properties of an employee and his project manager role (Fig 2a) are dependent on each other, therefore, a bidirectional intrinsic role for project manager should be used (as in Fig 6c).

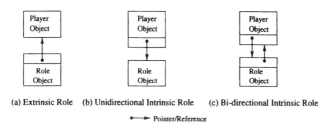

(a) Extrinsic Role   (b) Unidirectional Intrinsic Role   (c) Bi-directional Intrinsic Role

●——▶ Pointer/Reference

Fig. 6. Extrinsic and intrinsic roles.

The relationships between players and roles are either one-to-one or one-to-many, with roles dependent of players, i.e. a role cannot exist without a player. Since role classes cannot be instantiated without a player, players always exist first. An entity can play multiple roles at the same time, and play different sets of roles at different times.

The dependencies among players, roles, and associations have to be defined precisely in the system model to achieve system integrity.

6 An Application Example

Let us use our experience in implementation of our CoBase [Chu96] project as an example to illustrate the usefulness of the association class and role class. CoBase is a cooperative database interface which provides query relaxation (approximate answers), associative querying (provides relevant answers that the user does not explicitly ask for), and explanation that describes the relaxation process and its reasoning. A portion of its classes and associations are shown in Fig. 7, where RelaxEngine is for Relaxation Engine, AssocEngine is for Association Engine, and ExplanEngine is for Explanation Engine. These engines all work on a uniform internal query representation (QueryRep). Part of QueryRep component classes are shown in the left-hand side of Fig. 7.

There is a large class hierarchy for representing operands in SQL query conditions with our cooperative SQL (CoSQL) [CID96] extension. Engine modules of the system manipulate on a query representation (QueryRep) to achieve their functionalities. The CoBase system is developed incrementally. In traditional object-oriented way, many functions would have to be added gradually into the operand class hierarchy. It would cause endless recompilations of all the code and a fat interface that is the union of relatively independent functions for different modules. If we extend functions outside of the QueryRep, we have to use a long list of typecase tests to discriminate the types of the operands. Polymorphism is important in eliminating these long lists of cases.

To reduce the dependencies among RelaxEngine, AssocEngine, and ExplanEngine, we used the following mechanisms:

1. Extrinsic role classes for QueryCond classes are used for roles associated with RelaxEngine and AssocEngine to keep their states. Extrinsic roles make

their usage of `QueryCond` in `RelaxEngine` and `AssocEngine` independent of each other.

2. Extrinsic roles are used for the conditions that need to be explained in `ExplanEngine`. As a result, there are only dependencies of `ExplanEngine` on `RelaxEngine` and `AssocEngine`, but not the other direction.

3. Intrinsic associations are used for the associations on the `RelaxEngine`, `AssocEngine`, and `ExplanEngine`, so that the manipulation of these associations is direct from these respective engines.

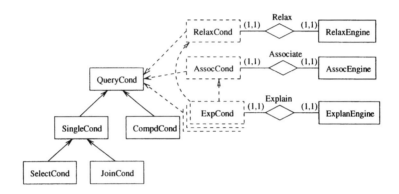

Fig. 7. Illustration of associations and roles in part of the CoBase system.

Our experience has revealed the association and role constructs not only increase expressive power, but more importantly, greatly simplify system development and maintenance.

7 Related Work

The association construct proposed in this paper is related to semantic data modeling, object modeling technique(OMT), multi-methods in functional OO languages, and traditional relational database integrity constraints.

The importance of supporting explicit relationships in object-oriented systems has long been recognized [Ditt90, Rumb87, Tan95]. There have been also several attempts in supporting relationships in object-oriented databases [AGO91, Brat91, Catt96, DG91, NQZ91]. In [Rumb87], Rumbaugh proposed relation as a construct to support associations. A relation is a collection of associations, but associations are not objects and cannot have methods. The relationship support proposed in [Brat91] is similar on this aspect. In [AGO91], an association is a set of distinct bindings, each of which is like a value tuple. Their association is more like our association extent, or an extension to relations for relationships in relational databases. The major difference is that our association also emphasizes the properties of individual association instances. ODMG-93 [Catt96] has a `relationship` prefix for instance variables that are for associations to maintain integrity constraints, but no special construct for associations. An association concept in OMT is proposed by Rumbaugh et al.[Rumb91] and used in object relationship modeling and translation into regular instance variables. These latter two proposals suffer some of the problems as pointed out in the introduction of this paper.

Our work is similar to those in semantic data modeling[Chen76, HK87, PM88, TYF86], which focuses on structural aspects of representing semantics in different constructs. However, we introduced behavior modeling with object-oriented constructs.

Multi-methods in OO languages[BK86, Cham92, MHH91] provide multiple polymorphism and is a well-studied topic for multiple polymorphism and dispatching. But they are not as well organized and have been criticized as not being object-oriented, since they are not tied with any objects. Association class construct makes multiple polymorphism a natural property of association instances, an extension to the current object-oriented model.

Object-role modeling [Bron95, SD96] allows bottom-up analysis, based on local relationship properties. Then the roles can be integrated into classes. Object with roles extension to object-oriented systems [GSR96, RS91, Pern90, Alba93, WCL97] aims at solving the object evolution problem, thus provides more flexibility to the class-based systems. We are unifying them under the entity-role-association scheme, combining the benefits from both.

8 Conclusions

We have proposed entity-role-association as basic constructs for supporting flexible applications and studied the properties and relationships of these constructs.

The ISA relationships among classes are subdivided into ISA and RoleOf relationships. ISA is used for static classification and RoleOf is for dynamic role-playing and object evolution.

A new association class construct is proposed. Its object-oriented features are presented. ISA relationship in association class hierarchy has its special features. Different implementation scheme of associations meet different needs. The intrinsic association allows easy referential integrity maintenance, while the extrinsic association allows easy extension for existing classes and objects. The extrinsic association also allows polymorphism without adding methods into role classes, which can improve the code dependencies among modules.

The role concepts from *object with roles* and *associations* are unified based on the observation that entities play roles in association with other entities. The roles are classified into extrinsic roles and intrinsic roles. Extrinsic roles provide easy extension to existing objects, while intrinsic roles allow players to adapt their behaviors based on the roles they are playing. The different role classification allow developers to choose suitable roles in their implementation.

The entity-role-association scheme supports bottom-up analysis and easy integration of submodels. The proposed constructs not only provide clear semantics, clear interdependencies, and guidance for the implementation with current

OO techniques, also can be supported as language constructs. Our experience shows that our proposed model provides useful software structure, and also results in easy software maintenance.

Acknowledgments

The authors would like to thank Brad Perry and Chih-Cheng Hsu of UCLA for their insightful comments during the writing of the paper.

References

[AGO91] Albano, A., Ghelli, G., and Orsini, R., A relationship mechanism for strongly typed object-oriented database programming language, in *Proceedings of the 17th VLDB conference*, Barcelona, Sept. 1991, pp.565-575.

[Alba93] Albano, A. et al. An object data model with roles, *Proc. 19th VLDB Conf.*, Dublin, Ireland, 1993, pp. 39-51.

[BK86] Bobrew, D. G., and Kahn, K. et al. CommonLoops: Merging lisp and object-oriented programming, In *Proceedings of ACM OOPSLA '86*, pp. 17-29.

[Booc94] Booch, G., *Object-oriented analysis and design with applications*, Benjamn/Cummings, Redwood City, CA, 1994.

[Brat91] Bratsberg, S. E., FOOD: Supporting explicit relations in a fully object-oriented database, in *Object-oriented databases: Analysis, design & construction (DS-4)*, Proceedings of the IFIP TC2/WG 2.6 Working Conference, Windermere, UK, July 1990, pp. 123-140.

[Bron95] Bronts, G.H.W.M. et al., A unifying object role modelling theory, *Information Systems*, Vol. 20, No. 3, 1995, pp. 213-235.

[Catt96] Cattell, R. G. G. (Ed.), *The object database standard: ODMG-93 Release 1.2*, Morgan Kauffmann Publishers, Inc. San Francisco, California, 1996.

[Cham92] Chambers, C., Object-oriented multi-methods in Cecil, in *Proceedings of ECOOP '92*, LNCS 615, pp. 33-56.

[Chen76] Chen, P. P., The entity-relationship model: toward a unified view of data, *ACM TODS* Vol.1, No.1, March, 1976, pp.9-36.

[Chu96] Chu, W. W., Yang, H., Chiang, K., Minock, M. Chow, G., Larson, C., CoBase: A Scalable and Extensible Cooperative Information System, *Journal of Intelligent Information Systems*, 1996.

[CID96] CoBase Internal Document, CoSQL Specification Report, CoBase Research Lab., Computer Science Department, UCLA, 1996.

[DG91] Diaz, O. and Gray, P. M. D., Semantic-rich user-defined relationship as a main constructor in object-oriented databases, in *Object-oriented databases: Analysis, design & construction (DS-4)*, Proceedings of the IFIP TC2/WG 2.6 Working Conference, Windermere, UK, July 1990, pp. 207-224.

[Ditt90] Dittrich, K. R., Object-oriented database systems: the next miles of the marathon, *Information Systems*, Vol. 15, No. 1, pp. 161-167, 1990.

[GHJV95] Gamma, E., Helm, R., Johnson, R. and Vlissides, J., *Design patterns: elements of reusable object-oriented software*, Addison-Wesley, Reading, MA, 1995, pp.331-344.

[GSR96] Gottlob, G., Schrefl, M. and Röck, B., Extending object-oriented systems with roles, *ACM TOIS*, Vol. 14, No. 3, July 1996, pp.268-296.

[HK87]   Hull, R. and King, R., Semantic database modeling: survey, applications, and research issues, *ACM Computing Surveys*, Vol. 19, No.3, Sept. 1987, pp. 201-260.

[Ing86]   Ingalls, D. H. H., A simple technique for handling multiple polymorphism, in *OOPSLA '86 Proceedings*, Sept. 1986, pp. 347-349.

[MHH91]   Mugridge, W. B., Hammer, J. and Hosking, J. G., Multi-Methods in a statically-typed programming language, in *Proceedings of ECOOP '91*, pp.307-324.

[NQZ91]   Nassif, R., Qiu, Y., and Zhu, J., Extending the object-oriented paradigm to support relationships and constraints, in *Object-oriented databases: Analysis, design & construction (DS-4)*, Proceedings of the IFIP TC2/WG 2.6 Working Conference, Windermere, UK, July 1990, pp. 305-330.

[Pern90]   Pernici, B., Objects with Roles, *Proc. ACM Conf. on Office Information Systems*, 1990, pp.205-215.

[PM88]   Peckham, J. and Maryanski, F., Semantic data models, *ACM Computing Surveys*, Vol.20, No. 3, Sept. 1988, pp. 153-189.

[Rat97]   Rational Software Corporation, UML semantics v1.0, Jan. 1997.

[RS91]   Richardson, J. and Schwarz, P., Aspects: Extending objects to support multiple, independent roles, *Proc. ACM SIGMOD '91 Conf.*, May 1991, pp. 198-307.

[Rumb87]   Rumbaugh, J., Relations as semantic constructs in an object-oriented language, in *OOPSLA '87 Proceedings*, Oct. 1987, pp. 466-481.

[Rumb91]   Rumbaugh, J. et al., *Object-oriented modeling and design*, Prentice-hall, Englewood Cliffs, New Jersy, 1991.

[SD96]   Snoeck, M. and Dedene, G., Generalization/specialization and role in object oriented conceptual modeling, *Data & Knowledge Engineering*, Vol. 19, 1996, pp. 171-195.

[Taiv96]   Taivalsaari, A., On the Notion of Inheritance. *ACM Computing Surveys*, Sept. 1996, Vol. 28, No. 3, pp.438-479.

[Tan95]   Tanzer, C. , Remarks on object-oriented modeling of associations, *JOOP*, Vol. 7, No. 9, Feb. 1995, pp. 43-46.

[TYF86]   Teorey, T. J., Yang, D. and Fry J. P., A logical design methodology for relational databases using the extended entity-relationship model, *ACM Computing Surveys*, Vol. 18, No.2, June 1986, pp.197-222.

[WCL97]   Wong, R. K., Chau, H. L., and Lochovsky, F. H., A data model and semantics of objects withdynamic roles. In *13th IEEE International Conference on Data Engineering*, April, 1997.

Property Covering: A Powerful Construct for Schema Derivations

Anastasia Analyti[1], Nicolas Spyratos[2], Panos Constantopoulos[1,3]

[1] Institute of Computer Science, FORTH, Heraklion, Crete, Greece
[2] Universite de Paris-Sud, LRI-Bat 490, 91405 Orsay Cedex, France
[3] Department of Computer Science, University of Crete, Heraklion, Greece

E-mail: {analyti, panos}@ics.forth.gr, spyratos@lri.fr

Abstract. Covering is a well-known relationship in semantic and object-oriented models that holds when a class is the union of a collection of subclasses. Covering has been studied in the past *only* for entity classes. In this paper, we study covering for properties, and we introduce a new relationship, called *property covering*. Property covering holds when a property is the union of a collection of subproperties. Property covering allows to (i) partition a property into subproperties, (ii) express property value refinement, and (iii) express a particular form of negative information. We demonstrate that property covering is a powerful conceptual modeling mechanism, and we use it to provide a set of inference rules for schema derivations.

1 Introduction

Information systems should provide (i) powerful semantic constructs to adequately represent real world situations at the schema level, and (ii) inference mechanisms for schema derivations. These two components form the basis for helping users determine their informational needs, by navigating through the conceptual schema and by querying the structure of the data. Many user queries seek knowledge from the conceptual schema and have little to do with the individual objects stored in the database [10].

Covering is a well-known relationship in semantic and object-oriented data models that holds when a class is the union of a collection of subclasses [11, 2, 8, 7, 3]. However, covering has been studied *only* for entity classes. In this paper, we investigate covering for *properties*. We introduce a new relationship among properties, called *property covering*. Property covering holds when a property, restricted to a given class, is the union of a collection of subproperties.

To get a feeling of property covering, refer to Figure 1. Assume that books are classified into humanities books, scientific books, and general-interest books. A humanities author is one that has written humanities books (but may have also written books other than humanities). A sciences author is one that has written sciences books, and a general-interest author is one that has written general-interest books. Finally, a scholarly author is one that has written humanities or scientific books, only. In the figure, property 1 relates authors to the books they

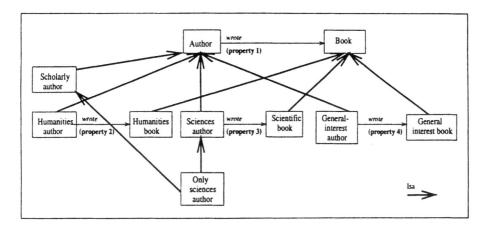

Fig. 1. Example of property covering

have written; property 2 relates humanities authors to the humanities books they have written; property 3 relates sciences authors to the scientific books they have written; and property 4 relates general-interest authors to the general-interest books they have written.

Now, let *a wrote b* be an instance of property 1, meaning that author *a* wrote book *b*. If the author *a* happens to be a scholarly author, then *b* will be either a humanities book or a scientific book. It follows that *a wrote b* will be an instance of property 2 or of property 3. In this case, we say that property 2 and property 3 *cover* property 1 *on* the class *Scholarly author*. Following a similar reasoning, we can say that properties 2, 3, and 4 *cover* property 1 on the class *Author*.

Property covering, together with class disjointness, provides a powerful conceptual modeling mechanism. To see this, refer to Figure 1. Assume that the class *Only sciences author* has no explicitly declared property, but has been declared as (i) subclass of *Scholarly author* and *Sciences author*, and (ii) disjoint from *Humanities author*. We have seen that property 2 and property 3 *cover* property 1 *on* the class *Scholarly author*. Let *a* be an only-sciences author and let *a wrote b* be an instance of property 1. As *a* is also an instance of *Scholarly author*, *a wrote b* should be an instance of property 2 or of property 3. However, as *Only sciences author* and *Humanities author* are disjoint, *a wrote b* cannot be an instance of property 2. Therefore, *a wrote b* is an instance of property 3. Therefore, property 3 covers property 1 on *Only sciences author*. This expresses that every book written by an only-sciences author is a scientific book, providing the end-user with more precise information about the semantics of the class *Only sciences author*.

The operational context of our work is the Semantic Index System (SIS) [4, 5, 6]. Intended applications of SIS include models for descriptive sciences, cultural documentation, thesauri, and other reference information and repository indexes.

The main contribution of this paper is the introduction of a new and powerful semantic construct, called property covering. Property covering has multiple applications, as it can be used to:

(i) partition a property into subproperties,

(ii) express property value refinement and differentiate between possible class semantics,

(iii) determine which subproperties of a property are inapplicable on a class,

(iv) express a particular form of negative information.

These claims are substantiated in the paper and further discussed in the concluding section.

The rest of the paper is organized as follows: Section 2 describes real world objects and their *In* and *Isa* relations. Section 3 contains the motivation and formal definition of property covering. Section 4 defines inapplicable properties and disjoint classes, and discusses how they contribute to the expression of negative information. Section 5 presents a comprehensive example of property covering. Section 6 contains related work and concluding remarks.

2   In and Isa Relations

Real world objects are distinguished with respect to their nature into individuals and arrows. An *individual* is a concrete or abstract object of independent existence, such as the concrete object *Camus*[4] or the abstract object *Author*. An *arrow* is a concrete or abstract property or binary relationship[5] from an object o to an object o', such as *Camus wrote "The Plague"* or *Author wrote Book*. The object o is called the *from* object of the arrow, and the object o' is called the *to* object of the arrow. In contrast to individuals, arrows do not exist independently: their existence presumes the existence of the *from* and *to* objects. The *from* object of an arrow a is denoted by $from(a)$ and the *to* object by $to(a)$[6].

The distinction of objects into individuals and arrows is based on their nature. Objects are also distinguished with respect to their concreteness into tokens and classes. A *token* is a concrete individual, such as *Camus*, or a concrete arrow, such as *Camus wrote "The Plague"*. A *class* is an abstract individual or an abstract arrow, in the sense that it refers collectively to a set of objects that are considered similar in some respect. Examples of classes are the abstract individual *Author* or the abstract arrow *Author wrote Book*.

Our distinction of objects into tokens and classes on one hand, and into individuals and arrows on the other, follows the structural part of the knowledge representation language Telos [9].

---

[4] Albert Camus is a French author.

[5] We do not make the distinction between property and binary relationship, as our approach is common to both. Thus, we use the term *arrow* to mean either a property or a binary relationship.

[6] In the present work, we consider only arrows whose *to* objects are individuals, while the *from* objects can be either individuals or arrows.

We assume that each object is defined by a set of constraints, called the *real world intension* of the object. For a class c, the real world intension determines the set of all objects to which c refers collectively. We call this set the *real world extension* of c. We assume that the real world extension of an arrow class a is a set of arrows from objects in the real world extension of $from(a)$ to objects in the real world extension of $to(a)$.

The fragment of the real world mapped in an information base is delimited by the needs of the user and by his imperfect knowledge of the real world. The latter implies that not all objects of interest are represented in the information base. We refer to the representation of the real world in the information base as *the model*. Though a real world object and its representation in the model are distinct, we will not differentiate between them in order to simplify our presentation.

Real world objects are related through the IN and ISA relations[7]. The IN relation expresses membership of an object in the real world extension of a class, and the ISA relation expresses inclusion between real world extensions of classes.

Definition 1. IN relation
If an object o belongs to the real world extension of a class c then we say that o is an *instance of* c, and we denote it by $IN(o, c)$. An object can be instance of zero, one, or more classes (multiple instantiation). ◇

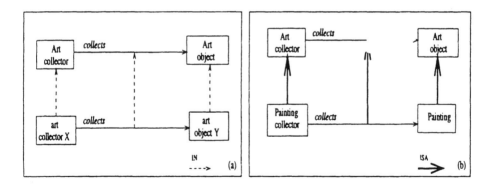

Fig. 2. Example of the IN and ISA relations

For example, in Figure 2(a), the individual token *art collector X* is instance of the individual class *Art collector*. Additionally, the arrow token *collects* from *art collector X* to *art object Y* is instance of the arrow class *collects* from the individual class *Art collector* to the individual class *Art object*. Note that every instance of an arrow class a is an arrow from an instance of $from(a)$ to an instance of $to(a)$.

---

[7] Throughout the paper, we use the term *relation* with its mathematical meaning.

As we mentioned earlier, not all real world objects and relations are represented in the model. We denote by In, the subset of the real world relation IN that is represented in the model. It follows that if $In(o, c)$ holds then $IN(o, c)$ holds, whereas the converse is not always true.

Definition 2. ISA relation
Let o, o' be two classes. We distinguish two cases:
Case 1: o and o' are individual classes.
We say that o is *subclass* of o', denoted by $ISA(o, o')$, if it holds that: for any individual x, if $IN(x, o)$ then $IN(x, o')$.
Case 2: o and o' are arrow classes.
We say that o is *subclass* of o', denoted by $ISA(o, o')$, if it holds that
(i) $ISA(from(o), from(o'))$, (ii) $ISA(to(o), to(o'))$, and (iii) for any arrow x, if $IN(x, o)$ then $IN(x, o')$.
In all other cases, ISA is undefined.
A class can be subclass of zero, one, or more classes (multiple specialization). ◇

For an example of ISA relation, refer to Figure 2(b). The arrow class *collects* from *Painting collector* to *Painting* is subclass of the arrow class *collects* from *Art collector* to *Art object* (meaning that every painting collected by a painting collector is an art object collected by an art collector)[8].

We define two classes o, o' to be *equivalent* if it holds that $ISA(o, o')$ and $ISA(o', o)$. Roughly speaking, equivalent classes can be seen as different ways of looking at the same set of objects. In the remainder of the paper, we shall talk of classes up to equivalence.

We denote by Isa, the subset of the real world relation ISA that is represented in the model. It follows that if $Isa(c, c')$ holds then $ISA(c, c')$ holds, whereas the converse is not always true.

We introduce a number of inference rules in the model, in order to reflect properties of real world relations. For example, ISA is transitive. Thus, we introduce in the model an inference rule that reflects ISA transitivity:
for all classes $c_1, c_2, c_3,$ $\quad Isa(c_1, c_2) \land Isa(c_2, c_3) \Rightarrow Isa(c_1, c_3)$.
This rule will allow us to *derive* $Isa(c_1, c_3)$ from $Isa(c_1, c_2)$ and $Isa(c_2, c_3)$.

The inference rules regarding Isa relations are called *Isa Rules* and are given in the Appendix.

3 Arrow Covering

The notion of *covering* is well-known in semantic and object-oriented data models. Roughly speaking, we say that a set of classes $c_1, ..., c_n$ covers a class c if (i) each of $c_1, ..., c_n$ is subclass of c, and (ii) every instance of c is instance of at least one of $c_1, ..., c_n$. For example, the classes *Male* and *Female* cover their superclass *Person*. However, covering in the literature refers only to individual classes.

---

[8] Intuitively, arrow subclasses correspond to what we have called "subproperties" in the Introduction.

In this paper, we consider covering for arrow classes and we demonstrate that it is a powerful conceptual modeling mechanism. Roughly, we say that a set of arrow classes $a_1, ..., a_n$ *covers* an arrow class a on a class c, if the following hold: (i) each of $a_1, ..., a_n$ is subclass of a, (ii) c is subclass of $from(a)$, and (iii) if x is instance of a', and $from(x)$ is instance of c then x is instance of at least one of $a_1, ..., a_n$.

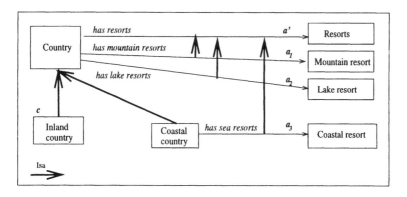

Fig. 3. Example of arrow covering

For example, in Figure 3, assume that the resorts of a country are classi-fied into mountain-resorts, lake-resorts, and sea-resorts. Then, the arrow classes a_1, a_2, a_3 cover the arrow a' on *Country*. As inland countries do not have sea-resorts, the arrow classes a_1 and a_2 cover a' on *Inland country*.

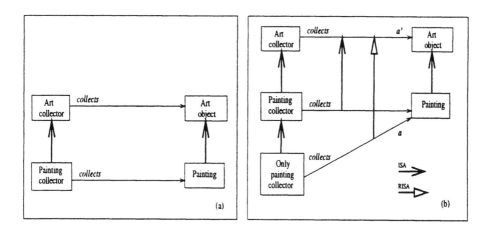

Fig. 4. Differentiation of class semantics through arrow covering

Arrow covering, in conjunction with *Isa*, can be used to differentiate between possible class semantics. For example, in Figure 4(a), an instance o of *Painting collector* acquires the property *collects* of *Painting collector* by being an instance of the class. However, as o is also an instance of *Art collector*, it also acquires the property *collects* of *Art collector*. This leads to two possible interpretations of *Painting collector*:

Option 1: A painting collector collects paintings but can also collect art objects other than paintings.
Option 2: A painting collector collects only paintings.

Arrow covering, together with *Isa*, can differentiate between Option 1 and Option 2, as follows: If we declare that *collects* of *Painting collector* is just subclass of *collects* of *Art collector*, then the semantics of *Painting collector* is as in *Option* 1. However, if we declare that *collects* of *Painting collector* covers *collects* of *Art collector* on *Painting collector* then the semantics of *Painting collector* will be as in *Option* 2.

We now give the formal definition of the arrow covering relation.

Definition 3. ACOV relation
Let $a_1, \ldots a_n$, a' be arrow classes and let c be a class. We say that the set $\{a_1, \ldots, a_n\}$ covers a' on c, denoted by $\text{ACOV}(\{a_1, \ldots, a_n\}, a', c)$, if the following hold:
(i) $\text{ISA}(a_i, a')$, for all $i \leq n$,
(i) $\text{ISA}(c, from(a'))$, and
(iii) for any arrow x, if $\text{IN}(x, a')$ and $\text{IN}(from(x), c)$ then $\exists\, i \leq n$ such that $In(x, a_i)$. ◇

In order to simplify notation, we write $\text{ACOV}(a, a', c)$ instead of $\text{ACOV}(\{a\}, a', c)$.

We denote by *Acov*, the subset of the real world relation ACOV that is represented in the model. The inference rules regarding *Acov* relations are called *Acov Rules* and are given in the Appendix. In section 5, we will see a comprehensive example of schema derivations using the *Acov* Rules.

3.1 Restriction Isa: A Special Form of Arrow Covering

A special case of arrow covering is of particular interest. It is the case where a single arrow a covers an arrow a' on $from(a)$. This form of arrow covering is called *Restriction* ISA, or RISA for short.

Definition 4. RISA relation
Let a, a' be two arrow classes. We say that a is a *restriction subclass* of a', denoted by $\text{RISA}(a, a')$, if $\text{ACOV}(a, a', from(a))$ holds. ◇

As the following proposition shows, the RISA relation can be seen as a stronger form of ISA, which is defined for arrow classes and expresses property value refinement.

Proposition 5. *Let a, a' be two arrow classes.* RISA(a, a') *holds iff the following hold:*

(i) ISA(a, a'), *and*

(ii) for any arrow x, if IN(x, a') *and* IN($from(x), from(a)$) *then* IN(x, a). ◇

For example, in Figure 4(b), assume that *Painting collector* has the semantics of Option 1, whereas *Only painting collector* has the semantics of Option 2. Then, the property *collects* of *Painting collector* is just subclass of the property *collects* of *Art collector* (denoted by a'), whereas the property *collects* of *Only painting collector* (denoted by a) is restriction subclass of a'. Intuitively, a refines a', as every instance of a' whose *from* object is instance of *Only painting collector* takes values in *Painting*.

We denote by *Risa*, the subset of the real world relation RISA that is represented in the model. Inference rules regarding *Risa* relations are called *Risa Rules* and are given in the Appendix. The reader is referred to [1], for further results on the interaction between ACOV and RISA, and their role in a formal treatment of inheritance.

4 Inapplicable Arrows and Disjoint Classes

In this section, we define inapplicable arrows and disjoint classes. Intuitively, inapplicable arrows allow to express that no instance of a class can have a given property.

Definition 6. Inapplicable arrow

Let a be an arrow class and let c be a subclass of $from(a)$. The arrow a is called *inapplicable on c*, if there can be no instance of a whose *from* object is instance of c.

An arrow a is called *inapplicable*, if a is *inapplicable on $from(a)$*. ◇

For example, the arrow *flying* of class *Bird* is inapplicable *on* the subclass *Penguin*.

We call *empty class*, denoted by $\perp$, the individual class whose real world extension is the empty set. Obviously, this class is unique (up to equivalence). Intuitively, the empty class corresponds to contradictory real world intensions. By convention, we assume that an arrow a is inapplicable iff its *to* object is the empty class, i.e., iff $to(a) = \perp$.

The inference rules regarding inapplicable arrows are called *Inapplicable Arrow Rules* and are given in the Appendix.

Inapplicable arrows allow to express "negative" information. For example, when we think of birds, we think of *flying* as being their basic property. This is so because *flying* is true for all birds, but for a few exceptions, such as penguins. Moreover, when we think of penguins, we think of *non-flying* as being their basic property. We can represent this situation by declaring that *flying* is inapplicable on *Penguin*.

In general, to declare that a' is inapplicable on a subclass c of $from(a')$, we do the following (see Figure 5(a)):

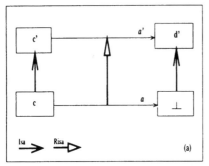
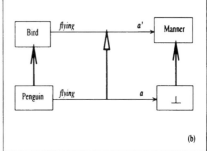

Fig. 5. (a) Declaring that a' is inapplicable on c, (b) Declaring that penguins do not fly

1. we create an arrow a from c to $\perp$ (inapplicable arrow), and
2. we declare a to be restriction subclass of a'.

For example, in order to declare that the arrow *flying* of *Bird* (denote it by a') is inapplicable on *Penguin*, we first create an arrow a from *Penguin* to $\perp$, and then declare $Risa(a, a')$, as shown in Figure 5(b).

Two classes are called *disjoint* if they can never have instances in common, i.e., if their real world extensions are disjoint.

Definition 7. DISJ relation
Two classes c, c' are called *disjoint*, denoted by DISJ(c, c'), if there is no object x such that IN(x, c) and IN(x, c'). ◇

We denote by *Disj*, the subset of the real world relation DISJ that is represented in the model. The inference rules regarding the *Disj* relation are called *Disj Rules* and are given in the Appendix.

5 A Comprehensive Example of Schema Derivations

In this section, we present a complex example (see Figure 6), illustrating the various concepts presented in this paper.

Angiosperm is the category of flowering plants. Flowers are either fertile or sterile. Fertile flowers are characterized as (i) male, if they have male components, e.g. stamens, and (ii) female, if they have female components, e.g. ovaries. Female flowers are either of a single sex (female-only flowers) or bisexual (both female and male). Similarly, male flowers are either of a single sex (male-only flowers) or bisexual.

In Figure 6[9], the class *Angiosperm* refers to the angiosperm plants. The class *Angiosperm with only fertile flowers* refers to the angiosperms that do not have sterile flowers. The class *Female angiosperm* (resp. *Male angiosperm*) refers to the

---

[9] The name of each of the arrows $a_3, ..., a_7$ is *has flowers*.

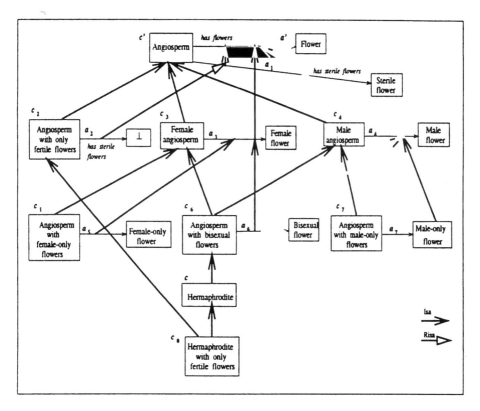

Fig. 6. Example of schema derivations using *Acov* relations

angiosperms that have female (resp. male) flowers. Note that an angiosperm may have both female and male flowers. The class *Angiosperm with female-only flowers* (resp. *Angiosperm with bisexual flowers, Angiosperm with male-only flowers*) refers to the angiosperms that have female-only flowers (resp. bisexual flowers, male-only flowers). The class *Hermaphrodite* refers to plants of species that have bisexual flowers but not single-sex flowers (they may have sterile flowers). The class *Hermaphrodite with only fertile flowers* refers to hermaphrodite plants that do not have sterile flowers.

In addition to the declarations shown in the figure, assume that the user has made the following declarations:

Isa Declarations

Isa(Sterile flower, Flower), Isa(Female flower, Flower),
Isa(Male flower, Flower), Isa(Female-only flower, Female flower),
Isa(Bisexual flower, Female flower), Isa(Bisexual flower, Male flower),
Isa(Male-only flower, Male flower)

Acov Declarations:

1. $Acov(\{a_1, a_3, a_4\}, a', c')$, expressing that all flowers of an angiosperm are sterile, female, or male.
2. $Acov(\{a_5, a_6\}, a_3, c_3)$, expressing that all female flowers of a female angiosperm are female-only or bisexual.
3. $Acov(\{a_6, a_7\}, a_4, c_4)$, expressing that all male flowers of a male angiosperm are male-only or bisexual.

Disj Declarations:

1. $Disj(c, c_5)$, expressing that a hermaphrodite plant does not have female-only flowers.
2. $Disj(c, c_7)$, expressing that a hermaphrodite plant does not have male-only flowers.

Using the inference rules of the Appendix, the following informative relations can be derived:

Derived Relations:

1. $Acov(\{a_1, a_5, a_6, a_7\}, a', c')$, expressing that all flowers of an angiosperm plant are sterile, female-only, bisexual, or male-only. Intuitively, this follows from *Acov* Declarations 1,2, and 3.
2. $Acov(\{a_3, a_4\}, a', c_2)$, expressing that all flowers of an angiosperm with only fertile flowers are female or male. Intuitively, this follows from *Acov* Declaration 1, and the fact that a_1 is inapplicable on c_2.
3. $Acov(a_6, a_3, c)$, expressing that all female flowers of a hermaphrodite plant are bisexual. Intuitively, this follows from *Acov* Declaration 2, and *Disj* Declaration 1.
4. $Acov(a_6, a_4, c)$, expressing that all male flowers of a hermaphrodite plant are bisexual. Intuitively, this follows from *Acov* Declaration 3 and *Disj* Declaration 2.
5. $Acov(\{a_1, a_6\}, a', c)$, expressing that all flowers of a hermaphrodite plant are sterile or bisexual. Intuitively, this follows from *Acov* Declaration 1 and Derived Relations 3 and 4 above.
6. $Acov(a_6, a', c_0)$, expressing that all flowers of a hermaphrodite plant with only fertile flowers, are bisexual. Intuitively, this follows from Derived Relation 5, and the facts that a_1 is inapplicable on c_2 and $Isa(c_0, c_2)$.

The formal derivations of the above relations are given in [1].

6 Related Work and Concluding Remarks

Covering of an entity class c by a set of subclasses cs is explicitly supported in many semantic and object-oriented data models [2, 11, 8, 7, 3]. In [2], covering appears in the form of union types where pre-existing types are combined to form a new (union) type. In [11, 2], a stronger form of covering is considered where the classes in cs have to be disjoint. In [8], a more general form of covering is proposed where the classes in *cs* are not necessarily subclasses of *c*, and *c* is *only* a subset of the union of the classes in *cs*. There, a set of sound and complete inference rules for covering is given. However, all of the above proposals consider covering only for entity classes, whereas covering on properties has not been studied before.

In this paper, we have introduced covering for property classes, through a new semantic construct, called *property covering*. We have demonstrated the expressive power of property covering by showing that:

1. It partitions a property into subproperties, thus providing finer descriptions at schema level (top-down). Additionally, it helps to better organize available schema information (bottom-up).
2. It expresses property value refinement, through a special form that we have called *Risa*. As we have seen in Section 3, *Risa* and *Isa* can be used to differentiate between possible class semantics.
3. It can determine which subproperties of a property are inapplicable on a given class. For example, in Figure 3, arrow covering tells us that the sub-property *sea resorts* is inapplicable on *Inland country*. This knowledge provides finer information on the semantics of *Inland country*.
4. It can express a particular form of negative information. For example, it can express that penguins do not fly. This allows us to express exception information explicitly, when such information is of interest.

Our conclusion is that arrow covering, together with disjointness and inapplicability, forms a powerful conceptual modeling mechanism, that merits further investigation. Specifically, it would be interesting to investigate the interaction between property covering and inheritance [1]. Another interesting research direction would be to investigate the interaction between property covering and property participation constraints (such as, total or optional properties). For example, in Figure 6, property participation constraints could be used to derive that a hermaphrodite plant *necessarily* has bisexual flowers, and *possibly* has sterile flowers.

References

1. A. Analyti, N. Spyratos, P. Constantopoulos, Property Covering: A Powerful Construct for Schema Derivations, Technical Report TR199, Institute of Computer Science, Foundation for Research and Technology-Hellas, June, (1997). Available from ftp.ics.forth.gr, cd tech-reports/1997,
   1997.TR199.Property_Covering_Construct_Schema_Derivations.ps.gz.
2. S. Abiteboul, R. Hull, IFO: A Formal Semantic Database Model, *ACM Transactions on Database Systems*, 12(4), 525-565 (1987).
3. C. Batini, S. Ceri, S.B. Navathe, Conceptual and Logical Database Design: The Entity-Relationship Approach, Benjamin/Cummings, 1992.
4. P. Constantopoulos, M. Doerr, Component Classification in the Software Information Base, O.Nierstrasz and D.Tsichritzis (eds.), *Object-Oriented Software Composition*, Prentice-Hall (1995).

5. P. Constantopoulos, M. Theodorakis, Y.Tzitzikas, Developing Hypermedia Over an Information Repository, *Proc. of the 2nd Workshop on Open Hypermedia Systems at Hypertext'96*, (1996).

6. P. Constantopoulos, Y.Tzitzikas, Context-Driven Information Base Update, *Proc. of the 8th Intern. Conference on Advanced Information Systems Engineering (CAiSE'96)*, 319-344 (1996).

7. M. Gogolla, U. Hohenstein, Towards a Semantic View of an Extended Entity-Relationship Model, *ACM Transactions on Database Systems*, 16(3), 369-416 (1991).

8. M. Lenzerini, Covering and disjointness constraints in type networks, *Proc. of the 3rd IEEE Intern. Conference on Data Engineering*, 1987.

9. J. Mylopoulos, A. Borgida, M. Jarke, M. Koubarakis, Telos - a Language for Representing Knowledge about Information Systems, *ACM Transactions on Information Systems*, 8(4), 325-362, (1990).

10. M.P. Papazoglou, Unraveling the Semantics of Conceptual Schemas, *Communications of the ACM*, 38(9), pp.80-94 (1995).

11. T.J. Teorey, D. Yang, J.P. Fry, A Logical Design Methodology for Relational Databases Using the Extended Entity-Relationship Model, *Computing Surveys*, 18(2), 197-222 (1986).

APPENDIX: Inference Rules

We denote by I, A, C, AC the sets of individuals, arrows, classes, and arrow classes, respectively.

ISA RULES

Rule 1: $\forall c \in C, \quad Isa(c,c)$

Rule 2: $\forall c_1, c_2, c_3 \in C, \quad Isa(c_1,c_2) \wedge Isa(c_2,c_3) \Rightarrow Isa(c_1,c_3)$

Rule 3: $\forall c \in IC, \quad Isa(c, \perp) \Rightarrow c = \perp$

ACOV RULES

Rule 1: $\forall a_1, ..., a_n, a' \in AC, c \in C \quad Acov(\{a_1, ..., a_n\}, a', c) \Rightarrow \forall i \leq n, Isa(a_i, a')$

Rule 2: $\forall a \in AC, c \in C, \quad Acov(\{a\}, a, c)$

Rule 3: $\forall a_1, ..., a_n, a' \in AC, c \in C$

$$Acov(\{a_1, ..., a_n\}, a', c) \wedge (Disj(from(a_n), c) \vee Disj(a_n, a')) \Rightarrow Acov(\{a_1, ..., a_{n-1}\}, a', c)$$

Rule 4: $\forall a_1, ..., a_n, a' \in AC, c, c_0 \in C$

$$Acov(\{a_1, ..., a_n\}, a', c) \wedge Isa(c_0, c) \Rightarrow Acov(\{a_1, ..., a_n\}, a', c_0)$$

Rule 5: $\forall a_1, ..., a_n, a', b_1, ..., b_m \in AC, c \in C$

$$Acov(\{a_1, ..., a_n\}, a', c) \wedge Acov(\{b_1, ..., b_m\}, a_n, from(a_n))$$
$$\Rightarrow Acov(\{a_1, ..., a_{n-1}, b_1, ..., b_m\}, a', c)$$

Rule 6: $\forall a_1, ..., a_n, a', b_1, ..., b_m \in AC, c \in C$

$$Acov(\{a_1, ..., a_n\}, a', c) \wedge Acov(\{b_1, ..., b_m\}, a_n, c) \Rightarrow Acov(\{a_1, ..., a_{n-1}, b_1, ..., b_m\}, a', c)$$

Rule 7: $\forall a_1, ..., a_n, a', a \in AC, c \in C$

$$Acov(\{a_1, ..., a_n\}, a', c) \wedge Isa(a, a') \wedge Isa(c, from(a)) \wedge (\forall i \leq n, Isa(a_i, a))$$
$$\Rightarrow Acov(\{a_1, ..., a_n\}, a, c)$$

RISA RULES

Rule 1: $\forall a, a' \in AC, \quad Risa(a, a') \Rightarrow Isa(a, a')$
Rule 2: $\forall a \in AC, \quad Risa(a, a)$
Rule 3: $\forall a_1, a_2, a_3 \in AC, \quad Risa(a_1, a_2) \wedge Risa(a_2, a_3) \Rightarrow Risa(a_1, a_3)$
Rule 4: $\forall a_1, a_2, a_3 \in AC,$

$$Isa(a_1, a_3) \wedge Risa(a_2, a_3) \wedge Isa(from(a_1), from(a_2)) \wedge Isa(to(a_1), to(a_2)) \Rightarrow Isa(a_1, a_2)$$

Rule 5: $\forall a_1, a_2, a_3 \in AC, \quad Isa(a_1, a_2) \wedge Isa(a_2, a_3) \wedge Risa(a_1, a_3) \Rightarrow Risa(a_1, a_2)$
Rule 6: $\forall a, a' \in AC, \quad Risa(a, a') \Leftrightarrow Acov(\{a\}, a', from(a))$

INAPPLICABLE ARROW RULES

Rule 1: $\forall a, a' \in AC, \quad to(a) = \bot \Rightarrow Disj(a, a')$

DISJ RULES

Rule 1: $\forall c_0, c, c' \in C, \quad Disj(c, c') \wedge Isa(c_0, c) \Rightarrow Disj(c_0, c')$
Rule 2: $\forall c, c' \in IC, \quad Disj(c, c') \wedge Isa(c, c') \Leftrightarrow c = \bot$
Rule 3: $\forall a, a' \in AC, \quad Disj(from(a), from(a')) \vee Disj(to(a), to(a')) \Rightarrow Disj(a, a')$

Inheritance Graph Hierarchy Construction
Using Rectangular Decomposition of a Binary Relation
and Designer Feedback

Mohamed M. GAMMOUDI[1,2], Jerônimo D. MENDES[1], Wilson S. PINTO[1],

(1) - Universidade Federal do Maranhão, DEEE/CT, Grupo de Ciência da Computação,
Campus do Bacanga, 65080-040 São Luís - MA
Fone: (098) 2178242, Fax: (098) 2178241
E-mail: gammoudi@bacanga.ufma.br or gammoudi@elo.com.br

(2) - Tunis University, Faculty of Sciences, Departement of Computer Science,
Campus Universitaire, Le Belvédère, 1060, Tunis, Tunisia.

ABSTRACT

Inheritance is the main theme of schema design for the object-oriented software and object-oriented database [10]. It supports class hierarchy design and capture the is-a relationship between a class and its superclass. Obviously, the designer needs tools to assist him to define his conceptual schema. However, very few approaches attempt to provide methods and tools for designing inheritance graph in object databases [29], and object software [1]. In this paper, we propose a semi-automatic method for generating inheritance graph hierarchy. This method is semi-automatic because it takes into account the feedback of the designer based on his expertise. It has a sound mathematical foundation and allows us to obtain a number of classes less than methods which uses Galois Lattice as a support to generate class hierarchy. Steps of our method are : **(i)** From a binary relation which represents the links between classes and their properties and methods, some heuristics generate a set of *Optimal Rectangles* (OR: group of classes which share the same properties and methods). **(ii)** The set of OR is organised by a partial order relation into a *Brut Inheritance Graph* (BIG). **(iii)** BIG is simplified and shown to the designer. **(iv)** The designer can modify, add or remove classes, attributes or methods in the binary relation and activates steps **(ii)** and **(iii)** until he obtains a proper class hierarchy or an *Optimal Inheritance Graph.*

KEYWORDS: Conceptual Schema, Class, Inheritance Graph Hierarchy, Binary Relation, Rectangular Decomposition, Optimal Rectangle.

1. INTRODUCTION

Inheritance is a powerful paradigm in Object Oriented Programming. This mechanism supports the class hierarchy design and capture the *is-a* relationship between a superclass and its subclass. It is also a promising programming tool with good properties to reduce the cost of software development and enhance software main theme of software reuse and object-oriented design. This property has been widely applied in object oriented software and object oriented databases [26].

There are two kinds of inheritance:

• *Simple inheritance*, where a class can have only one direct superclass. Its means a class inherits attributes and methods from only one class.

• *Multiple inheritance*, or *repeated inheritance* [12] means that a class inherits attributes and methods from more than one direct superclass.

In systems which support simple inheritance, classes form a hierarchy class. Systems which support multiple inheritance the classes form a *Rooted Directed Graph*, sometimes called a *Class Lattice* [12]. In fact, several research works use *Galois Lattice* structure as a support to define class hierarchy [29] or for interface hierarchy [18]. When we have to develop an object oriented system, we have to define classes, methods and all relationships between classes such as: aggregation (Part-of), specialisation / Generalisation (Is-a), and so on. It is very important that the designer has tools which helps him in his task, such as a tool for generating and displaying the inheritance graph, because it allows the designer to efficiently control the conceptual schema such as name-conflicting, redundant inheritance, redundant is-a relationship and cyclic inheritance [10].

In our approach, we introduce a semi automatic method for inheritance graph construction using the *Rectangular Decomposition of a Binary relation* (RDBR) [5] and the feedback of the designer. In fact, from a binary relation, we select a set of optimal rectangles by RDBR and organise them into a *Brut Inheritance Graph* (BIG) using the *partial order relation*. After removing the redundancy from the BIG, the system interacts with the designer to validate the graph and generates the *Optimal Inheritance Graph*.

This paper is organised as follows: section 2 shows related work and expose steps of our approach. In section 3, we present some mathematical foundation on which our method is based and which are necessary for its understanding. In section 4, we illustrate the Optimal Inheritance Graph generation step by step using an example. At the end we conclude with advantages and limits of our methods and mention future work.

2. RELATED WORK

Several research works are done for modelling and designing class hierarchy. Some of them are based on conceptual clustering methods and taxonomic reasoning in knowledge representation system such as the approach introduced by Michalski in [24]. This approach is considered as an alternative to the limitation of conventional techniques which are used to construct classification of a given set of objects and is based on cluster analysis and numerical taxonomy. Conventional techniques are inadequate because they organise objects into classes on the basis of a numerical measure [3]. Some other research works uses structural elements to generate inheritance hierarchies such as the structure of Galois Lattice. It is used to represent the inheritance hierarchy. It is understandable, since multiple inheritance is defined as a class lattice [11]. Galois Lattice is also used in several domains, such as in interface class hierarchy [19], [20], knowledge representation and learning theory[28] and in Class Hierarchy designing [29].

These methods are efficient and provide good results. However, they use a Galois Lattice structure which has a high number of classes compared to the initial number of given objects [29]. This high number of nodes in Galois Lattice implies a lot of redundancy. To remove the redundancy a lot of time processing is required. As an alternative to this limitation, we introduce a method which has a simple mathematical foundation and provides a number of nodes less than methods based on Galois Lattice structure. This is ensured by the use of the Optimal Rectangle notion. To generate a proper Inheritance Graph Hierarchy we proceed as follows:

• First, we use some heuristics to decompose a binary relation into a set of optimal rectangles which constitutes its minimal cover. This decomposition is an approximate solution of an NP-Complete problem;

• Second, the set of Optimal Rectangles is organised into a Brut Inheritance Graph (acyclic) using the partial order relation;

• Third, The Brut Optimal Graph is simplified by removing redundant entities or properties;

• Fourth, the system uses some inferences rules to analyse the BIG and shows it to the designer to be validated. The feedback of the designer allows us to obtain an Optimal Inheritance Graph avoiding problems of name-conflicting, redundant inheritance, and so on.

3. MATHEMATICAL FOUNDATIONS AND PRINCIPLES OF RECTANGULAR DECOMPOSITION OF A BINARY RELATION (RDBR)

A binary relation R on sets E and F is defined as a subset of the Cartesian product E x F. We can associate the following subsets of E and F with a given binary relation R: the *image* set of e is defined by : e. R = $\{e' \in F \mid e \, R \, e'\}$;

the *antecedents* of e' are defined by : R. e' = $\{e \in E \mid e \, R \, e'\}$;

the *domain* of R is defined by : dom(R)= $\{e \mid \exists \, e' \in F : e \, R \, e'\}$;

the *range* of R is defined by : Range(R) = $\{\acute{e} \mid \exists \, e \in E : e \, R \, e'\}$.

3.1 RECTANGLE

Let R be a binary relation defined on sets E and F. A *rectangle or rectangular relation* of R is a couple of sets (A,B) such that $A \subseteq E$, $B \subseteq F$, and $A \times B \subseteq R$. A is the domain of the rectangle (A,B) and B is its range.

Remarks:

The correspondence between rectangles (A_i, B_i) and the associated rectangular relations [6] $A_i \times B_i$ is a bijective one, except when $A_i = \varnothing$ or $B_i = \varnothing$. For instance, the rectangles $(\varnothing, B_1)$ and $(A_1, \varnothing)$ are both associated with the null rectangular relation $\varnothing$. The main reason for making a distinction between rectangles and rectangular relations is that the concept of a rectangle enables us to obtain a lattice structure.

3.2 MAXIMAL RECTANGLE
The notion of maximal rectangle is not new, it is found with different names such as: Complete couple in [19], or Concept in Wille [Wille 89]. Let (A,B) be a rectangle of a given relation R defined on sets E and F. The rectangle (A,B) is said to be *maximal* if whenever A x B $\subseteq$ A' x B' $\subseteq$ R, then A = A' and B = B'.

3.3 GAIN
With respect to storage space, the *gain* which is obtained by a given rectangle RE = (A,B) (or the associated rectangular relation A x B) (see fig. 3.2) is computed by the following function: g(RE) = $(\|A\|*\|B\|)-(\|A\|+\|B\|)$ where $\|A\|$ denotes the cardinality of the set A and $\|B\|$ the cardinality of the set B.

3.4 OPTIMAL RECTANGLE
A rectangle RE = (A,B) which contains an element (a,b) of a binary relation R is said to be *optimal* if it realizes the maximal gain g(RE) among all the maximal rectangles (see section 3.3) which contain (a,b). Fig. 3.1-a represents an example of a relation R. The fig.s 3.1-b, 3.1-c,and 3.1-d represent three maximal rectangles of R which contain the couple(y,3). The gains obtained, in the sense of memory space with these three maximal rectangles are respectively 1, 0, and -1. Then, the optimal rectangle which contains the couple (y,3) of R is the rectangle illustrated by fig. 3.1-b because it allows to realize the maximal gain.

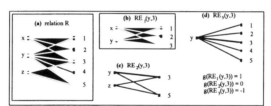

Fig. 3.1. Illustration of Optimal Rectangle and Gain Notions

3.5 MINIMAL COVER
Let R be a binary relation. The cover of R is a set of rectangles C = {RE_1, RE_2, . . ., RE_n} such that for each element (x,y) of R there exists REi $\in$ C which (x,y) $\in$ REi. The minimal cover of R is the smallest subset of C which covers it.

3.6 ELEMENTARY RELATION
Proposition 1: Let R be a finite binary relation , and (a,b) $\in$ R. The Union of rectangles which cover R and which contain the couple (a,b) is equal to the relation $\Phi_R(a,b)$ = I(b.R^{-1}) o R o I(a.R). The proof of this proposition can be found in [5], and [13]. We say that the relation $\Phi_R(a,b)$, is an *elementary relation* which contains the couple (a,b) of R. As an example, the fig. 32-d is the elementary relation containing the couple (a,1) of the initial relation R illustrated by the fig. 3.2a.

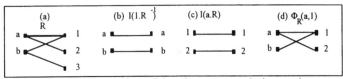

Fig. 3.2. Illustration of the elementary relation notion

3.7 PARTIAL ORDER RELATION
Proposition 2:
The relation defined below on the set of optimal rectangles of a binary relation R is a partial order relation:
$\forall$ (A_1, B_1) and (A_2, B_2) two optimal rectangles of R, $(A_1, B_1) \leq\leq (A_2, B_2) <=> A_1 \subseteq A_2$ and $B_2 \subseteq B_1$. The proof of this proposition can be found in [13].

3.8 OPTIMAL RECTANGULAR GRAPH
Let R be a binary relation defined on the sets E, F. Let G be a set of optimal rectangles obtained from the Rectangular Decomposition of R. $(G, \leq\leq)$ forms a graph. This graph has a supremum $(E,\varnothing)$ and an infimum $(\varnothing,F)$.

Remark :
In the case where G is a set of maximal rectangles, $(G, \leq\leq)$ forms a Galois lattice having as a supremum $(E,\varnothing)$ and as an infimum $(\varnothing,F)$ [5]. This notion is used to represent the Brut Inheritance Graph and the Optimal Inheritance Graph

3.9. GALOIS LATTICE
Let R be a finite binary relation defined on E and F, There is a unique Galois Lattice corresponding to R [17]. Each element of the lattice must be a maximal rectangle as defined in 3.2, noted (X,Y), composed of a set $X \in P(E)$ and a set $Y \in P(F)$.
Let f and g defined as following :
$Y = f(X) \mid f(X)= \{ y \in F \mid \forall x \in X, xRy \}; X= g(Y) \mid g(Y) = \{ x \in E \mid \forall y \in Y, xRy \}$
where the couple of functions (f, g) is said Galois Connection between P(E) and P(F) and the Galois lattice $(GL, \leq\leq)$ for the binary relation is the set of all maximal rectangles with the partial order relation defined in 3.7. The partial Order is used to generate the graph of the Galois lattice which is called Hasse Diagram. Galois lattice has a supremum $(E,\varnothing)$ and an infimum $(\varnothing,F)$, for more details on Lattice Galois the reader should consult [3].

4. OPTIMAL INHERITANCE GRAPH GENERATION

As shown in the fig. 4.1, in this section we treat the following points :
(1) how we generate the set of optimal rectangles from a binary relation using RDBR;

(2)   how the set of optimal Rectangle that forms nodes of the BIG is organised by a partialorder relation;

(3)   how the BIG is simplified and shown to the designer;

(4)   how the system interacts with the designer to refine BIG and to define a Proper Inheritance Graph or an Optimal Inheritance Graph (see fig. 4.1).

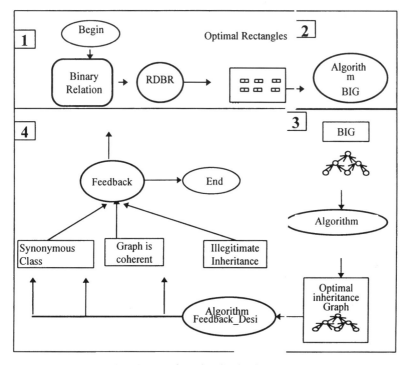

Figure 4.1: Steps of Optimal Inheritance Graph Generation

4.1. RECTANGULAR DECOMPOSITION OF A BINARY RELATION

In this section we just recall the principles of the RDBR method and we show how we apply it on an example to generate the Brut Inheritance Graph.

Let R be a finite binary relation: we mean by Rectangular Decomposition of R, the selection of a set of optimal rectangles which form a minimal cover of R. A binary relation R, from E to F defines edges of a bipartite graph on E ∪ F. Then, arectangle is a complete bipartite subgraph of the graph (E ∪ F, R). The problem of optimal rectangle selection containing an element (a,b) from a binary relation R can be seen as the choice of a subset of maximal rectangles which are selected. This problem is similar to a selection of a complete bipartite subgraph with maximal cardinality and which is contained in bipartite graph. Then it is NP-complete [Garey and al. 79]. Several research work on this subject have been done such as in [Bordat 92], [Godin and al. 89]. The proposed algorithms in [Belkhiter and al. 92] give an exact solution to the lattice construction problem, but they are of a combinatorial nature and are not suitable if the cardinality of a finite binary relation is increasing (more than 16 couples). Furthermore, we distinguish two currents which contributes to the Galois Lattice Construction. The first one include [Malgrange 62], [Guenoche 90], [Norris 78] and so on which are interesting on how to select the nodes of the Galois Lattice, and the second current which includes [Bordat 92], [Godin and al. 93], [Godin and al. 95] which introduce incremental algorithms to construct Galois Lattice. The problem is that the number of Galois Lattice nodes is high. As an alternative, we use the notion of optimal rectangle in the objective to optimise the number of nodes without lost of information. Rectangular Decomposition of a Binary Relation is defined as following:

(1)   Decompose R in p elementary relations $PR_1, PR_2, \ldots, PR_p$;
(2)   Select in parallel from each elementary relation PR_i the set of optimal rectangles;
(3)   Select the minimum of optimal rectangles from each elementary relation Pr_i which forms its covering;
(4)   Eliminate the maximum of redundant elements in the optimal rectangles.

Remarks: The study of the complexity of algorithms used in RDBR shows that their complexity are in the order of $O(n^3)$ in the worst. More details on the heuristics could be found in [13], [5], [15].

4.1.1. Construction of Brut Inheritance Graph

We assume that the designer uses one of the Design methods to define classes, attributes and methods, such as Booch Method [7] or OMT method, probably the

	Properties	1	2	3	4	5	6	7
Entities		Name	Credits	Salary	Vacation	Type of	Penalty	Type of viol
1	Staff	1		1				
2	Student	1	1					
3	Vacations student	1	1	1	1			
4	Training staff	1	1	1		1		
5	Bad staff	1		1				1
6	Bad student	1	1				1	1

Fig. 4.2. Binary matrix representing the relationship R between Entities and their properties.

a binary matrix which expresses the relationship between entities and their attributes and methods (see fig. 4.2).

This example is taken from [29] and [25]. It concerns the payment and fraud for staff and students.

Heuristics of the RDBR allow us to classify automatically all entities according into their common properties and obtain a set of optimal Rectangles. An optimal rectangle could be interpreted as a cluster where we find all entities which share the same properties. It is interesting to remark that the number of Optimal rectangles generated by RDBR is less than the number of maximal rectangles which constitutes the nodes of a Galois Lattice generated by Godin algorithm [29] corresponding for the same example (see following results).

The Minimal Cover obtained by RDBR is : MC ={ ({3},{1,2,3,4}), ({4},{1,2,3,5}), ({6},{1,2,6,7}), ({5,6},{1,7}) , ({2,3,4,6},{1,2}), ({1,3,4,5},{1,3})}.

However, using Godin algorithm, we obtain the following set of maximal rectangles:

{(({3},{1,2,3,4}), ({4},{1,2,3,5}), ({6},{1,2,6,7}), ({5,6},{1,7}) , ({2,3,4,6},{1,2}), ({1,3,4,5},{1, 3}), (**{1,3,4,5,6},{1}**), (**{3,4},{1,2,3}**), (**{5},{1,3,7}**))}.

These results shows nine nodes of Galois Lattice provided by Godin algorithm. With RDBR, we avoid the redundancy represented by three rectangles written in bold . Furthermore, we ensure that we do not lose information because RDBR computes the minimal cover of R. Another advantage of our method is that we realise an important gain in storage space when the cardinality of the binary relation is high. The proof that we obtain all times better results (in relation to the number of nodes) than methods used for generating Galois Lattice is expressed by the fact, that from a set of maximal rectangles which contains the same couple (a , b), we extract only the maximal rectangle which ensures maximal gain as is shown in section 3.4. In the bad case, we have for a given couple (a , b) of R only one maximal rectangle. Then the minimal cover of R is a set of maximal rectangles which could be organised into a Galois Lattice.

4.2 CONSTRUCTION OF THE BRUT INHERITANCE GRAPH (BIG)

The algorithm for building the Brut Inheritance Graph is presented. First, BIG means an optimal rectangular graph as defined in section 3.8 without infimum and is acyclic. From the set of optimal rectangles, we construct a graph where their nodes are the Optimal Rectangles and the links represent the partial order relation between them. We do not take into account links between the infimum and optimal rectangles, because the inheritance hierarchy can be represented as a tree and forms an acyclic graph [22].

In the BIG algorithm, we have 2 steps:
1. We organise all optimal optimal rectangles into a list of levels according into the cardinality of their domains;

```
Algorithm Brut_Inheritance_Graph (Set_of_Opt_Rectangles);/* BIG */
/*R: initial binary Relation */
BEGIN
    FOR ALL Opt_Rect in Set_of_Opt_Rectangles DO        /* Opt_Rect : Optimal Rectangle */
        IF Cardinality(Opt_Rect .Dom) NOT EXIST in  Cardinality_List /*Dom: Domain */
            THEN  Insert Cardinality(Opt_Rect.Dom) into Cardinality_List
        Insert Opt_Rect Into List_of_Opt_Rect _with_ Cardinality(Opt_Rect.Dom)
    NEXT
    Insert Supremum  Into List_of_Opt_Rect _with_ Cardinality(R.Dom)
                            /* R: initial Binary Relation */
                            /* Last_Level means level of the supremum */
    FOR Level_x:= First_Level TO Previous(Last_Level) DO
      FOR all Opt_Rect of Level_x DO
            FOR Level_y:= Next(Level_x) TO Last_Level DO
                FOR all Opt_Rect of Level_y DO
                    IF (Opt_Rect _x ≤≤ Opt_Rect _y) THEN
                        IF Level_x > first_Level then
                            IF list_Soon_of_ Opt_Rect _y is not empty
                                        Remove_cycle(Opt_Rect of Level_y,
                                        Opt_Rect of Level_x)
                            END-IF
                        END-IF
                        Link (Opt_Rect _x, Optimal_Rect _y)
                        Insert Id_Opt_Rect_x Into list_Soon_of_ Opt_Rect_y
                        Insert Id_Opt_Rect_y Into list_father_of_ Opt_Rect_x
                    END-IF
                END-FOR
            END-FOR
      END-FOR
    END-FOR
END. /*End of BIG */

Procedure Remove_cycle (Opt_Rect of Level_y, Opt_Rect of Level_x)
BEGIN
      FOR all Id_Opt_Rect in list_Soon_of_ Opt_Rect _y DO
            IF Id_Opt_Rect Exists in list_Soon_of_ Opt_Rect _x THEN
                    Remove_link (Id_Opt_Rect, Opt_Rect_y)
            END-IF
      NEXT
END.
```

2. We generate links between optimal rectangles using the partial order relation and avoiding the cyclic links.

The study of the complexity of this algorithm shows that it is in $O(n2)$ order. Unfortunately, it is not incremental, but some work is in progress. We did not use Godin or Bordat algorithms [8] which are incremental because they generate maximal rectangles that are different from the notion of Optimal rectangle.

4.3. SIMPLIFICATION OF THE BRUT INHERITANCE GRAPH (BIG)

After the generation of BIG shown in fig. 4.3, we remark that there are some necessary simplifications because for a given optimal rectangle (A,B) is included in another Optimal Rectangle (A', B') as defined in section 3.7, it is not necessary to have some redundancy such as elements of A, which are also in A' and elements in B'

294

which are also in B. The simplification consists into the deletion of elements of A
from A' and elements of B' from B, because they can be generated dynamically,
knowing that the optimal rectangle (A,B) is included in the optimal rectangle (A', B').
This operation is done on all levels of the BIG (see algorithm Simplify_BIG). As a
result we obtain an Optimal Inheritance Graph (see fig. 4.3 after removing elements in
bold).

```
Algorithm Simplify_BIG
BEGIN
   FOR k := First_Level TO Previous(Last_Level) DO
      FOR ALL Optimal_Rect_of_level_k DO
         Temp_Dom_Opt_rect_k := Optimal_Rect_of_level_k.Dom
         Temp_Range_Opt_rect_k := Optimal_Rect_of_level_k.Range
      NEXT
   END-FOR
   FOR k := First_Level TO Previous(Last_Level) DO
      FOR ALL Optimal_Rect_of_level_k DO
         FOR ALL Id_Opt_Rect_Father in list_father_of_ Opt_Rect_k DO
            Temp_Dom_Opt_rect_Father := Temp_Dom_Opt_rect_Father -
                                    (intersect(Temp_Dom_Opt_rect_Father
                                    Opt_Rect_k.Dom)
            Temp_Range_Opt_rect_k := Temp_Range_Opt_rect_k -
                                    (intersect(Temp_Range_Opt_rect_k,
                                    Opt_Rect_Father.Range)
         NEXT
      NEXT
   END-FOR
   FOR k := First_Level TO Previous(Last_Level) DO
      FOR ALL Optimal_Rect_of_level_k DO
         Optimal_Rect_of_level_k.Dom:= Temp_Dom_Opt_rect_k
         Optimal_Rect_of_level_k.Range:= Temp_Range_Opt_rect_k
      NEXT
   END-FOR
END. / * End of Simplify_BIG*/
```

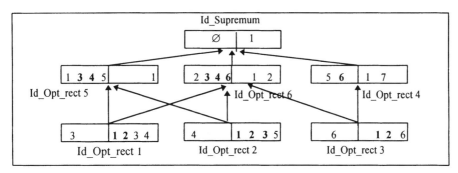

Fig. 4.3. Brut inheritance Graph

4.4. DESIGNER FEEDBACK

The difficult task of the designer in now reduced to take decision in function of the cases found in the Optimal Inheritance Graph. We detect three cases :

1. The cardinality of an optimal rectangle is equal to 1, then we can consider that the name of this entity is the name the class which has properties (the range of this optimal rectangle);

2. The cardinality of an optimal rectangle is superior to 1 than we find two possibilities: (1) Elements of an optimal rectangle does not exists in another optimal rectangle (there is no intersection); then we interpret that one of these entities can represent the other and then is indicated as the name of the class. We call these entities Synonymous classes. (2) There is an intersection between the optimal rectangle domain and other optimal rectangle domain, then designer has to verify and resolve the problem illegitimate inheritance [2], which means same entities inherit different properties.

Other cases could appear, they remain in charge of the designer whose is able to decide which modifications are necessary in the graph and does them in a tabular manner in the initial binary matrix. After doing modifications (eg. add new class, remove a class, or properties) he can interact with the system as explained in the fig. 4.1 until he obtains a proper inheritance graph (see fig. 4.4).

In the example, the class Object which corresponds to the suppremum of the optimal inheritance graph has as a property "Name". This case occurs when all classes that are linked with Class object (Staff, Student, and Bad_staff) has common properties, they are placed into the range of the supremum.

```
Algorithm Designer_Feedback
BEGIN
        FOR x := First_Level TO Previous(Last_Level) DO
                FOR ALL Optimal_Rect_x DO
                        IF Cardinality (Optimal_Rect_x.Dom) > 1 THEN
                                Display "Synonimous Class"+ Optimal_Rect_x.Dom
                        END-IF
                NEXT
        NEXT
        FOR x := First_Level TO Previous(Last_Level) DO
                FOR ALL Optimal_Rect_x.Dom DO
                        FOR ALL Class of Optimal_Rect_x.Dom DO
                                IF Class Exist in List_Class THEN
                                        Class_Occurrency := Class_Occurrency + 1
                                ELSE
                                        Insert Class in List_Class
                                        Class_Occurrency := 1
                                END-IF
                        NEXT
                NEXT
        NEXT
        FOR ALL Class in List_Class DO
                IF Class_Occurrency > 1 THEN
                        Display "Illegal Inheritance" + Class
                END-IF
```
```
        NEXT
END. /* End of Designer_Feedback */
```

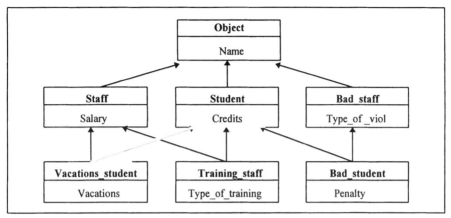

Fig. 4.4. Optimal Inheritance Graph.

5. CONCLUSION

We introduced a formal method for semi automatic generation of a proper inheritance Graph which represents the class hierarchy of an object oriented conceptual scheme. Our method has a mathematical foundation and allows us to obtain a number of classes less than the number of maximal rectangles given by methods which use Galois Lattice structure as a support. Some polynomial algorithms are introduced to generate, organise and clean Optimal Rectangles to construct a proper inheritance graph Hierarchy. The feedback of the designer which is crucial in the analysis and design steps is taken into account. It is interesting, if our algorithm of RDBR method and Optimal Graph construction are incremental such for Galois lattice construction by Bordat or Godin. This limitation constitutes one of our future work. The RDBR method is used in several domains such as Documentary database [15] and in Artificial Intelligence for automatic consensual rules from multiple experts [14].

6. BIBLIOGRAPHY

[1]   Ann L. Winblad, Samuel d. Edwaards, David R. King - "Object-Oriented Software": Addison-Wesley Publishing Company, Inc. 1990.

[2]   M. Armstrong ; Richard J. Mitchell, "Uses and Abuses of Inheritance"
       Journal Enginnering Software, Vol 9 Iss 1 19 - 26 pp., Jan 1994, Univ. UK

[3]   M. Barbut and B. Monjardet, "Ordre et classification", Algèbre et combinatoire, Tome II, 1970, Hachette.

[3]   H. Belaid and Ali Jaoua, "Abstraction of Objects by Conceptual Clustering", to appear in proceeding of Joint Conference on Information Sciences, 1997.

[4]   N. Belkhiter, C. Bourhfir, M.M. Gammoudi, A. Jaoua, N. Le Thanh, M. Reguig, "Architecture rectangulaire optimale d'une base documentaire indexée", Université Laval, Département d'Informatique (Rapport de Recherche), DIUL-RR-9201, 1992.

[5]   N. Belkhiter, C. Bourhfir, M.M. Gammoudi, A. Jaoua, N. Le Thanh, M. Reguig, "Décomposition Rectangulaire Optimale d'une Relation Binaire: Application aux Bases de Données Documentaires" Information Systems and Operational Research Journal, Février 32 (1): 33-54, 1994.

[6]   N. Belkhiter, J. Desharnais, G. Ennis, A. Jaoua, H. Ounalli, M.M. Gammoudi, "Formal Properties of Rectangular Relations", in Proceeding of the Ninth International Symposium on Computer and Information Science, ISCIS IX, Antalya, Turkey, November 7-9, 1994.

[7]   Booch Grady, "Object-Oriented Analisys and Design with Applications", Second Edition - The Benjamin/Cummings Publishing Company, Inc.1994.

[8]   J.P. Bordat, "Sur l'algorithmique combinatoire d'ordre finis", Thèse de Doctorat d'état mention Sciences de l'Université de Montpellier II, (USTL), 29 avril 1992.

[9]   John Daniels, "Objects Design Methods and Tools", IEEE London, UK, 1994 24 pp.

[10]   Ding-An Chiang ; Ming-Chi Lee, "Cyclic Inheritance Detection for Object-Oriented Database", IEEE New York, NY, USA, Vol 2 1047 pp., 1992, Univ. TAIWAM.

[11]   Chi-Ming Chung;   Lee M. C, "Inheritance-Based Object-Oriented Software Metrics", IEEE New York, NY , USA, 1992 Vol 2   1047 pp.

[12]   Chi-Ming Chung ; Chun-Chi Wang, Ming-Chi Lee , "Class Hierarchy Based Metric for Object-Oriented Design", IEEE New York, NY , USA, 1994 Vol 2 xxvii+1111 pp.

[13]   M. M Gammoudi. "Méthode de décomposition rectangulaire d'une relation binaire: une base formelle et uniforme pour le génération automatique des thesaurus et la recherche documentaire, Thèse de doctorat, Université de Nice Sofia Antipolis, Septembre 1993.

[14]   M.M. Gammoudi and S. Labidi "An Automatic Generation of Consensual Rules Between Experts Using Rectangular Decomposition of a Binary relation", in Proceeding of the XI Brazilian Symposium on Artificial Intelligence, Fortaleza, October 1994.

[15]   M.M. Gammoudi "heuristics for Clustering Method and Its use in Information Retieval System", in Proceeding of the International Conference SCCC'96, Valdivia, Chile, November 1996.

[16]   B. Ganter, "Two Basic Algorithms in Concept Analysis", Preprint 831, Technische Hochschule Darmstad, p. 28, 1984.

[17]   M. R. Garay, D. S. Jonhson, "Computer and Interactability : A guide of the theory of NP-Completeness.", W. H. Freeman, 1979.

[18]   R. Godin, Rokia Missaoui, Hassan Alaoui, "leraning Algorithms Using a Galois Lattice Structure", in Proceedings of the 1991 IEEE Int. Conf. On Tools for AI, San Jose CA-Nov, 1991

[19]   R. Godin and H. Mili, "Buildind and Maintaining analysis-level class hierarchies using Galois Lattice", OOPSLA-93 Washington DC, USA Oct 1993 ACM press pp. 394 - 410.

[20]   R. Godin and H. Mili, "Conceptual Clustering Methods based on Galois lattice ans aplications", French Revew on Artificial Intelligence, Vol 9 N 2, 1995 pp. 105- 137.

[21]   A. Guenoche, "Construction du treillis de Galois d'une relation binaire", *Math. Inf. Sci. hum.*, 28ème année, (109) : 41-53, 1990.

[22]   Jean, Mayrand and Guay, François and M. Merlo, Ettore. "Inheritance Graph Assessment Using Metrics", Proceedings of METRICS '96, 1996 IEEE.

[23]   E.M. Norris, "An algorithm for Computing the Maximal Rectangles in a Binary Relation", *Revue Roumaine de Mathématiques Pures et Appliquées*, 23(2) p. 243-250, 1978.

[24]   R. E. Stepp and R. S. Michalski, "Conceptual clustering: inventing goal-oriented classifications of structured objects", R. Michalski, J. Carbonnel, and T. Mitchell, (eds)., machine learning: An I.A. Approach. San Mateo, Calif. Morgan Kauffmann, 1986.

[25]   I. Schmitt and G. Saake, "Integration of inheritance trees as part of view generation for database federations", In proceeding of the 15th International Conference on Conceptual Modelling - ER'96. Cottbus, Germany, 7th - 10th October 1996, B. Thalheim (Ed.), LNCS No 1157, pp. 195-210.

[26]   Wei Sun ; Sha Guo ; Farah Arafi ; Shengru Tu, "Supporting Inheritance in Relational Database", IEEE Computing Soc. Press, Los Alamitos, CA , USA, 1992, xi+641 pp.

[27]   R. Wille, "Finite Distributive Lattices as Concept Lattices",
Atti Inc. Logica Matematica, (2) 1985.

[28]   R. Wille, "Knowledge Acquisition by Methods of Formal Comcept Analysis",
In E. Diday (Eds). Data Analysis, Learning Symbolic and Numeric Knowledge, New York : Nova Science, 1989.

[29]   A. Yahia, L. Lakhal, and Jean Paul Bordat, "Designing Class Hierarchies of Object Databse Schema", To appear in the Computer journal, 1997.

Towards an Object Database Approach for Managing Concept Lattices

Kitsana Waiyamai, Rafik Taouil and Lotfi Lakhal

Université Blaise Pascal – Clermont-Ferrand II,
Laboratoire d'Informatique (LIMOS), Complexe Scientifique des cézeaux,
24, av. des Landais, 63177 Aubière Cedex, France

Abstract. The concept lattice is a conceptual model firstly introduced by Wille in *formal concept analysis,* a theory of concept formation derived from lattice and order theory. Various concept lattice based applications have been reported in several domains such as conceptual clustering, conceptual knowledge representation and acquisition, and information retrieval. In this paper, we propose an object database approach for managing concept lattices in these applications. The goal of our work is two-fold. First, we extend the concept lattice model by basic operations supporting concept analysis. These operations allow to search and discover data directly from the concept lattice. Then, we present an approach for modeling and querying concept lattices within an object database framework.

1 Introduction

The concept lattice is a formal conceptual model firstly introduced by Wille [19] in *formal concept analysis* to represent the concepts' philosophical notions and their hierarchy. Various concept lattice based applications have been reported in the literatures. They are conceptual clustering [7], knowledge representation and acquisition [20, 21], knowledge discovery in databases [12], and information retrieval [13, 7]. However, all these research works are domain dependent. In our knowledge, there are also other three domain independent systems that have been proposed to support concept analysis: *Toscana* [17], *ConImp* [6], and *Tk-Concept* [15]. An abstraction mechanism, implemented in these systems provides the application designers with the ability to define and manipulate various kinds of concept lattices, and also helps them to concentrate on the domain specific part of such applications. However, searches in these systems, as well as in the above mentioned applications, are not done in a uniform way since sometimes they need to be performed from the context, sometimes from the concept lattice. For this reason, both context and its concept lattice often need to be stored. Moreover, none of these approaches addresses the problem of storing and accessing concept lattices using object database technology. In particular, in existing systems, concept lattices are often stored in files, and they are lack of sophisticated querying mechanisms. To manage complex and large size lattices, what is need is efficient tools, such as high level declarative query languages which provide users object description and manipulation languages.

In this paper, we propose an object database approach for managing concept lattices in concept lattice based applications. We are convinced that OODBMS technologies can bring a lot of benefit to concept analysis, e.g., object-modeling, high level declarative query languages, large databases of complex objects, persistence support. Our approach is related to recent works using database technology for advanced applications such as those of Abiteboul et al. [2], Cicchetti & Lakhal [9], Abiteboul et al. [1] and Gardarin & Yoon [11], concerning object database management of respectively files, statistical tables, structured documents, and hypermedia documents. While these research works have extended the query facilities for various data structures, they do not allow managing large amounts of data organized into concept lattices.

The goal of the work presented in this paper is two-fold. First, we extend the concept lattice model with basic operations supporting concept analysis, expressed directly on the concept lattice [18]. Second, we present an object database modeling and querying of concept lattices. Object database generic and specific schemas supported by the O_2 data model [14] for representing concept lattices, and an object query language $COQL$ based on the extensibility of OQL [3] are presented. The proposed concept lattice operations are considered as methods of generic classes in the object generic schema. Several examples of queries illustrate, from a practical point of view, the expressive power of the COQL language to search and discover, in a flexible manner, the concepts, entities and properties in the concept lattice. Throughout the paper, the context of an educational film "Living Beings and Water" [20] is used as an example, where living beings and their properties are considered as entities and properties of the concept lattice.

The rest of the paper is organized as follows: Section 2, gives a formal definition of the concept lattice model. The concept lattice model is then extended with basic operations supporting formal concept analysis. Section 3, introduces the O_2concept generic database schema for representing concept lattice, and presents an O_2concept specific database schema of concept lattice based applications. Section 4, describes the COQL language with examples of querying concepts, entities and properties of the concept lattice. Section 5, concludes the paper and presents future work.

2 Extending Concept Lattice Model

In this section, we first give a formal definition of the concept lattice model. We then extend it with basic operations supporting concept analysis, expressed directly on the concept lattice.

2.1 Concept Lattice Model

The *concept lattice model* is a form of knowledge representation that attempts to model the world as being composed of *entities* and *properties* within a specific *context*. From the context, the *concept lattice* is generated, where *concepts* are constructed as being subsets of entities and properties based on the notion of

Galois connection. Based on its structure, we try to interpret the dependencies between entities, properties, and both of them. Below, we give the basic definitions of *context*, *Galois connection*, *formal concept*, and *concept lattice*. For further details of this theory, reader who interests should consult [19, 10, 21].

Formal Context. *A formal context is a triple $(\mathcal{E}, \mathcal{P}, \mathcal{R})$, where $\mathcal{E}$ and $\mathcal{P}$ are finite sets of entities and properties, $\mathcal{R} \subseteq \mathcal{E} \times \mathcal{P}$ is a binary relation. We denote as $e\mathcal{R}p$ when the entity $e \in \mathcal{E}$ is in relation $\mathcal{R}$ to the property $p \in \mathcal{P}$, if the entity e has the property p (or the entity e verifies the property p).*

Example 1. In Table 1, the binary relation of the context which contains the basic knowledge underlying an educational film on "Living Beings and Waters" [20] is represented through a matrix. This matrix captures the relationships between eight entities (living beings) and their properties. The ith entity verifying the jth property is denoted by "1" at the case ij^{th} of the matrix, when a given entity has a given property. For instance, the "bream(br)" has four properties which are "needs water(A)", "lives in water(B)", "can move about(G)" and "has limbs(H)".

Table 1. Matrix representation of the binary relation of the context "Living Beings and Water".

entities(abbreviation)	A	B	C	D	E	F	G	H	I
leech(le)	1	1					1		
bream(br)	1	1					1	1	
frog(fr)	1	1	1				1	1	
dog(do)	1		1				1	1	1
spike-weed(sw)	1	1		1	1				
reed(re)	1	1	1	1		1			
bean(be)	1		1	1	1				
maize(ma)	1		1	1		1			

The properties have the following meaning: A:needs water, B:lives in water, C:lives on land, D:needs a chlorophyll to prepare food, E:two little leaves grow on germinating, F: one little leave grows on germinating, G:can move about, H:has limbs, I:suckels its offsprings.

Galois Connection. *Let $(\mathcal{E}, \mathcal{P}, \mathcal{R})$ be a formal context. For $E \subseteq \mathcal{E}$ and $P \subseteq \mathcal{P}$, we define $f(E) = \{p \in \mathcal{P} \mid \forall e \in E \cdot e\mathcal{R}p\}$, and conversely $g(P) = \{e \in \mathcal{E} \mid \forall p \in P \cdot e\mathcal{R}p\}$. That is, $f(E)$ is the set of all properties common to all entities in E, and $g(P)$ is the set of all entities which have all properties in P. The pair (f, g) forms a Galois connection between $2^{\mathcal{E}}$ and $2^{\mathcal{P}}$.*

Formal Concept. *A formal concept is a pair (Extent, Intent) where Extent $\subseteq \mathcal{E}$, Intent $\subseteq \mathcal{P}$ and $f(Extent) = Intent$ and $g(Intent) = Extent$. Let L be a set of all concepts formed from the formal context $(\mathcal{E}, \mathcal{P}, \mathcal{R})$, and let $c \in L$. Hence, c is formed by two parts: an extent represents a subset of entities, denoted as*

$Extent(c)$, and an intent represents the common characteristics between this subset of entities, denoted as $Intent(c)$.

Example 2. ({re,fr},{A,C,B}) is a concept of the binary relation in Table 1 where its extent is corresponding to {re,fr} and its intent is {A,C,B}. This means the fact that, there are no more than two living beings possessing *at least* all properties in {A,C,B} and sharing *at most* these properties in common.

Concept Lattice. *A concept lattice* $\mathcal{L} = (\mathcal{L}, \leq)$ *of a formal context* $(\mathcal{E}, \mathcal{P}, \mathcal{R})$, *is a complete lattice of formal concepts derived from the formal context. The lattice structure imposes:*

- *a partial order on concepts such that, for concepts* $c_1, c_2 \in \mathcal{L}$, $c_1 \leq c_2$, *iff* $Extent(c_1) \subseteq Extent(c_2)$ *(or, equivalently* $Intent(c_2) \subseteq Intent(c_1)$*),*
- *any concept subset of* $\mathcal{L}$ *has one greatest subconcept (the Meet element) and one least superconcept (the Join element).*

Theorem. *Let* $(\mathcal{E}, \mathcal{P}, \mathcal{R})$ *be a formal context, let* $\mathcal{L}$ *be a concept lattice of formal concepts derived from* $(\mathcal{E}, \mathcal{P}, \mathcal{R})$ *and* $S \subseteq \mathcal{L}$. *The* $Meet(1)$ *and* $Join(2)$ *elements are given as follows [19, 10, 21]:*

$$Meet(S) = (\bigcap_{c \in S} Extent(c), \ f(g(\bigcup_{c \in S} Intent(c)))) \tag{1}$$

$$Join(S) = (g(f(\bigcup_{c \in S} Extent(c))), \ \bigcap_{c \in S} Intent(c)) \tag{2}$$

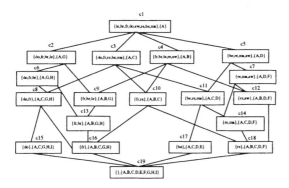

Fig. 1. Hasse diagram representing the concept lattice of the context in Table 1.

In a traditional representation for a concept lattice called the *Hasse diagram* (a *graph-oriented representation*) of lattice, nodes represent concepts and edges represent the sub-superconcept (specialization-generalization) relationship, forming hierarchy of concepts. An example of a Hasse diagram corresponding to our example is shown in Fig. 1.

2.2 Concept Lattice operations

In the following, we will first introduce the notion of *lattice Galois connection* (*Pconnect, Econnect*), equivalent to the *Galois connection* (f, g). Then a set of lattice operations reconsidered from partially ordered set operations are given.

Lattice Galois Connection. A concept lattice is derived from a context through which entities and properties are connected. Traditionally, entities connected to the set of properties, and conversely properties connected to the set of entities, are queried using the *Galois connection* (f, g). Since, these two functions are defined based on the context, all search operations cannot be done directly from the concept lattice but via the context which needs to be stored.

Here, we introduce the notion of *lattice Galois connection* (*Pconnect, Econnect*) equivalent to the Galois connection (f, g). The couple of connection functions are defined directly on the concept lattice without taking into account the context. The properties connected to the entity subset E, denoted as $Pconnect(E)$, are computed by joining the intents of all concepts containing at least the given subset E. In the same way, finding all entities connected to the property subset P, denoted as $Econnect(P)$ can be computed by joining the extents of all concepts containing at least the given subset P :

$$Pconnect(E) = \bigcup\nolimits_{c \in \{c \in \mathcal{L} \mid E \subseteq \mathrm{Extent}(c)\}} Intent(c),$$
$$Econnect(P) = \bigcup\nolimits_{c \in \{c \in \mathcal{L} \mid P \subseteq \mathrm{Intent}(c)\}} Extent(c)$$

Notice that $Pconnect(\emptyset) = \mathcal{P}$ is the set of all properties of the lattice, and $Econnect(\emptyset) = \mathcal{E}$, is the set of all entities of the lattice.

Proposition. *Let $K = (\mathcal{E}, \mathcal{P}, \mathcal{R})$ be a formal context, and (f, g) the Galois connection of K. Let $\mathcal{L}$ be a concept lattice derived from K, and (Pconnect, Econnect) the lattice Galois connection of $\mathcal{L}$. We have the following equalities $Pconnect(E) = f(E)$ and $Econnect(P) = g(P)$, for $E \subseteq \mathcal{E}$ and $P \subseteq \mathcal{P}$. The proof of this proposition is given in [18].*

Example 3. $Pconnect(\{\mathrm{sw,ma}\}) = \{\mathrm{A,D,F}\}$. This means the fact that *"needs water"*, *"needs a chlorophyll to prepare food"* and *"one little leave grows on germinating"* are common properties of *"spike-weed"*, and *"maize"*.

Lattice Operations. In the following, partially ordered set operations are expressed using the lattice Galois connection previously defined. These operations allow to search concepts within a sub-superconcept hierarchy.

UB: *Upper Bound.* Let $\mathcal{L}$ be a concept lattice, and $S \subseteq \mathcal{L}$. A concept $c' \in \mathcal{L}$ is a *superconcept* of S iff $Extent(c) \subseteq Extent(c')$ (or equivalently, $Intent(c') \subseteq Intent(c)$) for all $c \in S$. The set of common superconcepts to all concepts from S is denoted by $UB(S)$:

$$UB(S) = \{c' \in \mathcal{L} \mid (\forall c \in S) \; Extent(c) \subseteq Extent(c')\}$$
$$= \{c' \in \mathcal{L} \mid (\forall c \in S) \; Intent(c') \subseteq Intent(c)\}$$

LB: *Lower Bound.* Let $\mathcal{L}$ be a concept lattice, and $S \subseteq \mathcal{L}$. A concept $c' \in \mathcal{L}$ is a *subconcept* of S iff $Extent(c) \supseteq Extent(c')$ (or equivalently, $Intent(c') \supseteq Intent(c)$) for all $c \in S$. The set of common subconcepts to all concepts from S is denoted by $LB(S)$:

$$LB(S) = \{c' \in \mathcal{L} \mid (\forall c \in S) \; Extent(c) \supseteq Extent(c')\}$$
$$= \{c' \in \mathcal{L} \mid (\forall c \in S) \; Intent(c') \supseteq Intent(c)\}$$

Join. Let $\mathcal{L}$ be a concept lattice, and $S \subseteq \mathcal{L}$. The *Join* of concepts in S is the smallest common superconcept of all concepts from S. Its intent (the common properties of all concepts in S) is obtained by intersecting the intents of all concepts from S, while its extent is determined by finding all entities connected to all properties of the intent:

$$Join(S) = (Econnect(\bigcap_{c \in S} Intent(c)), \bigcap_{c \in S} Intent(c))$$

Meet. Let $\mathcal{L}$ be a concept lattice, and $S \subseteq \mathcal{L}$. The *Meet* of concepts in S is the greatest common subconcept of all concepts from S. Its extent (the common entities of all concepts in S) is obtained by intersecting the extents of all concepts from S, while its intent is determined by finding all properties connected to all entities of the extent:

$$Meet(S) = (\bigcap_{c \in S} Extent(c), Pconnect(\bigcap_{c \in S} Extent(c)))$$

Example 4. $UB(\{c_{16}, c_{17}, c_{18}\}) = \{c_1, c_3\}$ represents the set of superconcepts common to $\{c_{16}, c_{17}, c_{18}\}$, and $Join(\{c_{16}, c_{17}, c_{18}\}) = \{c_3\}$ is the smallest common superconcept of $\{c_{16}, c_{17}, c_{18}\}$.

3 Object Modeling of Concept Lattices

In this section, we consider the representation of concept lattices in the O_2 database system. We choose O_2 [4] because it is fully ODMG compliant [8] and in particular it is the first system that supports the ODMG query language OQL which can easily be extended. The object database generic schema called O_2 *Concept Generic Database Schema* which is supported by the O_2 data model [14] is proposed. Concept lattice structure is supported by O_2 concepts such as *inheritance* and *object identity* (OID), and O_2 object constructors such as *Set* and *Tuple*. In particular, the notion of object identity provided by the O_2 data model is very useful for the representation of concepts (as O_2 objects) because of the references to the entities and properties they possess. In the O_2 concept database schema, concept lattice operations are considered as methods in generic classes. Also, integrity constraints are introduced to capture concept lattice structure. This O_2concept generic schema is then integrated in an O_2 database schema of any concept lattice based application. The inheritance mechanism between application classes and generic classes of the generic schema is utilized to allow generic properties of concept lattices to be reused in application classes.

In the following, we first present the O_2concept generic database schema. Then an O_2concept specific database schema for concept lattice based applications is given. Translation from the concept lattice of the context "Living Beings and Water" into corresponding O_2 objects illustrates our modeling approach.

3.1 O_2 Concept Generic Database Schema

Let us first recall the formal definition of an O_2 *database schema*. An O_2 database schema is a representation of the structure, semantics, and constraints on the use of a database in the O_2 data model. Formal definition of an O_2 database schema is given in [18]. As described in the Sect. 3, there are two main components of concept lattice: the first one is the context from which a concept lattice is derived and the second one is the concept lattice structure. Here, the representation of the context is not considered, because it is not stored. All searches can be done directly from the concept lattice using the notion of lattice Galois connection (as described in 2.2). We propose to model concept lattice with two classes: the *GenConcept class* defines the type of formal concepts, and the *GenConceptLattice class* models the concept lattice structure. Let us look in more detail their descriptions:

GenConcept Class. A tuple constructor is used to represent a formal concept. A formal concept consists of a name, an extent, and an intent. Concept's name is defined as a string of characters. Concept's extent is a set of entities sharing a set of properties, represented by a set of references (object identifiers) pointing to instances of the O_2 *Object* class. Concept's intent is a set of properties sharing a set of entities, represented by a set of references pointing to instances of the O_2 *Object* class. It should be noted that, all O_2 classes inherit implicitly to the root class *Object*. Hence, in application specific classes, the O_2 generic *Object* class can be specialized to define specific types of entities or properties. Description of the *GenConcept* class using O_2C syntax is given in Fig. 2.

```
class GenConcept inherit Object public type
    tuple(name  : string,
          extent: unique set(Object),
          intent: unique set(Object))
end;
```

Fig. 2. O_2 definition of the *GenConcept* class.

GenConceptLattice Class. The *GenConceptLattice* class models a concept lattice as a complex object having its name and its set of concepts corresponding to a set of objects of *GenConcept* class. This means the fact that each concept in the lattice is represented as an O_2 object (object concept). Concept lattice operations we have defined previously (cf. 2.2) are considered as methods and implemented in this class. A concept lattice can be represented as *GenConcept-Lattice* class without losing the lattice structure by integrating two integrity constraints into class. A more detailed description of *GenConceptLattice* class using O_2C syntax is given in Fig. 3.

```
class GenConceptLattice inherit Object public type
    tuple(name: string,
          concepts: unique set(GenConcept))
method
    public VerifyConcept(GenConcept): Boolean,
           /* for concept constraint checking */
    public VerifyLattice(unique set(GenConcept)): Boolean,
           /* for lattice constraint checking */
    public UB(ens_concept: unique set(GenConcept)): unique set(GenConcept),
    public LB(ens_concept: unique set(GenConcept)): unique set(GenConcept),
    public Meet(ens_concept: unique set(GenConcept)): GenConcept,
    public Join(ens_concept: unique set(GenConcept)): GenConcept,
    public Econnect (ens_obj: unique set(Object)): unique set(Object),
    public Pconnect (ens_obj: unique set(Object)): unique set(Object)
end;
```

Fig. 3. O_2 definition of the *GenConceptLattice* class.

Concept Lattice Constraints. Concepts are stored in a set. The set of concepts is maintained by two integrity constraints ensuring that the set represents a concept lattice. These constraints are:

- *Concept constraint*: verifies that each concept of the lattice must be a complete pair according to the lattice Galois connection,
- *Lattice constraint*: asserts that any concept subset of the lattice has one greatest subconcept (the Meet element) and one least superconcept (the Join element).

At the present time, the integrity constraints are not available in the O_2 DBMS. From now on, we consider that these constraints are implemented by methods, and the system possesses all necessary modeling primitives. Formal definition of an O_2 *concept generic database schema* is given in [18].

3.2 O_2 Concept Specific Database Schema

Once the concept generic database schema is defined, it can be integrated into a database schema of any specific concept lattice based application. All application specific concept classes will be subclasses of the *GenConcept* class, and all application specific concept lattice classes will be subclasses of the *GenConcept-Lattice* class. This means that, the generic *GenConcept* class can be specialized to define specific types of formal concepts, and the generic *GenConceptLattice* class can be specialized to define specific concept lattices. The inheritance mechanism ensures that all the inherited classes will have the set of attributes and methods defined in the O_2 concept database schema as their own properties.

To enter the database, O_2 *named (or top-level) objects* are used as persistence *entry points*. The named objects are defined as sets of objects of the application entity and property classes, and objects of the application concept lattice classes. From these named objects, sub-objects (i.e, lattice elements), can be requested and explored by method invocation or using appropriate query language. Formal definition of an O_2 *concept specific database schema* is given in [18].
According to the example, there are four application classes (as we have only one concept lattice) which are *Being, Property, BeingProperty* and *BeingProperty-Lattice*. These classes represent respectively, entity and property types, formal concept type, and the concept lattice. The O_2 database contains three named objects. They are labeled as *Beings, Properties* and *BPL. Beings* and *Properties* are persistence root representing the set of all living beings and properties in the database. *BPL* is a persistence root representing the concept lattice. Descriptions of classes and named objects are given in Fig. 4.

```
class Being inherit Object public type
    tuple(name: string)
end;
class Property inherit Object public type
    tuple(name: string)
end;
class BeingProperty inherit GenConcept public type
    tuple(extent: unique set(Being),
          intent: unique set(Property))
end;
class BeingPropertyLattice inherit GenConceptLattice public type
    tuple(concepts: unique set(BeingProperty))
end;
Name Beings : unique set(Being);
Name Properties : unique set(Property);
Name BPL : BeingPropertyLattice;
```

Fig. 4. An O_2 concept database schema for representing the concept lattice of the context "Living Beings and Water".

4 Object Querying of Concept Lattices

In the previous section we have explained how concept lattices can be represented as complex objects in the O_2 object database. Once this is done the concept lattices can be queried using a high level object query language. Conventional query languages lack features that are essential for accessing lattice concepts such as partially ordered set operators and lattice Galois connection dealing with both entity and property access. To fit these needs, we extend the OQL [3] query language with the proposed concept lattice operations. OQL includes many useful primitives for querying concept lattices such as *select-from-where* clause, and set operators. Its semantics relies on a functional approach. OQL is defined by a set of basic operators and a way of building new operators through compositions and iterators. Thus, to enrich the set of predefined operators of the language, we rather to add new operators through methods [5]. Here, the concept lattice methods are defined and implemented in the *GenConceptLattice* class. The resulting query language called *COQL* allows complex selection and retrieval of lattice elements by retrieving them directly from the concept lattice without the presence of the context in a flexible manner.

In the following, we illustrate the expressive power of COQL language with example queries through the use of concept lattice operators we have implemented. This language provides (i) concept retrieval (ii) entity-property retrieval (iii) entity implications and property implications. We believe that these functionalities are useful for a variety of concept lattice based applications in an object database environment. The running example using the O_2 database is given in Fig. 4.

4.1 Querying Concepts

In this subsection, several examples of queries illustrate the functionalities of the language to retrieve lattice concepts. We illustrate the COQL queries exploring sub-superconcept hierarchy of concepts. This kind of queries will use the lattice operations previously defined.

The following query uses a *select-from-where* clause to retrieve concepts according to a given condition. The *where* clause is used to select the set of all concepts containing at least a given entity subset (or, a given property subset) in their extent (resp. their intent), and the *select* clause returns the corresponding concepts.

Query 1 Find all concepts containing at least "spike-weed(sw)","reed(re)" and "maize(ma)" in their extent.

```
select tuple(Extent: (select b.name
                      from b in Beings
                      where b in c.extent),
             Intent: (select p.name
                      from p in Properties
                      where p in c.intent))
from c in BPL.concepts
```

```
where (select b
       from b in Beings
       where b.name in set("spike-weed","reed","maize")) <= c.extent;
                           /* <= is an O2 set inclusion operator */
```

Query 2 Find the greatest common subconcept of all concepts that contain at least "bream(br)" in their extent.

```
/* element is an O2 operator for extracting the element of a singleton */
element(select c.name
        from c in BPL.Meet(select distinct c'
                           from c' in BPL.concepts
                           where (select b
                                  from b in Beings
                                  where b.name = "bream") <= c'.extent));
```

4.2 Querying entities and properties

In concept lattice based applications such as information retrieval and conceptual knowledge representation, we often need to access entities and properties of the lattice. In this subsection, several examples to query connections between entities and their properties, implications between properties and implications between entities are given.

Entity-property Retrieval. In the following, we give some COQL examples using lattice Galois connection to query the relationships between entities and properties of the lattice.

Query 3 Which are the common properties of "spike-weed(sw)" and "maize(ma)" ?

```
select p.name
from p in Properties
where p in BPL.Pconnect(select b
                       from b in Beings
                       where b.name in set("spike-weed","maize"));
```

Query 4 Which living beings "live in water(B)" and "on land(C)", that need "chlorophyll to prepare food(D)" or "suckle their offsprings(I)" ?

```
select b.name
from b in Beings
where b in (BPL.Econnect(select p
                        from p in Properties
                        where p.name in set("B","C"))
            intersect  (BPL.Econnect(select p
                                     from p in Properties
                                     where p.name = "D")
            union
```

```
BPL.Econnect(select p
             from p in Properties
             where p.name = "I")));
```

According to the above queries, it should be noted that COQL allows combination of operations to be used in query expressions, each method produces a result which can be used in another query.

Entity Implications and Property Implications. The concept lattice provides a basic analysis of a context (i.e., connection between entities and their properties), and an appropriate classification of entities (i.e., entities sharing a common set of properties are placed in the same concept). As noticed by Wille [19], a concept lattice can also be viewed as a representation of all implications between properties (via its intents) or between entities (via its extents). A *property implication* of a context $(\mathcal{E}, \mathcal{P}, \mathcal{R})$ is a pair of subsets of $\mathcal{P}$, denoted by $P_1 \to P_2$, for which $g(P_1) \subseteq g(P_2)$, i.e., each entity from $\mathcal{E}$ having all properties of P_1 has also all properties of P_2. An *entity implication* which is a pair of subsets of $\mathcal{E}$, denoted by $E_1 \to E_2$, is defined dually, i.e. each property from $\mathcal{P}$ which is common to all entities of E_1 is also common to all entities of E_2. By using the lattice Galois connection, the implication relations between the properties, and implication relations between the entities can be expressed as follows:

$$\forall P_1, P_2 \subseteq \mathcal{P}, \ P_1 \to P_2 \text{ iff } Econnect(P_1) \subseteq Econnect(P_2)$$
$$\forall E_1, E_2 \subseteq \mathcal{E}, \ E_1 \to E_2 \text{ iff } Pconnect(E_1) \subseteq Pconnect(E_2)$$

The following queries illustrate the power of COQL language to query implications between entities and between properties directly from the lattice.

Query 5 Does the properties which are common to "leech(le)" are also common to "frog(fr)" ?

```
BPL.Pconnect(select distinct b
             from b in Beings
             where b.name = "leech")
<= /* <= is an O2 set inclusion operator */
BPL.Pconnect(select distinct b
             from b in Beings
             where b.name = "frog");
```

Given such a query, the lattice will be browsed to check whether a given implication rule holds. The above query returns *true*, i.e. all properties which are common to *"leech(le)"* are also common to *"frog(fr)"*.

Query 6 Which properties are implied by the "has limbs(H)" property ?

```
select x.name
from x in Properties
where BPL.Econnect(select p
             from p in Properties
             where p.name = "H") < BPL.Econnect(unique set(x));
                   /* < is an O2 set inclusion operator */
```

This query returns the property subset {G,A}. This means that all living beings which *"have limbs(H)"*, they also *"need water(A)"* and *"can move about(G)"*. Such an implication can be also interpreted as *"has limbs(H)"* is the specialization of the properties *"need water(A)"* and *"can move about(G)"*.

5 Conclusion and Future Work

We have presented an approach using object database technology to manage data organized into concept lattices. We pointed out some lacking features in existing systems supporting concept analysis, e.g., (i) the context needs to be taken into account in order to perform searches, (ii) concept lattices are often stored in files, and (iii) the lack of sophisticated querying mechanisms. To answer (i), we introduced the notion of lattice Galois connection equivalent to the Galois connection allowing relationship between entities and properties to be retrieved directly from the concept lattice without the presence of its context. Then, to answer (ii) and (iii), we presented a generic database schema for representing the concepts lattices together with the COQL query language (based on the extensibility of OQL) to query them. COQL query facilities are archived by providing partially ordered set operators UB, LB, Join and Meet and lattice Galois connection dealing with both entity and property access. We believe that these features are very useful for a variety of concept lattice based applications.

We are currently implementing the querying methods for concept lattices on the top of the O_2 DBMS, using the O_2C programming language. To generate O_2 schemas and instances from a given context, an object database version of the *incremental concept formation algorithm* [16] will be implemented. In the future, we plan to extend this work in two directions. First, to allow the evolution of concept lattice based applications, algorithms for updating the object concepts in the database must be defined. Second, an other key aspect we think to do is to provide the means to visualize the concept lattices through a graph-oriented representation (Hasse diagram).

Acknowledgment. Thanks to A. Rungsawang for his reading and comments of this paper.

References

1. S. Abiteboul, S. Cluet, V. Christophides, T. Milo, G. Moerkotte, and J. Siméon. Querying documents in object databases. *Int. J. of Digital Libraries*, 1996.
2. S. Abiteboul, S. Cluet, and T. Milo. Querying and updating the file. In *Proc. of the 19th Int. Conf. on Very Large Data Bases (VLDB'93)*, pages 73–84, 1993.
3. F. Bancilhon, S. Cluet, and C. Delobel. A Query Language for O_2. In F. Bancilhon, C. Delobel, and P. Kanellakis, editors, *Building an Object-Oriented Database System: The Story of O_2*, pages 234–255. Morgan Kaufmann, 1992.
4. F. Bancilhon, C. Delobel, and P. Kanellakis, editors. *Building an Object-Oriented Database System: The Story of O_2*. Morgan Kaufmann, 1992.

5. E. Bertino, M. Negri, G. Pelagatti, and L. Sbattella. Object-oriented query languages: The notion and the issues. *IEEE Trans. on Knowledge and Data Engineering*, 4(3):223–237, 1992.

6. P. Burmeister. Formal concept analysis with *ConImp*: Introduction to the basic features. Technical report, Darmstadt, Germany, 1996.

7. C. Carpineto and G. Romano. A lattice conceptual clustering and its application to browsing retrieval. *Machine Learning*, (24):95–122, 1996.

8. R.G.G. Cattell. *The Object Database Standard: ODMG-93*. Morgan Kaufmann, San Francisco, CA, 1994.

9. R. Cicchetti and L. Lakhal. Matrix relation for statistical database management. In *Proc. of the Int. Conf. on Extending Database Technology (EDBT'94)*, volume 779 of *LNCS*, pages 31–42, 1994.

10. B.A. Davey and H.A. Priestley. *Introduction to Lattices and Order*. Cambridge University Press, 1990.

11. G. Gardarin and S. Yoon. Object-oriented modeling and quering of hypermedia documents. In *Proc. of the 4th Int. Conf. on Database Systems for Advanced Applications (DASFAA'95)*, pages 441–448, 1995.

12. R. Godin and R. Missaoui. An incremental concept formation approach for learning from databases. *Theoretical Computer Science: Special Issue on Formal Methods in Databases and Software Engineering*, 133:387–419, 1994.

13. R. Godin, R. Missaoui, and A. April. Experimental comparaison of navigation in a Galois lattice with conventional information retrieval methods. *Int. J. of Man-Machine Studies*, 38:747–767, 1993.

14. C. Lécluse, P. Richard, and F. Vélez. O_2, an Object-Oriented Data Model. In F. Bancilhon, C. Delobel, and P. Kanellakis, editors, *Building an Object-Oriented Database System: The Story of O_2*, pages 77–97. Morgan Kaufmann, 1992.

15. C. Lindig. *TKConcept Documentation Manual*. Technical University of Braunschweig, 1996.

16. R. Taouil and L. Lakhal. Construction Incrémentale du Treillis de Galois (Concepts) d'une Relation Binaire. Technical report, LIMOS, University of Clermont-Ferrand II, Clermont-Ferrand, France, 1996. Submitted for publication.

17. F. Vogt and R. Wille. *TOSCANA* - a graphical tool for analyzing and exploring data. In *Proc. of the DIMACS Int. Workshop on Graph Drawing (GD'94)*, volume 894 of *LNCS*, pages 226–233, 1995.

18. K. Waiyamai, R. Taouil, and L. Lakhal. Querying concept lattices in object databases. Technical report, LIMOS, University of Clermont-Ferrand II, Clermont-Ferrand, France, 1997. Submitted for publication.

19. R. Wille. Restructuring lattices theory: an approach based on hierarchies of concepts. In I. Rival, editor, *Ordered Sets*, pages 445–470. Dordrecht-Boston, 1982.

20. R. Wille. Knowledge acquisition by methods of formal concept analysis. In E. Diday, editor, *Data Analysis, Learning Symbolic and Numeric Knowledge*, pages 365–380. 1989.

21. R. Wille. Concept lattices and conceptual knowledge systems. In *Computers Math. Applications*, volume 23, pages 493–515. 1992.

An Experience of Integration of Conceptual Schemas in the Italian Public Administration

C. Batini[i] - G.Longobardi[ii] - S.Fornasiero[iii]

Abstract . *Large amount of data are managed by most organizations, available to be viewed and analysed from multiple perspectives, which becomes a fundamental resource to the effectiveness of the organizations. An organization can achieve full benefit from the available information by managing its data resource, through the planning of its exploitation and its maintenance. The concept of data repository fulfils these requirements, due to the fact that it contains the description of all types of data produced, managed, maintained and exchanged in an organization. Data descriptions should be organized in a repository to enable all the users of the information system to understand the meaning of data and the relationships among them.*

This paper deals with the problem of populating a data repository, using an existing methodology to build a repository of entity relationship data schemas.

In this paper the methodology is applied in a real case, concerning the information system of an Italian Public Administration (Ministry of Finance). One of the steps of the methodology concerns the strong integration of the data bases of the Department of Territory. The concrete applicability of the methodology for the data repository and for strong integration is discussed by means of the case study.

1. Introduction

The Italian Government's policy, in the past few years, was to improve the quality of services to the citizen, by gradually improving the information systems and databases of its agencies. However, the lack of co-operation among the departments led in the past to the establishment of heterogeneous and isolated systems. As a result, two main problems arise:

- duplicated and inconsistent information;
- difficult data access

Moreover, the Government efficiency depends on the sharing of information among the departments, due to the fact that many of them are usually involved in the same procedures.

Therefore it is necessary to achieve in the long term database integration; this will provide the spread of information within the government branches and will result in: a more easily accessible working environment, an increased quality of information management, and an improved state-wide decision making.

At this regard the "Information System Authority for Public Administration" (AIPA) was founded, in Italy, in 1993, mainly with the purpose to promote, to co-ordinate, to plan and to control the Public Administration information systems through the standardization, interconnection and integration of automated systems.

[i] AIPA – Information System Authority for the Public Administration, Italy EMAIL: carlo.batini@aipa.it

[ii] AIPA – Information System Authority for the Public Administration, Italy- EMAIL: guglielmo.longobardi@aipa.it

[iii] Andersen Consulting EMAIL: simona.fornasiero@ac.com

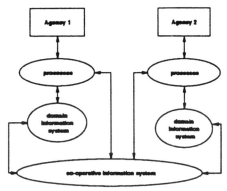

Figure 1: The co-operation architecture of the Information system of the Italian Public Administration

One of the first activities proposed by AIPA has been the project of building an inventory of existing information systems operating within the Central Public Administration in Italy. In this paper we concentrate on the activities performed on the database schemas collected (233 database schemas). The analysis of these schemas has shown that many departments manage flows of information dealing with the same or similar data. In order to avoid data inconsistencies and to improve service quality, it has been decided to achieve data sharing among the departments with the implementation of a loosely coupled architecture of systems that reconciles the autonomy and interoperability of departments. For this reason, AIPA performed in the last year a feasibility's study concerning the interconnection and the integration and the co-operation of information systems (Figure 1).

The first activity to be performed in the design of the co-operation architecture concerns the conceptual integration of database schemas of the organizational unit. The aim of this paper is to describe the experience performed. The methodology chosen for this activity has been proposed by one of the authors in a previous paper[1]. The final goal of the conceptual integration activity is the production of the "schema repository". By schema repository we mean an integrated description of the conceptual schemas managed by an organisation. In the paper, we will examine a proposed architecture of data repository and the methodology required to build it (including schema integration), and to test it with schemas from a governmental department. Seven schemas, located within the information system of the Land Department of Ministry of Finance, are therefore the starting point for the activity of repository design.

The paper is organised as follows:
- description of a repository structure (section 2);
- analysis of a methodology for the design of the repository, in which we show the steps performed (section 3);
- application of the methodology to the Land Department information system. (section 4);
- conclusions and discussion of open problems (section 5).

2. The Structure of a Repository

A repository can be defined as a set of conceptual schemas, each one describing all the information managed by an organisation area within the information system considered. In particular, the data repository referenced in this paper uses the Entity Relationship model to represent conceptual schemas. However a simple set of schemas does not display the relationships among schemas of different areas; the repository has to be organised in a more complex structure, through the use of the structuring primitives, described in the following section.

Structuring Primitives

The primitives are: refinements; views; integration. Refinements allow the description of the same reality at different levels of abstraction. This mechanism is fundamental for a data repository, since it helps the user to perceive a complex reality step by step, going from a more abstract level to a local one. Views are descriptions of fragments of a schema. They allow users to focus their attention just on the part of a complex reality of interest to them. Integration is the mechanism by which it is possible to build a global description of data managed by an organisation area starting from local schemas. By jointly using these structuring primitives we obtain a grid of schemas. Each column of the grid represents an organisation unit while each row stands for a different abstraction level. The left column contains the schemes resulting from the integration of all the other schemes belonging to the same row (views of the integrated schema). In figure 2 we show an example of grid, where the Production, Sales, Department Schemas are represented at different refinement levels respectively in the second, third and fourth column, while the Company schema in the first column is the result of their integration.

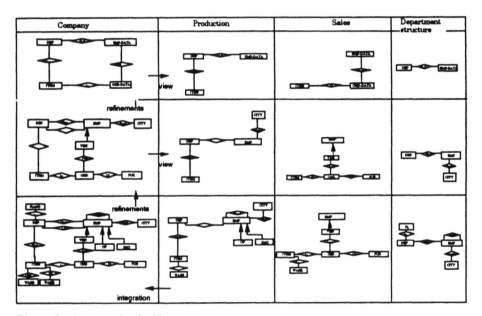

Figure 2 : An example of grid

3. A Methodology for the Design of the Data Repository

One possible strategy in order to fill the grid considered in the previous section is described in this section. First, local schemas representing the different organisation areas are integrated into a unique schema (see also figure 2). Second the required refinements for this integrated schema are the production of these refinement planes which are projected into local views corresponding to the starting local schemas. All those activities are now briefly described in order to better understand the subsequent application of the methodology to the real case. (A more detailed description of the methodology may be found in [1]).

Local Schemas Integration

The activity of schema integration can be divided in three main steps: conflict analysis; schema merging; enrichment and rearrangement.

Conflict Analysis

The aim of the first step is to discover and solve every type of conflict between data representations in different schemas. Two main activities may be distinguished:

name conflict analysis to establish naming correspondences for concepts. There are basically two sources of name conflict: synonyms and homonyms. The first ones occur when schema objects with different names represent the same concept while the second occur when the names are the same but different concepts are represented. Therefore, whenever synonyms or homonyms are detected a concept renaming is required to solve the conflict; structural conflict analysis, to discover conflicts between different representations of the same concept. The use of an entity and an attribute to represent the same concept in two different schema is a typical example of structural conflict. Each difference in representing the same reality can be solved by applying an equivalence transformation (a transformation which does not change the schema contents) to the schemas involved. At the end of this stage, we obtain a set of "amended schemas" that can be syntactically integrated, all the name and structural conflicts having been solved.

Schema Merging

The activity required in this step is a simple superimposition of common concepts belonging to the amended schemas, thus building the "global schema".

Enrichment and Rearrangement

This phase aims at detecting "interschema properties", corresponding to redundancies and cycles within the global schema, in order to build the final "integrated schema". In particular, with the term "interschema properties" we mean mutual constraints between concepts appearing in different schemas. Due to their cross-schema nature, in fact, these relationships have not yet been represented in the global schema and therefore require a specific analysis at this point of the methodology. After obtaining the integrated schema there are two different way to build the grid, according to the different policies to follow: strong integration; loose integration. In the first case the last row of the grid, corresponding to the most detailed level of abstraction, is filled with the integrated schema and the amended ones. On the contrary, in the second case the starting local schemas are kept within the grid and put in that row together with the integrated schema.

In the following we deal with a methodology for strong integration.

Production of refinements for the integrated schema

The purpose of this step is to build a chain of refinement planes for the schema obtained in the previous phase of the methodology. First of all, we have to split the integrated schema in a proper number of subschemas. Then, for each one we have to determine an abstract concept that suitably represents it and map these relationships between concepts and subschemas by means of macro-transformations. Finally, linking these concepts in a unique schema we obtain the most abstract refinement for the integrated schema. The simple iteration of the described activity leads to building the refinement planes required to fill the first column of the grid.

Production of local refinements

After producing refinement planes for the integrated schema and corresponding transformation sequences, we have to project the transformations over local schemas, in order to obtain local refinement planes. With these schemas we can therefore fill all the other columns of the grid, thus ending the design activity of the data repository structure. In order to obtain a data repository which can be really helpful to the user, a tuning activity may be required. This implies moving transformations within a sequence in order to achieve both concept and global balancing. The first property, concept balancing, requires that the number of new concepts deriving from each concept in a schema increases homogeneously within a sequence of refinements. The second property requires a homogeneous increase in the set of concepts in each refinement plane for each sequence of refinements.

4. Application of the methodology to the Land Department information system

We will concentrate our attention on the information system of the Land Department inside the Ministry of Finance. This Department is in charge of the valuation of real property so as to determine direct and indirect tax assessment and to issue real estate certifications. Moreover, this Department administers and records all state properties in regard to their financial affairs. Its responsibilities include: the acquisition of new state properties; the disposal of properties when authorised; the care and supervision of state properties; and the maintenance of an inclusive inventory. Seven databases have been located within the information system of the Land Department, each represented by one of the conceptual Entity Relationship schemas as follows. These seven schemas are therefore the starting point for the activity of data repository design. In applying the strong integration methodology to the conceptual schemas of the Land Department, we have tested the activities required to implement a data repository. Providing a description of every single step required by the method, however, would be too complex and heavy. The next figure provides a description of the schemas considered in the application of the methodology.

| level | Integrated Schema | General Land Office: | | | State Property Office | | | |
		urban database	land database	Mortgage Registry database	real estate database	property grant database	confiscated private database	private estate renting database
first	↑ ⇥							
second	⇥							
third	▸							
fourth								
fifth	⇤	Fig. 3	Fig. 4	Fig. 5	Fig. 6	Fig. 7	Fig. 8	Fig. 9

Table 1: The grid of schemas of Land Department of Ministry of Finance

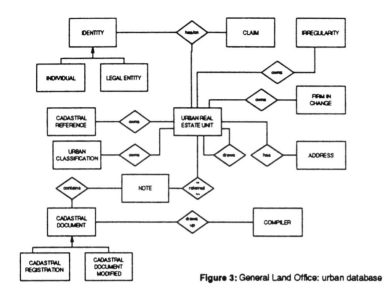

Figure 3: General Land Office: urban database

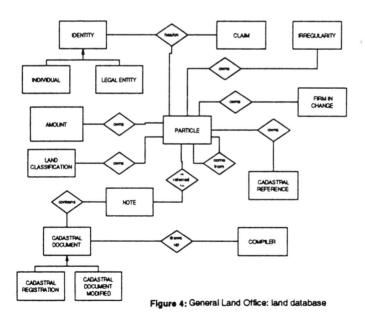

Figure 4: General Land Office: land database

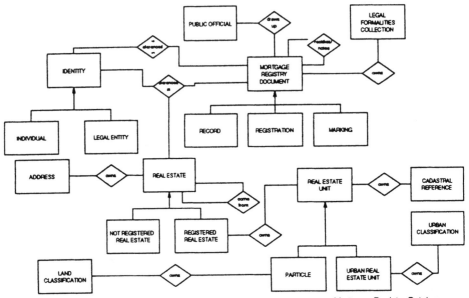

Figure 5: Mortgage Registry Database

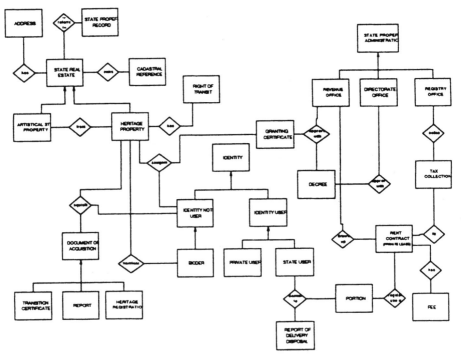

Figure 6: State Property Office:real estate database

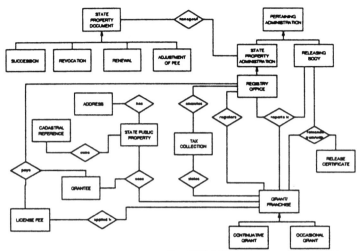

Figure 7: State Property Office:property grant database

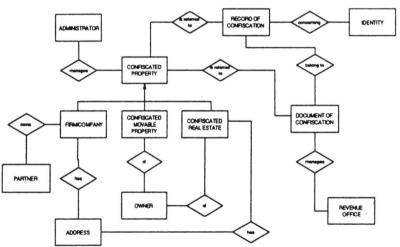

Figure 8: State Property Office: confiscated private database

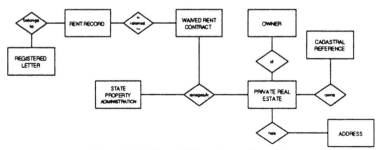

Figure 9: State Property Office:private renting database

5. Concluding remarks

In this paper we have applied a methodology for a data repository, to a small yet meaningful sample of the information system of the italian Ministry of Finance.

The most meaningful results of the experience concern the integration methodology and the grid approach.

Concerning the integration methodology we may say that: the methodology is very effective in showing redundancies and inconsistencies present in the local schemas at different detail levels, since the representation of the integrated schema is always kept coherent with local refinements. The designer may choose the starting abstraction level of the analysis, and then go up or down in checking specific aspects of the schemas. However, the methodology may look demanding because the first step concerns an integrated schema at the most detailed refinement level. During this building activity, the designer must overcome the difficulty of comparing entities that describe different domains at a very detailed and specific level.

Another possible strategy consists in producing the integrated schema at a more abstract level. Infact, when we go up in the grid, the level of detail is lower, but the most important concepts of the schemas survive. Once chosen a suitable level of abstraction for the local schemas, specific design activities can be performed with the responsible of each area. The second step leads to merge these local schemas in an integrated one. Following this approach, it is simpler to perform conflict analysis and to produce an integrated schema. This schema can be used as reference when later the integration of the most detailed schemas must be performed.

New experiment will be made in order to compare the different approaches.

Concerning the grid approach, we have seen that it can be used as a useful instrument of analysis, since: 1) it allows comparing the information contents of global views and local views 2) this comparison can be performed at different levels of abstraction.

When the set of schemas is very large, it is worthwhile to follow a different approach during the grid production. Infact, in performing the activity of grid production for the repository, due to the huge amount of integration activities, groups of schemas were integrated and abstracted at the same time, thus leaving void the grid in specific cells referring to integrated schemas.

As we said in the introduction, the integration activity on the seven schemas of the Department of Territory has to be seen as a small part of the wider activity on the repository of schemas.

The whole repository consists of a very large set of ER schemas (260 database schemas). The 233 local schemas (with 4164 entities and relationships) collected during the inventory are divided into 17 areas (financial resources, human resources etc.) as shown in figure 10.

The integration of the seven schemas dealt with in this paper needed about 1 person/year; so it is really critical to foresee with the available resources when the complete activity could be finished. We have presently completed a "weak integration" of the whole set of schemas, by performing a recursive integration of schemas (see figure 10), that in about 2 person/years led to build a pyramidal repository. Every schema produced is the joint result of an integration and an abstraction activity; first level integrated/abstract schemas are further integrated, finally producing a unique integrated schema, that represents at a very high level the most significant types of information used in Public Administration, i.e. Persons, Property, Territory, Documents, the Administration itself. The pyramid of schemas provides a natural representation of entities at different abstraction levels, and allows, with suitabile approximation, to find the common parts among databases pertaining to different agencies. First results in this direction have been presented in [3] and [4]. With regard to the methodology for data repository, we have to define suitable metrics for the activities performed in the process (e.g. number of transformations, number of interschema properties) and analyse the relationship between such metrics, the resources and tools involved in the process, and the levels of quality achieved. This activity is just at the beginning.

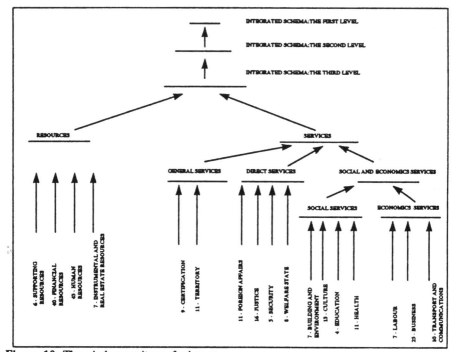

Figure 10: The whole repository of schemas.

References
[1] C. Batini, G. Di Battista, G. Santucci - Structuring primitives for a dictionary of entity relationship data schemas -IEEE Transactions on Software Engineering vol.19 no.4 April 1993.
[2] AIPA - Il Repository delle basi di dati della pubblica amministrazione - ottobre 1995 - (C. Batini G. Longobardi - I. Siciliani) (in italian)
[3] C. Batini, S. Castano, V. De Antonellis, M.G. Fugini, B. Pernici - Analysis of an Inventory of Information systems in the Public Administration - Requirements Engineering, 1996, 47-62
[4] C. Batini, S: Castano, B. Pernici - Tutorial on Reuse Methodologies and Tools - Entity Relationships International Conference, Cottbus, Germany, 1996.

Application-Oriented Design of Behavior: A Transformational Approach Using RADD

Meike Albrecht, Margita Altus, and Martin Steeg
{meike,altus} @ informatik.tu-cottbus.de, steeg @ iabg.de
Brandenburg Technical University of Cottbus
Research Group for Databases and Information Systems

Abstract. This paper presents an approach to support the design of 'dynamic' databases. The basis of our approach is formed by schemata of an extended entity-relationship model which are constructed in a modular way and can then be enriched by behavior specifications, functions, and view definitions. The goal is to derive the retrieval and update semantics from a given data schema as far as possible, such that we discover aspects in a not well-ordered design, inconsistencies, or behavior bottlenecks. These are eliminated in later steps using conventional design and implementation strategies, and database tuning measures. The conceptual database design optimizer of the database design toolbox RADD can be used to analyze applications of the resulting information system, such that alternative EER schemata with better behavior properties can be automatically inferred, and visualized to the database designer.

1 Introduction

A well-known problem of information system design is that consequences of the earlier modeling phases for the subsequent phase (conceptual, logical, and physical design) and the modeling's effects for database maintenance are almost not considered. Given today's graphical database design, such as an entity-relationship schema or an object model, operations have mostly been considered by either presupposing them (select, insert, delete, update in some ER design tools) or declaring their names and providing their signatures (object models). An advantage of object models that must not be ignored is that along with the design, the structuring of classes and methods is already given for the later implementation. However, entity-relationship as well as object models do not generally analyze the data, module, and method structuring's impacts according to *processing properties* of the resulting system. These properties describe the reaction of the database system to operations such as storing, updating, and retrieving the data or objects. To improve the reaction of the database system to such operations most tools force the designer to restrict their modeling view to graphical presented inheritance keys, declaration of dummy methods, or generation of content-less templates for triggers and database procedures. These give the designer the impression that many possibilities are available, but make a good design of graphical data or object models quite complicated. These schemata are – without adaptation and restructuring – not appropriate for database maintenance. Behavior, performance, and processing requirements often force the designer to completely redesign the schema. There are several reasons why processing information should be included in the earlier phases of database design:

- Low storage complexity is an objective of conceptual and logical design. Efficiency is the main database processing requirement. The latter goal is often in contradiction to the former which is realized by normalization.[1]
- Normalization is the typical approach to state there is no, or almost no redundancy in the schema. In consequence of redundancy, we have to cope with potential inconsistencies (update anomalies) as well as insertion and deletion anomalies. But, normalization algorithms may derive several schemata from the same attribute set and functional dependency set ([13]). Thus, we need to know which one is optimal.
- Structural well-designed schemata often imply operational bottlenecks. For different DBMSs different tuning principles are appropriate ([9]). Database structures for the most efficient implementation often cannot be derived directly from the given. Hence, external views may not be supported by the 'tuned' internal or logical schema.

RADD implements a strategy to incorporate requirements analysis and design impacts for the later database maintenance already into conceptual design. This makes database development more transparent, flexible, and consistent, but does not require the conceptual designer to refer to logical and physical design aspects, since these are inferred by the toolbox. Physical design aspects are highlighted in the conceptual design to notify the designer of possible mistakes.

The paper is organized as follows. Section 2 presents the ideas of graphical design transformations (design primitives) which are the prerequisite for a modular construction of EER schemata within RADD. Section 3 gives an overview on how the design is improved by behavior specifications, function and database application module definitions, and, how physical performance properties are derived from the schema. A special application that is discussed here is a database for companies' departments, projects, and staff. This is not a typical application for a *'dynamic'* database, but the approach can be easily extended to such databases too. The article concludes with prospects for the future.

2 Graphical Database Design

Design Strategies. By analysing known design strategies, primitive steps can be extracted. *These primitives are the basis for the strategy support in RADD.* The designer can choose his own strategy and compose the strategy from primitives. The system RADD supports this choice based on the user model, user preferences, and characteristics of the application. Thus, the designer can switch among bottom-up, top-down, modular, inside-out, and other strategies. The *controller* derives graph grammar rules for the maintenance of consistency and for guiding explanations. Strategy consultancy and error location are included in the user guidance tool. Apart from the primitives, each design strategy is related with a set of *checkpoints*. The designer applies a heuristic search method, such as the A^* algorithm using an estimation function. A normal user of a database design environment can be supported

---

[1] Notice that object models even make these design problems worse, since they consider neither efficiency nor performance.

by implementing such search techniques and by providing *evaluation functions* and *design primitives*. The evaluation function estimates what the most *plausible* next design step is according to the design goal, and it is based on several pieces of evidence: populations of data items, cardinality constraints, inclusion and exclusion constraints, additional functional and multivalue dependencies, i.e. semantics acquired and accumulated during earlier design steps and new discovered semantics as well as behavior information. The plausibility function of the evidence theory has been proposed to model the accumulation and evaluation of different pieces of evidence to support the *inductive design decision process*, [3]. Design primitives are used as *abstract operators* for moving from one design state to another. In the following, the term design strategy is used as a synonym for search method. The variety of different strategies is based on the dimensions of database design. Classical design strategies are well known such as top-down, bottom-up, mixed, inside-out, and modular design strategies, [12, 4]. Each design strategy is composed of different approaches (dimensions of database design), [12]: *the design direction, the control of the design, the modularity of the design*. An operational framework and *guidelines* for the construction of design modules on the basis of atomic design primitives are included in our database design environment, especially, the way to specify the content of database modules consistently and graphically. In the following, the term *unit* is used as a synonym for database design module. This style-of-working composes the new design methodology *design-by-units* that incorporates information hiding. Design primitives are considered to be transformations on the design database.

The system is based on the RADD extended entity-relationship model which allows the user to specify graphically the structure of an application, the integrity constraints which are valid in the given application, operations, and transactions which are necessary for the given application. This extension requires an easy-to-handle and advanced support for graphics. Furthermore, the editor enables the designer to visualize the complete design information. The user interface and the explanation component are adapted to skills, abilities, and intentions of the database designer. This tool allows customization of the user interface and the explanation component.

3 Database Design Optimization

RADD allows one to observe the conceptual database schema for inconsistencies and probable bottlenecks. We use the conceptual schema to

(a) derive internal database representations,

(b) compute on the internal representation behavior and performance properties of transactions, and

(c) discover aspects for more advantageous conceptual design,

in order to omit problems of database - implementation tuning – which often destroys or confuses semantic dependencies. The target of our approach is to develop a conceptual database schema that supports an efficient database application. Most times insufficient processing requirement fulfillments lead to later database tuning, see for example [11, 9]. We now show how performance properties can be inferred once a schema (entity-relationship schema or object model) is given, and how obvious bottlenecks of the designed system are used to restructure and improve the schema.

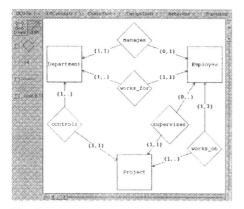

Fig. 1. Initially modeled *Company* schema.

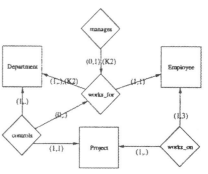

Fig. 2. Optimized *Company* schema.

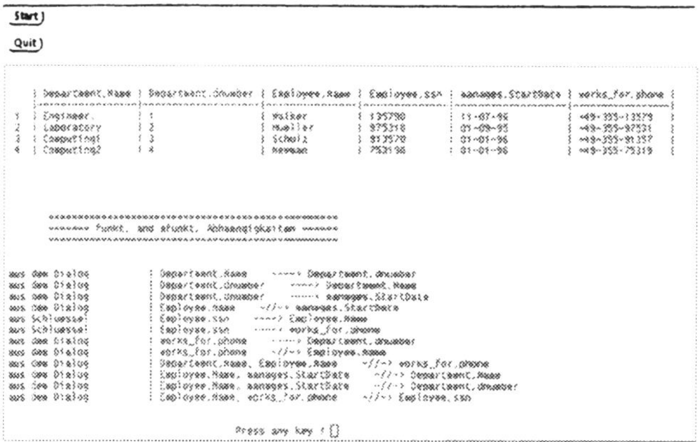

Fig. 3. Semantic acquisition of dependencies.

Tab. 1. Inclusion constraints which are *not* represented implicitly in the initial schema.

(1) If an employee *supervises* a project then the department *for* which he must *work* is *equal* to the department that *controls*.

(2) If an employee *supervises* a project then the set of projects he is *working on* includes at least this project.

(3) If an employee *manages* a department then at least this employee *works for* the same department (all managers are employees in the same department in which they work).

The Database Design Problem. Assume the user has modeled a *Company* schema comprising entities *Employee*, *Department*, and *Project* and relationships *manages*, *works_on*, *works_for*, *supervises*, and *controls*. The initial schema has been designed with a top-down strategy, but without an explicit set of functional dependencies. Functional dependencies are conceptualized by *many-to-one relationships* between the object classes. To determine the functional dependencies which are valid for the schema we have to carefully consider what the object classes (entity/

relationship types) mean. In this sense, dependencies are actually assertions about the real world. These assertions can be validated by examples using a component of RADD: semantic acquisition, Fig 3, [1]. The *optimized* company schema allows one to specify these constraints in a more efficient way. Fig. 2 shows how RADD restructures the conceptual schema of Fig. 1. The dependency *Department* $\longrightarrow$ *manages* $(CC(manages, Department) = (1, 1))$ is maintained and visualized in the optimized schema by the path-key constraint label K_2.

Considering Information System Dynamics. Knowing the information system dynamics supports the inductive design decision process. That means, we like to determine which parts of the schema need to be strongly normalized, and, which parts or sets of structures can be collapsed according to improvement of retrieval performance. Information system dynamics can be derived in part from population aspects which are acquired for the structures of the designed schema.

```
Tuple number for Type 'Employee' >> 760
Tuple number for Type 'Department' >> 4
Tuple number for Type 'Project' >> 17
Tuple number for Type 'manages' [4] >> 4
Tuple number for Type 'works_on' [>=760] >> 875
Tuple number for Type 'works_for' [760] >> 760
Tuple number for Type 'supervises' [17] >> 17
Tuple number for Type 'controls' [17] >> 17
```

In contrast to traditional textbooks [13, 14, 6, 8], collapsing (denormalized) structures, e.g. an entity and a relationship structure, can improve retrieval performance and insert/ delete/ update performance as well. For the considered *Company* schema and the population aspects (*Tuple number*, numbers of tuples), the internal schema containing an *Employee* structure with a repeating group of *Project*-references has better retrieval performance and update behavior properties than one with a separate *Employee*, *works_on*, and *Project* structure, respectively, [10]. It is clear that whether operational behavior is really a bottleneck of the schema depends upon the frequency and priority of the operations:

- if insert is an often required operation for *Employee, Department, works_for*, and *works_on* then the insert operation creates a crucial bottleneck;
- if it is necessary to frequently delete an *Employee, Department,* or *manages* record then the delete operation has higher complexity;
- the update operation is inefficient for the entity structures *Employee* and *Department* and the relationship structure *works_on*;
- and the retrieval operation for *works_on* is relatively complex.

According to the frequency of this operations the integration of explicit constraints in the schema is necessary:

- the relationship *manages* is a subtype of *works_for*, identifying the special role of department managers,
- the *Employee* who supervises the *Project* must work for the *Department* that *controls* the *Project*.

If the entity occurrence sets are not frequently changed then the aforementioned relationship structures should be grouped in the case in order that their update operations get a very high frequency and priority. The retrieval operation for type *works_on* should be considered as important in frequency and priority, i.e., information according to projects and their staff is frequently required; therefore, we can ask for criteria whether this type should be used to create a separate data file on the implementation level or not. Having a collapsed *Employee/works_on* structure on the implementation level (a repeating group in a hierarchical or relational database, a set-typed attribute in a network or object database) has the advantage that we can omit a join operation. According to our consideration of the database population aspects, from the fact that we have only 1.2 as many *works_on* objects as *Employees* we can infer that most of the *Employees* work on exactly one *Project*. The result of our schema optimization algorithm is shown in Fig. 2.

Adding Behavior Properties to the Graphical Design. In RADD, the designer has to specify error prevention options for each transaction *separately*. This improves the design and the maintenance of design specifications since normally, there is an arbitrary number of repair reactions, but four cases (behavior properties) are very common at the appearance of an error caused by data inconsistencies in the running database.

Tab. 2. Four common cases.

---

(1) *RESTRICT.* Roll-back of the transaction at appearance of data inconsistencies.
(2) *CASCADE.* Invoking *repair actions* at appearance of data inconsistencies. (e.g., missing or deleted items of the parent structure.)
(3) *SET NULL.* If the item of a parent structure for which child items still exist is deleted (or updated), then the corresponding child references are set to "null" (iff "null" is allowed).
(4) *SET DEFAULT.* On insert of some child items use a default as reference to the occurrence set of the parent structure. If the item of a parent structure is deleted (or updated) for which child items still exist, then set the corresponding child references to the default.

We have *default behavior rules* which are compiled into the conceptual database optimizer, and, in the user's specification frame, *general rules* which are identified by a 'General' section, and *special rules* for special integrity constraints ('Special' section). The following shows a specification frame for a part of the company schema:

```
General:                                   Special:
   On insert restrict;                        On insert("manages",m)
   On delete cascade;                         IF Not (m.Employee in "Employee")
   On update parent                           THEN insert("Employee",s) FI;
   IF nullable(child) THEN set null        For Reference "manages" TO "Employee":
                      ELSE set default FI;    On delete restrict;
   On update child cascade;
```

Adding Functions and Application Module Declarations to the Graphical Design. RADD allows *behavior specifications* with the help of user-defined database functions and IF-THEN-ELSE statements, such that transactions can be specified in a programmatical way. The conceptual database optimizer of RADD provides a functional language *(Csl, conceptual support language[2])* specification interface which is based on:

---

[2] Essentially, Csl re-implements a subset of the Standard ML of New-Jersey functional language, and adds database operations.

- *select, insert, delete,* and *update* as denoters for database operations – Csl uses operation terms[3], to evaluate transactions and necessary sub-transactions; the conceptual support language also considers group and aggregation functions, like *min, max, count, sum, avg,* and so forth;
- *entity, relationship, cluster, component,* and *tcomponent* as testing operations for the data context;
- *compatible, highcomplexity,* and *attrsize* as structure/operation property evaluators;
- *group, separate, nest, unnest,* and *clusterize* as schema transformation operations;
- and "+", "−", "∗", "/", " ˉ " (unary minus), and " ˆ " (string concatenation) as primitive operators, "=", "<", "<=", ">=", ">", and "<>" as comparison operators, and ":=" as assignment operator.

Values, i.e. constants, can be defined within Csl by expressions of the form:

"val" < *value* > "=" < *val* >

and functions by:

"fun" < *value* > < *par* > "=" < *val* > { "|" < *par* > "=" < *val* > }∗

where < *val* > is a constant, a Csl-defined value, or a Csl expression:

```
val ::= < const > | < value > | "fn" < par > "=>" < val > { "|" < par > "=>" < val > }∗ |
        "let" <decl> "in" <val> { ";" <val> }∗ "end" | "(" <val> { "," <val> }∗ ")" |
        ref < val >
```

In Csl, the symbol "fn" introduces the definition of a function, which has no own identification and is handled as a value only. The "fn" construct is used to specify pattern matching when defining curried functions as well. Based on the given ER schema, the type of all structures is assumed "struc", e.g.:

```
CSL> Employee;
it : struc = Employee
```

Besides "struc", Csl types are "unit", "bool", "int", "real", "number", "date", "string", "data_schema", the generic types "tuple", "list", and "set", and "function". Csl maintains the RADD types {*char, float, decimal*} by SQL-2 types{string, real, number}. Csl values can be used to specify "select" expressions:

```
CSL> fun avageolder year = select avg(truncyear(today() - Bdate))
CSL>     from Employee where truncyear(today() - Bdate)) >= year;
avageolder : int -> real = <function>
```

Thus, *avageolder* evaluates the average age of all *Employees* whose age is older than *year*. The Csl expression is compiled into an internal representation and the type of the internal representation is displayed. Note, that the primary intention of Csl is not to evaluate the database and the select expression, respectively, instead it is to provide an interface and a language to specify operations' requirements and evaluate a database design. However, the Csl-interface can evaluate arithmetic expressions as well.

A Csl module is defined as follows:

---

[3] e.g. *insert(Employee)* or *insert(Employee,(Name="Victor H.", Bdate="11-01-59",Salary=54000,...))*

```
moddecl ::= "class" <module> "=" [ "structures" { <struc> [ "=" <struc> ] }+ ]
            [ "knows" { <module> "." { "all" | <val> } }+ ] { <viewdecl> }• { <idxdecl> }•
            { <valdecl> | <fundecl> | <moddecl> }•
        "end"
```

where a module is introduced by the keyword "class". An example of a Csl module is:

```
CSL> class Demo =
CSL> structures Employee Dept = Department works_on
CSL> view manages = select Employee.Name ename,Dept.Name dname,mgrStartDate
CSL>        from Employee,Dept,works_on where works_on.Employee = Employee
CSL>     and works_on.Department = Dept and not mgrStartDate is null and mgrStartDate <= today()
CSL> val showDeptManages = fn dept => select * from manages where dname = dept
CSL> end;
Demo : ( manages : (ename:string,dname:string,mgrStartDate:date) = <view>
         showDeptManages : string -> (ename:string,dname:string,mgrStartDate:date) set ) = <module>
CSL> open Demo;
manages : (ename:string,dname:string,mgrStartDate:date) = <view>
showDeptManages : string -> (ename:string,dname:string,mgrStartDate:date) set = <function>
CSL> showDeptManages "Engineering";
{ ("Walker","Engineering","11-07-96") } : (ename:string,dname:string,mgrStartDate:date) set
```

Currently, we only support modules without instances, i.e., *proper modules*. We use the keyword "class" because we also plan to support modules with instances, i.e., *classes*. Csl modules are also compiled into an internal representation. Thus, the module code is executable. Csl modules are specified (implemented) conceptually, and they allow navigation at the physical database which is different from the conceptual schema. In this way, Csl modules are like database views which provide navigation, inserts, deletes, and updates to a physical realized database. This user-interface approach is an extension of the CoDO approach of [10]. It is to provide the user with facilities which allow him to implement and maintain the database by a high-level conceptual language without knowing (necessarily) the implementation details.

Automating the Design Transformation and Visualizing Database Transactions to the Conceptual Designer. As mentioned above, *group, separate, nest, unnest,* and *clusterize* are transformation primitives, which are used to automatically generate an internal database schema. An example for such a transformation rule is shown in Tab. 3 (for a relational schema). The symbol $MaxRepGrpSize$ is a global constant,

Tab. 3. Design Transformation Rule.

component(R_1,R_2)	$CC(R_1,R_2,(m,n))$
$m{\geq}1$ and ($n{=}1$ or attrsize($R_1,(m,n)$)<MaxRepGrpSize) $\to$ group($R_2,R_1,(m,n)$)	

used as reference to decide whether internal structures are to be grouped (collapsed). The generated internal schema is a different view to the database. Thus, structures have been grouped, splitted, or restructured, in order to derive efficient database applications (refer to [10]). The Cottbus Conceptual Database Design Optimizer *CoDO* has a generic cost model and also uses rules[4] to derive performance properties for the conceptual schema.

---

[4] The transformation and optimization rules are interpreted during run-time.

The applied transformation actions do not only refer to the transformation rules but also to the transaction and behavior properties which are specified for the schema. Thus, if there is a transformation rule which states to group two structures of the entity-relationship schema and there is also an ON-INSERT-CASCADE rule between the two structures, then the structures are not grouped.

Suppose, the database designer wants to specify an ON-INSERT-CASCADE rule for the reference from *works_for* to *Employee*:

```
CSL> For Ref works_for to Employee: On insert cascade;
Adding 1 new rules to schema Company.
```

Fig. 4. Visualizing Database Transaction Costs and Contents to the Conceptual Designer.

Then, RADD assumes that the designer does not want the structures *Employee* and *works_for* to be grouped. According to this, Fig. 4 shows how transactions and their costs which are evaluated on the basis of the internally generated schema, are visualized to the database designer.

Conceptual Database Design Tuning. The properties of the internal schema are used to optimize the conceptual schema since performance bottlenecks which are recognized on the internal schema are often caused by a not well-ordered conceptual design. An example for an optimization rule is shown in Tab. 4.

Tab. 4. Design Optimization Rule.

$$\frac{\text{highcomplexity}(\text{delete}(R_1)) \quad\quad \text{entity}(R_1)}{\text{and highcomplexity}(\text{delete}(R_2)) \quad\quad \text{and entity}(R_2)}$$

$$\frac{(\text{dcycle}(R_1, R_3, R_2, R_4) \text{ or } \text{dcycle}(R_1, R_4, R_2, R_3))}{\text{and compatible}(R_3, R_4)} \rightarrow \text{separate}(\text{group}(R_3, R_4, (.,.)), R_4)$$

4 Concluding Remarks and Prospects for the Future

Using our rule-based approach for conceptual schema tuning, we can improve the schema by collapsing and subsequently dividing conceptual schema structures. Consequently we restore the old structures, which the database design originally models, and delete and generate new relationship-entity references, such that we obtain a schema with lower operational complexities, easier implementation mapping, and better behavior. Further rules for (internal) schema optimization can be developed in accordance to tuning techniques of the chosen DBMS. Our approach versus classic database tuning, which is separated from conceptual and logical design, incorporates an optimization rule base, transformation primitives, specification of behavior *properties*, behavior specification using CSL which provides database view and module definitions. Thus, it is conceptual database design tuning using an extended entity relationship model. In [2], it is shown that the set of optimization rules is extendable. This makes database development more transparent, flexible, and consistent.

The development of the RADD components *schema editor* and *graphical design environment* [3], *semantic acquisition* [1], and *behavior estimator/conceptual database optimizer* [10] is already finished. Our mediate goals are (1.) to extend Csl modules (shown in Section 3) such that we also can support information hiding *(public, protected, private)* and inheritance, and (2.) to couple the RADD graphical database modules with Csl module specifications. We are currently working on the automatical generation of *FORMS* applications from Csl modules, which has been presented in the article [2]. In this way, RADD represents a *next-generation database design tool*, that is guiding the database designer through all steps of the database's development and animating the design for him in developing a complete and consistent design.

Acknowledgements. The authors would like to thank Prof. Bernhard Thalheim who initiated this work.

References

1. M. Albrecht, M. Altus, E. Buchholz, A. Düsterhöft, and B. Thalheim, The rapid application and database development (RADD) workbench - A comfortable database design tool. In: Proc. of the 7th International Conference, CAiSE 95 (Eds.: J. Ivari, K. Lyytinen, M. Rossi), LNCS 932, Jyväskylä, Finland, 1995, p.327–340. http://www.informatik.tu-cottbus.de/cs/dbis/radd/caise95/caise95.html.
2. M. Albrecht, M. Altus, and M. Steeg, Conceptual Data Modeling, Implementation Prototyping, Transformation, and Application Design - An Animating Approach using RADD. ADBIS'97 in St.-Petersburg, September.
3. M. Altus, Meta-Modelling of Conceptual Data Base Design Using a Plausibility Function. In: Procs of the 6th European-Japanese Seminar on Information Modelling and Knowledge Bases, May 28-31, 1996. http://www.informatik.tu-cottbus.de/~altus/node4.html.
4. C. Batini, S. Ceri, and S. Navathe, Conceptual database design, An entity-relationship approach. Benjamin Cummings, Redwood, 1992.
5. P. Bunemann and Atsushi Ohori. Polymorphism and Type Inference in Database Programming. *ACM ToDS*, 21(1):30 – 76, March 1996.
6. C.J. Date. *An Introduction to Database Systems.* Addison-Wesley, 6th edition, 1995.
7. R. Elmasri and S.B. Navathe. *Fundamentals of Database Systems.* Benjamin/ Cummings, 1994.
8. A. Raihä and H. Manila. *The Design of Relational Databases.* Addison-Wesley, 1992.
9. D.E. Shasha. *Database Tuning – A Principled Approach.* Prentice Hall, 1992.
10. M. Steeg. The Conceptual Database Design Optimizer CoDO – Concepts, Implementation, Application. In *Conceptual Modeling – ER'96*, October 1996.
11. S.S. Su. Processing-Requirement Modeling and Its Application in Logical Database Design. In S.B. Yao, editor, *Principles of Database Design*, volume 1: Logical Organization, pages 151 –173, 1985.
12. B. Thalheim. Fundamentals of Entity-Relationship Modelling. Springer-Verlag, 1996.
13. J.D. Ullman. *Principles of Database Systems.* Computer Science Press, Rockville, Maryland, 1988.
14. G. Vossen. *Datenmodelle, Datenbanksprachen und Datenbankmanagementsysteme.* Addison-Wesley, 1987. (in German).

A Java-Based Framework for Processing Distributed Objects*

Daniel Wu   Divyakant Agrawal   Amr El Abbadi   Ambuj Singh

Department of Computer Science
University of California, Santa Barbara
{danielw, agrawal, amr, ambuj}@cs.ucsb.edu

Abstract. The Alexandria Digital Library Project at UC Santa Barbara has been building an information retrieval system for geographically-referenced information and datasets. To meet these requirements, we have designed a distributed Data Store to store its holdings. The library's map, image and geographical data are viewed as a collection of objects with evolving roles. Developed in the Java programming language and the HORB distributed object system, the Data Store manages these objects for flexible and scalable processing. To implement the Data Store we provide a messaging layer that allows applications to distribute processing between the Data Store and the local host. We define a data model for Data Store repositories that provide Client access to Data Store objects. We finally provide support for specialized views of these Data Store items.

1   Introduction

In recent years, the need for distributed computing has spurred the introduction of distributed object packages such as CORBA[Sie96], COM[Rog97], and ActiveX[Cor97]. While these object systems provide access to remote objects they are limited in how they distribute processing and dynamically extend services. These systems are designed to be language and platform-independent; thus, though the *state* of an object may be transferred, its actual processing is still restricted to the host where it was created and where the implementation code resides. Hence, although, access to an object is distributed across many sites, via a global object reference, the processing of the object is not distributed.

To address these issues we present a Java-based dynamic object framework to distribute Java-based objects across multiple hosts. True object migration is supported so that an object (its implementation as well as its state) can be moved to a new site. In addition to migration services, we also provides dynamic binding facilities; that is, an object's methods may be extended or overridden at run-time to provide new services and resources across a network. An object method may, in fact, be shipped independently of an object so that new behavior can be defined and effected when the object arrives at some particular host.

---

* Work supported by research grants from NSF/ARPA/NASA IRI9411330 and NSF CDA-9421978.

As an application of this distributed object system, we have incorporated these services to develop a digital library project. The Alexandria Digital Library (ADL)[Smi96] project at the University of California, Santa Barbara, is building a digital library that distributes data and processing of its collections. The holdings in the Alexandria library include a myriad of maps, images, and geographical data sets collected from satellites, radar-imaging and remote-sensing devices. This vast collection of data poses a number of challenges due to its sheer bulk; Alexandria library holdings easily exceed 1,000,000 items, with some of the geographical images requiring over a gigabyte of disk space. With such large amounts of data available, heavy demands are made on its storage and management. For this reason, we have designed and prototyped a Data Store for Alexandria. Besides distributing the collection, the Data Store provides a data model for the items in the collection. In our design, each item in the Data Store can be viewed as an object. That is, a library document is no longer a passive entity, but an object that can be instantiated and processed through method operations. An image, for example, belonging to a LandsatImage class has as relevant methods: zoomIn(), getThumbnail(), queryElevation(), print(). By modeling objects in this manner, we seek to distribute their operations and their functionality using the Java-based dynamic object framework.

The paper is organized as follows: Section 2 presents the goals and motivations of a digital library based on objects; Section 3 describes object migration and extensibility within a message-passing layer; Section 4 describes the dynamic object access of the Data Store; Section 5 illustrates how dynamic views of Data Store objects are constructed; Section 6 concludes the paper.

2 Distributed Objects in an Information System

Within a distributed object-based digital library, data and resources can be scattered and co-located to several hosts. When processing of these resources take place, there are two basic alternatives: either transfer all the data items to a centralized access point for processing, or distribute the processing by visiting each host and executing a portion of the execution at the remote host. There are trade-offs to either approach depending on the size of the data items, and the amount of processing capability at each site. In our distributed system (Figure 1), where code and data mobility are primary considerations, we provide support for both forms of access and processing. We begin by discussing the basic requirements for true object distribution and extensibility in a digital library.

2.1 Object Migration

Consider a situation where a Client creates a large LandsatImage object at a Data Store Server and later that Server becomes so heavily loaded that it can no longer provide adequate performance. Rather than continue processing at the Server, the Client would like to download the object for local processing, or migrate that object to another less heavily-loaded Server. Alternately, consider a distributed network in which services and resources are available at

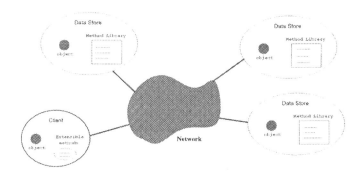

Fig. 1. Distributed objects propagated across Data Store Servers.

remote sites. Again, the need to migrate the object becomes evident. Current distributed technologies support object migration by transferring the state of an object between two different hosts. CORBA, for example, permits applications to transfer an object's state, but not its actual implementation. This restriction serves several purposes; it provides a framework for language-independent and host-independent implementations. The drawback, however, is that while the state of an object is migrated, its processing is not. An application still accesses the object's methods through a proxy; the execution is performed on the host where the operating code is stored. Thus, while information pertaining to the object may be distributed, its processing is still restricted to the target platform where the implementation code was registered.

To fully support object migration services, an object's methods, as well as its state must be shipped together as a single programming unit, so that the receiver may perform processing upon that object at the remote site. Providing this capability, though, forces many requirements upon the system. The receiver must be able to run the sender's object code, thus fixing the binary and run-time executable for the object implementation across disseparate machines. To achieve platform independence, we have chosen Java[AG96] as our implementation language because both its byte-code and Java Virtual Machine are designed to be machine-independent. Programming in Java adds a virtual programming layer upon the native operating environment. In addition, the Java programming architecture is standardized so that Java objects may be serialized into portable byte-code using JDK 1.1's Object Serializer[RWW96]. The choice of Java thus addresses many of the platform compatibility issues raised in implementing a distributed system.

2.2 Object Extensibility

Object roles and behavior[RS91] in a digital library evolve over time, and may need to be individually tailored to specific user requirements. Hence a distributed digital library must provide some means of dynamically extending an object's functionality. For example, the LandsatImage object supplies a locateVegetation() method to segment and outline the areas of vegetation growth. Suppose, though, that a particular Client would like a locateLivestock() method to identify bovine grazing areas. Rather than create a new object class with such functionality and register it into the Data Store repository, we need to provide the Client with the capability of extending an object's methods. The Client can write its own locateLivestock() method and ship it to the object, thus extending the object's available methods. This is an example of a Client providing its own private object extensions. The Data Store object is temporarily extended to a new object to satisfy a user's particular need. A trusted user (a librarian user), however, could introduce a new object into the Data Store by defining a new subclass in the Data Store repository; this would then result in a permanent and global change, visible to all Clients.

2.3 Dynamic Object Access

Another limitation found in current tools is the requirement of a static proxy to access a distributed object. In systems such as CORBA, an object is first created and registered into an interface repository and implementation repository. A Client program queries the interface repository to obtain a proxy to the remote object. Execution takes place by calling methods through the proxy. This manner of processing follows a rigid imperative style of programming, in which access is provided only after an object proxy has been located. For our system, we offer a more dynamic discovery-based form of access in which a Client can query Data Store repository records to determine the structure, format, and meta-data of Data Store objects. Upon discovering an object type of interest, the Client can instantiate the object directly without reference through a proxy. The Data Store repository can thus be viewed as an extended database in which data, object state, and object methods are stored in a distributed manner.

2.4 Dynamic Views of Distributed Objects

Just as each Data Store holds a repository of method programs, a digital library database should also let the Client build its own private repository to reflect its view of the relations among the Data Store items. By storing object instances and object methods within a migrating store, the Client can process its contents by visiting selected Data Store sites to collect new data and executable resources. The implementation of this view, however, requires additional programming facilities. For this reason, we introduce a programming model for Data Store applications that utilizes the Data Store's migration services. In this model, an application constructs a view of a mobile Data Store object. The program instructions direct the object to visit Data Store sites in the network, executing and processing data along each site. The goal of this model is to distribute resources and processing in the network so that an object completes a computational task by visiting a set of Data Store servers.

3   Object Migration and Extensibility

To transfer an object from one site to another, we must first have some means of preserving the state of the object as it is migrated to a remote host. In addition, we must also ensure that executable code is available to the object at the destination site in order to continue processing. In this section, we describe how object migration can be performed using Java as an underlying implementation language. Since we have developed an information system in a client/server architecture, we need a message passing abstraction for our system.

In our design, a message is not a passive message containing a enumerated value or string. Rather, the message is itself an object. Just as we viewed the data in the Data Store not as passive data items, but as active objects with structure and methods, we also view the messages between Client and Server not as mere tags or codes, but as full message objects. The **Message** object is passed from Client to Server, and processed at the Server. Unlike traditional approaches, no implementation code need be registered at the Server to handle the message. Rather, the message implements its own functionality, since it is an actual object. The Data Store server need only dispatch the message. We have developed our Messaging layer in Java and a distributed programming package called HORB[Sat96], that provides the basic remote invocation services between Client and Server; other applicable distributed programming packages for Java include RMI (Remote Method Invocation) [WRW96], and CORBA (Common Object Request Broker Architecture)[Sie96].

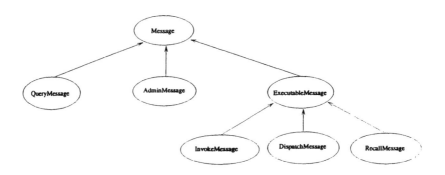

Fig. 2. Message Class Hierarchy

Figure 2 illustrates a hierarchy of different types of messages that can be sent from Client to Server. At the root of the hierarchy is the **Message** object. Different types of objects are derived from **Message**, namely, **QueryMessages**, **AdminMessages**, and **ExecutableMessages**.

QueryMessages are provided for a Client to query for information regarding the Data Store Server's collection and meta-data. **AdminMessages** provide administrative functions such as shutting down and restarting the Data Store, updating a data item, and defining a new Data Store class. It is the **Executable-Messages**, however, that are of primary interest. Clients send **ExecutableMes-**

sages to perform some action. Among these actions are the capability of invoking a method operation (InvokeMessages), of extending an object with new functionality (DispatchMessages), and of transferring processing from the Server site to Client site (RecallMessages).

Each ExecutableMessage defines a method called execute(). When the Server receives an ExecutableMessage from the Client, the Server processes the request by executing the message's execute() method, thus dispatching the ExecutableMessage. The ExecutableMessage then performs some operation upon the object. The operation can either be a class method of the object (in which case, the Java Reflections Package[Sun97] is employed to invoke the particular method), or the method can be some external method that extends the object's functionality. In the latter case, the executable code that provides this additional functionality must satisfy a Data Store Application Code interface called DSAppCode that defines a run() method; the executable code can either reside at the Server site, or be stored in a byte stream within the ExecutableMessage itself.

Upon completion of an operation, the Server returns a result to the Client in the form of an Extractable object. An Extractable object is any object that provides an extract() method to unserialize and retrieve an object out of the result.

Initially, all object data and methods are stored across the collection of Data Store servers. A Client queries a Catalog to locate a particular object at some Data Store. The Client downloads the object's Java implementation type from the Data Store Server and instantiates the Data Store object in two steps. First, the Client calls a system-wide *factory* object that downloads the byte-code of a Java class from the Server site, and constructs a Java object from the implementation class; this creates an initially empty object. Next, the Client passes the empty object to the Server and invokes a constructor method to create a Data Store object by initializing it with the instance data that resides at the server.

The following messages illustrate this process. We take, as an example, a scenario in which Client creates a Data Store LandsatImage of Santa Barbara County residing at the host ella, by calling the object factory DSFactory

```
DSFactory factory = new DSFactory ();
Object    sbCounty = factory.createObject ("LandsatImage",
           "horb://ella.cs.ucsb.edu");
```

The Client then issues ExecutableMessages to initialize and segment the sbCounty object.

InvokeMessages

The InvokeMessage class is the most basic of the ExecutableMessages. A Client sends an InvokeMessage to the Server, specifying some Data Store method to be executed, and supplies the message with a list of required arguments. The create() operation for the sbCounty instance is implemented by sending an InvokeMessage. When the Client wishes to specify the operation,

```
sbCounty.create ("SB-COUNTY-97-04-01");
```

an InvokeMessage is constructed and sent to the Data Store Server.

```
Arglist arglist = new Arglist ();
arglist.append ("SB-COUNTY-97-04-01");
ExecutableMessage mesg = new InvokeMessage (sbCounty, "create", arglist);

sbCounty = mesg.send ("horb://ella.cs.ucsb.edu");
```

The InvokeMessage message is created by specifying the instance, sbCounty, the name of method to invoke, create, and an argument list of relevant objects, in this case, the name of the image to instantiate (SB-COUNTY-97-04-01). Each object that is appended into the argument list is serialized using the Java Object Serializer. Likewise, the instance sbCounty is also serialized within the ExecutableMessage. Finally, the Client calls mesg.send(), which delivers the message to the specified Data Store Server through a HORB remote execution facility. The execute() method of InvokeMessage performs the bulk of the work, when it is executed at the Data Store Server site. It first unserializes the instance object (sbCounty) to recover the object, then it searches the Data Store for the code corresponding to the method create(). The program code is loaded using a Java class loader and dispatched upon the object. The result of this execution is then returned as an Extractable object back to the Client.

DispatchMessages

A DispatchMessage is used to extend a data object's functionality. To take an example, suppose after calling create(), the Client wishes to segment the image to identify city blocks and thoroughfare. Unfortunately, the sbCounty instance belongs to a simple class, which has no such segmentation method. Since the Data Store does not provide the method, it is up to the Client to extend the functionality for the class. To do this, the user running the Client program must first write a Java program that performs the segmentation.

```
public class Userdefined__segment implements DSAppCode {

        public Extractable run (DSObject instance, Arglist arglist) {
            // Code perform segmentation on the image.
        }
}
```

The user creates a program called Userdefined_segment.java, containing a Userdefined_segment class. This Userdefined_segment.java program implements the DSAppCode interface by supplying a method called run(). As we shall see, the Data Store relies on this structure to dispatch the Client's message.

The Client program then compiles the Userdefined_segment.java into byte-code, and stores the byte-code within a DispatchMessage that it sends to the Server.

```
Arglist arglist = new Arglist ();
ExecutableMessage mesg =
    new DispatchMessage (sbCounty, "Userdefined__segment", arglist);

sbCounty = mesg.send ("horb://satchmo.cs.ucsb.edu");
```

The DispatchMessage is constructed by specifying the name of the instance sbCounty, the Userdefined_segment byte-code, followed by the argument list. Note that the constructors for the InvokeMessage and the DispatchMessage have precisely the same signature. In both cases, the arguments supplied are the object instance, a string representing the name of an operation, and an argument list. Where the InvokeMessage and the DispatchMessage differ is that the middle argument represents the name of a Data Store class method in the former, while it represents the name of user-supplied program code in the latter.

Conceptually, the above DispatchMessage has the effect of a Client specifying the operation

```
sbCounty.Userdefined__segment ();
```

though the Userdefined_segment method is user-supplied, and not one of the usual methods found in the LandsatImage class. As discussed before, the DispatchMessage is sent to the remote Server, which then calls the message's execute() method. The Server processes this message by extracting the byte-code from the message and dynamically loading a DSAppCode instance from the byte-code. In executing the DispatchMessage, the Server calls the run() method of the DSAppCode instance to dispatch the client's Userdefined_segment routine.

After execution of the DispatchMessage, this Userdefined_segment method is discarded. If the Client wishes to retain Userdefined_segment so that it is always available at the Server, then it can modify the Data Store class hierarchy by introducing a new Data Store class (eg: SegmentableLandsatImage), and providing the class with this new segmentation method. Adding a new type to the Data Store, however, requires an AdminMessage which can only be sent by trusted Library Users.

RecallMessage

The last of the basic ExecutableMessages is the RecallMessage. This message allows the execution of an operation to be migrated between Client and Server. A RecallMessage is very similar to a DispatchMessage except that the execution takes place at the Client's site rather than at the Server site.

4 Dynamic Object Access

As geographical information constitutes the bulk of data in the Alexandria Digital Library, most of the objects that we encounter in the Data Store model geographical data types[Rob95]. We now describe the Data Store repository, which provides a dynamic and extensible type system for objects in the Data Store collection.

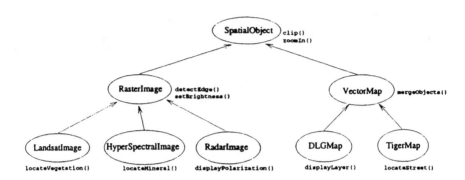

Fig. 3. DataStore Class Hierarchy

To motivate the discussion, we use as an example the class hierarchy of Figure 3. We briefly describe each data type presented in the figure: LandsatImages are high altitude, medium resolution images that are useful for terrain identification and analysis; HyperSpectralImages have hundreds of spectral channels and allow objects in the image to be identified by their component spectra; RadarImages are active-sensored data used for all-weather terrain imaging; TigerMaps combine maps of streets, cities, and counties along with census data to produce population and traffic studies; DLGMaps (Digital Line Graphs) present layers of transportation, hydrographic, and urban planning data for earth modeling and simulation.

To model the organization and relationships among these different types, we construct the following *Instance, ClassFormat,* and *ClassHierarchy* relations in Tables 1–3. Each entry in the *Instance Table*, consists of an instance name and a class name, corresponds to an object in the Data Store. The instance name refers to some static representation of the Data Store object. In the case of images, this representation is the bitwise pixel map of the image. A Data store object is created by first instantiating a Java-program object and then calling a Data Store constructor that converts the Java-level object into a Data Store object, initializing it by loading in its static representation.

The *ClassFormat Table* describes the behavior of each class by listing the available methods in the class; every method that a Client specifies in an Invoke-Message or RecallMessage must have a corresponding entry in the methodName column. Associated with the methodName is the location of the program code that the Server invokes on behalf on the Client to execute the operation. Runtime type checking information in the program code ensures that the appropriate method be applied upon an object for consistent execution.

The remaining table, the *ClassHierarchy Table*, describes the inheritance re-

class	parent
SpatialObject	Root
VectorMap	SpatialObject
RasterImage	SpatialObject
LandsatImage	RasterImage
HyperSpectralImage	RasterImage
RadarImage	RasterImage
DLGImage	VectorMap
TigerImage	VectorMap

Table 2. ClassHierarchy Table

instanceName	className
SB-COUNTY-97-04-01	LandsatImage
GOLETA-CITY-95-03-02	LandsatImage
UCSB-CAMPUS-96-05-07	DLGMap
SOLVANG-CITY-97-12-12	TigerMap

Table 1. Instance Table

className	methodName	executable
SpatialObject	zoomIn	SpatialObject__zoomIn
RasterImage	zoomIn	SpatialObject__zoomIn
RasterImage	detectEdge	RasterImage__detectEdge
VectorImage	zoomIn	VectorImage__zoomIn
VectorMap	mergeObjects	VectorMap__mergeObjects
LandsatImage	zoomIn	SpatialObject__zoomIn
LandsatImage	detectEdge	RasterImage__detectEdge
LandsatImage	locateVegetation	LandsatImage__locateVegetation
TigerMap	zoomIn	VectorImage__zoomIn
TigerMap	mergeObjects	VectorMap__mergeObjects
TigerMap	locateStreet	TigerMap__locateStreet

Table 3. ClassFormat Table

lationships among the Data Store classes. Just as in the usual object-oriented languages, implementation inheritance is supported in our model. Since a Tiger-Map is-a VectorMap, it inherits the mergeObjects method from VectorMap by re-using the VectorMap_mergeObjects program code for its method implementation.

These *Instance, ClassFormat,* and *ClassHierarchy* tables provide object management facilities for the Data Store. A Client application can issue database queries (via a QueryMessage) to browse the Data Store repository for meta-data and identify objects of interest. Upon locating a particular object representation, the Client instantiates the object dynamically by issuing ExecutableMessages to retrieve the object to the Client site.

In designing this data model, we have provided a schema that adheres to a relational model, in order to facilitate storage in a relational DBMS. Other approaches to decomposing and mapping objects into relational databases have been explored in Postgres [Sto86].

By providing the basic structure and methods of the Data Store in terms of a DBMS that allows Clients to dynamically execute methods, we no longer need a statically defined proxy for each object in the Data Store. Rather, the Client can dynamically discover relevant methods to execute on the objects of interest.

We note here the departure from the usual approach adopted by distributed object systems such as CORBA. Each CORBA distributed object is compiled into a proxy object, which in turn acts as a stub to provide remote access for the desired object. In the Data Store, there is no need to generate proxies for a Data Store object. A new object type such as WeatherMap can be introduced into the Data Store without having to provide a new proxy. We need only add new WeatherMap entries into the *Instance, ClassFormat,* and *ClassHierarchy* tables, and supply the required method programs that implement WeatherMap operations.

The benefit of this dynamic object access lies in the run-time time interpretation of the Data Store object model. The class format and inheritance relations of LandsatImage are defined statically. Once instantiated, a Java LandsatImage remains fixed. There are no provisions to extend or alter the LandsatImage class model within the Java language. Instead, we provide this dynamic extension through the Data Store's own data model.

5 Dynamic Views of Data Store Objects

With a collection of Data Store servers storing data and executable programs of Data Store objects, we now provide a means for constructing a specialized view of these Data Store items for Client applications. A Client constructs a view that is a result of processing various Data Store objects that are distributed around the network.

We begin by defining a new container object called a Data View Object; each *DataView* initially holds a Data Store object (also referred to as a *DataView Object*) and a set of instructions for this object. The goal is to distribute processing of the operations in the *DataView* across several Data Store Server sites. By visiting each site, the Data Store object can collect new data and perform a portion of its processing to obtain a new object state for the view. The *DataView* itself is built on top of the Messaging Layer. In order to migrate a *DataView* from Server to Server, the *DataView* itself is an ExecutableMessage object, albeit a programmable one.

To program the DataView, we define a set of instruction primitives that targets processing of the DataView object and of the DataView container. These instructions are *call, load, pull,* and *push.* A *call* operation invokes a Data Store method by sending an InvokeMessage on behalf of the Data Store object. The *load* instruction loads in the Client's program code in order to extend a method; the *load* is implemented by issuing a DispatchMessage to dispatch the operation code upon the object. The *pull* instruction downloads and executes program code from a remote Data Store by means of a RecallMessage.

A *push* differs from the others. While the previous *call, load,* and *pull* instructions operate on the Data View object, the *push* instruction operates on the DataView itself. The purpose of the *push* is to propagate the DataView to a new Data Store site, while the remaining three instructions operate on the object at each new site. A **push** instruction is created by specifying a target URL. When executed, the *DataView* contacts the **DSServer** at the new URL, and forwards the **DataView** to that new site for further processing. After processing each of its instructions, the **DataView** returns to the Client's site.

We illustrate this programming model with an example of a **DataView** that migrates across several Data Store sites. As shown in Figure 4, a **LandsatImage**

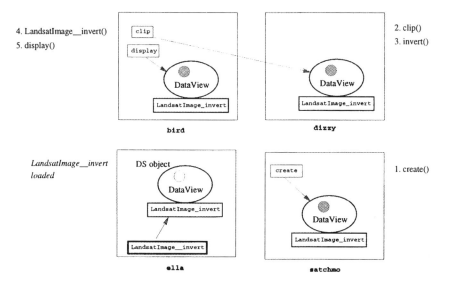

Fig. 4. Dynamic DataView over 4 machines

is created and stored in an **DataView** on a host named **ella**. There are four operations inserted into the **DataView**, and three push instructions.

instruction	operation	address
push		satchmo
call	create	
push		dizzy
pull	clip	bird
push		bird
load	LandsatImage__invert	
call	display	

The instructions are processed in two phases: the loading phase and the execution phase. In the loading phase, all load instructions are processed by loading in the program code from the Client site. Each of the instructions is then sequentially executed in the execution phase. Thus the **DataView** begins by loading a local program called LandsatImage_invert to dynamically extend the LandsatImage object's functionality. The DataView is then pushed to satchmo where the create constructor is invoked from the Data Store repository to conceptualize the Java program object into a Data Store object. Next, the DataView is propagated to dizzy where is sends a RecallMessage to bird to obtain the program code for the clip operation, so that a clip may be executed on dizzy. Finally, the DataView advances to bird, where it executes that LandsatImage_invert program that was originally loaded from ella, and then calls display to display the image.

The program code for this run is shown below:

```
DataView  dataview = new DataView ("LandsatImage", "ella");
dataview.push ("satchmo");

arglist = new Arglist ();
arglist.appendObj ("SB-COUNTY-97-04-01");
dataview.call ("create", arglist);

dataview.push ("dizzy");
arglist = new Arglist ();
arglist.appendObj (10);
arglist.appendObj (10);
arglist.appendObj (50);
arglist.appendObj (50);
dataview.pull ("clip", arglist, "bird");

arglist = new Arglist ();
dataview.load ("LandsatImage__invert", arglist);

dataview.push ("ella");
arglist = new Arglist ();
dataview.call ("display", arglist);

dataview.process(); // begin migration
```

We note from the program code how closely these instructions resemble assembly language. The *load, call,* and *pull* instructions correspond to immediate, direct, and indirect addressing modes of a traditional assembly language. While ordinary opcodes specify operations in which operands provide data and destination addresses, in our programming model, the opcode specifies the *addressing format* while the operands specify the operation and destination. This inversion reflects a difference between a procedural computational model and our distributed model. We program the DataView by specifying the manner in which operations are to be distributed and processed. As in a data-flow language, the operations are then targeted towards the location where the object resides. The state of the object is then updated at each Data Store site by performing one of programmed instructions upon the object.

6 Conclusion

We have designed and built a framework for a Data Store that distributes processing across multiple host sites, and also defines a dynamic object model to implement Client services. By building a messaging layer using HORB, we were able to obtain a dynamic and extensible distributed environment for Data Store objects. We show how the object instances and object methods can be selectively migrated to different sites for remote processing. We describe the Data Store repository's data model, and provide a programming model to build a dynamic DataView in which sequences of method executions are targeted at particular Data Store sites for distributing the processing. We have developed a prototype of the Data Store that exhibits these features, and are currently investigating other applications involving workflow and distributed database queries on federated databases using the DataView.

An expanded version of this paper is available as a Technical Report (TRCS97-14) at http://www.cs.ucsb.edu/TRs/TRCS97-14.html.

References

[AG96]   Ken Arnold and James Gosling. *The Java Programming Language*. Prentice-Hall, Reading, Mass., 1996.

[Cor97]   Microsoft Corp. *Automation Programmer's Reference : Using ActiveX Technology to Create Programmable Applications*. Microsoft Press, 1997.

[Rob95]   Arthur H. Robinson. *Elements of Cartography*. Wiley, New York, 1995.

[Rog97]   Dale Rogerson. *Inside COM*. Microsoft Press, 1997.

[RS91]   Joel Richardson and Peter Schwarz. Aspects: Extending object to support multiple independent roles. In *Proc. ACM SIGMOD Int. Conf. on Management of Data*, pages 298–307, May 1991.

[RWW96]   R. Riggs, J. Waldo, and A. Wollrath. Pickling state in java. In *2nd Conf. on Object-Oriented Technologies and Systems (COOTS)*, pages 241–250, Toronto, Ontario, June 1996.

[Sat96]   HIRANO Satoshi. *The Magic Carpet for Network Computing: HORB Flyer's Guide*. Electrotechnical Laboratory, http://ring.etl.go.jp/openlab/horb, 1996.

[Sie96]   Jon Siegal. *CORBA: Fundamentals and Programming*. Wiley, 1996.

[Smi96]   T.R. Smith. A digital library for geographically referenced materials. *IEEE Computer*, pages 54–60, May 1996.

[Sto86]   Michael Stonebraker. Object management in postgres using procedures. In *1986 International Workshop on Object-Oriented Database Systems*, pages 66–72, Pacific Grove, Calif., September 1986.

[Sun97]   Sun Microsystems, Inc., http://java.sun.com/products/jdk/1.1/docs/guide-/reflection/index.html. *Java Core Reflection API and Specification*, 1997.

[WRW96]   A. Wollrath, R. Riggs, and J. Waldo. A distributed object model for java. In *2nd Conf. on Object-Oriented Technologies and Systems (COOTS)*, pages 219–231, Toronto, Ontario, June 1996.

Fragmentation Techniques
for Distributing Object-Oriented Databases*

Elzbieta Malinowski[1] and Sharma Chakravarthy[2]

[1] Computer and Information Science School, University of Costa Rica, Costa Rica,
emalinow@cariari.ucr.ac.cr
[2] Database Systems Research and Development Center, Computer and Information
Science and Engineering Department, University of Florida, Gainesville FL 32611,
sharma@cise.ufl.edu

Abstract. Design of distributed object-oriented databases inherits the
design problems from the relational distributed databases and presents
additional difficulties related to schema represented by classes and their
possible complicated hierarchical structure. Unlike the relational case,
access to data by user-defined methods further complicates the problem.
This paper addresses fragmentation issues related to design of distributed
object-oriented databases. Specifically, this paper investigates vertical
fragmentation of objects as a generalization of previous work on relational databases.

1 Introduction

The relational distributed databases have been investigated for many years. According to [10] – I/O operations and data transfer – are the most important
factors that affect the performance of distributed database applications. The
performance of a DBMS can be improved if adequate distribution design including fragmentation, replication and allocation are applied. The relational approach distinguishes two kinds of fragmentation: horizontal and vertical. Also
the hybrid fragmentation is considered another way to partition the data. There
are many algorithms developed for horizontal and vertical fragmentation. Each
of them has its own metric to determine the best fragmentation scheme for the
relational system being considered [3, 4, 5, 11, 13, 14].

Ezeife and Barker [6] specify benefits of fragmentation in relational databases
and mention that they should be recognized in distributed object-oriented database
(DOODB), too. However, there is an important aspect that makes the development of the algorithms more complicated: for a relational approach the granularity of partition was easy to identify (attributes for vertical partitioning, in-
stances/tuples for horizontal). In contrast, in object-oriented databases, different
criteria could be considered for fragmentation: hierarchical structure, "affinity"

---

* This work is partly supported by the Office of Naval Research and the Navy Command, Control and Ocean Surveillance Center RDT&E Division, and by the Rome
Laboratory.

of classes, "affinity" of objects, frequency of usage of complex objects, and so forth.

Even though significant differences exist between relational and object-oriented databases, it should be clear that a relational approach can be viewed (ignoring, for simplicity, the existence of the methods) as a special case of an object-oriented system without a class hierarchy and complex attributes (attributes that include the reference to other object/attributes). From this viewpoint, many of the algorithms developed for relational databases can be generalized and applied to object-oriented databases as is presented in this paper: the problem of vertical fragmentation in distributed object-oriented databases. Vertical fragmentation can improve transaction processing cost by decreasing the communication cost for accessing remote attributes in a distributed environment.

1.1 Contributions

This paper makes several contributions to the vertical fragmentation in DOODB:

- A Partition Evaluator for Distributed Object-Oriented Database (termed PEOO) is presented. It is a generalization of Partition Evaluator (PE) for vertical partitioning used in a relational approach described by Chakravarthy et al. [2].
- The matrices that represent method and attribute usage are specified. Also, the rules for calculating the values of Attribute Usage Matrix for DOODB are presented.
- The distinction between update and retrieve operations are provided through the method-attribute usage matrix.
- Not only is the static information about the hierarchical structure of the object-oriented database system considered, but also the frequencies of used methods and attributes are used for establishing the fragmentation scheme.
- Different levels of granularity of vertical fragmentation are proposed.

This paper is organized as follows: Section 2 discusses the issues related to the vertical partitioning in object-oriented databases. In section 3 the process of development of the objective function for vertical partitioning is shown. Section 4 describes the information requirements and their representation for partitioning in object-oriented database systems. Several examples of small object-oriented schemes, their partitioning, minimum cost, and behavior of partition evaluator are presented in section 5. Section 6 contains the conclusions.

2 Fragmentation issues in OODB

Vertical partitioning allows the designer to group attributes

2.1 Related Work in OODB

In developing algorithms for horizontal partitioning, Ezeife and Barker [6] analyzed four separate cases of simple attributes and simple methods, simple attributes and complex methods, complex attributes and simple methods and complex attributes and complex methods. Karlapalem and Li [9] try to establish some common schemes for the fragmentation in object-oriented databases. They do not present specific algorithms for fragmentation, but propose some initial steps for each fragmentation scheme. Karlapalem et al. [10] describe some of the issues to be considered in an object-oriented distributed environment such as used data model, the method invocation important for allocation purposes, types of transparency, closeness of methods and attributes, inheritance hierarchy, and so forth. They do not present any algorithms for vertical partitioning, and affirm that the algorithm proposed in Navathe et al. [14] can be used for the simple method and value-based attributes.

2.2 Motivation for Vertical Partitioning in DOODB

In the relational approach [8, 7, 13, 14, 5, 3, 4] the fragmentation deals with algorithms that apply to attribute distribution. Depending on the kind of fragmentation, the information about transaction frequency, attribute usage, or predicate type is needed.

However, in the object-oriented approach the conceptual schema can be more complex and apart from the features presented in a relational approach, additional aspects have to be considered for fragmentation such as:

- Methods.
- Hierarchical structure.
- Complex attributes.

To the best of our knowledge, only fragmentation schemes presented by Ezeife and Barker [6] have been implemented. Also, none of the presented algorithms consider the relationship between relational and object-oriented approaches and the possibility of extending existing algorithms from relational to object-oriented databases. Even though Karlapalem et al. [10] propose the feasibility of using the fragmentation schemes existing in relational approach in object-oriented environment, they only describe this adoption in very general form.

Most algorithms for vertical partitioning in a relational database also use attribute affinity matrix as an input. This matrix can only express between pairs of attributes, and cannot express the "affinity" among *several (more than two) attributes*. Hence, our approach that uses only the attribute usage matrix can accurately reflect the real behavior of the system. Moreover, some existing algorithms declare themselves as the best and give different "optimal" fragmentation for the same input information. The result of one algorithm very often cannot be compared to the results of others. Therefore, the necessity of having a tool that can measure the "goodness" of presenting results is important.

3 The Objective Function for DOODBs

The goal of partitioning the attributes is to obtain the minimum processing cost for a given set of transactions and their usage of attributes. It is unlikely to achieve an ideal fragmentation scheme, where any transaction locally accesses

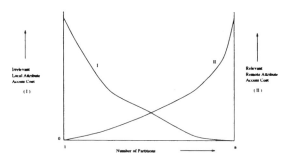

Fig. 1. Behavior of partition evaluator in relational approach

only the attributes that are needed and does not need to perform any remote accesses. The objective function proposed here tries to balance the cost of local and remote accesses for a given transactions. According to Chakravarthy et al. [2], the overall transaction processing cost in a distributed environment consists of two elements:

1. The first component, called irrelevant local attribute access cost, represents the cost of accessing irrelevant attributes when accessing the object in the local site, assuming that all data fragments required by a transaction are available locally, and

2. The second component, called relevant remote attribute cost, includes the cost of accessing the relevant attributes required by the transaction from remote sites.

Chakravarthy et al. [2] showed the expected behavior of the objective function using the above component. It is shown in Figure 1.

Individually, the irrelevant local attribute cost should have a maximum value for one fragment and equal to zero for a partition size (i.e. number of fragments in the partition) equal to the number of attributes. The relevant remote access cost should be zero and maximum values for these two extremes respectively. Moreover, as stated by the previously mentioned authors, the local cost should be more responsive to smaller partition sizes in contrary to the remote cost that should be more responsive to larger fragments in between these two extreme values.

As is evident, the partitioning evaluator for an object-oriented database should have the same behavior as the partitioning evaluator presented above for a relational database. However, the irrelevant local cost will have one additional component. Because the frequencies of attributes for the same transaction can be different, the penalty for accessing some relevant attributes more than others will be considered as a penalty for the local cost.

Our Partition Evaluator function for an object-oriented approach (PEOO) is given by

$$PEOO = E_L^2 + E_R^2 \qquad (1)$$

where,

$$E_L^2 = \sum_{i=1}^{M} \sum_{t=1}^{T} \left[\sum_{j=1}^{|S_{it}|} \left(f_{tj}^i - \frac{\sum_{p=1}^{|S_{it}|} f_{tp}^i}{n_i} \right)^2 + \sum_{j=1}^{|I_{it}|} \left(f_{tj}^i - \frac{\sum_{p=1}^{|S_{it}|} f_{tp}^i}{n_i} \right)^2 \right] \quad (2)$$

and

$$E_R^2 = \sum_{t=1}^{T} \Delta_{i=1}^{M} \sum_{k \neq i} \left[CC_{ik} * \sum_{p_k} (f_{tp_k}^k)^2 * \frac{|R_{itk}|}{n_{itk}^{rem}} \right] \quad (3)$$

Based on the analysis similar to presented by Chakravarthy et al. [2], the expected behavior of this partition evaluator is the same as the one shown in the Figure 1.

This formula is a generalization of the formula presented by Chakravarthy et al. [2] for relational distributed databases. With the suppositions $\sum_{p_k} = |R_{itk}|$, $f_{tp_k} = q_k$, and $CC_{ik} = 1$ for all sites concerning the relational approach, we obtain the same formula for Remote Access Cost as presented in the previously mentioned paper.

4 Modeling object hierarchy for partitioning

The goal of the modeling is to obtain the TAUM (transaction attribute usage matrix) that corresponds to AUM (attribute usage matrix) in relational approach. As was mentioned before, the only difference between these to matrices is in values for accessing attributes by specific transaction in contrast to AUM where these values are the same. For this TAUM we can apply PEOO and using an exhaustive search obtain the best fragmentation scheme.

4.1 Assumptions

The following assumptions are made:

1. Object-based and no values-based approach is applied.
2. The information of the classes including the methods and attributes used by methods is given.
3. The access to the attributes is done only through the methods following the principle of information hiding, encapsulation, and abstract data. This assumption facilitates the path expression allowing to have in it no more than two elements.
4. The information of accessing the method by specific transaction is given.
5. The frequencies of accessing transactions is specified.
6. The existence of the type tuple, set, and list are ignored.

4.2 Transaction, Method and Attribute Usage Matrices for DOODB

The information needed for partitioning can be represented in the form of the Transaction-Method Usage Matrix (TMUM), Method-Method Usage Matrix (MMUM) and Method-Attribute Usage Matrix (MAUM).

– Transaction-Method Usage Matrix (TMUM): the matrix of frequencies that indicates if the transaction calls specific methods. Used values are zero or one that represent no call or call of the specific method respectively.

$$
\begin{array}{lcccc}
trans \setminus methods & m_{i,j}^1 & m_{i,j}^2 & \dots & m_{i,j}^m \\
& & & & \\
tr_1 & fm_{1,1} & fm_{1,2} & \dots & fm_{1,m} \\
tr_2 & fm_{2,1} & fm_{2,2} & \dots & fm_{2,m} \\
\vdots & \vdots & \vdots & \vdots & \vdots \\
tr_T & fm_{T,1} & fm_{T,2} & \dots & fm_{T,m}
\end{array}
\tag{4}
$$

where
m Total number of methods in the system that is being partitioned.
$m_{i,j}^l$ Method j of class i, for l=1 to m.
T Total number of transactions that are under consideration.
tr_p Transaction p, for p=1 to T.
$fm_{p,r}$ Frequency that transaction p accesses method r (equal to 0 or 1).

– Method-Method Usage Matrix (MMUM): the matrix of frequencies that indicates the number of times that the method calls other methods (in the case of simple methods this matrix does not exist). Similar to the TMUM the values of zero or one represent the existence of nested calls. The value equal to two is presented only in the case when the method is called through the complex attribute.

$$
\begin{array}{lcccc}
methods \setminus methods & m_{i,j}^1 & m_{i,j}^2 & \dots & m_{i,j}^m \\
& & & & \\
m_{i,j}^1 & 1 & fmm_{1,2} & \dots & fmm_{1,m} \\
m_{i,j}^2 & fmm_{2,1} & 1 & \dots & fmm_{2,m} \\
\vdots & \vdots & \vdots & \vdots & \vdots \\
m_{i,j}^m & fmm_{m,1} & fmm_{m,2} & \dots & 1
\end{array}
\tag{5}
$$

where
m Total number of methods in the system that is being partitioned.
$m_{i,j}^l$ Method j of class i, for l=1 to m.
$fmm_{s,r}$ Frequency that method s calls method r (equal to 0, 1, or 2) .

– Method-Attribute Usage Matrix (MAUM): the matrix that represents the number of invocations of specific attribute in one execution of a method. There are possible three values:

- Zero - indicates that a method does not access an attribute.
- One - indicates that a method reads the value of an attribute (retrieve).
- Two - indicates that a method reads and writes the value of an attribute (update).

$$methods \setminus attr \quad at_{i,j}^1 \quad at_{i,j}^2 \quad \ldots \quad at_{i,j}^n$$

$$
\begin{array}{cc}
m_{i,j}^1 & fat_{1,1} \quad fat_{1,2} \ldots fat_{1,n} \\
m_{i,j}^2 & fat_{2,1} \quad fat_{2,2} \ldots fat_{2,n} \\
\vdots & \vdots \quad \vdots \quad \vdots \quad \vdots \\
m_{i,j}^m & fat_{m,1} \quad fat_{m,2} \ldots fat_{m,n}
\end{array}
\tag{6}
$$

where

n Total number of attributes in the system that is being partitioned.

$at_{i,j}^p$ Attribute j of class i, for p=1 to n.

$fat_{k,l}$ Frequency of accessing of attribute l by method k (equal to 0, 1, or 2).

The information specified above is typically given by the designer of the system. Additionally, in the same way as was done for relational approach, the frequency of using the specific transaction by applications is given. Frequencies of used transaction by applications (ftr):

$$
\begin{array}{l}
transaction \quad tr_1 \quad tr_2 \quad tr_3 \ldots tr_T \\
frequency \quad ftr_1 \; ftr_2 \; ftr_3 \ldots ftr_T
\end{array}
\tag{7}
$$

With TMUM, that contains the information of methods used by a specific transaction, and MAUM, that contains the frequencies of used attributes by a specific method, we can multiply them and obtain the matrix that represents the frequencies of used attributes by a specific transaction. These frequencies serves as a basis for the fragmentation scheme and correspond to the Attribute Usage Matrix (AUM) in the relational approach. Why not fragment methods and then assign the attributes to the adequate fragments? The reason is obvious. The methods as a piece of software can be easily copied, or duplicated without any problems (space, concurrency control, and so forth). The adequate distribution of the data, which optimizes data distribution (no unnecessary duplication) and gives good performance regarding the used transaction, is the main goal of the design in distributed databases systems, either relational or object-oriented.

5   Implementation and Results of the Experiments

To analyze the behavior of PEOO several tests were developed. According to the previous explanation the same behavior as presented by Chakravarthy et al. [2] regarding to local and remote costs was expected.

The cases of simple attributes and simple methods, and complex attributes and complex methods were tested. The case of simple attributes and complex methods gives only the additional matrix multiplication (TMUM and MMUM).

The number of classes and subclasses used in the experiments were limited to allow the readers to understand the process of fragmentation. The basic idea was to show the behavior of PEOO and compare the best fragmentation obtained from a theoretical analysis and a program run. The program written in C++ that calculates the values of local and remote costs for an object-oriented approach was run for all the possible combinations (4140) of attributes with the number of fragments varying from one to eight. The PEOO was applied for each of these combinations. During the program execution, each transaction is run on each fragment. Depending on the selected option (average, minimum or maximum) the value of PEOO is calculated. The optimal value with the partitioning scheme is presented as a result of the program.

We assume that if a transaction should be run on a fragment, then at least one attribute used by this transaction is present in this fragment. If this is not the case, the transaction is not run on this fragment.

Due to lack of the specific information about network, in most of the examples the real transmission cost is ignored taking a unit cost for each access to remote fragment. In these cases we will see the frequencies as a dominate feature to obtain best fragmentation scheme. Other experiments show that increasing the communication cost can change the fragmentation scheme considerably.

For the case of simple attributes and simple methods the following hierarchical class representation was used:

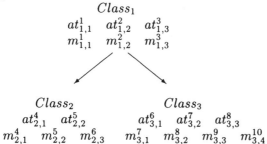

Because the access to the attributes are done through the methods following the principles of encapsulation and information hiding, the methods of each class can only use the attributes of their own class or superclasses.

For the case of complex attributes and complex method calls the following hierarchical representation of classes was used:

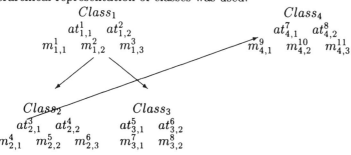

We assume the attribute $at_{2,1}^3$ to be the complex attribute that points to $Class_4$. Also, the method $m_{2,1}^4$ of the $Class_2$ calls the methods $m_{4,1}^9$ and $m_{4,3}^{11}$ of the $Class_3$ through this complex attribute $at_{2,1}^3$ and $m_{2,2}^5$ calls the method $m_{4,2}^{10}$ through the same attribute. This means, in some transactions method $m_{2,1}^4$ can have the call such as: $at_{2,1}^3.m_{4,1}^9$.

Because of a limited number of attributes that can be managed using an exhaustive partitioning algorithm, the presented classes have only two or three attributes each. Moreover, in the first part of the experiments, we assume that the desired granularity level covers all levels of classes presented in our examples. This allows us to consider all attributes for fragmentation. To see the effect of using different levels of granularity more attributes need to be used. The last three examples presented in this section were provided to show the feasibility of using our PEOO for different levels of granularity. In these three cases ten attributes and the following class representation were used:

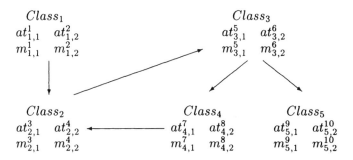

Here, two complex attributes are presented: $at_{2,1}^3$ and $at_{4,1}^7$. The following calls are made using these complex attributes:

- Method $m_{2,1}^3$ calls twice $at_{2,1}^3.m_{3,1}^5$
- Method $m_{2,2}^4$ calls once $at_{2,1}^3.m_{3,2}^6$
- Method $m_{4,1}^7$ calls once $at_{4,1}^7.m_{2,1}^3$
- Method $m_{4,2}^8$ calls twice $at_{4,1}^7.m_{2,2}^4$

Even though many experiments were developed, because of space limitation we will show the results of some of them.

For each example the TMUM shows the values obtained after multiplication of TMUM and frequencies of accessing of each transaction.

5.1 Simple Attributes and Simple Methods

. For this case several sub-cases were developed, which allow us to check the obtained fragmentation with the theoretical analysis previous to program run. Only two of them will be shown.

Example 1: Clear distribution of frequencies of accessing the methods by transaction.

The following TMUM was used:

	$m_{1,1}^1$	$m_{1,2}^2$	$m_{1,3}^3$	$m_{2,1}^4$	$m_{2,2}^5$	$m_{2,3}^6$	$m_{3,1}^7$	$m_{3,2}^8$	$m_{3,3}^9$	$m_{3,4}^{10}$
tr_1	25	25	25	0	0	25	0	0	0	0
tr_2	30	30	30	0	0	0	0	0	0	0
tr_3	0	0	0	80	80	80	0	0	0	0
tr_4	0	0	0	70	70	70	0	0	0	0
tr_5	5	0	0	0	0	0	5	5	5	5
tr_6	0	10	0	10	0	0	10	10	10	10

This matrix shows a clear clustering of higher frequencies and a separation of lower frequencies. This facilitates the prediction of the fragmentation scheme.

The used MAUM reflects the situation when the methods use the attributes only from their own class:

	$at_{1,1}^1$	$at_{1,2}^2$	$at_{1,3}^3$	$at_{2,1}^4$	$at_{2,2}^5$	$at_{3,1}^6$	$at_{3,2}^7$	$at_{3,3}^8$
$m_{1,1}^1$	2	0	0	0	0	0	0	0
$m_{1,2}^2$	0	2	0	0	0	0	0	0
$m_{1,3}^3$	0	0	1	0	0	0	0	0
$m_{2,1}^4$	0	0	0	1	0	0	0	0
$m_{2,2}^5$	0	0	0	0	2	0	0	0
$m_{2,3}^6$	0	0	0	2	1	0	0	0
$m_{3,1}^7$	0	0	0	0	0	2	1	0
$m_{3,2}^8$	0	0	0	0	0	1	2	0
$m_{3,3}^9$	0	0	0	0	0	0	1	2
$m_{3,4}^{10}$	0	0	0	0	0	0	1	2

The values in MAUM are zero, one, or two to reflect no access, only read (retrieve), or read and write (update) of the attributes. The values can be changed in case it is necessary. After multiplying the above matrices the resulted TAUM is as follows:

	$at_{1,1}^1$	$at_{1,2}^2$	$at_{1,3}^3$	$at_{2,1}^4$	$at_{2,2}^5$	$at_{3,1}^6$	$at_{3,2}^7$	$at_{3,3}^8$
tr_1	50	50	25	50	25	0	0	0
tr_2	60	60	30	0	0	0	0	0
tr_3	0	0	0	240	240	10	0	0
tr_4	0	8	0	210	210	0	0	0
tr_5	10	0	0	0	0	15	25	20
tr_6	0	20	0	10	0	30	50	40

In this TAUM matrix we can see that dominant values are presented in such a way that they should give the following grouping of the attributes:

- $at_{1,1}^1$, $at_{1,2}^2$ and $at_{1,3}^3$
- $at_{2,1}^4$ and $at_{2,2}^5$.
- $at_{3,1}^6$, $at_{3,2}^7$ and $at_{3,3}^8$.

Indeed, the result of the program, using the criterion of minimum, gave this fragmentation as the optimal one with the minimum cost equal to 5307.

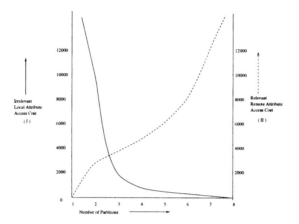

Fig. 2. Behavior of the components of PEOO for an example

The local, remote, and total costs for the optimistic approach with the minimum values and the corresponding partitioning schemes are given below. The results for minimum cost of each component and total cost are plotted in Figures 2 and 3.

$NFrag$	$LocCost$	$RemCost$	$PEOO$	$Partition$
1	165028	0	165028	(12345678)
2	10408	2862	13270	(123678)(45)
3	1966	3341	5307	(123)(45)(678)
4	863	4950	5813	(12)(3)(45)678)
5	676	6075	6751	(12)(3)(45)(6)(78)
6	613	8075	8688	(12)(3)(45)(6)(7)(8)
7	363	13800	14163	(1)(2)(3)(45)(6)(7)(8)
8	0	116175	116175	(1)(2)(3)(4)(5)(6)(7)(8)

The behavior of PEOO corresponds to the previous supposition: the minimum value of local cost is equal to zero for one fragment and maximum for eight fragments; the remote cost in these extremes has opposite values of maximum and minimum (equal to zero) respectively. In this case the communication cost between sites was equal to one for all the pairs of sites. To analyze the influence of the communication cost (CC) on the fragmentation scheme we run experiments with CC different from one, but equal the same value for all the sites. The following are the results:

CC_{ik}	$MinCost$	$Fragm.Scheme$
17	58763	(123)(45)(678)
18	61924	(123678)(45)
100	149040	(123678)(45)
105	150140	(12345)(678)
180	165028	(12345678)

Here, we can notice that increasing communication cost affects the optimal fragmentation scheme. For example, for communication cost varying from one to seventeen, the fragmentation scheme remains the same. The fragmentation scheme changes for $CC_{ik} = 18$. However, if we distribute the communication cost differently, such as

sites	s_1	s_2	s_3	s_4	s_5	s_6	s_7	s_8
s_1	0	13	10	11	8	7	3	4
s_2	13	0	6	14	10	3	5	9
s_3	10	6	0	11	3	2	8	6
s_4	11	14	11	0	10	2	1	5
s_5	8	10	3	10	0	6	9	12
s_6	7	3	2	2	6	0	13	11
s_7	3	5	8	1	9	13	0	6
s_8	4	9	6	5	12	11	6	0

even though the individual cost is not greater than 18 the fragmentation scheme changes to $(12)(3678)(45)$ with the minimum cost equal to 43261.

In each case, the behavior of PEOO was analyzed and was found similar to the PE behavior presented by Chakravarthy et al. [2] and expected for PEOO.

Example 2: Influence of dominant value of transaction frequency.

The partitioning scheme is sensitive to the presence of the significant values of the frequency of accessing method or attribute. For example, if we modify in the first example only one value for $m_{2,3}^6$ and $at_{2,1}^4$ in MMUM such as

	$at_{1,1}^1$	$at_{1,2}^2$	$at_{1,3}^3$	$at_{2,1}^4$	$at_{2,2}^5$	$at_{3,1}^6$	$at_{3,2}^7$	$at_{3,3}^8$
$m_{1,1}^1$	2	0	0	0	0	0	0	0
$m_{1,2}^2$	0	2	0	0	0	0	0	0
$m_{1,3}^3$	0	0	1	0	0	0	0	0
$m_{2,1}^4$	0	0	0	1	0	0	0	0
$m_{2,2}^5$	0	0	0	0	2	0	0	0
$m_{2,3}^6$	0	0	0	0	1	0	0	0
$m_{3,1}^7$	0	0	0	0	0	2	1	0
$m_{3,2}^8$	0	0	0	0	0	1	2	0
$m_{3,3}^9$	0	0	0	0	0	0	1	2
$m_{3,4}^{10}$	0	0	0	0	0	0	1	2

leaving the matrix TMUM without changes, we will obtain TAUM with the corresponding values:

	$at_{1,1}^1$	$at_{1,2}^2$	$at_{1,3}^3$	$at_{2,1}^4$	$at_{2,2}^5$	$at_{3,1}^6$	$at_{3,2}^7$	$at_{3,3}^8$
tr_1	50	50	25	0	25	0	0	0
tr_2	60	60	30	0	0	0	0	0
tr_3	0	0	0	80	240	0	0	0
tr_4	0	0	0	0	210	0	0	0
tr_5	10	0	0	0	0	5	25	20
tr_6	0	20	0	10	0	30	50	40

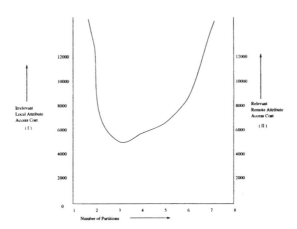

Fig. 3. Behavior of PEOO for an example

This example gives the best fragmentation $(123)(4)(5)(678)$, clearly putting the attribute $at_{2,2}^5$ in a different fragment than attributes $at_{2,1}^4$. This result was expected because the high frequency of accessing the attribute $at_{2,2}^5$ will increase the local cost (the part that corresponds to the accessing of relevant attributes with different frequencies) if these three attributes were together. This value changes from 1603 (with the total cost equal to 13794) for fragmentation $(12)(3)(45)(678)$ to 24566 (with the total cost equal to 25094) for the fragmentation $(123)(45)(678)$.

6 Conclusion

The extension of the Object-Oriented Partition Evaluator developed for relational model clearly indicates that the object-oriented case is indeed a generalization of the relational model, at least from the data modeling viewpoint. The concept of vertical partitioning when extended to the object-oriented database systems as presented in this paper opens the possibility to "flatten" the complicated hierarchical structure and present it in the form of matrices which are easy to manage for computational purposes. These matrices represent the relationship between transactions, methods and attributes. Moreover, the method-attribute usage matrix and the concepts of encapsulation and information hiding adopted from programming languages gives the designer the possibility to distinguish between retrieve and update operations without special modifications to the presented algorithms.

Our approach supports different levels of granularity thereby allowing the user to state additional restrictions regarding the partitioning of the classes, limiting it to the desired hierarchy level. Results of experiments that are not detailed in this paper can be found in [12].

The algorithm for vertical partitioning for complex attributes and complex methods represents the generalization for three other cases of simple attributes and simple methods, simple attributes and complex methods, complex attributes and simple methods. This means one general program can be used for vertical partitioning and each of the corresponding options can be seen as a special case of complex attributes and complex methods.

Experiments presented in this paperconfirm the expected behavior of PEOO and show feasibility of its use.

References

1. Ceri, S., and Pelagatti, G. Distributed Databases: Principles and Systems. McGraw-Hill, New York, 1984.
2. Chakravarthy, S., Muthuraj, J., Varadarajan, R., and Navathe, S.B. An Objective Function for Vertically Partitioning Relations in Distributed Databases and its Analysis. *Distributed and Parallel Databases*, Vol.2, No.1, 1993.
3. Chu Pai-Cheng. A Transaction Oriented Approach to Attribute Partitioning. *Information System*, Vol. 17, No.4, 1992.
4. Chu, W., and Ieong, I.T. A Transaction-Based Approach to Vertical Partitioning for Relational Database Systems. *IEEE Transactions on Software Engineering*, Vol. 19, No. 8, August 1993.
5. Cornell, D., and Yu, P. A Vertical Partitioning Algorithm for Relational Databases. *Proc. Third International Conference on Data Engineering*, February 1987.
6. Ezeife, C.I., and Barker, K. A Comprehensive Approach to Horizontal Class Fragmentation in a Distributed Object Based System. Technical report, Advanced Database Systems Laboratory, Department of Computer Science, University of Manitoba, Canada, October 1994.
7. Hammer, M., and Niammir, B. A heuristic Approach to Attributes Partitioning. *Proc ACM SIGMOD International Conference on Management of Data*. Boston, MA, 1979.
8. Hoffer, J. A., and Severance, D. G. The use of Cluster Analysis in Physical Database Design. *Proc. First International Conference on Very Large Data Bases*. Framingham, MA, September 1975.
9. Karlapalem, K. and Li, O. Partitioning Schemes for Object Oriented Databases. Technical report, University of Science and Technology, Department of Computer Science Clear Water Bay, Kowloon, Honk Kong. August, 1994a.
10. Karlapalem, K., Navathe, A.B., and Morsi, M. Issues in Distribution Design in M.T.Ozsu, U.Dayal, and P.Valduriez (eds.), *Distributed Object Management*. Morgan Kaufman Publishers, San Mateo, 1994b.
11. Lin, X., Orlowska, M., and Zhang, Y. A Graph Based Cluster Approach for Vertical Partitioning in Database System. *Data & Knowledge Engineering*, Vol. 11, 1993.
12. Malinowski, E. Fragmentation Techniques for Distributing Object-Oriented Databases, MS thesis, University of Florida, Database Systems R&D Center, Aug. 1996.
13. Navathe, S., Ceri, G., Wiederhold, G., and Dou, J. Vertical Partitioning Algorithm for Database Design. *ACM Transaction on Database Systema*, Vol.9, No.4, December 1984.
14. Navathe, S. and Ra, M. Vertical Partitioning for Database Design: A Graphical Algorithm. *ACM SIGMOD*, Portland. June 1989.

An Agent Based Mobile System

Niki Pissinou, Kia Makki, Mei Hong, Lusheng Ji, Ashok Kumar
The Center For Advanced Computer Studies
The University of Southwestern Louisiana, Lafayette LA

Abstract. In this paper we propose a new mobile system architecture, called the Client-Representative-Agent-Server (CRAS) architecture. While developing this architecture, an attempt is being made to keep CRAS compatible existing distributed object management frameworks and standards.

1   Introduction

Currently most database system architectures are not designed to support a mobile computing environment, and existing designs do not facilitate the simulation of such an environment. Furthermore there are no hardware and software platforms for mobile computing [4, 5]. Thus the pending needs are several [4, 5]: We need to design specifications for energy efficient data access methodologies and processing, strategies for processing location dependent queries, migrating locatity, data broadcasting and global name strategies due to mobility and disconnection, to name a few [6]. We also need to develop a software environment that builds on existing database system designs and platforms [5]. This will allow us to develop a wireless infrastructure by extending already existing database functionalities. In this way, the resources will not become yet another collection of wireless networks and devices, but a true system capable of supporting a wide variety of mobile applications and computing.

In view of the above, in this paper we introduce a new mobile system architecture, called the ClientRepresentativeAgentServer (CRAS). CRAS is designed to minimize the effects of frequent disconnection and to provide an intelligent medium on the fixed network platform to speed up the query processing. It is also designed to take into account mobile user's feedback while processing a query etc and support advanced features like mobile conferencing. While developing this architecture, an attempt is being made to keep the CRAS compatible to the distributed databases and distributed object management.

2   The Client-Representative-Agent-Server Architecture

In the CRAS architecture, a Client keeps a close contact with its Representative which takes care of the Client's mobile computational needs. The connection

* This work is partially supported by NSF/LaSER under grant number EHR-9108765, by LEQSF grant number 94-RD-A-39, and by NASA under grant number NAG 5-2842.

between a Mobile Unit and its Representative is wireless. There is a one-to-one connection between a Representative and a Mobile Unit. That is, a Mobile Unit gets only one Representative and a Representative exists to serve only one Mobile Unit. An overview structure of the CRAS architecture is shown in fig 1.

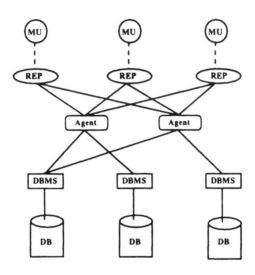

Fig. 1. CRAS Architecture

In the CRAS architecture, a Representative lies on the fixed network and it represents a Mobile Unit to the rest of the fixed network. (a typical example would look like as shown in 1, where one can infer that the things new to the conventional agent-based distributed database system are the Mobile Unit (MU), the Representative, and the Agent-Representative (ARS) server [2].)

A Representative employs agents to do the job. By an agent, we mean a program written in a high level language that allows internal parallelism [1]. An agent is a living entity residing in the fixed network. It has its own local data, a set of methods (both local and global methods), a set of dependency among methods, a set of break and relocation points for recovery [Ev95]. In CRAS, a Representative consists of a set of agents and a mechanism to control and coordinate the activities of these agents.

The basic functioning of the CRAS architecture is as follows. All queries from the Client are sent through the wireless channel and received by the base station, which passes the message to the corresponding Representative. The Representative pre-processes the query and requests an agent from the server (Intermediate Agent) for the proper assignment of the query to a cost-effective set

---

[2] For simplicity we use the words Client and Mobile Unit interchangeably.

of database server agents (Collection Agents). Further, the agent issued by the server (Intermediate Agent) gathers the results from the database server agents and propagates it back to the Representative. Then the Representative stores the results temporarily and passes it in an appropriate format to the Mobile Unit when the wireless connection between the Mobile Unit and the Representative is reliable (bandwidth is greater than a prescribed minimum threshold for reliable communication).

There are two types of servers in the CRAS system. The first type is the database server, which has data entries stored on and which responds to queries from agents and local users. The second type is the Agent-Representative-Servers (ARSs) which are the home servers for Clients and are responsible for regional database server information. ARSs keep a set of agents (Intermediate Agents) that the Representatives can also request.

2.1 The Representative

A Representative consists of a set of agents (User Interface Agent, Buffer Agent, Cache Agent) and a mechanism to control and coordinate the activities of these agents, as defined in the previous section. It has a data cache to keep the most frequently accessed data items by its Client, a store-and-forward data buffer, a pointer to the local ARS, a pointer to the home ARS, and a set of requests that it (the Representative) can send asking the local ARS to send agents (Intermediate Agents).

To the rest of the distributed system, the Representative acts like the regular client in a traditional sense because the rest of the distributed system receives queries only from the Representative (and not the Client). A Representative can follow the move of the Mobile Unit so that wireless communication between the Mobile Unit and the Representative is optimized. The Representative and the Mobile Unit keep close contact to ensure the reliability of connection.

A Representative is created when a Mobile Unit registers to one of the home servers. A Representative exists in the fixed network until the Mobile Unit signs off from the service. Because of the 1-to-1 mapping between the Mobile Unit and its Representative, every Mobile Unit-Representative pair is unique in the whole mobile database system. A unique session-id can be assigned to each pair. This session-id number will be included in every message passed between the Mobile Unit and the Representative. Using this id number, the base station can search for the Representative when a wireless message is received. Figure 2 shows the architecture of the Representative.

Let us understand the role of the Representative in the light of different phases of connections. There are three types of disconnections a Mobile Unit can have. One is "nice disconnection", which is a user-issued disconnection. In this type, the connection is broken only after the significant information exchange has taken place between the Mobile Unit and the Representative. An example of such an information exchange would be updating the Mobile Unit's cache objects. Two is "hand-off disconnection", which happens when the Mobile Unit moves from one wireless communication cell to another. This type of disconnection can be

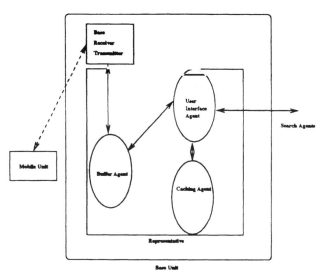

Fig. 2. A Representative in Action

detected by the control system of the cellular network so that the Representative can be informed and get ready. The third type of disconnection contains all the rest disconnections and is called "unexpected disconnection", which is a type of disconnection that neither the network nor the Representative can know in advance.

A Representative possesses the ability to detect the transmission error then either discard the corrupted message or ask for a re-transmission. Because of this functionality of the Representative, the final query coming out from the Representative is always correct and meaningful so that the fixed network does not have to carry those problematic messages at all. In addition to providing consistent state, this will also help reduce (undesired) data traffic in the fixed network.

After the first type of disconnection occurs, the Representative will change to "half-sleeping" state. In the "half-sleeping" state, the Representative stops contacting with the Mobile Unit but still listens to the incoming data from the fixed network and all unfinished transactions are still processed. If the unfinished transaction can be continued without involving the Mobile Unit, then it will continue till the transaction commits. Otherwise, the Representative will send out "abort" message to the serving agents to abort the transaction. All these processings will be recorded in a log so that when the Mobile Unit is connected back, the report can be sent to it. At this state, system updating messages will be buffered so that they can be processed after the Representative wakes up.

After all transactions by hand have been finished, the Representative will go to the "sleeping" state. Under this state, the Representative will stop processing transactions. However, all messages received will still be processed after the Representative wakes up. The Representative can be waken up from both "sleeping" and "half-sleeping" states. The Representative will be waken up by the "wake up" message from the same Mobile Unit when the Mobile Unit is turned back on. The first thing the Representative needs to do after it wakes up is to update its local data set. This update includes updating the log, updating the local ARS pointer if the location is changed, registering to the local ARS as a visiting Representative if not in the service range of its home ARS (the later two will not happen if the Representative wakes from "half-sleeping" state assuming that there is no location change in this case). Then the Representative needs to process the messages in its buffer. These messages can contain the updates of the data items stored in the Representative's local cache and the Mobile Unit's data cache as well as the other system changes.

It is possible that after being in the "sleep" state, the Representative wakes up in a new location if necessary. This happens when the Mobile Unit is turned on in a different communication cell from where the disconnection occurred. In this case, after the Representative receives the wake up call, it will copy itself to the new base station, then wake up and establish the connection with the Mobile Unit. After this, the old copy at the old location is removed. The same situation (location change of Mobile Unit) might happen when the Representative is under "half-sleep" state too. But it might not be a good idea to move the Representative under this case, because usually the time interval that the Representative stays in "half sleeping" is not long, and the distance that the Mobile Unit can move in this period will not be big either. Therefore, even if the communication between the Mobile Unit and the Representative has to go through the fixed link between the base station which has the Mobile Unit in its radio coverage, and the base station which has the Representative, the overall performance will not decrease too much. But if the user feels the performance becomes unsatisfactory, s/he can always exit nicely and log back into the system.

The second type of disconnection can be detected by the cellular network. The Representative can be informed of the change and the Representative can make necessary changes with respect to the new situation. In such a situation, the representative will change to "half sleep" state and will be waken by a message from cellular network controlunit saying that the Mobile Unit hand-off is finished.

The third type of disconnection can be detected by the Representative. Besides the data messages flying between Mobile Unit and the Representative, there are also some control messages. When the Representative detects that the Mobile Unit is unexpectedly disconnected, it will roll back to the point of the last check point after which there is at least one successful hand-shake with the Mobile Unit, and changes its state to "half-sleeping". Also, the Representative needs to take all unfinished transactions at that check point as unfinished transactions and mark all transactions issued after that check point as aborted. The Representative will wake up again if some message from the Mobile Unit is directed to it, or changes its state to "sleeping" state if nothing happened before it finished all unfinished transactions.

2.1.1 The Components of The Representative

Here a description of the component agents of a Representative is presented, which clarifies the interdependencies and collaboration between the agents.

A User-Interface-Agent (UIA) becomes active as soon as a Representative is assigned to a Mobile Unit. There is one and only one User-Interface-Agent associated with a Representative to meet the needs of its associated Mobile Unit. A User-Interface-Agent can be a prototype UIA or it can be of personalized type for a specific Mobile Unit. A User-Interface-Agent resides on the fixed network and it continuously interacts with other agents in the fixed network besides carrying out one particular Mobile Unit's requests. A User-Interface-Agent, for example, can inform the user of any significant changes of information on (the fixed network) database/information server. In order to do this, appropriate rules and event-based trigger mechanisms may be developed. Such a trigger-based mechanism can help identify the objects that have changed and thus incorporate those changed object's values into the outcome rather than processing an entire query all over again. This is useful because a query may be distributed widely over the network. However, in case of complicated queries, the queries may be resubmitted for evaluation if parts of those queries are dependent on the values of objects that have changed (and hence, have been detected by the trigger-mechanisms).

From the Mobile Unit's perspective, a User-Interface-Agent serves in two ways. First, upon receiving a query from the Mobile Unit, the User-Interface-Agent 'models' the query to the format understandable by the search agents and then, upon the successful completion of a query, it (the UIA) sends results to the user in the format 'understandable' by or appropriate for the Mobile Unit. Second, upon unsuccessful completion of a query or in case of a malformed query, the User-Interface-Agent sends the feedback to the feedback to the Mobile Unit and thus prompts the Mobile Unit to provide more information for that query (for e.g, subject, fact, item, document type text or image etc).

The Mobile Unit user can end any particular User-Interface-Agent feedback session as soon as he/she is satisfied with the outcome of a query. Thus, although the User-Interface-Agent provides for the feedback facility, it does not create an interminable loop. It is worth noting that a User-Interface-Agent depends on other agents to completely process a query. These agents lie on the fixed network in a sufficient quantity. An Intermediate Agent (IA) is contacted by a User-Interface-Agent to further propagate the query to the appropriate search agents (Collection Agents).

Thus the duty of an IA is to further 'model' the query/data to the format understandable by the Collection Agents, transfer the new query to the Collection Agents, wait for the results from the Collection Agents, again 're-model' the result to the format understandable by the User-Interface-Agent, and pass the result to the User-Interface-Agent. The most attractive feature of an IA is that it keeps in contact with a number of Collection Agents and is aware of the approximate time and cost of computation associated with a particular collection/query-processing. Thus, when the IA gets an input from the User-Interface-Agent, it can check if there are more than one collection agents free to do the same job at that time, and if so, it assigns the query to the set of Collection Agents that would incur the minimal processing cost.

There is a Collection Agent associated with each database repository. All the Collection Agents can handle searching within specific collections of text, images, graphics, audio and video. Associated with each Representative, there is also a Buffer Agent (BA). The Buffer Agent does its job 'silently' and its actions are not not visible to the Mobile Unit user. The functions of a Buffer Agent is to keep a vigilance on the quality of communication between the Mobile Unit and the fixed network Representative. The Buffer Agent has mechanisms to detect the status of bandwidth (low,high etc) of the wireless communication and report the same to the User-Interface-Agent. In turn, both the User-Interface-Agent and the Buffer Agent together decide how much of a query result is to be sent to the Mobile Unit without compromising the response time; and also as what transformations need to be done on the data so that the MU gets the result swiftly.

For example, depending on the bandwidth of the wireless communication, it might be desirable for the Representative's User-Interface-Agent to send to the Mobile Unit only necessary data of a file at a time, rather than the whole file. Another example might be that of sending to the Mobile Unit a monochrome and reduced image, not the larger colored image obtained as the result of a query, because of low bandwidth in the current cell. Thus the provision of a Buffer Agent makes a Mobile Unit free to move in non-homogeneous cells. Bandwidth variations are taken care of automatically by the agents without disturbing the response time.

To make the efficient use of the data acquired at the Representative node (as a result of queries etc), we provide caching. This caching would help the Mobile Unit to get quick response to queries involving the objects in the Representative's cache. We expect that a Representative's cache will typically hoard objects referenced by previous queries plus frequently or most commonly used objects pertaining to the local geography or location etc.

In such a situation it becomes imperative to employ a mechanism which would update the objects in the cache as they are updated on the network. A Caching Agent is proposed for this purpose. The Caching Agent will also be made to take care of the arrangement or indexing of objects in the cache.

In addition, the Caching Agent will also ensure that the objects in the cache are arranged in such a way that will help update the Mobile Unit's own cache quickly. Therefore, it would help be beneficial if objects are arranged at group levels with appropriate time-stamps. This would help to detect if (and which) object-groups in the Mobile Unit need to be updated. For example, it would be useful to keep in one group such data that reflect factual representation of a geographical area and are highly unlikely to change. A Mobile Unit's local cache would typically be updated upon connection to Representative, and also at such times when the Mobile Unit-user sends a prior notice to the Representative of its intended disconnection.

2.2 The Agent-Representative Server (ARS)

The ARS is a fixed node on the network. It is the home of Representatives. Every ARS keeps a list of Representatives which are created at this home base. Every time a Mobile Unit is registered to the mobile database system, an account is opened and a log is kept as well as a backup of the Representative from the last check point. Besides these native Representatives, ARS also keeps a list of all visiting Representatives; so it can provide service to these visiting Representatives too. If a Representative changes location after it wakes up, it will need to register to the local ARS as visiting Representative.

The ARS provides service to the Mobile Unit by keeping a fair amount of agents (ARS agents) that the Clients can request through their Representatives. After the Representative processes the query from the Client, it will determine the ARS agents it needs to request. Then it will first request the local ARS for those agents. If some ARS agents can not be sent by the local ARS, the request for these agents will be directed to this Representative's home ARS. All ARS agents requested will be sent to the database servers and query the database server agents for the results. After a query is finished , the ARS agent will send the results back to the requesting Representative.

In this architecture the Representative only needs to carry a set of agent requests, a pointer to the local ARS, and a pointer to the home ARS to request service. Because agents are sent by the ARS, the ARS will set the environment for the agents. This will help to get service from a local server if such a service is available.

2.3 Conferencing With Other Mobile Units

A Mobile Unit can communicate with another Mobile Unit via the fixed network only. When a Mobile Unit needs to conference with another Mobile Unit, it must know the id of that Mobile Unit. Typically an Mobile Unit "A" sends a 'conference-request' along with another Mobile Unit "B"s id to Mobile Unit A's Representative.

It is worth noting here that each Mobile Unit that will ever have an intention to conference with another Mobile Unit must inform the Representative of its intention. The default status would be a "NO" for a Mobile Unit to avoid undesired conferencings. Alternatively, we can check for a Mobile Unit's willingness to participate in a conference when there is a call from another Mobile Unit.

Let us consider the case of Mobile Unit "A" wishing to conference with Mobile Unit "B". Mobile Unit "A" sends this request along with Mobile Unit B's id to its (A's) Representative. This Representative then appropriately modifies this request and then forwards it to the network server to confirm the validity of the id of Mobile Unit-B; checks whether Mobile Unit-B is "alive" and whether Mobile Unit-B is willing to participate in the conferencing. These informations are gathered by the Representative-A and disclosed to Mobile Unit-A (subject to the extent and the format allowable by the security guidelines).

When "A" and "B" are to conference, their Representatives play a crucial role in receiving, buffering, transforming and formatting the data as per the status in the local cell (bandwidth status etc) or the specifics of the Mobile Unit (particular personalized input/output format). If the quality of the wireless communication falls below a certain threshold, the Representative must inform the parties of a possible (abrupt) termination of conferencing.

2.4 Invoked Methods For a Session

To provide a specific context to this architecture, in this section we provide the important methods that are typically invoked for any session. The VOID REGISTER_MOBILE_UNIT(INT REPRESENTATIVE_ID, CHAR REPRESENTATIVE _NAME, CHAR ADDRESS_OF_HOME_ARS) command is executed by the Mobile Unit requesting the fixed-node computer for a session. The parameters passed with this request are the name and id of Mobile Unit's Representative and the address of its home-ARS. (e.g., Register_Mobile_Unit(78435, MUREP9826Z, http://www.usl.edu).

Upon receiving this request, the fixed-node computer internally assigns a unit-number for this Mobile Unit and executes the SHORT INT VERIFY_VALIDITY (CHAR *ADDRESS_OF _HOME_ARS, INT REPRESENTATIVE_ID, CHAR *REPRESENTATIVE_NAME); command. This command validates the supplied parameters and returns a true/false value which is used in following. The Verify_Validity() command returns a 0/1, and subsequently the a VOID SIGNAL_MOBILE_UNIT (CHAR *MSG, INT MOBILE_UNIT_NUMBER); command is invoked. For example, Signal_Mobile_Unit("invalid inputs .. identity not established", 21) or Signal_Mobile_Unit("Identity established", 21);

The next step is to get the address of previous-ARS from the home-ARS of the Mobile-Unit which can be done via a CHAR *FIND_PREVIOUS_ARS(CHAR *ADDRESS_OF_HOME_ARS, INT REPRESENTATIVE_ID, CHAR *REPRESENTATIVE_NAME) command. This will return the address of the previous-ARS. The returned address would be verified through a SHORT INT VERIFY_PREVIOUS _ARS(CHAR *ADDRESS_OF_PREVIOUS_ARS); step and returns a 0 or 1. Upon completion of this step, a message would be sent to the control-mechanism of the previous ARS that the Mobile Unit is in a different cell and the (old) Representative needs to wind-up.(It is appropriate to mention that REGISTER_MOBILE _UNIT() is functionally overloaded and if the previous-ARS happens to be the current-ARS then, it will be considered a "wake-up" call for the Representative by the Mobile-Unit.

The parameters of the SHORT INT PREVIOUS_REPRESENTATIVE_WINDUP(CHAR *ADDRESS_OF_PREVIOUS_ARS, INT REPRESENTATIVE_ID, CHAR *REPRESENTATIVE_NAME, CHAR *ADDRESS_OF_PRESENT_ARS, CHAR *MESSAGE); include the address of the present ARS (that is, the address of the ARS in whose cell the Mobile Unit is residing currently), and a message (for example, "windup"). The control mechanism of the ARS will execute another set of commands, after getting this message, to take care of the intended winding up.

The fixed-node computer then creates a Representative for the requesting Mobile Unit via a INT CREATE_REPRESENTATIVE(INT REPRESENTATIVE_ID, CHAR *REPRESENTATIVE_ADDRESS, CHAR *ADDRESS_OF_HOME_ARS); request. This request creates a Representative for the requesting Mobile Unit and returns a session-id as the return value. This session-id is further used in all communications by the Mobile Unit and the Representative. This session-id is informed to the Mobile Unit so that it can include the session-id in all further communication. The session-id can be used for calculation of effective time of usage (of Mobile Computing services) by the Mobile Unit and it will help solve the billing problem. At the end of the session, the bill may be directed to the home-ARS of the Representative.

As a result of the above Create_Representative command, the following commands are executed.

1. CHAR *CREATE_USER_INTERFACE_AGENT(INT REPRESENTATIVE_ID, CHAR *REPRESENTATIVE_NAME); This will create a User-Interface-Agent and will return the User-Interface-Agent-Id back.
2. CHAR *CREATE_BUFFER_AGENT(INT REPRESENTATIVE_ID, CHAR *REPRESENTATIVE_NAME); This will create a Buffer-Agent and will return the Buffer-Agent-Id back.
3. CHAR *CREATE_CACHE_AGENT(INT REPRESENTATIVE_ID, CHAR *REPRESENTATIVE_NAME); This will create a Cache-Agent and will return the Cache-Agent-Id back.
4. INT CREATE_CONTROL_AGENTS_UNIT(INT REPRESENTATIVE_ID, CHAR REPRESENTATIVE_NAME, CHAR *UIA_ID CHAR *BUFFER_AGENT_ID, CHAR CACHING_AGENT_ID); This will create a method which will guard the activities of the User-Interface-Agent, the Buffer-Agent, and the Caching-Agent. It will control and coordinate the activities of these agents.

A typical command executed by the Cache-Agent initially is VOID HOARD _COMMON _OBJECTS(CHAR *CACHING_AGENT_ID, CHAR *CONTROL_AGENTS _UNIT_ID); This command will make the Caching-Agent contact the local ARS server and get the most frequently used common objects. Most of these objects would often pertain to factual information, for example, details of local hospitals, police-stations, emergency-lines etc. It is worth stressing that the Caching-Agent has a trigger mechanism to detect any changes in the hoarded objects and make necessary command execution to update those objects in its cache. It can be noted that cache-hoarding is not limited to only the initial hoarding. Further objects are hoarded as they are obtained as a result of user issued queries. This is done to exploit the locality of reference character of Mobile-Unit's queries and hence to expedite the response time of the overall system.

Another typical command issued by the Caching-Agent would be to update the Mobile-Unit's cache before a session is closed. The command is following : SHORT INT UPDATE_MOBILE_CACHE(INT MOBILE_UNIT_NUMBER, INT REPRESENTATIVE_ID, CHAR *REPRESENTATIVE_NAME); Similarly, a typical command executed by the Buffer-Agent is the following : VOID GET_MOBILE_STATUS(CHAR *BUFFER_AGENT_ID, CHAR *CONTROL_AGENTS _UNIT_ID); The Get_Mobile_Status command will get the status of the communication bandwidth and also possibly the approximate physical coordinate of the Mobile Unit. All these informations are passed to the User-Interface-Agent, in consonance with the coordination rules of the Control-Agents-Unit of this Representative.

Some of the typical commands executed by the User-Interface-Agent are the following :

1. VOID INFORM_MOBILE_USER(CHAR *MSG); An example of this would be to inform the user of bandwidth conditions, and the mode of file/object transfer, for example, only a monochrome picture is being transferred because of bandwidth conditions etc.
2. VOID GET_USER_QUERY(); will be executed by the User-Interface-Agent to obtain the Mobile-Unit's query and to prepare it to be further sent to the Intermediate-Agent. Every incoming query will be assigned a query-number by the User-Interface-Agent. This query-number will be used thoroughly in the query evaluation process by the User-Interface-Agent, the Intermediate-Agent, and the Collection-Agent.
3. VOID DO_TRANSFORMATIONS_QUERY(CHAR *QUERY_NUMBER); This will perform transformations, such as reducing the size of image, preparing big files to be sent in chunks, on the result of a query.

Some of the methods executed by the Intermediate-Agent are the following :

1. CHAR *GET_QUERY_UIA (CHAR *QUERY_NUMBER); This command is used to obtain a query from User-Interface-Agent. Upon receiving a query from the User-Interface-Agent, the Intermediate-Agent will send an acknowledgement to the former.
2. VOID DETERMINE_COLLECTION_AGENTS(); This will be executed by the Intermediate-Agent to determine the set of Collection-Agents to choose and to whom the query can be sent to.
3. CHAR *GET_QUERY_CA(CHAR *QUERY_NUMBER); This command will get the results from the Collection-Agents. This routine might have to wait for completion of parts of query from all the assigned Collection-Agents.
4. CHAR *SEND_QUERY_RESULT_UIA(); will send the result of the query to the User-Interface-Agent.

3 Implementation

For the implementation of the CRAS architecture, we have chosen ORBline 2.0 [2], a complete implementation of Object Management Group's (OMG) Common Object Request Broker Architecture (CORBA) [3]. Based on this, we assume that each Mobile Unit is the client, and the implementation of the Mobile Unit, Mobile Unit Manager and the Representative will reside on a server. We simulate frequent disconnections and mobile using a random time generator. An overview of this simulation is shown in the figure 3.

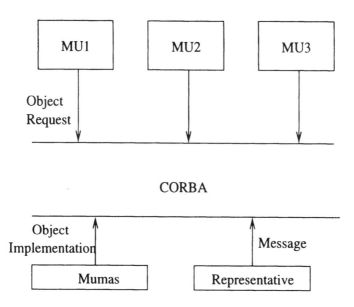

Fig. 3. Simulating Mobility Using CORBA

In what follows we showed a simplified version of the IDL definitions of our simulation. These are based on Orbeline 2.0. There are three global type definitions. Base station names, mobile unit names and representatives. i.e.,

```
#ifndef CRAS_IDL
#define CRAS_IDL
#typedef string BaseName;
#typedef string MobileName;
#typedef string RepName;
interface MobileUnit{ ........ }
interface Representative{ ........ }
interface MUManager{ ......... }
#endif
```

There are also three interfaces, namely Mobile Unit for mobile units, Representative for mobile unit representatives, and MU Manager for mobile unit managers, one at each base station. The base stations are connected through a fixed network, while the representatives are considered as software processes that run on stations. For each mobile unit there are three attributes: Repname for its representative name, Basename for the current base station name, status for its status. The interface for the Mobile Unit is as follows:

```
interface Mobile Unit{
 typedef short TimeInterval;
 enum status Type {off, on};
 attribute RepName repname;
 attribute BaseName currentbase;
 attribute statusType status;
 boolean move(in TimeInterval waitTime, in BaseName next Base);
 boolean send;
 boolean receive(in string message)};
```

We assume that the mobile unit can only send or receive messages when the status is on. Each mobile unit can perform three operations: move to simulate that it moves to a named destination base station after some randomly generated time period, send to send a message to the currently visited base station, and receive to reive a message from the currently visited base station. Each representative represents one and only one registered mobile unit by maintaining a profile for the unit. A representative's interface is as follows:

```
interface Representative{
  struct Profile{
    MobileName muname;
    BaseName currentBase;
    BaseName homeBase;
    MobileUnit muRef;};
    attribute Profile MyMu
    boolean send();
    boolean receive(in string message);
    boolean changeProfile(in BaseName currentBase); out BaseName lastBase);}
```

The profile records the name of the mobile unit muname, the name of the currently visited based station currentBase, the name of a home base station for the unit homeBase, and a reference to the unit muRef. The representative always sits on the home station of the unit it represents, whereas the unit itself can move around. There are three operations: "send" to send a message to the home base station, "receive" to receive a message from the home base station, and "changeProfile" to update the information of the current base station and output the last visited station.

In each base station there is one mobile unit manager which manges all the mobile units that are registered on this station, and their representative. In its implementation, the mobile unit manager maintains two lists, one is of type RegisteredMUList, which records all registered mobile units on this station, and the other is of type CurrentMUList, which records all mobile units that are currently visiting this station but may or may not be registered in this station. The interface for the MUManager is as follows:

```
interface MUManager{
  struct RegMUStruct{ MobileName muname; Representative repRef;};
```

```
struct MURefStruct{ MobileName muname; MobileUnit MURef;}};
typedef sequence<RefMUStruct>RegisteredMUList;
typedef sequence<RefRefStruct>CurrentMUList;
boolean muregister(in MobileName MUname, in RepName Repname);
boolean unregister(in MobileName MUname);
boolean moveIn(in MobileName MUname);
boolean moveOut(in MobileName MUname);
boolean receiveFromRep(in BaseName currentbase, in MobileName
Muname in string message);
boolean receiveFromMU(in MobileName MUname, in string message);
boolean receiveFromOtherBase(in MobileName MUname, in string message);}};
```

A manager has the following operations: "register" to register a mobile unit in this station and bind the unit to a representative. The unit must not be registered anywhere before, and the representative must not be used by other registered units; "unregister" to unregister a mobile unit that was registered in this station, and also free the representative for that unit; "movein" to record that the named mobile unit is moved into the service area of this station; "moveout" to record the named mobile unit is oved away from this station. The other three operations are related to message passing.

This section outlined the implementation of the infrastructure. Due to space limitations we have not outlined the implementation of the agents.

4 Conclusion

We are currently extending our work in several directions. First, due to a newly funded laboratory containing wireless and infrared network hubs, adaptors, a toshiba satellite and mobile units, as well as other wireless networking equipment, CRAS would also be implemented on this platform. There is also undergoing research on data broadcasting strategies, cache update algorithms due to frequent disconnections, data access methodologies and on a new data model.

References

1. F.C. Cheong, *"Internet Agents"*, New Riders Publishing, Indianapolis, IN, 1996.
2. PostModern Computing. Orbeline, http://www.pomoco.com, Sept. 1, 1995.
3. Object Management Group. *"Common Object Request Broker Architecture"*, OMG technical committee document 93-12-43, http://www.omg.org, December 1993.
4. R.Alonso and H. Korth, *"Database System Issues in Nomadic Computing"*, In Proceedings of the ACM SIGMOD International Conference on Management of Data, pp. 388-392, May, 1993.
5. T. Imielinski, and H. Korth (editors), *"Mobile Computing"*, Kluwer Academic Publishers, 1996.
6. D. Barbara and T. Imielinski, *"Sleepers and Workaholics: Caching Strategies in Mobile Environments"*, In Proceedings of ACM SIGMOD Conference on Management of Data, pp. 1-12, May, 1994.

Is the Future of Conceptual Modeling Bleak or Bright?

Moderator: Shamkant B. Navathe

College of Computing
Georgia Institute of Technology

Successful Practices in Developing a Complex Information Model

Patrick Thompson, Microsoft Corp
John W. Sweitzer Tivoli Systems (An IBM Company)

Abstract

The Desktop Management Task Force (DMTF) has recently announced the introduction of the Common Information Model (CIM). The primary objective of CIM is to facilitate the useful exchange of management information between different management applications and between management applications and the resources they are managing The information model defines the objects and their characteristics necessary for critical aspects of system, network, database, and application management.

CIM captures many common representations required for management applications. This paper argues that these common representations are similar to object oriented design patterns.

DMTF member organizations including Microsoft, IBM, SUN, Intel, Computer Associates, Hewlett Packard and Compaq have committed to support the model. For example, Microsoft's implementation of CIM will be in the form of an object manager that supports the basic CIM model together with compliant win32 extensions. This implementation will be a part of all future Microsoft operating systems.

This paper describes the basic model and many of the design decisions and trade-offs considered in producing the Common Information Model.

Introduction

Information models are a way to organize or structure information so multiple groups of people can perform common and related tasks. Information models are composed of two parts: (1) a meta-model - a set of statement types or syntax to represent the information and (2) model content - a collection of actual expressions of these statements. The Desktop Management Task Force's Common Information Model (DMTF 's CIM) is an information model developed by multiple companies to organize the information required to manage common aspects of complex computer systems. The primary objective of CIM is to facilitate the useful exchange of management information between management applications and between management applications and the resources they are managing.

There are numerous methodologies used to develop complex information models. These methodologies address many of the challenges associated with developing an information model. One of the unique challenges associated with developing the CIM is the diversity of companies directly involved (Microsoft, Tivoli Systems(IBM), Sun Microsystems, Intel, Computer Associates , Hewlett-Packard and Compaq) resulting in a very diverse set of requirements.

Similar industry initiatives have been attempted in the past but not with the same level of success. This paper discusses some of the reasons and methodologies that lead to this higher level of success. In particular, the paper discusses how the notion of design patterns allowed the participants to agree on high level principles and the paper presents many of the actual design patterns.

DMTF[1] Common Information Model (CIM)

The DMTF's Common Information Model uses object-oriented modeling statements that are expressible in UML [Booch]. The content of CIM is organized into three broad categories, core schema, common schemas, and extension schemas. The next two sections describe these areas and the model used to express them.

CIM Meta-Model

A complete description of the CIM Meta Model can be found in [DCIM]. The following provides a brief summary so the reader can understand the notation used in this paper.

A *Schema* is a group of classes with a single owner. A *Class* is a collection of instances that support the same type, that is, the same properties, associations and methods Classes can be arranged in a generalization hierarchy that represents subtype relationships between Classes. The generalization hierarchy is a rooted, directed graph and does not support multiple inheritance. A *Property* is a value used to characterize instances of a class. A Property can be thought of as a pair of "get" and "set" functions that, when applied to an object[2] return state and set state, respectively.

Classes can have Methods that represent the behavior relevant for that Class. A *Method* is a declaration of a signature (that is, the method name, return type, and parameters).

An *Association* is a subtype of Class that contains two or more *References* that represent a relationship between two or more objects. Since associations are subclasses of Class, any Association can be subclassed into other Associations. *References* are a type of Property that defines the role each object plays in an Association.

Properties and Methods have reflexive relationships that represent Property and Method overriding. A Method can override an inherited Method, which implies that any access to the inherited Method will result in the invocation of the implementation of the overriding Method. A similar interpretation implies the overriding of Properties.

Qualifiers are used to characterize elements of the schema (for example, there are Qualifiers that define the format of a Property or the key of a Class). Qualifiers provide a mechanism that makes the meta schema extensible in a controlled fashion. It is possible to add new types of Qualifier by the introduction of a new Qualifier name, thereby providing new types of meta data to processes that manage and manipulate classes, properties, and other elements of the schema.

---

[1] The Desktop Management Task Force or DMTF is a company consortium that focuses on defining standard management information and APIs. This organization sponsored the activities described in this document. More information about this organization can be obtained at www.dmtf.org.

[2] Note the equivocation between "object" as instance and "object" as class. This is common usage in object-oriented literature and reflects the fact that in many cases, operations and concepts may apply to or involve both classes and instances.

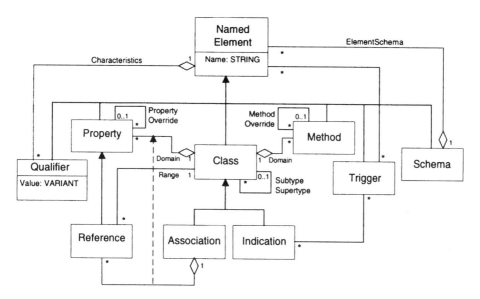

Figure 1 Metaschema

A *Trigger* is a recognition of a state change, such as create, delete, update, or access of a Class instance; and update or access of a Property. An *Indication* is an object created as a side effect of a Trigger. Because Indications are subtypes of Class, they can have Properties and Methods and be arranged in a type hierarchy.

CIM Content

The content of the CIM model is intended to capture the information required by a wide variety of management applications. The primary objective of CIM is to facilitate sharing management information between management applications supporting different tasks. This is accomplished by organizing the content of CIM in three broad categories: a core schema, common schema, and extension schemas.

The Common Schemas are the building blocks or organizing principles for management platforms and applications that support areas such as device configuration, performance management, and change management. The Common Schemas are represented by a set of abstract and concrete classes that define the basic characteristics of Systems, Networks, Applications and various groupings of statistical and other management related data.

CIM is structured in such a way that the managed environment can be seen as a collection of interrelated systems, each of which is composed of a number of discrete elements. The Common Schema includes Systems in the form of the Managed System Element hierarchy, Applications in the form of the Application Component hierarchy, and Networks in the form of the Network Component Hierarchy. Each of these areas represents aspects of the system that is expected to be a common focus for a wide range of applications.

The Core Schema is a framework for the class structures that make up the overall model and is expected to be very stable. In a sense the Core Model can be seen as an arbitrary structure. The fact that it is arbitrary is what lends it stability. Any attempt to challenge or change the core model can only be done on the basis of an alternate view that, by definition, is an alternative not a substitute.

The schema is provided as both an information model and as a framework for the development of an information model. The concept of a framework is becoming widely accepted in the object-oriented community. A framework is typically contrasted with a class library. In using a framework, developers "write framework code that gets called by the code they are reusing, instead of writing code that calls the code they are reusing." [CoSch] In the same way, schema designers are expected to extend the schema by establishing specializations of the provided classes. The specializations are required to follow the patterns established by the content of the Core Schema that establishes the basic terminology, types of associations and classifications available to the schema designer. In this way the Core Schema resembles a framework as it provides a compulsory structure that requires a common information modeling approach on the part of individuals extending the schema.

Representational issues that are unique to a particular technology (for example, a particular operating system like Microsoft's Windows NT or Sun's Solaris) are captured in Extension Schemas. Extension Schemas extend the Common Schema for a particular technology or implementation.

Design Patterns

Design patterns [Gamma] are a technique that captures reusable object oriented designs that experts extract out of recurring situations within object oriented implementations. A design pattern is a systematic way to capture a simple and elegant solution to a specific problem. Essentially, a good design pattern provides a novice object oriented designer with the insights of an experienced designer so they can develop flexible and durable implementations.

The motivation behind the creation of design patterns is not new to information modeling techniques. The development of the Entity-Relationship data model and its many extensions introduced a number of design patterns. For example, the introduction of weak and total relationships involved a type of design pattern that experienced modelers found re-occurring in many information models. In the case of a weak entity for example there are implications for the propagation of keys, cardinality of the associations and the life cycles of the objects involved.

In some cases, the CIM core model uses design patterns that were developed by others. For example, the Composite design pattern document in [Gamma] provided the basis for representing systems. The intent of the Composite design pattern is to represent part-whole hierarchies of objects so it is possible to manipulate individual objects and compositions of these individual objects in a common way.

Methodology

A significant portion of the CIM work involved developing design pattern like constructs to capture common representations of management information. The objective was not to develop reusable object oriented designs but to develop standards ways to represent common management information.

A common approach (for example, the View Integration process presented in [Batini]) to designing schemas or combining schemas is to systematically enumerate the information requirements that have to be supported by the schema. These requirements are defined in terms of the union of the requirements expressed by the applications that will have to use the schema.

Such approaches are based on two assumptions. Firstly, they assume that the set of applications that will use the schema is known and each of the applications is sufficiently well defined to be able to articulate its information needs clearly. Secondly, they assume that the applications will not change over time and no new applications will have to be supported by the schema.

For CIM, neither of these conditions apply. It cannot be known in advance what applications will be built against the schema. The applications currently deployed in the systems management arena are not in a position to clearly articulate their needs as they are typically evolving from release to release and cannot anticipate exactly what requirements will have to be met at some future date.

As a result it is necessary to formulate the information requirements in terms of the general characteristics of the system to be managed rather than the specific requirements of any particular management application. Developing CIM focused on capturing abstract and clearly articulated approaches to standard representational problems that occurred frequently for management applications.

CIM Design Patterns

CIM's Core Schema and Common Schemas implicitly propose a series of design patterns as a way to get agreement on fundamental representational issues. This section describes several of the key design patterns that were developed by the DMTF CIM Committee.

Pattern: Dependencies

Intent
Provides a unified way to express dependency between many elements.

Motivation
Most management applications need to understand how the components of a large computer system are interdependent. This is critical to determine whether individual components are properly configured, are failing because of other failing components, and so on. The challenge is balancing the specific details with the high level notion of one component being dependent on some other components. Some specific examples are:

- software runs on a computer system
- sound card is installed in a computer system
- a printer is connected to a computer system
- software uses a sound card and a printer

These specific situations have unique semantic meaning. However, they can be abstracted into the general notion of an element being dependent on other elements.

Applicability
Use the Dependency design pattern to aggregate a set of associations that have a common set of semantics in a higher context.

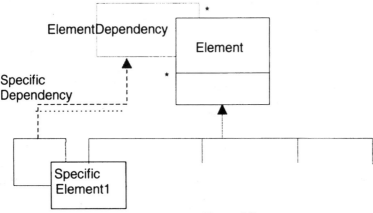

Figure 2 Structure

Participants
- Element: Uniquely identifies a type of element that has interdependencies.
- ElementDependency: Expresses the general notion of one element being dependent on another.
- Specific Element: Uniquely identifies element types that have dependencies that are only meaningful between it and dependent elements.
- SpecificDependency: Expresses a specific type of dependency between specific elements.

Collaboration
The Element class abstracts the components that can be interdependent. The dependencies that are "hidden" in more specific semantics (for example, software installed on a system) are captured with the Specific Dependency association. The classes that participate in these "hidden dependencies" are represented using Specific Element. The Specific Dependency associations are sub-classed associations of Element Dependency and the Specific Element classes are sub-classes of Element.

Consequences
This approach eliminates the need for a management application to keep track of all the dependencies that exist between components. This is especially important when an application does not deal with or have knowledge of the many specific dependencies that exist between specific components. Without having the Element Dependency as a common collector of the hidden dependency, an application needs to be aware of all known and future dependencies that exist within the model.

Pattern: Arrangements and Setting

Intent
Provides a consistent mechanism for capturing property values that are significant in the context of combinations of components.

Motivation
The components that make up a computer system are often reconfigured or changed as their usage changes. This occurs within the active stage of a resource. For example, mobile computers change their configuration when they are connected to a larger system or network. Replaceable hardware cards like PCMCIA cards can drastically change the capability of a system. For many of these components, they have capabilities that can be configured to different levels or are turned off or on depending on their actual uses.

Information models for management domains must capture detail information about what the elements of the system are capable of and identify which of these capabilities are being exploited in a particular system.

Applicability
Use Arrangements and Settings design pattern to capture a set of property that are meaningful within the context of a particular set of associations.

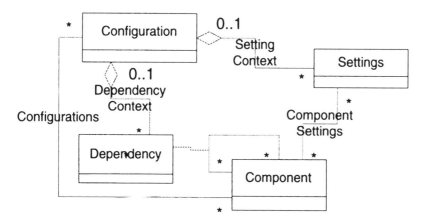

Figure 3 Structure

Participants
- Component
  Identifies the element having arrangements and the sub-elements of this element.
- Arrangement
  Stores specific dependencies and setting for a particular situation
- Component Arrangements
  Identifies the Arrangements a particular Component has for the sub-components in contains
- Dependency
  Describes the interdependency that exist between components.

- Arrangement Dependencies
  Identities the Dependencies used with a particular Arrangement
- Setting
  Declares a set of characteristics that describe what a particular component is capable of.
- Arrangement Settings
  Identifies the Settings used within a particular Arrangement.
- Component Settings
  Identifies the Settings that are defined for a particular component.

Collaboration

The Component class represents the elements that make up a decomposable component. In this context, the decomposable components can have Settings to represent the different ways they can be configured and can have Dependencies defined between them. A Component containing subcomponents can have Arrangements. Arrangements define a particular combination of the dependencies and related settings that are used together. Thus, Arrangements collect a subset of the dependencies and settings that exist for the sub-components.

Consequences

This approach is in direct contrast to an approach that attempts to establish a class hierarchy the captures the different capabilities. The problem with such as approach is the hierarchy does not allow the same object to have multiple values depending on its configuration.

Detailed Example

Managed System Elements have Element Settings, that is, operational parameters that may vary from time to time. Managed System Elements may have Dependency associations to other Managed System Elements. Both Settings and Dependencies may be specified in a context, the Setting Context and Dependency Context associations. The context is a Configuration.

As an example of the use of the configuration class, a Network Interface Card may have a TCP/IP configuration and an IPX configuration. Particularly if these configurations involved related settings for multiple Managed System Elements - for example a Driver object requiring different parameters depending on whether the network card was running IPX or TCP/IP - a Configuration object would be used to associate all of the objects that together make up the configuration.

Note that the Configuration object can be used to group both Dependencies and Settings, these taken together correspond to the traditional idea of a configuration.

So for the "at home" configuration, the workstation containing the Network Interface Card is connected to the network using TCP/IP, the element settings for the workstation are set to the TCP/IP settings. Likewise, for the "at work" configuration, the Network Interface Card is connected to the network using IPX, the element settings for the workstations are set to IPX.

Pattern: Root Class

Intent
The Root Class pattern provides a central class from which the generalization hierarchy grows. It is used to define a type for abstract associations that themselves provide association types that are expected to be common across the hierarchy. See for example the Dependency association on ManagedSystemElement.

Motivation
In the absence of a root class schemas tend to become fragmented and lack motivation for the introduction of commonality particularly with respect to associations. The presence of a root class tends to encourage the introduction of type hierarchies within the associations. These hierarchies of associations provide coherence and order to the model and facilitate both schema extension and schema navigation.

The Root Class provides a location for iteration. Iteration over the instances of the Root Class provides access to all of the objects in the type hierarchy

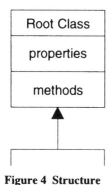

Figure 4 Structure

Applicability
The root class pattern should be used wherever a substantial simplification can be achieved by abstracting associations or properties out of a set of semantically related classes. The introduction of null values is an acceptable by-product of this abstraction on the basis that it is very difficult to find empirical generalizations that do not have exceptions.

Consequences
The use of the root class pattern results in the classes being arranged in semantically related groups. This is facilitated by the "aspects of an object" pattern that allows different aspects of an object to be categorized under different root class objects (see the discussion below).

Detailed Example
The ManagedSystemElement class represents all system component objects. Any managed object that is a component of a system is a descendant (or member) of this class. Examples of ManagedSystemElement descendants include software components, such as files; devices, such as disk drives and controllers; and physical components, such as chips and cards.

Pattern: Object Aspects

Intent
Multiple objects in the model may represent a given object in the managed environment. Each model object represents different aspects of the managed object.

Motivation
In natural classification schemes, objects do not adhere to a single type over the life of the object. It is also frequently difficult to determine some aspect of the state of an object. For example in the distinction between Logical and Physical aspects of the

ManagedSystemElement hierachy, it is commonly relatively inexpensive to obtain information about the logical state of an object. By contrast the physical state of an object frequently cannot be interrogated programmatically and can only be maintained through a complex manual auditing and inventory procedure. The separation of these two aspects of the object allows for the recognition of the differential costs and value of the physical and logical properties of the objects while maintaining the semantic integrity implied by the existence of a single underlying component in the managed environment.

Applicability

Object aspects should be considered wherever an object has a life cycle in which it appears to change state or where the properties or behavior of an object have natural groupings with representational significance. Object aspects are also very useful in dealing with time. One approach to the representation of a change in state over time is to provide the various temporal states as aspects of an object.

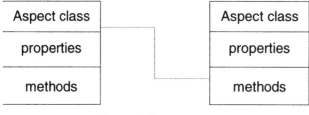

Figure 5 Structure

The relationship between the aspect classes as typically a directed dependency association based on an assumption that some aspect is more fundamental than another. For example the relationship between the Device class and the PhysicalElement classes is PhysicalDependency and defines the physical element that provides the implementation of the Device.

Consequences

The use of the Object Aspects pattern requires a clear understanding on the part of any users of the model of the underlying integrity implied. For example in order to delete an object from the system it is necessary to delete all of the aspects of the object. As a corollary the Object Aspects pattern also implies the use, under some circumstances of discovery algorithms that can consistently recognize situations where multiple aspects of an object are present. For example network discovery techniques may allow the generation of a population of objects that include network nodes, many of which may be aspects of a computer systems that can also be discovered from the system directory. It is essential for the realization of the full potential of the model for the system to be able to discover and relate these different aspects, allowing, for example, network traffic volumes evident in the network model to be related to apparent system performance visible in the computer systems model.

Related Patterns

This approach has been recognized in the development of interface based environments such as Java and COM. It is commonly contrasted with systems that support multiple inheritance in which the various aspects of an object are represented by the inheritance of the different aspects of the object from multiple superclasses. The disadvantages of multiple-inheritance are well-known [Carg] as it leads to cross dependencies in the class structure that make the extension and interpretation of the class hierarchy problematic.

Detailed Example

The classes LogicalElement and PhysicalElement are used to represent different aspects of the objects that make up a system. Typically systems are structured in terms of an architectural topology that has a vertical slicing by which the system is separated into functional units and a horizontal slicing whereby the system is separated into implementation layers.

For example data storage and retrieval can be understood in terms of different implementation layers. Databases provide the most sophisticated capabilities. Databases are based on the file system that has more basic capabilities. The file system in turn is based on devices such as logical disks. Logical disks are realized by some sort of physical packaging.

An essential aspect of the model is the ability to encapsulate the layers in such a hierarchy in such a way that it is possible to provide a variety of possible implementations. In the storage example, the Device level could be provided by a logical disk based on random access memory (RAM) rather than an actual disk drive.

This de-coupling of the functional aspects of the device from its implementation allows for the representation of situations such as multi-function cards, or functions that have no specific correspondence to a physical element of the system and is critically dependent on depicting various aspects of the managed object as different objects within the model..

Pattern: System

Intent

A system is a collection of managed objects that is viewed or handled as an independently identifiable, functional, and atomic whole requiring a single object that represents the identity of the system as a whole.

Motivation

The pattern is driven by the requirements of the applications using the model as well as the actual objects in the managed environment. The system is intended to provide a view of the top-level management objects. Obvious examples include servers and workstations and other discrete units such as network routers. Other not so obvious examples include such independently manageable units as network printers that have to be considered as systems in their own right.

The system pattern establishes a basis for the construction of management applications that are directed to functional areas. As such the objects that conform to the pattern will always be significant as top-level management objects.

Applicability

Anything which can only be managed in the context of another system is not itself a system. A text editor for example could not be considered a system on the grounds that it is always managed in the context of the system that hosts the text editor. A distributed database on the other hand is a system given that it can be managed independently of any given hosting server. Note again the Object Aspects pattern: One aspect of a database is the object that represents the database as an application. Another aspect is the database as a system service. Another is the database as a collection of Processes. Yet another aspect is the database as a System if the database is distributed.

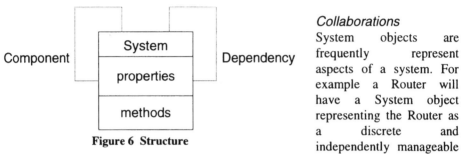

Figure 6 Structure

Collaborations
System objects are frequently represent aspects of a system. For example a Router will have a System object representing the Router as a discrete and independently manageable system. The router will also be a network node in the network model. Systems always have Dependencies and Components (both types of associations).

A functional system is defined as a collection of managed objects whose state of availability and performance, conforms to the specification of the work the system must provide. The Component association is critical to understanding the structure of the system. The Dependency association is critical to understanding the functionality of the system.

Consequences
The model classifies and presents information in a functional rooted graph with systems at the base. An application that chooses not to follow this scheme in presenting, manipulating or populating the model will have to devise its own scheme and either manage that scheme implicitly in structures private to the application or by populating and maintaining an extension to the model that represents the alternative scheme. This is likely to be an expensive process both in terms of development time and in terms of communicating the alternative scheme to the wider audience of developers and users.

Known Uses
The System class and its descendants all conform to this pattern. There are no other uses of the pattern and within the CIM model other uses are positively disallowed.

Detailed Example
In the CIM schema the System class represents a group of functioning logical and physical elements. A system can be composed of other systems because systems are themselves LogicalElements. Any grouping of logical elements that provides a functional whole that needs to be dealt with as a single independent unit for administration purposes is a descendent (or member) of this class.

In a CIM context a system is composed of physical elements, which make up the physical realization of the system, and logical elements, which provide the rules, processes and information needed to regulate and run the system. The emphasis of the system model is on providing base classes required to organize this level of information about any managed system and its components.

Numerous objects in the managed environment can be seen in the same light. Wherever there is a requirement to manage the object as a unit in this sense, it is sensible to establish an instance of the system class to represent the system aspect of the grouping in question.

Pattern: Object Capabilities

Intent
In a systems management context it is essential to separate the functional capabilities of an object from other aspects such as its configurations or its physical realization. The object capabilities pattern isolates the current functional state and operations that can be used to manipulate that state from these other aspects of the object.

Motivation
The separate representation of an object's capability follows the "divide and conquer" approach to systems design and implementation. By reducing the problem to a set of simpler component elements the overall problem becomes more tractable.

The separation of current functional state from other aspects of the object facilitates the development of applications that focus on the consistent maintenance of service for a system with respect to its users. Configuration, physical topology and current state each represent significant management problem domains and need to be separable in order to minimize the size of the modules that have to be deployed in order to accomplish management in the given area.

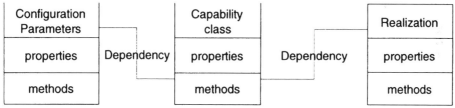

Figure 7 Structure

Applicability
Any case where an object has clearly distinguishable capabilities, configuration parameters and physical (or other realization) is a candidate for the use of this pattern.

Capabilities typically represent devices such as a modem, configuration parameters are represented in the CIM schema by the Setting class and its descendents. Realizations are either other devices (such as emulators for example) or physical components such as a PCMCIA card.

Consequences
The use of the object capability pattern implies a clear separation of the properties of the object. There is a set which is intrinsic to the object and represent the object's state at a given moment in time and a separate set of properties that represent the configuration parameters applicable to the object (see for example the Setting class in the CIM schema). It is critical to the integrity of the model that these property types not be confused.

Detailed Example

The Device class represents a unit of functionality associated with providing the basic capabilities of a system; such as input, output, or storage management. Devices may be directly expressed by a physical component, for example a keyboard. However, almost any device can be 'virtualized' either by simulation; for example, simulating a modem using main CPU cycles, by allocation of a single device to multiple physical components, or by allocation of more than one device to a single physical unit. Examples include a printer, mass storage devices or direct memory access devices, a modem or LAN adapter (note that both devices could share the same PCMCIA card).

Pattern: Physical Components

Intent

The Physical Components Pattern is a special case of the Root Class pattern. It provides a root class for all physically discrete objects. The pattern implies a structure in the model in which logical aspects of the overall domain are separated from the physical aspects.

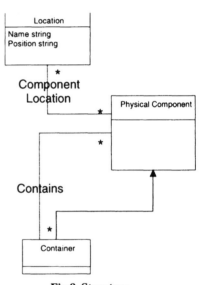

Motivation

The separation of the logical and physical areas, in the case of the systems management domain, is justifiable on the basis that logical components of a system can be instrumented in such a way that the component can be monitored and discovered programmatically. This approach allows a detailed picture of the current state of the logical environment to be maintained at a reasonable cost. Physical

Fig 8 Structure

components by contrast are generally not amenable to such a strategy and have to be monitored using costly manual procedures that have to be carefully implemented and audited if the data gathered is to have any reliability.

Location and containment associations are peculiar to the physical components. That is, in order to discover the physical location of a device (a logical component) it is necessary to traverse the dependency association between the device and its physical counterpart and from there traverse the association between the physical component and its associated location object. Note that containment and location are not the same and that location and containment are not considered to be types of Dependency or Component.

Applicability

The physical component pattern is principally used in the CIM schema in the form of the PhysicalElement subclass of ManagedSystemElement. The same pattern may apply to other components of the model. It is conceivable for example that non-system physical objects may be introduced (buildings for example).

Consequences

This distinction between the logical and physical can always be eliminated by the traversal of appropriate associations. It will be the case that in many instances an agent that returns a logical component is able to determine some aspects of its corresponding physical component (existence, type and name for example). This information may then have to be reconciled with the information introduced into the system by services and systems that specialize in the population of the physical side of the model. This again is a discovery problem and is analogous to the problem discussed elsewhere in this paper that arises from the dual representation of server and other devices as systems and network nodes with the resulting necessity of reconciling the two manifestations of the same object.

Detailed Example

The PhysicalElement class represents any system component that has a distinct physical identity. Any physical component, which can be defined in terms of labels that can be physically attached to an object, is a descendent (or member) of this class. Processes, files, records, and devices are not considered physical components. A card that implements a device, such as a modem is an example of a PhysicalElement. It is not possible to attach a label to a modem; it is only possible to attach a label to the card that implements the modem.

Pattern: Networks as circuits

Intent

Networks can be seen either as a topology defined by nodes and connections between nodes, or as a set of connections to a common medium with each connection point implying a potential communication capability with any other connection point attached to the common medium. This pattern is intended to model the second view of a network.

Motivation

Providing an explicit model of networks as circuits is essential as the model accurately reflects how most networks actually work. The structure and behavior of the model is sufficiently counterintuitive (given a point-to-point model of a network) that it is important to explicitly recognize and define the concepts required to model such a network. A point-to-point network could be modeled as a series of connected circuit networks, each circuit having two connection points and a bridge to the next connection point in the point-to-point network. This is in fact how wide area networks are generally structured, as bridged circuits with selective forwarding mechanisms across the bridging device.

The intent of the pattern is to facilitate modeling and management of a communications network and to allow the objects that represent the network to be smoothly integrated with the other objects that represent the other aspects of the managed environment.

Applicability

Direct application of the networks as circuits patterns is limited to the NetworkElement class and its descendents. However the interaction with the pattern by other elements of the model has wider possibilities. As noted earlier the objects in the network model (particularly the Endpoints) can frequently be seen as aspects of other objects in the model. The behavior of the overall system can only be understood as a combination of the behavior of the network and the behavior of other systems such as applications and servers.

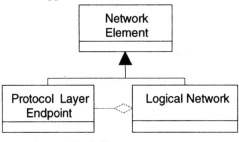

Fig 9 Structure

Consequences
Analysis of overall system behavior has to be performed in terms of the circuit model of a network. It would be perfectly reasonable to provide a view that gave a point-to-point topology for the network. It must always be understood that this point-to-point view is just an approximation and can shift dramatically from one point in time to another as various potential connections are activated or dropped depending on massage patterns across the circuit network. The topology of the network is a function of how the network is being used not of what is connected to what.

Detailed Example
A network as a communication medium is represented by the model in the form of the Logical Network object, representing the shared medium and network EndPoints representing the ability to place and receive messages on the network

This view of a network leads to a model in which rather than a set of connections between points, the network must be seen as a common medium with devices attached to it. This common medium is what the Logical Network class specified in the model describes. A bridge can be thought of as a device that has visibility to more than one logical network. For one device to communicate with another it is necessary for the two devices to either be attached to the same logical network, or for there to be a path between the logical networks they are attached to consisting of some number of bridging devices and associated logical networks.

The network itself can be thought of and managed as a system. The Network system object represents this aspect of the network. Network System is a type of system (and an aspect of a network). Other associated objects include the various types of network service such as ManagementAgents and NetworkForwardingServices. Protocols are represented separately as logical objects that have specialized types of settings associated with them indicating the configuration of the service responsible for running the protocol in the given context.

Pattern: Storage Hierarchy

Intent
The provision of mass storage capability is a critical, complex, and rapidly evolving aspect of computer systems. This pattern defines a general template for defining mass storage systems utilizing other aspects of the model and introducing some additional features.

Motivation
Mass storage, like the network area, is sufficiently complex that it is essential to provide a model that is intended to explicitly deal with this complexity.

The pattern is intended to be an accurate and economical representation of the structure and characteristics of the mass storage subsystem.

Applicability
Mass storage applies to any form of storage present on the system. This includes logical disks, so-called "physical" disks, other types of disks such as CDROM drives and zip drives, tapes and other streaming devices and various higher level mappings and realizations for mass storage such as network drives and memory mapped drives. The model also has to deal with the physical structure of the devices in the form of various types of RAID device and other physical storage configurations.

Collaborations
The pattern defines mass storage in terms of two specialized types of the Device class, namely LogicalStorage and MassStorage and assumes the Capabilities pattern (represented by Device) as well as the Object aspects pattern used to segregate the physical aspects of the model from the logical aspects.

Object aspects, Object Capabilities, Physical Components, Media

Consequences
The structure of the information represented by the complex of classes used to define mass storage requires consistent usage and presentation if it is to remain useful over time. In particular the distinction between LogicalStorage and MassStorage and between Device (Object Capabilities) and PhysicalElement is critical to proper extension of the model. Any schema desingner responsible for extending the model needs to clearly understand the motivation behind the classification scheme if the schema is to be extended correctly. This consideration of course applies to any extension to the schema but is particularly germane in this case given the very specific division of responsibility between the various classes involved in the pattern.

Known Uses
Modeling Disks, Diskettes, CDROMs and other random access devices, Tapes and other streaming devices. Modeling logical structures such as LogicalDisks, partitions and file systems.

Detailed Example
The LogicalStorage class represents a logical storage device on the system. LogicalStorage is distinct from MassStorage in that a LogicalStorage device is concerned purely with the provision of storage capacity and is not concerned with the way the capacity is provided. MassStorage on the other hand does represent information about how the storage capacity is realized.

The MassStorage class represents a mass storage device on the system. A MassStorgae device is a device that describes how storage capacity is provided by the system. Examples include Ram Drive, CDROM Drive, and Tape Drive.

MassStorage devices typically have complex organizing structures such as sectors and cylinders. They may also have surface organization structures such as Partitions and FileSystems. MassStorage devices need not map directly to physical structures but may, as in the case of Network Drives, only map indirectly to such structures.

Conclusion

There are numerous methodologies used to develop complex information models. This paper discusses the experiences of the team that developed Version 1.0 of the Desktop Management Task Force Common Information Model (DMTF CIM). By looking at the fundamental elements of CIM as design patterns rather than a merger of individual constructs, it was easier to get agreement on the fundamental elements of CIM. This was partly due to the fact that such an approach segmented the design, provided a better way to communicate the intent of the model, and focused on the high level principles that required agreement. This resulted in a valuable combination of object oriented design technique and classical data modeling techniques. As the CIM Version 1.0 evolves, we expect that a more rigorous and systematic application of design patterns will result in more commonality being established between the various stakeholders in the CIM schema.

Acknowledgments

Numerous individuals both inside and outside the DMTF have made substantial contributions to the development of the model. We would particularly like to mention past and current members of the DMTF CIM committee Winston Bumpus, Mike Gionfriddo, John Hemphill, Hal Jespersen, Trisha Johnson, John Keith, Bruce Nielsen , Jim Olsen, Doug Snapp, Peter Winter and a particular thanks to Ray Williams, who acted as chairman throughout the model development period.

References

[Batini] C. Batini, S. Ceri, S. Navathe, *Conceptual Database Design An Entity-Relationship Approach*, Benjamini/Cummings, California, 1992.

[Booch] Grady Booch and James Rumbaugh, *Unified Method for Object-Oriented Development Document Set*, Rational Software Corporation, 1996, http:llwww.rational.comlotluml.html .

[Carg] Cargill, Tom *C++Programming Style,* Addison-Wesley, Massachusetts, 1992

[CoSch]Coplein, James O., Schmidt, Douglas C (eds). *Pattern Languages of Program Design*, Addison-Wesley, Reading Mass. 1995 [DCIM] Desktop Management Task Force: Common Information Model (CIM).

[Gamma] Gamma, Erich et al, *Design Patterns: Elements of Reusable Object-Oriented Softwar*, Addison-Wesley, Massachusetts, 1995

Resolving Constraint Conflicts in the Integration of Entity-Relationship Schemas

Mong Li LEE   Tok Wang LING

Department of Information Systems & Computer Science
National University of Singapore
email: {leeml, lingtw}@iscs.nus.sg

Abstract. In this work, we address the problem of constraint conflicts while integrating the conceptual schemas of multiple autonomous databases modeled using the Entity-Relationship (ER) approach. This paper presents a detailed framework to resolve three types of constraint conflicts, domain constraint conflicts, attribute constraint conflicts and relationship constraint conflicts. There are two types of domain constraint conflict, convertible and inconvertible. We distinguish two types of convertible domain constraints conflict, reversible and irreversible, and present an algorithm to resolve domain constraint conflicts. We identify six factors that can contribute to conflict in attribute constraints: imprecise constraint design, domain mismatch, incomplete information, imprecise semantics, value inconsistency and set relation between object types. In relationship constraint conflict resolution, we examine the set relation between equivalent relationship sets and the functional dependencies that hold in these relationship sets. Our conflict resolution approach does not assume that equivalent entity types or relationship sets in two schemas model exactly the same set of instances in the real world. Furthermore, our approach enforces the most precise constraints and enables the retrieval of all the data in the local databases via the integrated schema.

1. Introduction

Schema integration involves merging several schemas into one integrated schema. More precisely, schema integration has been defined as "the activity of integrating the schemas of existing or proposed databases into a global, unified schema" [2]. With the current research into heterogenous databases, this process plays an important role in integrating export schemas into a global schema. [8] proposes an Entity-Relationship (ER) based federated database system where local schemas modeled in the relational, network or hierarchical models are first translated into the corresponding ER export schemas before they are integrated. In the integration of ER export schemas into a global schema, the following conflicts need to be resolved:

1. Naming conflict - Synonyms and homonyms are the two sources of naming conflicts. Renaming is a frequently chosen solution in traditional methodologies.
2. Type conflict - Same real world concept may be represented in two schemas using different modeling constructs. For example, the concept of Publisher may be modeled as an entity type in one schema and as an attribute in another schema.
3. Key conflict - Different keys may be assigned as the identifier of the same concept in different schemas. For example, attributes Ssno and Empno may be identifiers for the entity type Employee in two schemas. Given a precise known

correlation (1:1) between the two keys, this conflict is solved by asking the integrator which key to be used as the identifier in the integrated schema.

4. Constraint conflict - Two schemas may represent different constraints on the same concept. For example, an attribute Phoneno may be single-valued in one schema and multivalued in another schema. Another example involves different constraint on a relationship set such as Teach; one schema may represent it as 1:n (a course has one instructor) whereas the other schema may represent it as m:n (some courses may have more than one instructor).

Previous research has concentrated mostly on the resolution of type conflicts [1, 5, 6, 12]. Little attention has been paid to constraint conflicts. [13] identifies the roles of integrity constraints in database interoperation while [11] examines the integrity constraints that can be defined in an integrated schema. The global integrity constraints obtained can be used to optimise queries at the integrated schema level. We can reduce the average response time for global query processing by eliminating subqueries which yield empty results and formulating the global query into its optimised equivalent. Another possible use of global integrity constraints is in the validation of update transactions, preventing the formulation of subtransactions which will be rejected by the local transaction manager.

Two or more databases modeling the same real world situation, using the same data model and using the same data semantics may possess very different sets of integrity constraints based on the knowledge acquisition skills of their respective designers. We may even have conflicting constraints. This paper investigates how we can resolve the various constraint conflicts that occurs when we integrate ER schemas.

We have the following constraints in the ER model:
1. Domain (value set) constraints on the possible values that an attribute can take.
2. Attribute constraints, which specify whether an attribute of an entity type or relationship set is single-valued or multivalued.
3. Relationship constraint, which specify constraints on the participation of entity types in relationship sets.

Our approach to the resolution of these constraint conflicts is guided by the following principles:
1. Enforce the most precise constraints in the integrated schema.
2. Retrieve all the data in the local databases via the integrated schema.

Two entity types from two different schemas are *semantically equivalent* if they model the same real world concept. Real world concepts may be involved in a variety of associations called relationship sets. Two relationship sets from two different schemas are semantically equivalent if they model the same set of relationships involving the same real world concepts. The sets of instances of a pair of semantically equivalent object types (entity types or relationship sets) can be related in one of the following ways: *EQUAL, SUBSET, OVERLAP, DISJOINT.* For example, if the entity types Book from two schemas S1 and S2 model exactly the same set of books in the real world, then we have S1.Book EQUAL S2.Book. If S1 models Chinese books while S2 models English books, then we have S1.Book DISJOINT S2.Book. If S1 models all Chinese books while S2 models all Chinese and English books, then we have S1.Book SUBSET S2.Book. If S1 models all

Chinese and English books while S2 models all English and Japanese books, then we have S1.Book OVERLAP S2.Book.

The rest of the paper is organized as follows. Section 2 briefly describes the ER model. Sections 3, 4 and 5 describe the resolution of conflicts in domain constraints, attribute constraints and relationship constraints respectively.

2. The Entity-Relationship Approach

The ER approach introduced by Chen [4] attracted considerable attention in systems modeling and database design [3, 4]. The ER concepts correspond to structures naturally occuring in information systems which enhance the ability of designers to describe accurately a universe of discourse. The integration of databases in a federated database system is best performed at the conceptual model level using the ER approach [2, 10] because it has the semantics for defining all the desirable mappings.

The ER model incorporates the concepts of *entity type* and *relationship set*. An entity type or relationship set has *attributes* which represent its structural properties. An attribute can be *single-valued, multivalued* or *composite*. A minimal set of attributes of an entity type E which uniquely identifies E is called a *key* of E. An entity type may have more than one key and we designate one of them as the *identifier* of the entity type. A minimal set of identifiers of some entity types participating in a relationship set R which uniquely identifies R is called a *key* of R. A relationship set may have more than one key and we designate one of them as the *identifier* of the relationship set. If the existence of an entity in one entity type depends upon the existence of a specific entity in another entity type, then such a relationship set and entity type are called *existence dependent relationship set* and *weak entity type*. A special case of existence dependent relationship occurs if the entities in an entity type cannot be identified by the values of their own attributes, but has to be identified by their relationship with other entities. Such a relationship set is called *identifier dependent relationship set*. Existence dependent (EX) relationship sets and identifier dependent (ID) relationship sets are also called weak relationship sets. An entity type which is not a weak entity type is called a *regular entity type*. In the ER approach, *recursive relationship sets* and special relationship sets such as *ISA, UNION, INTERSECT* etc, are allowed. A relationship set which is not weak or special is called a *regular relationship set*. The structure of a database organized according to the ER model can be represented by a diagrammatic technique called an Entity-Relationship Diagram (ERD). The ERD has proven to be a useful database design tool. For more details, see [7].

3. Resolving Conflict in Domain Constraints

Conflicts in domain constraints are also known as *domain mismatch*. This occurs when we have conflict between the domains of equivalent attributes. For example, the value set for an attribute ExamScore may be in grades (A, B, C etc) in one database and in marks in another database.

There are two types of domain mismatch: *convertible* and *inconvertible* domain mismatch. While inconvertible domain mismatch is self-explanatory, we distinguish two types of convertible domain mismatch: *reversible* and *irreversible*. Examples of reversible domain mismatch (or scale differences) are 0° in Celsius corresponds to 32° in Fahrenheit, and 1 kilogram corresponds to 2.2 pounds. Mismatches of this type is easily resolved with a conversion function between the domains.

Attributes with irreversible domain mismatch are attributes whose domains are at various levels of explicitness. Examples include a grade of 'A' in one database being equivalent to a score in the range of 80 to 100 in another database, and a cuisine of 'Chinese' in one database versus 'Hunan' in another database. For mismatches of this type, each value in one domain, say A, is a sub-concept with respect to a value in another domain, say B. Hence each value in domain B corresponds to a set of values in domain A. The conversion between A and B is irreversible. We can convert from A to B, but not from B to A, denoted by $A \Rightarrow B$.

Example 1. Let entity types Restaurant in schemas S1 and S2 be semantically equivalent. Let r1 be an instance of S1.Restaurant and r2 an instance of S2.Restaurant such that r1 and r2 refer to the same real world restaurant. Let Cuisine be an attribute of Restaurant. We have r1.Cuisine = {Chinese} and r2.Cuisine = {Hunan, Cantonese}. Note that Hunan and Cantonese cuisines are Chinese cuisines. We have Domain(S2.Restaurant.Cuisine) $\Rightarrow$ Domain(S1.Restaurant.Cuisine) which indicates an irreversible domain mismatch. We can convert from the domain of S2.Restaurant.Cuisine to that of S1.Restaurant.Cuisine but not vice versa. We construct a domain mismatch hierarchy from the domains of the attributes Cuisine (Fig. 1). In the domain mismatch hierarchy, the domain of S2.Restaurant.Cuisine is at a lower level than that of S1.Restaurant.Cuisine. Note that no total order exists in the domain mismatch hierarchy.

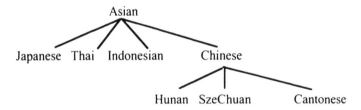

Fig. 1. Domain mismatch hierarchy for Cuisine

This irreversible domain mismatch in S1.Restaurant.Cuisine and S2.Restaurant.Cuisine can be resolved by considering the set relation between the equivalent entity types S1.Restaurant and S2.Restaurant. If S1.Restaurant EQUAL (or SUBSET) S2.Restaurant, then domain of Cuisine in the integrated schema will be that of S2.Cuisine. This ensures that we will be able to retrieve all the various cuisines via the integrated schema. On the other hand, if S2.Restaurant SUBSET S1.Restaurant, then domain of Cuisine in the integrated schema is the union of Domain(S1.Restaurant.Cuisine) and Domain(S2.Restaurant.Cuisine). This is because for all the real world restaurant instances r which are modeled in both S1.Restaurant and S2.Restaurant, r.Cuisine $\in$ Domain(S2.Restaurant.Cuisine). However, for restaurants r which are modeled in S1.Restaurant only, r.Cuisine $\in$ Domain(S1.Restaurant.Cuisine). Similarly, if S2.Restaurant OVERLAP (or DISJOINT) S1.Restaurant, then domain of Cuisine in the integrated schema is the union of Domain(S1.Restaurant.Cuisine) and Domain(S2.Restaurant.Cuisine).

The following algorithm resolves conflicts in domain constraints. If we have a reversible domain mismatch between two equivalent attributes, then it is immaterial which of the attributes' domain is used in the integrated schema. This is because a conversion function defines a one-to-one mapping between the attributes' domains.

Algorithm   Resolve_DomainConstraint

Let O_1 and O_2 be two semantically equivalent object types in different schemas and A be an attribute of both O_1 and O_2. O_1.A and O_2.A are semantically equivalent. Let O be the integrated object type of O_1 and O_2 and A be the integrated attribute of O_1.A and O_2.A.

Case 1: No domain mismatch.
　　Domain(O.A) is either Domain(O_1.A) or Domain(O_2.A).

Case 2: Convertible domain mismatch.
　　Case 2.1: Reversible domain mismatch.
　　　　Domain(O.A) is either Domain(O_1.A) or Domain(O_2.A).

　　Case 2.2: Irreversible domain mismatch.
　　　　Case 2.2.1: O_1 EQUAL O_2.
　　　　　　Without loss of generality, let Domain(O_1.A) $\Rightarrow$ Domain(O_2.A).
　　　　　　Domain(O.A) is Domain(O_1.A) to retrieve all values for attribute A via
　　　　　　the integrated schema.
　　　　Case 2.2.2: O_1 SUBSET O_2.
　　　　　　If Domain(O_1.A) $\Rightarrow$ Domain(O_2.A)
　　　　　　Then   Domain(O.A) is Domain(O_1.A) $\cup$ Domain(O_2.A) [1]
　　　　　　Else   /* Domain(O_2.A) $\Rightarrow$ Domain(O_1.A) */
　　　　　　　　Domain(O.A) is Domain(O_2.A) [2].
　　　　Case 2.2.3: O_1 OVERLAP O_2 or O_1 DISJOINT O_2.
　　　　　　Domain(O.A) is Domain(O_1.A) $\cup$ Domain(O_2.A).

Case 3: Inconvertible domain mismatch.
　　Domain(O.A) is Domain(O_1.A) $\cup$ Domain(O_2.A).

After we have determined the domain of an integrated attribute, we may face the possibility of *value inconsistencies*. Consider two databases DB_1 and DB_2 held by different booksellers. Both contain an entity type Book with attributes ISBN, Title, Publisher, Price. Assuming that any domain mismatch in the attribute Price has been resolved, the same book may be priced differently by the two booksellers. Inconsistency in the attributes' values arises because ISBN $\rightarrow$ Price is a *local constraint*, which is valid in the context of a specific database only. When we

---

[1] For all $t \in O_1$, clearly t.A $\in$ Domain(O_1.A). On the other hand, for all $t \in O_2$ and t $\notin O_1$, t.A $\in$ Domain(O_2.A). Therefore, Domain(O.A) is Domain(O_1.A) $\cup$ Domain(O_2.A).

[2] For all $t \in O_1$ implies $t \in O_2$ since we have O_1 SUBSET O_2. For all $t \in O_2$, clearly t.A $\in$ Domain(O_2.A). Therefore, Domain(O.A) is Domain(O_2.A).

integrate the two databases, ISBN → Price is no longer true. Instead, we derive the *global constraint* {ISBN, DB} → Price where DB is a new attribute whose domain is the set of database names.

We distinguish three approaches to handle conflict in attribute values depending on the semantics of the attributes.

1. Ignore
   This indicates a situation where we do not deal with possible value conflict. We can choose any of the values. For example, the publisher of a particular book can be retrieved from either one of the databases.
2. Avoid
   Choose one of the databases as the most reliable source of values for the integrated attribute.
3. Resolve
   Case 1: Single-valued attributes
   Value inconsistency is resolved by using a *resolution function* which derives a value(s) for the integrated attribute from the attribute values in the component databases. Examples of resolution functions include *MAX, MIN, AVERAGE, SUM* and *UNION*. For the function UNION, we may need to qualify each of the component attribute value by the database name. For example, given two booksellers' databases DB_1 and DB_2, a database integrator may choose to resolve value inconsistency in the attribute Price by keeping all the various booksellers' prices in the integrated attribute, in which case we will have the set of values {DB_1.Price, DB_2.Price} for the integrated attribute. Note that the UNION function will cause the integrated attribute to be multivalued.
   Case 2: Multivalued attributes
   Inconsistency in the sets of values for the equivalent attributes in the component databases can be resolved by using the UNION function.

4. Resolving Conflict in Attribute Constraints

Attribute constraints are also known as attribute cardinalities. A single-valued attribute can be 1:1 (one-to-one) or m:1 (many-to-one). A multivalued attribute can be 1:m (one-to-many) or m:m (many-to-many). Attribute constraint conflict occurs when two semantically equivalent attributes do not have the same cardinalities.

Conflict in attribute constraints is resolved in two phases:
Phase 1. Establish whether the integrated attribute is single-valued or multivalued.
Phase 2. Determine precisely which type of single-valued or multivalued cardinality for the integrated attribute, that is 1:1 versus m:1 or 1:m versus m:m.

We identify six possible factors that can lead to inconsistency in attribute constraints. We first illustrate these factors informally using an example. A detailed and precise algorithm is given later in the section. Let O_1 and O_2 be two semantically equivalent object types and A be an attribute of both O_1 and O_2. Let O be the integrated object type of O_1 and O_2 and A be the integrated attribute of O_1.A and O_2.A. Suppose O_1.A is single-valued and O_2.A is multivalued.

1. Imprecise constraint design
    If for all instances t in O_2 and t.O_2.A has exactly one value, then it is possible that the multivalued cardinality of O_2.A has been imprecisely designed. We should verify the constraint design with the database integrator. If the integrator is very sure that there may exist some instance t in O_2 such that t.O_2.A has more than one value, then O.A is multivalued. Otherwise, we change the constraint of O_2.A to single-valued and the conflict is resolved.

2. Domain mismatch
    Reversible domain mismatch does not contribute to attribute constraint conflict. If we have an irreversible domain mismatch such that Domain(O_2.A) $\Rightarrow$ Domain(O_1.A), then a value in Domain(O_1.A) may correspond to a set of values in Domain(O_2.A). That is, for all $t_1 \in O_1$, $t_2 \in O_2$ such that t_1, t_2 refer to the same real world instance, all the values in t_2.A can be converted to the same single t_1.A value. No actual constraint conflict exists and O.A is multivalued. If the domains of O_1.A and O_2.A are inconvertible, then O.A is multivalued.

3. Incomplete information
    If there exist some instance t in O_2 and t.A has more than one value, then O_1.A may contain incomplete information. This occurs when O_1.A and O_2.A have exactly the same semantics. For example, both O_1.A and O_2.A may model the name of a person. However, O_2.A includes the aliases of a person. In this case, O.A will be multivalued.

4. Imprecise semantics
    If O_1.A and O_2.A do not have exactly the same semantics, then we may not have any actual constraint conflict. For example, O_1.A may model the highest qualification of a person while O_2.A may model the set of qualifications of a person. If the integrator still choose to merge these two attributes, then O.A will be multivalued. Otherwise, O_1.A and O_2.A will not be integrated.

5. Value inconsistency
    As mentioned in the previous section, value inconsistency arise because of local constraints. The integrator may choose to take the union of all the values in the equivalent attributes. In this case, O.A will be multivalued.

6. Set Relation between Object Types
    If O_1 and O_2 do not model exactly the same set of objects in the real world, then we may not have any actual constraint conflict. For example, if O_1 SUBSET O_2, then O_1.A is more restrictive than O_2.A. This may indicate that for all $t_1 \in O_1$, $t_2 \in O_2$ where t_1, t_2 refer to the same real world instance, t_2.A is single-valued. However, for some $t \in O_2$ and $t \notin O_1$, t.A is multivalued. Hence, O.A is multivalued to enable retrieval of all information in O_1 and O_2 via O. Similarly, if O_1 DISJOINT (or OVERLAP) O_2, then t.A is single-valued for all $t \in O_1$ and $t \notin O_2$, and t.A is multivalued for all $t \in O_2$ and $t \notin O_1$. Therefore, there is no actual constraint conflict and O.A is multivalued.

Some of the factors such as set relation between object types, domain mismatch and value inconsistency are orthogonal. We can have more than one factors causing a constraint conflict. The order of checking for the possible factors is important because it affects the constraint of the integrated attribute. The following algorithm determines the cause(s) of an attribute constraint conflict and resolves it.

Algorithm   Check_Conflict_Cause

Let O_1 and O_2 be two object types and A be an attribute of both O_1 and O_2. Let O be the integrated object type of O_1 and O_2 and A the integrated attribute of O_1 and O_2. Let O_1.A be single-valued and O_2.A be multivalued.

Step 1.   Check O_2.A for imprecise constraint design.

      If $\forall\ t \in O_2$, t.A has exactly one value

          Then   Verify constraint design of O_2.A with database integrator.

              If integrator confirms imprecise constraint design
              Then   Change O_2.A to single-valued.

              O.A is single-valued. Goto Step 6.
              /* Conflict resolved. Just check for value inconsistency */

Step 2.   Check for domain mismatch.
      If the domains of O_1.A and O_2.A are inconvertible

          Then   O.A is multivalued. Goto Step 6.
          Else   /* Check for irreversible domain mismatch. Reversible domain mismatch do not cause conflict. */
              Let K be the identifer of O_1 and O_2.

              If for each $t_1 \in O_1$, $t_2 \in O_2$, t_1.K $= t_2$.K and all t_2.A values can be converted to the same single t_1.A value

              Then   O.A is multivalued. Goto Step 5.
                  /* Check if set relation between object type is also a cause of conflict. Check for value inconsistency in Step 6. */

Step 3.   Check for incomplete information.
      If O_1.A and O_2.A have exactly the same semantics

          Then   Inform integrator O_1.A contains incomplete information.

          O.A is multivalued. Goto Step 5.

Step 4.   Check for imprecise semantics.
      If O_1.A and O_2.A do not have exactly the same semantics

          Then   Inform integrator of the imprecise semantics.
              If integrator still want to integrate O_1.A and O_2.A

              Then   O.A is multivalued. Goto Step 5.
              Else O_1.A and O_2.A will not be integrated. Exit.

Step 5.   Check set relation between object types.
      If $(O_1$.A SUBSET O_2.A) or $(O_1$.A OVERLAP O_2.A) or
      $(O_1$.A DISJOINT O_2.A)

          Then   O.A is multivalued.

Step 6.   Check for value inconsistency.
      If there exists potential value inconsistency

Then   Ask integrator for the resolution function RF.
        If RF = UNION   Then O.A is multivalued.

Example 2   Consider again the databases DB_1 and DB_2 held by different booksellers. Suppose we have a constraint conflict in the attribute Price: DB_1.Book.Price is single-valued and DB_2.Book.Price is multivalued. Let DB.Book.Price be the integrated attribute. In the process of determining the cause(s) of the attribute constraint conflict, we discover the following facts:

Fact 1.   Cardinality of DB_2.Book.Price has been imprecisely designed because each book in DB_2 has only one selling price.

Fact 2.   There is a potential value inconsistency in DB_1.Book.Price and DB_2.Book.Price because the different booksellers may price the same book differently. This is because of the local constraint ISBN $\rightarrow$ Price. The integrator removes this attribute value inconsistency by taking the union of all the prices for the integrated attribute Price.

Fact 3. DB_1.Book OVERLAP DB_2.Book.

Fact 1 automatically resolves the constraint conflict which arises because of imprecise constraint design. Therefore, we do not need to consider the OVERLAP set relation between DB_1.Book and DB_2.Book. At this point, the integrated attribute DB.Book.Price is single-valued. However, Fact 2 alerts us to a potential value inconsistency because of the local constraint. If the integrator resolves this inconsistency by taking the average selling price for the integrated attribute (Step 6 in Algorithm Check_Conflict_Cause), then DB.Book.Price remains single-valued. However, if the integrator resolves the value inconsistency by taking the union of all the prices for the integrated attribute, then DB.Book.Price becomes multivalued.

In Phase 2, we want to determine a more precise type of single-valued or multivalued attribute constraint for the integrated attribute. Given two object types O_1 and O_2 and an attribute A of both O_1 and O_2. Let O be the integrated object type of O_1 and O_2. Both O_1.A and O_2.A are either single-valued or multivalued attributes. We denote the cardinality of an attribute A by Card(A) = x:y where x, y is equal to 1 or m. Let Card(O_1.A) = 1:y and Card(O_2.A) = m:y where y = 1 or m. We derive a more precise constraint for the integrated attribute O.A as follows:

If $\exists$ s, t $\in$ O_2 such that s $\neq$ t and s.A = t.A
        Then   Card(O.A) = m:y
        Else   Verify constraint design with the integrator.
                If integrator confirms imprecise constraint design
                Then   Card(O.A) = 1:y which is more precise
                Else   Card(O.A) = m:y.

Finally, if there is no conflict in the cardinalities of the equivalent attributes, then Card(O.A) is equal to either Card(O_1.A) or Card(O_2.A) since both cardinalities are the same. This is true except when the cardinalities of both O_1.A and O_2.A are either 1:1 or 1:m. If we have for O_1 SUBSET O_2 or O_1 OVERLAP O_2 or O_1 DISJOINT O_2, then the cardinalities of O_1.A and O_2.A are local constraints which valid in the context of their respective databases only. These constraints may not hold in the integrated database. For example, if we have O_1 DISJOINT O_2 and $Card(O_1.A) = Card(O_2.A) = 1:1$, then $Card(O.A) = m:1$ (Fig. 2).

Fig. 2. The mappings from O_1 and O_2 to A are both 1:1.

We can similarly resolve any cardinality conflicts of attributes A_1 and A_2 should they belong to relationship sets R_1 and R_2 of two databases respectively. Note that our approach attempts to determine the most precise constraints in the integrated schema without compromising the retrieval of information from the local databases.

5. Resolving Conflict in Relationship Constraints

Next we proceed to resolve conflicts in relationship constraints. These are cardinality constraints on the participating entity types in a relationship set which actually indicate functional dependencies in the relationship set. Conflicts in these constraints occur when the same participating entity types of a relationship set have different cardinalities in the different databases.

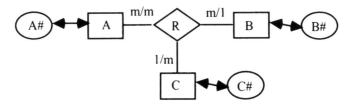

Fig. 3: A relationship set R can have more than one cardinality constraints which indicate more than one functional dependencies in R.

Fig. 3 shows a relationship set R with participating entity types A, B and C with identifiers A#, B# and C# respectively. R has two constraints as follows:
1. The first constraint where the cardinalities of A, B and C in R are m, m, 1 respectively implies that the functional dependency {A#, B#} → C# holds in R.
2. The second constraint where the cardinalities of A, B, and C in R are m, 1, m respectively implies that the functional dependency {A#, C#} → B# holds in R.

In general, each functional dependency in a relationship set represents a cardinality constraint on its participating entity types. If the identifier of a participating entity type E of a relationship set R appears on the left hand side of a functional dependency in R, then E has a cardinality of m in R with respect to that cardinality constraint in R. Otherwise, if the identifier of E appears on the right hand side of a functional dependency in R, then E has a cardinality of 1 in R with respect to that cardinality constraint in R. There is no functional dependencies in R if the cardinality of each of the participating entity types in R is m. However, the cardinality constraint of 1:1

between entity types A and B in a binary relationship set actually represents two functional dependencies A# → B# and B# → A#.

Example 3   Consider the two schemas given in Fig. 4a and Fig. 4b which models the ternary relationship between student, subject and teacher.

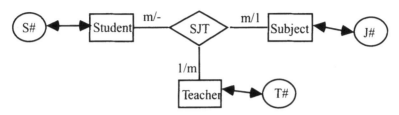

Fig. 4a: Schema S1

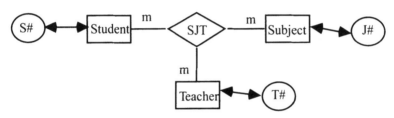

Fig. 4b: Schema S2

The following constraints apply in the relationship set S1.SJT:
  1. For each subject, each student of that subject is taught by only one teacher.
  2. Each teacher teaches only one subject.
From the first constraint, we have {S#, J#} → T#. From the second constraint, we have T# → J#. These functional dependencies are reflected by the two sets of cardinality constraints in S1.SJT. A dash "-" in the cardinality of the entity type Student means that it is not involved in the second constraint. We have no cardinality constraint or non-trivial functional dependency in the relationship set S2.SJT. That is, the cardinality of each of the participating entity types in S2.SJT is m.

When we integrate these two schemas, we need to reconcile these two diffferent relationship constraints. Our resolution approach will enforce the most precise constraints in the integrated schema and enable the retrieval of all the data in the local databases via the integrated schema. We examine the set relation between these two relationship sets and the functional dependencies that hold in these relationship sets. Let F_1 and F_2 be the sets of functional dependencies that hold in S1.SJT and S2.SJT respectively. $F_1 = \{\{S\#, J\#\} \to T\#, T\# \to J\#\}$ and $F_2 = \emptyset$.

Case 1: S1.SJT EQUAL S2.SJT
  The integrated relationship set needs to enforce all the constraints from both S1.SJT and S2.SJT. The set of functional dependencies that hold in the integrated relationship set is $F_1 \cup F_2 = \{\{S\#, J\#\} \to T\#, T\# \to J\#\}$ which is more precise. S1 is the integrated schema. We also conclude F_1 holds in S2.

Case 2: S1.SJT OVERLAP (or DISJOINT) S2.SJT

In order to retrieve all the data in the databases modeled by S1 and S2 via the integrated schema, the integrated relationship set needs to enforce the least restricted constraints. The set of functional dependencies in the integrated relationship set is $F_1^+ \cap F_2^+$ which contains no non-trivial functional dependencies, F^+ denotes the closure of F [Maie83]. The integrated schema is S2 and there is no real constraint in the integrated relationship set. All the participating entity types in the integrated relationship set have cardinality m.

Case 3: S1.SJT SUBSET S2.SJT

A relationship in S1.SJT will need to satisfy the constraints in $F_1 \cup F_2$ while a relationship in S2.SJT but not in S1.SJT will need to satisfy the constraints in F_2 only. Therefore, in order to retrieve all the data in the databases modeled by S1 and S2, the integrated relationship set needs to enforce the constraints in F_2 only, which is the set of functional dependencies in the superset relationship set S2.SJT. The integrated schema is S2 and there is no non-trivial functional dependency in the integrated relationship set.

Case 4: S2.SJT SUBSET S1.SJT

As in Case 3, the integrated relationship set contains the same set of functional dependencies as the superset relationship set. The integrated schema is S1 and the set of functional dependencies $\{\{S\#, J\#\} \rightarrow T\#, T\# \rightarrow J\#\}$ holds in the integrated relationship set. We can also conclude that S2.SJT should have the more precise functional dependencies $\{\{S\#, J\#\} \rightarrow T\#, T\# \rightarrow J\#\}$.

From the set of functional dependencies that hold in the integrated relationship set, we can obtain the cardinality constraints of the participating entity types in the relationship set. It is easy to obtain $F_1 \cup F_2$. However, it may not be so obvious how we can obtain the cardinalites of the participating entity types from $F_1^+ \cap F_2^+$. Note that we cannot simply take the intersection of F_1 and F_2. For example, given two sets of functional dependencies $F_1 = \{A \rightarrow B, B \rightarrow C\}$ and $F_2 = \{A \rightarrow C\}$, then $F_1 \cap F_2 = \emptyset$. But $F_1^+ \cap F_2^+ = \{A \rightarrow C\}^+$.

The following proposition summarizes the resolution of relationship constraint conflicts. We assume any erroneous or imprecise constraint designs have been detected by examining the databases.

Proposition 1: Let R_1 and R_2 be two semantically equivalent relationship sets. Let F_1 and F_2 be sets of functional dependencies that hold in R_1 and R_2 respectively. Let F be the set of functional dependencies that hold in the relationship set R obtained by integrating R_1 and R_2. Each pair of semantically equivalent participating entity types from the two schemas will be merged into an entity type in the integrated schema.

Case 1: R_1 EQUAL R_2 Then $F = F_1 \cup F_2$.

Case 2: R_1 SUBSET R_2 Then $F = F_2$.

Case 3: R_1 OVERLAP R_2 or R_1 DISJOINT R_2 Then $F = F_1^+ \cap F_2^+$.

Proof: Each functional dependency in F represent a cardinality constraint among the participating entity types in the integrated relationship set.

Case 1: If R_1 EQUAL R_2 then R_1 and R_2 contain the same relationships at all points in time. A relationship r in the integrated relationship set R can be found in both R_1 and R_2. Therefore r needs to satisfy all the constraints that hold in R_1 and R_2. Hence, we have $F = F_1 \cup F_2$.

Case 2: If R_1 SUBSET R_2 then all the relationships in R_1 also exists in R_2. A relationship in R_1 will need to satisfy all the constraints in $F_1 \cup F_2$ while a relationship in R_2 but not R_1 will need to satisfy the constraints in F_2 only. Hence, we have $F = (F_1 \cup F_2) \cap F_2 = F_2$. Note that if $F_1 \subset F_2$, then clearly the set of functional dependencies in F_1 is imprecise. That is, F_2 should also hold in R_1.

Case 3: If R_1 OVERLAP R_2 or R_1 DISJOINT R_2 then a relationship r in the integrated relationship set R can be found in either R_1 or R_2. Therefore r needs to satisfy either F_1 or F_2. R will contain the least restrictive constraints which is the set of functional dependencies common in both R_1 and R_2. Hence, we have $F = F_1^+ \cap F_2^+$.

Note that unlike the resolution of attribute constraint conflicts, the resolution of relationship constraint conflicts do not require us to consider factors such as domain mismatch, incomplete information, imprecise semantics and value inconsistency. This is because these factors are either not applicable or do not influence the constraint resolution.

6. Conclusion

In this paper, we have focused on the resolution of constraint conflicts in the integration of ER schemas. We have given a detailed framework to resolve conflicts in domain constraints, attribute constraints and relationship constraints. There are two types of domain mismatch, convertible and inconvertible domain mismatch. We distinguished two types of convertible domain mismatch, namely reversible and irreversible domain mismatch. We gave an algorithm to resolve these domain constraint conflicts. We also distinguished three approaches to handle value inconsistency or conflict in attribute values depending on the semantics of the attributes.

In the resolution of attribute constraint conflicts, we identified six factors that could contribute to the conflict: imprecise constraint design, irreversible domain mismatch, incomplete information, imprecise semantics, value inconsistency and set relation between object types. We developed an algorithm to check for these various conflict causing factors and showed that the order of checking for these factors is important. In the resolution of relationship constraint conflicts, we examined the set relation between the equivalent relationship sets and the functional dependencies that hold in these relationship sets. Our conflict resolution approach does not assume that corresponding equivalent entity types or relationship sets in two schemas model exactly the same set of instances in the real world. Our approach enforces the most precise constraints and enables the retrieval all the data in the local databases via the integrated schema.

References

[1] Batini, C. and Lenzerini, M., A Methodology for Data Schema Integration in the Entity-Relationship Model, IEEE Trans.Software Engineering, SE-10, pp 650-664, 1984.

[2] Batini, C., Lenzerini, M. and Navathe, S.B., A Comparative Analysis of Methodologies for Database Schema Integration, ACM Computing Surveys, Vol 18, No 4, December 1986, pp 323-364.

[3] Chan, E.P.F. and Lochovsky, F.H., A Graphical Data Base Design Aid using the Entity-Relationship Model, in Entity-Relationship Approach to Systems Analysis and Design, North Holland, 1980, pp 295-310.

[4] Chen, P.P., The Entity-Relationship Model: Toward a Unified View of Data, ACM Transactions on Database Systems vol 1, no 1, 1976, pp 166-192.

[5] Larson, J., Navathe, S. and Elmasri, R., A Theory of Attribute Equivalence in Database with Application to Schema Integration, IEEE Trans. on Software Engineering, 15:449-463, 1989.

[6] Lee, M.L. and Ling, T.W., Resolving Structural Conflicts in the Integration of Entity Relationship Schemas, Proc. 14th Int. Conference on Object-Oriented and Entity-Relationship Modeling, 1995.

[7] Ling, T.W., "A Normal Form for Entity-Relationship Diagrams", Proc. 4th International Conference on Entity-Relationship Approach, 1985.

[8] Ling, T.W. and Lee, M.L., Issues in an Entity-Relationship Based Federated Database System, in Proceedings of the International Symposium on Cooperative Database Systems for Advanced Applications, Japan, 1996.

[9] D. Maier: Theory of Relational Databases, Computer Science Press, 1983.

[10] Navathe, S.B., Elmasri, R. and Larson, J., Integrating User Views in Database Design, IEEE Computer 19, 1, 1986, pp 50-62.

[11] Reddy, M.P., Prasad, B.E. and Gupta, A., Formulating global integrity constraints during derivation of global schema, Data & Knowledge Engineering 16, 1995.

[12] Spaccapietra, S., Parent, C., and Dupont, Y., Model independent assertions for integration of heterogenous schemas, VLDB Journal, (1), 1992, pp 81-126.

[13] Vermeer, M and Apers, P.M.G., The Role of Integrity Constraints in Database Interoperation, Proc. of the 22nd VLDB Conference, India, 1996.

A Formal Framework for ER Schema Transformation

Peter McBrien and Alexandra Poulovassilis

Department of Computer Science, King's College London,
Strand, London WC2R 2LS.
alex,pjm@dcs.kcl.ac.uk

Abstract. Several methodologies for semantic schema integration have been proposed in the literature, often using some variant of the ER model as the common data model. As part of these methodologies, various transformations have been defined that map between ER schemas which are in some sense equivalent. This paper gives a unifying formalisation of the ER schema transformation process and shows how some common schema transformations can be expressed within this single framework. Our formalism clearly identifies which transformations apply for any instance of the schema and which only for certain instances.

1   Introduction

When data is to be shared or exchanged between heterogeneous databases, it is necessary to build a single integrated schema expressed using a common data model (CDM) [13]. Conflicts may exist between the export schemas of the component databases, which must be removed by performing transformations on the schemas to produce equivalent schemas.

In this paper we examine the behaviour of the schema transformations commonly found in the literature within a new formal framework, and distinguish in a precise manner between schema transformations which are dependent on knowledge about the instances associated with the schema, and those which are not. This distinction has the benefit of precisely defining what assumptions are made when a database object is transformed or is considered to have the same "real world state" [8] as some other object.

Previous work on schema transformation has either been to some extent informal [2, 7, 6], has formalised only transformations that are independent of database content [10, 11], or is limited to certain types of transformation only [3, 8, 14, 5]. The latter cases assume that specific types of dependency constraints are employed to limit the instances of schemas in order that the schemas can be regarded as equivalent. In contrast, our approach allows arbitrary constraints on instances to be specified as part of the transformation rules. A similar approach has recently been adopted in [6] where the notion of a database "context" constrains instances so that schemas can be considered equivalent.

In common with much previous work on semantic schema integration [1, 2, 4], we use a variant of the ER model as the CDM, namely a binary ER model with subtypes. This model supports entity types with attributes, subtype relationships between entity types, and binary relationships (without attributes) between entity types. Subtype relationships give sufficient modelling expressiveness for representing object-oriented schemas. By omitting generalisation hierarchies, aggregations and n-ary relationships for n > 2, some alternate representations of the universe of discourse are avoided. There is no loss of modelling expressiveness since there are obvious transformations that can be applied from these more complex structures into our CDM (see, for example, [9]).

Similarly to [1], in our CDM each relationship, r, between two entity types, e_1 and e_2, has associated with it a pair of cardinality constraints, $l_1 : u_1$ and $l_2 : u_2$, where $l_1 : u_1$ ($l_2 : u_2$) indicates the lower and upper cardinalities of the participation in r by each instance of e_1 (e_2). Each association between an entity type and an attribute similarly has a pair of cardinality constraints associated with it. If not explicitly stated, a cardinality constraint of $1 : 1$ should be assumed.

The main tasks of database schema integration are **pre-integration, schema conforming, schema merging** and **schema restructuring** [2]. The last three of these tasks involve a process of **schema transformation**, and Figures 1-3 illustrate some of the common transformations used. In practice, schema conforming transformations are applied bi-directionally and schema merging and restructuring ones uni-directionally. For each of these transformations, the original and resulting schema obey one or more alternative notions of schema **equivalence** [12, 1, 8]. This paper presents a unifying formalism for the schema transformation process, including all of the transformations of Figures 1-3.

In Section 2 we define the notions of ER schemas, instances and models. In Section 3 we define the notion of schema equivalence which provides the semantic foundation of schema transformation in our approach. In Section 4 we define a set of primitive transformations and explore their properties with respect to schema equivalence. We then extend these transformations into "knowledge-based" versions, which allow conditions on instances to be expressed. Section 5 demonstrates the expressiveness of our primitive transformations by showing how they can be used to define all the transformations of Figures 1–3. In Section 6 we give our concluding remarks.

2   ER Schemas, Instances and Models

Our definitions of schemas, instances and models (Definitions 1-3 below), assume the availability of two disjoint sets: $Vals$ (values) and $Names$ (names of entity types, attributes and relationships). The distinguished constant $Null$ is a member of $Names$. $Seq(Vals)$ is the set of sequences of values of finite length. P is the powerset operator. $Cards$ is the set of cardinality constraints, a cardinality constraint being a pair $l : u$, where l is a natural number and u is either a natural number or N (denoting no upper limit). For any function f, $Range(f)$ denotes the range of f.

Definition 1. An **ER schema**, S, is a quadruple $\langle Ents, Incs, Atts, Assocs \rangle$ where:

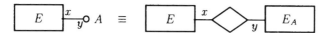

(a) Entity/attribute equivalence

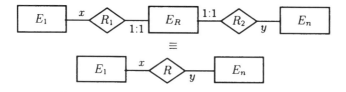

(b) Entity/relationship equivalence

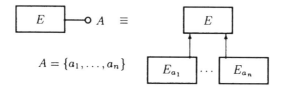

(c) Attribute/subtype equivalence

Fig. 1. Schema Conforming Transformations

- $Ents \subseteq Names$ is the set of entity type names.
- $Incs \subseteq (Ents \times Ents)$, each pair $\langle e_1, e_2 \rangle \in Incs$ representing that e_1 is a subtype of e_2. We assume that $Incs$ is acyclic.
- $Atts \subseteq Names$ is the set of attribute names.
- $Assocs \subseteq (Names \times Names \times Names \times Cards \times Cards)$ is the set of **associations**.

  For each relationship between two entity types $e_1, e_2 \in Ents$, there is a tuple $\langle rel\_name, e_1, e_2, c_1, c_2 \rangle \in Assocs$, where c_1 indicates the lower and upper cardinalities of instances of e_2 for each instance of e_1, and c_2 indicates the lower and upper cardinalities of instances of e_1 for each instance of e_2. rel_name may be $Null$ if there is only one relationship between e_1 and e_2. Similarly, for each attribute a associated with an entity type e there is a tuple $\langle Null, e, a, c_1, c_2 \rangle \in Assocs$, where c_1 indicates the lower and upper cardinalities of a for each instance of e, and c_2 indicates the lower and upper cardinalities of instances of e for each value of a.

Definition 2 below defines an instance, I, of a schema, S, to be a set of sets. The extent of each item in S (*i.e.* each entity, attribute and association) is derived by means of an expression over the sets of I expressed in some mapping language

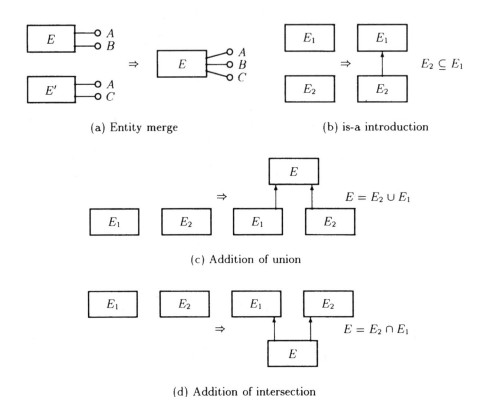

(a) Entity merge

(b) is-a introduction

(c) Addition of union

(d) Addition of intersection

Fig. 2. Schema Merging Transformations

L (point (i) below). In order to support updates to I, this mapping should be reversible (point (ii)). The instance I respects the subtype relationships in S (point (iii)) and the domain and cardinality constraints (point (iv)).

Definition 2. Given an ER schema $S = \langle Ents, Incs, Atts, Assocs \rangle$, let

$$Schemes = \{\langle n_0, n_1, n_2 \rangle \mid \langle n_0, n_1, n_2, c_1, c_2 \rangle \in Assocs\}$$

An **instance of** S is a set $I \subseteq P(Seq(Vals))$ such that there exists a function

$$Ext_{S,I} : Ents \cup Atts \cup Schemes \rightarrow P(Seq(Vals))$$

where:

(i) each set in $Range(Ext_{S,I})$ is derivable by means of an expression in L over the sets of I;

(ii) conversely, each set in I is derivable by means of an expression in L over the sets of $Range(Ext_{S,I})$;

(iii) for any $\langle e_1, e_2 \rangle \in Incs$, $Ext_{S,I}(e_1) \subseteq Ext_{S,I}(e_2)$;

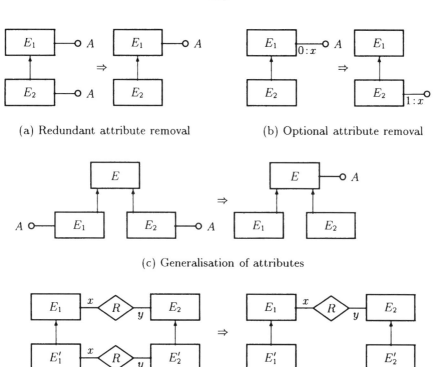

(a) Redundant attribute removal

(b) Optional attribute removal

(c) Generalisation of attributes

(d) Redundant relationship removal (1)

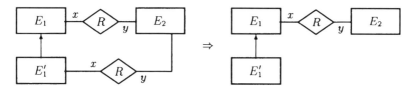

(e) Redundant relationship removal (2)

Fig. 3. Schema Restructuring Transformations

(iv) for every $\langle n_0, n_1, n_2 \rangle \in Schemes$, $Ext_{S,I}(\langle n_0, n_1, n_2 \rangle)$ satisfies the appropriate domain and cardinality constraints *i.e.* the following two conditions hold:

(a) each sequence $s \in Ext_{S,I}(\langle n_0, n_1, n_2 \rangle)$ contains two, possibly overlapping, subsequences s_1, s_2 where $s_1 \in Ext_{S,I}(n_1)$ and $s_2 \in Ext_{S,I}(n_2)$; we denote by $n_1(s)$ and $n_2(s)$ these subsequences of s;

(b) if the cardinality of $\langle n_0, n_1, n_2 \rangle$ is $\langle l_1 : u_1, l_2 : u_2 \rangle$ then
$\forall s_1 \in Ext_{S,I}(n_1).l_1 \leq | \{n_2(s) | s \in Ext_{S,I}(\langle n_0, n_1, n_2 \rangle) \wedge n_1(s) = s_1\} | \leq u_1$
and

$$\forall s_2 \in Ext_{S,I}(n_2).l_2 \leq |\ \{n_1(s)|s \in Ext_{S,I}(\langle n_0, n_1, n_2 \rangle)) \wedge n_2(s) = s_2\} \ | \leq u_2$$

Such a function $Ext_{S,I}$ is termed an **extension mapping** from S to I.

Definition 3. A **model** is a triple $\langle S, I. Ext_{S,I} \rangle$ where S is a schema, I is an instance of S and $Ext_{S,I}$ an extension mapping from S to I.

3 Schema Equivalence

Definition 4. $Inst(S)$ denotes the set of instances of a schema S. A schema S **subsumes a schema** S' if $Inst(S') \subseteq Inst(S)$. Two schemas S and S' are **equivalent** if $Inst(S') = Inst(S)$.

For example, the top half of Figure 4 shows a schema S consisting of an entity 'person' with an attribute 'dept', a database instance I consisting of three sets $\{john, jane, mary\}$, $\{compsci, maths\}$ and $\{\langle john, compsci \rangle, \langle jane, compsci \rangle, \langle jane, maths \rangle, \langle mary, maths \rangle\}$, and the function $Ext_{S,I}$ defined as follows:

$$Ext_{S,I}(\text{person}) = \{john, jane, mary\}$$
$$Ext_{S,I}(\text{dept}) = \{compsci, maths\}$$
$$Ext_{S,I}(\langle Null, \text{person}, \text{dept}\rangle) = \{\langle john, compsci \rangle, \langle jane, compsci \rangle,$$
$$\langle jane, maths \rangle, \langle mary, maths \rangle\}$$

The bottom half of Figure 4 shows another schema S' consisting of two entities 'person' and 'dept' and a relationship 'works_in' between them. S' subsumes S in the sense that any instance of S is also an instance of S'. In particular, we can define $Ext_{S',I}$ in terms of $Ext_{S,I}$ as follows:

$$Ext_{S',I}(\text{person}) = Ext_{S,I}(\text{person})$$
$$Ext_{S',I}(\text{dept}) = Ext_{S,I}(\text{dept})$$
$$Ext_{S',I}(\langle \text{works\_in}, \text{person}, \text{dept}\rangle) = Ext_{S,I}(\langle Null, \text{person}, \text{dept}\rangle)$$

By a similar argument, it is easy to see that S subsumes S', and so S and S' are equivalent. This is an example of the entity/attribute equivalence of Figure 1(a). We can generalise the definition of equivalence to incorporate a condition on the instances of one or both schemas:

Definition 5. $Inst(S, f)$ denotes the set of instances of a schema S that satisfy a given condition f. A schema S **conditionally subsumes (c-subsumes)** a schema S' w.r.t. f if $Inst(S', f) \subseteq Inst(S, f)$. Two schemas S and S' are **conditionally equivalent (c-equivalent) w.r.t** f if $Inst(S, f) = Inst(S', f)$.

For example, in Figure 5 the schema S and the instance I are as in Figure 4. The schema S' now consists of three entities 'person', 'mathematician' and 'computer scientist', with the last two being subtypes of the first. I can be shown to be an instance of S' only if the domain of the 'dept' attribute consists of two values. In this case this is indeed so, the two values being *compsci* and *maths* and we can define $Ext_{S',I}$ in terms of $Ext_{S,I}$ as follows:

$$Ext_{S',I}(\text{person}) = Ext_{S,I}(\text{person})$$
$$Ext_{S',I}(\text{mathematician}) = \{x \mid \langle x, maths \rangle \in Ext_{S,I}(\langle Null, \text{person}, \text{dept} \rangle)\}$$
$$Ext_{S',I}(\text{computer scientist}) = \{x \mid \langle x, compsci \rangle \in Ext_{S,I}(\langle Null, \text{person}, \text{dept} \rangle)\}$$

Conversely, we can define $Ext_{S,I}$ in terms of $Ext_{S',I}$ as follows:

$$Ext_{S,I}(\text{person}) = Ext_{S',I}(\text{person})$$
$$Ext_{S,I}(\text{dept}) = \{maths, compsci\}$$
$$Ext_{S,I}(\langle Null, \text{person}, \text{dept} \rangle) = \{\langle x, maths \rangle \mid x \in Ext_{S',I}(\text{mathematician})\} \cup$$
$$\{\langle x, compsci \rangle \mid x \in Ext_{S',I}(\text{computer scientist})\}$$

Thus S and S' are c-equivalent with respect to the condition that $\mid Ext_{S,I}(\text{dept}) \mid = 2$. This is an example of the attribute/subtype equivalence of Figure 1(c).

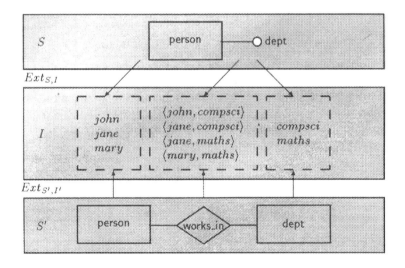

Fig. 4. Two equivalent schemas

4 Transformation of ER Models

We now propose a set of primitive transformations on ER models and explore their properties with respect to schema equivalence. Each primitive transformation takes an argument and a model and returns a new model. The instance component of the input model is left unchanged, only the schema component

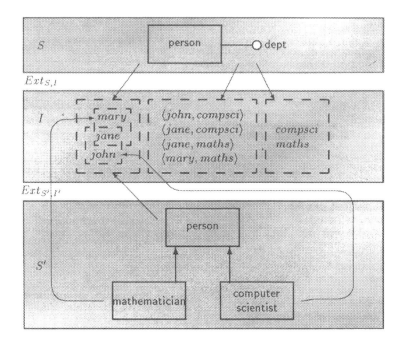

Fig. 5. Two c-equivalent schemas

and the extension mapping are changed. Each primitive transformation has one or more provisos associated with it. If these are not met then the transformation returns an "undefined" value, denoted by $\emptyset$. The result of applying a primitive transformation to $\emptyset$ is $\emptyset$.

Definition 6 below lists the primitive transformations, giving their name and the type of their first argument and explaining their effect. Their full formal definition can be found in [9]. In Definition 6, *Queries* is the set of queries expressible in the mapping language L. Such queries will be applied to items of the input schema (*i.e.* to members of $Ents \cup Atts \cup Schemes$) and will return a set which is the extent of the new item.

Definition 6. The following are the primitive transformations.

1. $rename_X (Names \times Names)$ renames a schema item, where X may be E, A or R, denoting entity, attribute or relationship, respectively.
   $rename_X$ takes a pair $\langle fromName, toName \rangle$ and a model and returns a new model in which all occurrences of $fromName$ in the schema have been replaced by $toName$. **Proviso:** $toName$ is not already the name of an entity, attribute or relationship in the schema.
2. $expand(Names \times Names \times Names \times Cards \times Cards)$ expands a constraint. It takes a tuple $\langle n_0, n_1, n_2, c_1, c_2 \rangle$ and a model, and replaces the old cardinality constraint on this association by the new, relaxed, constraint $c_1 : c_2$.

Provisos: $\langle n_0, n_1, n_2, oc_1, oc_2 \rangle$ is an existing association for some oc_1 and oc_2, $oc_1 \subseteq c_1$, and $oc_2 \subseteq c_2$.

3. $contract(Names \times Names \times Names \times Cards \times Cards)$ contracts a constraint. It similarly takes a tuple $\langle n_0, n_1, n_2, c_1, c_2 \rangle$ and a model, and replaces the old cardinality constraint on this association by the new, stricter, constraint $c_1 : c_2$. **Provisos:** $\langle n_0, n_1, n_2, oc_1, oc_2 \rangle$ is an existing association for some oc_1 and oc_2, $c_1 \subseteq oc_1$, $c_2 \subseteq oc_2$, and $Ext_{S,I}(\langle n_0, n_1, n_2 \rangle)$ satisfies c_1 and c_2.

4. $add_E(Names \times Queries)$ adds a new entity. It takes a pair $\langle e, q \rangle$ and a model, and adds e to the entity set of the schema. e's extent is given by the value of the query q. **Proviso:** e is a new entity.

5. $del_E(Names)$ deletes an entity. It takes an entity e and a model, and removes e from the schema. **Provisos:** e has no attributes and participates in no relationships, and property (ii) of Definition 2 is not violated by setting $Ext_{S',I}(e)$ to be undefined.

6. $add_R(Names \times Names \times Names \times Cards \times Cards \times Queries)$ adds a new relationship. It takes a tuple $\langle r, e_1, e_2, c_1, c_2, q \rangle$ and a model, and adds $\langle r, e_1, e_2, c_1, c_2 \rangle$ to the set of associations of the schema. The extent of this relationship is given by the value of the query q. **Provisos:** entities e_1 and e_2 exist, r is a new relationship between them and its extent satisfies the appropriate domain and cardinality constraints.

7. $del_R(Names \times Names \times Names)$ removes a relationship. It takes a tuple $\langle r, e_1, e_2 \rangle$ and a model, and removes this relationship from the schema. **Provisos:** this relationship exists, and property (ii) of Definition 2 is not violated by setting $Ext_{S',I}(\langle r, e_1, e_2 \rangle)$ to be undefined.

8. $add_A(Names \times Names \times Cards \times Cards \times Queries \times Queries)$ adds an attribute to an entity type. The attribute may either already exist in the schema or may be a new attribute. It takes a tuple $\langle e, a, c_1, c_2, q_{att}, q_{assoc} \rangle$ and a model, and adds $\langle Null, e, a, c_1, c_2 \rangle$ to the set of associations of the schema. The queries q_{att} and q_{assoc} respectively give the extents of the attribute and the association. **Provisos:** entity e exists and does not already have an attribute a, and the extent of the association satisfies the appropriate domain and cardinality constraints.

9. $del_A(Names \times Names)$ removes an attribute from an entity type. It takes a pair $\langle e, a \rangle$ and a model, and removes this association from the schema. **Provisos:** this association exists, and property (ii) of Definition 2 is not violated by setting $Ext_{S',I}$ to be undefined for $\langle Null, e, a \rangle$ and for a.

10. $add_I(Names \times Names)$ adds a subtype relationship. It takes a pair of entities $\langle e_1, e_2 \rangle$ and a model, and adds this subtype relationship to the schema. **Provisos:** entities e_1 and e_2 exist, $\langle e_1, e_2 \rangle \notin transitiveClosure(Incs')$ and $Ext_{S,I}(e_1) \subseteq Ext_{S,I}(e_2)$.

11. $del_I(Names \times Names)$ removes a subtype relationship. It takes a pair of entities $\langle e_1, e_2 \rangle$ and a model, and removes this subtype relationship from the schema. **Proviso:** this subtype relationship exists in the schema.

We note that the above primitive transformations are syntactically complete, in the sense that without their associated provisos they could be used to transform any ER schema into any other ER schema. With the addition of the provisos, the transformations become semantically sound *i.e.* they output a valid model.

We also note that for all input models with the same schema, the models output by a primitive transformation also all have the same schema. We denote by $Schema(t, S)$ the schema that results from applying the primitive transformation t to any model of the schema S.

Definition 7. A primitive transformation t is **schema-dependent (s-d) w.r.t. a schema** S if t does not return $\emptyset$ for any model of S, otherwise t is **instance-dependent (i-d) w.r.t.** S.

It is easy to see that if t is s-d w.r.t. S then $Schema(t, S)$ subsumes S. Thus, if a schema S can be transformed to a schema S' by means of a series of s-d primitive transformations, and vice versa, then S and S' are equivalent. Similarly, if t is i-d w.r.t. S with associated proviso f then $Schema(t, S)$ c-subsumes S w.r.t. f. Thus, if a schema S can be transformed to a schema S' by means of a series of s-d or i-d primitive transformations with an overall proviso f, and vice versa, then S and S' are c-equivalent w.r.t f.

For each of the primitive transformations of Definition 6 we now define a new transformation that takes as an extra argument a condition which must be satisfied in order for the transformation to be successful. We call such transformations **knowledge-based (k-b)** ones. We use the same name for both the 2-parameter and the 3-parameter versions of the primitive transformations since the number of arguments distinguishes which version is being used. Each 3-parameter version, op, is defined in terms of the 2-parameter one as follows:

$$op\ arg\ f\ m\ =\ \text{if } f(m) \text{ then } (op\ arg\ m) \text{ else } \emptyset$$

We note that, semantically, there is no difference between i-d and k-b transformations since both require instances to satisfy a condition.

5 Expressiveness of the primitive transformations

We now show how the transformations of Figures 1-3 can be expressed using sequences of our primitive transformations.

Entity/Attribute Equivalence. If a schema S contains an attribute a, an entity e, and an association $\langle Null, e, a, c_1, c_2 \rangle$, then the following sequence of s-d primitive transformations converts a to a new entity e_a:

$$add_E\ \langle e_a, a \rangle;\ add_R\ \langle r, e, e_a, c_1, c_2, \langle Null, e, a \rangle \rangle;\ del_A\ \langle e, a \rangle$$

Conversely, if a schema S' contains an entity e_a whose only association is $\langle r, e, e_a, c_1, c_2 \rangle$, then the following sequence of s-d primitive transformations converts e_a to a new attribute a of e:

$$add_A\ \langle e, a, c_1, c_2, e_a, \langle r, e, e_a \rangle \rangle;\ del_R\ \langle r, e, e_a \rangle;\ del_E\ e_a$$

Thus, by the remarks in Section 4, S and S' are equivalent.

Entity/Relationship Equivalence. If S contains an entity e_R for which the only associations are $\langle r_1, e_1, e_R, c_1, 1:1 \rangle$ and $\langle r_2, e_R, e_2, 1:1, c_2 \rangle$, then the following sequence of s-d primitive transformations transforms e_R into a new relationship r:

$$add_R \; \langle r, e_1, e_2, c_1, c_2, \{ \langle e_1(s_1), e_R(s_1), e_2(s_2) \rangle \mid s_1 \in \langle r_1, e_1, e_R \rangle \wedge s_2 \in \langle r_2, e_R, e_2 \rangle$$
$$\wedge e_R(s_1) = e_R(s_2) \} \rangle; \; del_R \; \langle r_1, e_1, e_R \rangle; \; del_R \; \langle r_2, e_R, e_2 \rangle; \; del_E \; e_R$$

Conversely, if S' contains a relationship $\langle r, e_1, e_2, c_1, c_2 \rangle$, then the following sequence of s-d primitive transformations transforms r into a new entity e_R and new relationships r_1, r_2:

$$add_E \; \langle e_R, \langle r, e_1, e_2 \rangle \rangle; \; add_R \; \langle r_1, e_1, e_R, c_1, 1:1, \langle r, e_1, e_2 \rangle \rangle;$$
$$add_R \; \langle r_2, e_R, e_2, 1:1, c_2, \langle r, e_1, e_2 \rangle \rangle; \; del_R \; \langle r, e_1, e_2 \rangle$$

Thus, S and S' are equivalent.

Attribute/subtype equivalence. If S contains an attribute a, an entity e, and an association between them $\langle Null, e, a, m_1 : n_1, m_2 : n_2 \rangle$, then we can create n subtypes of e, and remove a, where the condition f is ($Ext_{S,I}(a) = \{a_1, \ldots, a_n\}$):

$$add_E \; \langle e_1, \{ e(s) \mid s \in \langle Null, e, a \rangle \wedge a(s) = a_1 \} \rangle; \; \ldots;$$
$$add_E \; \langle e_n, \{ e(s) \mid s \in \langle Null, e, a \rangle \wedge a(s) = a_n \} \rangle;$$
$$add_I \; \langle e_1, e \rangle; \; \ldots; \; add_I \; \langle e_n, e \rangle; \; del_A \; \langle e, a \rangle \; f$$

Conversely, if S' contains entity types $e, e_1, \ldots, e_n$, where $e_1, \ldots, e_n$ are subtypes of e and participate in no associations, then we can replace $e_1, \ldots, e_n$ by a new attribute a of e:

$$add_A \; \langle e, a, m_1 : n_1, m_2 : n_2, \{a_1, \ldots, a_n\}, \cup_{i=1 \ldots n} \{ \langle x, a_i \rangle \mid x \in e_i \} \rangle \; f';$$
$$del_I \; \langle e_n, e \rangle; \; \ldots; \; del_I \; \langle e_1, e \rangle; \; del_E \; e_n; \; \ldots; \; del_E \; e_1$$

where the condition f' is:

$$(\forall x \in Ext_{S',I}(e).m_1 \leq \mid \{e_i \mid x \in Ext_{S',I}(e_i)\} \mid \leq n_1) \wedge$$
$$(\forall e_i \in \{e_1, \ldots, e_n\}.m_2 \leq \mid Ext_{S',I}(e_i) \mid \leq n_2)$$

Thus, S and S' are c-equivalent w.r.t. the condition $f \wedge f'$.

Entity merge. We can rename an entity e' to an existing entity e if they have the same extent, and their common associations also have the same extents:

$$rename_E \; \langle e', e \rangle \; (Ext_{S,I}(e) = Ext_{S,I}(e') \wedge$$

$(\forall \langle n, e, to \rangle \in Schemes.$

$(\langle n, e', to \rangle \in Schemes \Rightarrow Ext_{S,I}(\langle n, e, to \rangle) = Ext_{S,I}(\langle n, e', to \rangle)) \wedge$

$(\langle n, to, e' \rangle \in Schemes \Rightarrow Ext_{S,I}(\langle n, e, to \rangle) = Ext_{S,I}(\langle n, to, e' \rangle)))) \wedge$

$(\forall \langle n, to, e \rangle \in Schemes.$

$$(\langle n, e', to \rangle \in Schemes \Rightarrow Ext_{S,I}(\langle n, to, e \rangle) = Ext_{S,I}(\langle n, e', to \rangle)) \wedge$$
$$(\langle n, to, e' \rangle \in Schemes \Rightarrow Ext_{S,I}(\langle n, to, e \rangle) = Ext_{S,I}(\langle n, to, e' \rangle))) \wedge$$
$$(\forall \langle n, e, e \rangle \in Schemes.$$
$$(\langle n, e', e' \rangle \in Schemes \Rightarrow Ext_{S,I}(\langle n, e, e \rangle) = Ext_{S,I}(\langle n, e', e' \rangle))))$$

This transformation is reversible by a sequence of s-d transformations which recreate the entity e', re-attach all its original attributes and relationships and detach the necessary attributes and relationships from e'. So the original and transformed schemas are c-equivalent.

Introduction of a union or intersection entity. If S contains two entities e_1, e_2, the following sequence of s-d primitive transformations creates a new entity e as the union of e_1 and e_2:

$$add_E \ \langle e, e_1 \cup e_2 \rangle; \ add_I \ \langle e_1, e \rangle; \ add_I \ \langle e_2, e \rangle$$

Conversely, if S' contains entities e, e_1, e_2 and subtype relationships $\langle e_1, e \rangle, \langle e_2, e \rangle$, and e participates in no associations in S', then we can apply to following sequence of primitive transformations to obtain S, provided $Ext_{S',I}(e) = Ext_{S',I}(e_1) \cup Ext_{S',I}(e_2)$:

$$del_I \ \langle e_2, e \rangle; \ del_I \ \langle e_1, e \rangle; \ del_E \ e$$

Thus S and S' are c-equivalent w.r.t the above proviso. Similar remarks apply to the introduction of an intersection entity $e_1 \cap e_2$ into S, and to its removal from S' provided $Ext_{S',I}(e) = Ext_{S',I}(e_1) \cap Ext_{S',I}(e_2)$.

The rest of the transformations we give here are reversible by s-d transformations and so give rise to c-equivalent schemas:

Subtype relationship introduction. If S contains entities e and e', then $add_I \ \langle e', e \rangle$ introduces a subtype relationship between them provided $Ext_{S,I}(e') \subseteq Ext_{S,I}(e)$.

Redundant attribute removal. If the extent of an association between a sub-entity e' and an attribute a is subsumed by the extent of the association between a super-entity e and a, then a can be removed from e':

$$del_A \ \langle e', a \rangle \ (Ext_{S,I}(\langle Null, e', a \rangle) = \{s \mid s \in Ext_{S,I}(\langle Null, e, a \rangle) \wedge e(s) \in Ext_{S,I}(e') \})$$

Optional attribute removal. An attribute a with cardinality $\langle 0 : x, c \rangle$ can be moved from an entity e to a set of its subtypes $e_1, \ldots e_n$ if a is only ever associated with these subtypes and is a mandatory attribute for these types:

$$add_A \ \langle e_1, a, 1 : x, c, a, \{s \mid s \in \langle Null, e, a \rangle \wedge e(s) \in e_1 \} \rangle$$
$$(Ext_{S,I}(e_1) \subseteq \{e(s) \mid s \in Ext_{S,I}(\langle Null, e, a \rangle) \});$$

$$\cdots$$

$$add_A \ \langle e_n, a, 1 : x, c, a, \{s \mid s \in \langle Null, e, a \rangle \wedge e(s) \in e_n \} \rangle$$
$$(Ext_{S,I}(e_n) \subseteq \{e(s) \mid s \in Ext_{S,I}(\langle Null, e, a \rangle) \});$$
$$del_A \ \langle e, a \rangle \ (\{e(s) \mid s \in Ext_{S,I}(\langle Null, e, a \rangle\} = \cup_{i=1 \ldots n} Ext_{S,I}(e_i))$$

Generalisation of attributes. If entities $e_1, \ldots e_n$ have a common super-entity e and their extents cover the extent of e, then an attribute a common to $e_1, \ldots, e_n$ can be moved to e:

$$add_A \ \langle e, a, c_1, c_2, a, \cup_{i=1\ldots n}\langle Null, e_i, a\rangle\rangle \ (\cup_{i=1\ldots n} Ext_{S,I}(e_i) = Ext_{S,I}(e));$$
$$del_A \ \langle e_1, a\rangle; \ \ldots; \ del_A \ \langle e_n, a\rangle$$

The values c_1, c_2 in the above transformation can be computed either from the constraints on the sub-types or from the extent information.

Redundant relationship removal. As illustrated in Figure 3(d):

$$del_R \ \langle r, e'_1, e'_2\rangle \ (Ext_{S,I}(\langle r, e'_1, e'_2\rangle) =$$
$$\{s \mid s \in Ext_{S,I}(\langle r, e_1, e_2\rangle) \wedge e_1(s) \in Ext_{S,I}(e'_1) \wedge e_2(s) \in Ext_{S,I}(e'_2)\})$$

and in Figure 3(e):

$$del_R \ \langle r, e'_1, e_2\rangle$$
$$(Ext_{S,I}(\langle r, e'_1, e_2\rangle) = \{s \mid s \in Ext_{S,I}(\langle r, e_1, e_2\rangle) \wedge e_1(s) \in Ext_{S,I}(e'_1)\})$$

6 Concluding Remarks

In this paper we have proposed a formal framework for ER schema transformation. We have defined a set of primitive transformations and have demonstrated their expressiveness by showing how they can be used to define the schema transformations commonly found in the literature. The notion of schema equivalence which underpins our primitive transformations is based on formalising a database instance as a set of sets. We have distinguished between transformations which apply for any instance of a schema and those which only apply for certain instances. Our work is novel in that previous work on schema transformation has either been informal, or has formalised only transformations that are independent of the database instance, or is limited to specific types of transformation. A detailed theoretical treatment of our notion of schema equivalence can be found in [9], as well as a discussion of how our approach can be applied to the overall schema integration process.

Our work has practical application in the implementation of tools for aiding schema integration. Our primitive transformations can be used as a "programming language" for the specification of new schema transformations to suit particular environments. The distinction between s-d, and i-d and k-b transformations serves to identify which transformations need to be verified against the data, and possibly other knowledge about the database (*e.g.* semantic integrity constraints), to ensure that they can be applied. For future work we wish to investigate further the applicability of our formalism to the wide range of schema integration methodologies that have been proposed.

References

1. C. Batini and M. Lenzerini. A methodology for data schema integration in the entity relationship model. *IEEE Transactions on Software Engineering*, 10(6):650–664, November 1984.

2. C. Batini, M. Lenzerini, and S. Navathe. A comparative analysis of methodologies for database schema integration. *ACM Computing Surveys*, 18(4):323–364, 1986.

3. J. Biskup and B. Convent. A formal view integration method. In *Proceedings of ACM SIGMOD International Conference on Management of Data*, pages 398–407, Washington, 1986. ACM.

4. C. Francalanci and B. Pernici. View integration: A survey of current developments. Technical Report 93-053, Dipartimento di Elettronica e Informazione, P.zza Leonardo da Vinci 32, 20133 Milano, Italy, 1993.

5. P. Johannesson. *Schema Integration, Schema Translation, and Interoperability in Federated Information Systems*. PhD thesis, DSV, Stockholm University, 1993. ISBN 91-7153-101-7, Rep. No. 93-010-DSV.

6. V. Kashyap and A. Sheth. Semantic and schematic similarities between database objects: a context-based approach. *VLDB Journal*, 5(4):276–304, 1996.

7. W. Kim, I. Choi, S. Gala, and M. Scheeval. On resolving schematic heterogeneity in multidatabase systems. In *Modern Database Systems*. ACM Press, 1995.

8. J.A. Larson, S.B. Navathe, and R. Elmasri. A theory of attribute equivalence in databases with application to schema integration. *IEEE Transactions on Software Engineering*, 15(4):449–463, April 1989.

9. P. McBrien and A. Poulovassilis. A formalisation of semantic schema integration. Technical Report 96-01, King's College London, ftp://ftp.dcs.kcl.ac.uk/pub/tech-reports/tr96-01.ps.gz, 1996.

10. R.J. Miller, Y.E. Ioannidis, and R. Ramakrishnan. The use of information capacity in schema integration and translation. In *Proceedings of the 19th International Conference on Very Large Data Bases*, pages 120–133, Trinity College, Dublin, Ireland, 1993.

11. R.J. Miller, Y.E. Ioannidis, and R. Ramakrishnan. Schema equivalence in heterogeneous systems: Bridging theory and practice. *Information Systems*, 19(1):3–31, 1994.

12. J. Rissanen. Independent components of relations. *ACM Transactions on Database Systems*, 2(4):317–325, December 1977.

13. A. Sheth and J. Larson. Federated database systems. *ACM Computing Surveys*, 22(3):183–236, 1990.

14. S. Spaccapietra, C. Parent, and Y. Dupont. Model independent assertions for integration of heterogenous schemas. *The VLDB Journal*, 1(1):81–126, 1992.

A Generative Approach to Database Federation

UWE HOHENSTEIN & VOLKMAR PLESSER

Corporate Research and Development, Siemens AG, ZT AN 4, D-81730 München
(GERMANY)
E-mail: <Firstname>.<Lastname>@mchp.siemens.de

Abstract. This paper introduces a comprehensive, specification-based approach to database federation, supporting an integrated ODMG-93 conforming access to object-oriented and relational databases. Central point is a set of intuitive specification languages. These languages allow defining ODMG-93 views of existing databases, and building system-spanning federated views thereupon. Given concrete specifications defining those views, ODMG schemas are generated automatically due to a generative approach. Heterogeneous databases can be plugged into a federation without implementing adapters for any schema again and again. The generative nature provides flexibility wrt. schema modification of component databases, as new views are implemented automatically. Furthermore, the approach is one of the first to support manipulating federated data seamlessly in C++.

1 Introduction

Federated DBSs provide flexible solutions to give an integrated access to data stored in several autonomous DBSs [ShL90]. A federation framework gives a user the illusion of a homogeneous "database system" by means of a unified, database spanning, and transparent access. In particular, the local organization of data is hidden and users are protected from system-specific data models, access interfaces, query languages, paradigms etc. A unified and consistent view of the stored data resolves discrepancies [SCG92] and conflicts [SpP94] between database schemas, which result from representing real world situation in different ways. And finally, users are not aware of the location of items in a particular system. With all that, the autonomy of the constituent systems is preserved. Each DBS still exists, and especially existing applications are not affected.

Research in the field of federated DBSs has brought up several prototypes [REC+89, RAD+91, BFN94] and results that tackle fundamental problems [LiM91, KRS91, HNS92, IMS93] such as integration methodologies [RPRG94, Joh93, ScS96], languages for view definitions [KDN90, CzT91, KLK91], global transaction management, global query processing and optimization. In spite of the variety of approaches, some important points are often neglected.

1. Only few approaches incorporate object-oriented systems, and if they do, they use an own system instead of arbitrary commercial ones (cf. Pegasus [RAD+91]). IRO-DB [BFN94] is one exception as it incorporates the commercial systems O_2 and Ontos. Indeed, plugging object-oriented systems in a federation

framework is certainly not so trivial as it seems to be. For instance, it is not clear how to handle databases that use advanced modeling concepts such as versioning. There are no solutions discussed so far for that case.

2. The adapters [HFBK94, Rad95] for incorporating existing databases must be hand-coded for any database again and again. Some proposals are able to import relational tables into an object-oriented schema [AAK+93]. However, the imported part consists of tables whithout using any object-oriented features.

3. A lot of approaches rely on querying [KDN90] only, or use own stand-alone manipulation languages. For example, Pegasus uses an extension of OSQL, the language of HP's object-oriented system for manipulation. Data manipulation embedded in a standard language such as C++ is neglected. There are two important points that cause trouble: First, federated schemas must be represented in the programming language. This is quite critical in C++, because its semantics is sometimes odd. Second, problems with view updates must be avoided. In IRO-DB [BFN94] federated views are defined by means of OQL queries. It is extremely doubtful, whether data can be manipulated via those views.

Our research prototype FIHD (**F**lexible **I**ntegration of **H**eterogeneous **D**atabase Systems) provides a comprehensive solution to all these aspects. FIHD is a federation framework that is open wrt. commercial systems. We use ODMG-93 [Cat96] as a basis because it is the emerging standard for object-oriented DBSs. Relying on ODMG-93, it is easy to plug in ODMG conforming DBSs. Moreover, ODMG-93 defines C++ interfaces to query and manipulate data. This is especially important in view of manipulating federations in C++.

The overall approach of FIHD is generative. Section 2 describes how generators homogenize databases, i.e., produce adapters that provide ODMG conforming manipulation and query facilities. Those adapters are implemented automatically on top of the component systems. An additional generator creates federated schemas that define system-spanning views and provide a uniform access. Federated schemas are implemented on top of the homogenized schemas.

The generators require input to produce homogenized and federated schemas. This is done by means of logic-based languages. Section 3 is concerned with languages to homogenize relational and object-oriented databases. A specification language for relational databases enables remodeling relational tables in the ODMG-93 object model, thereby using object-oriented concepts intensively in order to express semantics directly. Concepts developed in the context of reverse engineering [HTJC93, CBS94, PrB94] are incorporated. It is very important to specify the correct and precise semantics because wrong database semantics could lead to inadequate and defective federated schemas. Furthermore, homogenizing commercial object-oriented DBSs is discussed. A specification language handles database concepts that are not available in ODMG-93.

Having defined ODMG views of existing databases and generated ODMG layers put on top of them, the next step consists of providing integrated views of databases and a corresponding uniform access. Section 4 presents a specification language for defining federated schemas, i.e., integrated ODMG views.

In the conclusions, we summarize our ideas and outline some future work.

2 Generative Approach to Database Federation

According to [ShL90], two steps in our architecture are essential. *Homogenization* eliminates syntactic heterogeneity resulting from different data models and access interfaces. Each local schema, expressed in the native data model of the system, is translated into a *canonical* data model. Hence, data represented by homogenized schemas can be handled by one manipulation language uniformly.

Data integration then deals with integrating such homogenized schemas into *federated* ones. A federated schema provides a unified, consistent, and transparent view of all the integrated data. Particularly, semantic heterogeneity such as discrepancies between homogenized schemas – owing to independent designs – are eliminated. Federated schemas are again defined in the canonical model.

From a functional point of view, homogenization requires adapters that convert local data into the canonical model and map operations onto the local DBSs. Other federation approaches generally require implementing a *hand-coded* adapter for each database. Data integration has to support special operational aspects such as global transaction management and global query processing.

Our federation approach is now characterized by the following points.

- We rely on ODMG-93 [Cat96] as canonical model. Hence, the schema layers conform to this emerging standard for object-oriented DBSs. This is advantageous if DBSs support ODMG-93. Then no real homogenization is necessary.

- Homogenization and schema integration are done in a *generative manner*, i.e., the code of homogenized and federated schemas is generated automatically. Nevertheless, we require user input to define schemas by means of corresponding specification languages.

- Homogenizing relational systems is combined with *semantic enrichment* [Cas93, HoK95]. Relational DBSs, since having rather primitive modeling structures, do not carry much semantics. This is rather bad, since data integration is a complex and ambitious task, as it requires a deep knowledge about the semantics of data. Any support that can be provided previously is useful to let the integration concentrate on its real task. Hence, tables are not just converted to object types that possess the simple table structure. Instead implicit knowledge is expressed explicitly by using higher modeling concepts.

We adopt the Object Definition Language ODMG ODL and extend it to capturing explicit information according to the respective purpose. A language ODL_R defines semantic enrichment for relational databases. In fact, the advantage of our approach lies in the fact that semantic enrichment is explicitly – *precisely* – specified. This gives us the opportunity to remodel schemas in object-oriented terms in various ways. Given as input any ODL_R semantic enrichment specification, a schema including operations is produced automatically by a corresponding generator GEN_R. Similarly, ODL_{oo} specifications homogenize schemas of any object-oriented system oo. Consequently, Interface$_R$ and Interface$_{oo}$ are generated that allow manipulating local databases according to ODMG-93: Homogenization yields adapters, ODMG wrappers. Please note Interface$_R$ provides an adequate view of relational data due to semantic enrichment.

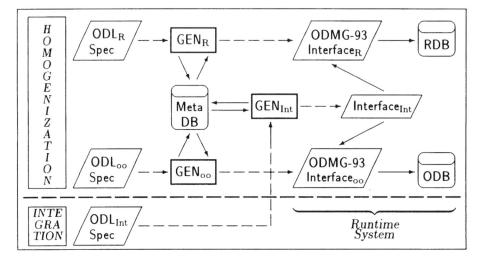

Fig. 1. *Generative Approach*

Federated schemas are specified in an integration language ODL_{Int} that provides means to merge homogenized schemas into federated ones. A specification defines a system-spanning view of federation. A generator GEN_{Int} produces a corresponding interface $Interface_{Int}$ to operate on the federation.

Figure 1 illustrates the process of generation. Each generator parses a specification and stores information about local schemas, how homogenized schemas are related to local ones, and how federated schemas are composed of homogenized ones, into a meta database. The real kernels of the generators take the meta information as input and generate the ODMG-93 conforming interfaces. The outcome consists of C++ classes including methods for manipulations. Naturally, the implementations of $Interface_R$ and $Interface_{oo}$ must call the original component DBSs, while $Interface_{Int}$ is implemented on both.

Homogenization already provides local adapters for local databases. Please note these adapters are sufficient to access several databases in parallel with one single manipulation language. However, the individual databases must be handled separately according to the respective schemas. An application must open the databases, must understand the semantics of homogenized schemas, and can access the databases in a homogeneous way. It is the task of federated schemas to provide a system-spanning view with an integrated interface in addition. $Interface_{Int}$ allows handling so far disjoint databases in an integrated manner and provides global transaction management and global query processing.

3 Homogenization

3.1 Homogenizing Relational Databases with Semantic Enrichment

Converting relational tables into ODMG schemas, we take benefit from semantic enrichment and data reverse engineering [HTJC93, NNJ93, CBS94, PrB94]: It is our overall goal to make explicit any semantics that is implicitly given in tables, by using object-oriented concepts extensively. The price we pay for comprehensive remodelling capabilities is an *explicit* specification. We consider this matter not so bad, because automatic types of reverse engineering and knowledge detection do not always produce satisfactory results; there is a danger of expressing wrong semantics, a fact we definitively want to avoid.

We propose a logic-based specification language ODL_R the syntax of which bridles the horse from the back: It is specified what object types are the outcome and how they correspond to tables. This is advantageous, because an object type is generally made up of several tables. Moreover, the syntax remains intuitive and easily understandable, since the object types are immediately visible.

Figure 2 gives an example. It presents a relational schema defining a part hierarchy. Table A contains atomic parts and C complex ones that are composed of atomic or complex ones. A and C possess a foreign key father that refers to the pid of the father part in C. Machines are stored in table M. A part is produced by a machine. Similarly, foreign keys machine refer to the machine table.

Semantic enrichment should produce the presented ODMG schema with object types PART, MACHINE etc. Atomic and complex parts are organized in a *subtype hierarchy*. Obtaining a supertype PART, subtypes ATOMIC and COMPLEX inherit all the properties of its supertype, attributes as well as methods and relationships. The composition hierarchy of parts is modeled by means of a *multi-valued* relationship Components and a single-valued relationship PartOf. Each part belongs to at most one complex part. The directions Components and PartOf model the same semantic relationship from different perspectives. They are *inverse*; both directions are kept consistent and referential integrity is guaranteed.

Figure 2 also presents a corresponding ODL_R specification. Object types are defined by interface declarations, as usual in ODMG ODL. But there are some extensions to ODL that define the association to the relational database.

The clause from relation relates object types to tables. The essential semantics we assign to that clause is to define in what relation the extent of a type is found. COMPLEX : PART from relation A[pid] means that subtype COMPLEX of PART is built from table C directly. [pid] is the relational key of C. Each tuple, which is uniquely identified by its key value, refers to one object. We presuppose a key for each relation, because it is necessary to constitute object identifiers for manipulations. Composite keys are possible and denoted as (pid,name,...). If a table does not possess a key, it cannot represent an object type. But it may be a structure (without object identity), which can be nested into a type.

PART from relation A[pid] + C[pid] defines a type PART, the extent of which is obtained by computing the union ('+') of tuples in A and C. [...] again denotes the key in order to constitute object identifiers of PART.

An equation String Assembly = C.assembly connects an object type's attribute Assembly to a relational attribute assembly directly. In PART, Id = A.id + C.id identifies semantically equivalent attributes in tables A and C. Equations can also combine several relational attributes to predefined ODMG types such as Date, e.g., Date BuildDate = (A.day,A.month,A.year) + (C.day,C.month,C.year).

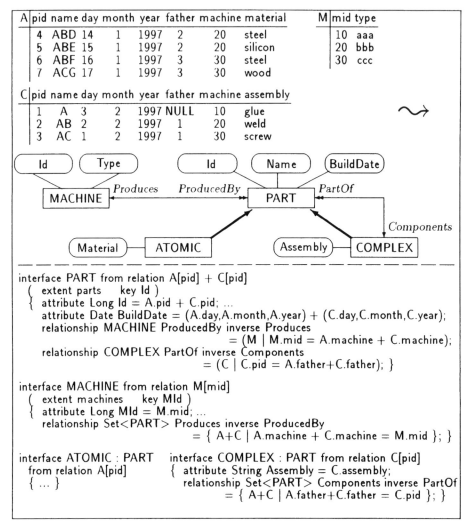

Fig. 2. *Specification for Semantic Enrichment*

The relationship Produces of MACHINE is expressed by Set<PART> Produces = { A + C | A.machine + C.machine = M.mid }. The set of produced parts consists of those tuples in A and C that have the machine's mid as value of machine. The inverse relationship ProducedBy is analogously computed: The machine is that tuple in M that has a mid equal to the machine value in A or C. Round brackets convert a tuple in M into a corresponding object of type MACHINE, while curly brackets convert a set of tuples into a set of objects. Composite attributes are again possible to establish associations.

When designing the specification language, we put emphasis on two points: *Expressiveness*, i.e., to provide powerful mechanisms to derive object types from tables in various ways. Secondly, we have to avoid problems with *view updates*. This is important because we automatically generate object-oriented operations

```
d_Database* db = new d_Database; db->open( "PartsDB");
d_Transaction t; t.start();
d_Ref<ATOMIC> a8 = new(db) ATOMIC (8,"abc");
d_Ref<ATOMIC> a9 = new(db) ATOMIC (9,"def");
d_Ref<MACHINE> m40 = new(db) MACHINE (40);
a8->ProducedBy = m40;
m40->Produces.insert_element(a9);
/* all the machines that produce components of a part named "abc" */
d_OQL_Query q = "select m from m in machines where exists p in m.Produces:
                (p->PartOf->Name == \"abc\");"
d_Set<d_Ref<MACHINE>> resultSet;
d_oql_execute(q,resultSet);
d_Ref<MACHINE> m;
d_Itr<d_Ref<MACHINE>> mItr = resultSet.create_iterator();
while (mItr.next(m)) {
        cout << "Machine " << m->Id << " with produced parts:" << endl;
        d_Ref<PART>> p;
        d_Itr<d_Ref<PART>> pItr = m->Produces.create_iterator();
        while (pItr.next(p)) cout << p->Id << endl;
}
m40->Produces.delete_element(a8);
t.commit(); db->close();
```

Fig. 3. *ODMG-93 Standard*

the effects of which must be unambiguous when operating on tables. For more details about the specification language, the reader is referred to [HoK95, Hoh96].

Having homogenized the relational database in such a way, manipulation can be done in an ODMG conforming manner, We support the *C++ binding* of ODMG-93. This binding defines a C++ representation of object types and possesses an Object Manipulation Language (OML) that provides manipulation features. Figure 3 presents a short C++ application program using the OML.

d_Database and d_Transaction are predefined C++ classes that manage database and transaction handling. After opening a database "PartsDB", a transaction is started. The basis for handling objects are so-called *references* given by a d_Ref template. They are able to refer to transient *and* persistent objects. Particularly, attribute access and method invocation is done via '->', as in C++. Here, objects of type ATOMIC with Ids 8 and 9 as well as a machine m40 are created in the database db. m40 should produce parts 8 and 9. This can be done either by assigning m40 to the ProducedBy relationship of a8, or by inserting a9 into the Produces relationship, because ProducedBy and Produces are inverse. A special method d_oql(q, resultSet) allows invoking associative queries. The parameter q contains a string that defines the query in an Object Query Language (OQL). OQL enhances SQL in an orthogonal manner with object-oriented features such as inheritance and traversal along relationships.

The result can be processed as a set of machines (Set<Ref<MACHINE>>), e.g., iterators can be created to handle a collection element by element. Similarly, the set of produced parts (i.e., relationship Produces) is handled.

Anyway, programs act according to the ODMG view and can take full benefit from object-orientation; the underlying relational tables are not visible.

3.2 Homogenization of Object-Oriented Databases

Homogenizing object-oriented databases is also done in a generative manner. An ODL_{oo} specification defines an ODMG schema and its association to the original database. Naturally, the specification language is simpler than ODL_R since it is easy to express how ODMG object types are built from existing object types.

But every object-oriented DBS provides special modeling and manipulation concepts that are not available in ODMG. Even if commercial systems completely support the ODMG standard, they will surely offer specific add-ons in order to beat competitors. Those advanced constructs certainly cause trouble. There may be existing databases that made use of those concepts, e.g., versioned objects. In order to be able to plug in those databases, we must find ODMG ways to remodel peculiarities adequately without falsifying semantics. In fact, versioning and other concepts possess a specific semantics that must be maintained by ODMG operations at the homogenized level!

In the following, we discuss some problems that occur when homogenizing the commercial object-oriented DBS Objectivity/DB. However, the critical points are similar for other systems. We present how the specification language ODL_{Objy} reflects advanced concepts in ODMG-93.

Storage hierarchy. Objectivity has a storage hierarchy that consists of federated databases [1], containers, and objects. A federated database contains several databases that share a common schema. The databases can be located on different sites in a network. Databases are partitioned into containers. Newly created objects are assigned to one of the containers. Containers are useful for clustering objects physically.

Concerning homogenization, federated databases and databases do not give rise to problems. An Objectivity application program can open only one federated database in a process. Consequently, the names of a database and its associated federated database can be considered together as a database name from an ODMG point of view. Opening a database at the ODMG level requires then opening a federated database and the database.

But containers cause some trouble. If we did not support containers, we would give up clustering, an important aspect of tuning object-oriented databases. Creating new objects can then only be done into one, pre-fixed container.

We suggest establishing a predefined type d_Container as a subtype of ODMG type d_Database: Each container becomes an instance of d_Container. Containers can thus be created and deleted dynamically, as in Objectivity. Being objects of supertype d_Database, containers can be used instead of db when creating objects with new(db). Clustering becomes possible. Moreover, d_Container inherits the typical d_Database functionality such as open and close, now defining the specific container semantics. Certainly, we have slightly extended ODMG, as there is a new predefined type, but the real user-defined schema is not affected. Supporting clustering is worth it anyway.

---

[1] Please note that the term "federated database" is here used in an Objectivity context.

Complex objects. Objectivity allows one to define propagation of operations copy, delete, and lock. This is done by means of specifiers that are associated with relationships: The operation is propagated to objects related by that relationship.

If propagation is not supported at the ODMG level, the semantics of an Objectivity database may be violated: Propagation of delete can define an integrity constraint; an object cannot exist without participating in a relationship.

We suggest no propagated copy and lock, because ODMG does not support any explicit copy and lock operations; otherwise we would extend OML. But a propagated delete can be achieved by changing the effect of ODMG delete_object. The ODL$_{Objy}$ syntax should indicate propagation so that propagation does not come unexpected for users when deleting an object.

> interface ARTICLE from object type Article
> { relationship ORDER OrderedBy = Article.ordered_by : propagate delete; }

This is just an extension to ODL (as we frequently did for relational enrichment), not affecting the database schema.

Versioning. In Objectivity, any object in the database may occur in several versions. Versionable classes do not need to be defined in the schema. Objects can dynamically become versionable by invoking a method setVersStatus(on/off). If versioning is enabled for an object, any invocation of ooUpdate (explicit notification of update, comparable to ODMG's mark_modified) creates a new version. A version graph maintains all versions of an object and possesses predefined relationships to navigate in the graph, i.e., going to previous or next versions. There exists a predefined *Genealogy* class the objects of which are surrogates for version graphs. Besides normal relationships pointing to a concrete version of an object, it is possible to establish relationships referring to genealogies, i.e., whole version graphs. Those relationships are *floating* in a certain sense. The target of a relationship being a genealogy, it is always possible to access the current version within the graph by means of predefined methods. Fortunately, versioning does not possess additional semantics, e.g., for querying data.

We cannot omit the concept of versioning if there are existing databases containing versioned objects and floating relationships. We propose a predefined class VersionGraph. This class supports special methods to handle versions, e.g., to turn versioning on and off, to designate a current referenced version in a version graph etc. Any versionable type must inherit from VersionGraph. Thus, objects inherit methods to access previous or subsequent versions. Furthermore, it is possible to designate relationships as floating. Finally, the semantics of mark_modified is altered to create new versions if versioning is switched on. Since all these points affect the "semantic enrichment" of object-oriented database systems, ODL$_{Objy}$ must reflect them in the following way.

> interface ARTICLE : VersionGraph from object type Article ...
> interface ORDER from object type Order
> { ... relationship Set<ARTICLE> Orders = Order.orders floating; }

Please note neither the schema nor OML is really extended. The whole functionality is concentrated in one additional predefined class.

Object manipulation. Emulating ODMG OML onto Objectivity, differences in manipulation languages must obviously be bridged. But again, there are advanced Objectivity manipulation concepts that exceed ODMG-93. Omitting those manipulation features causes a lack of Objectivity functionality. Anyway, this will not exclude existing databases from a federation. Hence, we propose omitting functions that do not endanger usability, e.g., copy propagation.

Sometimes simulating operations is easily possible (propagational delete with delete_object, creating new versions with mark_modified). Keeping advanced functionality can also be done by adding new methods to existing types or by defining new classes. The latter one is preferable because the extensions are encapsulated in classes, staying outside the original OML. This principle has been applied previously to supporting versioning and containers, e.g., classes VersionGraph and d_Container. Furthermore, we introduce a subclass d_LongTransaction of d_Transaction to support Objectivity's checkIn/checkOut functions. And we add an additional parameter to the start of d_Transaction method that denote a "Multiple Reader, One Writer" transaction.

We strictly avoid introducing new OML methods. Hence, we do not support scoped queries in the sense that searching objects can be done in a particular container, in one database, or in the whole federation. This would require a new type of query method in ODMG.

4 Data Integration

A flurry of activities define methodologies to develop integrated views [RPRG94, ScS96] and languages to specify them. However, most proposals rely on relational and functional canonical models [DAT87]. They do not handle important aspects such as subtype hierarchies. Others do rely on object-orientation, but present only simple examples [Rad95], not showing how to mix subtype hierarchies, as discussed in [ScS96] from a methodological point of view. Some approaches seem to be too powerful wrt. view updates. For example, [BFN94] use ODMG OQL queries to describe federated schemas, a natural and flexible mechanism. Although they claim in [HFBK94] to support ODMG OML, it is not clear how they map updates on views onto local databases. As far as we perceived, updates are a general problem of federation approaches. Queries are often preferred, sometimes adopting the style of a programming language such as Smalltalk [CzT91]. What is neglected, is how to represent federated views in a language such as C++, and how to embed object manipulation.

These points led us carry on our language approach, designing a good compromise that is powerful enough, but is also able to support updates invoked from C++. ODMG-93 helps us since it defines a C++ binding for the OML. What we still have to do is to care for a C++ representation of federated views.

The specification language ODL_{Int} we propose provides syntactic constructs to handle typical problems and aspects of schema integration such as homonyms/synonyms, type conflicts of attributes, scaling conflicts (Dollar vs. DM), structural discrepancies [KLK91, SpP94], objectification of values and relationships [BFN94], generalization and others [BLN86, RPRG94]. The language follows the way we pursue for homogenization. Given an ODL_{Int} specification as input, object classes that represent the federated schema and provide OML are automatically generated.

In the following, we stress important aspects that are mainly centered around subtyping. We feel subtyping not investigated enough, especially because C++ possesses an odd semantics in this respect that impedes a class representation.

Suppose PART (of schema S1) and ARTICLE (of schema S2) are disjoint, and we want to generalize them to one type PART_ART (receiving all objects):

```
interface PART_ART from PART@S1 + ARTICLE@S2
    ( extent part_arts )
    { attribute No = PART@S1.Id + ARTICLE@S2.No; ... }
```

The basic bricks are existing types (related to homogenized schemas by means of '@'), means to identify objects ('[ ]'), and set operators '+' (disjoint union), '∪', and others. Similar to ODL_R, the from part defines how to compute the extent of PART_ART. Equations decide which attributes and relationships should be part of PART_ART, which are semantically equivalent etc. If PART and ARTICLE should be disjoint wrt. Id and No values, we will just add key specifiers [ ]:

```
interface PART_ART from PART[Id]@S1 + ARTICLE[No]@S2
```

Let us now suppose PART and ARTICLE overlapping: Parts that are stored in both databases should possess the same Id and No. The following interface definition is sufficient at a first glance:

```
interface ALL_PART from PART[Id]@S1 ∪ ARTICLE[No]@S2 ...
```

'∪' now allows non-disjoint unions, in contrast to '+'. [Id] and [No] specify how to relate identical parts in PART and ARTICLE.

PART_ART and ALL_PART allow handling all parts uniformly, independently of their location. But it is not possible to access only the parts in one database, since homogenized schemas are not automatically part of the federated schema in our approach. But corresponding interfaces can be added in order to access all parts, the parts in S1 (as PART_S1), and the parts in S2 (as ARTICLE_S2), too.

```
interface PART_S1    : ALL_PART from PART@S1 ...
interface ARTICLE_S2 : ALL_PART from ARTICLE@S2 ...
```

But this specification is only partly correct, owing to the odd semantics of C++: Subtypes are always disjoint in C++ wrt. real instances. Even if PART and ARTICLE contain common objects, the federated view is not aware of them. There is no means in OML, no object type, to insert instances that are common to PART_S1 and ARTICLE_S2. This problem can be solved by introducing an additional subtype P_A:

```
interface P_A : PART_S1,ARTICLE_S2 from PART@S1[Id],ARTICLE@S2[No] ...
```

P_A is now the type to insert common objects; it has the purpose to hold the intersection of PART and ARTICLE. Hence an identification [ ] of objects in both types is demanded. ALL_PART contains the instances that are neither parts nor articles, PART_S1 contains the real parts (that are not articles), ARTICLE_S2 the real articles, and P_A all the parts that are also articles. Other approaches [BFN94, Rad95] that also rely on ODMG-93 do not discuss this important fact!

Only approaches that use their own manipulation language such as [KDN90] can make things easy to handle disjoint and overlapping generalizations.

Mixing several subtype hierarchies is another problematic case that require special concepts. The literature contains methodologies how to mix hierarchies [ScS96]. But less effort has been spent on languages to define mixed subtype hierarchies and their relationships to the original ones. Let us assume two databases: A university library (UN1) contains a type PUBLication with a subtype JOURNAL and corresponding extents { 1,2,3,4 } and { 2,3 }, respectively. A computer science library (CS2) has a type PUBL with an extent { 2,3,4 } possessing a subtype PROCeedings with an extent { 3,4 }. Obviously, the following conditions hold wrt. extents:

PUBL@UN1 $\supseteq$ PUBL@CS2 $\supseteq$ JOURNAL@UN1,

PUBL@UN1 $\supseteq$ PUBL@CS2 $\supseteq$ PROC@CS2, and JOURNAL@UN1 $\cap$ PROC@CS2 $\neq \emptyset$

The following specification defines an integrated subtype hierarchy that covers these conditions, again using multiple inheritance. Furthermore, types of different schemas are put in a subtype relationship by "join" conditions such as [isbn=PUBL@UN1.isbn]. This is necessary to access inherited attributes.

interface UNI_PUBL from PUBL@UN1 ...

   interface CS_PUBL : UNI_PUBL from PUBL@CS2 [isbn=PUBL@UN1.isbn] ...

     interface JOURNAL : CS_PUBL from JOURNAL@UN1 [isbn=PUBL@CS2.isbn] ...

     interface PROC   : CS_PUBL from PROC@CS2 ...

      interface J_P : JOURNAL,PROC from JOURNAL@UN1[isbn],PROC@CS2[isbn] ...

The definition of federated schemas must obviously be done in accordance with the extents of the existing types. In principle, we can derive different federated schemas from one and the same set of subtype hierarchies. Methodologies such as [ScS96, SpP94] help finding the right semantics.

To sum up, ODL$_{Int}$ has the power to to handle complex situations. The above examples can certainly give only an impression of the power and flexibility of our approach. Anyway, the semantics is completely compatible with C++ so that manipulations become possible.

5 Conclusions

In this paper, we suggested a comprehensive approach to database federation. The approach is based on a set of specification languages. A first class of languages is concerned with homogenization. Each object-oriented database system acquires a language of its own due to the diversity of systems and concepts. Relational systems are handled by one single language. Particularly relational schemas can be given real object-oriented views in the sense of semantic enrichment [Cas93]. An additional language allows one to merge the homogenized schemas to federated ones. A federated schema defines a system-spanning, integrated and consistent view of all the databases.

Corresponding generators produce code to provide the schemas with an ODMG-93 conforming object manipulation [Cat96]. Defining a homogenization specification, a generator produces a schema-dependent adapter that automatically maps ODMG-93 operations and queries onto the database. Each adapter can be used stand-alone. For instance, the adapter for a relational database provides an object-oriented access to relational data. A set of generated ODMG adapters can be used to access several, heterogeneous databases in parallel, without implementing any glue! A programmer just needs to compile and link the homogenized schemas into an application program in order to operate in an ODMG manner on the databases. However, there is no database-spanning view, and no support of global querying and transaction management. But plugging adapters in a global federation framework provides full functionality.

The generative nature of database federation has a significant advantage with regard to schema evolution: Any time a local schema is modified, the corresponding generator produces a new adapter for the local database without any implementational effort. Just the specification has to be adapted.

Future work will be dedicated to other types of data, particularly file systems. Furthermore, we have to care for external schemas, which expose data to an application in a data model different to ODMG-93. Finally, we feel that comfortable graphical support for defining schemas is needed [HoK95].

References

[AAK⁺93] J. Albert, R. Ahmed, M. Ketabchi, W. Kent, M.-C. Shan: *Automatic Importation of Relational Schemas in Pegasus.* In [IMS93]

[BFN94] R. Busse, P. Fankhauser, E. Neuhold: *Federated Schemata in ODMG.* Proc. of 2nd East/West Database Workshop 1994

[BLN86] E. Batini, M. Lenzerini, S. Navathe: *A Comparative Analysis of Methodologies for Database Schema Integration.* ACM Comp. Surveys 1986, 18(4)

[Cas93] M. Castellanos: *Semantic Enrichment of Interoperable Databases.* In [IMS93]

[Cat96] R. Cattell (ed.): *The Object Database Standard: ODMG-93.* 2nd edition, Morgan-Kaufmann Publishers, San Mateo (CA) 1996

[CBS94] R. Chiang, T. Barron, V. Storey: *Reverse Engineering of Relational Databases: Extraction of an EER model from a Relational Database.* Data&Knowledge Engineering 12, 1994

[CzT91] B. Czedjo, M. Taylor: *Integration of Database Systems Using an Object-Oriented Approach.* In [KRS91]

[DaA87] K.H. Davis, A.K. Arora: *Converting a Relational Database Model into an Entity-Relationship Model.* In [ERA87]

[DAT87] S.M. Deen, R.R. Amin, M.C. Taylor: *Data Integration in Distributed Databases.* IEEE Transactions on Software Engineering 13 (7), 1987

[ERA87] S. March (ed.): 6th Int. Conf. on *Entity-Relationship Approach,* 1987

[ERA93] 12th Int. Conf. on *Entity-Relationship Approach.* Karlsruhe 1993

[HNS92] D.K. Hsia, E.J. Neuhold, R. Sacks-Davis (eds.): Proc. of the IFIP WG 2.6 Database Semantics Conf. (DS-5) on *Interoperable Database Systems,* Lorne (Australia), 1992

[HFBK94] G. Huck, P. Fankhauser, R. Busse, W. Klas: *IRO-DB: An Object-Oriented Approach towards Federated and Interoperable DBMS.* In: Advances in Databases and Information Systems (ADBIS'94), Moscow 1994

[Hoh96] U. Hohenstein: *Bridging the Gap Between C++ and Relational Databases.* In: Proc. of 10th European Conf. on Object-Oriented Programming (ECOOP'96), Linz (Austria) 1996, Springer LNCS 1098

[HoK95]   U. Hohenstein, C. Körner: *A Graphical Tool for Specifying Semantic En-richment of Relational Databases.* In: 6th IFIP WG 2.6 Work. Group on Data Semantics (DS-6) "Database Applications Semantics", Atlanta 1995

[HTJC93]   J.-L. Hainault, C. Tonneau, M. Joris, M. Chandelon: *Schema Transforma-tion Techniques for Database Reverse Engineering.* In [ERA93]

[IEEE95]   *Legacy Systems.* Special Issue of IEEE Software 12(1), 1995

[IMS93]   Proc. of Conf. on Research Issues in Data Engineering: *Interoperability in Multidatabase Systems* (RIDE-IMS'93). Vienna 1993

[Joh93]   P. Johannesson: *A Logical Basis for Schema Integration.* In [IMS93]

[KDN90]   M. Kaul, K. Drosten, E. Neuhold: *ViewSystem: Integrating Heterogeneous Information Bases by Object-Oriented Views.* In: Proc. 6th Int. Conf. on Data Engineering, Los Angeles 1990

[KLK91]   R. Krishnamurthy, W. Litwin, W. Kent: *Language Features for Interope-rability of Databases with Schematic Discrepancies.* In: [KRS91]

[Kap+94]   G. Kappel et al.: *COMan – Coexistence of Object-Oriented and Relational Technology.* In: 13th Int. Conf. on Entity-Relationship Approach,

[KRS91]   Y. Kambayashi, M. Rusinkiewicz, A. Sheth (eds.): Proc. of 1st Int. Work-shop on *Interoperability in Multidatabase Systems* Kyoto (Japan), 1991

[LiM91]   Q. Li, D. McLeod: *An Object-Oriented Approach to Federated Databases.* In [KRS91]

[LPL96]   L. Liu, C. Pu, Y. Lee: *An Adaptive Approach to Query Mediation Across Heterogeneous Databases.* Proc. of Int. Conf. on Cooperative Information Systems, Brussels 1996

[MaM90]   V. Markowitz, J. Makowsky: *Identifying Extended ER Object Structures in Relational Schemas.* IEEE Trans. on Software Engineering 16(8), 1990

[NNJ93]   B. Narasimhan, S. Navathe, S. Jayaraman: *On Mapping ER and Relational Models into OO Schemas.* In [ERA93]

[PBT95]   E. Pitoura, O. Boukres, A. Elmagarid: *Object-Orientation in Multidata-base Systems.* ACM Computing Surveys 27(3), 1995

[PrB94]   W. Premerlani, M. Blaha: *An Approach for Reverse Engineering of Rela-tional Databases.* Communications of the ACM 37(5), May 1994

[RAD+91]   R. Rafii, R. Ahmed, P. DeSmedt, B. Kent, M. Ketabchi, W. Litwin: *Mul-tidatabase Management in Pegasus.* In [KRS91]

[Rad95]   E. Radeke: *Efendi: Federated Database System of Cadlab.* In: ACM SIG-MOD Conf. on Management of Data 1995, SIGMOD RECORD 24(2)

[REC+89]   M. Rusinkiewicz, R. ElMasri, B. Czejdo, et. al: *OMNIBASE. Design and Implementation of a Multidatabase System.* In: Proc. of 1st Annual Symp. in Parallel and Distributed Processing, Dallas 1989

[RPRG94]   M. Reddy, B. Prasad, P. Reddy, A. Gupta: *A Methodology for Integration of Heterogeneous Databases.* IEEE Trans. on Knowledge and Data Engi-neering 8(6), 1994

[SCG92]   F. Saltor, M. Castellanos, M. Garcia-Solaco: *Overcoming Schematic Dis-crepancies in Interoperable Databases.* In [HNS92]

[ScS96]   I. Schmitt, G. Saake: *Integrating of Inheritance Trees as Part of View Ge-neration for Database Federations.* In: 15th Int. Conf. on Conceptual Mo-deling (ER'96), Cottbus 1996, Springer LNCS 1157

[ShL90]   A. Sheth, J. Larson: *Federated DBSs for Managing Distributed, Heteroge-neous and Autonomous Databases.* ACM Comp. Surveys 1990, 22(3)

[SpP94]   S. Spaccapietra, C. Parent: *View Integration: A Step Forward in Solving Structural Conflicts.* IEEE Trans. on Knowledge & Data Engin. 1994, 6(2)

[YaL92]   L.-L. Yan, T.-W. Ling: *Translating Relational Schema With Constraints Into OODB Schema.* In [HNS92]

A Virtual Reality Interface to an Enterprise Metadatabase

Lester Yee
Department of Computer Science
The University of Hong Kong
Pokfulam Road, Hong Kong
Email: yeel@cs.hku.hk

Cheng Hsu
Decision Sciences and Engineering Systems
Rensselaer Polytechnic Institute
Troy, NY 12180-3590
Email: hsuc@rpi.edu

Abstract. A variety of semantic data models are inherently three dimensional (3D), yet are popularly presented in 2D diagrammatic outline form. A system called the VIU-2, a second generation prototype of a 3D information visualization system for metadata is presented. Employing a virtual reality (VR) toolkit, VR hardware and a Metadatabase, the system visualizes an enterprise's conceptual model in 3D interactive space. Enterprise users in turn navigate and interact with the model as a means to facilitate information management tasks. Presented are the underlying concepts to this research work and its particular implementation methods.

1 Introduction

Information models such as extended E-R, object-oriented, DFD, and other decomposition-based models are inherently three dimensional. A Metadatabase (enterprise data and knowledge repository) [11, 14, 16] serves to store such model representations as a means for managing them and their corresponding information resources. Modeling tools and repository interfaces typically sport the traditional graphical user-interface (GUI); providing 2D outline diagrams for viewing conceptual models and tables for data. The use of such techniques as multiple windows and GUI controls of pull-down lists, menus, icons, and scroll-bars, the interface facilitates enterprise users' understanding of information.

There are some inherent problems associated with the above user-interface method for viewing enterprise information, specifically the fragmented presentation of the information, lack of guidance in the user-interface, and static presentation of complex information. In GUI, the user is allowed to view 2D "planes" of information that is but a horizontal slice of its inherent 3D representation. Basic functions of panning and zooming found in the GUI interface trades off global views, local details, and object constancy in helping a user to comprehend information. [24]. Lacking is the natural presentation of enterprise information as models, smooth navigation for global context and local details, interactivity as a means to request for supporting information, and the use of dynamic coding to convey relationships.

Using the latest advances in virtual reality development toolkits, a VR-based user-interface has been developed for a Metadatabase. The information resources represented in the Metadatabase is visualized using the Two-Stage Entity-Relationship (TSER) modeling methodology [10]. Geometric forms conforming to the TSER modeling methodology has been given to the multiple abstraction layers of enterprise information resources; making them visual and identifiable. Further a universe paradigm and globe metaphor [12] has been employed as a means to logically organize the models in the information space.

This paper reports on conceptual modeling foundations for the VR-based user-interface for the Metadatabase and its implementation methods for addressing the deficiencies of the GUI. A prototype system called the Visual Information Universe II (VIU-2) utilizing VR concepts and tools is presented.

2 Implementation Methods

In the development of the Visual Information Universe II system, a number of established research components were employed and named above. Specifically, 1) TSER Methodology for integrative modeling, 2) Metadatabase for managing enterprise information resources, and 3) Universe Paradigm and Globe Metaphor as the model for the visualization environment. A synopsis of these three methods is presented in the context of the VIU-2 system. Further details on each can be obtained in a number of publications [14, 15, 16].

2.1 The TSER Methodology

The Two-Stage Entity-Relationship (TSER) methodology was developed to integrate the dichotomy of modeling methods associated with semantic-level and data-level modeling methodologies. Composed of a two-stage definition with a proper mapping mechanism (algorithm) from the functional (or Semantic Entity-Relationship - SER) model to the data-structure (or Operational Entity-Relationship - OER) model. The methodology served to create a holistic data modeling approach integrating the so-called top-down design and bottom-up synthesis approaches for database/information systems development (Fig. 1). The focus of TSER is on the functional role of data and hence is more concerned with localized (user) views of data and the declaration of its inter-relationships (e.g., functional dependencies).

SER

The Semantic Entity-Relationship (SER) modeling level for hierarchical conceptual modeling composes of two constructs: 1) *Subjects* which are like objects, capture localized user views of data and 2) *Contexts* that serve to related Subjects. Subjects capture data semantics such as data items, functional dependencies and business rules. Contexts contains information such as data equivalence and integration rules. The Subject construct can further be decomposed into lower level SER diagrams.

OER

The Operational Entity-Relationship (OER) modeling component follows closely with the traditional E-R modeling methodology with a more rigorous requirement for cardinality-oriented (normalized) representation. Four modeling constructs (one entity and three types of relationships) are used for its definition. An enterprise OER model can be created to represent the data abstraction layer for a whole organization.

The OER model can be automatically derived from an SER model through rigorous mapping algorithms.

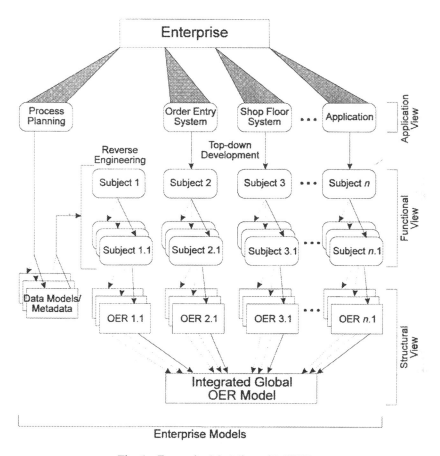

Fig. 1. Enterprise Modeling with TSER

The TSER Methodology has been shown to be suitable as generic meta-modeling method where a variety of modeling methodologies (object-oriented, relational, and E-R) can be mapped to it as a common base [17]. Further the models can also be integrated by references to shared data objects, thus creating a unified enterprise model. The TSER methodology has been in use world-wide for a number of years since its inception in 1985. A CASE tool called the Information-Based Modeling System (IBMS) is an implementation of the TSER methodology, and is available as educational freeware (http://viu.eng.rpi.edu).

2.2 Metadatabase

The Metadatabase is an on-line enterprise data and knowledge repository for information integration and management. The Metadatabase itself employs a generic meta-structure, the Global Information Resource Dictionary (GIRD) model (Fig. 2)

439

[11, 13, 15]. The GIRD, which can be considered an extended Information Resources Dictionary System (IRDS) [8], abstracts the enterprise metadata resources (functional views, data models, and implementation definitions) into an implemented Metadatabase. The structure itself, as well as the global and visual representation of local models as metadata instances, is developed using the TSER methodology. Thus the Metadatabase can capture entirely an enterprises multiple information models/resources and its integration definitions. The Metadatabase has been well documented in a number of papers [14, 16]. (Note: The IBMS CASE tool also provides a function to instantiate a Metadatabase for a given TSER model.)

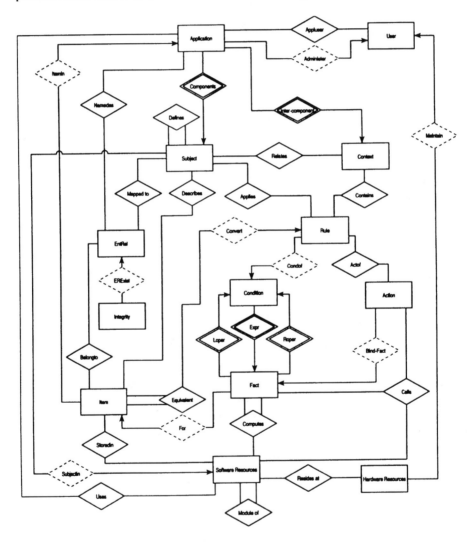

Fig. 2. The GIRD Model

2.3 Visual Information Universe (VIU)

As with many user-interface approaches, there necessary needs to be a operating metaphor to organize and manipulate information in a user-interface presentation. For the GUI, it is the windows/desktop metaphor. In information visualization using VR techniques, this typically involves a spatial metaphor. Thus for the visual interpretation of enterprise information and its management, a visualization paradigm characterizing the four-dimensional (4-D) field of space and time, has been conceived as the Visual Information Universe (VIU). It uses the notion of the Universe in which we both physical live and logically conceptualize our existence as the basic paradigm [12, 19]. In brief, the Universe paradigm represents the information space where a user interacts (communicates) with visualized information. Information is organized in the universe as globes (the metaphor) representing domains of information. The globe surface represents user's needs of the interface, such as applications, management, and other utilization of these information contents for the enterprise. Information resources visualized within the globe are given specific physical forms appropriate for its cognitive comprehension (e.g., TSER models for enterprise information). The VIU model is incorporated into the visualization environment.

3 The VIU-2 System

The VIU-2 System has been developed on a high-performance Silicon Graphics VR platform at Hong Kong University and uses the replicated Metadatabase from Rensselaer Polytechnic Institute. Details of its architecture, visualized information, system functions, and unique features are presented.

3.1 The Basic Architecture

The key components of the VIU system are depicted in Fig. 3.

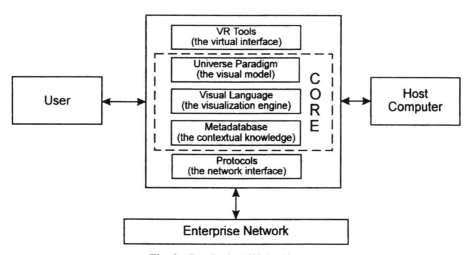

Fig. 3. The Basic VIU Architecture

The three components in the core and their connections to virtual reality (VR) tools and the common network protocols comprise the basic VIU architecture. The user front-end is the virtual interface to the VIU core, and the back-end is a host-computer linked through an enterprise network (e.g., the National Information Infrastructure for a global enterprise). Within the core component, the universe paradigm is the interface model matched with a set of communication/navigation operators that define its interactive visual language. The core is complete with the incorporation of contextual knowledge from the enterprise metadatabase to drive the visualization.

3.2 The Visualized Metadata

The visualized enterprise model has been given the following geometric forms (Fig. 4) re essentially four abstraction layers of information: 1) applications (highest level SER model), 2) semantic models (SER), 3) data models (OER), and 4) data items. These four layers are logically related and thus visual links in the form of "lines" and "light rays" relate the decomposition hierarchy.

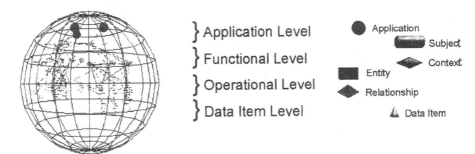

Fig. 4. Metadata Visualization definitions.

3.3 The System Functions

Two general enterprise information management functions are presently implemented in the VIU-2 system: 1) metadata browsing, and 2) distributed query language generator. For these two modes of operation, the visualization of the Metadatabase is the same; just the interaction mode (visual language) for each function is different. Mode changes between browsing and query building is done through the VR interface device of the Spaceball (and alternate mouse controls). In the case of the query building state, system controls allow for the selection/de-selection of objects to be involved in the query.

Enterprise Information Browsing

In enterprise information browsing, we can expect executive users needing to understand the state of operations and what information resources are used across the enterprise. This level of browsing activity does not require a particular goal, and can be a free-form exploration of an enterprise's information resources. Thus a user can expect to: 1) navigate through the Metadatabase model, 2) follow the logical links, 3) observe the inter-relationships, and 4) select objects in the visual model for additional contextual information. Interaction is by selection of information objects with the corresponding system responding by highlighting/de-highlighting related abstractions of the model. For example, selection of the "Order Processing" application object will highlight the SER model, OER model, and all its data items. With this self guided navigational tour, an executive users can have a good understanding of the information infrastructure that can be used to help in management decision making.

Distributed Query Generator

Beyond the browsing capabilities of the Metadatabase through the VIU-2, the next level of function is the application of a query building function. Thus, a second order interaction mode with the visualized enterprise model will be for selection of objects that are to be involved in a query request. The output of this function is a query language, the Metadata Query Language (MQL) for distributed information access [4] (Fig. 5).

```
FROM OE/PR WO_SEQ GET
    WO_ID;
FROM OE/PR PART GET
    PART_ID
    PART_NAME
    DESCRIPTION;
```

Fig. 5. Example of MQL generated by VIU-2

Since the metadatabase model represents real information resources available in the enterprises, additional information such as the method of storage (database relation/file, network location, access methods, etc.) represent additional knowledge that is usable for executing the retrieval of distributed data. A global query system (GQS) has been developed for the Metadatabase with this capability [4]. Therefore the VIU-2 generates MQL expressions that can be submitted to the GQS engine for execution. (Note: The GQS Engine resides at Rensselaer Polytechnic Institute, and can process distributed queries to Oracle DBMS, dBase, Btrieve, and an OO-DBMS. Remote integration of the two system is being looked into for the future.)

3.4 Special Features

Beyond the two basic functions of the VIU-2 system, there are five distinctive features of the VIU-2 that provides an advantage over GUI-based user-interfaces.

Knowledge-Based System

The interactivity of the user to the information universe is guided by the contextual knowledge within the Metadatabase. As the user interacts with the visualized information, the actions trigger transactions to the Metadatabase for additional information based on the user context (Fig. 6). That is, rather than encapsulate behavior within the VIU-2, system behaviors are defined within the Metadatabase. A benefit is the reduction of the high system overhead typical for a large enterprise model. The system will sacrifices some performance in speed, and is somewhat compensated for by the use of a fast-response transaction system (Oracle 7 with Transaction Processing capability). Furthermore, the information presented through the VIU-2 represents the most current information defined in the Metadatabase.

Visualization of Integrated Information

One of the characteristics to enterprise information systems is that it implicitly refers to information that is integrated. That is multiple systems can be related at the functional or data level through common/shared data objects. This integration information is captured by the support of an equivalence meta-relation in the Metadatabase. Thus if an information manager would like to know how the multiple systems in his enterprise are integrated, this information is visualized with links (arcs) between the data objects (Fig. 7).

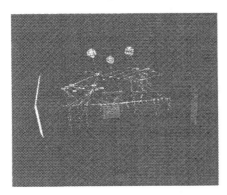 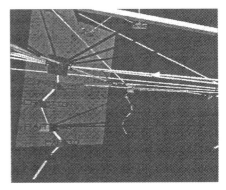

Fig. 6. An application model highlighted by contextual knowledge in Metadatabase

Fig. 7. The data item *PART_ID* shows equivalence relationships with visible arcs

User-Centered Presentation

An objective of the VIU-2 system is for the system to accommodate the user rather than the other way around. Thus in the context of user browsing, information will automatically appear or orient itself for the users' comprehension. Consider that text labels orient themselves for readability to the user, regardless of the user's spatial orientation (Fig. 7). Greater detail is resolved for the user-view as objects appear closer (e.g., icons representing additional information appear as the user approaches objects in the model) (Fig. 8).

Text labeling of entities is a popular way to convey enterprise information models and is supported in VIU-2. Text has its limitation as it is subject to vague labeling and reduction in speed of identifying information objects. The use of multimedia as an alternate (or primary) object identification channel is a method towards moving away from this dependency of text; hence specific national languages. One cannot expect to completely do away with national languages, but a direction for reducing this dependency is an objective of the VIU-2.

Thus as the user navigates through the model and gets within a close proximity to certain entities/objects, icons may appear (pop-up) on the surface allowing for drilling of additional information (Fig. 8). The icons can represent sound clips, images, and video segments. The user need only to select any of these icons, and the multimedia element will appear or play (Fig. 9). These multimedia elements are related to the information objects by registering (and relating) them in the Metadatabase - they are by no means pre-established or manually authored for the visualization. The visualization system will transact for these multimedia items for all visualized objects if they exist.

Fig. 8. Pop-up icons for multimedia information.

Fig. 9. Selection of the video icon starts a film clip.

4-D Dynamism

Space compression techniques such as fish-eye views, multiple window views, etc. has been used as a means of displaying vast amounts of information [20]. Rather than distort or fragment information that is inherently related and vast into snapshots or frames, translation dynamics is used to communicate such information. The visualized Metadatabase automatically rotates in the user's view when it first appears in the VIU system startup view, thus serving to communicate the whole model as a continuum.

This manner of information compression through the use of time-order expressions, is defined in the VIU context as integrals. These integrals represent visual expressions for the purpose of communications. A formal definition of integrals in this context can be found in [18]. An integral is communicated to the user on first viewing of the Metadatabase model within a globe (the domain metaphor). The model automatically cycles through the multiple-systems (3 systems in the example manufacturing enterprise model) by cycling different colors for each system (Fig. 10). This communicates to the user the segmentation of each application in relation to the entire enterprise model, along with its points of integration.

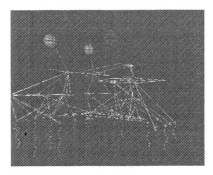

Fig. 10. An integral rotating the model to reveal extent.　　**Fig. 11.** A user interfacing with the VIU-2 system.

3.5 The Development Tools

The VIU-2 implementation is based on a client-server design. The system itself was written in the C-language using the Sense8 WorldToolkit for the Silicon Graphics (SGI) platform. The Metadatabase was implemented with the Oracle v7 database management system on a Sun Unix server. Using this configuration, the client-server connection between the two environment was managed through Oracle SQL*Net software for both platforms. The Oracle Pro*C library for SGI was used to develop the Metadatabase transaction calls from the VIU-2.

To provide a historical perspective to VIU-2, a first generation prototype called VIU-1 [18] was developed in early 1994 using Oracle 6 Server and General Electric's LYMB object-oriented visualization system [21] on an IBM RS/6000 workstation. Providing wire-frame views and mouse controls, it was an exploration of the basic ideas that are reflected in the higher performing VR-based VIU-2. The VIU-2 system thus provides a more engaging interactive environment using the VR hardware (Fig. 11) and software.

4　Analysis and Experiences

A brief comparative analysis is used to highlight the basic advantages and capabilities of the VIU-2 over traditional GUI/diagrammatic interface methods for enterprise information management. Additionally, some user-trials and responses have been recorded and their comments summarized.

4.1 A Comparative Analysis

A primary objective of the VIU-2 is the movement away from static and fragmented views of information typifying the windows of information in the GUI. User-interface strategies such as relying on multiple windows, zoom capabilities, and panning by scroll-bars interrupt the user efforts in comprehending the multitude of enterprise information. The VR environment of the VIU-2 overcomes this by integrating and synthesizing the visual presentation of information in a continuous navigational environment. The information visualization is dynamic for the purposes of communicating extent as well as multiple coding of logical associations. Rather than employ information compression techniques such as distortive fish-eye views [20] to show macroscopic views of the enterprise, dynamics is used without distortions [12, 24].

The movement away from text-based visualizations [27] and towards conceptual modeling constructs (e.g., the TSER methodology) takes advantage of the simplicity and logical nature of the methodology [9, 25]. The use of an extensible user-interface operating model such as the universe paradigm and globe metaphor provides a recursive and extensible environment that is logically supportive of spatial representations of enterprise information [18].

An objective in using a 3D, interactive, and continuous spatial environment is to move part of the cognitive load to the perceptual vision system. By doing so, it takes advantage of our highest bandwidth of communication - vision. Additionally, the navigational interface proposes to provide an operating environment that is memorable and friendly with only a limited number of natural controls (navigation and interactivity) - congruent in simplicity to the ease-of-use of today's Web browsers.

4.2 User Trials

Though no formal user-interface experiments was done for this research prototype, the VIU-2 system was exposed to 30 students in a university-level database class. Students were given the opportunity to trial run their TSER database models from a data modeling assignment and generate their own Metadatabase for the VIU-2. The metadata for their model was created with the IBMS CASE tool.

Overall comments received were very positive, as students were able to see and interact with their own model in fully visualized 4D (time-ordered 3D). Students have created their original TSER model through the traditional 2D diagrammatic modeling facility of IBMS. Specific comments were received on 1) the ease of recognition and comprehension of their own visualized model in stereo-view, 2) freedom to navigate and zoom through their model, and 3) see their model respond to their interactions.

Comments for improvement were particularly directed towards the VR interface hardware and some limitations for the VR software. Specifically, the adjustments to obtain the stereoscopic view from the Crystal Eyes Shutter glasses. Due to the parallax errors of the 3D generation, frequent adjustments had to be made depending on the zoom level. Other comments referred to the difficulty in using the navigational controls and slow responsiveness of the Spaceball 3D input device. Switching over to the alternate mouse control (mapped for 3D navigation) provided better user responses.

5 Related Work

A brief review on some related research in this area. The research underlying the VIU-2 falls within the field of information visualization - a field targeting the visualization of logical information and databases. Though few efforts have been devoted to the domain of metadata, conceptual models or for purposes of information resources management [6, 23]. Efforts presented here are representative of related work.

Ahlbert and Wistrand's work on IVEE (Information Visualization and Exploration Environment) [1] is one related work for query access of multiple databases. Their visualization approach utilizes geographical information system methods and visual presentation types of "starfield", scatter-plot, and 3-D bar charts. Users interact with GUI sliders to vary parameters in their query formulation.

Internet information resources have been visualized as a text tree diagrams for browsing purposes [7]. Incorporated in their system is a technique for cluster mapping of related words in a concept analysis of retrieved homepages. Internet resource visualizations are recently becoming a popular phenomenon [2, 22].

Xerox PARC's seminal work on the Information Visualizer and 3D-Rooms metaphor is a system well acknowledged [3, 24]. Using a matrix of rooms as a macro arrangement of information, each room provides a spatial boundary for classes of information. Each room can support a variety of animated information visualization methods (e.g., Cone Tree, Cam Tree, Perspective Walls, etc.)

A commercial product call CA-UniCenter TNG (The Next Generation) by Computer Associates [5] provides a VR user-interface for managing information systems. The interface system provides more physical representation of systems ranging from 3D models of world geography to specific computer hardware components. Logical databases are included as well, but represented as monoliths within a landscape. Similar logical representation of databases or files as objects in the landscape can be found in the File System Navigator (FSN or Fusion) by Silicon Graphics [26].

6 Conclusion and Future Work

The VIU-2 is based on established research work in the areas of integrative information modeling, Metadatabase, global query system architecture, and 4D information visualization. This paper presents the implementation of the VR-based user-interface designed for Metadatabase management (browsing and global query formulation) using information visualization.

Taking the argument that a primary reason why Data Flow Diagrams, E-R diagrams, and OO models have been so popular is due to their simplicity in approach and their universal communication ability for the full range of users (end-users, systems analysts, and executives). The Two-Stage Entity-Relationship (TSER) methodology can be similarly justified. The TSER constructs provided the geometrical basis for the visualized enterprise conceptual model. The VIU-2 as an implementation succeeds over traditional GUI/diagrammatic interfaces in terms of the knowledge-supported interactive environment, navigational interface, 4D visualizations, and reduced cognitive overhead (shift to human perceptual system) in its use.

With the progression of Internet technology for enterprise-wide information management, we are evaluating technologies such as VRML and Java and their viability to the VIU methods. We believe a future direction is towards enterprise-wide access for a suite of VR-based information management functions that is accessible from a WWW/Intranet browser. Further investigation of providing greater coverage of information management functions to the VIU-2 system such as information modeling, simulation, and decision support are further being investigated as well.

References

[1] Ahlberg, C., and E. Wistrand, "IVEE: An Information Visualization and Exploration Environment," Proc. of 1995 Information Visualization, pp.66-73, 1995

[2] Andrews, K., "Visualizing Cyberspace: Information Visualization in the Harmony Internet Browser," *Proc. of 1995 Information Visualization*, pp.97-104, 1995.

[3] Card, S. K., G.G. Robertson, and J.D. Mackinlay, "The Information Visualizer, an Information Workspace," *Proceedings of CHI'91*, ACM, New York, (1991), 181-188.

[4] Cheung, W., and C. Hsu, "The Model-Assisted Global Query System," *ACM Transactions on Information Systems*, vol.14, 4 (Oct. 1996), pp.421-470.

[5] Computer Associates, "Unicenter: The Next Generation (TNG)," 1996. (References available at www.cai.com/products/unicent/tng_ov.htm).

[6] Fairchild, K.M., "Information Management Using Virtual Reality-Based Visualizations," in *Virtual Reality Applications and Explorations*, Ed. Alan Wexelblat, pp.45-74, 1993.

[7] Gershon, N., J. LeVasseur, J. Winstead, J. Croall, A. Pernickc, and W. Ruh, "Visualizing Internet Resources," *Proc. of 1995 Information Visualization*, pp.122-128, 1995.

[8] Goldfine, A. and P. Konig, "A Technical Overview of the Information Resources Dictionary System (Second Edition)," *NBS Special Publications NBSIR 88-3700*, National Bureau of Standards, Gaithersburg, MD, Jan. 1988.

[9] Haber, E., Y. Ionannidis, and M. Livny "OPOSSUM: A Flexible Schema Visualization and Editing Tool," *CHI '94 : Human Factors in Computing Systems - Conference Companion*, ACM Press, (1994), 321-322.

[10] Hsu, C., "Structured Databases Systems Analysis and Design Through Entity-Relationship Approach," *Proceedings of the 4th International Conference on Entity Relationship Approach*, pp. 56-63, 1985.

[11] Hsu, C., M. Bouziane, L. Rattner, and L. Yee, "Information Resources Management in Heterogeneous, Distributed Environment: A Metadatabase Approach," *IEEE Trans. on Softw. Eng.*, vol.17, 6 (1991), 604-625.

[12] Hsu, C. "Towards the Next Generation User Interface: A Universe Paradigm Using the Globe Metaphor for Enterprise Information Visualization," *Proc. IEEE Conf. on Systems, Man, and Cybernetics*, Oct. 1994.

[13] Hsu, C., M. Bouziane, W. Cheung, Javier Nogues, L. Rattner, and L. Yee, "A Metadata System for Information Modeling and Integration, " *Proceedings of the First*

International Conference on Systems Integration, IEEE Computer Society, April 1990, pp. 616-624.

[14] Hsu, C., G. Babin, M. Bouziane, W. Cheung, L. Rattner, A. Rubenstein, and L. Yee, "The metadatabase approach to integrating and managing manufacturing information systems," *J. of Intelligent Manufacturing*, 5, (1994), 333-349.

[15] Hsu, C. *Enterprise Integration and Modeling: The Metadatabase Approach*, Kluwer Academic Publishers, Boston, MA, (1996).

[16] Hsu, C., G. Babin, M. Bouziane, W. Cheung, L. Rattner, and L. Yee, "Metadatabase Modeling for Enterprise Information Integration," *J. of Systems Integration*, vol.2, 1, (1992), 5-37.

[17] Hsu, C., Y.C. Tao, M. Bouziane, and G. Babin, "Paradigm Translation in Integrating Manufacturing Information Using a Meta-Model: The TSER Approach," *Information Systems Engineering*, vol.1, 3, (1993), 325-352.

[18] Hsu, C. and L. Yee, Visual Information Universe. *Enterprise Integration and Modeling: the Metadatabase Approach*, Kluwer Academic Publishers, Norwell, MA, (1996), 215-236.

[19] Hsu C, and L. Yee, "Four-Dimensional Information Visualization: An Illustration," *Proceedings of the ACME V International Conference*, Minneapolis, MN, (August 1995), 123-133.

[20] Jerding, D.F., and J.T. Stasko, "The Information Mural: A Technique for Displaying and Navigating Large Information Spaces," *Proc. of 1995 Information Visualization*, pp.43-50, 1995.

[21] Lorensen W., and B. Yamrom, "Golf Green Visualization," *IEEE Computer Graphics & Application*, vol.12, 4 (1992), 35-44.

[22] Mitchell, R., D. Day, and L. Hirschman, "Fishing for Information on the Internet," *Proc. of 1995 Information Visualization*, pp.105-111, 1995.

[23] Nilan, M. S. Cognitive Space - Using Virtual Reality For Large Information Resource Management Problems. *J. of Communication*, vol.42, (Autumn 1992), 115-135.

[24] Robertson, G.G., S.K. Card, and J.D. Mackinlay, "Information Visualization using 3D Interactive Animation," *Commun. of the ACM*, vol.36, 4 (1993), 57-71.

[25] Rogers, T.R., and R. Catell, "Entity-Relationship Database User-Interfaces," *Proceedings of the 6th International Conference on Entity-Relationship Approach*, New York, (1987), 323-336.

[26] Strasnick, S., and J. Tesler, "3D Information Landscapes," Silicon Graphics Inc., Mountain View, CA, 1992. (Software available at ftp://sgi.sgi.com/sgi/fsn/.)

[27] Wise, J.A., J.J. Thomas, K. Pennock, D. Lantrip, M. Pottier, A. Schur, and V. Crow, "Visualizing the Non-Visual: Spatial analysis and interaction with information from text documents," *Proc. of 1995 Information Visualization*, pp.51-58, 1995.

[28] Yee, L., and C. Hsu, "A Metadata Visualization User-Interface for Enterprise Information Management," *Proc. of the IASTED/ISMM International Conf. on Intelligent Information Management Systems*, pp.100-106, 1996.

A Fully Flexible CAME in a CASE Environment

A.N.W. Dahanayake, H.G. Sol, J.L.G. Dietz
Delft University of Technology
The Netherlands
E-mail : A.N.W.Dahanayake@is.twi.tudelft.nl

Abstract

A comprehensive solution is presented in this paper to the environment problem by integrating the concept of CAME into CASE, where attention is paid to a conceptual model of such an environment that is designed to avoid the confusion around integration issues, and to meet the specification of user requirements concerning flexible method support. An outline of the motivations behind this research, the philosophy, architecture, functionality and future developments are presented.

1   Introduction

In spite of the fact that CASE (Computer Aided Systems Engineering) environments have been around since the 70's, there are still many problems with these environments. Among the problems of CASE environments are a lack of conceptual models to help understand the technology, the poor state of user requirements specification, inflexible method support and complicated integration facilities, contribute to the dissatisfaction in CASE users.

During the 90's there has been a growing need to provide a more formal basis to the art of software development and maintenance through standardized process and product models. The importance of CAME (Computer Aided Method Engineering) in CASE led to the development of CASE shells, MetaCASE tools or fully customizable CASE environments, that were intended to overcome the inflexibility of method support. The declining cost of computing technology and its increasing functionality, specifically in graphic user interfaces has contributed to the present re-invention of CASE environments.

CASE research in the last decade has addressed issues such as method integration, multiple user support, multiple representation paradigms, method modifiability and evolution, and information retrieval and computation facilities. Considerable progress has been made by isolating particular issues and providing a comprehensive solution with certain trade-offs on limited flexibility, but to date the CAME solutions have failed to address the requirements for full flexibility when supporting an arbitrary modeling technique.

The theory formulation and development of a prototype for a next generation of CASE environments is presented in this paper. A comprehensive solution is sought to the environment problem by paying attention to a conceptual model of such an environment that has been designed to avoid the confusion around integration issues, and to meet the specification of user requirements concerning flexible method support.

As a CAME environment the MetaCAME provides a fully flexible environment for method specification, integration, and can be use for information systems design activities. An outline of the motivations behind this research, the philosophy, architecture, functionality and future developments is given in this paper.

2 The Theory Formulation

There are a number of approaches that can be used when attempting to develop a better understanding of CASE technology to support systems engineering activities. Models based on integration issues such as given in [Was90] provide a view whereby integration can be thought of as a set of characteristics of a CASE environment. This multidimensional view of integration is somewhat problematic. It is not clear what is meant by: "the dimensions are orthogonal" and whether they can, or should, be considered separately.

A generic framework for CASE environments with all types of integration is presented in [BCM+94], and combined in a coherent manner with the NIST/ECMA Frameworks Reference Model [BEM92]. This is a result of the joint standardization efforts of ECMA (European Computer Manufactures Association) and NIST (National Institute for Standardization and Technologies). The environment framework does not take into consideration that different CASE environments have different facilities and categorization of requirements. In addition, different CASE environments have their own way of defining interactions between requirement categories. Although this framework describes a basic architecture for standardization, its focus is more or less on an inventory list of approaches. It is not easy to acquire exact requirements to describe a flexible architecture, little is said about the requirements for integration at the semantic level.

A view that is focused on a central repository as a key mechanism for data integration in CASE environments is preferred by many people, and has formed the basis of several efforts to develop environments. There are a number of CASE environments offering repository based models. For example, PCTE(Portable Common Tool Environment) and its Object Management Services. Some other examples include proprietary tools, such as IEW and IEF, Object Management Workbench, software through pictures, research based Daida, and Ithaca. There is a belief that a repository of some sort placed at the heart of a CASE environment should be the primary means of tool integration. At the schema level there have been a number of attempts to define generic models that can be used as the basis for semantic agreement between tools across an application domain. A great deal of research is taking place in this area, with 'enterprise modeling and integration' being the phrase that unites much of this work. To date, none of these generic schemata has achieved wide success, although the IBM AD/Cycle Information Model [IBM89], and ISO Information Resource Dictionary Systems (IRDS) [ISO90], represent extensive efforts in this area.

Current MetaCASE tools based on repository models called CASE shells, MetaCASE tools or fully customizable CASE environments have given rise to a number of improvements in the CAME arena. The main goal behind these achievements is to embed a method engineering capability in a CASE environment. Several studies such as [WKvD91, Wij91] discuss the importance of CAME in CASE. There are many products that claim method support and flexibility. These commercial as well as research tools such as MetaEdit+, Decamerone, Customizer, VSF, Paradigm, RAMATIC, ConceptBase and MetaView provide various forms of integration of MetaCASE with their environment.

Most MetaCASE initiatives enable modification of diagram elements and associated storage and manipulation functionality, and their efforts have been based on providing method component libraries, method reuse and run time adaptability. Modification of advanced aspects such as consistency verification, diagram techniques definition according to the requirements of an arbitrary technique and generation or model execution are still non-existent. The existence of a schema, or a meta model within an environment is not adequate, even though meta model integration leads to increased flexibility [Ver93]. There are many issues that need to be resolved. These issues fall into two main categories: syntax issues, e.g. naming, notation, convention, and semantic issues, e.g. what is stored, where is it stored, and what does it means?.

Summarizing, the Information Systems Development (ISD) process needs to address issues involved in an integrated modeling environment, regardless of the available technology. The basic question 'What does this environment do?' can be answered when the services correspond to an abstract description of the functionality of the environment that is offered to its users [BCM+94]. The conceptual model, as opposed to actual models, the service descriptions tend neatly to partition the functions of an environment. When an actual environment is examined, however, these neat conceptual groupings are seldom found [BEM92, DBFW92]. The likelihood of this functional overlap is the reason why a conceptual model is necessary: one of the principle values is that it provides a common conceptual basis with which to define problem specific CASE environments.

2.1 An Object Oriented Service Model

The research discussed in this paper follows the philosophy of a design context, the process that the environment must support in terms of a service based conceptual model distinguishing conceptual issues, the services, from implementation issues. ISD is the *process* that is crucial to this study, and central to this process are the *services* available to the users of environment. The *mechanisms* are a way of implementing the services concerned with the available technology and the techniques that can be applied to connect different service components. Opposed to this, the process encodes the set of goals of a project, providing the context in which the services must be related. The integration can then be regarded as the specification of which services are provided by the environment, and how these services relate to each other, this is similar to the approach adopted in [BCM+94].

A framework based on an object-oriented approach is presented in [DBFW92]. This service model is used to formulate the conceptual model of a CASE environment that provides method flexibility. The approach is advantageous, as the object concept allows modularity. When a model increases in modularity, it enables a flexible architecture which can be modified more easily to support maintenance and reuse of design techniques.

The general idea is that a particular repository is a 'configuration' of functionalities, where such a functionality can be expressed as a service with its associated concepts and behavior, called a 'Service Object'. Each service object interacts with the world outside the environment as well as with the other service objects around it. It is not necessary for each CASE environment to offer all the services defined by this object model. Any actual CASE environment has the freedom to decide on its service objects and its services. The repository object is a configuration of service objects and gives the capability to model the interfaces such that they satisfy the service users' demands without having to redefine the service. Figure 1 represents the service model of this CASE environment.

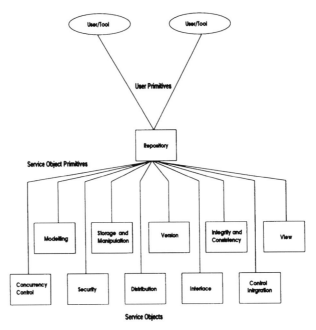

Figure 1: Service model of a CASE environment

2.2 Basic CAME Services

The overall functionality of the CAME environment is to provide the services necessary to define the required design tools. The environment should not only support different methods, it should also be able to support integration of modeling techniques within a method as well as the models developed by these different modeling techniques. Therefore, it is necessary for the environment to be able to support independent modeling techniques in a consistent manner. The framework given in [DBFW92], was used to identify the basic services of a CAME environment, limiting the attention to the services, Modeling, Storage and Manipulation, Integrity and Consistency, Views, and Interfaces. These are considered to be the basic services that are important for this research. Eventually, these basic services were formalized using PSM [Hof93], LISA-D [Hof93], Task Structures [Hof93] and Graphic Structures [HVWN92], to a meta model of a CAME environment. A detailed specification of this CAME meta model can be found in [Dah97]. An informal description of the conceptual model of the CAME environment is presented in the next section.

3 The Architecture

The global philosophy behind the construction of a problem specific CAME environment prototype is that such an environment has to provide the required design tools according to the chosen method particular to a problem situation. The CAME environment has to function as a service based object oriented MetaCASE environment, which offers services required for modeling tools by a mechanism interpreting the required modeling knowledge and changing the visual representations to the required form with the use of a graphic object binding mechanism. Further, this environment offers mechanism for population of models specified according to such designed tools.

The environment is a layered database architecture based on the principle of service objects. This approach differs from other MetaCASE approaches which focus more on the representation of the methods as first order logical theories, or graphical behavior of design objects. The approach has some similarity to the MetaEdit+ [KLR96] approach from the viewpoint of conceptual modeling where the design of a method specification is akin to the development of a conceptual schema of a software repository, and the design of a CASE tool resembles the design of an external view to a conceptual schema [ANS75]. A specific difference of this approach with respect to the MetaEdit+ approach is the ability to define process description and to support process specification which is important for selecting the suitable method or its parts for a specific problem area. Following this direction the solution presented can achieve the design goals of a better, improved, fully flexible open architecture.

When using this environment two types of activities can be identified (see figure 2): the *method engineering* activities which make use of the *Meta model Editor* and *Tool Editor* and *systems engineering* activities which make use of the *CASE Tool Editors* and *Population Editors*. Firstly, the method engineering activity of *method definition* use the *Meta model Editor* to specify meta models of design tools according to problem specific design activities. When the meta model of a particular modeling technique is ready the *tool generation* activity associates the required graphic representations to the modeling concepts and constraints using the *Tool Editor*. The second type of activities are *systems designing* using generated *CASE Tool Editors* and the *population* of the models with the help of the *Population Editor*.

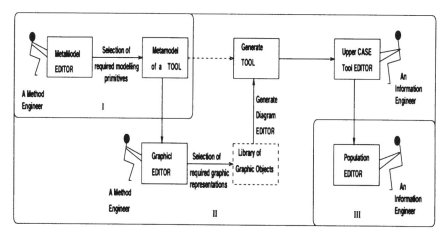

Figure 2: The main support functions of the CAME environment

The five basic *Service Objects* describe the *meta-meta model* of the CAME environment and form the *schema description layer* of the Object base. The *meta models* that describe the process and product knowledge of modeling techniques constructed by the *Meta model Editor* forms the *schema layer* of the object base. The *data models* constructed with the *CASE Tool Editors* according to the graphic representations specified by *Tool Editor* forms the *data model layer*. The data models' associated populations constructed by the *Population Editor* forms the *operation data layer*. This way the description of the information systems design process is embedded in the layered database architecture. The description of the service objects associated with the IS design process are used as the actual architectural building blocks of the flexible information systems modeling environment. The prototype based on this generic model is implemented on NeXTstep/Objectvie C platform, integrating the research areas of MetaCASE and object-oriented service specifications.

3.1 The Meta Model Editor

The Meta model Editor forms the kernel of the CAME environment. The object model of each module discussed under the functional description of the CAME meta model provides the important architectural building blocks. The Meta model Editor supports the construction of meta models according to the constructs of the *Modeling Service Object*.

3.1.1 Modeling Service Object

The Modeling Service Object describes a *range of concepts* required in design tools to model problem areas, guaranteeing that there is *full flexibility* in supporting the design and generation of an arbitrary modeling technique used in IS design activities providing *method integration*, *method modifiability* and *evolution* for future problems and requirements.

Using PSM, the modeling service is described as a tuple *Object Structure*, *Graphic Constraints* and *Interactions*.

Informally an *Object Structure* is a non-empty finite set of *Object types*, which is a finite disjoint union of *Label types*, *Entity types*, *Set types*, *Sequence Types*, *Schema types* and *Relationship types*. *Label types* can be represented directly on a communication medium to provide for properties such as names. A many-sorted algebra *D* instantiates *Label types* and a set of operations. A function *Dom* yields the domains of the *Label types*. *Entity types* depend for their representation on *Labels* and are called abstract object types. *Entity types* are required for the representation of independent objects for example Process in a DFD or an Entity in an ERD. *Set types* are Composite *Object types* which represent the elements of the composition. *Sequence types* represent an ordering in which elements appear in a composition. A function *Elt* yields the Elements of *Set types* and *Sequence types*. *Schema types* which are composite *Object types* are useful to represent meta models of modeling techniques. A relation *schema* describes the Elements in *Schema types*. *Relationship types* consisting of *roles* denote the way *Object types* participate in an association. For example, a *Relationship* is a data flow in a DFD and *roles* define the way in which objects participate in specific *Relationship*. For example, *roles* of a data flow *Relationship* can be 'to' or 'from' part of the flow. A function *Base* specifies that the base of a *role* is the related *Object type*. *Specialization* and *Generalization* are provided as follows: a relation *Spec* on *Object types* express specialization and a relation *Gen* on *Object types* express generalization. The *Graphical Constraints* are a set of commonly occurring constraints that can be represented graphically.

There are 15 such PSM constrains (for details see [Dah97]) associated as constraints of the modeling service. They play an important role in determining the behavior of the method and are vital for defining the flexibility of the environments' method specification service.

The basic *interactions* of the modeling service results in the *addition* of an instance, or *deletion* of an instance of one of the components of *Object Structure* or of *Graphic Constraints*. These actions correspond to the development of a meta model of a method. By doing so, we produce a population of an *Object Structure*, which is again a *Schema* in PSM terms. Figure 3 is an example of a simple DFD meta model designed according to the modeling service.

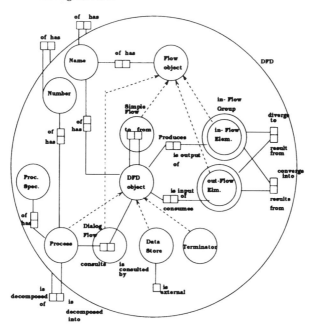

Figure 3: A DFD meta model designed with the use of modeling services

The Meta model Editor has primarily to edit a meta model using the modeling concepts of *Object Structures* and *Graphical Constraints*. The developed models correctness is controlled according to the *Population Derivation Rules*.

3.1.2 User Interface Service Object

This service provides different kinds of host languages or user interfaces to facilitate the variety of representation paradigms such as graphical diagrams, matrices, and tables to provide multiple method support. Most existing CASE tools operate on only one, graphic diagrams. When other representation forms are needed they are generated by some triggered operations that generate a report, or allow the choice of specific tool editors from a tool set which offers only limited syntactic and graphical modifications. Some CAME environments adopt hypertext support for semi-structured and non-structured linking of design objects in different representation formats or models [KLR96]. The graphic object representation supports independent modeling concepts of a method and makes CASE tools adaptable to differing representational demands. Therefore, representationally independent graphic object support is provided with the use of *Graphic Structures, Graphic Constraints* and *Interactions.*

A *Graphic Structure* consists of sets of *Graphic Object types,* a set of *Pointer names,* a relation called *Pointer* that describes which *Pointer types* are assigned to which *Graphic Object types* and a set consisting of *Standard Interaction Object types* to associate object types such as windows, menus, and editors, which provide the overall interaction for the *Graphic Structures.* A function *Representation* is used to denote the instantiation of *Graphic Object types.* A function *Graf* is defined as relating to the *meta model level Object types* and *Graphic Object types* forming the relationship between the modeling concept and its graphical shape. Generalized Object types are not assigned a Graphic Object type, and the graphic representation of a subtype is determined by the representation of associated pater familas; therefore, the subtypes are not assigned a Graphic Object type. A function *Graf_Inst* is defined at the *application level* to relate *meta model level object instances* to *graphic object instances.* Object instances that occur in the instantiation of non-generalized Object type have a common Graphic Object. A function *Pointer_Instance* is defined to realize the actual assignment of a set of points to specific pointer instances.

The *Graphic Constraints* of *Graphic Structures* allow the specification of constraints over *pointer types* to provide *positioning rules.*

The basic *interactions* of this service results in *Standard interactions* of the form Open, Close, Delete and New which operate on *Standard Interaction Object types* and, *Addition* or *deletion* of *Graphic Object types* and their respective *Graphic Constraints.*

The user interface of the CAME environment is based on layers of interfaces (see figure 4). The highest layer called the MAIN is provided for the user to communicate with the tool using menus. When MAIN is started, a menu will appear on the screen with some items to choose from: Repository, Population, Representation, Hide, Quite etc. The Repository item gives access to the Meta model Editor. The Population item gives access to the Population Editor and the Representation item gives access to the Tool Editor. The top part of the MAIN window shows the type of the next level editors and an image to indicate the MAIN. There are two types of editors that can be activated from the MAIN: *Object structures* (OSE) and *Task Structures* (TSE). A Group Editor (GED) can be created by dragging and dropping the OSE_icon on to the bottom part of the repository window. Similarly by dragging and dropping the GED_icon number of DED's can be created for editing meta models. A Diagram Editor (DED) provides the graphical interface to meta model editor. Since the modeling service object already takes care of methodical constraints, DEDs need to be concerned only with the *Graphic Structures* and *Graphic Constraints,* and the mapping of user actions for providing *User Interface Service.*

3.1.3 Storage and Manipulation Service Object

When design tools are developed, well defined *storage* specifications are required to store such models. Such stored data needs to be *accessed and manipulated* with a suitable *query facility.* This service *Storage and Manipulation Structure* is described in LISA-D (Language for Information Structure and Access Description) [Hof93] and fulfills all the requirements for the generation of data populations of all types of models, and a query facility for manipulation of such data. The basic *interactions* are defined as the LISA-D *updates* and *assignments.* All the data of the Meta model Editor will be stored in a central Repository. This central repository should supply a

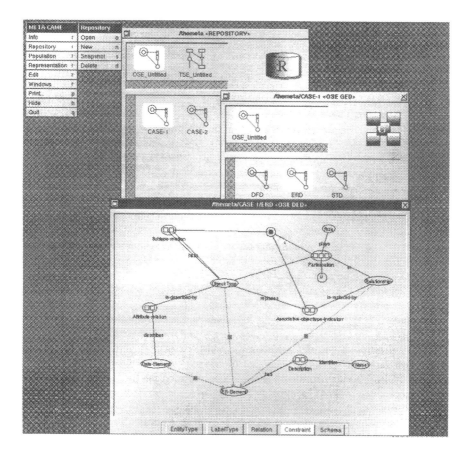

Figure 4: The Meta model Editor's User Interface Structure

simple *store-query-add-delete-read* mechanism providing facilitates for the developed models and modeling components to be stored and manipulated as described under the *Storage and Manipulation Service Object*.

3.1.4 Integrity and Consistency Service Object

When data is created, be it tools' meta models or operational models, this service provides the *Transaction* definitions and supports the process of information passing, and the maintainance of the overall integrity and consistency of the CAME database. This service is defined as an *Integrity and Consistency Structure* using the *Transaction* definition based on Task Structures [Hof93] as the nature of this process needs concepts capturing dynamic aspects of activities involved in these services. The basic *interactions* of this service are *Atomic* and *Nested Transactions* that express the process dependencies via *transaction tasks*.

3.1.5 View Service Object

In a CAME environment one has to deal with different levels of data (meta-meta, meta, data, operation) to support multiple methods and integration of models and data. Therefore, the CAME environment needs to be able to support view definition and its manipulation, and to provide a multi-tool and multi-user support.

View definition at different levels is an important aspect for such integrated development activities. The view definition service is involved mainly in definition of PSM Schemas. The populations of Schema Type are valid instances of a Schema. In this way it is possible to define views at type level as a meta model of a tool, and at the instance level as the data model designed by that specific tool. Both these views are, by definition, populations of PSM Schemas. Since view is a Schema type, it can have, by definition, overlapping compositions, it can be combined, and it can have generalization as well as specialization hierarchies. View manipulation is concerned with the creation of views to represent meta models of tools. It requires dynamic changing of the representations of modeling concepts to arrive at the required diagrammatic representation. The concept of *View Structure* is introduced as an environment has to keep track of the defined views.

The *view structure* consists of: A set *View type*, where it's *Object Structure* is derived from the *Schema type* it relates to, because each meta as well as data model of a method is a population of a *Schema type*, and it is also a view of the modeling primitives needed for a specific method; and a set *View* containing the associated Schema restricted to *Object types* in *View type*. Views defined on shared data need to be maintained for consistency of overall data of the repository. This is apparently handled under the derivation rules of *Schema type* defined for *Object Structures*. Therefore by considering a view as a *Schema type* we do not have to consider special types of constraints for views. This consideration provides the opportunities for defining multiple tools, as well as multiple user support.

The basic *interactions* of the view service results in the *addition* or *deletion* of a meta or data model view. These actions correspond to the definition of an *View Structure* that is associated with the *Object Structure* population of the modeling service.

3.2 The Population Editor

The *Population* item in the MAIN gives access to the instance generation part of the CAME environment. The editor is started by selecting the *Edit Population* item in this *Population* sub menu (see figure 4). The main part of the Population Editors can be reached through the *Edit Population* button. When a new object is selected the *Pop Editor* and *Add Instance Dialog* windows are updated automatically.

The population Editor extends the kernel object model of the Meta model Editor to support generation of populations. The important architectural building blocks extensions are as follows: the *Storage and Manipulation Structure* is provided with an *Object browser* enabling the user to select Object types that need to be populated and gives access to all objects in the active repository defined under a meta model. An object *PopManager* is required to store an object's population and to provide access to it. Each type of object that may be populated has its own type of PopManager, because each type of object needs different services from its PopManager. The *Graphic Structure* is extended with a *Pop editor* that allows the user to add instances to database populations and with an *Instance dialog* to provide basic update interactions. The

Integrity and Consistency Structure is extended with an object *PopManContrMPoint* for taking over the information passing process and an *Instance Validation checker* to maintain consistency according to *pre- post conditions*.

3.3 The Tool Editor

The item *Representation* of the *MAIN* menu gives access to the components of the Tool Editor. The Tool Editor supports the binding of visual representations to the meta model components to arrive at the necessary representational requirements according to the specified modeling technique. This stage is simply the generation of CASE tools. The Tool Editor extends the *graphic Structure* for this purpose by providing: A *Library of Graphic Objects* containing the required Graphical representations according to the specifications of the modeling technique. An editor *Edit Representation* for selecting the required meta model of the CASE Tool. An editor *Select Representation* for selecting and binding graphic objects to modeling concepts described under the meta model of the modeling technique. The required Graphic representation can be typed or selected with the use of the *Help* button that gives access to a browser which provides a visualization of the available Graphic Object types. *Draw Representation* for selecting the required CASE tool and to assign a name. A *Diagram Editor* with a PopUpList that acts as the required CASE tool (see figure 5).

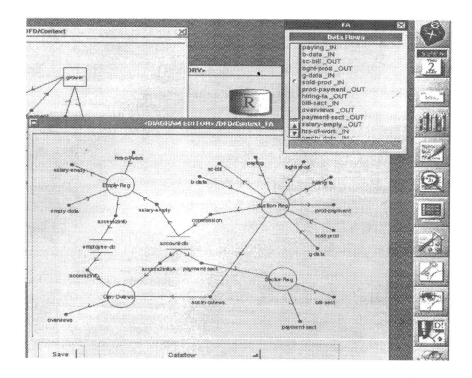

Figure 5: A Diagram Editor window

3.4 Discussion and Conclusions

The lack of tailorable automate support at the level of the information systems design stage according to the information modeling needs of a problem situation continues to pose a considerable challenge to both academics and practitioners. This paper outlines how a CAME environment prototype was designed to deal with this situation. A platform has been developed to try out a tool construction principle based on high level specification of methods with a powerful, easy to use method specification language. The environment is represented as a configuration of service objects representing the major functionalities of information design activities. The specifications of these service objects are used as the architectural building blocks of the prototype. The mapping of service object architecture to an object-oriented technology that has demonstrated the possibility of using an object-oriented architecture to design and implement a MetaCASE tool that can function as a CAME environment. The prototype, which is based on the service object base theory, demonstrated that it is possible to develop an automated method engineering environment for information systems design work by mapping the service object description into an available object oriented technology. A Number of tests were conducted using case studies to evaluate the theory and its technical feasibility.

The first test case was the designing of an information architecture for the Financial and Administration sector of the Dutch Flower Auction. The expert involved in this project was a final year masters student who decided to use the YOURDON's [You89] systems design and analysis approach. The first series of tests involved designing and development of simple ERD, DFD and STD meta models as well as producing data models of the problem using the CAME environment. In the second series of tests we increased the number of modeling concepts as well as the constraints of the DFD and ERD meta models and found that the environment is extremely flexible in supporting the process of modeling. In a third series of tests the three techniques; ERD, DFD and STDs were integrated and tests were carried out to check the integration of these three methods at the meta model integration level. These tests proved that the environment was extremely flexible for generating these common methods and for method integration. The use of the meta-meta model allows the environment to become flexible and gives an ability to evolve the specification of the process of modeling and its use in a manner not found in any other CAME environment.

The second test case was the designing of an Object model of the automobile map system using the OMT method [RBP+91]. The three techniques Object Modeling, Dynamic Modeling and Functional Modeling were generated according to the method specifications given in [RBP+91]. The flexibility of the environment in supporting OO modeling techniques was tested. A number of repositories were created and within each repository a number of groups were created using a GED, with each group in a GED giving access to three DEDs with the meta models of Object Model, Dynamic Model and Functional Model with a slightly varying composition of meta models along the groups in GED and along the Repository, creating a number of Object Models, Dynamic Models and Functional Models. Again each method specification was used to develop a number of data models at the data modeling level. The results showed this multi-user and multi-tool support provided successful consistency control, where the changes within one group are propagated, and indicated directions for an effective concurrency control facility.

The third test case was used to test the ability of the environment to support an uncommon arbitrary modeling approach. For this the modeling approach DEMO

(Dynamic Essential Modeling of Environments) [Die96] was chosen to model the transactions of the communication processes required for a hotel's booking and reception facilities. The techniques, Communication Modeling and Process Modeling were generated and models were designed for this particular case study. The unusual modeling style as well as the concepts were supported successfully by the CAME environment and proved its ability to support an arbitrary modeling technique.

The modeling tools required to structure the production process of three large production organizations were generated in the fourth test case[Vro96]. This was conducted first by modeling the schema description of the the the production process and generating six tools to represent the data in the required form. These six tools were 0-IDEF schema that has a close resemblance to SADT modeling technique, three types of tree structures(Organization structure, Activity structure and Information structure) and two types of matrices (Create-use and Task distribution). The database was populated with the real information from the production processes of these organizations and each database contained around 2500 object instances. Performance was low but reliable, as the experiment was conducted with an index structure instead of an OO database. This experiment proved the ability of the environment to support multi-methods and reinforced the method integration claim and showed a reliable information retrieval and computational facility. At the same time the degree of representation independence was shown by providing, O-IDEF graphic representation as well as matrices and tree structures. The novel method specification and generation mechanism answered the needs of the highly diverse representational paradigms and information processing needs which are demanded of systems engineering environments.

The service object based architecture which separates the conceptual specification and the representational differences of tools conveys a high level object-oriented application program interface for tool repository interactions. The integrity and consistency of repository data during concurrent access by different tools is guaranteed in the architectural specifications of the environment. The meta meta model of this environment can be used as the basis for the future evolution of CASE environments, which can lead to fully automated support along the phases of information systems development. We are at present working on adding incremental functionality as service objects to the CASE environment and working towards full life-cycle support in systems development.

To conclude, this research has addressed many flaws found in current CAME environments and has introduced a basis for a common terminology to allow useful scientific and commercial initiatives to take place. In this respect this paper provides a major paradigmatic revision of how CASE environments are conceived and implemented providing considerable benefits for systems designers with the easily adaptable generic services that adequately address flexible support for information systems design activities.

References

[ANS75]   ANSI. Study Group on Data Base Management Systems: Interim Report 75-02-08. Technical Report 7(2), ACM SIGMOND Newsletter, 1975.

[BCM+94]   A.W. Brown, D.J. Carney, E.J. Morris, D.B. Smith, and P.F. Zarrella. *Principles of CASE tool Integration*. Oxford University Press, New York, 1994.

[BEM92]   A.W. Brown, A.N. Earl, and J.A. McDermid. *Software Engineering Environments. Automated Support for Software Engineering.* The McGraw-Hill, 1992.

[Dah97]   A.N.W. Dahanayake. *An Environment to Support Flexible Information Systems Modeling.* PhD thesis, Delft University of Technology, The Netherlands, 1997.

[DBFW92] A. Dahanayake, J. Bosman, G. Florijn, and R.J. Welke. A Framework for Modelling Repositories. In *Proceedings of the 3rd Workshop On NEXT Generation of CASE Tools*, Manchester, UK, May 1992.

[Die96]   J.L.G. Dietz. *Introductie tot DEMO : van informatietechnologie naar organisatietechnologie.* Samsom, 1996.

[Hof93]   A.H.M. ter Hofstede. *Information Modelling in Data Intensive Domains.* PhD thesis, Katholic University of Nijmegen, The Netherlands, 1993.

[HVWN92] A.H.M. ter Hofstede, T.F. Verhoef, G.M. Wijers, and E.R. Nieuwland. Specification of Graphical Conventions in Methods. In *Proceedings of the Next Generation of CASE Tools*, 1992.

[IBM89]   IBM. *Systems Application Architecture - AD/Cycle Concepts*, first edition, September 1989.

[ISO90]   ISO/IEC. Information Resource Dictionary System Framework, 1990.

[KLR96]   S. Kelly, K. Lyytinen, and M. Rossi. MetaEdit+ A fully Configurable Multi-User and Multi-Tool CASE and CAME Environment. In *Proc. of 8th International Conference CAiSE'96, Advanced Information Systems Engineering*, Greece, June 1996. Springer-Verlag.

[RBP+91] J. Rumbaugh, M. Blaha, W. Premerlani, F. Eddy, and W. Lorensen. *Object-Oriented Modeling and Design.* Prentice-Hall, 1991.

[Ver93]   T.F. Verhoef. *Effective Information Modelling Support.* PhD thesis, Delft University of Technology, Delft, The Netherlands, 1993.

[Vro96]   R.W. Vroom. A general example model for automotive suppliers of the development process and its related information. *Computers in industry*, (31):255–280, 1996.

[Was90]   A. Wasserman. Tool Integration in Software Environments. In F. Long, editor, *Software Engineering Environments. Lecture Notes in Computer Science*, number 467, pages 138–150, Berlin,Germany, June 1990.

[Wij91]   G.M. Wijers. *Modelling Support in Information Systems Development.* PhD thesis, Delft University of Technology, Delft, The Netherlands, 1991.

[WKvD91] R.J. Welke, K. Kumar, and H.G. van Dissel. Methodology Engineering: een voorstel om te komen tot situationeel specifiek method-ontwikkeling. *Informatie*, 33(5):322–328, 1991.

[You89]   E. Yourdon. *Modern Structured Analysis.* Prentice-Hall, Englewood Cliffs, New Jersey, 1989.

A Rapid Development Model for Meta-CASE Tool Design

Maokai Gong, Louise Scott, Yingping Xiao, and Ray Offen

CSIRO-Macquarie University Joint Research Center
for Advanced Systems Engineering
Macquarie University, Sydney, NSW 2109, Australia
e-mail: gmk@mpce.mq.edu.au

Abstract. This paper presents a rapid development model for meta-CASE (Computer Aided Software Engineering) toolset design that can be customised to specific CASE tools. In this model, we address the methodology customisation through direct graph manipulation. Rapid prototyping modelling is employed to support this design with an easy to learn and use Graphic User Interface (GUI). It also emphasizes the ability to be an integrated platform for users to dynamically plug their own functionality into existing tools. Large and complex methodologies and projects can be supported due to the hierarchical design mechanism and flexible type definition method of the model. The use of powerful GUI classes of the model can greatly lighten developer work load. Through the implementation, our design model is verified and the results are satisfactory.

1 Introduction

Meta-CASE tools are software tools that support the design and generation of CASE tools[1]. In general, meta-CASE tools should provide generic CASE tool components that can be customised and instantiated into particular CASE tools. The intent of meta-CASE tools is to capture the specification of the required CASE tool and then generate the tool from the specification[2]. Meta-CASE tools address the particular needs of organisations, projects and individuals without the high cost of building customised CASE tools from scratch.

There are three important aspects that need to be addressed in a meta-CASE tool. They are the repository, the GUI, and the functionality of CASE tools. The repository must be customisable to support data structures for capturing design information, the GUI should be able to support user defined representations for design data via various graph-driven tools, and it should be possible to add or customise the functionality of the tools to the customers' needs. In this paper we concentrate on the last two aspects to provide a customisable meta-CASE tool design environment. We call it MetaBuilder.

Some commercial meta-CASE products are available now. Before our project started, several popular meta-CASE research projects and tools[1–8] were analysed. Generally speaking, most of these meta-CASE tools have some common functions. They

1. support a variety of object modeling, software process and method notation.
2. employ a language-based specification notation for describing the iconic syntax and composition semantics of the Software Design Methodology (SDM) supported in the target tools.
3. allow the specification or redefinition of user interface functionality.
4. support at least one design editor (graph editor) for which strong graph editing functions are provided. Some of them have graphical, table, and matrix editors to cater for various user's demands.
5. provide multiple layouts of graphic information.

On the other hand, most of them also have some common weaknesses:

1. The possibility for method customisation based on graphical modelling is limited, comparing to the text-based environments[8]. The field of conceptual modelling is well established and has therefore provided sound principles for the modelling of concepts, but the field of graphics has not provided similar principles for graphical modelling. Software engineers must integrate user interface development and modern software development within the context of a unified methodology. Because diagrams give a concise and accessible means of describing a methodology the graphical modelling must be addressed in a meta-CASE tool design.
2. They are hard to learn and use. meta-CASE tool users, especially those from the application domains often complain that meta-CASE is a complex technique. They have to spend a long time studying not only the meta-CASE tools but also the principles of design methods before they can use these tools to design their own projects. They find that the GUI of current meta-CASE tools are rigid, sophisticated, and cannot shorten their study periods. The quality of meta-CASE GUI is an important part of meta-CASE tools and is considered to be one of the areas in which current tools are deficient.
3. They have very limited ability to let users add their own functionality. A meta-CASE tool cannot be expected to have all the functionality needed by every specific CASE project. Also when a new tool is generated, in order to support a specific methodology, it is necessary to have knowledge about the designed component and their relationships (what should it look like?) on the one hand, and about the underlying modelling process (how should it work?) on the other. As the result, sometimes users must add new functionality which is developed by themselves or the third party products to address special needs. A good meta-CASE toolset, as an integrated platform, must have strong "plug and play" ability to extend itself.

MetaBuilder is not designed to address every issue in Meta-CASE research and provide all functionality possible in CASE tools. Instead, our research work focuses on the above problems and tries to find a new solution, and verifies the power of our hypernode data model supporting software methodology design.

In Sect. 2, after the research issues are discussed, the concept model of MetaBuilder is presented. From Sect. 3 to 5, the details of the model are described. Finally, the implementation of MetaBuilder and the conclusions are given in Sect. 6.

2 The Architecture of MetaBuilder

2.1 Graphic Hypernode Data Model

MetaBuilder is built on a graphic hypernode data model developed by ourselves. The detail description of graphic hypernode theory can be found in some papers[9, 10]. In summary, the graphic hypernode data model supports:

1. nested directed-graphs for storing both methodological information and design information. All information is stored in hypernodes as either nodes or edges.
2. unique node labelling mechanism so that one node in a database has only one name but may have many different visual representation in different tools.
3. powerful HyperNode Query Language (HNQL) and interface classes for querying and manipulating hypernode structures.
4. strong ability for capturing semantics by well designed type definition.

A Hypernode/Edge Type is an abstraction of a group of hypernodes/edges which have the same symbolic representations, semantic specifications and constraints. On the one hand, every hypernode or edge must be an instance of a specific hypernode/edge type and every hypernode can be defined as a type and be given specifications and constraints again. A diagram of hypernodes and edges is a hypernode and can be defined as a new hypernode type as well. On the other hand, a hypernode type is a hypernode. A diagram of hypernode type is also a hypernode and can be a hypernode type again. The significance of such a definition is that it provides a very flexible way to define a sophisticated methodology. In contrast, in many current tools mentioned in section 1, an object can be a property of another object but an existing property can not be extended to an object.

The hypernode type level defines the ways how information modelling processes may be performed and which products may result from those information modelling processes. The hypernode level is an instantiation of the type level. It concerns on the information which results from CASE tools for specific CASE applications.

2.2 Research Issues

Our research work concentrates on the following issues of meta-CASE tool development environment design:

1. Support methodology customisation through graph manipulation rather than script language or forms. Every design methodology should have its own notations and rules governing the graphical display of design information. A customisable GUI must support the user definition of methodological notations and rules.

2. The development of a rapid CASE tool design environment which can maximum lighten user's design work. There is no re-compilation needed for new CASE tool development. Results of design can be incorporated and seen immediately. This makes the tool easy to understand and use by both information engineers and application engineers, shortening their learning periods and creating their specific CASE tools quickly. Using this approach users can focus on their task rather than study the usage of meta-CASE tool.

3. The design of an integrated platform for users to plug their own functionality (programs) into MetaBuilder. This means new functionality, new GUI components, and even third party products can be added into MetaBuilder without re-compiling the whole system. Such new artefacts become parts of MetaBuilder and can be used in new CASE tool design immediately.

4. Incremental extension of MetaBuilder. There are no pre-defined symbols, design components, methodologies, or CASE tools in the MetaBuilder repository at the initial state. As CASE tools are created, any symbol, design component, or functionality created for them remains in repository for use in other CASE tools. In this way MetaBuilder gradually increase its abilities as a meta-CASE tool and encourages reuse of CASE concepts and tailoring of previously defined concepts, rather than complete redefinition of commonly used concepts.

5. The desire to provide a consistent GUI design mechanism, style, generic and powerful GUI classes. Unlike other tools in which the methodologies and specific project diagrams are developed in separate environments, a unique graph editor can be used for both development. The GUI classes should be powerful enough to cater for various design requirements for CASE tool design. Users can directly call these classes when they develop their own functions that can greatly lighten their developing burden.

6. Hierarchical design mechanism and flexible type definition. Through hierarchical object-oriented design, users can break their complex task into simpler sub-tasks and can work more effectively. MetaBuilder should provide flexible navigation functions to let users create and view a hierarchically designed repository easily.

The conceptual model of MetaBuilder is developed to cater for above requirements.

2.3 The Conceptual Model of MetaBuilder

Fig. 1 shows the conceptual model of MetaBuilder. MetaBuilder interacts with a hypernode repository for data storage. The hypernode conceptual model is a key part of our meta-CASE tool, but it only handles the data storage component whereas MetaBuilder handles tool environment construction. The repository and MetaBuilder are connected by a graphical hypernode data access interface layer which means that CASE tools built by MetaBuilder access the repository only through this layer. This results in a simple interface between the two.

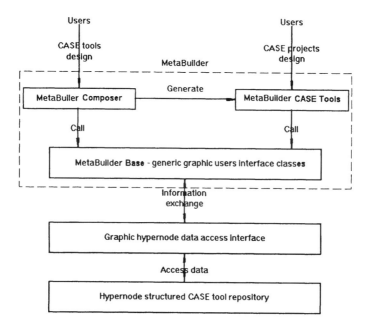

Fig. 1. The conceptual model of MetaBuilder

MetaBuilder is based on an object-oriented design paradigm. Important principles of object-oriented design, especially encapsulation and inheritance that encourage reuse and customisation of components and concepts, are well suited to this kind of project. Hence MetaBuilder consists of a collection of object-oriented classes and tools for customising to particular CASE tools.

MetaBuilder comprises three major parts:

1. MetaBuilder Base: a group of generic GUI classes that can be reused by all CASE tools. These classes provide links to the meta-CASE tool repository as well as have strong functionality for the graphical manipulations of design information.

2. MetaBuilder Composer: built on the MetaBuilder Base, provides several integrated tools that can be used together to develop specific CASE tools interactive and rapidly. A prototype CASE tool is provided for users to customise to a new one. Users can add their own functionality to the tool to cater for different applications.

3. CASE Tools: created by using MetaBuilder. The CASE tools can be modified again via MetaBuilder even as they are being used.

In the following sections the details of these three parts of MetaBuilder will be presented respectively.

3 MetaBuilder Base

The MetaBuilder Base has three major functions:

1. It separates the MetaBuilder from the underlying hypernode structured repository. In this way users need not to know the internal structure of the database. New tools are added into MetaBuilder by calling these generic classes.
2. These generic GUI classes can be used by all design tools to provide maximum GUI components reuse. The tools built on the MetaBuilder Base can share design resources and work cooperatively.
3. Every tool should only concern its own work and let the MetaBuilder Base control the consistency of information access, exchange, and display in every tool and every work window in the tools.

In MetaBuilder Base design, we focus on two important issues:

1. Separate the concept aspect from the graphical aspect in these classes. In MetaBuilder Base the concept part of a class describes the conceptual attributes of a class - data and some operations which do not relate to visual aspect of the class, whilst the graphical part describes how an object can be seen or operated through the GUI. Only the graphical part relies on specific GUI developing tools on various system platforms while the concept part is written in standard C++ language. As the result the modification of one part does not affect another.
2. Make these classes more generic and more flexible to provide the best reuse. Users should not build their CASE GUI (menus, dialogues, tables, and matrix) from such basic components as a button, a text field, a scroll bar, or so on. The MetaBuilder Base classes should be at higher level. They are really customisable CASE tool GUI components. These classes should be customised and overridden to give different appearances and reactions. Users can also use the combination of these classes to finish very complex interactive design.

MetaBuilder Base comprises five generic class sets: document classes, widget classes, edit classes, view classes, and control classes.

1. Document classes are responsible for the temporary storage of information and transfer between MetaBuilder tools and the hypernode structured repository. MetaBuilder tools call document classes for the information stored in the repository, then document classes transfer information by loading it from the database and mapping it to the format which can be understood and used by tools. On the other hand, tools save their data by calling document classes to map these data into the format which hypernode data structure can accept and store.
2. Widget classes comprise the generic GUI components such as windows, menus, dialogues, toolbar, their combination, and etc. These classes can

be reused by tools through inheriting these classes and setting different attributes so that a quite different appearance can be realised from one widget. Some special widgets, such as generic node type dialogue, symbol drawing editor, user defined function palette, CASE tool palette, textual table, and matrix, are also included in widget classes. Users can build their own interface for specific functionality by customising these generic widgets that will greatly lighten their GUI developing burden.

3. Edit classes are responsible for the graph manipulation of all CASE tools. Some generic edit functions, which are supposed suitable for most CASE tools (eg. select, highlight, cut, copy, paste, zoom, move, grid, multi-layer layout, mouse and cursor control, and so on), were carefully selected. These edit functions can be considered generic for various applications because our graphic operations base on hypernode structure which is also suitable for textual table and matrix structures.

4. View classes are responsible for the graphic representations of nodes and edges on various graphical windows and text on various textual windows. Every graphic hypernode can have different graphic representation (eg. different positions, size, and color) on different tool windows for different purposes, so view classes are specially designed to cater for this. When a window is covered by other windows and exposed again, or a window is moved/scaled, view classes are also responsible for redrawing the diagrams in the window.

5. Control classes maintain all opened windows in all tools, save necessary information about these windows, maintain the process sequence of these windows, and control the consistency of information displayed in every tool and every window. When a user modifies the content in one window and saves it, control classes will analyse the changes and instruct all related windows to modify their display. For example, if a node's graphical representation is changed, control classes will be called to inform all windows to change the shape of related node.

The information transfer among these classes is described in Fig. 2.

4 MetaBuilder Composer

Being a generic CASE tool builder, MetaBuilder Composer comprises several editors and tools for designing new CASE tools. These tools are Hypernode Type Editor, Edge Type Editor, Symbol Editor, type checking function, User Defined Function Editor and Repository Navigator.

4.1 Hypernode/Edge Type Editor

Hypernode Type Editor provides functionality to create, view, and modify the types of hypernodes stored in the repositories. Examples of them may be 'Data Flow Diagram', containing 'Process' and 'Data Store' nodes, or 'Class Diagram', containing 'Class' nodes.

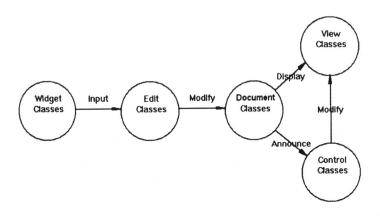

Fig. 2. Information flows within MetaBuilder Base

Edge Type Editor provides functionality to create, view, and modify the types of edge which manage connections between nodes in diagrams. Examples of these edge types are 'Flow' in Data Flow Diagrams, or 'Message Connection' in Object Diagrams.

A hypernode/edge type should comprise at least a Name (label) to uniquely identify this type and an Attached Symbol to show the graphic features of this type. These two components are necessary for any hypernode/edge type. Then there are several selectable properties that can be used for further description. They are Behaviours, Constraints, and Description. The Behaviours component provides an interface for users to assign some activities to the type if this kind of hypernode/edge is selected and focuses on the internal activities of a hypernode. The Constraints component focuses on the relationship of one node with other nodes and diagrams, such as cardinality (how many times this type of node can appear in a kind of diagram), outDegree and inDegree (how many times this type of node can connect to another specific type of node in a kind of diagram) and so on.

4.2 Symbol Editor

Symbol Editor specifies notations that are used to distinguish the graphic representation of each hypernode/edge type from others. MetaBuilder allows alternative equivalent notations for one modelling concept. On the other hand similar graphical and textual topologies can represent different types of modelling concepts. The symbol library maintains the storage and reuse of defined symbols. Symbol Editor defines the abstract topological arrangement of graphic primitives (eg. 'Line', 'PolyLine', 'Circle', 'Curve', 'Rectangle', 'RoundRectangle', 'Arrow', and 'Text') which are assigned to this symbol, and how this graphic information will be viewed in CASE tools.

There are two types of symbols: node type symbols and edge type symbols corresponding to hypernode type and edge type respectively. The design of them are somewhat different.

The key issue is that no restriction should be given on how these graphic primitives can be arranged and connected to form a symbol. Users simply draw various primitives showing the possible shape of a node/edge, then the graph vector features should be automatically extracted and saved in a symbol library by Symbol Editor. But how can we extract these graph vector features automatically? For a hypernode type symbol, it may be very complex and scalable. For an edge type symbol, its 'edge' (maybe 'PloyLine' or 'Curve') direction and length should be changeable. What is more, sometimes there are one or two small widgets such as 'Arrow' or 'Dot' attached at the ends or middle of an edge. These widgets must keep good connection with the 'edge' no matter what changes happen to the 'edge'. Fig. 3 explains the above problem.

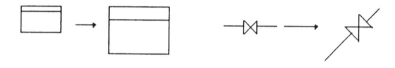

Fig. 3. Demonstration of the changes of symbols

An algorithm was developed to solve this problem. For edge type symbol, the drawn primitives are divided into extendable ('edge') and unextendable (widgets). The positions (ends or middle of an 'edge') and angles of these widgets connected to the edge are calculated. This information is extracted when users draw the sample figures via symbol editor and stored in the repository. When an edge is being drawn in a diagram the information will be recalculated according to current positions and angles of the edge.

4.3 Type Checking

We explore the use of typing to check whether the structural and behavioural constraints may be expressed and maintained in MetaBuilder. Unlike instantiation, these operations simply map a source hypernode to a target one, the type checking can help to check whether the structural relationships contained in the target diagram (project diagram designed by specific methodology) satisfy the constraints of the source diagram (methodology).

The type definition diagram is employed to define what hypernode types and edge types make up the artefacts in the methodology and the rules governing the way these artefacts relate to each other. These artefacts can also be type definition diagrams. Every hypernode may have different constraints in different methodologies. This provides a better way to portray the relationship among these artefacts.

4.4 User Defined Function Editor

The User Defined Function Editor provides an interface that lets users easily add their own functionality to MetaBuilder Composer (and generated CASE tools). Users can do some programming to add new functionality to realise specific semantic descriptions and graphic simulation for a specific methodology. MetaBuilder Composer provides sockets to let users plug in their new programs. The reason for this is that we do not intend to develop a full functionality meta-CASE tool, and actually, we could not do that because we can not predict all the requirements users propose. 'Plug and play' functionality will give users the chance to integrate their own programs into MetaBuilder. These new functions should be dynamically linked by their name and used during run time. They can be written in a different language and can call our MetaBuilder Base GUI classes and graphic hypernode classes. New GUI components, such as new dialogues and toolbars can also be added to the MetaBuilder Composer.

In implementation the Microsoft Dynamic Link Library (DLL) technique is used in our MetaBuilder to dynamically link users' function library (DLL files). A user defined function palette with customisable buttons is provided as a socket for users to plug their own functions in (attaching a function to a specific button). The information about user defined functions (eg. the names of function and DLL file) is stored in the repository and will be checked when the specific button is pushed. Then the executable function is dynamically loaded into memory and run. Users also can change the bitmap on every button using any image editor. Different CASE tools may have different user defined functions. So the user defined function palette changes automatically when a different CASE tool is selected.

4.5 Repository Navigator

The Repository Navigator is a tool for viewing and editing the contents of the repository and for presenting various project related design information to the users in different formats. The heart of the meta-CASE tool is the repository. All information in the meta-CASE tool is stored in the repository, including methods, diagrams, matrices, objects, properties, and even colour selection in a unique data structure. When the repository is very large, an effective navigator is necessary for the user. The navigator must be easily understood and operated. Navigation from diagram to diagram, diagram to text, text to diagram and text to text is supported.

4.6 The Integration of Editors

MetaBuilder Composer has an effective prototype CASE tool for users to customise. Several editors are seamlessly integrated into this prototype tool that supports new CASE tool creation. With this prototype CASE tool, users who have little experience with meta-CASE can easily and quickly design their own CASE tools. What is more, MetaBuilder Composer lets users know their design results and use these results immediately, so it is a true rapid prototyping approach.

Users create a new CASE tool by using the following design procedures:

1. Use existing CASE tools if their is one suitable for their project. If existing tools do not satisfy their requirements, do the next steps.
2. Design the necessary graphic symbols for the notation that will be used in the new CASE tool via the Symbol Editor.
3. Create the necessary hypernode types and edge types via Hypernode/Edge Type Editors and attach specific symbols to these types to show their graphic representation in diagrams. These types are added to the repository for use in other CASE tools as well as the one being created now.
4. Customise any existing CASE tool (or prototype tool) by adding the necessary hypernode/edge types from the repository and removing some unnecessary types from the existing tool to form a new CASE tool.
5. Draw the type definition diagram (methodology) using the hypernode and edge types selected. Through this hierarchical diagram, the structural relationship and rules of all design artefacts (types) involved in this methodology can be well defined. This information will be used to check the structures of design diagrams produced by this CASE tool.
6. This new CASE tool is now functional and can be used to create design diagrams immediately. Diagrams can be checked against the type definition diagram using the type checking facility automatically whenever a new design component is added.
7. Nodes in a diagram can be decomposed into sub-diagrams in a hierarchical fashion. In this way, large and complex projects can be defined and effectively managed.
8. If desired, add new functionality or tools to the new CASE tool by dynamically linking the user's own function library via User Defined Function Editor. These new functions can be used immediately.

The above scenario describes the use of MetaBuilder as a fast prototyping tool for creating methodology specific CASE tools. It is also envisaged that for more sophisticated projects (such as those within our own research centre), the meta-CASE toolset can be used as a component library to build CASE tool support. Utilising the object-oriented design, new CASE components could be derived from the tool components and new functionality could be added. Much development effort on user interface and database aspects could be saved.

5 Prototype CASE Tool

Prototype CASE Tool is the first CASE tool created by MetaBuilder. It can be used for hypernode model based projects design and can be customised to a new

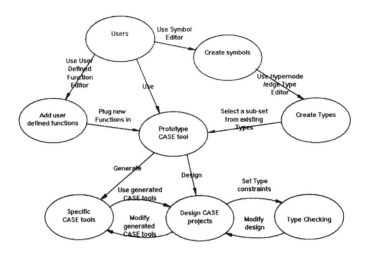

Fig. 4. Integration of editors in MetaBuilder Composer

CASE tool. Several editors are integrated into it seamless so that these editors can be used together to create new CASE tools. It provides various kinds of generic functions to cater for a wide range of methodological notations.

The prototype CASE tool comprises the following generic functions which may be used by every CASE tool.

1. several data input/output functions such as New, Open, Save, Close, and Print diagrams or a CASE tool.
2. general graph edit functions for editing nodes and edges such as Copy, Cut, Paste, and Del.
3. diagram explosion functions to form multi-layer hierarchical structures (nested graphs).
4. general viewing functions for whole or parts of diagrams, such as Zoom In/Out, set Grid, Snap, Show/Hide some GUI components and some parts of the diagram.
5. several editors, such as Symbol Editor, Hypernode Type Editor, Edge Type Editor, Type Constraint Editor, CASE Tool Editor, User Defined Function Editor, Type Checking tool, and Navigator are integrated seamless.

The prototype CASE tool is not only a real CASE tool itself and provides generic functions suitable for all CASE tools, but a visual demonstration for how to create a CASE tool to new user of MetaBuilder. Whenever users want to create a new CASE tool, rather than customise an existing one, this prototype CASE tool is automatically generated by MetaBuilder for users to customise. Users can create their own CASE tool (methodology) by simply changing the content of the CASE tool palette, designing a type definition diagram, and hooking users' own functions to the user defined function palette. Users manipulate their design directly on the tool they are customising and see the result of their every modification immediately. So it provides the simplest and easiest way to create a new tool.

6 Conclusions

MetaBuilder is implemented on IBM PC platform, under Windows NT3.51, with Visual C++4.0 and Versant database, totalling about 20,000 source code lines. Our hypernode data model, which is not introduced in this paper, is built on Versant, an object-oriented database. Through the implementation, our research proposals are verified and the results are satisfactory. All figures shown in this paper are drawn by MetaBuilder itself.

Fig. 5 shows the implemented interface of a customised CASE tool. The CASE tool bar at the left side contains the necessary hypernode/edge types for this CASE tool. The palette near the right-top corner is the user defined function palette.

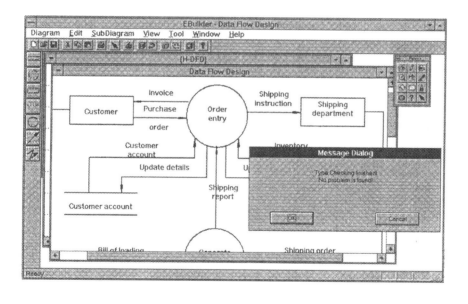

Fig. 5. The implemented interface of a customised CASE tool

MetaBuilder is a generic graph-driven CASE tool builder provided for users to develop their own CASE tools, software development methodologies, and CASE projects. MetaBuilder is not a full functionality MetaCASE tool. We are, however, extending its functionality by cooperating with several research projects which are processing in our centre. This kind of integration will enrich MetaBuilder functionality and verify our design methodology further.

In the approach of MetaBuilder, we address some important issues in meta-CASE tool design: methodology costumisation through direct graph manipulation, rapid prototyping modelling with an easy to learn and use GUI, the ability to be an integrated platform for users to dynamic plug their own functionality into existing tools, and the support for large and complex methodology and project design via the hierarchical design mechanism and flexible type definition method.

References

1. Bashar Nuseibeh: Meta-CASE support for method-based software development. Proc. of 1st Int. Congress on Meta-CASE, Sunderland, UK, January (1995)
2. Albert Alderson: Meta-CASE technology. Lecture Notes in Computer Science, Software Development Environments & CASE Technology **509** (1991) 81–91
3. Piotr Findeisen: The Metaview system. Research Report, Software Engineering Group, Computing Science Department, the University of Alberta, Canada (1994) http://www.cs.ualberta.ca/softeng/Metaview/doc/
4. MetaEdit+ version 2.0 evaluation manual. MetaCASE Consulting Company (1996)
5. Graphical Designer user's manual. Advance Software Technologies, Inc. (1997) http://www.advancedsw.com/
6. A. H. M. ter Hofstede and T. F. Verhoef: Meta-CASE: Is the game worth the candle? Info Systems J. **6** (1996) 41-68
7. Michael Amberg: An architecture for a MetaCASE tool. Research Report, Department of Information Systems, University of Bamberg, Germny (1995) http://elwood.seda.sowi.uni-bamberg.de/forschung/metacase/meta-e.htm
8. Steven Kelly, Kari Smolander: Evolution and issues in MetaCASE. Information and Software Technology **38** (1996) 261–266
9. Levene M., Poulovassilis A.: The hypernode model and its associated query language. Proc. of the 5th Jerusalem Conf. on Information Technology, Oct. (1990) IEEE Press, 520–530
10. Louise Scott: Hypernode model support for software design methodology modelling. Proc. of Software Technology and Engineering Practice 97 (STEP97) IEEE Press, London July (1997)

Author Index

D. Agrawal	333	A.G. Merten	1
M. Albrecht	323	V.B. Mišić	243
M. Altus	323	D. Moody	184
A. Analyti	271	S. Moser	243
L. Bækgaard	127	S.B. Navathe	375
C. Batini	313	R. Offen	464
A.C. Bloesch	113	A. Olivé	57
M.L. Brodie	183	Y. Oohara	198
S. Chakravarthy	347	Y. Ooshima	198
W.W. Chu	257	M.T. Özsu	71
P. Constantopoulos	271	R.J. Peters	71
D. Costal	57	I. Petrounias	43
A.N.W. Dahanayake	450	W.S. Pinto	285
H. Dalianis	215	N. Pissinou	361
D. Dey	102	V. Plesser	422
J.L.G. Dietz	450	A. Poulovassilis	408
A. El Abbadi	333	C. Pu	169
S. Fornasiero	313	S. Purao	30
M.M. Gammoudi	285	M.R. Sancho	57
M. Gong	464	S. Sarkar	102
I.A. Goralwalla	71	K.D. Schewe	141
T.A. Halpin	113	M. Schrefl	155
U. Hohenstein	422	L. Scott	464
M. Hong	361	J. Sekine	198
T. Hruška	229	A. Singh	333
C. Hsu	436	H.G. Sol	450
S. Iyengar	85	N. Spyratos	271
L. Ji	361	M. Steeg	323
P. Johannesson	215	V.C. Storey	2, 30
A. Kitai	198	M. Stumptner	155
P. Kolenčík	229	S. Sundaresan	2
A. Kumar	361	J.W. Sweitzer	376
L. Lakhal	299	D. Szafron	71
M.L. Lee	394	R. Taouil	299
T.W. Ling	394	P. Thompson	376
L. Liu	169	H. Ullrich	2
M. Lloyd-Williams	16	K. Waiyamai	299
G. Longobardi	313	D. Wu	333
K. Makki	361	Y. Xiao	464
E. Malinowski	347	L. Yee	436
P. McBrien	408	G. Zhang	257
J.D. Mendes	285		

Springer
and the
environment

At Springer we firmly believe that an international science publisher has a special obligation to the environment, and our corporate policies consistently reflect this conviction.

We also expect our business partners – paper mills, printers, packaging manufacturers, etc. – to commit themselves to using materials and production processes that do not harm the environment. The paper in this book is made from low- or no-chlorine pulp and is acid free, in conformance with international standards for paper permanency.

Lecture Notes in Computer Science

For information about Vols. 1–1262

please contact your bookseller or Springer-Verlag

Vol. 1263: J. Komorowski, J. Zytkow (Eds.), Principles of Data Mining and Knowledge Discovery. Proceedings, 1997. IX, 397 pages. 1997. (Subseries LNAI).

Vol. 1264: A. Apostolico, J. Hein (Eds.), Combinatorial Pattern Matching. Proceedings, 1997. VIII, 277 pages. 1997.

Vol. 1265: J. Dix, U. Furbach, A. Nerode (Eds.), Logic Programming and Nonmonotonic Reasoning. Proceedings, 1997. X, 453 pages. 1997. (Subseries LNAI).

Vol. 1266: D.B. Leake, E. Plaza (Eds.), Case-Based Reasoning Research and Development. Proceedings, 1997. XIII, 648 pages. 1997 (Subseries LNAI).

Vol. 1267: E. Biham (Ed.), Fast Software Encryption. Proceedings, 1997. VIII, 289 pages. 1997.

Vol. 1268: W. Kluge (Ed.), Implementation of Functional Languages. Proceedings, 1996. XI, 284 pages. 1997.

Vol. 1269: J. Rolim (Ed.), Randomization and Approximation Techniques in Computer Science. Proceedings, 1997. VIII, 227 pages. 1997.

Vol. 1270: V. Varadharajan, J. Pieprzyk, Y. Mu (Eds.), Information Security and Privacy. Proceedings, 1997. XI, 337 pages. 1997.

Vol. 1271: C. Small, P. Douglas, R. Johnson, P. King, N. Martin (Eds.), Advances in Databases. Proceedings, 1997. XI, 233 pages. 1997.

Vol. 1272: F. Dehne, A. Rau-Chaplin, J.-R. Sack, R. Tamassia (Eds.), Algorithms and Data Structures. Proceedings, 1997. X, 476 pages. 1997.

Vol. 1273: P. Antsaklis, W. Kohn, A. Nerode, S. Sastry (Eds.), Hybrid Systems IV. X, 405 pages. 1997.

Vol. 1274: T. Masuda, Y. Masunaga, M. Tsukamoto (Eds.), Worldwide Computing and Its Applications. Proceedings, 1997. XVI, 443 pages. 1997.

Vol. 1275: E.L. Gunter, A. Felty (Eds.), Theorem Proving in Higher Order Logics. Proceedings, 1997. VIII, 339 pages. 1997.

Vol. 1276: T. Jiang, D.T. Lee (Eds.), Computing and Combinatorics. Proceedings, 1997. XI, 522 pages. 1997.

Vol. 1277: V. Malyshkin (Ed.), Parallel Computing Technologies. Proceedings, 1997. XII, 455 pages. 1997.

Vol. 1278: R. Hofestädt, T. Lengauer, M. Löffler, D. Schomburg (Eds.), Bioinformatics. Proceedings, 1996. XI, 222 pages. 1997.

Vol. 1279: B. S. Chlebus, L. Czaja (Eds.), Fundamentals of Computation Theory. Proceedings, 1997. XI, 475 pages. 1997.

Vol. 1280: X. Liu, P. Cohen, M. Berthold (Eds.), Advances in Intelligent Data Analysis. Proceedings, 1997. XII, 621 pages. 1997.

Vol. 1281: M. Abadi, T. Ito (Eds.), Theoretical Aspects of Computer Software. Proceedings, 1997. XI, 639 pages. 1997.

Vol. 1282: D. Garlan, D. Le Métayer (Eds.), Coordination Languages and Models. Proceedings, 1997. X, 435 pages. 1997.

Vol. 1283: M. Müller-Olm, Modular Compiler Verification. XV, 250 pages. 1997.

Vol. 1284: R. Burkard, G. Woeginger (Eds.), Algorithms — ESA '97. Proceedings, 1997. XI, 515 pages. 1997.

Vol. 1285: X. Jao, J.-H. Kim, T. Furuhashi (Eds.), Simulated Evolution and Learning. Proceedings, 1996. VIII, 231 pages. 1997. (Subseries LNAI).

Vol. 1286: C. Zhang, D. Lukose (Eds.), Multi-Agent Systems. Proceedings, 1996. VII, 195 pages. 1997. (Subseries LNAI).

Vol. 1287: T. Kropf (Ed.), Formal Hardware Verification. XII, 367 pages. 1997.

Vol. 1288: M. Schneider, Spatial Data Types for Database Systems. XIII, 275 pages. 1997.

Vol. 1289: G. Gottlob, A. Leitsch, D. Mundici (Eds.), Computational Logic and Proof Theory. Proceedings, 1997. VIII, 348 pages. 1997.

Vol. 1290: E. Moggi, G. Rosolini (Eds.), Category Theory and Computer Science. Proceedings, 1997. VII, 313 pages. 1997.

Vol. 1291: D.G. Feitelson, L. Rudolph (Eds.), Job Scheduling Strategies for Parallel Processing. Proceedings, 1997. VII, 299 pages. 1997.

Vol. 1292: H. Glaser, P. Hartel, H. Kuchen (Eds.), Programming Languages: Implementations, Logigs, and Programs. Proceedings, 1997. XI, 425 pages. 1997.

Vol. 1293: C. Nicholas, D. Wood (Eds.), Principles of Document Processing. Proceedings, 1996. XI, 195 pages. 1997.

Vol. 1294: B.S. Kaliski Jr. (Ed.), Advances in Cryptology — CRYPTO '97. Proceedings, 1997. XII, 539 pages. 1997.

Vol. 1295: I. Prívara, P. Ružička (Eds.), Mathematical Foundations of Computer Science 1997. Proceedings, 1997. X, 519 pages. 1997.

Vol. 1296: G. Sommer, K. Daniilidis, J. Pauli (Eds.), Computer Analysis of Images and Patterns. Proceedings, 1997. XIII, 737 pages. 1997.

Vol. 1297: N. Lavrač, S. Džeroski (Eds.), Inductive Logic Programming. Proceedings, 1997. VIII, 309 pages. 1997. (Subseries LNAI).

Vol. 1298: M. Hanus, J. Heering, K. Meinke (Eds.), Algebraic and Logic Programming. Proceedings, 1997. X, 286 pages. 1997.

Vol. 1299: M.T. Pazienza (Ed.), Information Extraction. Proceedings, 1997. IX, 213 pages. 1997. (Subseries LNAI).

Vol. 1300: C. Lengauer, M. Griebl, S. Gorlatch (Eds.), Euro-Par'97 Parallel Processing. Proceedings, 1997. XXX, 1379 pages. 1997.

Vol. 1301: M. Jazayeri, H. Schauer (Eds.), Software Engineering - ESEC/FSE'97. Proceedings, 1997. XIII, 532 pages. 1997.

Vol. 1302: P. Van Hentenryck (Ed.), Static Analysis. Proceedings, 1997. X, 413 pages. 1997.

Vol. 1303: G. Brewka, C. Habel, B. Nebel (Eds.), KI-97: Advances in Artificial Intelligence. Proceedings, 1997. XI, 413 pages. 1997. (Subseries LNAI).

Vol. 1304: W. Luk, P.Y.K. Cheung, M. Glesner (Eds.), Field-Programmable Logic and Applications. Proceedings, 1997. XI, 503 pages. 1997.

Vol. 1305: D. Corne, J.L. Shapiro (Eds.), Evolutionary Computing. Proceedings, 1997. X, 307 pages. 1997.

Vol. 1306: C. Leung (Ed.), Visual Information Systems. X, 274 pages. 1997.

Vol. 1307: R. Kompe, Prosody in Speech Understanding Systems. XIX, 357 pages. 1997. (Subseries LNAI).

Vol. 1308: A. Hameurlain, A M. Tjoa (Eds.), Database and Expert Systems Applications. Proceedings, 1997. XVII, 688 pages. 1997.

Vol. 1309: R. Steinmetz, L.C. Wolf (Eds.), Interactive Distributed Multimedia Systems and Telecommunication Services. Proceedings, 1997. XIII, 466 pages. 1997.

Vol. 1310: A. Del Bimbo (Ed.), Image Analysis and Processing. Proceedings, 1997. Volume I. XXII, 722 pages. 1997.

Vol. 1311: A. Del Bimbo (Ed.), Image Analysis and Processing. Proceedings, 1997. Volume II. XXII, 794 pages. 1997.

Vol. 1312: A. Geppert, M. Berndtsson (Eds.), Rules in Database Systems. Proceedings, 1997. VII, 214 pages. 1997.

Vol. 1313: J. Fitzgerald, C.B. Jones, P. Lucas (Eds.), FME '97: Industrial Applications and Strengthened Foundations of Formal Methods. Proceedings, 1997. XIII, 685 pages. 1997.

Vol. 1314: S. Muggleton (Ed.), Inductive Logic Programming. Proceedings, 1996. VIII, 397 pages. 1997. (Subseries LNAI).

Vol. 1315: G. Sommer, J.J. Koenderink (Eds.), Algebraic Frames for the Perception-Action Cycle. Proceedings, 1997. VIII, 395 pages. 1997.

Vol. 1316: M. Li, A. Maruoka (Eds.), Algorithmic Learning Theory. Proceedings, 1997. XI, 461 pages. 1997. (Subseries LNAI).

Vol. 1317: M. Leman (Ed.), Music, Gestalt, and Computing. IX, 524 pages. 1997. (Subseries LNAI).

Vol. 1318: R. Hirschfeld (Ed.), Financial Cryptography. Proceedings, 1997. XI, 409 pages. 1997.

Vol. 1319: E. Plaza, R. Benjamins (Eds.), Knowledge Acquisition, Modeling and Management. Proceedings, 1997. XI, 389 pages. 1997. (Subseries LNAI).

Vol. 1320: M. Mavronicolas, P. Tsigas (Eds.), Distributed Algorithms. Proceedings, 1997. X, 333 pages. 1997.

Vol. 1321: M. Lenzerini (Ed.), AI*IA 97: Advances in Artificial Intelligence. Proceedings, 1997. XII, 459 pages. 1997. (Subseries LNAI).

Vol. 1322: H. Hußmann, Formal Foundations for Software Engineering Methods. X, 286 pages. 1997.

Vol. 1323: E. Costa, A. Cardoso (Eds.), Progress in Artificial Intelligence. Proceedings, 1997. XIV, 393 pages. 1997. (Subseries LNAI).

Vol. 1324: C. Peters, C. Thanos (Eds.), Research and Advanced Technology for Digital Libraries. Proceedings, 1997. X, 423 pages. 1997.

Vol. 1325: Z.W. Raś, A. Skowron (Eds.), Foundations of Intelligent Systems. Proceedings, 1997. XI, 630 pages. 1997. (Subseries LNAI).

Vol. 1326: C. Nicholas, J. Mayfield (Eds.), Intelligent Hypertext. XIV, 182 pages. 1997.

Vol. 1327: W. Gerstner, A. Germond, M. Hasler, J.-D. Nicoud (Eds.), Artificial Neural Networks - ICANN '97. Proceedings, 1997. XIX, 1274 pages. 1997.

Vol. 1328: C. Retoré (Ed.), Logical Aspects of Computational Linguistics. Proceedings, 1996. VIII, 435 pages. 1997. (Subseries LNAI).

Vol. 1329: S.C. Hirtle, A.U. Frank (Eds.), Spatial Information Theory. Proceedings, 1997. XIV, 511 pages. 1997.

Vol. 1330: G. Smolka (Ed.), Principles and Practice of Constraint Programming - CP 97. Proceedings, 1997. XII, 563 pages. 1997.

Vol. 1331: D. W. Embley, R. C. Goldstein (Eds.), Conceptual Modeling - ER '97. Proceedings, 1997. XV, 479 pages. 1997.

Vol. 1332: M. Bubak, J. Dongarra, J. Waśniewski (Eds.), Recent Advances in Parallel Virtual Machine and Message Passing Interface. Proceedings, 1997. XV, 518 pages. 1997.

Vol. 1333: F. Pichler. R.M. Díaz (Eds.), Computer Aided Systems Theory - EUROCAST'97. Proceedings, 1997. XI, 626 pages. 1997.

Vol. 1334: Y. Han, T. Okamoto, S. Qing (Eds.), Information and Communications Security. Proceedings, 1997. X, 484 pages. 1997.

Vol. 1335: R:H: Möhring (Ed.), Graph-Theoretic Concepts in Computer Science. Proceedings, 1997. X, 376 pages. 1997.

Vol. 1336: C. Polychronopoulos, K. Joe, K. Araki, M. Amamiya (Eds.), High Performance Computing. Proceedings, 1997. XII, 416 pages. 1997.

Vol. 1337: C. Freksa, M. Jantzen, R. Valk (Eds.), Foundations of Computer Science. XII, 515 pages. 1997.

Vol. 1338: F. Plášil, K.G. Jeffery (Eds.), SOFSEM'97: Theory and Practice of Informatics. Proceedings, 1997. XIV, 571 pages. 1997.

Vol. 1339: N.A. Murshed, F. Bortolozzi (Eds.), Advances in Document Image Analysis. Proceedings, 1997. IX, 345 pages. 1997.

Vol. 1341: F. Bry, R. Ramakrishnan, K. Ramamohanarao (Eds.), Deductive and Object-Oriented Databases. Proceedings, 1997. XIV, 430 pages. 1997.